EDUCATIONAL
and
PSYCHOLOGICAL
MEASUREMENT
and
EVALUATION

eighth edition

Kenneth D. Hopkins
University of Colorado, Boulder

Allyn and Bacon
Boston • London • Toronto • Sydney • Tokyo • Singapore

To Jackson and Christine

Senior Vice President, Publisher: Nancy Forsyth
Editorial Assistant: Cheryl Ouellette
Editorial-Production Administrator: Joe Sweeney
Editorial-Production Service: Walsh & Associates, Inc.
Composition Buyer: Linda Cox
Manufacturing Buyer: Suzanne Lareau
Cover Administrator: Suzanne Harbison

Internet: www.abacon.com
America Online: keyword: College Online

Library of Congress Cataloging-in-Publication Data

Hopkins, Kenneth D.
    Educational and psychological measurement and evaluation / Kenneth
D. Hopkins.—8th ed.
        p.   cm.
    Includes bibliographical references and indexes.
    ISBN 0-205-16087-5
    1. Educational tests and measurements.   2. Psychological tests.
    I.   Title.
    LB3051.H72   1998
    371.26—dc21   97-18264
                                                                            CIP

Printed in the United States of America

10   9   8   7   6   5   4   03 04 05

Contents

PART II
THE DEVELOPMENT OF EDUCATIONAL MEASURES

7 **GENERAL PRINCIPLES OF TEST CONSTRUCTION: ACHIEVEMENT MEASURES   157**

8 **CONSTRUCTING AND USING ESSAY TESTS   184**

9 **CONSTRUCTING OBJECTIVE TESTS   213**

10   ITEM ANALYSIS FOR CLASSROOM TESTS   254

11   THE ASSESSMENT OF AFFECTIVE VARIABLES   273

12   GRADING AND REPORTING   302

PART III
STANDARDIZED MEASURES

Preface

Since 1941 this book has been a standard textbook in educational measurement. We are gratified that the reception of the book is sufficient to warrant an eighth edition, giving it a longer life span than any other textbook in educational or psychological measurement—a classic of sorts.

This eighth edition is a revision, not a new book. As in the previous editions, the selection and treatment of topics were guided by two general considerations: (1) knowledge and skills that are necessary for the development of valid evaluation measures and (2) knowledge and competencies that are required for a proper interpretation of teacher-made and standardized tests.

The book is divided into three major parts: (I) Basic Concepts, (II) The Development of Educational Measures, and (III) Standardized Measures. To afford flexibility in the selection of chapters to fit various curricular objectives, most chapters are essentially self-contained. Part III can be ignored when the course's emphasis is entirely on test development. The chapter on grading and reporting is an option branching off from the thoroughfare of the other chapters. For certain courses in classroom and educational testing, Chapter 15 (Standard Interest, Personality, and Social Measures) may be skipped without disruption.

The eighth edition differs from the seventh in minor respects. The content has been updated in terms of recent research and assessment trends, such as the use of portfolios in educational evaluations.

Naturalistic assessment approaches have been given more emphasis than in previous editions. Because of the positive feedback we received, we have continued to use the innovation (among measurement texts) of interspersing self-instruction reinforcement into the usual narrative treatment of statistical concepts that was introduced in the fifth edition. The purpose of this strategy is to reduce the inordinate amount of time frequently devoted to statistics in introductory measurement courses so that the course does not become a watered-down statistics course. The primary objective of the statistics is conceptual, not computational, although of course the two interact.

The treatment of test development represents a balanced view, reflecting both norm-referenced and criterion-referenced aspects. Mastery tests follow each chapter; these are designed to be of diagnostic value to students as well as to reinforce their understanding.

The book is not trendy. The learner is viewed as having intelligence and deserving respect; the content is not watered down to cater to the lowest common denominator. The question that determines the content is, "What should an educational professional know about measurement theory, procedures, and instruments in order to properly select, develop, use, and interpret assessment measures and have literacy for research and evaluation studies that utilize such measures?"

Basic Concepts

1

Measurement: Its Nature and Function

1.1 ASSESSMENT AND MEASUREMENT

Many people have erroneous notions about the nature of measurement. *Measurement involves a process by which things are differentiated and described.* It is not limited to the use of highly developed and refined instruments. Certainly, thermometers, yardsticks, and stopwatches can be used to measure temperature, distance, and time. But these variables can also be measured informally by observation—by the "trained eye." Skilled printers using only sight and touch are said to be able to assess (measure) the thickness of a film of ink to an incredible degree of precision—millionths of an inch! Our senses are our yardsticks for assessing the environment around us. When these observations are expressed using the language of numbers, the process of measurement has been completed.

We do not need a thermometer to tell whether it is "hot" or "cold" today, even though the thermometer can measure more accurately and purely (i.e., without the confounding effects of humidity, wind, etc.) than our impressionistic assessment. The point is that any differentiation among members of a class of things that is expressed numerically illustrates a process of measurement, be the things objects, days, schools, dogs, or persons. Of course, the validity of the differentiation is a direct reflection of the quality of the measuring instrument or procedure. Indeed, there is a close correspondence between the scientific maturity of a discipline and the degree to which the relevant variables in that discipline can be measured objectively and accurately.

1.2 HOW MUCH PRECISION IS NEEDED?

If you estimate (measure by observation) how much each of your classmates weighs, the resulting "measurements" would have some validity, but not as much as if a bathroom scale had been used. However, even the weights (measurements) yielded by the scale would contain some degree of measurement error because no measuring instrument is perfect. This need not discourage us; the degree of precision needed in a measurement depends on its purpose. Physicists and chemists need to measure temperature to hundredths of a degree, but do you care whether it reaches 82.6° or 82.3° today? Or whether you are not actually 67.5 inches tall but only 67.47 inches? Or whether you can correctly spell 43.76 percent, and not 44 percent, of the words in *Webster's Collegiate Dictionary*? The appropriate degree of precision of measures in education and the behavioral sciences is usually less than that required in engineering and the physical sciences. Further, the precision required in a measurement differs when it is used to compare group means, as in research and evaluation studies, than when important decisions are to be made about an individual. *The degree of accuracy needed in a measurement is related to the purpose served by the measurement.*

1.3   VARIABLES THAT ARE NOT DIRECTLY OBSERVABLE

Some variables, such as age, height, blood pressure, and sex, can be observed directly. Many other variables, especially in the behavioral and social sciences, cannot be observed directly but instead must be inferred from a *sample* of indirect indications. Adequate measurements of the latter type are much more difficult to obtain and usually will contain a greater degree of measurement error than variables that can be directly assessed. Musical aptitude, reading ability, and self-concept cannot be measured with the same reliability as height, the amount of weight you can bench-press, and penmanship. Cognitive and affective variables such as reading ability, writing ability, and attitude toward education can be assessed, but they lack the common *yardsticks* possessed by height, weight, and age. They are, and must be, assessed continually by instructors during the process of education. The more accurate the assessments are, the more valid the decisions based on those assessments can be. A goal of this book is to enable you to better understand the degree of accuracy in various measures in order to estimate and improve the reliability and validity of important educational and psychological assessments.

1.4   OBSERVATION AND QUANTIFICATION

How does every student in a first-grade class know that the "blue birds" are the best readers in the class and the "yellow birds" are the poorest readers, even if no formal reading test has been administered? They do so because observation itself is a process of assessment. Even now, as you read this chapter, you are implicitly or explicitly monitoring (assessing) many variables—how long you have been reading (time), how well the material is written, the level of vocabulary being used, the degree of interest you have in the material, your fatigue, and so forth. If the situation required it, you could quantify these perceptions, for example, on a scale from 1 to 5, and thereby translate them into measures.

But *the process of assessment does not necessarily involve the use of numbers* (quantification); it becomes measurement when the language of numbers is used. As you study a classmate, you assess, consciously or casually, the age, sex, attractiveness, friendliness, and many other variables of that person. Perhaps the result of this assessment process is that the person is, to you, a "young, attractive, friendly female." Although we have quite a clear notion of the meaning of "female," what is "young," "attractive," and "friendly"? These variables do not have a precise, uniform semantic meaning from one observer to another—they are to some extent dependent on "the eye (or ear) of the beholder." By your yardstick, "young" might mean less than 25 years of age, but by my yardstick "young" could include persons in their 50s. In other words, words contain much ambiguity—there is uneven calibration from one person to another. Indeed, a speaker and a listener often do not realize that the meaning of the information *sent* is not identical with the meaning of the information *received*. "We're having a cold winter day" means one thing in Florida but something else in Alaska.

When the results of observation can be quantified and expressed in numbers, this source of error, semantic ambiguity, can be reduced greatly. "I'm tall and skinny" means something; "I'm 6 feet 4 inches tall and weigh 160 pounds" means much more. Is the latter expression dehumanizing because it uses numbers? You are far too clever to be taken in by such fatuous, *knee-jerk* associations.

Quantification is not an end in itself; it is employed because it allows information to be communicated and interpreted with less ambiguity and less subjectivity than would otherwise be the case. In addition, the tools of statistical methods become available when numerical coding of information is used. Educational and psychological tests and inventories are simply attempts to obtain information regarding personological variables in a systematic manner and to express these results with a minimum of ambiguity—a point that has eluded many critics of educational and psychological tests.

1.5   THE PARADOX OF TESTING

> There is a paradox in educational measurement today. While assessments of achievement and competence are being more urgently called for and more widely employed than ever before, tests are, at the same time, being more sharply criticized and more strongly opposed. (Ebel & Frisbie, 1986)

Many people are opposed to measurement and evaluation yet at the same time favor excellence, which is facilitated by, and can be identified only through, measurement and evaluation. You will probably agree that assessment, measurement, and evaluation are in the best interests of students in particular and society in general—that educational decisions are only as good as the quality of the information on which they are based.

Anti-testing crusades have often been ignited by first- or secondhand contact with a poor test, poor test items or tests that have been inappropriately used and interpreted, or by persons who misconstrue the intent of a test or other measure. These "straw persons" that are often attacked are not defended by reputable measurement specialists; nor are they accurate representations of the way things are. Indeed, the testing profession has a tradition of pulling-no-punches critiques of every published test via the *Mental Measurements Yearbooks*, begun in 1936 by the late O. K. Buros. Journalistic exposés can make a cogent case on the evils of testing, especially standardized testing, only if the audience is uninformed and lacks an understanding of the fundamentals of measurement.

Particularly unfortunate is an unfair and naive book, *The Myth of Measurability*, in which tests and those who develop them are vilified. Here are some quotes from the book: "I feel emotionally toward the testing industry as I would toward any other merchants of death." "[Tests] are polluting the whole atmosphere of education." "One serious disadvantage of the present use of tests is that they let the wrong sort of people take control of testing." Ralph Nader, in a periodical, *The Fair Test Examiner*, is shockingly unfair. Speaking of the SAT, Nader asserts, "60 years of idiocy is enough," and "Standardized tests are a specialized form of fraud." He charges that ". . . most tests in common use incorporate the arbitrary, elitist standards of a racist society. . . ." Nader's contention that "curriculum is blatantly shaped and distorted to conform to the limited content of what a standardized multiple-choice test measures" shows a remarkable lack of familiarity with empirical research on the issue (Gullickson, 1984). Such outlandish and emotionally charged language may make interesting reading, but it does not serve the best interests of education (Millman, 1981b); it is not professionally responsible. The choice is not between (a) current tests, many of which are excellent, and (b) superior alternatives kept back by people who are bent on subverting education. Non-test assessment procedures are being recognized by evaluators as being of critical importance (Gullickson & Hopkins, 1987). Most test publishers are private enterprise operations that offer their wares in a competitive marketplace; they are not sinister organizations. The substance of various anti-testing criticisms will be considered in the appropriate contexts in later chapters of this book.

The attacks on testing represent misunderstandings about the nature and purposes of tests; how they are developed; what *norms, reliability*, and *validity* mean; how tests should be used and interpreted; and the emotional effects they have on examinees. Of course, the fact that a test is standardized and published is no guarantee of quality or professional endorsement—"there is much chaff amongst the wheat." In addition, any test or non-test assessment procedure can be misused and become a weapon rather than a tool, but to fail to make this critical distinction creates much confusion in the minds of the general public, who often lack the background for an independent assessment of the issues being contested.

Providing an understanding of these and related issues is a basic objective of this book. Some of the issues in the anti-testing movement are addressed in a position paper (APGA, 1972) developed by the American Personnel and Guidance Association (APGA), the Association for Measurement and Evaluation in Guidance (MEG), and the National Council on Measurement in Education (NCME):

WHAT TESTING IS[1]

Testing is not a policy nor a set of beliefs or principles. Testing is a technique for obtaining information. Its special virtue is that this information is provided in organized form, and that the technology of testing also provides methods for determining how dependable or undependable the information is.

As a technique, testing itself is neutral. It is a tool that serves the ends of the user. The better he understands the technology of testing, the better it meets his needs. The less well he

---

[1]Reprinted by permission from "The responsible use of tests," in *Measurement and Evaluation in Guidance*, Vol. 5, Falls Church, Va.: American Personnel and Guidance Association, 1972, pp. 385–388.

grasps this technology, the greater the risk that inadvertently (and perhaps unknowingly) he may work at cross-purposes to his own goals.

In schools and colleges, the principal needs served by testing include the providing of information (a) to teachers, as an aid to the improvement of instruction; (b) to students and, in the case of younger students, to their parents, as an aid to self-understanding and to both educational and vocational planning; and (c) to administrators, as a basis for planning, decision-making, and evaluating the effectiveness of programs and operations.

In business, industry, government service, and other walks of life, the general goal of testing is that of improving the match between persons and jobs, whether they be manual or managerial, personal contact or professional. Tests serve either to verify claimed knowledge or competence (e.g., a typing test) or to appraise readiness to master the training needed in order to perform the job. They may be used either competitively (to aid in selecting the best qualified and to avoid political or racial favoritisms), or as a standard (to avoid placing on the job persons whose work would likely be unsafe or uneconomic). Not every job nor every selection situation is equally likely to benefit from the use of tests, of course.

In these terms, testing as such would seem hard to criticize and quite unlikely to arouse antagonism or draw complaints from anyone. Yet it has been the target of bitter attacks, by members of some minority groups and by others in their behalf. The attacks usually result from one, or from a combination of two, of these three factors:

1. The use of tests, more or less competently, by administrators and others with whose goals and values the attackers disagree.
2. Side effects of testing, unintended results obtained when tests are used incompetently or without due regard for their technological strengths and limitations.
3. Misunderstandings of the role played by testing—the tendency to attribute to the tool shortcomings of its user, often accompanied by the simplistic assumption that if use of the tool is forbidden, things will somehow get better, if not be entirely all right. . . .

1.6   THE *RESPECTFUL* USE OF TESTS

Good testing is marked by

Respect for the Individual

In educational and clinical testing, all the work is undertaken for the benefit ultimately of those who are tested, not of the institutions and agencies doing the testing.

In employment testing, the primary benefit may be the employer's—but in the long run no selection program can be of genuine value to the employer if it is not so designed and conducted as to also benefit the employees and the applicants.

Respect for the Instrument

It is an abuse of the instrument, as well as disrespectful of the individual's needs and rights, to use a test for a purpose inappropriate to those characteristics and limits that make it a test. Test directions, stimulus material, verbal or other content, time limit, and supporting data, all must be considered in the decision to use a particular measure with particular individuals for a particular purpose under particular circumstances.

Decisions of this kind may be quite clear and easy to make but often are neither; frequently the *purpose* is the crucial consideration. It may, for example, be both fair and useful to give an individual examination in English to a child or adult whose native language is another when the purpose is simply to appraise his readiness to profit from lectures given in English; yet the same activity clearly is indefensible if the test score is to be used as an estimate of his all-around intellectual capability.

Fix the tools?

It is very tempting to think that if only better, "fairer," more nearly perfect tests were made, all will be well. But better tests will not solve the social ills they reflect. Indeed, as John W. Gardner pointed out years ago in his book entitled *Excellence*, the more adequately tests do what they are supposed to do, the *more, not the less*, they will provide disturbing information when the underlying social, economic, and educational conditions are not those of equality.

Better tests can and will be made—but while seeking perfection, we cannot wait for its realization. Even though imperfect and incomplete, the information tests provide is essential to realistic handling of our educational and personnel problems—whether they are those of learning or of teaching, of hiring a worker or of getting a job.

Ban testing?

The role of measurement is too central, too fundamental to the conduct and improvement of education and sound personnel practices in business and industry for a ban to be a realistic alternative. For some years it was illegal to request information as to race on applications for admission or employment; forbidding the recording of such information was thought to work toward the abolition of discrimination. Now the trend is reversed; organizations are required by law to obtain and report the very information that they once were forbidden to ask. What vanished under the ban was not discrimination but the ability to tell whether and to what extent colleges or employers were doing what most persons now agree they should do. The same cycle may be predicted if we try to deal with the present problem by doing away with tests; the ostrich approach does not lead to the effective solution of problems. Organizations and persons committed to changing educational or social systems, no less than those seeking to preserve a system, will need the information that measurement provides.

1.7   MEASUREMENT AND EVALUATION IN THE EDUCATIONAL PROCESS

Measures, such as standardized tests of achievement, intelligence, interest, and aptitude, have become a part of the contemporary culture. Many millions of standardized tests are administered each year in the United States, in addition to perhaps 500 million classroom tests. The process of education depends extensively on assessment and measurement and on a related procedure—*evaluation*. The word *evaluation* designates a summing-up process in which value judgments play a large part, as in grading and promoting students, whereas the development, administration, and scoring of assessment procedures constitute the *measurement* process. Interpreting such scores is part of the process of evaluation.

A simple illustration may clarify the distinction. Miss Jones gives her class a standardized spelling test consisting of 25 difficult words. She finds that the number of words spelled correctly ranges from 6 to 25, and that the average number correct is 15. Will Miss Jones stop here? The mother of one of her students may ask, "How *well* is David doing in spelling?" Miss Jones may show her his test and explain that he spelled 16 words correctly out of 25 on the test. David's mother may press for an evaluation of measurement (i.e., the score of 16) by replying, "Nine words wrong, 64 percent right; is that as terrible as it sounds?" If Miss Jones answers, "More than half the students missed a greater number than he did," she is confining her remarks to the distribution of scores on the test, that is, staying within the area we call measurement. If, however, she agrees that 16 is indeed a "poor" score, or if she insists that in view of his aptitude David is spelling about as well as can be expected, then Miss Jones is evaluating the score.

We consider the conversion of test scores and other information to grades such as *A, B, C, D, F; Excellent, Good, Fair, Poor;* or *High, Average, Low* as evaluation rather than measurement—value judgments are implicit in such conversions. Important decisions are made in selecting the items and the time and method of giving the test and scoring it, but the process of attaching value judgments to *performance* on the measure is uniquely evaluation. Whether a student's score is good or bad for a given purpose cannot be determined solely from the score itself. An interpretation must be made. The test score is often interpreted in terms of fixed standards, such as 80–89 percent receives a grade of *B*, in terms of the student's rank on the test in the class, or the student's score in relation to his or her academic aptitude. Throughout this book the distinctions among assessment, measurement, and evaluation that we emphasize are not always sharp or meaningful—their colors run together.

1.8   SUBJECTIVITY AND OBJECTIVITY

Subjectivity in a measurement or evaluation is the extent to which the results depend on *who* is doing the evaluation rather than on *what* is being evaluated. Little subjectivity is involved in determining the fastest runner in Mr. Smith's fourth-grade class, but considerable subjectivity is involved in *deciding* who should receive the best citizenship award. If a rating remains constant irrespective of the rater, the rating is said to be *objective*. The extent to which a measurement or evaluation is subjective is the degree to which it is vulnerable to personal bias and prejudice. It is desirable to increase the objectivity of testing, interviewing, rating, and similar enterprises that often are pursued quite subjectively.

Increasing the objectivity of the assessment and evaluation of human behavior is a major goal of this book. We are interested in increasing objectivity not for its own sake but because, as later chapters will make clear, the validity of a measure or evaluation is usually enhanced as it becomes less subjective.

1.9   EDUCATIONAL DECISIONS FOUNDED ON EVALUATION

If we view assessment and measurement narrowly as the preparing, administering, scoring, and evaluating of objective tests, we are likely to overlook important ways in which evaluation supports the entire educational system. Why do we have schools? Obviously, society has decided that without them many people would probably not acquire essential knowledge, understanding, skills, and attitudes. Schools are organized the way they are because, on the basis of much experience, current patterns appear to be successful—at least in the eyes of those who make educational decisions. Why is a particular school built where it is, as large as it is, and with certain facilities? Why are some teachers hired to staff it and not others? What determines salaries, the choice of textbooks and other instructional aids, grades, promotions, reports to parents, grouping patterns, the community's reactions to the school and its products, and recommendations for college and jobs? All of these decisions involve evaluations. Objective assessment and measurement are usually essential for sound evaluation, but they are by no means sufficient.

Most educators consider that a school's main business is promoting *growth* toward desirable individual and societal objectives; fewer agree on who should judge the desirability of these objectives. However, since all schools focus on student progress as the ultimate criterion, it is important to evaluate the status and gains of students expertly. How well are Mary and Paolo doing? Should they be doing better?

Assessment, measurement, and evaluation encompass such subjective aspects as the judgments made by teachers and administrators. Let us not fall into the trap of asking whether we should use teacher judgments *or* test scores. Faced by complex problems of assessment and evaluation of student growth and the factors that influence it, we cannot reject any promising resource. Various sorts of information *complement* each other.

Are today's educators being equipped adequately for the performance of their evaluation responsibilities? Studies have found that graduates of teacher-training institutions rarely demonstrate a satisfactory level of measurement competence and that most teachers have only minimal training in test and evaluation techniques. The unsatisfactory quality of the majority of teacher-made tests no doubt reflects this inadequacy in training. Not surprisingly, teachers who have had little preparation in measurement and evaluation tend to underemphasize the use of tests—teacher-made and standardized—for instructional purposes. We tend to shy away from areas in which we lack confidence in our abilities. *The role of measurement and testing in quality education are far too important to be left to chance.*

1.10   ESSENTIAL KNOWLEDGE AND SKILLS

What should school personnel know about measurement and evaluation, and what abilities do they need in this area? Figure 1–1 presents the three primary components of the educational process—a process for changing the behavior and attitudes of students.

First, educational goals are established either explicitly or (more often) implicitly. Learning experiences are then designed to promote the attainment of those goals. Finally, an evaluation is conducted to determine the extent to which the objectives have been attained. The results of the evaluation may affect the objectives (e.g., modify the goals) or the instruction (e.g., plan for remediation). The two-way arrows of Figure 1–1 indicate the interacting nature of the entire system. If evaluation procedures are poor, then the quality of the information on which decisions must be based will also be inadequate. "Appropriately used educational tests, whether created by classroom teachers or other agents, are potent educational tools which enhance the educational process . . . Appropriate test usage means that testing is an integral part of the instructional method or process" (Nitko, 1988).

The measurement and evaluation skills needed depend partly on the position one holds. Many of the skills needed for kindergarten and primary school teachers differ from

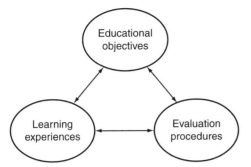

FIGURE 1–1 A graphic representation of the three interacting components of the educational process.

those needed by high school physics and English teachers. Principals, counselors, and school psychologists need certain competencies besides those that are essential for teachers.

Fortunately, *certain concepts, principles, and skills are useful at all levels* and in nearly all contexts. Even parents and others who are not professionally concerned with individual appraisal would benefit from a clear understanding of such concepts as *validity, reliability, IQ,* and *norms.* By concentrating on fundamental concepts and skills, we present in one textbook the basic measurement and evaluation *essentials* for most test users. Ebel (1961, p. 68) has outlined six requisites for competence in assessment (although phrased for *tests,* the principles apply to the development of other kinds of measures as well):

1. Know the uses, as well as the limitations, of tests.
2. Know the criteria by which the quality of a test (or other measuring instrument) should be judged and how to secure evidence relating to these criteria.
3. Know how to develop a test and write the test questions to be included in it.
4. Know how to select a standardized test that will be effective in a particular situation.
5. Know how to administer a test properly, efficiently, and fairly.
6. Know how to interpret test scores correctly and fully, with recognition of their limitations.

Throughout this book these six fundamentals are carefully illustrated with examples from various age and grade levels.

Users of evaluation information need to know how to perform certain aspects of measurement and evaluation, such as constructing tests, giving grades, and administering and interpreting standardized achievement and scholastic aptitude tests. They should know where they can find critical reviews of published instruments, and they should know how to select from the many available tests, inventories, questionnaires, rating scales, checklists, and the like that are most suitable for a particular purpose. *Educational and Psychological Measurement and Evaluation* is designed to help you achieve these important objectives.

1.11   THE GOALS AND FUNCTIONS OF TESTING

Tests serve a variety of functions. The purpose for which a test is given determines not only the appropriate *type* of test but also some of the test's *characteristics* (e.g., difficulty and reliability). A measure designed for a precise assessment of individual differences in arithmetic fundamentals requires very high test reliability, whereas a much shorter (and, hence, less reliable) test might suffice for program evaluation. The purposes served by assessments in education can be classified into four interrelated categories: (1) instructional, (2) administrative, (3) program evaluation and research, and (4) guidance. Standardized measures provide the basis for most of the guidance and administrative test roles, whereas locally constructed measures are used principally for instructional functions. Both types of measures are common for research and evaluation purposes.

1.12   INSTRUCTIONAL FUNCTIONS

The Process of Constructing a Test Encourages the Clarification of Meaningful Course Objectives.   If teachers are continually reminded of their destination, they are more apt to stay on course. As Bloom (1961, p. 60) observed three decades ago:

> Participation of the teaching staff in selecting as well as constructing evaluation instruments has resulted in improved instruments on one hand, and on the other hand it has resulted in clarifying the objectives of instruction and in making them real and meaningful to teachers. . . . When teachers have actively participated in defining objectives and in selecting or constructing evaluation instruments they return to the learning problems with great vigor and remarkable creativity. . . . Teachers who have become committed to a set of educational objectives which they thoroughly understand respond by developing a variety of learning experiences which are as diverse and as complex as the situation requires.

Tests Provide a Means of Feedback to the Instructor and the Student.   Feedback from tests can help the teacher provide more appropriate instructional guidance for individual students as well as for the class as a whole. "Linking testing and instruction is a fundamental and enduring concern in educational practice" (Burstein, 1983, p. 99). The students of teachers who incorporate systematic measurement and data-evaluation procedures into their instructional design tend to have considerably higher achievement than students whose teachers do not use these procedures (Fuchs & Fuchs, 1986b). Well-designed tests are useful for self-diagnosis by students—assisting them in identifying specific strengths and weaknesses. Teachers, however, acknowledge uncertainty as to how to improve the quality of classroom tests and other kinds of educational assessments (Stiggins & Bridgeford, 1986). The extent to which achievement tests contribute to improved learning and instruction is dependent on the quality of the tests (Linn, 1983).

Properly Constructed Tests Can Motivate Learning.   As a general rule, students pursue the mastery of objectives more diligently if they expect to be evaluated. In the intense competition for a student's time, courses without examinations are often *squeezed* out of high-priority positions. When queried, students have consistently reported greater study and learning with periodic testing. Frequent short tests are a far more effective learning aid than infrequent long tests.

Tests Can Facilitate Learning.   "Evaluation is a dominating aspect of educational practice. *It strongly influences what students attend to*, how hard they work, how they allocate their study time, and what they can afford to get interested in" (Sadler, 1983).

The anticipation of a forthcoming evaluation may also affect students' set to learn. Humans have the ability to be selective in the stimuli to which they attend and respond. When learners know they will subsequently be evaluated on content, they retain the information better than students who are in a different set. Expecting to be tested on material seems to encourage receptivity to learning and the shift into the "intention to remember" mental mode. One study found that students expecting a final examination perform much better than comparable students in the same classes who thought they had been exempted from the final. Students who expected to be tested following a videotaped lecture learned more from the lecture than a control group of students who were not told that they would be tested immediately following the lecture (Williams & Ware, 1976). Students are more attentive and retain more when they know they are going to be accountable for the content. Furthermore, when questions pertain to higher order levels of understanding, improved levels of conceptual understanding tend to be forthcoming (Hamaker, 1986).

Examinations Are a Useful Means of Overlearning.   When we review, interact with, or practice skills and concepts even after they have been mastered, we are engaging in what learning psychologists call *overlearning*. Even students who correctly answer every question on a test are engaging in behavior that is instructionally valuable *apart from the evaluation function being served* by the test. Scheduled examinations not only stimulate review (relearning and overlearning) but also foster overlearning through the process of reacting to test questions that assess content that has already been mastered. The value of overlearning for long-term retention is apparent in Figure 1–2, which presents the results of the classic study by Krueger (1929). The degree of retention of the meaning of a learned set of nouns

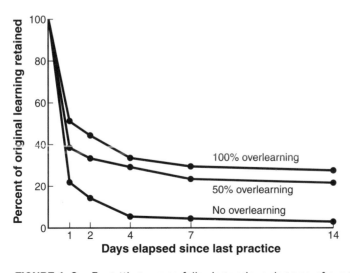

FIGURE 1–2   Forgetting curves following various degrees of overlearning.

was very slight for the no-overlearning group (bottom line), whereas the overlearning groups had a much superior degree of retention. The evidence that such continued review positively influences retention is so strong that it cannot be dismissed.

Although most of the research on overlearning has been based on rote learning and the learning of mazes, it is probable that the forgetting curves for meaningful materials follow a similar but less dramatic pattern. "The best way of mitigating forgetting is to give immediate feedback of results" (Wood, 1977, p. 201). Many studies have shown that immediate knowledge of results enhances learning (McMillan, 1977; Nitko, 1988).

1.13 ADMINISTRATIVE FUNCTIONS

Tests Provide a Mechanism of "Quality Control." National or local norms can provide a basis for assessing certain curricular strengths and weaknesses. At least three-fourths of the American public believe that standardized tests are useful (Millman, 1981b); the perception of teachers is similar (Kellahan, Madaus & Airasian, 1983). If a school district does not have a means for periodic self-evaluation, instructional inadequacies may go unnoticed. The evidence suggests that when tests identify a curricular deficiency, "substantial improvement typically has occurred when the school staff sets a specific improvement goal in a subject field" (Klausmeier, 1982, p. 11).

The quality control function of testing is illustrated in Figure 1–3, which shows some of the data on which the much-discussed national "achievement decline" is based. Note that the test data also corroborate *grade inflation*—GPAs increased in the 1970s, leveled off in the 1980s, and are increasing still further in the 1990s. Test scores declined sharply, bottomed out in the mid-1970s, changing little until the mid-1980s, and have shown a slight increase in more recent years.

Quality control is the major purpose of the National Assessment of Educational Progress (NAEP, 1978), which monitors the educational achievement of American students in most curricular areas in three- to five-year cycles (see Section 14.14).

Tests Facilitate Better Classification and Placement Decisions. Grouping children by their ability levels is an example of classification for which tests can be of value. Reading readiness tests can be helpful for placing first-grade students in the proper classes, sections, or groups. An English placement test for college freshmen serves the same purpose.

Tests Can Increase the Quality of Selection Decisions. Scholastic aptitude and achievement test scores have repeatedly demonstrated their value in identifying students who are or are not likely to succeed in various colleges. Certain jobs require special skills that are best assessed by well-designed tests. Tests serve as principal criteria for identifying gifted, learning-disabled, or retarded children.

A test designed especially for a particular selection purpose may have quite different characteristics than one used for classification. For example, selection of the sixth-grade students who are proper candidates for a special remedial reading program would not require a test that reliably detects differences between average and superior readers. However, *classification* of all students into high, average, and low reading groups would require a test

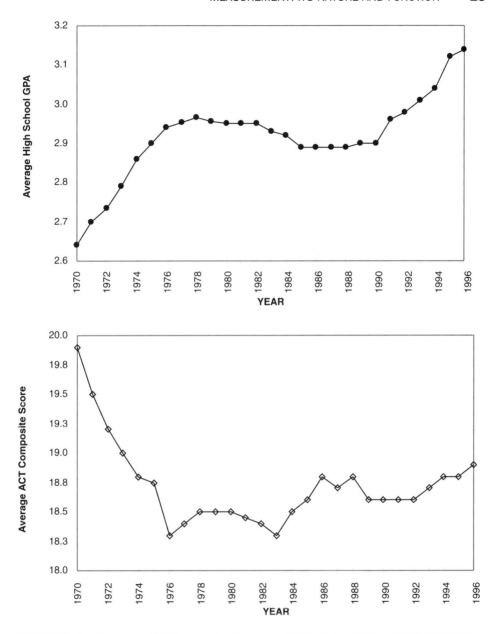

FIGURE 1–3   Trends in ACT Composite Scores and High School GPAs, 1970–1996 (Data provided by the ACT and is expressed in original ACT metric).

that reliably differentiates among students along the entire reading ability continuum. Classification is the process of deciding which "treatment" a person should receive, whereas the selection decision is concerned with whether the person should be treated, employed, admitted, or the like. The distinguishing feature of selection decisions is that some persons are rejected. A test that identifies kindergarten students who will have difficulty reading (selection) may not be helpful in deciding which instructional strategy is best for a given student (classification).

Tests Can Be a Useful Means of Accreditation, Mastery, or Certification (Jaeger, 1988). Tests on which standards of performance have been established allow the demonstration of competence or knowledge that may have been acquired in an unconventional way. The examinee may thereby receive some deserved credit or authorization. Measurement can help reduce some artificial barriers to the degree or credential. For example, the Tests of General Educational Development (GED tests) were designed to allow persons returning from military service to receive formal credit for demonstrated proficiency in various areas of academic achievement. This provision expedited the acquisition of a high school diploma for thousands of World War II veterans, migrant farm workers, and drop-outs (Campa, Mena & Clinton, 1987).

Students who have taken college-level courses in secondary schools can receive advanced placement in college if they demonstrate adequate competence on the Advanced Placement Program (AP) examinations of the College Board. Research indicates that students who pass the AP tests actually do better in subsequent courses in that discipline than college students who took the introductory course (Casserly, 1986).

In 1966 the College Board began an extensive College Level Examination Program (CLEP) based on the principle of credit by examination. Its goal was to provide a national program of general and subject examinations so that people who have reached a college level of achievement outside the classroom can receive college credit or placement.

Perhaps the most common example of a test that serves as a means of certifying knowledge is the test one must pass to obtain a driver's license. Additional examples are the state board examinations for physicians, dentists, lawyers, and psychologists.

1.14   RESEARCH AND EVALUATION

Tests Are Useful for Program Evaluation and Research.   Outcome measures are necessary to determine whether an innovative program is better or poorer than the conventional one in facilitating the attainment of specific curricular objectives. Standardized achievement tests have been the key sources of data for evaluating the success of federally funded programs, although several other criteria are required for any comprehensive evaluation.

Much of teaching consists of searching for better ways to help students learn. For example, if three different methods for aiding seventh-graders to solve arithmetic reasoning problems are readily available to the teacher, which one or ones should be used? Is one of the methods superior to the other two for all seventh-graders, or is one of them better for slow learners and another better for fast learners? This question suggests an experiment in which nine groups are used, representing all combinations of three levels of ability (low, medium, and high) with the three methods. Tests would play a prominent part in such a study, but experimentation involves much more than testing.

More generally, how does one evaluate the effects of new curricula and various "social reforms"? (see Campbell, 1969; Cook & Campbell, 1979) An innovation such as "experiential education," computer-assisted instruction, compensatory preschool education, an 11-month school year, or a radically different physics course may seem obviously promising to those who propose it, but skeptics will demand more evidence of its effectiveness than mere enthusiasm.

1.15   GUIDANCE FUNCTIONS

Tests Can Be of Value in Diagnosing an Individual's Special Aptitudes and Abilities. Obtaining measures of scholastic aptitude, achievement, interests, and personality is often an important aspect of the counseling process. The use of information from standardized tests and inventories can be helpful for guiding the selection of a college, the choosing of an appropriate course of study, the discovering of unrecognized abilities, and so on. Of course, there are poor tests just as there are good ones—they can be misused and misinterpreted, and in the wrong circumstances a test can become a weapon rather than a tool. If we achieve our objectives in this book, the chances that you will misinterpret or misuse tests will be greatly reduced. As the president of the American Federation of Teachers has written:

> Tests are not perfect; they are subject to error and misinterpretation. We will seek to improve our methods of testing and measurement. But we cannot wait until there are perfect and infallible measures—there never will be. As professionals, we will use the best measurements we have available to us . . . The worst possible approach is to suggest prohibition of any standardized tests. Such a position only convinces the public that teachers are merely trying to cover their own shortcomings. (Shanker, 1977)

SUMMARY

Tests and other measures play important roles in today's schools and other aspects of life. Thus, users of tests and other quantitative information must know how to employ and interpret measurements correctly.

Tests provide objective measurements on which educational decisions are based. Tests and other assessment devices can provide a means for improving and enhancing feedback, motivation, learning set, and overlearning. They facilitate "quality control" and improve classification and placement, selection, accreditation, mastery, and certification decisions. All behavioral research and evaluation studies use measures of some type. Tests can also be useful in diagnosing special aptitudes and abilities.

The aim of this book is to provide the necessary tools for proper selection and use of these various types of tests. However, it is up to you to make your competency in educational measurement a reality.

We hope that this book will contribute to your understanding and actions. You should finish it with much more *knowledge* about the special concepts and principles of measurement and evaluation than you may now possess. You will learn to *apply* your knowledge to new problems that confront you, to *analyze* situations efficiently, to *synthesize* (put ideas together creatively), and to *evaluate* soundly on the basis of internal evidence (e.g., within a test itself) and outside information (e.g., published standards for tests).

This book is valuable to you only to the extent that you actively and consistently interact with its content. A continuous growth in your measurement and evaluation skills in future years is the ultimate criterion.

In this chapter you have glimpsed a few of the ways in which measurement and evaluation function in the educative process. The ideas and operations that we have mentioned will receive detailed treatment in the chapters that follow.

Educational and Psychological Measurement and Evaluation contains three main sections: The first six chapters deal with fundamental principles and concepts of measurement and evaluation; the next six chapters are concerned with the construction, evaluation, and use of measuring instruments; and the final three chapters pertain to the use of various types of standardized tests and other measures. The appendix offers resources for the development and selection of measuring instruments for many educational and psychological variables.

IMPORTANT TERMS AND CONCEPTS

assessment	classification	evaluation
measurement	objectivity	overlearning
quantification	selection	subjectivity

CHAPTER TEST

1. What is the process by which the members of a class of things are differentiated?
   a) counting
   b) measurement
   c) quantification
   d) evaluation

2. Which one of the following terms *least* belongs with the other two?
   a) assessment
   b) measurement
   c) evaluation

3. Which one of the following adjectives *least* belongs with the other two?
   a) objective
   b) impressionistic
   c) subjective

4. Place the following processes in the temporal order in which they normally occur: evaluation, quantification, assessment.

5. Which one of the following variables is *not* directly observable but instead is a psychological construct that must be inferred from indirect behavioral indications?
   a) age
   b) intelligence
   c) strength
   d) high-jumping ability
   e) height

6. The measurements of which one of the variables listed in Question 5 would be expected to contain the *most* measurement error?

7. The principal function of quantification is best summarized as
   a) an essential in the measurement process.
   b) an essential in the evaluation process.
   c) reducing inefficiency.
   d) reducing ambiguity.

8. Which one of the following statements represents evaluation?
   a) Jim's score on the test was 98.
   b) Chang's score was at the 98th percentile of national norms.
   c) Pierre's IQ is very high.
   d) Sherry answered 100 percent of the questions correctly.
   e) Dale did well on the test.

9. Which one of the following is *not* a direct *instructional* function served by tests and evaluation?
   a) motivating learning
   b) facilitating a mental set for learning
   c) overlearning
   d) selection decisions

10. Which one of the following is *not* a direct function served by tests and testing?
    a) to help evaluate students
    b) to help evaluate teachers
    c) to help in curriculum evaluation
    d) to help in selection and classification decisions
    e) to help identify an individual's special aptitudes

ANSWERS TO CHAPTER TEST

1. b
2. c
3. a
4. assessment, quantification, evaluation

5. b
6. b
7. d
8. e

9. d
10. b

2

Communicating Numerical Information: Interpretation of Quantitative Data

2.1   INTRODUCTION

If information is important, it should be communicated as accurately as possible. Numbers are used in the reporting and interpretation of quantitative information. Numbers lend themselves to the language and procedures of statistics and mathematics. Many variables can be described more precisely by using numbers rather than words. Unfortunately, the impression is often given that the use of numbers in describing individuals is dehumanizing. The view is a red herring—reports of a performance and characteristics of persons or schools, whether reported in terms of numbers, letters, or words, have precisely the same function—to convey information in a correct and accurate manner. One cannot be a literate and intelligent consumer of quantitative information without understanding some basic statistical concepts and measures.

Increasingly, educated citizens are expected to interpret information using concepts of central tendency, variability, percentiles, standard scores, reliability, and validity. Some understanding of these concepts is essential for proper use and interpretation of classroom assessments and standardized tests. In addition, at least a rudimentary grasp of basic statistical concepts is required for comprehending much of the current educational and psychological literature. Some aspects of quantitative reasoning that were once assumed to belong in rather specialized technical courses must now be considered part of general cultural education. Even to be an intelligent reader of newspapers and newsmagazines, one frequently needs knowledge of certain statistical concepts, such as mean, median, mode, percentile, correlation, and range. But it is neither appropriate nor practical to devote a *major* portion of a measurement course to statistics.

We have tried to solve this problem in several ways. In addition to the usual narrative presentation, we have interspersed sequences of programmed material throughout our sections on statistics. This type of material lends itself especially well to self-instructional methods. This dual presentation—approaching the concepts using two different instructional strategies—should reduce the amount of classroom time required for mastery of these concepts. It is the *concepts* that are critically important; the principal function of the computation is to illuminate the meaning of the concepts. When one needs statistical computations, hand calculators and especially spreadsheets such as *EXCEL* are readily available.

Following each chapter is a carefully designed mastery test to help you assess your grasp of basic concepts and assist you in identifying topics that need further study. A summary of the most common statistical terms and symbols is given at the end of each chapter.

Despite these aids, most students will probably find that they cannot read this chapter quickly and easily. It will require the same sort of careful study that you would use in studying mathematics. This effort will be rewarded by increased confidence and ability to understand and communicate information that is expressed quantitatively.

Numbers can communicate data accurately and succinctly. In describing a distribution of scores, the two most informative characteristics are summarized by measures of central tendency and variability.

2.2 FREQUENCY DISTRIBUTIONS, CENTRAL TENDENCY, AND SKEWNESS[1]

1. Many people have the mistaken notion that one must have a good mathematical background and high quantitative ability to learn and to use statistics. Whether we are aware of it or not, we all use statistics frequently. All empirical disciplines use certain statistical concepts. When discussing topics such as average rainfall, temperature, and income, we are dealing with information that is expressed statistically by using the mean, median, or mode. When the weather report gives a new high or low temperature for a given day of the year, it is conveying statistical information about the range, another statistical concept. When students' reading achievement is evaluated in relation to their IQ scores, the statistical concept of correlation is implicit. So although we may not be statisticians, we all use _____ to communicate quantitative information in our work and daily activities.

statistics

2. Statistics have many functions. They summarize and simplify kinds and quantities of data that would otherwise be unwieldy. They help to bring order out of chaos. For example, suppose you obtained a raw score of 15 on a 20-word spelling test. Of

---

[1]To obtain the maximum benefit from the programmed instruction, cover the answer, which appears in the right-hand margin, and view it only after you have responded to the item.

course, we can determine that your score was 75 percent; that gives us some information. But we can evaluate your performance much better if we know something about the difficulty of the test. If the test was composed of words like *occasion, parallel, vacuum,* or *misspell,* your score of 75 percent would mean something quite different than if the words were *travel, measure,* or *interpretation.* Your score of 15 may have been the best or even the poorest in the class. When we examine the scores of a class of 30 students, your score begins to acquire more meaning. Suppose those 30 scores were 13, 12, 15, 13, 14, 18, 13, 13, 12, 14, 16, 17, 14, 15, 11, 16, 15, 14, 19, 14, 16, 17, 11, 9, 18, 12, 17, 16, 15, and 20. It can be sensed that your score of 15 is somewhere near the middle of the group. Your score can be interpreted more accurately if these raw scores are tallied into a frequency distribution. A frequency distribution shows the number of persons (frequency, or f) who obtained each score (X). If we list each score (X) with the number of times it was obtained, we are constructing a _____ _____.

frequency
distribution

3. The spelling scores from the preceding frame are partially tallied in the following frequency distribution. Complete the distribution.

X	f				
20	/				
19	/				
18	//				
17	///				
16	////				
15	////				
14	~~////~~				
13	////				
—	—		12 ///		
—	—		11 //		
—	—		10		
—	—		9 /		

4. The frequency distribution provides a backdrop for a more meaningful interpretation of your score. We can see at a glance that the lowest score was 9 and the highest score was _____ , resulting in a difference or *range*[2] of _____ points.

20, 11

5. The range gives us some idea of the variability of a set of scores, but information regarding where the scores tend to cluster (or tend centrally) is also useful. There are three commonly used measures of central tendency: *mean, median,* and *mode.* The score that occurs most frequently is called the *mode.* From the frequency distribution of the spelling scores, we can see that more students earned the score of _____ than any other single score; therefore, the _____ of this distribution is _____.

14, mode, 14

---

[2]To obtain the range, simply subtract the lowest score from the highest score.

6. We can determine the mode of a distribution by finding the score that has the greatest _____. The mode of the distribution in Frame 3 is _____.

frequency, 14

7. The mode of the following set of scores {1, 3, 4, 4, 4, 5, 6} is _____.

4

8. Another measure of central tendency is the *median*. The median is the point that divides the distribution of scores of the examinees into two equal halves. The median is another name for the fiftieth percentile (50th percentile or P_{50}) because 50 percent of the scores fall below it. The median of the following set of scores {11, 12, 12, 13, 14, 15, 17} is _____ , but the mode is _____.

13, 12

9. The simplest way to determine the median is to rank order the raw scores and then count up to the middle score—that is, to the point that exceeds one-half of the scores. The median for the following distribution of scores {52, 59, 61, 66, 68, 75, 77, 84, 88} is _____. (Scores at the median are considered to be half above and half below the median; hence, 50 percent of the $N = 9$ scores, i.e., 4.5 scores, fell below the median.)

68

10. In the distribution of scores in Frame 9, there were _____ scores above the median and _____ scores below the median. Another name for the median is the _____ percentile.

$4\frac{1}{2}$, $4\frac{1}{2}$, 50th

11. When there is an even number (N) of scores, the median is halfway between the two middle-most scores of ranked data. For example, the median of the set of scores {21, 23, 24, 25} is _____. The median of the distribution in Frame 3 is _____.

$23\frac{1}{2}$, $14\frac{1}{2}$

12. If one additional score, 30, were added to the distribution in Frame 11, the median would become _____.

24

13. If one additional score, 50, were added to the distribution in Frame 9, the median would become _____.

67

14. For the following frequency distribution, the mode is _____. How many scores of 6 were there? _____ From the frequency column we can determine that N, the number of scores in the distribution, is _____. The median of the distribution is _____.

7, 2, 9, 7

X	f
9	1
8	2
7	3
6	2
5	1

15. You have demonstrated your understanding of the mode and median. Even though the median is best for most descriptive purposes, the most widely used measure of central tendency, however, is the mean or average. The *mean* is simply the sum of the scores divided by the number of scores. The procedure for computing the mean is defined by the following formula:

$$\text{Mean} = \mu = \frac{\Sigma X}{N}$$

where
Σ is a symbol meaning "the sum of,"
X represents scores, and
N is the number of scores.

This formula is simply a shorthand way of saying that the mean equals the _____ of the scores divided by the _____ of scores.

sum, number

---

16. Let's try an example. Find the mean of these scores: {2, 3, 5, 7, 8, 9}.

$\Sigma X = 2 + 3 + 5 + 7 + 8 + 9 =$ _____ , and $N =$ _____ ; therefore,

mean $= \dfrac{34}{6}$ or 5.67.

34, 6

For the following set of scores {3, 2, 5, 8, 2},
$\Sigma X =$ _____ , $N =$ _____ , and mean = _____ .

20, 5, 4

---

17. Let's review. There are three commonly used measures of central tendency. Usually the scores will cluster around the most frequently occurring score, which is called the _____. The point that separates the frequency distribution into equal-sized groups (i.e., halves) is called the _____. The most dependable or stable measure of central tendency tends to be the _____.

mode, median, mean

---

18. The mean is sensitive to the value of every score in the distribution; this is not true of the mode or the median. To illustrate this characteristic, consider the distribution given in Frame 14. If, for example, a score of 3 had been incorrectly recorded as a score of 6, when the correction is made, the values of the _____ and _____ would not change, whereas the value of the _____ would decrease.

median, mode, mean

---

19. Many distributions are approximately symmetrical and rather bell-shaped. The distributions of many human traits, such as height, weight, IQ score, and reaction time, tend to show this pattern. Theoretical distributions that are precisely symmetrical and have a certain mathematically specified bell shape are termed *normal* distributions. In a true normal distribution, the mode, median, and mean have the **same** value. Since IQ scores tend to be approximately normally distributed with a mean IQ of 100, the median and the mode of IQ scores are also approximately _____.

100

20. If the mean and the median of a distribution differ considerably, the shape of the distribution is not symmetrical and therefore cannot be _____. (All normal distributions are symmetrical, but many symmetrical distributions are not _____.)

normal, normal

21. The shape of a distribution can provide some useful clues about the adequacy of a test. These unimodal (one-mode) asymmetrical distributions, such as the one in the following diagram, are said to be *skewed* (it appears as if a normal curve has been pushed to one side). When the tail points to the left, the curve is said to be skewed negatively or skewed to the left. In this distribution there were many rather _____ scores but relatively few _____ scores; the distribution would be described as being _____ negatively. Scores on mastery or criterion-referenced (see Chapter 7) tests are often negatively skewed.

high, low, skewed

Low   High
 −   +
              Scores

22. A test may be so difficult that there are many low scores and few high ones. Such a distribution would be described as being skewed _____. Draw a distribution with positive skewing. (Low scores are always plotted to the left and high scores to the right, just as in the preceding frame.)

positively

23. When skewing is present and the number of scores is large, the three measures will differ systematically. As shown in the following figures, the mean is always *pulled* most toward the tail and the mode the least; the median is between the mean and the mode. Since the height of the curve represents frequency, the highest point in the curve indicates the _____ of the distribution. On a very easy test, like the one represented in Frame 21, the median will be greater than the _____ but less than the _____.

mode, mean, mode

       Md Mo   Mo Md
       Mean   Mean

24. If the mean is considerably greater than the median, the distribution is probably skewed _____. If the mean has the lowest value of the three measures of central tendency, the distribution is probably skewed _____; if the mean, median, and mode have the same value, the shape of the distribution may be _____.

positively, negatively, symmetrical

25. Which of the following four terms *least* belongs with the other three?
normal   skewed   bell-shaped   symmetrical

skewed

26. Let's return to the common situation in which a test was very easy for a given group of examinees. The actual shape of the curve for the group of test scores will be skewed _____. The measure of central tendency with the largest value is the _____; the measure of central tendency with the smallest value is the _____.

negatively, mode, mean

One line shows actual distribution of scores on an *easy* test; the other shows the distribution of *true ability*.

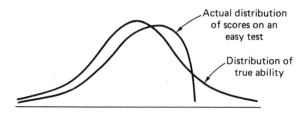

27. The measurement of ability differences with the easy test in Frame 26 was adequate for examinees of low ability, but true differences in ability were obscured for the more capable examinees since the test lacks an adequate ceiling. A test with an inadequate ceiling is like a high-jump apparatus that does not allow the crossbar to go beyond a certain height, a height that is below the jumping ability of several participants. (The psychological effect on the talented may be similar in both situations; that is, challenge and motivation for improvement may be decreased.) The reliability of the test is related to the extent to which the distribution of observed scores and the distribution of the examinees' true abilities are similar. Distributions of true abilities are rarely substantially skewed unless one is assessing knowledge of recently studied content that is primarily factual rather than conceptual or process oriented. A rough indication of skewness can be obtained by comparing the measures of central tendency, especially the mean and the median. (The mode is quite unreliable unless the number of scores is very large; consequently, it is not very useful for indicating skewness.) If the mean and the median are close in value, the distribution is probably not seriously skewed. For example, if the mean IQ for a class is found to be 110 and the median 100, the distribution is probably skewed _____. If a class had a mean of 89.3 and a median of 90.1, does skewing appear to be negligible? _____

positively, yes

28. Sketch a distribution that has a mean of 70, a median of 65, and a mode of 55. (The median is usually closer to the mean than it is to the mode.[3]) The distribution is skewed _____.

positively

Mo | *Mean*
Md

29. If the mean of a large distribution is 40 and the median is 50, the mode is probably
_____ than 50.   greater

With this introduction, the concepts of central tendency and skewness and other related concepts will now be developed in narrative style.

2.3 CLASSIFICATION AND TABULATION

Test scores and other quantitative data can be understood and interpreted more clearly if they are organized and summarized in an orderly manner. Table 2–1 shows the results of a test administered to a class of 20 students. However, the scores are difficult to interpret unless they are organized. For example, we can tell only with some difficulty whether Rosa, with a score of 80, is a very superior student or just average when compared with her peers. Knowing that the maximum score was 100 is of some value, but of less value than people often assume because the difficulty of a test is arbitrary—it is easy to ask simple or difficult questions about the same material.

TABLE 2–1 Test Scores for 20 Students

Name	Score	Name	Score	Name	Score	Name	Score
Rosa	80	Bruno	95	David	75	Stacey	75
Maxine	66	Derek	78	Jackson	81	Jonathan	81
Pierre	87	Barbara	70	Christine	81	Annie	71
Ila	84	Alfred	83	Kenda	89	Beata	85
Reuben	85	Rachel	96	Sherry	89	Cynthia	85

2.4 THE UNGROUPED FREQUENCY DISTRIBUTION

An "ungrouped" frequency distribution can be a useful way of presenting test data. If we start with the highest score and list every possible score with its frequency (if any) until we have included the lowest score, we have constructed an ungrouped *frequency distribution*. (see Table 2–2) The various scores are arranged in order of size (here, from 96 to 66), and to the right of each score the number of times it occurs is tallied. The total of the frequency column is N, the total number of scores (in this case, $N = 20$).

---

[3]In distributions based on many cases, the median tends to be twice as far from the mode as it is from the mean.

TABLE 2–2 Scores from Table 2–1 Tabulated into an Ungrouped Frequency Distribution

Score	Frequency
96	/
95	/
94	
93	
92	
91	/
90	
89	//
88	
87	/
86	
85	///
84	/
83	/
82	
81	//
80	/
79	
78	/
77	
76	
75	//
74	
73	
72	
71	/
70	/
69	
68	
67	
66	/

2.5 CENTRAL TENDENCY AND VARIABILITY

The two most important statistical concepts that apply to test data are central tendency and variability. These concepts are useful in summarizing the main features of a mass of data. It is possible to understand them at a conceptual level without having the computational details at your fingertips. The computations serve to enrich the understanding of the statistical concepts.

The tendency for the scores to be concentrated about some *center* is characteristic of most frequency distributions, as is typified to some extent by the data shown in Table 2–2.

An important statistic is the center around which the scores tend to be grouped or clustered—*central tendency* measures. The purpose of measures of central tendency is to give a succinct summary that represents the whole distribution.

We might want to compare the performances of several schools or classes on a certain test. To accomplish this, we would compute an average for each school and then note which had the highest average and which the lowest. There are three common measures of central tendency: the median, the mean (short for arithmetic mean), and the mode.

2.6   THE MEDIAN

The median is a widely used measure of central tendency. The median is the *point* that divides the distribution into halves. Of the 20 scores in Table 2–2, half (10) are 84 or above; the other half are for scores of 83 or below. Thus, the midpoint of the distribution is between 83 and 84, or 83.5. This is the same point that we would arrive at by arranging the 20 test papers in decreasing order by score (96, 95, 91, ... , 70, 66) and then counting halfway down the pile. The average of the score on the tenth test paper (84) and the score on the eleventh test paper (83) is 83.5, the point in the test score distribution above and below which half of the scores lie. This point is called the *median*.

In an ungrouped distribution, when N is an odd number, the middle-most score is the median. For example, if 31 students took a test, the sixteenth-highest score would be the median—15 scores would be above it and 15 scores below it. Strictly speaking, when N is an even number, there is no middle score. In that case the middle pair of scores is averaged, as was done in the example given in Table 2–2. As noted, the median of the distribution of the 20 scores shown in Table 2–2 is 83.5 (the average of the middle pair of scores). Since the median is the point that divides a distribution of scores into two equal-sized groups, 50 percent of the scores are below the median and 50 percent of the scores are above the median. Stated differently, *the median is always the 50th percentile.*[4]

The median is often used as a reference point for describing the location of individual students in a distribution. A student in the upper half is said to be "above the median," one in the lower half "below the median." If John received a score of 29 on a test with a median of 26, he scored in the upper half of the class.

If scores are ranked (as in an ungrouped frequency distribution), the median can be easily obtained by counting up (or down) to the point below (or above) which half of the cases fall. For most purposes, the median is the most useful, descriptive measure of the *central tendency*.

2.7   THE MEAN

The most common measure of central tendency is the *mean*. When *average* is used in ordinary conversation or in newspapers in such statements as "average temperature," "average

---

[4]The percentile is the percent of a distribution or set of scores that falls below a particular score.

rainfall," "average height for a given weight," and "average income," ordinarily the mean is indicated.

If you place dimes at 1, 3, and 8 inches on a 12-inch ruler, it would balance with a fulcrum placed at 4 inches. The torque (or force to rotate) on one side of the mean is equal to that on the other side: $8 - 4 = (4 - 3) + (4 - 1)$. By thinking of frequencies as weights, we see immediately that any score distribution balances (center of gravity) at its mean, not at its median or mode—except, of course, when they are equal to the mean. *Note also* that $(1 - 4) + (3 - 4) + (8 - 4) = -3 + (-1) + 4 = 0$: The sum of the deviations around the mean is *always* zero.

The mean can be computed simply by summing the scores and dividing by the number of scores. The number so obtained is the value that each individual would have if all shared equally. Unlike the median, the mean is affected by the *magnitude* of every score in the distribution. Increase any score by 10 points and you increase the mean by $10/N$ points. Increase the highest score in a typical distribution (where $N > 2$) or decrease the lowest score all you please, the *median* will not be changed. On well-constructed tests designed to measure individual differences, the mean will usually differ little from the median.

When N includes all persons in the group to be described (i.e., when it is *not* a sample), the symbol μ is used for the mean of the entire group of interest (known in statistics as the population). If the mean is based on only a sample, the symbol $\overline{X}$ denotes the mean of the sample. For classroom purposes, the class is a population and the appropriate symbol for the mean is μ. If one has access to a spreadsheet, the mean, median, and mode are pre-programmed functions that do the computations instantaneously. The formula for the mean is presented in Equation 2.1.

EQUATION 2.1

$$\mu = \frac{\Sigma X}{N}$$

where
   X represents scores,
   ΣX represents the sum of all scores, and
   N is the number of scores.

Using the data given in Table 2–2, we find that ΣX, the sum of all 20 scores, is 1646. Substituting these values into the formula for the mean, we find that

$$\mu = \frac{\Sigma X}{N}$$

$$= \frac{1646}{20} \text{ or } 82.3$$

You will notice that in our example the mean (82.3) and median (83.5) are quite close in value. This will be the case in any approximately symmetrical distribution. One of the most important symmetrical distributions is the *normal distribution*, often called the *normal curve*. Approximations of this type of distribution describe many human characteristics and abilities. The normal distribution is discussed later in this chapter and in Chapter 3.

2.8   THE MODE

The most frequently occurring score is called the *mode*. It is determined by inspecting the frequencies. In Table 2–2 the mode of the scores is 85 because more students (three) obtained this score than any other score. The mode is not very stable, especially with small groups. In the example in Table 2–2, changing even one score could shift the mode considerably. If one of the students who scored 85 had scored 75, the mode would decrease from 85 to 75. Largely because of its instability, the mode is not a very useful measure of central tendency on quantitative variables for small groups. One can, however, use the mode even with categorical variables such as ethnicity or college major.

2.9   COMPARISONS OF THE MEAN, MEDIAN, AND MODE

Which average is best? The mean is greatly influenced by skewness (see Frame 23), so for *descriptive* purposes the median is usually best. For example, if a test is very difficult, there may be several zero or chance scores; if a test is very easy, there may be several perfect scores. But in neither case are individual differences among the students at the extremes measured accurately. The median is often the best or most descriptive measure of central tendency. (With skewed distribution, it is possible for 60 percent, 70 percent, or more of the scores to be below average[5]) The median income of families in the United States is more informative than the mean; perhaps 60 percent of families have incomes below the average because of the extreme influence of the extremely wealthy on the mean. As an example:

> In professional sports, the distribution of salaries tends to be highly skewed positively (due to the extremely high salaries of the superstars). Consequently the players' union prefers to report the median salary for the players, whereas the owners prefer to report the mean salary. The median is usually the best single measure, although each average conveys some complementary information. The "average" household contribution to charity might be $0 or $2000, depending on whether the mode or the mean was used. Obviously, no single measure of central tendency is adequate unless distributions are normal (or symmetrical). Fortunately, we need not choose one but can report two or three different measures of central tendency as needed to summarize the distribution accurately. In order to adequately describe a distribution, in addition to measures of central tendency, measures of heterogeneity or variability are also needed.

---

[5]For example, if 24 of the 25 students in a class get perfect scores on a test, 24 of the 25 students (or 96%) will be above average!

2.10   MEASURES OF VARIABILITY

30. Although measures of central tendency indicate the values about which the scores tend to cluster, they provide no information on the degree of individual differences or variability that exists among students. We have already been introduced to one measure of variability—the difference between the highest and the lowest scores— called the _____.

range

31. To illustrate why measures of variability are needed, consider the following normal distributions, which could depict IQ scores from the students at two different schools. Both distributions have identical means, modes, and _____. Although their central tendencies are the same, they differ greatly in their degree of dispersion or _____.

medians,
variability

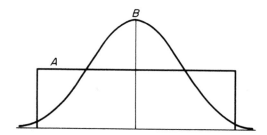

32. In the preceding frame, the more heterogeneous class (the one with the greater degree of individual differences) is class _____. The more homogeneous class (the one with the lesser variability in scores) is class _____.

B, A

33. Since the range is a crude, undependable indicator of variability, more refined measures of dispersion have been devised. The most widely used is the *standard deviation*, which is symbolized for a population by the Greek letter σ (sigma), or for a sample by the symbol s. We know now that the mean, median, and mode are measures of central tendency, while the range, variance, and standard deviation are measures of _____.

variability

34. A simple example will illustrate the direct computation of the variance. The formula for the variance[6] is

$$\sigma^2 = \frac{\Sigma x^2}{N}$$

where
   σ^2 is the variance of the distribution of scores,
   N is the number of scores, and
   Σx^2 is the sum of the squared deviation of each of the N scores from the mean, μ, i.e., $x = X - \mu$.

For example, suppose the scores of five examinees on a test were 40, 35, 30, 25, 20.

X	x	x^2
40	___	___
35	___	___
30	___	___
25	___	___
20	___	___
$\Sigma X =$ ___	$\Sigma x^2 =$ ___	

Recall that to compute the mean, you find the sum of the raw scores and divide that sum by the number of scores; thus, $\mu = \dfrac{\Sigma X}{N}$,

$\mu = ($___$)/($___$)$, or $\mu =$ _____.   150, 5, 30

---

35. Since x is the deviation of X from μ, we simply subtract μ from each raw score; that is, $x = X - \mu$. For the score of 40, compute x.

$x = ($ $) - ($ $)$ or ___.   40, 30, 10

---

36. For the score of 20, $x = 20 - ($ $)$ or ___.   30, –10

---

37. Enter the x-values (deviations) for 40 and 20 in the column of Frame 34. The x-values for the three other scores (25, 30, and 35) are _____ , _____ , and _____ , respectively.   –5, 0, 5

---

38. The x^2-column represents the *square*[7] of the deviation, x. The deviation, x, for the score of 40 was found to be 10; therefore, the square of 10 is entered in the corresponding row in the x^2-column; $10^2 =$ _____. The deviation, x, for the score of 20 is (-10); the square, $(-10)^2$, is _____. Since the square of a negative number is always positive, the values in the x^2-column are always positive.   100, 100

---

39. The corresponding x^2-values for scores 35, 30, 25, and 20 are _____ , _____ , _____ , and _____.   25, 0, 25, 100

---

[6]Since in typical classroom applications, the class of students includes all persons about whom we wish to make an inference (i.e., we do not wish to generalize beyond the set of obtained scores to any larger group (population) the symbol σ is appropriate—σ is a descriptive (not inferential) statistic. If one is viewing a set of scores as a sample of a larger population, then N–1 (rather than N) is used in the denominator of Equation 2.2, and the symbol s (rather than σ) is employed. The computation of s using N–1 rather than N as the denominator of Equation 2.2 makes s a better estimate of the population standard deviation, σ, but even then s tends to slightly underestimate the parameter, σ, although the bias is trivial except when N is very small (Hopkins, Hopkins & Glass, 1996, p. 61).

40. The formula calls for Σx^2 and N; in this problem, $N =$ _____.

5

---

41. Since the symbol, Σ, means "the sum of," Σx^2 is the total of the x^2-column. For the data in Frame 34, $\Sigma x^2 =$ _____.

250

---

42. Let's plug in our numerical values for N and Σx^2 into the formula:

$$\sigma^2 = \frac{\sum x^2}{N} = \frac{(\underline{})}{(\underline{})} = (\underline{})$$

250/5, 50

---

43. Although the variance is widely used in statistical inference, it is not a good descriptive statistic. Its square root[8], the *standard deviation*, is used extensively in interpreting test performance. To obtain the square root of 50, enter 50 into a hand calculator and hit the square root key ($\sqrt{}$). This yields approximately 7.07, therefore $7.07 \times 7.07 \approx$ ____.

50

---

44. In summary: The mean (μ) of the distribution with which we have been working (40, 35, 30, 25, 20) is _____ , its variance (σ^2) is _____, and its standard deviation (σ) is _____.

30, 50,
7.07 (or 7.1)

---

45. Let's review the steps in the computation of the standard deviation, σ.

1. Compute the mean (μ).
2. Find the deviation (x) of each score from the mean ($x = X - \mu$).
3. Square these deviations.
4. Find the average of these squared deviations (i.e., divide their sum (Σx^2) by the number of scores, N). This average is the variance, σ^2.
5. The square root of the variance is the standard deviation of the distribution and is denoted by the symbol _____.

σ

---

46. In Frames 46–50, you will compute the standard deviation for the following distribution of scores {4, 7, 3, 0, 2, 3, 2}:

---

[7]Recall that when a number is squared, it is multiplied by itself, thus $3^2 = 9$, and $(-3)^2 = 9$. Stated differently, the square root of a number X is that number which multiplied by itself equals X. The square root of 49 is 7 because $7 \times 7 = 49$.

[8]You once learned, and then mercifully forgot, the barbarous procedure for calculating the square root of a number. The computations are so onerous that square root tables were once common in measurement textbooks. Now, hand calculators and spreadsheets give square roots instantly and painlessly! Many hand calculators are programmed to compute the mean and standard deviation of a distribution.

X	x	x^2	
7	—	—	
4	—	—	
3	—	—	
3	—	—	
2	—	—	
2	—	—	
0	—	—	
$\Sigma X = $ ____			21

47. The mean (μ) of the distribution is ____. The deviations in column x, from top to bottom are 4, 1, 0, 0, –1, ____ , and ____.

3, –1, –3

48. The corresponding x^2-values from top to bottom are 16, 1, 0, 0, 1, ____ , and ____. The value for $\Sigma x^2 = $ ____.

1, 9, 28

49. The variance (σ^2) of the distribution is ( )/( ) = ____.

28/7, 4

50. The standard deviation is the square root of the variance: $\sigma = \sqrt{4}$ or __.

2

Now that we have computed the standard deviation, you are probably asking, So what? We will soon see how the standard deviation is used in interpreting performance, especially on standardized tests.

Central tendency and variability convey important information about the quality of a measure such as a test. Central tendency depicts a test's level of difficulty, and variability indicates the degree of individual *differences* among the scores. Let's now review and overlearn these concepts.

2.11 THE MEANING OF VARIABILITY

No distribution is adequately described solely by a measure of central tendency. The mean intelligence in two classes may be the same, and yet the classes may be very dissimilar— the ability level in one class may vary all the way from students with borderline mental retardation to students who are gifted, but the individual differences among members of another (homogeneously grouped) class can be much less. Obviously, these two classes, with equal means, present very different instructional strategies because of differences in variability. *Variability* is the extent to which the scores of a group tend to differ or spread above and below a central point in the distribution. Clearly, it is important to have some convenient method of describing the variability of a group. Two common measures of variability are the *range* and the *standard deviation*. Whereas measures of central tendency are points, these measures of variability are expressed as differences; the larger their values, the greater the variability (scatter, spread, heterogeneity, dispersion) in the distribution of scores.

2.12   THE RANGE

The *range* is simply the difference between the highest score and the lowest score. From the data given in Table 2–2, the range can be determined readily:

Range = the highest score (96) minus the lowest score (66) = 30 points.

Since the range depends solely on the two most extreme scores, it conveys limited information as a measure of variability. A shift in a single score may greatly alter the range. In addition, the range is highly dependent on the number of scores in the set. As the size of the group increases, the range will tend to increase; therefore, the ranges of groups of unequal size cannot be meaningfully compared. For example, we would expect the range for a random sample of 50 scores from an infinite population of normally distributed scores to be twice that of a set of five scores (Hopkins, Hopkins & Glass 1996, p. 63). Nevertheless, the range does convey some useful information about the degree of heterogeneity in a set of scores.

2.13   THE VARIANCE AND STANDARD DEVIATION

A second measure of variability, which has many uses in educational and psychological measurement, is the *standard deviation*, represented by the Greek letter sigma, σ. It is defined as the square root of the variance—the mean of the squared deviations of the scores from their mean.

Let us illustrate the computation of the standard deviation of a set of test scores. Equation 2.2 shows the standard deviation to be the square root of the variance, σ^2:

EQUATION 2.2

$$\sigma^2 = \frac{\Sigma x^2}{N} = \frac{\Sigma(X - \mu)^2}{N}$$

Using the 20 scores of Table 2–2, whose mean we already know to be 82.3 (see Section 2.7), the variance is:

$$\sigma^2 = \frac{(96 - 82.3)^2 + (95 - 82.3)^2 + \ldots + (66 - 82.3)^2}{20}$$

$$= \frac{(13.7)^2 + (12.7)^2 + \ldots + (-16.3)^2}{20}$$

$$= \frac{187.69 + 161.29 + \ldots + 265.69}{20} = \frac{1240.2}{20} = 62.01$$

The standard deviation (σ) is the square root of the variance.

$$\sigma = \sqrt{62.01} \text{ or } 7.87$$

In practice, when the computation of the standard deviation is needed, a hand calculator or spreadsheet is useful. Unless you wish to estimate test reliability or validity, you will not need to compute σ. The principal use of the standard deviation is in the interpretation of performance when norms are available, as we will see in the next chapter. For example, in a normal distribution, approximately two-thirds of the scores fall within one standard deviation of the mean. On most intelligence tests, the standard deviation of IQ scores is 15 points. Since the mean IQ is 100, approximately two-thirds of the IQs fall between 85 and 115. Because the distribution of IQ scores tends to be symmetrical, the remaining one-third of the scores is split evenly below 85 and above 115; approximately one-sixth of the IQ scores exceed 115 and approximately one-sixth fall below 85.

2.14 WHICH MEASURE IS BEST?

The standard deviation is an important measure of the variability of test scores. A small standard deviation indicates that there is little heterogeneity with a group—that is, it is relatively homogeneous with respect to the characteristic in question. A large standard deviation indicates great heterogeneity. As used in measurement, the standard deviation is considered the best and most useful measure of variability; the range is of some interest but is a crude measure of variability.

The standard deviation is of interest chiefly because it is used a great deal by test publishers and educational researchers. On standardized tests the position of a student in a distribution is often expressed in terms of standard deviation units, as we shall see in Chapter 3. Part of the next chapter is devoted to a study of information from test manuals, for which an understanding of the mean and standard deviation will serve you well.

SUMMARY

The following is an outline of some concepts that are useful in connection with test scores and other quantitative data:

I. *Central tendency and skewness*
   A. The *mean*, μ, or average, is obtained by adding all the scores and dividing their sum, ΣX, by the number of scores, N. It is the most widely employed measure of central tendency and usually the most reliable.
   B. The *median (Md)* is the point above which half of the scores lies and below which the other half lies; it is the 50th percentile. The median is easier to interpret than the mean, especially with skewed distributions. Scores tend to be closer to the median than to the mean or mode; it is the most useful measure of central tendency for descriptive purposes.

    C. The *mode* is the most frequent score and is a rather crude measure of central tendency unless the number of scores is very large.

    D. In symmetrical distributions, the mean, median, and mode are equal.

    E. In skewed distributions the mean is *pulled* toward the elongated *tail* and the median falls between the mode and the mean. The mean will have the lowest value in negatively skewed distributions and the highest value in positively skewed distributions. The median tends to be closer to the mean than to the mode.

  II. *Variability*

    A. Like the mean, the *standard deviation*, σ, is influenced by the value of every measure in the distribution. Approximately two-thirds of all scores in a normal distribution lie within plus or minus one standard deviation from the mean.

    B. The *range* is the distance between the highest score and the lowest score. It is a crude measure of variability and should be used primarily as a supplement to the standard deviation.

IMPORTANT TERMS AND CONCEPTS

central tendency	positive and negative skewness	standard deviation (σ)
mean (μ)	variability	frequency distribution
median	range	normal distribution
mode	variance (σ^2)	symmetrical distribution

CHAPTER TEST

Questions 1–6 refer to the following distribution of scores:

1, 1, 1, 2, 2, 3, 5, 8, 12, 20.

1. Find the mode.

2. Find the median.

3. Find the value of N.

4. Find the value of ΣX.

5. Find the mean.

6. What is the shape of the distribution?

7. In a negatively skewed distribution, which measure of central tendency tends to have the smallest value? The largest value?

8. In skewed distributions, which one of the three measures of central tendency tends to fall between the other two?

9. Which measure of central tendency is the 50th percentile? Do 50 percent of the scores fall below the median even in extremely skewed distributions?

10. Which term *least* belongs with the others?

a) mode
b) median
c) most popular score
d) most frequent score

11. In a distribution of scores for which the mean = 65.5, median = 64, and mode = 60, it was found that a mistake had been made on one score. Instead of 70, the score should have been 90. Consequently, which of these measures of central tendency would certainly be changed?
a) mean
b) mode
c) median
d) Two or more of the above would certainly change.

In Questions 12–16, match the verbal and graphic descriptions.

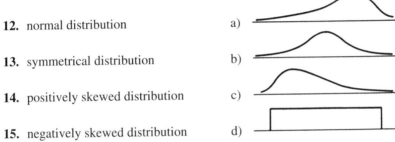

12. normal distribution

13. symmetrical distribution

14. positively skewed distribution

15. negatively skewed distribution

16. Which two distributions in Questions 12–15 are symmetrical?

In Questions 17 and 18, indicate whether the skewing in the distributions will be positive or negative.

17. U.S. household income in dollars for the last year.

18. Age at graduation from college

19. If most students in this class have mastered this chapter thoroughly so that they know the answers to almost all questions on this mastery test, the distribution of scores would probably be
a) symmetrical
b) skewed negatively
c) skewed positively
d) rectangular
e) normal

Questions 20–23 pertain to two measures of variability; select range *or* standard deviation.

20. Which is easy to understand?

21. Which tends to become much larger as sample size increases?

22. Which is simple to calculate?

23. Which is widely used on standardized tests?

Questions 24–28: In a sixth-grade class of 30 students, a "Guess Who" sociometric technique was administered to assess the degree of positive peer relationships for each of the students. Construct a frequency distribution for the scores for the 30 students.

0, 1, 1, 1, 1, 1, 2, 2, 2, 2, 3, 3, 3, 4, 4, 5, 5,
7, 8, 8, 9, 10, 11, 12, 13, 15, 17, 28, 33, 41

24. Describe the distribution
   a) symmetrical
   b) skewed positively
   c) skewed negatively.

25. Determine the range.

26. Find the mode.

27. Find the median.

28. From the values for the mode and median, the mean would be expected to be:
   a) greater than 4.5
   b) less than 4.5

29. Which of the following is *not* characteristic of a normal distribution?
   a) symmetry
   b) unimodal (having one mode)
   c) skewed
   d) bell-shaped

ANSWERS TO CHAPTER TEST

1. 1	16. b and d
2. 2.5	17. positive
3. 10	18. positive
4. 55	19. b
5. 5.5	20. range
6. positively skewed	21. range
7. mean, mode	22. range
8. median	23. standard deviation
9. median, yes	24. b
10. b	25. 41
11. a	26. 1
12. b	27. 4.5
13. b	28. a
14. c	29. c
15. a	

3

The Meaning and Application
of Norms

INTRODUCTION

Measurement and assessment are needed in individual and school appraisals. Obviously their purposes can be served only if they are interpreted correctly. The interpretation of educational and psychological tests is less straight forward than that of measurements in the physical sciences. Knowing that a child's score on a math test is 82 is less informative than knowing that the child's weight is 82 pounds. Measures of length, weight, and time are very refined; they represent *absolute* scales—scales with an absolute zero and equal units of measurement. The weight of 82 pounds is twice the weight of 41 pounds, but does a math score of 82 represent twice the knowledge of a score of 41? Obviously not.

Expressing test scores as percent-correct is useful but is often misinterpreted. Suppose the score of 45, converted to a percentage, is 90 percent. Does this high percentage certify excellent achievement or performance? It might represent high achievement, or the test could have been made up of very easy questions. The items on the mastery test at the end of the previous chapter could have been selected so that virtually everyone would score 100 percent. The meaning of test scores is enhanced when they can be viewed in relation to the performance of an appropriate *reference group*. When Mary tells her father that she got a score of 19 on a test, what is his first question? "Out of how many?" His next question is likely to be "How did the class as a whole do?" The question illustrates the usefulness of backdrop data from a reference group for enriching the meaning of test scores and other performance measures.

Norms are nothing more than information regarding the performance of a particular (reference) group to which an examinee's score can be compared. Norms can be useful with almost all measures—for example, height, blood pressure, cholesterol level, typing speed, reading comprehension, spatial ability, reaction time, or attitude toward mathematics. For example, suppose Henry, a 10-year-old boy, is 50 inches tall and weighs 80 pounds. Is his weight *about right* for his height? Who knows without norms (or at least informal norms based on experience)? If we use norms based on a national sample of 10-year-old boys, we will find that Henry appears to have a serious weight problem; he is at the 5th percentile in height but at the 75th percentile in weight. Data on a relevant reference group (i.e., norms) enrich the meaning of a direct measurement even when measurements are on an absolute scale like height, weight, and time; but norms are especially useful with measurements of educational and psychological performance resulting from measures that have neither an absolute zero point nor equal units of measurement.

3.2   NORMS ARE NOT STANDARDS

It is important to distinguish clearly between a *norm* and a *standard* because these terms are frequently misused. The confusion doubtless arises in part because norms are used with *standardized* tests and the development of norms is part of the process of standardization. Test norms are based on the actual performance of a group of persons, not on predetermined levels or standards of performance. Since many adults are overweight, the ideal weight (the standard) is well below the average weight—the norm (mean) would differ from the standard. For older adults, *normal* vision (20/20) is not the norm.

Standardized tests and measures have undergone the process of standardization. The best standardized tests have defined the *universe* carefully. Each item has been carefully scrutinized and evaluated using criteria based on content relevance (see Section 4.2), clarity, and appropriateness of vocabulary, in addition to statistical information regarding the item. This process eliminates most poor items. Further refinement results from field testing that allows the items to be evaluated empirically. In addition , the method of administration has been standardized and explicit directions have been formulated, with fixed time limits and instructions. The method of scoring also has been standardized. Finally, tables of norms have been provided to facilitate interpretation of the scores on the test. These norms are merely transformations of the raw scores into a more meaningful scale based on the performance of a large sample of persons selected to be nationally representative. Thus, norms are not standards but, instead, describe performance in relation to the reference (norm) group.

The word *standard* implies a goal or objective to be reached. *A norm is not necessarily a criterion of what is desired or what ought to be*—that is, a norm is not a goal—but a measure of what is (i.e., the *status quo*). If the average score for a school or class is at the national median on a standardized test, is there cause for rejoicing? Whether this level of performance is satisfactory cannot be determined from the norms themselves. The fact that the class average corresponds to the 50th percentile in the norm group does not of itself establish anything other than that the performance is similar in central tendency to that of the norm group. It is obvious that a group of students with superior opportunities and capabilities should be expected to perform better than a representative group (the norm group), whereas it would be exceptional for a group of students with impoverished educational opportunities to do as well as a typical group of students.

Most current standardized tests give age or grade norms based on a nationally based reference group. Some provide norms by sex, geographic region, type of school (e.g., large-city schools, public versus private schools, Title I schools), or for other subsets of the population. For achievement tests, the meaningfulness of a reference group is enhanced by the co-standardization of scholastic aptitude and achievement tests. When these tests are normed on the same group of students, there is a sounder basis for evaluating achievement in relation to measured scholastic aptitude. (The evaluation of achievement in relation to aptitude is considered more extensively in Chapter 14.)

Definitive standards, or goals of attainment, are almost altogether lacking in education. An adequate method for establishing meaningful standards has yet to be devised; such a process is inherently difficult (Jaeger, 1988; Shepard, 1980). The process of building norms, although time-consuming and expensive, is conceptually simple and straightforward. An understanding of the way norms are determined should make it obvious that norms for the general population are not, and should not be, goals of performance.

The point that norms should not be viewed as standards does not preclude such use when the standards have been established on some other basis. For example, persons who did not graduate from high school can obtain a certificate of equivalency, which is generally accepted as a high school diploma, if proficiency equivalent to the average of a representative group of high school graduates is demonstrated on the *General Educational Development Tests* (*GED*) (Graff, 1965). For example, using a standard based on a norm on the GED, a high school equivalency program for migrant farm workers has been established (Campa, Mena & Clinton, 1987). In this instance, a certain predetermined norm value is a minimal standard of performance. The validity of the standard has been supported by studies showing that people who receive high school accreditation via GED tests perform as well as regular high school graduates in industrial and public employment and almost as well in college work (Peters, 1956; Tyler, 1956; Farley, Wienhold & Crabtree, 1967). Similar procedures have been employed on the highly useful examinations of the Advanced Placement Program, in which college credit can be obtained by demonstrating competence (Casserly, 1986). Without norms of some sort, there would have been no definitive way of establishing the equivalent level of proficiency acquired outside the school setting.

Many colleges and universities participate in the *College Level Examination Program* (*CLEP*), whereby students have an opportunity to obtain college credit by examination. Examinations are available in any of approximately 50 subject areas. The examinee's performance is reported in terms of norms, but each institution establishes its own standard—the level of performance required to receive credit. The more reputable "external-college degree programs" (college credit without residence) use the CLEP tests extensively in awarding college credit.

Another example of the use of norms to define standards is illustrated in several states that require a minimum standard of a ninth-grade achievement level (defined by national norms) in reading, math, and writing in order to receive a state-approved high school diploma. Many states also use standardized tests in mandated teacher-competency examination programs (Lehmann & Phillips, 1987). Obviously, norms and standards are arrived at in very different ways and serve different purposes. The current "minimal competency" testing efforts that have used arbitrary "logical" standards have not met the challenge of criticisms very successfully (Glass, 1978a, 1978b).

In order to understand and use normative information, you must become familiar with the normal distribution and its interrelationships with the concepts of central tendency and variability introduced in Chapter 2. These concepts are needed to properly interpret the norms provided by standardized tests.

3.3   THE NORMAL DISTRIBUTION

The *normal distribution* is defined by a mathematical formula.[1] The formula is a stern taskmaster; no empirical distribution of scores meets its requirements fully. However, many random (chance) events tend to closely approximate a normal bell-shaped distribution, and so do many physical, psychomotor, and cognitive characteristics such as height, running speed, and IQ scores.

The normal curve is symmetrical; it has a single mode (identical in value to both the median and the mean) located in the middle of the distribution. In theory, the tails of this theoretical distribution would approach, but never quite intersect, the baseline. Obviously, no finite distribution of observations could ever perfectly describe such a curve. Nevertheless, many distributions of scores obtained by administration of carefully devised measures approximate the normal distribution sufficiently well to make it a useful model for interpretation.

---

1. The scores on most standardized aptitude and achievement tests (and measures of many other human characteristics) are approximately normally distributed. To properly interpret many types of norms, it is necessary to be familiar with characteristics of the normal curve. Look at the normal curve below. It is unimodal (the scores cluster around a single point) and symmetrical (if the portion to the left of the mean were folded over the right half, there would be an exact "fit"). Notice that the tails never quite touch the baseline, although they continue to approach it more closely as one moves _____ from the mean.   farther

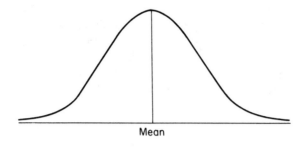

Mean

---

2. We learned previously that in normal distributions the mode, _____, and _____ are   median, mean
identical in value.

---

[1]For the formula and detailed explanations about the normal curve and its use, see Glass and Hopkins (1996) or Hopkins, Hopkins, and Glass (1996).

3. If we begin at the mean and mark to the left and to the right in units of one standard deviation, we find that a normal distribution spans approximately __ standard deviations (see curve below). That is, very few scores lie more than __ standard deviations above or below the mean.   6
3

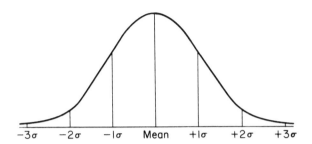

4. Since the curve is symmetrical, the area to the left of the mean equals the area to the _____ of the mean. Therefore, the area between the mean and one standard deviation above the mean is the same as that between the _____ and one standard deviation below the mean.   right
mean

5. Remembering that the height of the curve at a given point denotes the frequency of scores at that point, we can say that in a normal distribution there are as many scores that are one standard deviation above the mean as there are scores that are _____ standard deviation below the mean   one

6. It should be clear that the area under the curve between two points represents the number or frequency of scores falling between those two points. In a normal distribution 34 percent of the scores falls between the mean and one standard deviation above the mean; therefore, between the mean and one standard deviation below the mean falls __ percent of the scores.   34

7. In the following normal curve the percent of the area (or the percent of the cases) falling in the shaded area between one σ below the mean *and* one σ above the mean is __ percent + __ percent, or __ percent.   34, 34, 68

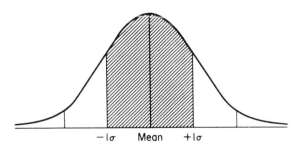

8. The area under the curve from 1σ below the mean to 1σ above the mean includes approximately two-thirds of the scores; therefore, about one-_____ of the scores falls outside this range, that is, below -1σ or above $+1\sigma$ from the mean.

third

9. We have seen that approximately one-third of the scores lies more than one standard deviation from the mean. Consequently, about one-_____ of the scores are more than 1σ above the mean, and one-sixth falls more than _____ standard deviation below the _____.

sixth
one
mean

10. The mean IQ on intelligence tests is 100, and the standard deviation is 15 (on Wechsler tests) or 16 (on the Stanford-Binet, see Figure 3–1) points. Assuming a normal distribution and $\sigma = 15$, from what we have just learned about the normal curve we can say that about two-thirds of all IQ scores fall between 85 and __, one-sixth of the IQ scores is above __, and one-_____ is below 85.

115
115, sixth

11. In Frame 10 we described the distribution of IQs in terms of approximate fractions. To be more precise (see Figure 3–1), assuming the IQ scores to be normally distributed, we would say that __ percent of the examinees obtain IQs between 85 and 115, __ percent have IQs above 115, and 16 percent have IQs below __. Eighty-four percent have IQs above __.

68
16, 85
85

12. A common method of reporting test scores is in terms of percentile norms. An IQ score of 85 exceeds the scores of 16 percent of the population—that is, the score is at the 16th percentile; the percentile *rank* of 85 is 16. An individual who obtains an IQ score of 100 exceeds __ percent of the population and therefore is said to be at the _____ percentile. An IQ score of 115 is one standard deviation above the mean, and since the percent of the IQs that fall between the mean and one standard deviation from it is __, that score exceeds __ percent more scores than are exceeded by an IQ of 100. Therefore, the percentile rank of this IQ score is __.

50
50th

34, 34
84

13. Find the percentile parts and complete the fractions that approximate the portions of the normal curve that correspond to the parts marked by the standard deviations. Only about 2 percent of the cases in a normal distribution fall below the point -2σ, two standard deviations below the mean. The corresponding percentile equivalent of -2σ to be inserted in the appropriate blank below this point on the curve is 2. Since the curve is symmetrical, can you determine the corresponding percentile value for $+2\sigma$? If 2 percent of the population falls below -2σ, then __ percent falls above $+2\sigma$. Consequently, $+2\sigma$ exceeds 98 percent of the scores and is at the __ percentile.

2
98th

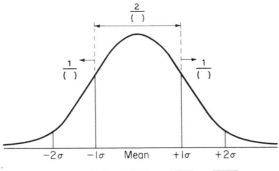

Percentile rank: ____ ____ ____ ____

---

14. One criterion for determining mental disability is an IQ score below 70 on an individual intelligence test. If the IQ distribution exactly followed the normal curve, about __ percent of the population would meet this criterion for mental disability.

2

---

15. Remembering that for a representative sample of children on the Wechsler intelligence tests the mean IQ score is __ and the standard deviation is __, insert the missing percentile ranks and corresponding IQs in the rows provided below the normal curve.

100, 15

2, 16, 50, 98
70, 85, 115,
130

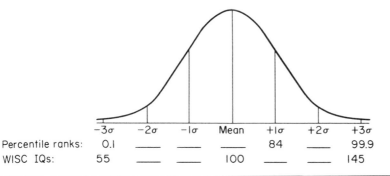

	-3σ	-2σ	-1σ	Mean	$+1\sigma$	$+2\sigma$	$+3\sigma$
Percentile ranks:	0.1	____	____	____	84	____	99.9
WISC IQs:	55	____	____	100	____	____	145

---

16. Assuming that IQ scores are normally distributed, for 100 randomly selected children we would expect approximately

__50__ percent to have IQ scores above 100
____ percent to have IQ scores above 100
____ percent to have IQ scores above 100
____ percent to have IQ scores above 100
____ percent to have IQ scores above 100
____ percent to have IQ scores above 100
____ percent to have IQ scores above 100

16
84
16
98
98
68

_____ percent to have IQ scores above 100   48
_____ percent to have IQ scores above 100   96
_____ percent to have IQ scores above 100   2
_____ percent to have IQ scores above 100   82
_____ percent to have IQ scores above 100   99.9

---

17. On a certain standardized reading test, the mean grade-equivalent (GE) score at the beginning of the third grade is 3.0. The corresponding standard deviation of the GE scores on this reading test is 1.0. Assuming a normal distribution, what are the GE scores that correspond to the points one and two standard deviations above, and below, the mean?

1.0 2.0 3.0 4.0 5.0

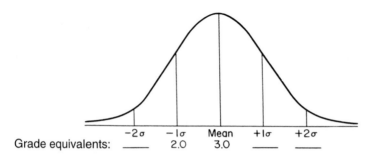

Grade equivalents: _____ -2σ -1σ Mean $+1\sigma$ $+2\sigma$
                              2.0   3.0   _____   _____

---

18. The curve in Frame 17 shows that at the beginning of grade 3, 50 percent of the pupils obtain a grade-equivalent score of __ or better. Bob's GE score on the test is 3.0, which has a percentile rank of __. Approximately one-sixth of the children receive scores above __. About 1 student in six obtains a score below __. A score of 4.0 is the __ percentile; a score of 2.0 is the __ percentile. In a typical class of 30 students, approximately 5 students will have GE scores above __ and another 5 will score below __. A grade-equivalent score of __ places a student at the 98th percentile. This score means that the student scored higher than __ of every 100 students across the nation who are entering grade 3. The middle two-thirds of a typical class will probably receive grade-equivalent scores between __ and __.

3.0
50
4.0, 2.0
84th, 16th
4.0
2.0, 5.0
98

2.0, 4.0

---

19. On the standardized reading test just described, the average beginning fourth-grade student would be expected to receive a score of __. Approximately __ percent of beginning third-grade students obtain higher scores than the average score of the beginning fourth-grade student.

4.0, 16

---

20. The _average_ student entering third grade would score higher than what percent of the students in grade 4? __

16

---

21. If the standard deviation at grade 4 were the same as that for grade 3 (it is actually slightly larger), and if the top, middle, and lower thirds of typical students in grades 3 and 4 form reading groups, as a group, which students are probably the better readers?

a) the third-grade students in the high reading group
b) the fourth-grade students in the low reading group

a

22. Suppose a student received a score of 72 on a 100-item test. Does this really give a good indication of the quality of his or her performance? This could be the highest or the lowest score for the group of examinees. What additional information is needed to give the score of 72 more meaning? You are probably thinking that knowledge of the mean or median would help, and of course it would. Suppose the mean on the test was 62. You now know that a score of 72 is a better than average score; but how much better? It is probably between the 51st and 99.9th percentiles, but at what point within this interval? It is evident that in addition to information on central tendency we also need data on _____.

variability

23. You remember that the mean is a common measure of central tendency; its companion measure of variability is the _____ _____. If we know these two measures, we can evaluate the score of 72 more accurately. Assume that the distribution of test scores was approximately normal in form (which is common on well-constructed tests) and that the standard deviation was 5. Since the mean was 62 and the student's score was 72, the score is __ standard deviations above the mean. This is equivalent to a percentile rank of __. Now the score of 72 has taken on more meaning.

standard
deviation

2
98

24. Fortunately, statisticians and psychometricians have devised a system of reporting test scores on standardized tests so that the interpreter always knows the mean and the standard deviation. Scores of this type are called *standard scores*. Regardless of what the raw score mean and standard deviation on a given test happen to be, they are converted to a fixed mean and a fixed standard deviation. The raw scores are then expressed in terms of a standard score scale; hence, they are called standard scores. Since the standard score mean and the standard deviation are known and fixed, any given score automatically takes on meaning. Standard scores are especially useful for standardized tests. It is impractical for a teacher to refer back continually to a test manual for the values of the mean and the standard deviation. Scores expressed in terms of a standard, constant mean and a standard, constant standard deviation are called _____ _____.

standard
scores

25. Look at Figure 3–1, which shows the normal curve. Notice the section illustrating typical standard scores. The z-scale is simply a standard score in which a raw score is expressed in terms of the number of standard deviations it deviates from the mean. A raw score one standard deviation above the mean is equivalent to a z-score of +1; that is, the raw score is $+1\sigma$ above the mean raw score. If, for example, a score is one-half of a standard deviation below the mean, the corresponding z-score is −.5. A minus value for a z-score indicates that the score falls below the _____. A z-score of +2 is two _____ _____ above the mean.

mean
standard
deviations

26. A score of 72 on a test with a mean of 62 and a standard deviation of 5 is __ standard deviations above the mean. Expressed as a z-score, the score of 72 is __.

2
+2

27. Obviously, the mean deviates not at all from itself; therefore, the mean z-score is __,   0
and the z-score of the mean is __.   0

---

28. By definition, the standard deviation of the z-score distribution is __. If the mean of a   1
raw score distribution is 80 and the standard deviation is 12, a score of 68 expressed
as a z-score will be __.   −1

---

29. The z-score system itself is not widely used in reporting test results, but it does
enable us to understand better the standard scores that are. Notice the T-score row of
Figure 3–1. The T-score type of standard score has a mean of __. If we move to a   50
point one standard deviation above the mean, we can see that the standard deviation
of the T-score system is __, since we move up 10 units in going from the mean (50)   10
to one standard deviation above the mean (60).

---

30. Recall that a score at the 2nd percentile is about __ standard deviations below the   2
mean. Expressed in T-score units, this would be __, since it is two standard devia-   30
tions (or $2 \times 10 = 20$) below the T-score mean of __.   50

---

31. If two tests report results using T-scores, an examinee's relative level of performance can be compared directly without any additional information, since the mean
and the _____ _____ for both sets of scores will be the same.   standard
deviation

---

32. Consider the following example, which illustrates the advantages of standard score
norms: Miss Martin teaches sixth grade. Suppose one of her students, Tommy,
obtained an IQ of 130 on a group intelligence test and a grade-equivalent score of 7.6
on a reading test. Is his reading relatively better or poorer than his performance on
the intelligence test? Miss Martin no doubt knows that an IQ of 130 is a high score
and that 7.6 is a good reading score, but are they equally good? Is a grade-placement
score of 7.6 relatively better or poorer than an IQ of 130? Are their percentile ranks
equivalent? As it stands, Miss Martin has no way of knowing without obtaining information on the central tendency and variability of the respective tests. Suppose she
obtains the following information from the test manuals:

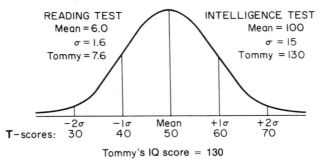

READING TEST INTELLIGENCE TEST
Mean = 6.0 Mean = 100
$\sigma = 1.6$ $\sigma = 15$
Tommy = 7.6 Tommy = 130

T−scores: −2σ −1σ Mean +1σ +2σ
30 40 50 60 70

Tommy's IQ score = 130

Tommy is __ standard deviations above the mean on the intelligence test, which   2
would be equivalent to a T-score of __. On the reading test, he is only __ standard   70, 1

deviation above the mean, which is equivalent to a *T*-score of __. Now, it is obvious that his reading performance is not nearly as outstanding as his performance on the intelligence test, although he is well above average on both measures.

    60

---

33. Notice that the teacher needed to go to the test manuals to determine the relative status of 130 and 7.6. If both tests had used the same standard scoring system, such as *T*-scores, the relative status would have been apparent at a glance. Since the standard deviation for the *T*-score type of standard score is 10, the *T*-score of __ on the intelligence test would exceed the *T*-score on the reading test of __ by 10 points, or 1σ.

    70
    60

---

34. It is evident that Miss Martin's task of comparing scores would be much easier and more accurate if the results on all the tests were expressed in _____ scores.

    standard (or *T*-)

---

35. Assume in a distribution with a mean of 33 and a standard deviation of 12 that a given raw score was 45. The score of 45 would be __ standard deviation above the mean, which would place it at the __ percentile. This would be equivalent to a *z*-score of __ and a *T*-score of __.

    1
    84th
    1, 60

---

36. Most, but not all, intelligence tests report IQs that are also a type of standard score called deviation IQs. Referring again to the normal curve in Figure 3–1, we can see that the mean IQ on the Wechsler Intelligence Scale is __ and the standard deviation is __. From Figure 3–1 we see that the mean IQ on the Stanford-Binet Intelligence Scale is 100 and its standard deviation is __. If a person scores one standard deviation below the mean of his or her age group, that person's Wechsler IQ is __, and and his or her Stanford-Binet IQ is __. If one is three standard deviations above the mean on the Wechsler, one's IQ score is __, whereas a score three standard deviations above the mean on the Stanford-Binet results in an IQ score of __.

    100
    15
    16
    85
    84
    145
    148

---

37. Let's review some of the characteristics of standard scores. A given standard score has a fixed mean and a fixed _____ _____. Because of this, individual scores on different tests can be compared directly and interpreted easily. A disadvantage of standard scores is that many users have not been introduced to them and consequently do not understand them, which is unfortunate since they are used in virtually all standardized tests.

    standard
    deviation

---

38. Suppose Jon had the following percentile ranks (*PR*) on five standardized tests:

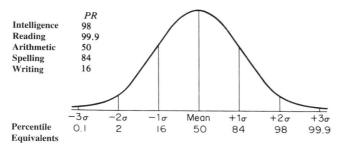

	PR
Intelligence	98
Reading	99.9
Arithmetic	50
Spelling	84
Writing	16

	−3σ	−2σ	−1σ	Mean	+1σ	+2σ	+3σ
Percentile Equivalents	0.1	2	16	50	84	98	99.9

Look at the normal curve with the accompanying percentile equivalents marked off in standard deviation units from the mean. From Jon's percentile ranks it might appear that he performed at about the same relative level on the intelligence and reading tests, whereas the difference in standard deviation units is actually as great as the difference between the intelligence and spelling tests. In both instances there was a difference of __ standard deviation; yet in percentile units the difference was only 1.9 in the first comparison, but __ in the second—again illustrating that equal differences in standard scores (or raw scores) do not yield equal differences in the corresponding percentile ranks.

1

14

39. Consider another example: If Jon improved his writing score by two standard deviations, his percentile rank would increase __ percentile units; the same improvement in spelling would cause an increase of only __ percentile units.

68

15.9

40. If, on the other hand, the scores had been expressed in standard score norms, no such problem of interpretation would have been present. Using T-scores, Jon's test scores would have been as follows:

	PR	T-score	
Intelligence	98	70	
Reading	99.9	__	80
Arithmetic	50	__	50
Spelling	84	__	60
Writing	16	__	40

41. We have mentioned two specified types of standard scores: z-scores and T-scores. Even though we are not among the proponents of a third type, *stanines,* we will mention them briefly since they are used on several standardized tests. Notice from Figure 3–1 that the stanine is a standard score in which the mean is 5 and the standard deviation is 2. If a person scores at the 84th percentile (one standard deviation above the mean), his or her stanine score is __.

7

42. Notice from Figure 3–1 that the stanine units are 0.5σ in width except in stanines 1 and __. Referring to Figure 3–1, indicate Jon's test performance using the stanine scale. Notice that information is lost in exchange for the simplicity of a single digit for reporting results.

9

	PR	Stanine	
Intelligence	98	__	9
Reading	99.9	__	9
Arithmetic	50	__	5
Spelling	84	__	7
Writing	16	__	3

43. To convert a raw score (X) to a z-score, we express the difference between the mean and X in standard deviation units.

$$z = \frac{X - \mu}{\sigma}$$

If $\mu = 32$, $\sigma = 5$, and $X = 30$

$$z = \frac{(\quad) - (\quad)}{5} \quad \text{or} \quad \underline{\quad}$$

30, 32, −.4

---

44. To transform a z-score to a T-score, multiply the z-score by 10 and add 50.

$$T = 50 + 10z$$

The raw score of 30 in Frame 43 was equivalent to a z-score of −.4. Hence, in T-score units

$$T = 50 + 10(\quad)$$
$$= 50 - \underline{\quad} \quad \text{or} \quad \underline{\quad}$$

−.4, 4, 46

The concept and use of the normal distribution and standard scores will now be presented in conventional narrative form.

3.4   MANY MEASURES REPORT SCORES THAT ARE BASED ON THE NORMAL CURVE

If a cognitive test is neither very easy nor very difficult for a large group being tested, the scores will usually be approximately normally distributed (Lord, 1955)—that is, the frequency distribution will be similar to the bell-shaped pattern shown in Figure 3–1. Notice that the normal curve is symmetrical (the left half is the mirror image of the right half) and unimodal (there is just one mode). In any symmetrical unimodal distribution, the mean, median, and mode are equal. The normal curve is a special kind of symmetrical unimodal distribution that is mathematically specified. (If you are curious, you can find the mathematical formula in most statistics books, e.g., Glass & Hopkins, 1996, p. 82.)

In a normally distributed set of scores, the 16th percentile lies at a point one standard deviation below the mean, and the 84th percentile lies one standard deviation above the mean. You can readily see this in Figure 3–1. Similarly, a score two standard deviations above the mean has a percentile rank of approximately 98. The corresponding percentile ranks for −3σ and +3σ are 0.13 and 99.87, respectively. The areas under various portions of the normal curve have been tabled in detail by Hopkins, Hopkins, and Glass (1996) from −6σ to +6σ. From these tables we can readily ascertain the distance from the mean in standard deviation units (z-scores) that corresponds to any percentile rank, from zero deviation, which corresponds to a *PR* of 50, to -4σ to $+4\sigma$, which are at the 0.003th and 99.997th percentiles, respectively. It should be borne in mind that the distribution in Figure 3–1 is a true normal curve based on an infinite number of observations. A set of actual test scores, being finite, never conforms exactly to this distribution, although the approximation between -2σ and $+2\sigma$ is often very good. For example, the highest IQ score possible on most intelligence tests is less than 160 ($+4\sigma$); so, the .003 percent of IQ scores exceeding 160 "predicted" by the normal curve obviously cannot agree with the observed distribution of IQs.

3.5   STANDARD SCORES ARE USEFUL IN DESCRIBING PERFORMANCE

We have already examined the limited meaning of a raw score on a cognitive or affective measure. The use of a standard score is a common way of expressing performance on standardized measures—to express the score as a deviation from the mean in standard deviation units. For example, if the mean of a normal distribution is 62, a score of 74 is 12 points above the mean, how "high" is it? It could be the highest score if the standard deviation were small ($\sigma = 3$ or 4); it would be the 84th percentile if the scores were normally distributed and standard deviation was 12. Sixteen percent of the students would score above 74. On almost all standardized tests, the deviation of a score from the mean ($X - \mu$) is divided by the standard deviation to obtain a standard z-score, which indicates how many standard deviations above or below the mean the raw score falls.

3.6   Z-SCORES

The basic standard score, the building block for all standard scores, is the z-score, defined in Equation 3.1.

EQUATION 3.1

$$z = \frac{Score - Mean}{Standard\ Deviation} = \frac{X - \mu}{\sigma}$$

As illustrated in Section 2.7, the sum (and therefore the mean) of a full set of deviation ($X - \mu$) scores is always zero. It is apparent from Equation 3.1 that the same is true for a full set of z-scores. If a test had a mean of 62 and a standard deviation of 12, a raw score of 74 would be equivalent to a z-score of 1.0 because it is one standard deviation above the mean. In other words, z-scores are simply raw scores expressed in standard deviation units from the mean. Therefore, the standard deviation of a full set of z-scores is 1.0. If we plot the distribution of z-scores, we find that it has exactly the same shape as the distribution of the original raw scores. Computing z-scores does *not* change the shape of the distribution; it just re-scales the numbers so that their mean is 0.0 and their standard deviation is 1.0. Skewed distributions remain skewed; symmetrical distributions remain symmetrical, and so forth.

In order to have adequate precision when using z-scores, scores are expressed to one or two decimal places—the scores are decimal fractions. In addition, scores below the mean are negative numbers. Decimals and negative numbers are drawbacks to the use of z-scores.

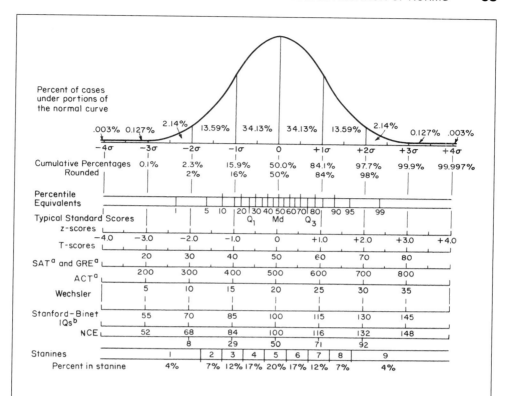

THE NORMAL CURVE, PERCENTILES AND STANDARD SCORES

Distribution of scores of many standardized educational and psychological tests approximate the form of the NORMAL CURVE shown at the top of this chart. Below it are shown some of the systems that have been developed to facilitate the interpretation of scores by converting them into numbers which indicate the examinee's relative status in a group.

The zero (0) at the center of the baseline shows the location of the mean (average) raw score on a test, and the symbol σ (sigma) marks off the scale of raw scores in STANDARD DEVIATION units.

Cumulative percentages are the basis of the PERCENTILE EQUIVALENT scale.

Several systems are based on the standard deviation unit. Among these STANDARD SCORE scales, the z-score, the T-score and the stanine are general systems which have been applied to a variety of tests.

The others are special variants used in connection with tests of the College Entrance Examination Board, the Graduate Records Examination, and other intelligence and ability scales.

Tables of NORMS, whether in percentile or standard score form, have meaning only with reference to a specified test applied to a specified population. The chart does not permit one to conclude, for instance, that a percentile rank of 84 on one test necessarily is equivalent to a z-score of +1.0 on another; this is true only when each test yields essentially a normal distribution of scores and when both scales are based on identical or very similar groups of people.

Most of the scales on this chart are discussed in greater detail in *Test Service Bulletin No. 48*, copies of which are available on request from the Psychological Corporation, 304 East 45th St., New York, N.Y. 10017.

[a]Score points (norms) on the scales refer to university students and not to general populations.
[b]Standard-score "IQs" with $\sigma = 16$ are also used on several other current intelligence tests; e.g., California Test of Mental Maturity, Kuhlmann-Anderson Intelligence Test, and Lorge Thorndike Intelligence Test.

FIGURE 3–1   Types of standard score scales

SOURCE: Adapted from *Test Service Bulletin No. 48,* The Psychological Corporation, New York. Reprinted by permission of The Psychological Corporation.

We can avoid negative scores and decimals simply by (1) setting up a standard score scale with a mean sufficiently greater than zero to avoid negative numbers, and (2) selecting a value for the standard deviation that is sufficiently greater than one to make decimals unnecessary.

The general formula for converting any z-score to any other standard score is stated in Equation 3.2.

EQUATION 3.2

$$\text{Standard score} = M + S(z)$$

where,

M is the mean of the standard score scale, and

S = the standard deviation of the standard scores.

Wechsler's intelligence tests use the following standard score form (see Figure 3–1):

$$\text{IQ score} = 100 + 15(z)$$

The 1987 *Stanford-Binet Intelligence Scale* has this standard score form (see Figure 3–1):

$$\text{IQ score} = 100 + 16(z)$$

Is a score of 145 on the *Wechsler Adult Intelligence Scale* (*WAIS*) as rare as a score of 145 on the *Stanford-Binet*? It is even rarer because $z = (145 - 100)/15$ or 3 on the WAIS is greater than $z = (145 - 100)/16$ or 2.81 for the *Stanford-Binet*.[2]

The *Graduate Record Examination* (*GRE*) and the College Board's *Scholastic Aptitude Test* (*SAT*) report results on a scale in which the mean is 500, with S set at 100. The principal competitor to the *SAT*, the *American College Testing Program* (*ACT*), used a μ of 20 and $\sigma = 5$ in its original standardization.[3] These standard scores were selected in part to prevent confusion with percentages or percentiles.

3.7   THE *T*-SCALE

The *T*-scale is a standard score procedure that employs a mean of 50 and a standard deviation of 10. This scale has all the properties of the z-scale without the awkwardness result-

---

[2]Small differences in σ become very significant at the extremes. For example, if scores are normally distributed, we would expect 0.13 percent (13 per 10,000) of the scores to exceed 145 on the Wechsler, whereas on the Stanford-Binet we would expect almost twice as many (0.25 percent, or 25 per 10,000) IQ scores to exceed 145.

[3]Some tests, such as the ACT, SAT and the GRE, serve an important function in the assessment of trends or changes in student ability or aptitude; hence, it is desirable to keep the scaled-score norms based on the same reference group even though the percentile norms are updated. This fixed meaning of the scaled scores on the College Boards quantify the "achievement decline" noted in Figure 3–3 and Figure 14–11. However, in 1995 the SAT was readjusted so that its mean is 500 and its standard deviation is 100 (see Figure 3–3).

ing from negative scores and decimal fractions. The T-score[4] is used for reporting performance on several standardized measures. Any score can be converted to a T-score by using Equation 3.3.

EQUATION 3.3

$$T = 50 + 10z$$

An important advantage of using standard scores results from the fact that one is always aware of the mean and the standard deviation of the distribution, and the mean and standard deviation are uniform within all tests in a battery, therefore, an examinee's relative performance on various tests (e.g., GRE verbal, quantitative, and analytic tests) can be easily compared. Why not just report performance using percentile ranks? The marked inequality of percentile units makes the comparison of performance less precise (see Figure 3–1). For example, the difference between the 84th and 98th percentiles (a difference of 14 percentile units) is as great as the difference between the 50th and 84th percentiles (34 percentile units).[5]

3.8   STANINES

Another standard score system that is used on some standardized tests is the *stanine*[6] scale. This standard score was developed and used extensively by the U.S. Air Force during World War II. Stanines are ordinarily normalized standard scores with a mean of 5 and a standard deviation[7] of 2. Consequently, all stanines except 1 and 9 span an interval of one-half a standard deviation in width. The nine stanines (1, 2, 3, 4, 5, 6, 7, 8, 9) are shown in Figure 3–2 in relation to the normal curve. Corresponding z-score and T-score limits are also given in this figure.

---

[4]As originally conceived, the T-scale was a *normalized* standard score. Scores from skewed and other non-normal distributions can be forced to approximate a normal distribution by a process of *normalizing*. When scores are normalized, the resulting scores will approximate the normal distribution as closely as possible. Normalized T-scores are obtained by (1) converting raw scores to percentile ranks, (2) converting these percentile ranks to the corresponding z-scores that are associated with those percentiles in a normal distribution, and then (3) using Equation 3.3. Currently the use of T-scores is not limited to normalized standard scores. There are differences of opinion as to whether the distribution of scores on standardized tests should be normalized (Angoff, 1971; Petersen, Kolen & Hoover, 1988). Scores on most standardized tests are not normalized. On well-constructed standardized cognitive tests, normalized and non-normalized T-scores will differ little.

[5]The difference between the 98th percentile and the 99.9th percentile (2 percentile units) also represents a difference of the same magnitude.

[6]Short for *sta*ndard scores with *nine* categories.

[7]The standard deviation of normalized stanine scores is not exactly 2.0, but 1.96, as shown by Kaiser (1958), who suggested a slight modification that would yield a standard deviation of precisely 2.0. For practical purposes the difference in the resulting scores is inconsequential.

THE MEANING AND APPLICATION OF NORMS

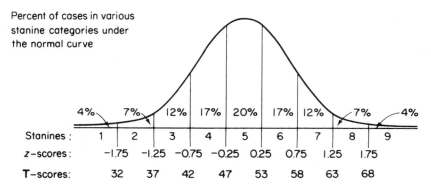

Percent of cases in various
stanine categories under
the normal curve

Stanines :	1	2	3	4	5	6	7	8	9
	4%	7%	12%	17%	20%	17%	12%	7%	4%

z-scores: −1.75 −1.25 −0.75 −0.25 0.25 0.75 1.25 1.75

T-scores: 32 37 42 47 53 58 63 68

FIGURE 3–2 The stanine scale related to *T*-scores, *z*-scores, and the normal distribution.

To convert raw scores into normalized stanine scores, one arranges the scores in rank order from the highest to the lowest. The top 4 percent of scores are assigned a stanine score of 9. The next 7 percent (see Figure 3–2 for the percents falling in each stanine[8]) receive a stanine score of 8, the next 12 percent fall in stanine 7, and the next 17 percent in stanine 6. Then, counting up from the bottom of the distribution, the bottom 4 percent are assigned a stanine score of 1, the next 7 percent receive stanine scores of 2, the next 12 percent fall in stanine 3, and the next 17 percent receive a stanine score of 4. The remaining 20 percent fall in stanine 5. Does this sound simple? With a little practice, it is. Any conscientious clerk can obtain stanine scores in this way, and at the same time the scores are being *normalized*. Normalizing occurs when we "force" the raw scores to fit the normal curve as closely as possible. Normalization is justified when any non-normality in the shape of the distribution of scores results from deficiencies in the test itself. Normalizing is not appropriate when the distribution of the underlying ability of the sample is non-normal in form (see Anastasi, 1976, p. 84).

Some have advocated the use of the stanine scale as the standard general system of reporting results from all standardized tests. Although the stanine scale offers the advantage of a single-digit index, a high price is paid for this convenience—namely, significant loss in precision. For example, if intelligence test results were reported in stanines, we would not be able to distinguish among people with IQ scores above 127, nor among persons with scores below 73—a significant shortcoming, since the identification of students who are gifted or students with disabilities has been an important function of standardized intelligence tests.

While it is true that the stanine scale helps convey the important concept that scores on a test should be viewed as *bands* rather than *points*, the fixed bands of the stanine scale

---

[8]When greater accuracy is needed, the percentages of scores assigned to the stanines are 4.01, 6.55, 12.10, 17.49, 19.74, 17.47, 12.10, 6.55, and 4.01 for stanines 1 through 9, respectively.

are the appropriate bandwidth only for those examinees who scored near the middle of the stanines. Some examinees will earn scores that differ by two stanines when their performance on two tests varies only slightly more than $.5\sigma$, whereas other students whose performance differs by $.9\sigma$ (or even much more if stanine 1 or 9 is involved) will have stanine scores that differ by only one. Although the stanine scale is a widely used standard score, we feel that its distinct disadvantages are such that it is definitely inferior to the T-score.

3.9   NORMAL CURVE EQUIVALENT (NCE) SCORES

Certain federal funding agencies (e.g., ESEA "Chapter 1") require school districts to use *NCE*s in reporting results to the federal government. The *NCE* scale yields a standard score with a mean of 50 and a standard deviation of 21 (actually 21.06). The scale was selected so that the *NCE* standard scores would approximate their corresponding percentiles as closely as possible. Note in Figure 3–1 that, indeed, *NCE*s and percentiles are in agreement for 1, 50, and 99 but differ greatly at other points (e.g., an *NCE* of 29 corresponds to a percentile of 16). *NCE*s are naturally easily confused with percentiles, so we do not recommend them.

3.10   NORMS PROVIDE A MEANS OF COMPARISON WITH A REFERENCE GROUP

The strengths and weaknesses of an examinee, school, or school district are illuminated when the performance is viewed in terms of a larger, representative reference group. Figure 3–3 depicts the results of students in a large high school who took the *Scholastic Aptitude Test* (*SAT*) of the College Entrance Examination Board over a period spanning more than two decades. The widely publicized decline[9] is evident in the national norms on both the verbal and math sections of the *SAT* (see Figure 14–11); note that the decline is greater on the verbal (≈ 50 points, $.5\sigma$) than on the math (≈ 25 points, $.25\sigma$). Notice also that the decline in scores appears to have bottomed around 1980, with some recovery in math scores since then.

   The pattern for Fairview High School is less consistent than the national patterns. Even though its verbal and math scores remain much above the national averages, there is a trend for the math scores to increase up to 1973 and to decrease somewhat thereafter. The verbal scores reflect a slightly larger decline beginning in 1975.[10]

---

[9]Part of the decline may be an artifact due to an increase in the proportion of high school seniors who take the *SAT* (Congress of the United States, 1987).

[10]Although a common practice, *SAT* scores cannot be used to compare states because the proportions of students taking the *SAT* varies *greatly* among the states. In ten states, 5 percent or fewer of high school graduates take the *SAT*, whereas in eleven states more than 50 percent of the graduates take the *SAT*. The correlation between the state's mean and the proportion taking the test is extremely high ($r = -.85$, Page & Feifs, 1985), in other words, the states with the high averages are the states in which fewer students take the tests and vice versa. The percentage of a state's population that are ethnic minorities also correlates negatively ($r = -.36$, Page and Fiefs, 1985; $r = -.38$, Taube & Lilnden, 1989) with the state's average *SAT* score.

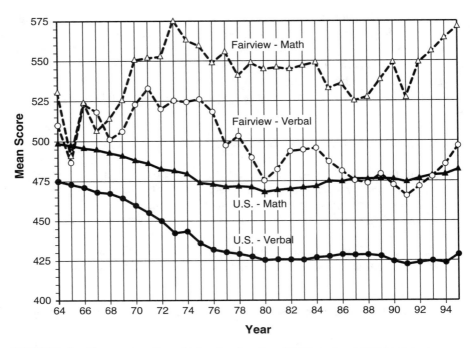

FIGURE 3–3   The results of one high school on the *SAT Verbal* and *SAT Math* tests compared to the national averages (norms). Note that the *SAT* norms were readjusted in 1995. (The authors are grateful to George Kretke for providing these data.)

The identification of an individual student's instructional accomplishments and needs likewise can be expedited via appropriate, properly used standardized tests, as we will see later in the chapter (Figure 3–4).

3.11   A REPRESENTATIVE SAMPLE IS NEEDED FOR ACCURATE NORMS

The size of the group on which norms are established is much less important than the degree to which it is representative of the relevant population. On measures of scholastic aptitude and achievement, there are significant differences associated with geographic region, socioeconomic status, urban versus rural residence, and so on. Norms based on one million persons from a "grab" sample are much less useful than norms based on a representative sample of 1000 persons.[11] Samples for standardization purposes are often selected

[11]Most of Gallup's surveys are based on a representative sample of 1500 persons, which is less than .001 percent of the population. It is the representativeness and size of the sample that are important, not the proportion of the population that is included in the sample (Hopkins, Hopkins & Glass 1996, pp. 144–145).

to correspond to the total population with respect to geographic region, sex, age, urban versus rural residence, community size, father's occupational and educational level, and/or ethnic group membership.

Data regarding the norm sample used in the 1986 standardization of the widely-used *Stanford-Binet Intelligence Scale* is given in Table 3–1 (Thorndike, Hagen & Sattler, 1986). The various boxes in Table 3–1 illustrate the comparability of the *Stanford-Binet* standardization sample with the national population. Although fewer than 400 persons were tested at most age levels, the sample was carefully selected to be representative; note the close correspondence between the norm sample and the population with respect to geographic region, size of community, gender, ethnicity, parental occupation, and parental education. Norms from tests that have been carefully standardized like the *Stanford-Binet* can be interpreted with much greater confidence than norms based on a much larger group with uncertain representativeness.

Most standardized group tests (tests on which several examinees can be tested at the same time) have norms based on more than 5000 persons at each age or grade level, yet the norms are less accurate than those on the *Stanford-Binet*, which are based on less than 10 percent as many students. For example, the mean IQ score from the *Stanford-Binet* norm sample of 400 will almost certainly (95 percent confidence) be not more than 1.5 points from the mean for the entire population.[12] We are much less certain of the accuracy of the norms on most other standardized achievement, aptitude, interest, and personality tests. Even though they have much larger standardization samples, the procedures used to obtain the samples allows some bias in the norms. For example, a substantial portion of school districts selected for norming purposes refused to participate, and those that refused probably differ in important ways from districts that participate. The size of the standardization sample is much less critical than its representativeness.

National norms are the most common type used in education and psychological testing. Some states and provinces, however, have established state or provincial norms on various achievement tests. Many school districts use their own local achievement norms in addition to national norms. Figure 3–4 shows the test performance of Pat Warren, a beginning sixth-grader, using national grade-equivalent and percentile norms as well as local percentile norms.

Notice that although Pat's composite score is better than those of four out of five beginning tenth-graders in the nation (i.e., national percentile rank of 80), it is just above the average for college bound students (50th percentile—column B). Pat's performance in mathematics was excellent (93rd percentile), but not strong in social studies reading. The "xxxxx" confidence bands to the right of the national percentiles help us attach the

---

[12]If you have taken an elementary statistics course, you may recall that the 95 percent confidence interval for the population mean is a band spanning the interval: the sample mean $(\overline{X}) \pm 2\sigma_{\overline{X}}$, where $\sigma_{\overline{X}} = \sigma/\sqrt{N}$. For the *Stanford-Binet*, $\sigma_{\overline{X}} = 16/\sqrt{400}$ or less than one (.8) IQ point. The .95 confidence interval is based on the assumption that the sample was selected completely at random from a population of normally distributed scores. The stratified sample described in Table 3–1 would further reduce the value of the standard error, which makes it very improbable that the mean of the norm sample differs more than one point from the mean that would have resulted if the entire national population of children at that age level had been tested.

TABLE 3–1   Comparison of a Standardization Sample with the U.S. Population*

*The standardization was conducted from January through July 1985. Approximately 500 examiners tested more than 5000 subjects in 160 testing centers from 47 states and the District of Columbia.

Representation of the Standardization Sample by Geographic Region

Geographic Region	Sample Percent	U.S. Population Percent
Northeast	16.7	21.7
North Central	29.3	26.0
South	31.9	33.3
West	22.1	19.0
Total	100.0	100.0

Representation of the Standardization Sample by Community Size

Community Size	Sample Percent	U.S. Population Percent
Large Cities		
1,000,000 or more	10.7	8.5
300,000 to 999,999	7.6	10.0
100,000 to 299,999	12.1	9.2
Cities		
25,000 to 99,999	24.3	20.8
Small towns		
2,500 to 24,999	23.1	25.2
Rural areas		
Less than 2,500	22.2	26.3
Total	100.0	100.0

Representation of the Standardization Sample by Gender

Gender	Sample Percent	U.S. Population Percent
Male	48.3	47.2
Female	51.7	52.8
Total	100.0	100.0

Representation of the Standardization Sample by Race/Ethnic Group

Race/Ethnic Group	Sample Percent	U.S. Population Percent
Native American	1.7	0.6
Hispanic	6.3	6.4
Black	14.4	11.5
White	74.6	79.6
Asian/Pacific Islander	2.5	1.5
Other	0.5	0.4
Total	100.0	100.0

Representation of the Standardization Sample by Parental Occupation

Parental Occupation	Weighted Sample Percent	U.S. Population Percent
Managerial/Professional	20.0	21.8
Technical/Sales	29.7	29.7
Service Occupations	13.9	13.1
Farming/Forestry	3.1	2.9
Precision Production	13.2	13.0
Operators, Fabricators, Other	20.1	19.5
Total	100.0	100.0

Representation of the Standardization Sample by Parental Education

Parental Education	Weighted Sample Percent	U.S. Population Percent
College Graduate or Beyond	15.1	19.0
1 to 3 Years of College	17.0	15.3
High School Graduate	38.1	36.5
Less Than High School Graduate	29.8	29.2
Total	100.0	100.0

SOURCE: R. L. Thorndike, E. P. Hagen, and J. M. Sattler, *Stanford-Binet Intelligence Scale,* 4th ed., Technical Manual, pp. 16, 22–24. Reprinted with permission of the Riverdale Publishing Company, 8420 W. Bryn Mawr Avenue, Chicago, IL 60631. Copyright 1986.

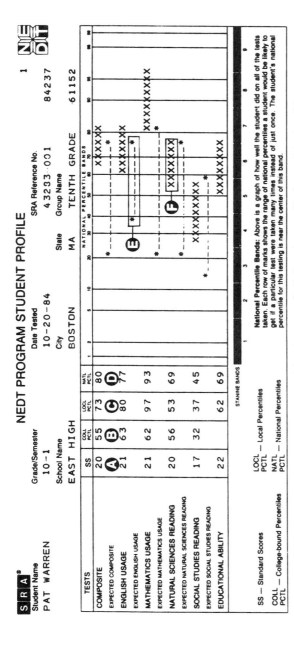

FIGURE 3–4 Simulated individual student profile report on Pat Warren, a beginning tenth-grade student at East High on the SRA National Educational Development Tests (NEDT).

appropriate degree of precision to our interpretation. Notice that the composite score is more precise (i.e., has a smaller "xxx" confidence band) than any of the separate tests—the length of a test is an important determiner of its precision and reliability, as will be seen in greater detail in Chapter 5.

3.12   NORMS SHOULD BE RELEVANT

A score on a standardized test can be compared with any number of different norm groups. In addition to national norms, standardized tests sometimes offer separate norms for special subgroups, for example, by sex, race, year, or region. In Figure 3–4 Pat Warren's achievement performance is compared to that of two norm groups, his local school peers (the local percentiles in column C), and his national grade-level peers (the national percentiles in column D). We see that his performance is somewhat higher relative to that of his local peers than to that of his national peers. The two sets of norms complement each other and when used together give a better evaluation of Pat's achievement. Both sets of norms are relevant and allow his performance to be viewed from two different perspectives. On the tests Pat took, norms are also available for large-city schools, Title I schools, affluent suburban schools, small-city and rural schools, and church-related schools. Are all of these norms relevant for evaluating Pat's performance? Some probably are but only if Pat is a member of that particular subgroup or needs to be compared to that subgroup.

    The relevant norm group is sometimes a highly select group of persons rather than the population at large. Scaled-score norms on the *ACT, SAT,* and *Graduate Record Examination (GRE)* are based not on the performance of a representative sample of the nation's population but on an educationally select group.[13] A mean score of 500 on the *GRE* represents greater ability than does the mean on a college admissions test, which in turn represents considerably higher abilities than an IQ score of 100 on general intelligence tests such as the *Stanford-Binet Intelligence Scale* or the *Wechsler Adult Intelligence Scale (WAIS).* For example, in one study (Pallas & Alexander, 1983) the *SAT* was administered to the entire senior class of several high schools, and it was found that the mean was 60 points ($.6\sigma$) below the average of the self-selected group of seniors who take the *SAT.* It is obvious why the information in Figure 3–1 cannot be used to estimate an IQ score directly from scores on the *SAT, ACT,* or *GRE.*

    The importance of the nature of the reference group is illustrated by the *GRE* data in Tables 3–2 and 3–3. Table 3–2 gives recent percentile norms for each of the three *GRE* tests. Table 3–3 includes the same data for the verbal and quantitative tests three decades earlier. (Table 3–3 also gives separate norms for each sex.) Using Table 3–2 and the "total" norms

---

[13]The *GRE* scaled-score norms are based on the performance of 2095 volunteer graduating seniors in the spring of 1952 at 11 colleges that were generally representative of schools that normally administer the *GRE* to their students. Test content is continuously revised by the inclusion of approximately one-sixth new items among the scored items in each *GRE* testing. Thus, normative data are obtained on the new items so that they may replace older items with the same statistical characteristics (item difficulty and reliability).

TABLE 3–2 1984–87 Percentile Norms on the Aptitude Tests of the Graduate Record Examinations (Based on the Performance of Examinees Tested at National Administrations between October 1, 1984, and September 30, 1987)

	Percent of Examinees Scoring Lower Than Selected Scaled Scores		
Scaled Score	*Verbal Ability*	*Quantitative Ability*	*Analytical Ability*[a]
800	99+	98	99
780	99	96	98
760	99	93	97
740	98	90	95
720	96	86	93
700	95	82	91
680	93	78	88
660	91	74	84
640	88	70	80
630	85	65	76
600	82	61	71
580	78	55	66
560	73	51	60
540	68	46	55
520	63	41	48
500	57	36	43
480	52	31	37
460	46	27	32
440	40	23	26
420	34	19	22
400	28	16	18
380	24	12	14
360	18	10	11
340	14	7	8
320	10	5	6
300	7	4	4
280	5	2	3
260	3	2	2
240	1	1	1
220	1		1
Mean	475	549	519
Standard Deviation	126	140	128

Number of Examinees	844,960		
Percent Women	49		
Percent Men	51		

SOURCE: From 1988–89 *Guide to the Use of the Graduate Record Examinations Program.* Copyright © 1988 by Educational Testing Service. All rights reserved. Reprinted by permission.

[a]In 1977, the GRE subtests were restructured to include a measure of "analytical ability" (ability to recognize logical relationships, draw conclusions from information, etc.). Performance on the analytical ability section correlates substantially with performance on the two original verbal and quantitative sections ($r_{VA} = 0.66$, $r_{QA} = 0.68$, whereas $r_{VQ} = 0.46$).

TABLE 3–3   1965–68 Percentile Norms on the Aptitude Tests of the Graduate Record Examinations[a]

| | Percent of Students Scoring Lower Than Selected Scaled Scores | | | | | |
| | Verbal | | | Quantitative | | |
Scaled Score	Men	Women	Total	Men[b]	Women[b]	Total
800				99		99
780	99	99	99	96		97
760	98	97	98	94	99	96
740	96	96	96	90	98	93
720	94	94	94	86	97	90
700	92	91	91	81	96	87
680	89	87	88	78	94	84
660	86	83	85	73	92	80
640	82	79	81	68	90	76
620	77	74	76	63	87	72
600	73	69	71	58	84	67
580	67	63	66	53	80	63
560	62	57	60	48	76	58
540	56	51	54	43	70	53
520	50	45	48	38	65	47
500	44	40	43	34	60	43
480	38	34	37	29	54	38
460	33	29	31	24	48	33
440	27	24	26	20	41	27
420	22	19	21	16	35	23
400	18	15	17	12	28	18
380	14	12	13	9	22	14
360	10	9	10	6	17	10
340	8	7	7	5	13	8
320	6	5	5	3	9	5
300	4	4	4	2	6	3
280	2	2	2	1	4	2
260	2	2	2		2	1
240	1	1	1		1	

SOURCE: *Guide to Use of Graduate Record Examination.* Copyright © 1968 by Educational Testing Service. All rights reserved. Reproduced by permission.
[a]Scaled score on the aptitude tests can range from 200 to 900. The data are based on the performance of a group consisting of graduate students and applicants for admission to graduate school tested from May 1965 through April 1968.
[b]The gender difference may have decreased slightly over the past two decades (see Table 3–4).

in Table 3–3, can you determine the change in average performance on the verbal test between 1965–68 and three decades later? A scaled score of 500 on the verbal test exceeded the scores of only 43 percent of the examinees in 1965–68, but the same score (500) exceeded 57 percent of those tested in 1984–87, reflecting an "achievement decline" during the three decades. Stated differently, three decades ago a score of 500 was at the 43rd percentile, whereas the same score today corresponds to the 57th percentile. Note, however, that for the quantitative test, little or no change has occurred in the norms during that same time period. For example, a scaled score of 500 in the quantitative test was equivalent to a percentile rank of 43 three decades ago and is also equivalent to a percentile rank of 43 today.

Note in Table 3–3 that, instead of the "total" group, a reference group of males or females can be employed. If your scaled score of 500 on the Quantitative subtest was compared to those of other people of the same sex, the percentile rank would be 34 or 60, depending on whether you reference the men's or women's norm group.[14] From Table 3–3, can you estimate the median scores on the *GRE* Verbal subtest? (The men's median is 520; but the women's is almost 540.) Repeat the task on the quantitative subtest. (The medians approach 570 and 470 for men and women, respectively.)

For decisions pertaining to graduate study, norms by major field of study are relevant (see Table 3–4). (see ETS, 1988, for more complete normative data) Note that a scaled score of 600 on the verbal test would be quite high relative to that of most of the reference groups represented in Table 3–4 but would be about average for the classical language subgroup. Similarly, a quantitative score of 700 would be excellent in relation to almost all reference groups but only about average for the field of physics. The implications of these normative data for vocational and academic counseling are obvious.

In addition to showing the large differences among major-field means, the large standard deviations reveal how extremely variable examinees are in verbal and quantitative ability *within* each major field of study. This fact should reduce our penchant for stereotyping by field of study.

Note also that the *numbers* of persons vary greatly among the various fields. Although the classical language group had the largest percent of people with high verbal ability (for example, persons obtaining scores of 600 or above) on the verbal test, the field of education probably contains many more persons with very high verbal ability. Assuming that the scores are approximately normally distributed with a standard deviation of 100, about 51 percent or 217 persons in the classical language group $(.51 \times 425 = 217)$ had scores above 600 while about 7 percent or 1839 persons in education $(.07 \times 26,266 = 1839)$ attained scores of 600 or higher. It is obvious that for a correct interpretation of any test, the precise nature of the reference group and the kinds of norm used must always be borne in mind.

3.13   NORMS SHOULD BE CURRENT

Society in general and education in particular are continually undergoing change. The norms in Table 3–3 are no longer representative of current students. For norms to be rep-

---

[14]At least some of this discrepancy results from the fact that, as a group, females less frequently elect courses that use mathematics and quantitative reasoning (Pallas & Alexander, 1983; Rigol, 1989).

TABLE 3–4 GRE Means of seniors and non-enrolled college graduates by intended graduate major field of study (1984–1987)

Field of Study	N	Means		
		Verbal	Quantitative	Analytical
Agriculture	3,126	453	533	526
Anthropology	2,041	553	526	557
Arts (Subtotal)	8,887	496	497	534
Behavioral Sciences	63,143	509	526	544
Bioscience (Subtotal)	19,922	507	582	570
Chemistry	6,263	507	637	590
Classical Languages	425	606	561	587
Computer Science	16,593	482	653	591
Dentistry	208	450	562	511
Economics	5,609	504	612	568
Education (all fields)	26,266	453	483	511
Engineering (Subtotal)	35,954	477	677	582
English	10,315	578	518	566
Health Sciences (Subtotal)	33,123	467	505	523
Journalism	3,265	512	498	534
Languages (and humanities)	32,620	542	532	556
Law	1,012	468	480	516
Mathematics	3,890	508	679	616
Medicine	1,236	484	571	549
Music	3,625	489	507	540
Philosophy	1,839	599	586	602
Physics	4,468	545	698	624
Psychology, Clinical	15,169	502	512	540
Religion	4,860	502	512	538
Sociology	2,386	483	497	513
Speech	846	470	475	526
Statistics	1,007	477	660	589
Females[14]	111,865	487	499	522
Males	97,640	487	585	536

resentative of current populations, they must be continually updated. The *Wechsler Intelligence Scale for Children* (*WISC*) was originally normed in 1949. The question of interest is not how intelligent a child is in relation to children of the same age in 1949 but rather in relation to his or her contemporaries. That is why the test is periodically updated.

SUMMARY

Raw scores and percentage scores are greatly influenced by the difficulty of the achievement items, which is arbitrary. Therefore, "percent correct" scores cannot be rigorously interpreted as an absolute scale such as "percent of mastery."

Standardized tests are tests in which the content and conditions of administration (e.g., directions, allotted time) are held constant.

The meaning of test scores is enhanced if the scores are expressed in relation to a *reference* or *norm* group.

The norms on standardized tests describe the performance of the reference group (norm sample). The reference group should be a representative sample of the current relevant population.

Norms are not standards or goals but represent the status quo. They provide a means for comparing an examinee with a reference group. *Percentile* norms are widely used and relatively easy to understand but have the disadvantage of very unequal units.

Many standardized tests make use of the normal distribution and standard score norms to describe an examinee's status. All standard scores express performance in terms of standard deviation units from the mean. The most "basic" standard score is the *z*-scale, which has a mean of 0 and a standard deviation of 1.

T-scores have a mean of 50 and a standard deviation of 10, thereby avoiding negative scores and decimal fractions that occur with *z*-scores. The *stanine* scale is a standard score with a mean of 5 and a standard deviation of 2. It has the advantage of single-digit reporting, but the disadvantage of being less precise, especially at the extremes.

There are many different kinds of norm groups—age, grade, sex, national, state, local—some of which are treated in later chapters together with the types of tests for which they are used. The relevant reference (norm) groups are those with which an examinee's score can be compared meaningfully. To remain accurate, norms need to be updated periodically.

IMPORTANT TERMS AND CONCEPTS

absolute scale	local norms	normal distribution
standard scores	standard	standardization sample
percentile norms	T-score = 50 + 10z	standardized test
stanine	Normal Curve Equivalent	reference (norm) group
z-score	(NCE)	
national norms		

CHAPTER TEST

Suppose Mary obtained the following percentile ranks on five subtests of the *McCarthy Scales of Children's Abilities*:

Subtest	Percentile
Verbal	98
Perceptual	99.9
Quantitative	50
Memory	84
Motor	16

Use Figure 3–1 as needed to help answer Questions 1–4. Assume that the scores are normally distributed.

1. If Mary's motor performance improved by 1σ, the percentile equivalent would increase from 16 to _____—a gain of _____ percentile units.

2. If the verbal score improved by 1σ, the percentile equivalent on the verbal tests would increase from 98 to _____—a gain of _____ percentile units.

3. In *standard deviation units*, is the size of the *difference* between Mary's verbal and perceptual tests the same as the difference between her motor and quantitative scores?

4. If expressed in *T*-scores, would the change in percentile units of 34 and 1.9 in Questions 1 and 2 represent the same amount of change?

5. Grading on the normal curve was popular in some circles a few decades ago. The most common method used the following conversion:

Grade	*z*-score
A	Above 1.5
B	.5 to 1.5
C	−.5 to + .5
D	−1.5 to −.5
F	Below −1.5

Using this system, estimate the percent of *A*s, *B*s *C*s, *D*s, and *F*s expected with a normal distribution of scores. (Use Figure 3–1.)

6. Occasionally you may encounter another measure of variability, the *quartile deviation* (also known as the semi-interquartile range), *Q*, which is one-half the distance between the first quartile (the 25th percentile), Q_1, and the third quartile (the 75th percentile), Q_3. In other words: $Q = (Q_3 - Q_1) \div 2$. Using Figure 3–1, estimate the value of *Q* for IQ scores on the Wechsler tests.

7. Small changes in *z*-scores near the mean (e.g., from 0 to .5) correspond to _____ (large or small) changes in percentile equivalents; but large *z*-score changes near the extremes (e.g., 2.0 to 3.0) correspond to _____ (large or small) changes in percentile equivalents.

For Questions 8–17 information on certain standardized intelligence and achievement tests is given in the following table. Assume that the scores are normally distributed.

IOWA TEST OF BASIC SKILLS Grade-Equivalent (GE) Scores[15]

			Reading		Math
	WISC IQ	**Grade 3**	**Grade 5**	**Grade 8**	**Grade 5**
μ	100	3.0	5.0	8.0	5.0
σ	15	1.0	1.4	1.9	1.1

8. An IQ score above 115 is obtained by what percent of the population?

9. If a fifth-grade student obtains a percentile rank of 84 in reading, what is the student's grade-equivalent score?

10. What is the GE score for the same relative performance (84th percentile) in math at grade 5?

11. Jack obtained a GE score in reading of 6.1 when he entered grade 8. If his Wechsler IQ is equivalent to the same percentile rank, what is it?

12. If Jack's score in Question 11 is valid, he reads better than about what percentage of the children in his grade?

13. Upon entering grade 3, about what fraction of third-grade children
    a) obtains a reading GE score of 4.0 or better?
    b) obtains a reading GE score of 5.0 or better?

14. On the reading test, what percent of beginning third-grade students score at least as high as the *average* fourth-grade student?

15. At grade 5, is a GE score of 6.0 relatively better (i.e., does it have a higher percentile rank) in math than in reading?

16. In reading, what percentages of third-grade students score below GE scores of 2.0, 3.0, 4.0, and 5.0, respectively?

17. How much reading "growth" in GE units is required during the five-year span between grade 3.0 and grade 8.0 to
    a) maintain a percentile rank of 50?
    b) maintain a percentile rank of 84?
    c) maintain a percentile rank of 16?

---

[15]The meaning of grade-equivalent (GE) scores is developed fully in Chapter 14; a GE score of 3.0 is the average performance at the beginning of grade 3; or a GE score of 6.4 is viewed as the average score for students at the fourth month of grade 6.

18. Given $\mu = 163$, and $\sigma = 26$, express the score, $X = 176$, as:
   a) a z-score
   b) a T-score
   c) a percentile rank
   d) a stanine

19. In a school district of 10,000 students, how many could be expected to qualify for a gifted program that required an IQ score of at least 130 on the Wechsler test, assuming a normal distribution? (*Hint*: Obtain proportion from Figure 3–1.)

20. Estimate the percentage of IQ scores that fall between 90 and 110.

21. Which one of the following is *not* characteristic of a normal distribution?
   a) symmetrical
   b) unimodal
   c) skewed
   d) bell-shaped

22. Which one of the following represents the *poorest* performance on a test?
   a) 10th percentile
   b) $z = -1.5$
   c) $T = 30$
   d) stanine 2

23. The heights of U.S. men are approximately normally distributed with a mean of 69.5 inches and a standard deviation of approximately 2.5 inches. Estimate the percent of men more than six feet tall.

Items 24–27 are based on Figure 3–4.

24. The national percentiles are given for Pat Warren in Figure 3–4. Use Figure 3–1 to express his Natural Science Reading score as
   a) a z-score
   b) a T-score
   c) a stanine
   d) a NCE

25. Based on the norms for college bound students (column B in Figure 3–4), Pat's performance is best in _____ and poorest in _____.

26. Does college seem to be a realistic goal for Pat?

27. Pat's school district is achieving at a level (a) above or (b) below that of the national reference group. (Compare the national and local norms.)

28. Which of these scores represents the *highest* level of performance?
   a) $z = 1.0$
   b) $T = 55$
   c) stanine 5
   d) 35th percentile
   e) NCE $= 50$

29. In Question 28, which score represents the *lowest* level of performance?

Here are four conclusions pertaining to norms:

a) Norms are not standards.

b) Raw scores do not represent an absolute scale.

c) Percentile refers to percent of the reference group, not percent of items.

d) The reference group should be relevant.

Each of the statements in Questions 30–34 represents a misunderstanding of one of these conclusions. Identify the conclusion that is misunderstood in each statement.

30. No first-grade child who is reading below the national grade equivalent (2.0) should be promoted to the second grade.

31. Using chimpanzee norms, I have an IQ of 200.

32. I guess I did poorly on the test; I scored at the 65th percentile—don't all scores below 70 percent get an F?

33. I guess I know all there is to know about standard scores—I got 100 percent on the test.

34. Jerry got a score of 40 percent, whereas Mary got a score of 80 percent; that makes Mary twice as smart as Jerry.

ANSWERS TO CHAPTER TEST

1. 50, 34
2. 99.9, 1.9
3. yes, 1σ in each case
4. yes, T-scores increase by 10 in each instance
5. approximate answers: A: 7 %; B: 24 %; C: 38 %; D: 24 %; F: 7 %
6. $Q = (110 - 90)/2$ or 10
7. large, small
8. 16%
9. 6.4
10. 6.1
11. 85th
12. 16%
13. a) 1/6, b) 1/50
14. 16%
15. yes
16. 16 %, 50 %, 84 %, 98 %
17. a) 5.0, b) 5.9, c) 4.1

18. a) $z = .50$, b) $T = 55$, c) approx. 69th %ile, d) 6
19. (2.14 % + .13 %) = 2.27 %; .0227(10,000) = 227
20. 50 %
21. c
22. c
23. 16 %
24. a) .5, b) 55, c) 6, d) 60 or 61
25. English Usage, Social Studies Reading
26. yes
27. a
28. a
29. d
30. a
31. d
32. c (also a)
33. b
34. b

4

Test Validity

4.1 INTRODUCTION

The *validity* of a measure is how well it fulfills the function for which it is being used. Regardless of the other merits of a test, if it lacks validity, the information it provides is useless. The validity of a measure can be viewed as the "correctness" of the inferences made from performance on the measure. These inferences will pertain to (1) performance on a *universe* of items (content validity), (2) performance on some criterion (criterion-related validity), or (3) the degree to which certain psychological traits or constructs are actually represented by test performance (construct validity).

It should be evident that validity is not a simple concept. In Chapter 1 several different uses of tests were described. The extent to which a test provides correct information is the extent to which it provides useful information and, hence, has validity for this purpose. The common question "Is the test valid?" is an ambiguous statement. Indeed, in a real sense a test possesses many validities; it may be valid for one purpose but not for others. The question of the validity of a test (or other measure) is always limited and particularized; it can be answered only in relation to a given purpose for a given set of examinees.

A joint committee of the American Psychological Association (APA), American Educational Research Association (AERA), and National Council on Measurement (NCME) in Education has prepared a set of recommendations to improve the quality of validity data and other information on published tests. In this chapter validity is classified into three subtypes: content, criterion-related, and construct, as outlined in the APA-AERA-NCME recommendations. The three types subsume the three principal purposes for which tests are used.

4.2 CONTENT VALIDITY

The relevant type of validity in the measurement of academic achievement is *content* validity. In assessing the content validity of an achievement test, one asks, "To what extent does the test require demonstration by the student of the achievements that constitute the objectives of instruction in this area?" For a test to have high content validity, it should be a representative sample of both the *content/topics* and the *cognitive processes/abilities* objectives of a given course or unit—the test should contain a representative sample of the content and uses to which the content is to be applied.

Figure 4–1, from the handbook accompanying the *Sequential Tests of Educational Progress* (*STEP*), illustrates both the content and the skills sampled on the *STEP* science test. Even more explicit information on a test's content validity is illustrated in Figure 4–2, in which specific instructional objectives and topics are referenced to test items across the various levels of the *Metropolitan Achievement Tests*. This kind of information is very helpful in assessing the test's content validity for a given curriculum and for diagnostic evaluations of curricular and special programs.

An achievement test should *re*-present the content universe about which one wishes to make an assessment. It is axiomatic that the content validity of a test must always be viewed in relation to the particular objectives to be assessed.

How does one determine the content validity of a measure? Content validation is primarily a process of logical analysis. By means of a careful and critical examination of the test items in relation to the course objectives and instruction, one must make the following professional judgments:

1. Does the test content parallel the curricular objectives in content and processes?
2. Are the test and curricular emphases in proper balance?
3. Is the test free from prerequisites that are irrelevant or incidental to the present measurement task? (For example, are the reading level of the science or math tests appropriate for the examinees?)

It is crucial that each of the points in question be studied carefully before selecting a standardized test. School districts too often make only a cursory examination of published tests before formulating their district-wide testing programs. Small wonder, then, that teachers complain, "The test doesn't measure what we're teaching." The teachers (especially high school teachers) feel that the test does not "mirror" the curriculum. The teachers' objections may, or may not, be correct. Some teachers think it is unfair to include any item that is not covered in the course of study for the class—a very narrow view of an appropriate content universe for a standardized test. Nevertheless, those who select standardized tests for a district testing program are often much too casual. A systematic study of the available standardized tests will rarely identify a test that is a perfect "fit" for a specific curriculum; only tests constructed carefully by a special team of curriculum and test experts (an expensive task) can approach this objective. However, some of the published tests will be more relevant for the district's objectives than others—even though none will measure all of the cognitive objectives, not to mention the affective objectives. This and related problems are considered more extensively in Section 14.4.

Besides providing norms, standardized achievement tests differ from locally constructed tests in at least two important respects: (1) Standardized tests measure a wider span of content because they are administered at intervals of a year or more, and (2) standardized achievement tests attempt to measure general, broad objectives and minimize any special local,

ITEM CLASSIFICATION

SCIENCE, FORM 3A

Item Number	Right Answer	Grade 7 % Right	Grade 8 % Right	Grade 9 % Right	Knowledge Biology	Knowledge Chemistry	Knowledge Physics	Knowledge Earth Sciences	Comprehension Biology	Comprehension Chemistry	Comprehension Physics	Comprehension Earth Sciences	Application Biology	Application Chemistry	Application Physics	Application Earth Sciences	Higher Abilities Biology	Higher Abilities Chemistry	Higher Abilities Physics	Higher Abilities Earth Sciences	Item Number
1	D	88	91	94												X					1
2	C	75	86	92	X																2
3	A	66	76	88											X						3
4	C	88	89	92												X					4
5	D	74	79	86								X									5
6	C	77	83	86				X													6
7	D	72	79	88						X											7
8	B	94	94	95					X												8
9	A	55	65	72					X												9
10	D	87	91	94								X									10
11	A	53	60	58								X									11
12	D	62	68	74												X					12
13	C	58	67	73									X								13
14	C	55	63	68						X											14
15	A	61	72	77	X																15
16	D	48	58	63									X								16
17	B	35	49	65		X															17
18	C	40	54	66	X																18
19	C	54	59	60											X						19
20	C	45	55	64													X				20
21	B	58	63	72					X												21
22	D	40	49	58					X												22
23	B	54	62	67									X								23
24	B	49	53	63										X							24
25	C	32	45	58													X				25
26	A	48	55	61												X					26
27	A	42	54	63	X																27
28	C	46	57	66															X		28
29	B	65	70	76														X			29
30	D	31	37	39								X									30
31	C	49	54	60									X								31
32	C	46	50	54											X						32
33	D	39	52	57		X															33
34	D	48	56	60									X								34
35	D	32	36	43										X							35
36	C	34	38	38																X	36
37	A	28	41	44									X								37
38	A	25	32	40										X							38
39	C	31	39	51										X							39
40	A	31	36	40	X																40
41	D	29	34	39												X					41
42	A	34	41	43									X								42
43	D	32	34	40													X				43
44	A	25	33	50										X							44
45	D	53	62	69						X											45
46	C	38	45	49										X							46
47	B	33	38	43										X							47
48	B	66	73	81	X																48
49	A	59	67	73									X								49
50	D	52	63	69								X									50

SCIENCE ITEM CLASSIFICATION CATEGORIES

Skill

Knowledge, the ability to recall ideas, material, or phenomena. (22% of the items)

Comprehension, the ability to translate ideas or material from one method of expression to another; to interpret material presented, or to extrapolate from it. (20% of the items)

Application, the ability to use learned information in answering an unfamiliar question or solving a new problem. (46% of the items)

Higher level skills, analysis, the ability to break down material into its constituent parts and to detect the relationships among them and the way they are organized; synthesis, the ability to combine parts to produce a new pattern or structure; evaluation, the ability to make purposeful judgments of ideas and solutions. (12% of the items)

Content

Biology, includes development, ecology, evolution, heredity, morphology, physiology, and taxonomy. (40% of the items)

Chemistry, includes atomic structure and bonding, kinetic-molecular theory, the chemistry of particular substances, energy considerations, and fundamental terms and calculations. Some questions are laboratory oriented. (16% of the items)

Physics, includes atomic and nuclear physics, electricity and magnetism, heat and kinetic theory, mechanics, optics, and waves. (24% of the items)

Earth Sciences, includes astronomy, geology, and meteorology. (20% of the items)

FIGURE 4–1   An illustration of topic and process grid on a standardized achievement test.

SOURCE: *The Sequential Tests of Educational Progress, STEP Series II Science Test,* Form A, Level 3, p. 104. Reprinted by permission of Educational Testing Service. Copyright © 1971 by Educational Testing Service. All rights reserved.

MATHEMATICS OBJECTIVES

For the following Mathematics objectives, item numbers on the Survey and Instructional tests are combined within the same chart, but are separated by a slash mark (⬜▱). For example, Numeration Objective 01 is tested by items 1, 2, and 3 on the Primer Numeration Test (Mathematics Instructional Tests), and by item 1 on the Mathematics Test of the Survey Battery. Preprimer and Advanced 2 are Survey only.

Instructional / Survey

Objective — NUMERATION	Preprimer	Primer	Primary 1	Primary 2	Elementary	Intermediate	Advanced 1	Advanced 2
01 Can count groups of objects to 10	/ 12	1,2,3 / 1						
03 Can associate the numerals 1-10 with the correct number of objects	/ 13	7,8,9 / 3						
11 Can determine ordinal position through 10		19,20,21 / 6	7,8,9 / 3					
18 Can count by 2's, 5's, and 10's			16,17,18 / 6	16,17,18 / 6	7,8,9 / 3			
28 Can associate the correct number-words with numerals (through millions)					25,26,27 / 9	19,20,21 / 14		
30 Can complete a simple number sequence when pattern must be discovered						13,14,15 / 12	1,2,3 / 7	
34 Can convert between standard and exponential notation							13,14,15 /	/ 31
GEOMETRY & MEASUREMENT								
08 Can tell time to the hour		25,26,27 / 23	10,11,12 / 14					
19 Can determine the amount of change due on purchases of one dollar or less				28,29,30 / 20	25,26,27 / 18	1,2,3 / 18		
22 Can determine the perimeter of squares, rectangles, and triangles					16,17,18 / 16	13,14,15 / 21		
PROBLEM SOLVING								
1SD Can solve a simple problem, dictated by the teacher, involving addition (Basic Facts: Sums to 10)	/ 25	13,14,15 / 25,26	1,2,3 / 20					
9SR Can solve a word problem, read by the pupil, involving one of the four basic operations, with no limit on the computation involved						16,17,18 / 6	13,14,15 / 3	16,18
OPERATIONS: WHOLE NUMBERS								
A4 Can find sums of two-digit numbers, and sums of two-digit and one-digit numbers, where no regrouping is required			10,11,12 / 33,34	16,17,18 / 36,37	1,2,3 / 40			
M5 Can multiply two-digit and one-digit numbers where regrouping is required					25,26,27 / 48	10,11,12 / 36	10,11,12 / 36	
D5 Can divide a two-digit number by a one-digit number, with remainder						19,20,21 / 39	19,20,21 / 39	
OPERATIONS: LAWS & PROPERTIES								
12 Knows the *Associative Properties of Addition and Multiplication* and can use them						13,14,15 / 28	1,2,3 / 15	
13 Recognizes multiplication and division as inverses						22,23,24 / 29	4,5,6 /	
14 Knows the rules for *order of operations* in algebraic sentences and can use them							7,8,9 / 16	

FIGURE 4-2   Illustrative mathematics objectives for the *Metropolitan Achievement Tests* classified by test level.

(Continued)

Objective OPERATIONS: FRACTIONS & DECIMALS	Test Level		
	Intermediate	Advanced 1	Advanced 2
01 Can add fractions with like denominators where *no reducing* is required	1,2,3 46		
04 Can subtract fractions with like denominators, with *reducing*	10,11, 12	7,8,9	
05 Can multiply two fractions where *no reducing* is required	19,20, 21	25,26, 27 46	
06 Can draw inferences from tabled data	7,8,9	4,5,6 26	
07 Can determine the average (mean) of data from a table		7,8,9 27	
08 Can interpret a frequency distribution		10,11, 12	
16 Can compute with percents		43,44, 45 50	12,13
17 Can multiply fractions and mixed numbers			8
GRAPHS & STATISTICS			
09 Can determine the probability of an independent event *not* occurring and the combined probability of independent events		22,23, 24	
10 Can determine a linear equation in two unknowns from a graph			47
11 Can determine slopes and intercepts for graphs of linear equations in two unknowns			48
12 Can determine graphs for quadratic equations			50

FIGURE 4–2 Continued

state, or regional emphases. Consequently, standardized tests are more process-oriented and less topic-oriented than is typical of teacher-made tests. Standardized achievement tests are not substitutes for teacher-developed tests; rather, the two types of measures are complementary.

It is impractical to conduct an *extensive* content validity analysis like those represented in Figures 4–1 and 4–2 on all or even most teacher-constructed tests, but the teacher should systematically examine each classroom test before its administration to ensure a good representative sampling from the content universe. The teacher should ask:

1. Are all the important instructional topics represented in about the correct proportions on the test?
2. Is there a proper balance of cognitive processes required, or is there an overemphasis on rote knowledge?
3. Are all of the questions relevant?
4. Are there trivial items that should be eliminated?

Such elementary questions as these, if raised systematically by teachers at all educational levels, would greatly improve the quality of educational measurement.

Content validity should not be confused with *face* validity; face validity lacks the systematic rational analysis required in the assessment of content validation. A test is said to have face validity if, on first impression, it appears to measure the intended content or trait. It is important that tests have face validity; otherwise, students may feel that they are being unfairly assessed. Typically, a content-valid test will also have face validity, but it is possible to have one without the other. Essay tests usually have high face validity, especially for people who are unfamiliar with research on the topic, but they may lack reliability (Chapter 5), an indispensable prerequisite for valid measurement of individual differences. Conversely, a test item that is not presented in a practical context may actually measure an important concept or ability, but it may lack face validity for some examinees. For example, consider the following item:

> Which of these *least* belongs with the other three?
> a) 84th percentile, b) $T = 60$, c) stanine = 8, d) $z = 1.0$

The item requires knowledge of the normal curve in relation to percentiles and some understanding of standard scores of the T, z, and stanine types as well. Options *a, b,* and *d* describe the identical point in a normal distribution, whereas stanine 8 falls above this point. Some students might respond, "If that's what you wanted to know, why didn't you ask?" If the item were recast into the form, "Which one of the following is *not* one standard deviation above the mean in a normal distribution?" much of the cognitive synthesis and induction of the item would be reduced, and hence its potential for measuring higher levels of understanding would be attenuated.

When properly used, the kind of item that requires the student to find the concept being assessed as well as the answer *can* measure a high level of conceptual comprehension and application. Such items may lack face validity for examinees who are unsophisticated in measurement but have face validity for more knowledgeable examinees. Face validity is important for the test's clientele, be they students or job applicants. Examinees should feel they are being treated fairly. Tests with good content validity *usually* have face validity; the reverse, however, is much less likely to be true.

Content validity is relevant not only for achievement tests but also for psychological, psychomotor, and behavioral measures. Are the items on the instrument a representative sample of the domain of content to which an inference is being made? If a performance measure in tennis required no use of a backhand stroke, its content validity would be impaired—the sample of tasks assessed would not be representative of the content universe. A teaching proficiency measure that pertains exclusively to interpersonal relationships with staff and students would be a non-representative sample of tasks within the job description of a teacher. Some general intelligence tests are composed entirely of vocabulary and verbal stimuli; the content validity of such tests is weaker than that of intelligence tests that also include pictorial, numerical, spatial, and abstract-reasoning items. *The content validity of a test is the degree to which the items of that test are a representative sample of the content universe and/or behavior of the domain being assessed.* The generalization from test scores to the domain of intelligence behavior is only as good as the representativeness of the sample of tasks (items) employed. The concept of content validity will be discussed further in Chapter 7 (course-oriented achievement tests) and Chapter 14 (standardized achievement tests).

4.3 CRITERION-RELATED VALIDITY

In contrast to content validity, which is based almost entirely on rational analysis, *criterion-related validity* is purely an empirical matter. There are two subclasses of criterion-related validity. The more common of these is *predictive validity*, in which the test has the task of predicting some subsequent performance on a criterion. For example, a university wishes to identify which applicants are most likely to complete a degree program if admitted to the university. The university is not concerned primarily with whether the test is a representative sample of some universe (content validity) or a measure of some psychological trait (construct validity); the university wishes to select the applicants who are good risks and reject those who are poor risks. Although unlikely, but just to make the point, if people who indicate that they prefer strawberry to vanilla ice cream are more likely to drop out, then this could be a relevant item in a selection test because it has predictive validity. The item fulfills its function—to increase the accuracy decision for the selection task at hand. In practice, logical validity and predictive validity usually are found together but not always.

A measure's predictive validity, then, is how well its predictions agree with subsequent outcomes. The type of validity for which the *Scholastic Aptitude Test* (*SAT*) is used is predictive validity (Boldt, 1986). The extent to which scores on the tests are related to various measures of success in college is the extent to which the test fulfills its predictive function. The accuracy of the predictions is described by the *correlation coefficient* between test scores and a subsequent empirical criterion. This correlation is a validity coefficient because it defines the degree of criterion-related validity of the test. Decisions involving selection (e.g., to admit or hire an applicant) are predictive in nature. Insurance companies set their rates based on variables that predict a subsequent outcome. Car insurance costs less for students with good GPAs because GPA has predictive validity for criteria that represent safe driving—criteria that have cost ramifications to the company. The extent to which the use of tests and other measures can improve the accuracy of predictions of performance on subsequent criteria is the extent to which the tests can be of value. Medical histories are a routine part of medical care because many of the questions have predictive validity for relevant health criteria.

The meaning of correlation and correlation coefficients is essential to an understanding of criterion-related validity.

4.4   CORRELATION AND PREDICTION

1. Most people have a general understanding of the meaning of correlation (i.e., co-relationship or covariation). Two traits are correlated if they tend to "go together." If high scores on variable X tend to be accompanied by high scores on variable Y, then the variables X and Y are correlated, since the scores "covary." For example, there is a tendency for tall people to weigh more than short people. Since height and weight tend to covary, they are said to be _____.   correlated

2. We can describe the degree of correlation between variables by terms such as *strong, low,* or *moderate,* but these terms are not sufficiently explicit. A more precise method is to compute a coefficient of correlation between the sets of scores. A coefficient of correlation is a statistical summary of the degree of relationship or "going-togetherness" between two variables. Correlation coefficients range in magnitude from +1.0 to −1.0. A positive correlation coefficient means that high scores on one measure tend to be associated with high scores on another measure, and low scores

on one tend to be associated with low scores on the other. For example, there is a tendency for individuals with high scores on a scholastic aptitude test to receive better marks than those with low scores. The correlation coefficient for this example would be _____ (positive or negative).

positive

3. On the other hand, for adults, age correlates negatively with certain psychomotor abilities. The sign (+ or −) of the correlation coefficient indicates the *direction* of the relationship. When low scores on variable A are accompanied by low scores on variable B, and high scores on A by high scores on B, r_{AB} (the coefficient of correlation between A and B) is _____ ; if high scores on A are associated with low scores on C (and vice versa), r_{AC} would be _____.

positive
negative

4. The sign of r does not indicate the strength of a relationship. For example, if test scores correlate −.3 with number of days absent for a group of third-grade students, then the correlation between tests scores and days present would be _____.

+.3

5. The numeric value of r denotes the degree of the relationship; the higher the absolute value (the value irrespective of the sign), the stronger the relationship. If $r_{AB} = +.55$ and $r_{AC} = -.70$, there is a stronger relation between variable A and variable ___ than there is between variable A and variable ___.

C
B

6. When $r = +1.0$ or -1.0, there is a perfect relationship between the two variables. In both cases a knowledge of one of the variables makes it possible to predict the second variable without error. With $r = +1.0$, the z-scores of each individual would be the same on both measures. With $r = -1.0$, the highest score on one measure would be associated with the lowest score on the second measure, and so on. Any pair of z-scores would be identical in value but opposite in sign, for example, +1.3 and −1.3. If two tests correlate +1.0 and Ann ranked third on test A, she would rank _____ on test B. If her z-score on test A is +1.8, her z-score on test B would be _____.

third
+1.8

7. Although a correlation coefficient cannot be interpreted as the percent of agreement, it does reflect the *expected* percentage of deviation from the mean of the second variable. For example, in the general population, fathers' or mothers' IQs tend to correlate about 0.5 with offsprings' IQs. The .5 correlation indicates that the best prediction we can make of a child's IQ score is that it will be only 50 percent as far from the population mean as the father's. If a representative sample 100 fathers scoring 130 on an intelligence test was selected, and then one child of each father was tested, the children's mean IQ would be expected to be only one-half (. 5) as far from the population mean (100) as were the fathers'. The mean of the children would be expected to be about _____.

115

8. On the other hand, if we selected a group of fathers with IQ scores of 80, and then examined their fathers, we would expect the mean IQ score of the fathers to be about _____.[1]

90

9. It is important to bear in mind that a correlation coefficient expresses the ratio of the average or *expected* deviation from the mean on the predicted variable (Y) to the *known* deviation from the mean on the predictor variable (X) in standard deviation units. The following regression equation makes this clear.

$$z'_Y = rz_X$$

where
z'_Y is the expected or predicted z-score on variable Y,
r = the correlation between variables X *and* Y, and
z_X = the known z-score on variable X.

If the distances that a group of children can high-jump and long-jump correlate .6, then we can say that, on the average, those who are two standard deviations from the mean in long-jumping average _____ standard deviation(s) above the mean in high-jumping. If a child has a z-score of –1.0 in high-jumping, a z-score of _____ in long-jumping is predicted for that child.

1.2

–.6

10. Grade point average (GPA) at most colleges correlates approximately, $\rho = 0.4$ with the verbal subtest of the *Scholastic Aptitude Test* (*SAT-V*). For College A, suppose you have the following information:

	SAT-V	GPA
μ	500	2.8
σ	100	.6

$$\rho = .4$$

A certain student has an *SAT-V* score of 600, which is 1.0 standard deviation above the mean; $z_X = 1.0$. Predict her GPA. Her GPA z-score is expected to be only 40 percent as far from the mean as is her *SAT-V* score: $z'_Y = $ (____)(1.0) = .4, or a GPA that is .4 standard deviations above the mean GPA. Therefore, her predicted GPA is:

2.8 + (____)(____) = 3.24

0.4, 0.4, 0.6

11. The hand computation of r (the Pearson product-moment coefficient of correlation) is cumbersome, but is an option on all spreadsheets and available on many hand calculators. The Spearman rank correlation coefficient, r_{ranks}, is a very close relative of r, and its value differs little[2] from r. The computation of r_{ranks} is straightforward, and the process of computation illuminates the meaning of correlation. The value of r_{ranks} and r for the same set of data will differ _____ (very little, or greatly).

very little

---

[1] An erroneous conclusion, often drawn when one is first introduced to this "regression toward the mean" (be it illustrated with IQ scores, height, or any other variable), is that successive generations become less variable. This is not the case. There are enough individual exceptions to the general trend to preserve the equality of the standard deviations for the two groups. In our example you will note that $\sigma = 15$ for both fathers and children; hence, the children are not more homogeneous in IQ scores than their fathers. The regression operates both ways; for example, had we selected 100 children with IQs of 130 and then tested their fathers, the mean IQ of the fathers would be expected to be 115.
[2] For example, using the data in Frame 12: $r_{ranks} = .18$ vs. $r = .19$; for the data in Frame 14: $r_{ranks} = .68$ vs. $r = .67$.

12. Correlation can be viewed simply as the degree to which persons maintain the same relative positions or ranks on two variables. If there is much change, the correlation coefficient will be low; if there is little change, the coefficient will be high. A correlation coefficient can be obtained between any two variables if scores are available on both. For example, two of the tests from the *Primary Mental Abilities Tests* (*PMA*), Verbal Meaning (VM) and the Word Fluency (WF) tests, were given to the students in a measurement class. To simplify our illustration, only 11 pairs of scores will be used to illustrate the computation of the Spearman rank correlation coefficient, r_{ranks}. To compute the Spearman rank correlation:

1. Rank the individuals on the first variable (e.g., VM) from the highest score (a rank of 1) to the lowest score (a rank of *N—N* is the number of *pairs* of scores, in this example, 11). The VM score of 50 (see table) is the highest score, thus receives a rank of 1; 49 is the next-highest score and receives a rank of 2, and so on; the lowest VM score is 35 and has a rank of 11.
2. Rank the individuals on the second variable (e.g., in the same way. The highest WF score is 67, which receives a rank of 1, and so on; the lowest WF score is 25, which has a rank of 11.
3. Find the difference between ranks for each individual, putting this value in the column headed "Rank Difference" (*D*). (The *sign* of the difference is unnecessary, since all values will be squared.)
4. Square each rank difference (*D*) value and place the result in the column, D^2.
5. Sum the values in the D^2 column to obtain[3] ΣD^2.

Person	Score		Rank		Rank Difference	
	VM	WF	VM	WF	D	D^2
A	50	51	1	5	4	16
B	49	56	2	4	2	4
C	48	59	3	2	1	1
D	47	48	4	6	2	4
E	46	37	5	9	4	16
F	45	32	6	11	5	25
G	44	58	7	3	4	16
H	43	44	8	8	0	0
I	42	34	9	10	1	1
J	41	61	10	1	9	81
K	35	46	11	7	4	16

$$\Sigma D^2 = 180$$

---

[3]Recall that "Σ" means "the sum of."

6. Compute r_{ranks}, using the formula:

$$r_{ranks} = 1 - \frac{6\Sigma D^2}{N(N^2 - 1)}$$

$$= 1 - \frac{6(180)}{11[(11)^2 - 1]}$$

$$= 1 - \frac{1080}{11(121 - 1)} = 1 - \frac{1080}{11(120)} = 1 - \frac{1080}{1320} = 1 - .82$$

$$r_{ranks} = \underline{\qquad} .$$

.18

13. The low relationship (.18) between the VM and WF scores can be illustrated graphically by a *scatterplot*—a plot that shows the pattern of relationship between the two variables. Complete the following scatterplot by (1) finding the person's rank on the horizontal axis (VM in this example), (2) then move up vertically from that point until you intersect with the rank on the vertical variable (WF in this example). Those persons with ranks of 1, 2, and 3 on VM have already been entered. Complete the plot of the corresponding ranks.

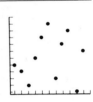

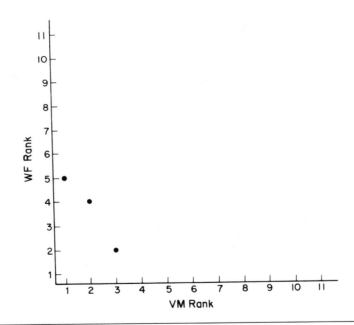

14. Complete the table and compute the rank difference correlation coefficient between math and IQ scores using the 10 pairs of scores given in the following table:

Person	Score Math	Score IQ	Rank[4] Math	Rank[4] IQ	Difference D	Difference D²	
A	30	105	6	—	—	—	8, 2, 4
B	38	120	—	3	—	—	2, , 1, 1
C	16	83	—	—	—	—	10, 10, 0, 0
D	37	137	—	—	—	—	3, 1 , 2, 4
E	32	114	—	5	—	—	5, , 0, 0
F	25	96	—	—	—	—	8, 9, 1, 1
G	19	107	—	—	—	—	9, 7, 2, 4
H	45	117	1	—	—	—	, 4, 3, 9
I	33	108	4	—	—	—	, 6, 2, 4
J	29	130	—	—	—	—	7, 2, 5, 25

$\Sigma D^2 =$ ____   52

$$r_{\text{ranks}} = 1 - \frac{6\Sigma D^2}{N(N^2 - 1)} = 1 - \frac{6(\underline{\quad})}{(\underline{\ })(10^2 - 1)} = 1 - .32 = .68$$

52, 10

4.5   THE CONCEPT OF CORRELATION

Almost a century ago, Sir Francis Galton (a cousin of Darwin) and the pioneer English statistician Karl Pearson succeeded in developing the theory and mathematical basis for what is now known as *correlation*. They were concerned with developing a quantitative description of the degree of relationships between two variables, for example, height and weight. It is obvious that above-average height tends to go with above-average weight. Height and weight vary together (correlate positively), though the relationship is certainly not perfect; tall and slender persons and short and heavy persons can also be found.

Let's examine some other variables that tend to be associated. There is a substantial positive correlation between academic aptitude test scores in high school and grades earned during the freshman year of college. The higher the test score obtained by a student, the higher the grades are *likely* to be. The lower the score is, the lower the grades the student will *probably* obtain. This relationship has been found with all sorts of cognitive tests for students of all ethnic groups since such tests first became available commercially, shortly after the end of World War I, including the physically handicapped (Bejar & Blew, 1981; Bennett, Rock & Kaplan, 1987; Donlon, 1984; Lavin, 1967).

---

[4]The computation of r_{ranks}, in this example has no tied scores. When ties occur, all scores receive the *average* of the ranks that are involved. Suppose two persons tied for the highest math score; the ranks for each of the two scores is $1.5 = (1 + 2)/2$. If three persons tied for the next-highest score, the ranks involved are 3, 4, and 5; each of the three persons has a rank of $4 = (3 + 4 + 5)/3$.

Husbands and wives *tend* to be much more like each other with respect to age, amount of education, and many other factors than they are like people in general. The sons of tall fathers tend to be taller than average, and the sons of short fathers tend to be shorter than average. Children resemble their own parents in intelligence more closely than they resemble other adults. Some degree of positive correlation between members of families is usually found for almost any characteristic, such as personality, attitude, interest, or ability.

To quantify Galton's the degree of *co*-relationships between traits, Pearson devised as a measure of relationship the *coefficient of correlation*, r. It is widely used in all social and behavioral sciences. College graduates lack minimal competency in quantitative literacy if they do not understand the correlation coefficient and measures of central tendency.

Pearson's *r* summarizes the *magnitude* and *direction* of the degree of relationship between two variables, such as height and weight on the *same* persons, or between the same variable on *pairs* of persons, like the fathers and sons. A *correlation coefficient* can be obtained for any set of paired observations (e.g., speaking ability and writing ability, speed of running the 100-yard dash and skill in playing the violin, school attitude and IQ, etc.). The correlation coefficient, *r*, can have values that range from –1 for a perfect inverse (negative) relationship, through 0 for no systematic correlation, to +1 for a perfect positive relationship. The *r*s between radically different pairs of variables can also be compared. For example, it is meaningful to say that reading ability and intelligence are more closely related than height and weight. Consider this more interesting example (Glass & Hopkins, 1996, p. 109): Whereas the IQ scores of identical twins reared apart are more highly correlated than the IQ scores of fraternal twins reared together; the pattern for scholastic achievement (e.g., GPA) is reversed— the *r* between scholastic achievement for fraternal twins reared together is higher than the *r* for identical twins reared apart. Although correlation coefficients are concise statistical summaries of relationships, their meaning is more evident and enhanced by the relationship depicted graphically using scatterplots.

4.6   CORRELATION AND SCATTERPLOTS

The scatterplot enables one to study the nature of the relationship between two variables. Each dot of the scatterplot indicates the intersection of the two measures, *X* and *Y*, for one individual. The scatterplot reveals whether the relationship between the two variables is linear. The relationship between two variables is *linear* if a straight line more closely fits the dots of the scatterplot than any curved line does. A perfect positive linear relationship ($r = 1.0$) is shown in Figure 4–3A—note that all of the dots fall on a straight line from low *X*-low *Y* to high *X*-high *Y*. A perfect negative relationship ($r = -1.0$) is illustrated in the scatterplot in Figure 4–3B. In practice, *r*s of 1.0 and –1.0 are rare; nevertheless, they help us to understand the meaning of perfect linear relationships.

In Figure 4–3C there is no relationship between the two variables *X* and *Y*; the value *r* is 0. Knowledge of persons standing on one measure does not help predict their standing on the other measure. Regardless of a person's standing on *X*, the best prediction of *Y* is the mean of *Y*. Intermediate values for *r* = .30, .60, and .90 are illustrated in Figures 4–3D, 4–3E, and 4–3F.

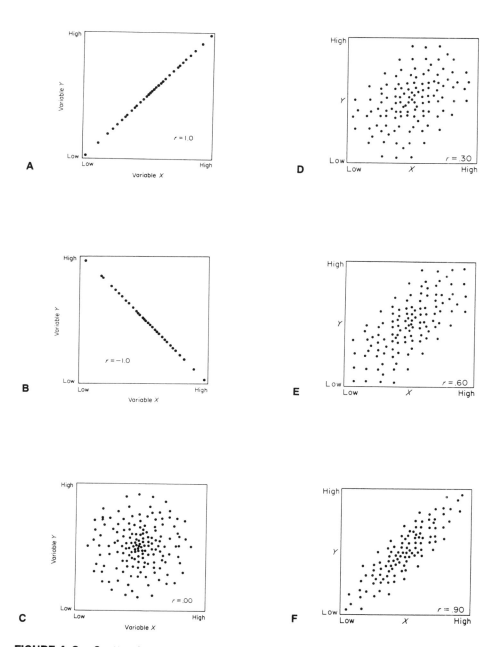

FIGURE 4–3 Scatterplots depicting various correlation coefficients.

Some variables are related, but not linearly related. A curvilinear (or non-linear) relationship is shown in Figure 4–4. Although the figure shows that there is no linear relationship between *X* and *Y,* if an individual's score is known on measure *X,* one can predict the score on the second measure *Y* with considerable accuracy despite the fact that if the value of *r* were computed, it would be zero. For scatterplots of this sort, *r* will greatly underestimate the degree of relationship between the two measures, and therefore is not an appropriate measure of relationship if the relationship is not linear. An actual scatterplot with a curvilinear relationship is given in Figure 10–2; if *r* were computed, its value would be near 0, yet a visual scan of the plot reveals a definite nonlinear (curvilinear) relationship.

4.7 INTERPRETING CORRELATION COEFFICIENTS

In interpreting a coefficient of correlation, several factors must be considered. The first is the *sign* of the coefficient; the second is the *magnitude* of the coefficient. The sign (+ or −) indicates the *direction* of the relationship. Positive coefficients indicate direct relationship, that is, the tendency for higher scores on *X* to be associated with higher scores on *Y*, and vice versa. High values in one column are associated with high values in the other column; low values in one column are associated with low values in the other column; and so on. Negative *r*s indicate and "upside-down" relationship—a tendency for the two scores to vary in opposite directions—high values on one variable are associated with low values on the other variable, and vice versa.

The magnitude of the value of *r* indicates the *degree* or closeness of the relationship. If there is no relationship between *X* and *Y*, the value of *r* is 0. A perfect relationship is denoted by an *r*-value of +1 or −1; if *r* is either 1.0 or -1.0, the exact value of *Y* can be pre-

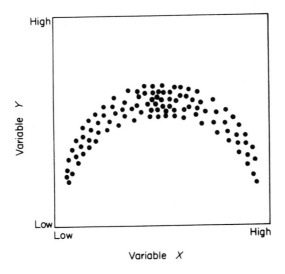

FIGURE 4–4 An illustration of a substantial curvilinear relationship.

dicted from knowledge of *X*. Similarly, all other values of the same size, such as −.50 and .50, indicate the same degree of relationships—the size, not the sign, of the coefficient indicates the closeness of degree of relationship.

Certain cautions should be observed. First, *r cannot be interpreted directly as a percent in the usual sense.* The value of *r* can be interpreted as a percent if standard deviations are used. Suppose traits *X* and *Y* correlate .60 (r_{XY} = .60). The .60 correlation indicates that examinees tend to be only 60 percent as far from the *Y* mean as they are from the mean of *X* (in standard score units, e.g., *z*). In other words, examinees who are one standard deviation above the mean on *X* (z_X = 1), tend to be only 0.6 standard deviation above the mean on *Y* (z_Y = 0.6) on the average. The interpretation is simplified when dealing with variables when the two standard deviations are equal, that is, $\sigma_X = \sigma_Y$. For example, the correlation between the height of a mother (or father) with the adult height of their sons (or daughters) is 0.5; this means that if a mother is 4 inches taller than average, then her sons will average 2 inches taller than average. The correlation between the IQ scores of one parent with the IQ scores of the children is also .5; this means that, on the average, children are only one-half as far from the mean of 100 as are the parents. In other words, fathers who receive IQ scores of 90, have daughters who have an average IQ score of 95. There is much variation in the scores of the daughters, but their mean will be only 50 percent as far from the mean as were their fathers.

The relationship between scores on *Graduate Record Examinations Analytical* (*GRE-A*) test and their subsequent composite scores in an elementary statistics course (expressed as *T*-scores) is graphically depicted in the scatterplot in Figure 4–5. Although there is a definite relationship (*r* = .58) for the 112 students, there are many individual exceptions to the

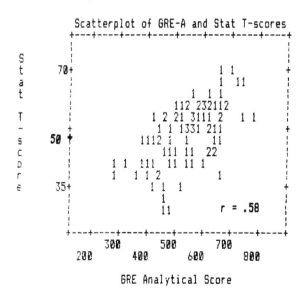

FIGURE 4–5 A computer-produced scatterplot of *Graduate Record Examination—Analytical* scores and composite scores in an elementary statistics course (expressed as *T*-scores) for *N* = 112 graduate students.

general trend, shown by the *line of best fit*—if the sample was extremely large, this line would connect the mean values of *Y* for each value of *X*.

Notice, for example, that some students with *GRE-A* scores above 500 did not do well, whereas others performed exceptionally well. Notice that no student with a very low *GRE-A* score did very well in statistics. Of the six persons with a *GRE-A* score below 400, only one had a score above 50 (the mean), whereas the other five were well below (about 1σ) average. Observe that, even though the *GRE-A* has some predictive validity, we should not lose sight of the fact that many individuals depart substantially from the general trend. Note that one student with a very high *GRE-A* score of 660 was a full standard deviation below the class average (i.e., performed at approximately the 16th percentile).

4.8   CORRELATION VERSUS CAUSATION

It is critical to understand that because two variables correlate does not necessarily mean that there is a *causative* relationship between the two. Another variable other than the two under consideration may be responsible for the association. Furthermore, problems in the social sciences, the field in which correlation is most often employed, are usually too complex to be explained in terms of a single cause. The fact that people who have taken driver training have fewer automobile accidents than those without such training is a far cry from establishing a causal relationship between accidents and lack of driver training.

Let us take several examples. It is probably true that in the United States there is some positive correlation between the average salaries of teachers in various high schools and the percentages of the schools' graduates who go on to college. But to say that these students attend college *because* their teachers are well paid is as inaccurate as to say that their teachers are well paid *because* many of the graduates attend college.

It has been found that the percentage of dropouts occurring in high schools varies inversely (is negatively correlated) with the number of books per student in the libraries of those schools. But common sense tells us that merely piling more books into the library will no more affect the dropout rate than hiring a better attendance officer will bring about a magical increase in the number of books. If only common sense always served us so well!

Attributing causation to correlation is a very common error. Students from homes having encyclopedias tend to have somewhat higher achievement than students without this resource. But this is true even for first grade students and others who virtually never consult the encyclopedia. Underlying and causing may be the culture of the home regarding the value of education, the amount of parent-child reading, and the like.

For criterion-related validity, causation is not the issue but forecasting. If college applicants who score well on the *SAT* subsequently tend to have high GPAs in college, the *SAT* can be said to have criterion-related validity for this purpose. The degree of criterion-related validity is usually denoted by a correlation coefficient, r.[5]

4.9   INFLUENCE OF SAMPLE SIZE, *n*

The size of the sample on which the correlation coefficient was determined is another factor important in interpreting correlation coefficients. For example, consider the correlation between IQ and height with a sample of two ($n = 2$). The computed *r* can only be either +1.0

or −1.0. The higher-ranking person in IQ will be either the taller of the two (hence, $r = 1.0$) or the shorter of the two (hence, $r = −1.0$).

To keep us from being misled by high correlation coefficients resulting from small samples, statisticians have developed procedures to assist in determining whether a given correlation coefficient can be attributed to chance (sampling error) or whether a genuine relationship exists. If a correlation is *statistically significant*, we can be confident that there is some degree of true relationship between the two variables. For example, if you encountered in your reading of professional literature a statement such as "For first-grade boys the correlation between height and achievement was statistically significant," it would mean that it is very unlikely that the true correlation is zero. Hence, we can be quite confident that some genuine relationship exists between the two variables.[6] A common error in interpreting such *statistically significant* relationships is to assume that because they are statistically significant that they are therefore *large* relationships. "Statistically significant" indicates that one can be confident that the true correlation in the population (i.e., the parameter, ρ) is not 0. If the sample size is very large, a relationship may be statistically significant and yet be trivial. For example, the relationship between height and IQ, though statistically significant, is too low to be of value for practical purposes.

To guard against the error in interpreting statistically significant relationships as strong relationships, *confidence intervals* should be used. These intervals give the upper and lower limits for the value of the true correlation coefficient in the population. For example, a highly significant correlation of $r = .32$ was observed between study habits and scholastic aptitude for 172 ninth-grade boys. How much error is there in the value of .32? The confidence interval around r gives a reasonable estimate as to how high or how low the value of the correlation coefficient might be if the entire population in question were included in the sample. In this instance the 95 percent confidence interval is (.16, .44), consequently, we can be "95 percent confident" that, in spite of the n of only 172, the true correlation coefficient in the population is at least .16, and perhaps as high as .44. If our sample is representative and if we repeatedly use this strategy, we will be correct 95 percent of the time. Stated another way, in the long run, the true correlation, ρ, will lie within the 95 percent confidence interval, in 95 percent of the intervals.

Since high or low values for r are much more likely to occur by chance with small ns, high values of r are required for statistical significance when n is small. Table 4–1 shows that (1) correlation coefficients based on small samples are not very reliable, and (2) that very weak relationships can be statistically significant with a very large n.

Table 4–2 was constructed to illustrate the influence of sample size on the precision of the rs. Since height is a variable that we can observe directly, it serves as a good illustration. We know that tall parents are more likely to have children who are taller than average. The correlation coefficient between the heights of parents and their children quantifies this relationship. The confidence interval makes allowances for sampling error (chance); it is the "band" of values within which we can expect the true correlation—that is, the parameter, ρ—to lie. Since the sample on which the value of .51 is based was quite large ($n = 374$), the con-

---

[5]In statistics, the correlation coefficient for the entire population, i.e., the parameter, is denoted by the Greek letter ρ (rho).

[6]Of course the average age of the taller boys will be greater, thus age may account for the relationship.

TABLE 4–1 Minimum Values of r Required to be Statistically Significant at the .05 Level for Various Sample Sizes (n)[7]

n	Minimum r for Statistical Significance
5	.878
10	.632
25	.396
100	.197
1000	.062

TABLE 4–2 Typical Correlation Coefficients and Confidence Intervals, Using Height as an Illustration

	r	N	.95 Confidence Interval for ρ
Identical twins reared together	.96	83	(.93, .97)
Identical twins reared apart	.94	30	(.88, .97)
Height at age 3 vs. height at maturity (males)	.75	66	(.62, .84)
Height at age 3 vs. height at maturity (females)	.70	70	(.56, .77)
Fraternal twins	.58	235	(.49, .66)
Siblings	.50	853	(.45, .55)
Parent and child	.51	374	(.43, .59)
Husband and wife	.34	320	(.24, .43)
Grandparent and grandchild	.32	132	(.18, .47)
First cousins	.24	215	(.11, .36)
Height and IQ	.20	4061	(.17, .23)

fidence interval is not very wide (.43, .59). As you recall, $r = .51$ means that, on the average, a child tends to be only about half as far from the mean height of the peers as the parents are from the mean heights of their age and sex peers.

4.10 VALIDITY COEFFICIENTS

The criterion-related validity of a test is quantified by the correlation coefficient between the test and the criterion. Predictive validity is criterion-related validity when there is a time

---

[7]These values are from Table J in Glass and Hopkins (1996, p. 641). The corresponding values of the rank correlation r_{ranks} required for statistical significance are very similar. (See Table K in Statistical methods in Education and Psychology, Glass & Hopkins, 1996, p. 642.)

interval between the test (*X*) and the criterion (*Y*). Percentile rank-in-class in high school graduating class correlates approximately .5 with the GPA in college—the *predictive validity coefficient* is .5.

4.11 SOME EXAMPLES OF CRITERION-RELATED VALIDITY

What can validity coefficients tell us about the usefulness of tests for selection purposes? Colleges that use the *SAT* or *ACT* are particularly interested in the average grades that selected students will attain. Figure 4–6 illustrates the average grades that would be expected at a typical college.

Figure 4–6 is a composite illustration based on the typical distributions of *SAT* test scores and GPAs found at 159 colleges (ETS, 1980a). Figure 4–6 indicates that there is a substantial relationship between *SAT* scores and college grades; students with higher *SAT* scores typically earn higher grades in college, and vice versa. Figure 4–6 also demonstrates that there are many exceptions to the general trend—there is considerable variation in the GPAs obtained by students having the same *SAT* score. The "boxes" in Figure 4–6 show the GPAs for the middle

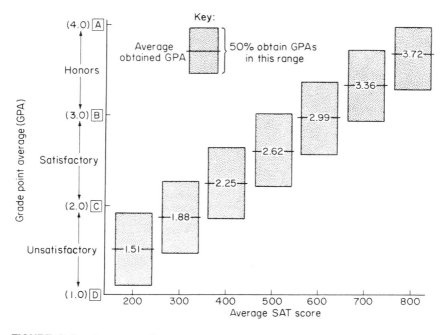

FIGURE 4–6 Average college grades for students with different *SAT* scores. Typical *SAT* score—college GPA correlation = .40, based on data from 159 validity studies in 1974.

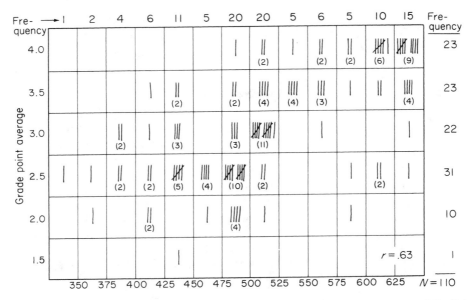

FIGURE 4–7   Scatterplot depicting the criterion-related validity of the *Test of English as a Foreign Language* (*TOEFL*) for predicting grade point averages of 110 first-semester foreign graduate students.

SOURCE: Data courtesy of Vera Santos and David Williams.

50 percent of the students at each *SAT* score value. *Notice,* 25 percent of the students have GPAs above the box, and another 25 percent have GPAs falling below the box.[8]

Virtually all universities in the United States require applicants from non-English-speaking countries to take an English proficiency test, the *Test of English as a Foreign Language* (*TOEFL*), to demonstrate competence in English. But do scores on the *TOEFL* have anything to do with academic success as a student? Are minimum scores for admission being set too low or too high on the *TOEFL*? Figure 4–7 displays the relationship between *TOEFL* scores and subsequent grades in the first semester of work for 110 foreign graduate students.

Note that the predictive validity of the *TOEFL* is substantial (*r* = .63); for example, of the 29 students with *TOEFL* scores below 475, 20 (69%) achieved a GPA of 2.5 or less and only 3 (10%) achieved a GPA above 3.0 (the usual standard for satisfactory progress). Conversely, note that for the 25 students with *TOEFL* scores of 600 or above, only 5 (20%)

---

[8]The *r* = 0.40 of Figure 4–6 is a conservative estimate of the *SAT*'s predictive validity because it does not reflect what the correlation would have been for the full range of applicants—it seriously underestimates the relationship that would occur if all applicants were admitted (see Sec. 4.17). Rank in high school graduating class has somewhat higher predictive validity for college GPA than *SAT* scores, but if both are used, the predictive validity is higher than for either used alone.

had a GPA below 3.0. Stated differently, the mean GPA for students scoring below 475 was 2.60, whereas students with *TOEFL* scores above 600 had a mean GPA of 3.76. The implications of these data for the selection of graduate students as well as academic counseling are obvious.

4.12   ANOTHER EXAMPLE OF PREDICTIVE VALIDITY

The principal function of the reading readiness tests administered in kindergarten or early in grade 1 is to identify (predict) those students who are likely to perform well, or not so well, in reading in the first grade. The purpose of the test is to assist the teacher in deciding which children are ready to begin reading and which should continue to engage in readiness activities for some time.

Figure 4–8 shows the predictive validity of scores on a reading readiness test given to 157 kindergartners for predicting reading performance on a standardized reading test at

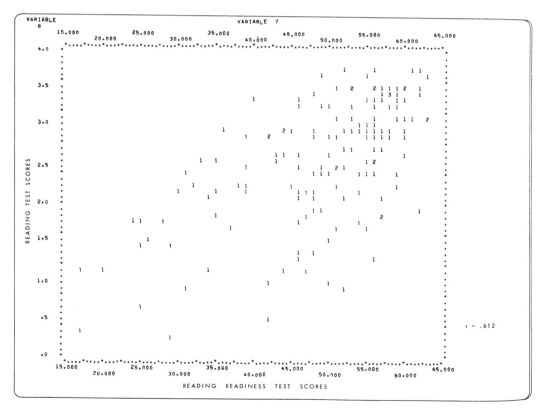

FIGURE 4–8   A scatterplot of the criterion-related validity of a reading readiness test for predicting subsequent scores on an end-of-year standardized reading test.

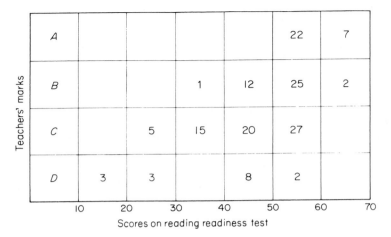

FIGURE 4–9   Scatterplot showing the criterion-related validity of reading readiness test scores at the beginning of grade 1 for predicting teachers' marks at the end of grade 1 (*N* = 157).

SOURCE: Based on data from K. D. Hopkins and E. C. Sitkic, "Predicting grade one reading performance: Intelligence vs. reading readiness tests," *Journal of Experimental Education, 37* (1969), 31–33.

the end of grade one (*r* = .61). Notice that, as a general rule, high scores on the readiness test (the predictor) are associated with good performance on the reading test (the criterion).

Figure 4–9 also shows the predictive validity of the reading readiness test, but it uses a different criterion for reading success: teachers' marks. Figure 4–9 shows that the students with low scores on the reading readiness test did not read well at the end of grade 1, as evaluated by their teacher. Only one of the 28 pupils with a score below 40 received a grade of *B*. The students with high scores generally read well, but there were some students with good readiness scores who did not perform well in reading in grade one. Of the 76 students with readiness scores between 50 and 60, there were 22 (29%) who received *A*s, 25 (33%) who received *B*s, 27 (36%) who received *C*s, and 2 (3%) who received a grade of *D* in reading. From Figure 4–8 (as well as from Figure 4–5), it is evident that failure was more predictable than success, a fact that is not evident from the correlation coefficient alone, but apparent from a study of the scatterplots.

The predictive validity of a test is always in relation to a *particular* criterion. Teachers' marks may be influenced by factors that are not associated with performance on the standardized reading test (such as deportment and effort); thus, to some extent marks may represent different factors. The two criteria depicted in Figures 4–8 and 4–9 correlated substantially (*r* = .75), but they are not interchangeable.[9] By studying both criteria we get a more complete picture than we could by considering only one.

[9]Some of the lack of correlation between the two criteria is due to errors of measurement (unreliability). If the reliability of each of the criterion is available, the extent to which the two criteria measure different factors, apart from measurement error, can be estimated (see Sections 4.12 and 13.18, and Glass & Hopkins, 1996, pp. 123–126.)

4.13 HOW LARGE DOES A VALIDITY COEFFICIENT NEED TO BE?

Obviously, the higher the validity coefficient is, the better the prediction. But how large must the coefficient be before it provides useful information? In certain situations, even tests with relatively low validity coefficients can be extremely useful.

Figure 4–10 displays the results of a study of the validity of the *GRE* Advanced Tests (special achievement tests in the student's major) for predicting whether students attain the Ph.D. degree. Note, for example, that in spite of the rather low validity coefficient of the advanced test in psychology ($r = .34$), that approximately 50 percent of students with a stanine score of 8 or 9 attain the Ph.D., whereas virtually none of those in stanine 1 or 2 does so. Studies have found the *GRE* tests to have validity for predicting quality criteria in graduate programs in virtually all fields, although the correlation coefficients are not high (partly due

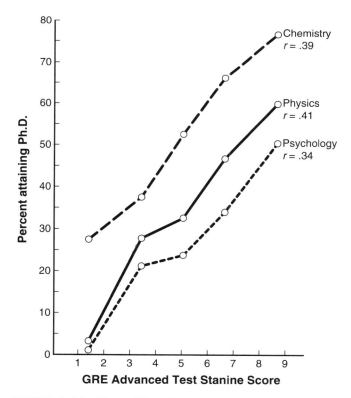

FIGURE 4–10 The validity of the *Graduate Record Examination* (Advanced Tests) for predicting attainment of the Ph.D. in chemistry, physics, and psychology.

SOURCE: *GRE Technical Manual.* Copyright © 1977 by Educational Testing Service. All rights reserved. Reprinted by permission of Educational Testing Service, W. W. Willingham, and the American Association for the Advancement of Science. © 1974 by the American Association for the Advancement of Science.

to the use of the test in the selection process—see Section 4.17), and there is considerable variation among institutions and fields.

4.14   EXPECTANCY TABLES

Predictive validity can be represented and interpreted meaningfully if an *expectancy table* is used, even for persons who are not familiar with correlation coefficients. In Figure 4–9, if frequencies within each score interval are converted to proportions, we obtain probabilities for various levels of performance on the criterion for any test score. For example, if a student earned a score of 45 on the reading readiness test, it is extremely unlikely that he or she would receive an end-of-year reading mark of *A* in grade one; the probabilities of receiving a grade of *B*, *C*, or *D*, is .30 (12 of 40), .50 (20 of 40), and .20 (8 of 40). A similar expectancy table is found in Figure 13–16, in which the criterion of success for vocational training (watch repair) is predicted from a special aptitude test (spatial ability).

4.15   CONCURRENT VALIDITY

Criterion-related validity is not limited to the relationships between tests and performance on criteria obtained after some interval of time. Occasionally our purpose is to describe the relationship between a test (such as a new test) and another test (such as an established test). In this situation, little or no interval is desired between the administration of the new test and the established test or criterion. It would be quite useful to find a short, inexpensive reading test that would correlate highly with a valid individual (and, hence, costly) test. The new test would be said to have *concurrent* validity to the extent that it correlates with the established test or some other concurrently obtained criterion. For example, standardized achievement test scores have been found to correlate highly (and, therefore, have high concurrent validity) with the independent teachers' assessments of students' abilities, especially in math, reading, and language arts (Hopkins, George & Williams, 1985). In this study, the purpose was not to predict future teachers' ratings but to determine the extent to which the test results and the professional assessments agree. Some critics of standardized tests contend that they are simply "guessing games," but if that is true, how does one account for the substantial relationship they have with the assessments of their teachers based on months of classroom performance.

Concurrent validity is sometimes the initial step in establishing predictive validity. In the early development of the *Strong Vocational Interest Blank*, studies of concurrent validity demonstrated that the interest scores could, for example, differentiate physicians from the general population. Only after 20 years of additional research could Strong provide evidence that interest scores of college freshman correlated with their adult occupations (although the predictive validity coefficients were not high) (Campbell, 1968).

4.16   VALIDITY CONSEQUENCES OF THE RELIABILITY OF THE CRITERION

The quality of the criterion has a major influence on a test's criterion-related validity. *To be predictable, a criterion must be reliable.* Even if a test is highly relevant and reliable, it cannot accurately predict a criterion that is full of measurement error (i.e., lacks reliability—

the concept of reliability is developed in the next chapter). If a criterion does not correlate with itself—that is, lacks reliability—it cannot be predicted by any other variable. This is the principal reason that the many attempts to predict teacher success have been so fruitless. The measures of teacher success are typically quite unreliable and, therefore, essentially unpredictable. For example, Walberg (1967) found only a .21 correlation between supervisor and principal ratings of the teaching success of 280 teacher trainees. A similar correlation has been observed between principal and parents' ratings of teachers (Epstein, 1985); other studies have reported comparable results (Quirk, Witten & Weinberg, 1973). This is, no doubt, an important reason why logically relevant factors such as student-teaching ratings, GPA, and subject-matter competence have yielded such low correlations with ratings of teacher effectiveness.

The present predictability of grades in college is probably about as high as it can be without an improvement in the reliability of the criterion. The reliability of a grade in a single course is rather low; one study estimated single-grade reliability for freshman-level courses to be only $r = .44$ (Etaugh, Etaugh & Hurd, 1972). Goldman and Slaughter (1976, p. 14) studied the predictive validity of tests for predicting GPA and concluded, "In sum, we believe that the validity problem in GPA prediction is a result of shortcomings of the GPA *criterion* rather than the tests that are used as predictors."

It is a statistical fact that the reliability coefficient of a test sets limits on its criterion-related validity—the accuracy with which a test predicts a criterion. The *maximum* criterion-related validity for any criterion is the square root of the reliability coefficient of the criterion. The reliability coefficient (Chapter 5) describes the degree to which measurement error contaminates a measure.

4.17   THE EFFECT OF RESTRICTED VARIABILITY ON CRITERION-RELATED VALIDITY

When a test is used for selection purposes, such as admission to college or an employment decision, much of its predictive value is capitalized upon at that point. The correlation of test scores within the selected group with a subsequent criterion will greatly underestimate the test's predictive validity, that is, its value as a selection measure. In the reading readiness test example in Figure 4–9, suppose that no student with a readiness score below 40 was admitted to grade 1; instead, all had to repeat kindergarten. Notice in Figure 4–9 that if the scores falling below 40 were excluded, the resulting scatterplot is much *fatter,* hence, the correlation coefficient for those with scores of 40 and above would be much less than the coefficient for the total group. In fact, the validity coefficient of $r = .61$ for the entire group drops to only $r = .44$ if the examinees scoring below 40 are excluded. If only students scoring 50 or more were included, the value of r would be lower still.

Figure 4–11 is an illustration of the common phenomenon of "range restriction" and its effects on validity coefficients.

Note the relative "roundness" in the shape of the corresponding scatterplot for the selected group versus the entire group. There is only a moderate correlation between the criterion and test scores within the selected group (shaded area), yet there is a substantial relationship for the entire group. Many studies substantially underestimate the predictive value of the *SAT, ACT, GRE* (Linn, 1983), and related measures like the *Medical College Admission*

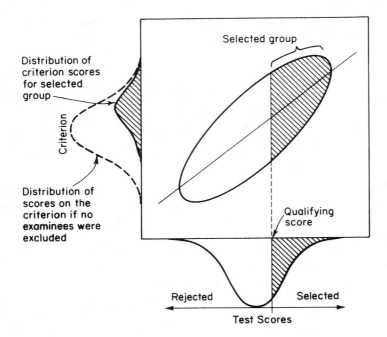

FIGURE 4–11 An illustration of the effect of selection on the correlation between test scores and a criterion. The validity coefficient *within* the selected group underestimates the actual predictive value of the test.

Test (MCAT) because they have failed to be cognizant of this important point. If test scores correlate, for example, only *r* = .3 with subsequent GPAs for the admitted group, Figure 4–10 demonstrates that the test may still be of great value for admission purposes (especially when the limited reliability of the criterion is borne in mind).[10]

Recall, for example, that Figure 4–7 depicted the relationship (*r* = .63) between scores on the *TOEFL* and subsequent GPA for graduate students for whom English was not their first language. Note that for the entire group the *TOEFL* had substantial predictive validity (*r* = .63). But what would the correlation of the *TOEFL* and GPA have been if a minimum score of 500 had been required for admission? Cover all *TOEFL* scores below 500 in Figure 4–7 and observe how much "rounder" the shape of the scatterplot for those 61 students with scores above 500 becomes. Indeed, the correlation of *r* = .63 for the unselected group drops to *r* = .39 when considering only students scoring above 500. For another example, suppose in Figure 4–5 that a *GRE-Analytical* score of 500 were required in order to take the statistics course; the predictive validity coefficient in Figure 4–5 would have dropped

---

[10]Few low-*SAT* applicants gain admission to a highly selective college. Those who do have something "special" to offer: excellent high school grades, athletic talent, alumni parent, or the like. The low-scoring *SAT* enrollees with excellent high school grades tend to vitiate the predictive validity of the *SAT* for freshman GPA.

from $r = .47$ to $r = .30$. Obviously, the criterion-related validity of a measure is greatly under-estimated if some portion of the examinees is excluded because of low scores on the test. The full predictive value of a test can be assessed only if no applicants are eliminated on the basis of their test performance.

The effect that restricting the range of scores has on the validity coefficient obtained was dramatically illustrated by Thorndike (1949), who compared the validity coefficient for a total group ($n = 1031$) of aspiring pilots to the coefficient for the group that was success-ful ($n = 136$). The validity coefficient for the composite score on the predictors was $r = .64$ for the total group, but a correlation of only $r = .18$ remained within the group for those who qualified.[11]

4.18   CONSTRUCT VALIDITY

When a test is used to describe the degree to which an individual manifests an abstract psy-chological trait or ability, the *construct validity* of the measure is the relevant concern (Cron-bach and Meehl, 1955). Psychological constructs are unobservable, postulated variables that have evolved either informally or from psychological theory. Intelligence, anxiety, mechan-ical aptitude, musical ability, critical thinking, ego strength, dominance, and achievement motivation are examples of commonly used constructs. *Construct validation* is the system-atic analysis of test scores designed to assess whether there is a basis for validity. The analy-sis has both logical and empirical components.

If a test is designed to measure emotional stability, what kinds of evidence are nec-essary before we can be confident that the information provided by the test reflects this vari-able? A logical analysis of the content of the test must confirm that the kinds of questions included are relevant for emotional stability. If the questions used are suspect ("Do you like to play football?") or use esoteric vocabulary, the test's claim for construct validity is reduced. In the empirical component of construct validation, certain predictions are made that should be correct if, indeed, the test does measure the construct in question. For exam-ple, if the scale actually measures emotional stability, one would expect (1) some correla-tion between inventory scores and peer ratings (perhaps from sociometric measures, Section 15.28), (2) some difference between scores of people who are in mental hospitals and people who are not, (3) some relationship between teachers' ratings in citizenship and social relationships and inventory scores, and so on. However, we might expect little or no relationship between inventory scores and gender, IQ, GPA, and the like. In a true sense, every bit of information about a test has relevance for construct validity—in establishing what it does and does not measure. In construct validation there is no single criterion, as there is with criterion-related validity; many criteria are required to confirm what the test does and does not measure.

---

[11]There are procedures to estimate the correlation for the entire group from the correlation within the selected group (Glass & Hopkins, 1996, pp. 121–123; Hopkins, Hopkins & Glass, 1996, p. 112–115), but these estimates are often quite imprecise unless n is very large (Gullickson & Hopkins, 1976; Linn, 1983).

The measurement of intelligence provides a classic example of the process of construct validation. Early attempts to measure "intelligence" using reaction time, auditory memory, sensory discrimination, and other psychomotor and psychophysical measures were discarded because performance on these measures did not correlate with other behavioral evidence of intelligence, such as school grades. The expected and logical relationships between relevant variables were not confirmed. Later, the French physician-researcher Alfred Binet constructed tasks that were logically related to intelligence (had content validity) and required complex cognitive abilities, such as logical reasoning. Many of Binet's tasks were found to be related to other variables in the manner expected of a measure of intelligence and, hence, to possess a degree of construct validity.

Gradually, through a continual process of research and revision, intelligence tests (at least the best tests such as the *Stanford-Binet* and *Wechsler* scales) yielded scores that agreed substantially with logical and theoretical expectations: (1) The mental age scores correlated positively with chronological age until maturity; marital age then reaches a plateau in the manner of other directly measurable human abilities; (2) the scores had substantial relationship with academic achievement; (3) children who repeated grades scored much lower on these measures than those who were promoted; (4) the IQ scores yielded by these tests showed some stability over a period of years; (5) persons with clinical types of mental disability (e.g., Down syndrome) performed poorly on the tasks; and (6) the correlation of identical twins was extremely high—much higher than for fraternal twins, even when the identical twins were reared separately. Such information illustrates the incremental procedure inherent in construct validation.

Certain tests such as the *Stanford-Binet* became accepted as having substantial validity as measures of intelligence (except for persons having atypical environmental backgrounds) because persons who obtained high scores on the test tended to behave intelligently in situations in which such behavior was required. Although certain predictions may be made regarding future performance from tests designed to measure psychological constructs, their primary function is to assess the degree of some variable or trait that is present within the individual at a given point in time.

If two students are achieving at the same level but one has an IQ score of 90 and the other a score of 130, we may be relatively satisfied with the educational success of the one but quite concerned about that of the other who appears to have more scholastic aptitude. However, if our sole task is to predict subsequent performance, there would be no point in administering intelligence tests; achievement tests usually predict subsequent achievement better than intelligence tests (Bracht & Hopkins, 1970b; Churchill & Smith, 1966). Intelligence or scholastic aptitude tests are one of the most common types of tests taken by virtually all Americans for which validation rests primarily in the construct validity domain.

The process of developing a measure of a psychological construct and establishing its validity can be summarized as follows:

1. Develop a set of tasks or items based on theory—a rational analysis of the construct.
2. Deduce testable predictions regarding the relationship between the construct and other empirical measures; for example, if the test measures anxiety, we should expect to find some relationship between test scores and clinical ratings of anxiety level, physiological indicators of anxiety, and so on.

3. Obtain the data required to investigate these predicted relationships empirically.
4. Eliminate items or tasks that operate contrary to theory (or revise the theory) and proceed again with steps 2 and 3.[12]

When measuring constructs, content and criterion-related validity are subsumed by construct validity (Messick, 1989; Shepard, 1993); everything that is known about a test—its content, its correlations with other relevant (and irrelevant) variables—helps establish what the test does, and does not, measure. The converse does not follow, however; if designing a measure to predict who is at risk for dropping out of school, who will succeed in a particular vocation, who should be paroled, and so on, it is criterion-related validity that irrelevant, regardless of whether the test content is under-girded by a psychological construct. The same can be said for content validity, as Cronbach (1989, p. 24) has observed, "saying that planning a test begins with "specifying a construct is a bit lofty," and "debases intellectual currency" by distorting the meaning of a construct—the American Civil War is not a construct, indeed, much of history, law, literature does not lend itself to construct validation.

SUMMARY

The need for an objective and precise measure to describe the degree of relationship between two variables is obvious. The Pearson correlation (r for a sample or ρ for a population) and the Spearman rank correlation (r_{ranks}) are such measures. The values for r_{ranks} and r will usually be quite comparable, especially if n is large.

The degree of relationship can vary from perfect but negative (–1.0) through 0 to perfect but positive (+1.0). The magnitude of the relationship is indicated by the absolute value of the correlation coefficient. The sign (+ or –) of a coefficient only indicates the *direction* of the relationship. A coefficient of 0 indicates no correlation between two variables.

A positive correlation indicates that high numbers on X (i.e., scores above the mean) are associated with high numbers on Y, and that low numbers on X (i.e., scores below the mean) are associated with low numbers on Y.

The correlation coefficient describes the degree of association between the variable X and the variable Y only when X and Y are linearly related; the actual degree of association may be seriously underestimated if a curvilinear relationship exists between X and Y. Scatterplots allow a rough visual check of linearity. The computed correlation coefficient will be accurate only if it is based on a representative sample and a sufficiently-large sample—the larger the n, the smaller the sampling error ($r - \rho$).

We have discussed three rather distinct classes of validity. *Content validity* is most critical for achievement testing; it consists of a logical study of the relationship of the topics and

---

[12]The interested reader should be informed of the more elaborate scheme for construct validation using a multitrait-multimethod matrix proposed by Campbell and Fiske (1959). From a matrix of correlation coefficients that describe the relationships among the same and different traits using a variety of assessment methods, certain criteria are suggested for establishing the validity of a construct and its measurement.

processes included on a test to the corresponding curricular objectives and instruction. *Predictive validity* is basic to selection decisions and is determined from an empirical study of the extent to which performances on a test (or some other measure) and performance on a subsequent criterion measure are related. *Construct validity* refers to the extent to which a test reflects an abstract psychological trait (construct). Both logical and empirical means are used to establish the validities of a test. All three types of validity are crucial for certain, although different, purposes. In a real sense, content and criterion-related validity are subsumed by construct validity; everything that is known about a test—its content, its correlations with other relevant (and irrelevant) variables—helps establish what the test does, and does not, measure.

IMPORTANT TERMS AND CONCEPTS

correlation
correlation coefficient, *r* and ρ
expectancy table
scatterplot
criterion-related validity

predictive validity
construct validity
statistically significant
linear and nonlinear correlation

confidence interval
content validity
concurrent validity
range restriction
reliability of the criterion

CHAPTER TEST

1. Which one of the following correlation coefficients indicates the strongest relationship?
   a) .55
   b) .09
   c) −.77
   d) .1

2. Using the options given in item 1, which coefficient shows that scores *below* the mean on one variable tend to be associated with scores that are *above* the mean on the other variable?

In Questions 3–7, select the scatterplot that best matches the relationships described.

Value of r	Description of Linear Relationship	Scatter Diagram
3. +1.00	Perfect direct relationship	(a)
4. About +.50	Moderate direct relationship	(b)
5. .00	No relationship	(c)
6. About –.50	Moderate inverse relationship	(d)
7. –1.00	Perfect inverse relationship	(e)

8. Indicate whether the expected correlation of the two designated variables X and Y would be positive, negative, or zero. (Assume that the population for items *a–d* is all U.S. students in grade 10.)

   a) X: height in inches, Y: weight in pounds
   b) X: reading grades, Y: grades in math
   c) X: shoe size, Y: teachers' ratings of "citizenship"
   d) X: social security numbers, Y: IQ scores
   e) X: miles traveled by a car, Y: year in which the car was manufactured
   f) X: maximum daily temperature, Y: amount of water used per day

9. If you obtained an r of +1.3, you would know for certain that
   a) the relationship is extremely strong.
   b) the relationship is positive.
   c) both *a* and *b* are true.
   d) a computational error has been made.

   One study found the importance of eight morale factors as ranked by employees and employers, as indicated in the following table: (Questions 10 and 11)

	Rank	
Factor	Employers	Employees
A. Credit for work done	1	7
B. Interesting work	2	3
C. Fair pay	3	1
D. Understanding and appreciation	4	5
E. Counseling on personal problems	5	8
F. Promotion based on merit	6	4
G. Good working conditions	7	6
H. Job security	8	2

10. Compute r_{ranks} between the rankings.

11. Which two factors contributed most to the negative correlation?

    The data in the following table show the relationship between IQ scores on verbal and non-verbal intelligence test with scores on standardized achievement tests in reading and mathematics. At each of the three grade levels, each correlation is based on approximately 2500 nationally representative students. On the basis of the data in the table, indicate whether each of Statements 12–14 is: true *or* false.

	Verbal IQ			Nonverbal IQ		
	Grade			Grade		
	3	5	7	3	5	7
Reading	.68	.76	.81	.53	.65	.67
Math	.66	.72	.74	.61	.68	.71

12. The correlation between the intelligence and achievement measures appears to increase with grade level.

13. The nonverbal IQs correlate as highly with achievement as do verbal IQs.

14. The correlation between both measures of achievement and both measures of intelligence is substantial at each of the three grade levels.

15. Complete the sentence: Verbal IQs tend to correlate slightly higher with _____, whereas nonverbal IQ scores correlate slightly higher with _____.

16. In the content/skill grid of the *STEP II* Science Test depicted in Figure 4–1, which science content is represented most heavily?
    a) biology
    b) chemistry
    c) physics
    d) earth sciences

17. If a school district's science curriculum deals primarily with the physical sciences at the grade level for which Form 3A of *STEP II* is designed,
    a) the *STEP II* content validity does not appear to be strong.
    b) the item norms (percent passing) would be especially important for evaluating a school district's performance.
    c) no useful information could be obtained from this test.
    d) More than one of the above

Use Figures 4–1 and 4–2 in answering Questions 18 and 19:

18. Which test allows a more explicit study of the test content validity in terms of topics covered?
    a) *STEP II*
    b) *Metropolitan Achievement Test*

19. Which test provides more information on the type of cognitive process required by the item?
    a) *STEP II*
    b) *Metropolitan Achievement Test*

20. Which type of test is better able to reflect the *specific* content and objectives of a particular course?
    a) standardized
    b) teacher-made

For Items 21–28, which type of validity is most important for the following measures?:
    a) Content Validity
    b) Criterion-Related Validity
    c) Construct Validity

21. An algebra test

22. A test to select job applicants for employment

23. A test of learning style

24. The *GRE*, *SAT*, and *ACT*

25. A self-concept test

26. A final examination based on this book

27. A new short, "cheapie" test designed to replace a long, expensive test

28. The extent to which this test measures the topics and objectives of this chapter

29. Among Items 21–28, which item best represents concurrent validation?

30. Suppose that for a sample of 25 people you obtained an $r = .3$ between a measure of obnoxiousness and a measure of garrulousness. Is an r of .3 large enough (see Table 4–1) to be statistically significant? If you increased your sample size to 100, would a computed r of .3 be statistically significant?

31. If colleges represented in Figure 4–7 began to require all foreign students to have a *TOEFL* score of at least 500, what effect would you expect this to have on the *TOEFL*'s validity coefficient in subsequent studies?

32. Suppose that colleges and universities adopted a new practice of assigning grades that required more frequent testing, more careful evaluation, greater use of the full range of grades (*A–F*), and so on, such that the reliability of GPA is increased. Other things being equal, what effect would this have on the predictive validity coefficients for tests such as the *GRE*, *SAT*, and *ACT*?
    a) r would increase.
    b) r would remain unchanged.
    c) r would decrease.

33. Refer to the expectancy table in Figure 4–9. For beginning first-grade students obtaining a score of 35, what is the most probable grade they will receive in reading?
    a) *A*
    b) *B*
    c) *C*
    d) *D*

34. If in Figure 4–11 the test scores represent scores on a college admissions test (*SAT* or *ACT*) and the criterion is performance on the *Graduate Record Examination*, the criterion-related validity coefficient of the *SAT* or *ACT* would be *least* at
    a) highly select institutions (a score of one σ or more above μ required for admission).
    b) moderately select institution (minimum score is the mean).
    c) an "open door" university.

35. From Figure 4–6, determine
    a) the average GPA for persons scoring 600 on the *SAT*.
    b) the percent of students with scores of 500 who earn a *B* average or better.
    c) the percent of examinees with *SAT* scores of 200 who fail to achieve a *C* average.

Questions 36–40: Based on a national sample of almost 23,000 cases, the correlations of the *SAT-Verbal* and *SAT-Math* with the *GRE-Verbal* and *GRE-Quantitative* taken four or more years later were extremely high: .858 and .862, respectively (Angoff & Johnson, 1990). Based on *this information*, it can be concluded that:

36. *GRE-Verbal* and *-Quantitative* scores can be predicted quite accurately from *SAT-Verbal* and *SAT-Math* scores. *[T or F]*

37. The *SAT* test must have high reliability coefficients. *[T or F]*

38. The *GRE* test must have high reliability coefficients. *[T or F]*

39. The correlations between true (universe) scores would be even higher. *[T or F]*

40. On the *SAT-Verbal* and the *GRE-Verbal* tests, $\mu \approx 500$ and $\sigma \approx 100$ ($\approx$ means "approximately equal to"). Therefore, for persons who obtained an *SAT-Verbal* of 600, the average score earned on the subsequent *GRE-Verbal* is _____.

ANSWERS TO CHAPTER TEST

1. c
2. c
3. c
4. d
5. e
6. a
7. b
8. a) positive, b) positive, c) zero, d) zero, e) negative, f) positive
9. d
10. $r_{ranks} = -.095$
11. A and H
12. True
13. False
14. True
15. reading, math
16. a
17. d
18. b
19. a
20. b
21. a
22. b
23. c

24. b
25. c
26. a
27. b
28. a
29. 26
30. No; Yes
31. Decrease
32. a
33. c
34. a
35. a) 2.99 or 3.0, b) about 25%; c) about 80%
36. T
37. T
38. T
39. T
40. 586 (The *r* of .86 shows that on the criterion, on the average, scores are 86% as far from the mean on the criterion as they were from the mean of the predictor: .86 × 100 = 86, 500 + 86 = 586

5

Test Reliability

5.1   INTRODUCTION

Anyone who regularly plays a sport such as golf, basketball, or track is acutely aware of the variability in human performance. No one operates at his or her personal best on all occasions, be the domain one of physical activity or mental activity. Quantification of the consistency and inconsistency in examinee performance constitutes the essence of reliability analysis (Feldt & Brennan, 1988).

To do its job well, a measure must yield accurate results. A test has little value if Alfred's score today is quite different from the score it would yield for him under similar conditions tomorrow. It is theoretically possible, however, for a test to yield highly consistent results from day to day without having any validity. A highly reliable measure of reaction time may be useful for predicting the quickness with which one applies an automobile brake, but it is has no validity for indicating how well one reads or solves math problems. The Foolproof Emotional Adjustment Test (FEAT) may have high reliability but no validity whatsoever. *Reliability is the extent to which the FEAT measures consistently, whatever it does measure.* What is measured may or may not be what is desired. In other words, *a measure can be reliable without being valid.* As we shall see, however, a measure cannot have any validity if totally unreliable. One of the unsolved problems in the current movement toward the use of portfolios in educational assessment is their low reliability that is associated with their evaluations (Koretz, Stecher, Klein & McCaffrey, 1994).

The concepts of reliability and validity (Chapter 4) are central to the theory and practice of educational and psychological measurement and evaluation. This chapter offers an overview of the classical theory of test reliability. Methods of estimating the reliability of a test, inventory, or measure are also considered, together with the implications for test interpretation. This chapter is the most conceptually challenging in the entire book; expect to read it two or three times before the material is well understood.

Suppose we wish to develop a simple inventory to measure the trait of honesty. Let's call it the *Honesty Inventory (HI)*. We will develop a series of questions that appear to sample honesty behavior, such as "Do you ever deliberately distort the truth?" "When you have had the opportunity, have you ever cheated on a test?" "If a clerk makes a mistake and gives you too much change, do you ignore the error?" Suppose the *HI* were administered to 100 persons. Are the *HI* scores reliable and valid? If we re-administered the *HI* to the same group a week later, do you think the two sets of scores would correlate highly? The correlation coefficient between the two sets of *HI* scores (i.e., the first score with the second score) is a test-retest reliability coefficient. The coefficient may range from 0 to +1; the reliability coefficient might be .9, or even higher. If each person answered all the questions exactly the same way both times, can we be sure that the answers were truthful? The reliability coefficient could be 1.0, yet the *HI*'s validity is the extent that the reported answers are truthful answers. It is unlikely, but possible, that the least honest person has the best *HI* score. The least honest person may wish to conceal his imperfections; thus, validity of the *HI* could be nil even if the reliability of the *HI* is perfect. If the examinees took the *HI* anonymously, the *HI*'s validity would probably increase greatly—people are unlikely to distort the truth unless a dishonest answer is perceived to be self-serving.

The point is that *reliability* (measurement precision) *is necessary, but not sufficient, for validity*. If repeated measurement yields disparate scores, we cannot have confidence in their validity. Reliability is an essential prerequisite for validity.

If the *HI* contained a representative sample of honest behavior, it would be viewed as having good content validity; but if the conditions under which the *HI* was administered did not disarm examinees of all incentives to "fake it," the inventory would lack construct validity (i.e., the extent to which scores on the test represent the examinees' standing on the trait or construct of honesty). The criterion-related validity of the *HI* is the extent to which *HI* scores correlate with some observed criterion measure (e.g., anonymous honesty ratings given by peers, teachers, or supervisors) or more direct behavioral measures (e.g., "cash shortages" for clerks).

Suppose that the *HI* does not have norms. Does that make its validity or reliability suspect? Norms have no necessary relationship with either validity or reliability. Norms simply enable us to interpret scores more meaningfully, by allowing us to compare the score to the distribution of scores from the norm group. A psychomotor measure, such as a handwriting scale (see Figure 8–1) or a measure of reaction time, can be made quite reliable (perhaps .95); the scores, however, may not correlate with variables that we wish to predict, such as college grades, job success, or running speed. The test may be useful for predicting this same type of psychomotor ability at some other time (i.e., it may possess reliability), but it may or may not be useful for predicting other criteria (and, therefore, lack criterion-related validity). In other words, a certain psychomotor test could have very high reliability but low predictive validity for the criteria of interest. And, of course, validity is the real aim of the testing; we are interested in reliability because it is a necessary, but not sufficient, condition for validity.

An Example of Reliability without Validity.

At the turn of the century, the first statistical study designed to predict academic success in college was conducted (Wissler, 1901). Using a test of reaction time (which can be measured very reliably), he obtained a validity coefficient of only –.02! Obviously, the high reliability does not guarantee validity, although *validity does guarantee some degree of reliability*.

5.2   ERRORS OF MEASUREMENT AND RELIABILITY

Assume that Form I of a 100-item multiple-choice reading vocabulary test of Chinese characters is given to your class. All students are required to attempt all 100 items, each of which has five options. Theoretically, scores can range anywhere from 0 to 100, but (assuming that no student has any reading vocabulary in Chinese) the class mean will probably be about 20 ($\frac{1}{5}$ of 100, i.e., a chance score); the theoretical standard deviation is four points.[1] Suppose your score is 28, very high in this group untutored in Chinese. If you were asked to take Form II of the test, would you expect your score on Form II to be 28? Not if you know much about the laws of chance and the reliability of random guessing. In this example all deviations in scores are due to chance. The best estimate of your score on Form II (and the score of each of your classmates) is 20, regardless of the score obtained on Form I. Your "good luck" score on Form I was 8 (28–20) and is technically termed the *measurement error*.

Errors of measurement can be positive or negative, that is, your observed score can be too high or too low; errors of measurement theoretically have a mean of 0 and are normally distributed. The best bet is that your error of measurement on Form II will be 0 and that your "expected" score will be 20.

For a large group of examinees, the correlation between the scores on Forms I and II of this random-marked test will be about 0, that is, the test scores will have zero reliability. Are the scores useful for predicting students' ages? IQs? Knowledge of English grammar? Anything at all? Most assuredly not. If scores on Form I will not predict scores on Form II, they cannot possibly predict anything else. A test wholly lacking in reliability cannot predict any variable more accurately than chance alone. Thus, the lowest possible reliability coefficient is zero and the highest possible reliability coefficient is 1.0. Between these two points lie the reliability indices for all tests and measures.

5.3   RELIABILITY AND TRUE SCORES

"An investigator asks about the precision or reliability of a measure because he wishes to generalize from the observation in hand to some class or universe of observations to which it belongs" (Cronbach, Rajaratnam & Gleser, 1963, p. 144). Rarely does a test measure all of the information of interest—a test should ordinarily be viewed as a *sample* of items or tasks from a *population* or *universe* of such items or tasks. There are many other sets of similar items that could have been employed. Suppose we randomly select 20 words (Form I) from the *Oxford American Dictionary* for a vocabulary test—the *Oxford Vocabulary Test*. Our principal interest is not in the percent of the *sample* of 20 words contained in Form I that the student knows; rather, it is in the percent of words in the *universe* of content (the dictionary) that is of interest. If we randomly select another 20 words from the dictionary for Form II of the test, few students will receive the identical scores on Forms I and II (i.e., rarely is the measurement error precisely the same on both forms).

---

[1]The standard deviation of the chance scores(σ_c) equals $\sqrt{k\pi(1-\pi)}$, where k is the number of items, and π is the chance probability of correctly guessing the correct answer. For this example, the standard deviation of the chance scores is $\sqrt{100(.2)(.8)} = \sqrt{16}$ or 4.

TABLE 5-1 Two Forms of the Hypothetical
Oxford Vocabulary Test

Form I	Form II
1. assess	1. assured
2. breakable	2. bred
3. cilium	3. circularize
4. cranny	4. crease
5. dissipated	5. distinguished
6. excretory	6. exhaustion
7. friendless	7. frontage
8. hart	8. hateful
9. indisposed	9. indulgence
10. latakia	10. laughable
11. maze	11. meant
12. niece	12. newspeak
13. parishioner	13. parse
14. powerhouse	14. prayerful
15. rebellion	15. receiver
16. sailfish	16. salivary
17. silverfish	17. signorina
18. stereophonic	18. stickball
19. tent	19. tern
20. visit	20. vitriol

Table 5–1 gives two random samples of 20 words (i.e., parallel forms of a test) from the content universe of approximately 32,000 words in the *Oxford American Dictionary*. Look over the words in Form I of the test, checking all the words in your vocabulary. Since there are 20 words, multiply your score by 5 to convert it to a percent. This percent is an *estimate* of the percent of the 32,000 words in the content universe (the entire dictionary) that are in your vocabulary (that is, your *true* or *universe*[2] percent score). But how closely does your observed score agree with your universe or true score? This is the central concern of reliability—*the correlation of observed scores on a test with corresponding universe scores is the test's index of reliability.*

Most examinees will, by chance, be familiar with a few more words on one form than on another form. Our greatest interest is in what an examinee's mean percent score would be on many (theoretically, an infinite number) forms containing 20 randomly selected words each. This average is known technically as the universe percent score—the percent score in the universe of content. Universe scores are free from the good or bad *luck* (measurement error) that results from chance factors in the sample of the items that appear on a given form,

---

[2]The term *true score* is conventionally used in classical test theory. We will use *universe* and *true* score interchangeably; although the former is more descriptive and less apt to be misinterpreted, the latter is more common. The term *true score* invites mental slippage from reliability to validity—*true* and *valid* are similar in meaning in common parlance but are not necessarily related in classical test theory.

as well as from other random sources of variation. In classical test theory a person's obtained score is said to be composed of two independent parts: the universe (or true) score and an error of measurement; the mean of the latter is 0 and its standard deviation is denoted by σ_e. Suppose Form I were given to a large representative sample of the U.S. adult population, and the mean and standard deviation were found to be 70 percent and 10 percent, respectively. The upper graph in Figure 5–1 depicts this distribution. The lower graph represents the hypothetical distribution of observed scores on many randomly "parallel" forms from one repeatedly tested examinee, Jane, whose universe score is 75 percent.

Occasionally Jane was *lucky*—the form included more words in her vocabulary, and she scored 80 percent or more; sometimes she knew less than 70 percent of the words on the test. Obviously, our principal interest is not in what percent of the 20 words on a given form that she knows, but in Jane's general word knowledge (i.e., her universe score). In Figure 5–1 we see that the mean of Jane's obtained scores (her universe score) is 75 percent, and all deviations from this score are called *errors of measurement*. When percent correct or standard scores are used, as the reliability of the measure increases, the errors of measurement decrease.

Distribution of scores for *all* students on Form I of the *Oxford Vocabulary Test*

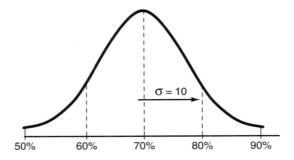

Distribution of scores on many parallel forms of the *Oxford Vocabulary Test* for a student having a true score of 75% (reliability coefficient = 0.80)

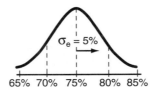

FIGURE 5–1 The distribution of scores for all students on one form of a test, and the theoretical distribution of scores for one student on many parallel forms of the test, assuming that the examinee has a universe score of 75%.

5.4   TRUE SCORES

Figure 5–2 depicts the interrelationship among universe scores, obtained scores, and errors of measurement, using IQ scores as an example. Recall that a person's true IQ score is a theoretical construct; it is the *average* IQ score that would result if that person were tested an infinite number of times on an infinite number of parallel forms of the test. Universe scores are given along the horizontal axis (*X*-axis) and obtained scores along the vertical axis (*Y*-axis). The correlation between true and obtained scores is termed the *index of reliability*.

Figure 5–2 shows that on this hypothetical intelligence test, the obtained IQ scores for those examinees with universe IQ scores of 100 do have a mean of 100 but with some variation above and below 100. What is the standard deviation of obtained scores for a given universe score, or equivalently, what is the standard error of measurement? In this example, as indicated in Figure 5–2, it is about 5 points. This σ_e of 5 indicates that about two out

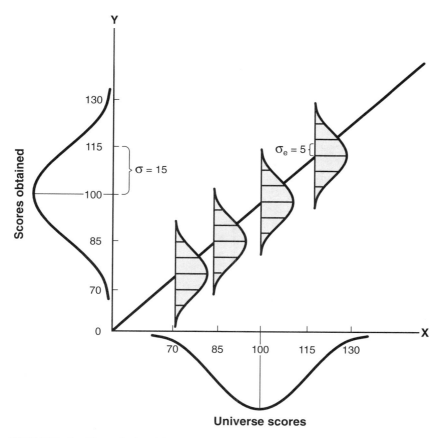

FIGURE 5–2   The relationship among universe scores, obtained scores, and standard error of measurement, illustrated by using an IQ test with a reliability of .90.

of three examinees (68 percent) will obtain IQ scores that fall within 5 points of their universe IQ score. Approximately half of the examinees will have an obtained score above their true score, and vice versa. About 95 percent would receive IQ scores that are within 10 points ($\pm 2\sigma_e$) of their universe scores. The σ_e helps us know how much elasticity should accompany our interpretations of test scores.

It is important to remember that a true score is not necessarily a perfectly *valid* score. True scores represent the average score a person would obtain on an infinite number of parallel forms of a test, assuming that the person is not affected by taking the tests (i.e., assuming no practice or fatigue effect).

5.5   THE STANDARD ERROR OF MEASUREMENT

The standard deviation of these errors of measurement is called the *standard error of measurement* (σ_e). Because the standard error of measurement is a measure of the discrepancies between obtained scores and true scores, it is very useful in test interpretation. Approximately two-thirds of the examinees on any test will have obtained scores that differ by one σ_e or less from their universe scores; only about 5 percent of the examinees will obtain scores that deviate by $2\sigma_e$ or more from their universe scores.

The concepts of reliability and the standard error of measurement are closely associated, as Figure 5–3 illustrates. The figure shows that when the standard deviation of a test remains constant (e.g., by the use of standard scores), the value of the standard error of measurement is completely determined by the test's reliability index, and vice versa. The figure also illustrates that this relationship is not linear. A change of .1 in a test's reliability index has a much greater effect on the standard error of measurement when the coefficient is large than when it is small. In the IQ metric, an increase in the index of reliability from .8 to .9 decreases σ_e from 2.5 points (or $\sigma/6$), but an increase from .1 to .2 decreases σ_e by only about .23 points (or $\sigma/65$).

5.6   THE STANDARD DEVIATION (σ) AND THE STANDARD ERROR OF MEASUREMENT (σ_e)

Figure 5–3 also indirectly depicts the relationship among a test's standard deviation (σ), standard error of measurement (σ_e), and reliability index. If a measure has no reliability, then σ and σ_e are equal; that is, individual differences on the test are totally the result of errors of measurement (as on the Chinese vocabulary test). When reliability is perfect, all differences in scores are due entirely to differences in universe scores. Between these extremes are found all tests and other empirical measures.

The reliability index of a test indicates how highly the distribution of obtained scores correlates with the distribution of universe scores. If the measure had a reliability index of 1.0, the obtained scores that it would yield would be true scores. If the reliability is 0, there is only a chance relationship between the examinees' universe scores and the obtained scores—all individual differences would be due solely to measurement error.

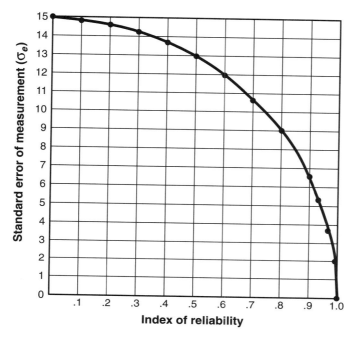

FIGURE 5–3 A graphic illustration of the relationship between the index of reliability of an intelligence test ($\sigma = 15$) and its standard error of measurement.

5.7 SOME TEST THEORY

In classical test theory an observed score is viewed as being composed of two independent parts, the universe score and the measurement error:

EQUATION 5.1

Observed score = True score + Measurement error; or X = T + e

Rearranging the equation, we see that $T = X - e$. Notice that the smaller the measurement error, e, the less the values of T and X differ. The average measurement error over the set of examinees (or within a given examinee taking many parallel forms) is zero. For half of the examinees, the observed score (X) will be higher than the true score (T)—they had good *luck* and a positive error of measurement; for the other half, the obtained scores will be less than the universe scores—they had bad *luck* and a negative error of measurement. In other words, the odds that X is greater than T are equal to the odds that T is greater than X.

The index of reliability, ρ_{TX}, quantifies and describes the closeness of the relationship between the Ts and Xs—it is the correlation between the Ts and Xs for the set of examinees. If ρ_{TX} is 1.0, all Xs and Ts are equal.

The measurement of the weights of a group of students on a given day using a good scale would have a reliability index that approaches 1.0, perhaps .99. Why wouldn't it be 1.0? Why is there any measurement error at all? If an $18 bathroom scale were used, the reliability would probably drop to perhaps .98 or .96 because there would be more measurement error—the effects of standing in a different location on the scale, leaning, errors in reading the register (e.g., different angles, rounding errors). If one person is weighed repeatedly many times (see Figure 5–1), the measurement errors average out (the mean of the *es* is 0); hence, the mean observed score would equal the universe score. Likewise, for a group of persons the measurement errors balance out so that the mean observed score equals the mean universe score.

The formula for the standard error of measurement, σ_e, for a *population* of examinees is

EQUATION 5.2

$$\sigma_e = \sigma\sqrt{1 - \rho_{TX}^2} \text{ or } \sigma_e = \sigma\sqrt{1 - \rho_{XX}} \text{ (since } \rho_{TX} = \rho_{XX}, \text{ Section 5.8)}$$

Imagine the measurement error involved in measuring the length of newborn infants. Often they are in no mood to cooperate with persons who are pulling on their legs, and so on. Let's estimate the standard error of measurement in the measures of length for newborn infants. The standard deviation is .92 inches, and the measures have a reliability coefficient of only approximately .75.

$$\sigma_e = .92\sqrt{1 - (.75)} = .92\sqrt{.25} = .92(.5) \text{ or } .46, \text{ about one-half inch.}$$

With a standard error of measurement of one-half inch, the recorded length is within ± 0.5 inches of the true length for about two-thirds (68 percent) of the infants. Approximately one infant in 20 (5%), however, will have a true length that differs from the true length by an inch or more.[3]

Applying the same theory to any measure, we can say that 68 percent of the obtained scores are within one standard error of measurement (σ_e) of the corresponding universe scores and that 95 percent are within $2\sigma_e$ of their respective universe scores. In interpreting results, the value of σ_e should be used as a margin for error to convey the appropriate degree of precision to scores. For example, for students who obtain an IQ score of 105 on a test with a standard error of measurement of 5 points, we infer that the corresponding universe IQ scores for most (68 percent) fall somewhere between 100 and 110. Only one student in six with an obtained score of 105 will have a universe IQ below 100. Conversely, one student in six will have a universe score above 110. Notice that if a confidence band of $\pm\sigma_e$ is set around a score, a much safer and more appropriate interpretation of performance results.[4]

---

[3]As you might guess, measures of weight of infants is much more reliable than the measures of length.
[4]Confidence intervals or bands have the same meaning and interpretation here as they do in statistics. In measurement, the universe score is the parameter, and $X \pm \sigma_e$ yields the .68 confidence interval for T; $X \pm 2\sigma_e$ approximates the .95 confidence interval. Even smaller confidence intervals (greater precision in estimating true scores) would result if predicted true scores (Equation 5.4) were used (Glutting, McDermott & Stanley, 1987), but this is not standard practice. The gain in precision is not great for highly reliable tests, but it is considerable for tests of moderate reliability (Feldt & Brennan, 1988).

5.8   INDEX OF RELIABILITY VERSUS RELIABILITY COEFFICIENT

Although the *index of reliability describes the correlation of observed scores with universe scores*, the *reliability coefficient* is more commonly reported. The reliability coefficient is the correlation between two sets of observed scores on parallel forms of a test. For example, the correlation between examinees' scores on Form I with their scores on Form II of the *Oxford Vocabulary Test* (see Table 5–1) is the *reliability coefficient*. Although the reliability coefficient is less interesting than the index of reliability, both convey the same information, expressed in different ways, since the index of reliability is the square root of the reliability coefficient. If Forms I and II of the *Oxford Vocabulary Test* are parallel, an examinee's true score is the same on both forms. Stated differently, what is the correlation between universe scores on Form A and universe scores on Form B? Obviously, the correlation is 1.0. If, on the other hand, the scores on one (and only one) form contain measurement error, the resulting correlation (i.e., the index of reliability) will be less than 1.0. If both Form A and Form B contain measurement error, the correlation (i.e., the reliability coefficient) decreases further. Stated more precisely, the square root of a test's reliability coefficient equals the test's index of reliability.

The relationship between a test's reliability index and reliability coefficient is graphically depicted in Figure 5–4. Note that the index of reliability is numerically larger than the corresponding reliability coefficient (except at 0 and 1.0). Obviously it is a simple matter to convert a reliability coefficient (ρ_{XX}) into a reliability index (ρ_{TX}):

EQUATION 5.3

$$\rho_{XX} = \rho_{TX}^2 \text{ or } \rho_{TX} = \sqrt{\rho_{XX}}$$

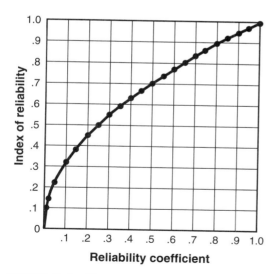

FIGURE 5–4   The relationship between reliability coefficients and reliability indices.

5.9   REGRESSION TOWARD THE MEAN

In classical measurement theory, an individual's score is considered to be composed of two independent parts, a universe (true) score and random measurement error. An obtained score is used to estimate the universe score. A difficulty arises, however, because obtained scores above the mean tend to have positive errors of measurement (*es*) and scores below the mean tend to have negative *es*. In addition, very high and very low obtained scores tend to have larger *es* than scores near the center of the distribution. These two facts lead to a phenomenon called *regression toward the mean*.

When a group of examinees is retested with a parallel form of a measure, the very high scorers on the first form will tend, on the average, to be not quite as high (though still high) on the retest. The initially low scorers will tend to increase their scores on the retest because their errors the first time were negative. These results occur because errors of measurement on the first test are uncorrelated with errors of measurement on the second. Therefore, obtained scores tend to underestimate true scores for the bottom half of the distribution and overestimate universe scores for the top half of the distribution. By how much? That depends on the reliability of the test. If scores on Form A were perfectly reliable ($\rho_{XX} = 1.0$), there would be no regressing toward the mean on parallel Form B because the scores would contain no error. Test scores on a perfectly unreliable test would be expected to regress all the way to the mean on the retest; that is, the expected score obtained on Form B would be the same for all examinees, irrespective of standing on Form A. (In this case, σ_e would equal σ.)

In other words, the obtained score of an examinee is the best estimate of the corresponding universe score only when $\rho_{TX} = 1.0$ (except when X = mean). If Mary obtained an IQ score of 140, her universe IQ score is probably less than 140, perhaps 136. Conversely, Billy's true IQ score is probably higher than his obtained IQ score of 80. There is a tendency for universe scores to be closer to the mean than the corresponding obtained scores. Thus, the standard deviation of true scores, σ_T, is less than the standard deviation of obtained scores, σ; this is always the case unless the reliability is 1.0 (hence, there is no measurement error).

Is this regression toward the mean just an abstract theoretical possibility, or does it really occur in practice? Figure 5–5 gives a scatterplot of IQ scores for 354 students on two forms of an intelligence test. The shaded boxes denote the areas in which scores on both forms fall within the same score interval. If there were no tendency for scores to regress toward the mean, the scores in each column would have a mean falling in the shaded boxes. But *note* that there is a tendency for high-scoring examinees on Form 1 to obtain scores on Form 2 that fall below the shaded boxes. This trend becomes more pronounced for scores deviating substantially from the mean. For example, notice that for the 32 examinees scoring 120 or above on Form 1, only 2 scored higher than 120 on Form 2. At the other (lower) end, the trend is reversed: 24 of the 29 students scoring below 80 on Form 1 improved their scores on Form 2 (i.e., their scores fell above the shaded boxes).

5.10   ESTIMATING TRUE SCORES FROM OBSERVED SCORES

The universe score for a given obtained score can be estimated from the reliability coefficient, ρ_{XX} (the square of the index of reliability). The reliability coefficient is the ratio of

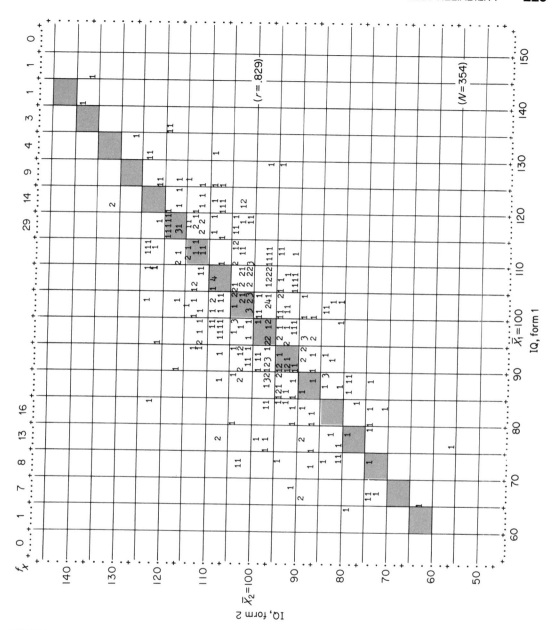

FIGURE 5–5   Scatterplot of IQ scores for 354 students on two forms of an IQ test.

SOURCE: Based on data from K. D. Hopkins and M. Bibelheimer, "Five-year stability IQs from language and nonlanguage group tests," *Child Development, 42* (1971), 645–649.

deviation of the universe score from the mean (*T*–mean) to the deviation of the obtained score from the mean (*X*–mean), averaged over the examinees. Thus, for a test with a reliability coefficient of .9, the universe scores tend to deviate from the mean only 90 percent as far as the corresponding obtained scores.

EQUATION 5.4

$$Estimated\ true\ score = \mu + \rho_{XX}(X - \mu)$$

For example, Mary obtained an IQ score of 140; what is the best estimate of her true score? Using Equation 5.4:

$$Estimated\ true\ score = 100 + (.90)(140 - 100) = 136.$$

Figure 5–6 illustrates this phenomenon graphically using IQ scores as an example. The graph allows us to estimate the universe IQ score corresponding to any obtained IQ score for tests with reliability coefficients of 1.0, .9, .75, .5, .2, and 0. If Mary obtained an IQ score of 140 on a test with a reliability coefficient of .9, her expected universe IQ score is 136. If ρ_{XX} is not .9 but .75, the expected universe IQ score is 130—the true score would

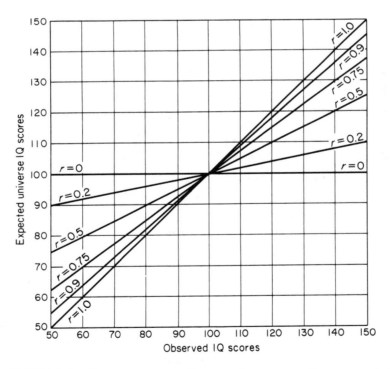

FIGURE 5–6   Expected universe IQ scores for observed IQ scores as influenced by test reliability, for tests having reliability coefficients of .0, .2, ..., .9, 1.0.

be expected to deviate only 75 percent as far from the mean (100) as the obtained score. Likewise, the expected universe IQ score for an obtained IQ score of 80 is 82, 85, or 90, depending on whether the test's reliability coefficient is .9, .75, or .5.

Estimated universe scores are always closer to the mean than obtained scores because all tests contain some measurement error. But the differences between obtained and true scores are relatively small for tests with high reliability. Indeed, on well-constructed standardized tests with reliability coefficients of .9 or higher, there is little need to estimate T because it differs little from X. But the concept of regression toward the mean needs to be kept in mind; otherwise, school boards and officials will wonder what's wrong with the gifted program—as a group their performance will decline when they are retested (see high scores on Form 1 in Figure 5–5). At the same time, the program for slow learners will appear very successful, since most of these students will earn higher scores on the retest (see lower scores on Form 1 of Figure 5–5); gains in obtained scores will result even without any true improvement in universe scores because, as a group, low scorers (on Form 1) tend to have had bad *luck* (Xs tend to be below Ts—es tend to be negative), whereas high scorers tend to have had good *luck* (Xs tend to be above Ts). Since *luck* at time 1 will not be correlated with *luck* at time 2, our best prediction of obtained scores on test 2 are universe scores.

5.11   TEST LENGTH, RELIABILITY, AND THE SPEARMAN-BROWN PROPHECY FORMULA

Test length has a very significant effect on both its reliability and its standard error of measurement. Short tests are usually not very reliable. Fortunately, the effect of changing the length of a test on a test's reliability can be predicted quite accurately using the Spearman-Brown formula (Equation 5.5), where ρ_{XX} denotes the reliability coefficient of the original test and $\rho_{XX'}$ is the reliability coefficient of the "new" test, which is L times as long as the original test (i.e., L is the ratio of the "new" length to "old" length). (It is assumed that the additional items and the original items are parallel samples of items from the same universe of items.)

EQUATION 5.5

$$\rho'_{XX} = \frac{L\rho_{XX}}{1 + (L - 1)\rho_{XX}}$$

If a test is doubled in length (i.e., $L = 2$), the Spearman-Brown formula simplifies to Equation 5.6.

EQUATION 5.6

$$\rho'_{XX} = \frac{2\rho_{XX}}{1 + \rho_{XX}}$$

Thus, if a test with a reliability of .50 is doubled in length, using Equation 5.6 we can predict the new increased reliability coefficient to be

$$\rho'_{XX} = \frac{2(.50)}{1.50} \text{ or } .67.$$

5.12   TEST LENGTH AND σ_e

Lord (1959b) and Kleinke (1979) have shown that a reasonably accurate estimate of the standard error of measurement of a test is given by Equation 5.7.

EQUATION 5.7

$$\sigma_e = .43\sqrt{K}$$

where K is the number of items composing a test and σ_e is expressed in raw score units.

Thus, if $K = 25$, $\sigma_e = .43\sqrt{25} = .43(5)$ or 2.15, but if $K = 100$, $\sigma_e = 4.3$.

Does it surprise you that σ_e increases as the length of a test increases? Note that this is the case only when raw score units are used. When scores are expressed as standard scores or percent-correct scores, σ_e decreases as K increases. When raw scores are converted into percents, the standard error of measurement of the percent scores, $\sigma_{e\%}$, is given by Equation 5.8.

EQUATION 5.8

$$\sigma_{e\%} = \frac{43}{\sqrt{K}}$$

Thus, if $K = 25$, $\sigma_{e\%} = \frac{43}{5} = 8.6\%$, but if $K = 100$, $\sigma_{e\%} = 4.3\%$.

Note in Figure 5–7 that on a typical 20-item test, $\sigma_{e\%}$ will be approximately 10%, but if $K = 50$, $\sigma_{e\%} = 6\%$. Using Figure 5–7, how long would a typical test need to be to yield a $\sigma_{e\%}$ of 5%[5]? It is evident that the percent-correct scores on very short achievement tests will be crude estimates of universe percent scores.

5.13   ESTIMATING RELIABILITY: THE TEST-RETEST METHOD

There are several methods for estimating the reliability of a test (or other measuring instrument). The Test-retest reliability coefficient is the correlation between scores on a measure with scores on the same measure administered at a later time. How stable are the individu-

---

[5]About 75 items.

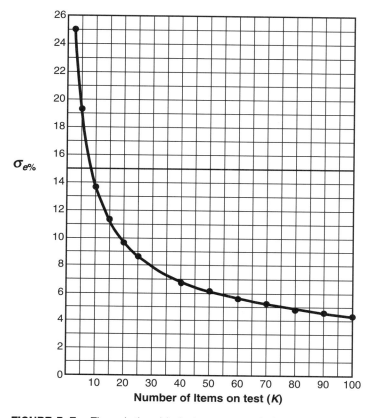

FIGURE 5–7   The relationship between a test's length and its standard error of measurement expressed as percents.

als' scores between the testing and retesting when the same questions or the same apparatus is used? The test-retest method is appropriate for determining the reliability of measures of strength, speed, cholesterol level, blood pressure, pap smears, body mass, and the like.

The test-retest method has drawbacks for estimating the reliability of an educational or psychological test. If the test-retest method were used to estimate the reliability of Form I of the *Oxford Vocabulary Test* (Table 5–1), the chance factors (sampling errors) involved in the particular set of 20 items would be constant on both occasions. Perhaps 40 percent of the words in the dictionary are scientific terms. On a given form of a test of 20 words, the percent of scientific words might vary from 20 percent to 60 percent.[6] If

---

[6]The standard deviation, (σ_p), of the proportion of scientific words that would be found on 25-item tests ($K = 25$), assuming that the words were selected randomly from a large unabridged dictionary, in which technical words represented 40 percent ($\pi = 0.4$) of the entries, is $\sigma_p = \sqrt{\pi(1 - \pi) / K} = \sqrt{(0.4)(0.6) / 25} = \sqrt{0.0096} = 0.098$, or approximately 10%. Notice that on a longer test there would be less difference among forms: If $k = 100$, $\sigma_e = 5\%$.

Form A has 45 percent scientific terms, examinees whose scientific vocabularies are greater than their general vocabularies will be overrated; *Lady Luck* was good to them as she assembled form A. If Form A is given a second time, the test content is fixed; hence, the consistency between scores is higher than it would be if different forms were administered. Therefore, the stability coefficient tells only the test-retest stability of performance for different administrations of this particular test, which may be much less interesting and relevant than the stability of performance on other parallel tests. On measures composed of a set of items, test-retest reliability coefficients are usually higher than parallel-form reliability coefficients because the latter permit a fresh sample from the same content universe.

Figure 5–8 shows two parallel forms of a test, A and B, equally representative of the same universe of content. The test-retest method of estimating reliability does not permit a new sample of items to be used in the second testing. Therefore, the test-retest reliability coefficients, ρ_{AA} and ρ_{BB}, will be higher than the parallel-form reliability estimate ρ_{AB} or ρ_{BA}, in which different random samples of items have been selected from the same item universe. Forms A and B are both random samples from the universe of content, yet ρ_{AA} will be greater than ρ_{AB} because the sample of test content is not allowed to vary in the test-retest method.

An important point in evaluating reliability coefficients is illustrated in Figure 5–8. If the procedure used to estimate reliability does not allow certain factors to vary (e.g., sampling variation in item selection), then, of course, they are constant and cannot be categorized as measurement error, even though they should be. Figure 5–8 also demonstrates that the term reliability coefficient is explicit only when the method used to estimate it is

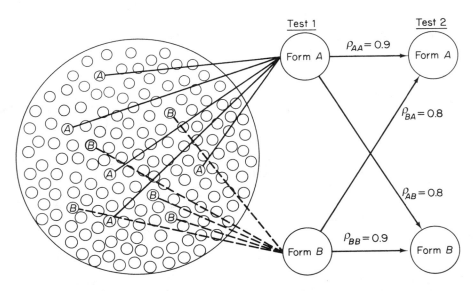

FIGURE 5–8   Graphic illustration of test-retest reliability (ρ_{AA} and ρ_{BB}) and parallel-form (ρ_{BA} and ρ_{AB}) reliability estimates.

reported. For example, one should report the "test-retest reliability coefficient is . . .", not "the reliability coefficient is . . ." (For further discussion, see Stanley, 1971b; Feldt & Brennan, 1988.) There are better ways of estimating reliability of educational and psychological tests than the test-retest method.

5.14   PARALLEL-FORM RELIABILITY

Reliability coefficients estimated from parallel-forms of a test are preferred to test-retest reliability coefficients. As evident in Figure 5–8, a parallel-form reliability coefficient is simply the correlation coefficient between the obtained scores on two parallel forms of the test.

Examinees' true scores are the same on the parallel forms. The standard errors of measurement for the two forms are also equal ($\sigma_{e1} = \sigma_{e2}$). Determining the parallel-form reliability coefficient of a test requires that two forms of the test be administered to the same group of examinees. For many purposes this is impractical. It not only requires the development of two forms of the test, it requires two administrations of the test (like the test-retest method). Lack of cooperation, motivation, fatigue, and boredom by examinees on a second administration of a test present additional drawbacks in using these methods to estimate reliability. Fortunately, there are methods of estimating a test's reliability that require only one administration; these methods are commonly employed in practice (and are the only practicable method for teacher-made tests).

As mentioned earlier, certain variables such as height, weight, blood pressure, and reaction time can be measured directly—the issue of sampling of items is not involved. Ascertaining the reliability of measures of variables like these requires a two-administration design such as test-retest. Other methods are, however, available for cognitive and affective (and other) measures that employ a sample of items or tasks from the universe of items or tasks.

5.15   THE SPLIT-HALF METHOD

To avoid the practical difficulties associated with two test administrations, a power (unspeeded) test can be split into two parts. For example, one might put the odd-numbered items (1, 3, 5, …) into half A and the even-numbered items (2, 4, 6, …) into half B. From a single test administration, a score for each half can be obtained for each examinee, and the half-scores can be correlated to obtain a coefficient that can be labeled $\rho_{X_A X_B}$, that is, the "parallel-form reliability" of a *half-length test*. Fortunately, one can estimate the ρ_{AB} of the full test from $\rho_{X_A X_B}$ via the Spearman-Brown formula (Equation 5.6):

$$\rho_{XX} = \frac{2\rho_{X_A X_B}}{(1 + \rho_{X_A X_B})}.$$

For example, if the Pearson correlation between the half-test scores on the odd versus the even items is $\rho_{X_A X_B}$ then the estimated reliability of the full-length test is predicted to be

$$\rho_{XX} = \frac{2(.6)}{(1 + .6)} = \frac{1.2}{1.6} = .75.$$

The halving process is called the *odd-even* or *split-half method*, and the stepped-up coefficient is usually referred to as a "corrected" split-half reliability[7] coefficient. Although historically the split-half correlation with Spearman-Brown correction has been the most commonly used procedure for estimating reliability, and it has been shown empirically to yield accurate results when its assumptions are satisfied, the method proposed by Flanagan (1937) is computationally simpler because it does not require either the computation of a correlation coefficient or the use of the Spearman-Brown formula. In addition, it is preferable because it does not assume that the two halves have equal standard deviations, an assumption of the Spearman-Brown formula. Flanagan's formula is

EQUATION 5.9

$$\rho_{XX} = 2\left(1 - \frac{\sigma_A^2 + \sigma_B^2}{\sigma^2}\right),$$

where σ_A^2 and σ_B^2 are the variances of halves A and B and σ^2 is the variance of the total scores on the test. For example, if $\sigma_A^2 = 5$, $\sigma_B^2 = 6$, and $\sigma = 10$, then

$$\rho_{XX} = 2\left(1 - \frac{5^2 + 6^2}{10^2}\right) = 2\left(1 - \frac{61}{100}\right) = 2(.39) \text{ or } .7.$$

The Flanagan method and the split-half correlation with the Spearman-Brown correction method usually yield reliability estimates that agree very closely. Indeed, they will yield identical coefficients when $\sigma_A = \sigma_B$; otherwise, the Flanagan method yields a slightly lower value.[8]

5.16   RELIABILITY VIA INTERNAL CONSISTENCY

Many years ago, Kuder and Richardson (1937) devised a procedure for estimating the reliability of a test without splitting it into halves. The rationale for Kuder and Richardson's most commonly used procedure, Kuder-Richardson formula 20, is essentially equivalent to (1) finding the mean correlation among the K items in the test, (2) considering this to be the reliability coefficient of the typical item in the test, and (3) stepping up this average r with the Spearman-Brown formula to estimate the reliability coefficient of a test consisting of K

---

[7]Thorndike and Hagen (1977) note that split-half estimates tend to exceed parallel-form estimates by 0.03 0.11 because the latter includes the influence of changes in the ability of the examinees over a time interval.

[8]The Flanagan formula is algebraically equivalent to a formula devised by Rulon (1939): $\rho_{XX} = 1 - (\sigma_d^2/\sigma^2)$, where σ_d^2 is the variance of the *difference* in scores on the two halves (it is also a direct estimate of σ_e^2). The ratio σ_d^2/σ^2 is an estimate of the proportion of the total variance that is due to error, and ρ_{XX} is the proportion of the variance that is *not* due to error (i.e., is true variance). Thus, we see that the reliability coefficient of a test is said to be the portion of the total variance that is "true" or (universe) variance, that is, $\rho_{XX} = 1 - (\sigma_e^2/\sigma^2) = \sigma_T^2/\sigma^2$ which is the reliability coefficient.

items (see Stanley, 1957). Since there are 300 possibly different inter-item correlations[9] even for a 25-item test, it is fortunate that we do not actually have to compute these rs but can estimate the reliability coefficient fairly easily from data on the items and the variance of the scores.

5.17   KUDER-RICHARDSON FORMULA 20

Even when the average inter-item correlation, r, of items is rather small, the internal consistency reliability of the test can be high if the test is composed of a fairly large number of items. When the average correlation among the 20 items in a test is .10, the ρ_{KR20} coefficient for the test will be approximately .74 as estimated by the Spearman-Brown formula (Equation 5.5).[10] For 50 items, other things being equal, the reliability coefficient is 0.85. The more items, the higher the ρ_{KR20} coefficient. Of course, other things being equal, *longer tests are more reliable that shorter tests.*

 A desirable property of the ρ_{KR20} reliability estimate is that it is the mean of all possible Flanagan split-half reliability estimates (Cronbach, 1951; Novick & Lewis, 1967). ρ_{KR20} has also been shown to be a good estimate of parallel-form reliability on unspeeded tests (Cronbach & Azuma, 1962). Its computation is straightforward. The formula for ρ_{KR20} is

EQUATION 5.10

$$\rho_{KR20} = \frac{K}{K-1}\left(1 - \frac{\Sigma pq}{\sigma^2}\right),$$

where p is the proportion passing a given item, and q is the proportion *not* passing that item ($q = 1 - p$). The pq values are summed over all K items to obtain Σpq. Note that item scoring must be dichotomous—that is, an item is either answered correctly or incorrectly (omitted items are scored as incorrect).

 To illustrate the computation with a simple example, suppose that for a three-item test the proportions of correct answers were .8, .7, and .5 and the standard deviation of the total scores as $\sigma = .9$. The value of $\Sigma pq = (.8)(.2) + (.7)(.3) + (.5)(.5) = .62$; hence

$$\rho_{KR20} = \frac{K}{K-1}\left(1 - \frac{\Sigma pq}{\sigma^2}\right) = \frac{3}{3-1}\left(1 - \frac{.62}{9^2}\right) = 1.5(1 - .765) = .35$$

---

[9]There are $k(k-1)/2$ inter-item correlations among k items.
[10]Stanley (1957) showed that if $\bar{r}$ is the average inter-item correlation among the k items, then the reliability coefficient estimated via the Kuder-Richardson formula is very nearly that yielded by the general Spearman-Brown formula (Equation 5.5). Thus, for a 25-item test, if the reliability of a single item (average $\bar{r}$ between items) is .1, the reliability of the 25-item test is

$$\rho = \frac{25(.1)}{1 + (.25 - 1)(.1)} = \frac{2.5}{1 + 2.4} = \frac{2.5}{3.4} = .74$$

5.18   COEFFICIENT ALPHA

The ρ_{KR20} is a special case of a more general reliability coefficient, alpha, developed by Cronbach (1951).

EQUATION 5.11

$$\rho_\alpha = \frac{K}{K-1}\left(1 - \frac{\Sigma\sigma_K^2}{\sigma^2}\right),$$

where $\Sigma\sigma_k^2$ is the sum of the variances of scores on the K parts (usually items) of the test. When the parts are individual items, $\rho_\alpha = \rho_{KR20}$. When the parts are halves, ρ_α is the split-half reliability coefficient yielded by the Flanagan formula.

Suppose the standard deviations to five 10-item quizzes are $\sigma_1 = 2, \sigma_2 = 3, \sigma_3 = 2, \sigma_4 = 1, \sigma_5 = 2$; the sum of the variances of the $K = 5$ parts ($\Sigma\sigma_k^2$) is $2^2 + 3^2 + 2^2 + 1^2 + 2^2 = 22$. If the standard deviation of the total scores (the sum of the scores on the five quizzes), σ, is 8; $\sigma^2 = 64$. The reliability estimate (coefficient alpha) of the composite score is then

$$\rho_\alpha = \frac{5}{5-1}\left(1 - \frac{22}{64}\right) = 1.25(1 - .344) = 1.25(.656) \text{ or } .82.$$

An important point for classroom evaluation is illustrated in this example. The reliability of a composite score can be high even if the component parts do not possess high reliability.[11]

5.19   KUDER-RICHARDSON FORMULA 21

Because computing ρ_{KR20} by hand is tedious if K is large, Kuder and Richardson (1937) proposed a second formula, Kuder-Richardson formula 21, that is somewhat less accurate but is simple to compute. It requires only the test mean, the variance (σ^2), and the number of items (K) on the test; it assumes that all items are of equal difficulty:

EQUATION 5.12

$$\rho_{KR21} = \frac{K}{K-1}\left[1 - \frac{\mu(K - \mu)}{K\sigma^2}\right]$$

---

[11]Using the Spearman-Brown formula (Equation 5.5) "in reverse," we can estimate the reliability of a 10-item test from the reliability of, for example, a 50-item test with $\rho_{xx} = .82$. In this case $L = 10/50$ or .2, so

$$\rho'_{xx} = \frac{.2(.84)}{1 + (.2 - 1)(.82)} = \frac{.164}{1 + (-.8)(.82)} = \frac{.164}{.344} \text{ or } .48.$$

For example, on a 50-item test ($K = 50$) where the mean[12] (μ) equals 30 and σ^2 equals 100,

$$\rho_{KR21} = \frac{50}{50-1}\left[1 - \frac{30(50-30)}{50(100)}\right] = \frac{50}{49}\left[1 - \frac{600}{5000}\right] = \frac{50}{49}(1 - .12) \text{ or } .90$$

The value of ρ_{KR21} is always less than (and less accurate than) the corresponding value of ρ_{KR20}, but the differences are usually not great on well-constructed tests (Cronbach & Azuma, 1962; Lord, 1959a; Payne, 1963). Figure 5–9 depicts the high relationship between Cronbach alpha ρ_α (or ρ_{KR20}) and ρ_{KR21} on 668 standardized tests and subtests (Betebenner & Hopkins, 1997); ρ_α consistently exceeds ρ_{KR21}, but usually by .03 unit or less if ρ_{KR21} is .60 or greater. The higher the reliability, the less ρ_{KR21} and ρ_α differ. Kuder-Richardson formula 21 assumes that the items on the test are equally difficult; it is lower than ρ_α to the extent that item difficulty varies within a test. On mastery criterion-referenced[13] or teacher-made tests that have many very easy items, ρ_{KR21} becomes more conservative (Cronbach & Azuma, 1962). On unspeeded tests, ρ_α is often given as a lower-bound (minimal) estimate of reliability. Using Figure 5–9, one can make a reasonable estimate of ρ_α from ρ_{KR21}. For example, if $\rho_{KR21} = .8$, ρ_α can be expected to be .83; if $\rho_{KR21} = .6$, ρ_{KR20} may be .66.[14]

Internal consistency reliability methods are not useful in situations such as the measurement of height, in which the items are not viewed as making up a representative sample from a universe of behavior. The ruler is a near-perfect scale for measuring height. To find the error of measurement, we need a second, *independent* measurement of height. Physical measurement is usually more reliable than educational and psychological measurement, because the units and scales of psychological measurement—the items themselves—are subject to much larger errors of measurement.

5.20   SPEEDED TESTS

Split-half and internal consistency procedures are appropriate only for *power* tests, tests in which every student has adequate time to complete the test. These procedures are not proper for speeded tests, tests for which not all the examinees have enough time to respond to all questions. If a test begins with items that are so easy that nearly everyone marks them correctly and ends with items that are so difficult that nearly everyone misses them, it may not be speeded even though not all students attempt all the items. When questions are ordered by degree of difficulty, a student may run out of ability long before completing the test.

---

[12]On classroom tests, the entire population of interest is represented so that the symbol, μ, is appropriate.

[13]Criterion-referenced tests are treated in Chapters 7 and 8. Livingston (1972) has shown that the classical concepts of reliability can be refined in a more general form that will apply to criterion-referenced measures. (See Stanley, 1971b.)

[14]Research (Betebenner & Hopkins, 1997) had demonstrated that ρ_a can be quite accurately predicted from ρ_{KR21} using the equation: $\rho_a = .883\rho_{KR21} + .115$. For example, if $\rho_{KR21} = .40$, $\rho_a = .883(.40) + .115 = .47$.

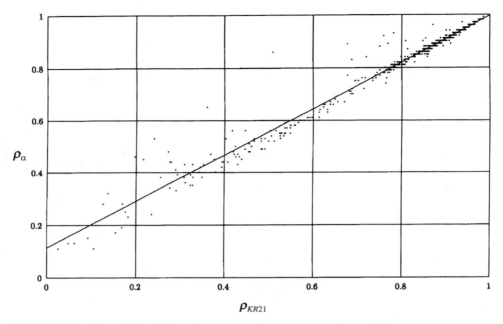

ρ_{α}

ρ_{KR21}

FIGURE 5–9   The relationship between reliability coefficients estimated by Kuder-Richardson Formula 21 and Cronbach's alpha for 668 tests (Betebenner & Hopkins, 1997).

Most standardized ability tests are not heavily speeded, but rarely is a standardized educational test strictly a pure power test. Educational tests usually contain elements of both speed and power. Some students do not have time to answer (or even to read) some of the items that they could answer correctly (see Section 6.7). Tests will yield spuriously high reliability coefficients when split-half or internal consistency methods are employed if they contain a significant speed component. To assess the reliability of a speeded test, one should administer separately timed comparable halves and use the Flanagan or another split-half procedure. Of course, the test-retest and parallel-form methods of estimating reliability are also legitimate for speeded tests.[15]

5.21   WHAT IS A HIGH RELIABILITY COEFFICIENT?

Obviously, we want tests to be highly reliable. Standardized tests need to be more reliable than classroom tests, since standardized test results must stand alone, whereas scores from quizzes and classroom tests are usually aggregated into a composite "score" that will have much higher reliability than the individual components. Standardized tests such as those used for college admission or special education placement should have reliability coeffi-

---

[15]For methods of estimating the reliability of speeded tests, see Feldt and Brennan, 1988.

cients of at least .90. For most purposes the standard error of measurement is a more meaningful indication of measurement precision. It is useful on both norm-referenced and criterion-referenced tests (CRT).[16] Recall that $\sigma_e = \sigma\sqrt{1 - \rho_{XX}}$.

The reliability coefficients for a CRT measure (and other tests on which there are minimal individual differences among examinees) can be low, even if the standard error of measurement is small. For example, the reliability of standardized achievement tests for a high-ability class will ordinarily be much lower than the reliability of the same test for a more heterogeneous class of students, even though the σ_e is the same in both instances.[17]

On criterion-referenced tests or other minimum-competency measures, the standard error of measurement conveys the degree of measurement precision far more meaningfully than the reliability coefficient does. To take an extreme example, suppose a 20-item mastery test for telling time was given to groups of first-graders, with these results: mean = 18, $\sigma^2 = 2$, and $\sigma_e^2 = 1$. The reliability coefficient is only .50, (see footnote 10) even though observed scores differ little from corresponding universe scores. In other words, virtually all students are answering 80 percent or more of the items correctly. If $\sigma_{e\%}$ is 5 percent or less, the test will ordinarily have very high measurement precision regardless of ρ_{XX}, that is, the universe scores are within 5 percent of the obtained scores for most (68 percent) of the students.

SUMMARY[18]

What are the qualities of a good measuring instrument? The two most important qualities are *validity* and *reliability*. The first consideration in educational and psychological testing is always validity. Measurement precision (reliability in some sense) is a crucial prerequisite for validity, but it is only a means toward that end.

When a test is administered to an examinee, a score is obtained. If the examinee had been tested on some other test or occasion, the exact same score probably would not have been earned. The score that would be earned, *on the average*, if the examinee had been tested at various times under the same testing conditions is called the *true* or *universe score*. Although we can never actually know universe scores, we can be aware of the magnitude of the discrepancies between obtained scores (which we know) and universe scores (which we do not know). This difference, the obtained score minus the true score, is called *measurement error*.

---

[16]Norm-referenced tests are designed to measure individual differences as reliably as possible; most standardized tests are examples of norm-referenced tests. Criterion-referenced tests are used to certify some level of mastery of certain skills. They are treated in Chapter 7.

[17]Note in the following reliability formula below that ρ_{XX} will decrease when σ decreases, even if σ_e remains constant: $\rho_{XX} = 1 - (\sigma_e^2/\sigma^2)$.

[18]The NCME Instructional Module, *Understanding Reliability* (Traub, 1991) provides an excellent, concise review of the concepts of this chapter. The methods described in this book are those needed for constructing classroom tests and interpreting standardized tests. There are measurement procedures used in large scale testing, namely item response theory, that are beyond the scope of this book. An excellent overview comparing classical test theory with item response theory can be found in Hambleton and Jones (1993).

The standard deviation of the errors of measurement is the *standard error of measurement* (σ_e or $\sigma_{e\%}$). About two-thirds of the examinees will have obtained scores that are within one σ_e of their universe scores. Only about one person in 20 will obtain a score that varies from his or her universe score by as much as $2\sigma_e$.

The *reliability index* of a test is the correlation between universe scores and obtained scores. The index of reliability is the square root of the test's correlation coefficient, that is, $\rho_{TX}^2 = \rho_{XX}$. Observed scores tend to deviate from the mean more than corresponding universe scores, which accounts for the phenomenon of regression toward the mean.

There are several methods for estimating the reliability of a test. The test-retest and parallel-form methods have the practical disadvantage of requiring two administrations, and the latter requires the construction of two forms. Although the parallel-form method is theoretically preferable, the split-half and internal consistency methods are more common because only one test and one administration are required. However, these one-form methods are inappropriate for speeded tests; they give inflated reliability estimates to the extent that speed rather than power influences test scores. Split-half (often odd-even) reliability estimates tend to be slightly higher than those yielded by the Kuder-Richardson formulas. Kuder-Richardson formula 20 is essentially the average of all possible corrected split-half coefficients and is usually a good estimate of parallel-form reliability. Kuder-Richardson formula 21 yields conservative reliability estimates for power tests, but its computation requires only the number of items on a test, the mean, and the variance. If ρ_{KR21} is .70 or above, ρ_{KR20} tends to be .05 or less higher. The higher the ρ_{KR21} value, the less it tends to differ from the corresponding ρ_{KR20} value.

Even though a test produces valid and reliable scores, it may not be functional because of some practical problem. If the test is too expensive, requires too much time to administer or score, or is difficult to interpret, its real value is reduced accordingly.

IMPORTANT TERMS AND CONCEPTS

coefficient alpha (ρ_α)
index of reliability (ρ_{TX})
measurement error
reliability coefficient (ρ_{XX})
sample
split-half method
test-retest reliability
universe of content
Flanagan reliability formula

Kuder-Richardson formulas (ρ_{KR20} and ρ_{KR21})
parallel-form reliability
regression toward the mean
Spearman-Brown formula
standard error of measurement (σ_e and $\sigma_{e\%}$)
universe (true) score
variance

CHAPTER TEST

1. Can a test be highly reliable and yet have no validity?
2. Can a highly valid test lack measurement precision?

3. If on both Forms A and B of a handwriting test, your penmanship ratings were very good, but otherwise your handwriting is poor, does the handwriting test appear to possess *reliability*?

4. Does the handwriting test just described appear to have validity?

5. Which of these is the classical term for universe score?
   a) real score
   b) valid score
   c) true score
   d) correct score

6. If σ_e is less than σ, the test
   a) is perfectly reliable.
   b) has a reliability index of 1.0.
   c) has a reliability index greater than 0.
   d) has a reliability index of 0.
   e) has a negative reliability index.

For Questions 7–20, suppose that there were many parallel forms of this mastery test. You took them all; assume no practice effect from the test. The distribution of your scores had a mean of 84 percent and a standard deviation of 6 percent.

7. Estimate your universe score.

8. You obtained scores between 78 percent and 90 percent on approximately two out of _____ tests.

9. How frequently did your score exceed 90 percent?

10. How frequently did your score fall below 78 percent?

11. How frequently did your score fall within the 72-96 percent interval?

12. The mean and standard deviation of your class on this mastery test were 80 percent and 10 percent, respectively. Using this and other given information, estimate the reliability coefficient of the test using the formula $\rho_{XX} = 1 - (\sigma_e^2/\sigma^2)$.

13. From the reliability coefficient, ρ_{XX}, estimate the index of reliability, ρ_{TX}.

14. What is the correlation between the obtained scores and the corresponding universe scores on the test?

15. If a second, parallel form were given to the class, estimate the correlation between the two sets of obtained scores.

16. Except when $\rho_{XX} = 0.0$ and 1.0, ρ_{TX} will have a (**larger, smaller**) value than ρ_{XX}.

17. If the mastery test were doubled in length,
    a) ρ_{XX} would increase.
    b) ρ_{TX} would increase.
    c) $\sigma_{e\%}$ would decrease.
    d) Two of the above
    e) All of the above

18. Suppose Mark scored 60 percent on this mastery test (recall that $\mu = 80\%$, $\sigma = 10\%$, and $\rho_{XX} = .64$); his universe score would be expected to be
   a) less than 60%.
   b) 60%.
   c) greater than 60%.

19. Estimate Mark's universe score. (Recall that the universe score is expected to deviate less from the mean than does the obtained score.) More specifically the relationship is: *Expected deviation* $= (\rho_{XX})(X - \mu)$.

20. Does Mark appear to have one of the lowest scores in the class?

21. Jill obtained an IQ score of 120; using Figure 5–6, estimate her universe IQ score
   a) if the test had a reliability coefficient of 0.9,
   b) if the test had a reliability coefficient of 0.75,
   c) if the test had a reliability coefficient of 0.5.

22. On highly reliable tests Xs will differ (**little, greatly**) from universe scores.

23. An obtained score will equal the estimated universe score when
   a) $X = \mu$.
   b) $\rho_{XX} = 0$.
   c) $\rho_{XX} = 1.0$.
   d) both *a* and *c*.

24. What is the principal disadvantage of the parallel-form method as compared to the test-retest method of estimating reliability?

25. Practical considerations aside, which method of estimating reliability is generally preferable?
   a) parallel-form
   b) test-retest
   c) split-half
   d) internal consistency

26. Which statistical measure describes the test-retest and parallel-form reliability?
   a) μ
   b) σ
   c) ρ or r

27. Which formula is used to estimate the reliability of a test if its length is changed?
   a) Flanagan formula
   b) Spearman-Brown
   c) ρ_α
   d) ρ_{KR20}
   e) ρ_{KR21}

28. Which of these tends to yield the lowest reliability coefficient for unspeeded tests?
   a) ρ_α
   b) corrected split-half
   c) ρ_{KR20}
   d) ρ_{KR21}
   e) test-retest

29. Which of these methods of estimating reliability requires the computation of a correlation coefficient?
   a) Flanagan formula
   b) Kuder-Richardson formula
   c) coefficient alpha
   d) All of the above
   e) None of the above

30. Which of the procedures in Question 29 are appropriate for speeded tests?

31. When would ρ_{KR20} and ρ_{KR21} be identical?

32. When the "parts" of a test are items, are ρ_α and ρ_{KR20} identical?

33. Which one of the following ρ_{KR21} values will be the best estimate of the corresponding ρ_{KR20} value?
   a) .40
   b) .50
   c) .60
   d) .70
   e) .90

34. Using Figure 5–9, if ρ_{KR21} is .75, which of these is probably a good estimate of the corresponding ρ_{KR20} value?
   a) .70
   b) .75
   c) .80
   d) .85
   e) .90

35. For interpreting an individual's score, which one of the following is most informative?
   a) ρ_{XX}
   b) σ_e
   c) σ

36. If σ_e remains constant but σ increases, ρ_{XX} and ρ_{TX} will
   a) increase.
   b) remain unchanged.
   c) decrease.

37. Most intelligence tests have a standard error of measurement of approximately five IQ points. For a very homogeneous class (e.g., $\sigma^2 = 50$), estimate the test's reliability coefficient. (*Hint*: See formula in Question 12.)

38. In the preceding question, for a typical class ($\sigma = 15$), the same test would be expected to yield a reliability coefficient of _____.

39. If a test has a reliability of .60, estimate its reliability if the test is doubled in length using the Spearman-Brown formula (Equation 5.6).

40. Using Equation 5.7, estimate σ_e of the raw scores for the following tests:
   a) a test of 25 items
   b) a test of 100 items

41. If raw scores are expressed as percent-correct, does $\sigma_{e\%}$ decrease as test length increases? Use Equation 5.8 to find the value of $\sigma_{e\%}$ for
    a) $K = 25$.
    b) $K = 10$.

42. If a test of 80 items had a $\sigma_{e\%}$ of 5 percent, estimate $\sigma_{e\%}$ if the test is reduced to 20 items. (Note the relationship between length and $\sigma_{e\%}$ in Question 41.)

43. What is L as defined by the Spearman-Brown formula, Equation 5.5, if the number of items is increased from 25 to 100?

44. Given the 25-item test with $\rho_{XX} = .50$, estimate the reliability of the 100-item test.

Other things being equal, as test length is increased, the standard error of measurement decreases (T or F) when

45. raw scores are used.

46. percent scores are used.

47. standard scores are used.

ANSWERS TO CHAPTER TEST

1. Yes	25. a
2. No	26. c
3. Yes	27. b
4. No	28. d
5. c	29. e
6. c	30. None, unless the halves are separately
7. 84%	timed, in which case *a* (and *c* if "parts"
8. three	are halves) is appropriate.
9. on about 1 test in 6	31. Only if all items were equal in (about
10. on about 1 test is 6	95 percent) difficulty
11. on about 19 tests in 20	32. Yes
12. $\rho_{XX} = 1 - (5^2/10^2) = .64$	33. e
13. $\rho_{TX} = \sqrt{\rho_{XX}} = \sqrt{.64} = .80$	34. c
14. $\rho_{TX} = .80$	35. b
15. .64	36. a
16. larger	37. $\rho_{XX} = 1 - (5^2/50) = .50$
17. e	38. $\rho_{XX} = 1 - (5^2/15^2) = .89$
18. c	39. .75
19. $80 - .64(20) = 67.2$	40. a) 2.15 b) 4.3
20. Yes, since he is 2σ below the mean, which ordinarily will be at about the second percentile.	41. Yes a) 8.6% b) 4.3%
	42. 10%
	43. 4
21. a) 118 b) 115 c) 110	44. $\rho'_{XX} = .80$
22. little	45. F
23. c	46. T
24. Two forms of the test are required.	47. T

6

Extraneous Factors That Influence Performance on Cognitive Tests

6.1   INTRODUCTION

Cronbach (1970) distinguished between measures of *maximum performance* (achievement, intelligence, and aptitude tests) and measures of *typical performance* (attitude, interest, and personality inventories). The goal of cognitive measurement is to obtain an examinee's best, maximum, and highest level of performance. The purpose of affective measurement, on the other hand, is to assess an examinee's usual, representative, and typical behavior. The measurement problems are very similar among measures within each of the two categories but are quite different between the classes. In this chapter we discuss the influences of certain irrelevant factors on the measurement of maximum performance.

Another, similar way to distinguish between two classes of psychometric instruments is to talk of "ability tests" versus "self-report or other-report inventories." In principle, one can fake a high score on the latter, which is not really a "test," but not on the former, which we call a cognitive test. Consider these two questions: "What does esoteric mean?" (ability-test item) versus "Do you like classical music?" (self-report item). One cannot pretend to know the meaning of a difficult word about which he or she is ignorant, but anyone is free to lie or be self-deceived about preferences, interests, values, attitudes, opinions, and the like.

In addition to the trait, knowledge, proficiency, ability, or aptitude that is to be measured, many other factors may affect an examinee's performance on a cognitive test. To evaluate the test results properly, one should not only be aware of the existence of extraneous variables but also be able to make appropriate allowances for such factors in the interpretation of the results.

6.2   TEST SOPHISTICATION, PRACTICE, AND COACHING

General know-how of test taking can affect test performance. *Test-wiseness* has been defined as the ability to use the characteristics and format of the test or the test-taking situation to increase the number of items answered correctly (Millman, Bishop & Ebel, 1965). Examinees who are unfamiliar with objective or essay tests usually perform somewhat more poorly than persons who have considerable experience with such tests.

The most basic factors in test-wiseness (American College, 1978; Millman, Bishop & Ebel, 1965; Miller, Fagley & Lane, 1988; Millman & Pauk, 1969) for objective tests are summarized in Table 6–1. (Test-wiseness as it applies to essay tests is treated in Chapter 8.)

It has been shown that test-wiseness increases progressively in grades 5 through 11 (Slakter, Koehler & Hampton, 1970) as, of course, does mental age. It has also been demonstrated that pupils can be taught test-wiseness practices (Bajtelsmit, 1977; Moore, Schutz & Baker, 1966; Nilsson, 1975; Wahlstrom & Boersma, 1968). Such test-taking skill usually improves the score of "naive" examinees on poorly constructed test items, although little

TABLE 6–1   Common Behaviors of Test-Wise Examinees

On objective tests, test-wise examinees tend to employ the following strategies:

1. Pay careful attention to directions and ask examiner for clarification when necessary.
2. Have more than one pencil ready in case one breaks.
3. Work as quickly as possible without being reckless; pace their test-taking rate in relation to the allotted time; try to allow enough time to attempt every item.
4. Guess on all unknown items if only right answers are scored, or if the penalty for guessing is simply a "correction for chance" (it almost always is), but don't waste time—guess quickly.
5. Guess at items that will require a disproportionate amount of testing time; place a check-mark by these items so that they can be returned to if time permits.
6. Use any time remaining to double-check answers, especially those about which there is some doubt.
7. Use deductive reasoning–the process of elimination; eliminate incorrect and implausible options; choose from among the remaining options.
8. Reject options that imply the correctness of each other, for example, 24 ounces and 1.5 pounds.
9. Utilize relevant information from other items on the test.
10. Put themselves in the shoes of the test constructor; consider the intent of the test and test constructor; adopt the level of sophistication that is intended.
11. Use relevant and extraneous clues to help identify the correct option. The correct answer is more likely to be qualified more carefully or longer, represent a different degree of generalization, or be composed of textbook or stereotyped phraseology.
12. Learn the test constructor's tendencies to use certain response positions more (or less) frequently, such as the middle position, or to include a disproportionate percentage of false (or true) items.
13. Recognize the use of specific determiners and clues from grammatical construction (e.g., subject-verb agreement, parallelism).
14. Recognize that true-false items using such terms as "always" or "never" are more likely to be false than to be true.

effect is typically found on well-constructed items (Bajtelsmit, 1977; Keysor & Williams, 1977; Pike, 1978) unless examinees are in the primary grades (Callenbach, 1973).

Since poor items are found on almost all teacher-made tests and on many standardized tests, test sophistication is probably a factor on most tests. It apparently is a major factor only with naive examinees on poorly constructed tests or on tests given under speeded conditions. A study by the College Board (Powers & Alderman, 1983) found that an orientation booklet, *Taking the SAT*, which provides students with detailed information about the test, including sample items, did not significantly influence SAT performance.

6.3   PRACTICE

Several studies provide information regarding the effects of taking a test on the examinee's subsequent performance on that test or a parallel form of that test. Almost all studies consistently show a general "improvement" in score on the retest. Most such studies have used intelligence tests; the gains are usually reported in IQ units.

A one-week practice effect of only 1.1 IQ points was found for verbal IQ scores on the *Lorge-Thorndike Intelligence Tests*; the corresponding value for nonverbal IQs (3.3 points) was only slightly larger ($.2\sigma$) (Thorndike & Hagen, 1974). A mean practice effect of 3.03 IQ points (about $.2\sigma$) has been observed on the Stanford-Binet (Jensen, 1980; Terman & Merrill, 1937). Kreit (1968) observed a practice factor of 7 IQ points (about $.4\sigma$) when third-grade students were administered four intelligence tests over a five-month interval. More recent studies have yielded comparable results (Kulik, Kulik & Bangert, 1984).

The practice factor on tests used for admission to college or graduate school is especially important to note. Levine and Angoff (1958) investigated the effect of repetition on the College Board's *Scholastic Aptitude Test* (*SAT*) for high school juniors and seniors. They found an average gain of only 10 points ($.1\sigma$) for the first retest after a two-month interval on either the *SAT* verbal or math test; an additional gain of 10 points was found for the second retest, but no further gain for a third retest. Angoff (1971) and Cole (1982) provide detailed information about changes in *SAT* scores over various time periods. Students who volunteer to take the *SAT* in May of their junior year and December of their senior year have an average gain of less than 25 points (about $.25\sigma$) from the aggregate of six months of learning and practice. Messick (1980) reported practice effects of 12 to 17 points (less than $.2\sigma$), although, as might be expected, more able students benefit somewhat more from practice than do less able students (Kulik, Kulik & Bangert, 1984; Bond, 1988). The legislated disclosures of copies of the *SAT* appear to have had no discernible effect on *SAT* averages (Stricker, 1984). Campbell, Hilton, and Pitcher (1967) compared the performance of a large group who had repeated the aptitude sections of the *Graduate Record Examination* after a three-month interval. These examinees had repeated the test on their own initiative; some apparently felt that the first test score did not accurately reflect their abilities. An average gain of only approximately 20 points ($.2\sigma$) was observed on the verbal aptitude section, and the same on the quantitative section; thus, it appears that the practice effect is not a major factor on these important tests. A similar gain of 25 points ($.25\sigma$) was observed for medical school applicants on the *Medical College Admission Test* (*MCAT*) (Schumacher & Gee, 1961). The practice effect is greater for persons with limited test-taking experience, for example, a greater practice effect was evident for Mexicans than for Americans on the *Cattell Culture Free Intelligence Test* (Knapp, 1968). The practice effects were much larger when speed was a factor.

The review of these related studies of the practice effect on cognitive tests, including the meta-analysis[1] of Kulik et al. (1984) supports the following generalizations:

1. Practice effects are more pronounced for examinees of limited educational background and test-taking experience.
2. The effects are greater on speeded tests as opposed to untimed, power tests.
3. The effects are much greater (usually twice as large) on a repeated test than on a parallel form of the test.
4. The greater the interval between tests, the smaller the effect. There appears to be little <u>practice</u> effect for an interval greater than three months with children, although some of the effect is sustained with adults.
5. Other things being equal, the effects appear to be slightly greater for examinees of high mental ability, especially when the identical test is repeated.
6. Practice effects appear to be somewhat greater for group tests than for individually administered tests.
7. Practice effects tend to be greater for nonverbal and performance (apparatus) tests than for verbal tests.
8. For a group of typical examinees, the average practice effect is usually $.2\sigma$ or less in magnitude.

6.4   COACHING

The topic of coaching is difficult to treat because of the great latitude in what may be represented by the term. It can mean anything from drill on specific items that were missed on a test to a general course in vocabulary development, math review, and instruction and practice in test taking. In addition to the kind of coaching given, the amount of time spent varies considerably in the published studies from a single session to instruction over a period of several months. Indeed, the amount and type of coaching instruction is hard to distinguish from certain other remedial or developmental instruction (Bond, 1988). Consequently, the results of coaching studies are quite varied. The following results for a study using the *Stanford-Binet* are representative. Three groups of schoolchildren were compared. The control group, which received no coaching (practice effect only), gained on the average 2 to 3 IQ points (about $.2\sigma$) on the retest. A second group received two hours of training on material that was similar but not identical to that on the test; this group had an average gain of 7 to 8 IQ points (about .4 to $.5\sigma$). A third group, which was coached on identical material, reflected a mean gain of about 30 points (about 2σ)! These differences declined with time over a three-year period, at which time no coaching advantage remained. The typical combined effect of both coaching and practice is approximately 9 IQ points.

---

[1]A meta-analysis (Glass, McGaw & Smith, 1981) is a statistical analysis that integrates all of the available research studies on a particular topic.

Several commercial enterprises have developed over the past several years, based on the claim that special coaching workshops can produce substantial gain on academic admissions tests. Several empirical studies have been conducted on the effect of coaching on the *SAT* (CB, 1968; Alderman & Powers, 1980; Bond, 1988) and the *GRE* (Powers, 1985). Most studies reveal a small 10 to 25 point (.1 to .25σ) gain from special coaching, although the effects are greater for long-term, intensive coaching (Bagert-Drowns, Kulik & Kulik, 1983). Frankel (1960) compared students who took a commercial coaching course with a group matched on initial *SAT* score who merely repeated the test. The coached students gained less than 10 points (.1σ) more than the matched group. Special secondary school programs designed specifically to improve student performance on the *SAT* verbal averaged only 7 points (less than .1σ) gain (Alderman & Powers, 1980). Similar findings have been reported for the *GRE* (Powers, 1985). The long-term focused coaching courses do seem to result in greater test improvement than does sustained instruction in broad academic skills (Anastasi, 1981; Bagert-Drowns, Kulik & Kulik, 1983).

From the results of these and related studies (Wood, 1977), we can make the following generalizations pertinent to the effects of coaching on test performance:

1. Short-term coaching usually results in small gains in test performance, over and above that accruing from the practice effect unless the training is extensive and over a substantial time period.
2. The magnitude of the gain rarely exceeds .2σ unless the examinees have been coached on the actual test items. Somewhat larger gains (often .3σ) result on achievement tests for those examinees who have not had recent association with the content area.

As long as the objective questions are reasonably straightforward, the amount of improvement typically brought about by coaching and/or practice is not great (Wood, 1977) and is not consistent with the claims made by expensive test-preparation courses.[2]

6.5 ANXIETY AND MOTIVATION

A poorly motivated student cannot be expected to make maximum effort on a test. Most examinees are intrinsically motivated to succeed in academic test situations, although the degree of motivation varies widely among ethnic and socioeconomic groups (Anastasi, 1968, p. 551). The problem is magnified when students see no direct relationship between test performance and their self-interest (as in state assessment programs). Trying to get students to give their best efforts when the exam doesn't have important direct consequences for them becomes an especially thorny problem. On the other hand, incentives such as cash, grades, and special urgings have little or no effect on typical students who are already motivated to do well. When the test content is not intrinsically interesting or examinees are not

---

[2]Owen's (1985) account of the effectiveness of the Princeton Review coaching clinic makes for interesting journalism, but the anecdotal reports given are highly nonrepresentative of the findings of disinterested researchers.

ego-involved with their performance, the effects of incentives can be moderate to sizable especially on group tests with students in the primary grades (Taylor & White, 1982).

If examinees are too ego-involved with their performance on a test, they may become anxious. There have been dozens of research studies relating anxiety and test performance. Almost all of this research is consistent in showing a small to moderate negative ($-.1$ to $-.4$) correlation between paper-and-pencil self-report test anxiety measures and performance on cognitive measures such as academic aptitude and achievement tests. Too often these findings have been interpreted incorrectly; that is, they have been assumed to show that test anxiety depresses ability test performance. Correlation may reflect causation, but it does not *necessarily* do so. One would be equally unjustified in concluding from the negative correlation, that "poor performance on ability tests generates high test anxiety." A brief look at some of the items used on the self-report scales designed to measure test anxiety (Sarason et al., 1960) will show that both explanations are logically plausible:

1. When the teacher says she is going to find out how much you have learned, does your heart begin to beat faster?
2. While you are taking a test, do you usually think you are not doing well?
3. After I take a test, I try to stop worrying about it, but I just can't stop.

As French (1962, p. 555) stated, "Evidence that anxiety is usually found to accompany low test scores proves nothing about the part that anxiety plays in bringing about the low scores." In a few studies, researchers have attempted to ascertain experimentally whether high anxiety impairs test performance. In these studies, subjects were randomly assigned to various anxiety-inducing or anxiety-reducing treatments. The evidence obtained thus far has failed to support the common contention that such experimentally induced anxiety depresses test performance (Allison, 1970; Chambers, Hopkins & Hopkins, 1972; French, 1962; Silverstein et al., 1964). However, in tests requiring psychomotor performance in addition to cognitive performance (such as mazes), anxiety-inducing instructions did cause more errors to be made by high-anxiety examinees (Sarason, Mandler & Craighill, 1952).

It can be concluded that although measured test anxiety is inversely associated with cognitive test performance, the available research fails to establish a causative relationship with the usual kind of cognitive test of maximum performance. This generalization does not necessarily apply to degrees of anxiety beyond those that can be investigated experimentally, to psychomotor measures, or even to individual tests in which the examiner plays a more active role in the testing process. Some evidence suggests that there is a curvilinear relationship (see Figure 4–4) between anxiety and test performance—that anxiety actually facilitates performance up to a point, after which it becomes progressively debilitating (Atkinson, 1983; Lens, 1983).

6.6   RESPONSE STYLES

Response sets or *response styles* are test-taking habits that cause people who are equal in ability (or whatever the trait being measured) to obtain different scores on a test or inventory (Cronbach, 1946, 1950, 1970). Many examinees bring to a test stereotypical patterns of test-taking behavior that influence performance but are unrelated to the trait being measured (Sesnowitz, Bernhardt & Knain, 1982) and, hence, can attenuate the validity of the scores (Powers, 1985).

6.7   THE SPEED-VERSUS-ACCURACY SET

Some examinees have a test-taking habit that causes them to work slowly and carefully; others have a tendency to work quickly and with less caution. The correlation between ability and working rate on tests has been shown to be very low. Some examinees respond more slowly than others irrespective of item difficulty or test content. Some examinees tend to skip over more difficult items and come back to them if time permits (Rindler, 1980).

There is an abundance of research that shows that there is little or no relationship between the order in which examinees finish a test and the scores on the test (e.g., Bridges, 1985; Burack, 1967; Michael & Michael, 1969). When tests are unspeeded (i.e., power tests), the effects from the speed-versus-accuracy response style are negligible. (On pure power tests, ample time is provided for all examinees to demonstrate their maximum performance.) Speeded achievement tests tend to be less valid (Traub & Hambleton, 1972) except in those areas where speed is intrinsically relevant to course objectives (e.g., typing). When achievement tests are speeded, scores are confounded with the speed-versus-accuracy response style.

Teacher-made and standardized tests often have inadequate time limits for students who tend to work for accuracy rather than with speed, allowing the irrelevant effects from the speed-versus-accuracy response set to contaminate the validity of test scores. If tests are speeded, the magnitude of the practice effect is also increased. Several studies have found that tests may measure different mental functions when administered under power and speed conditions (Lord, 1956; Myers, 1960; Mollenkopf, 1960). Older people tend to work more slowly, a factor in some early studies that led to a gross overestimate of the degree of intellectual decline with age.

Except for those educational objectives for which speed of response is an important objective (e.g., reading speed), standardized tests should be constructed and administered so that virtually all examinees (at least 90 percent) complete the examination. In classroom testing, periodic announcements of the time remaining for the test may help pace the examinees and reduce the contamination resulting from the speed-versus-accuracy set. Every standardized cognitive test should report the extent to which speed is a factor on the test (AERA-APA-NCME, 1985).

6.8   THE ACQUIESCENCE SET

If one is uncertain about a true-false item, there is a significant tendency to choose the "true" option (Cronbach, 1950). Gustav (1963) found that 63 percent of a group of college students had marked more items "true" than there were true items on the test. This is particularly interesting since some instructors have a tendency to include more "true" than "false" items on their tests (Metfessel & Sax, 1957). The acquiescence set allows more people to get undeserved credit for true items than for false items; which probably accounts for the fact that true-keyed items tend to be easier and less discriminating than items in which the correct answer is "false" (Storey, 1968). Rarely is the acquiescence set apt to be consequential on a cognitive test, although its effects on affective (personality, attitude, and interest) measures is usually substantial.

6.9   THE POSITIONAL-PREFERENCE SET

When examinees are ignorant of the answer to an item, their habits of taking tests are such that they do not choose among the alternatives entirely at random. The center position in a set of three-to-five options may be favored by habits of reading or attention (Guilford, 1965, p. 490). The research on the positional-preference response set has not yielded consistent findings. A few studies have found it to be a small factor on certain tests (Gustav, 1963; Ace & Dawis, 1973), but most studies have failed to find any significant examinee preference for certain response positions (Hopkins & Hopkins, 1964; Jessel & Sullins, 1975).

There does appear to be a tendency for examinees *not* to respond in a random manner (Wood, 1977). To a greater extent than random events, they tend to avoid repeating the same response position on consecutive items (e.g., *BB* or *CCC*). They also tend to use backward-series response sequences (e.g., *EDC*) more often than would be expected by chance (Rabinowitz, 1970).

The response position of the correct answer on teacher-made tests often reflects a bias toward certain positions, with fewer correct answers for the initial and, to a lesser extent, final response options (Carter, 1986). Standardized tests are less likely to have keying biases. The research evidence suggests that positional preference appears to have negligible consequences on test performance of motivated examinees..

6.10   THE OPTION-LENGTH SET

There is some evidence (Carter, 1986; Chase, 1964; Strang, 1977) that when students do not know the answer to an item, there is a response style toward favoring the longest option on difficult multiple-choice tests related, perhaps, to the fact that the longest option is more often the correct answer on teacher-constructed tests (Carter, 1986). This response set can easily be removed by inserting some long incorrect options on easy items early in the test.

6.11   THE SET TO GAMBLE

The undesirable effects from guessing on objective tests has been a continuing concern since this type of test was introduced early in this century. The problem results from the fact that not all students of equal ability guess with equal frequency. There are great differences among examinees in the tendency to guess on test items; these differences are reliable within a test, and they are generally consistent from one test to another (Jackson, 1955; Slakter, 1967, 1969; Swineford, 1938, 1941; Ben-shakhar & Sinai, 1991). The tendency to gamble varies from persons who will not guess even when told that they must answer every question to the gambler who attempts almost every item regardless of penalties or directions (Waters, 1967). In general, females have been shown to be less likely to guess when in doubt than males, a factor that accounts for some of the gender difference on objective tests (Ben-shakhar & Sinai, 1991).

The effect from the gambling response style is magnified when students are warned that there is a "penalty[3] for guessing." There are a few examinees, however, who omit some items even when they are assured of no penalty; some mistakenly assume they are being rash if they make wild guesses. Less able examinees tend to disregard "Do not guess" instructions more often than do more able examinees (Hopkins, 1964a; Wood, 1976, 1977), consequently the use of "Do not guess" instructions are not recommended.

Most standardized tests do not employ a correction for chance, thus, the gambler receives an unwarranted advantage over the more deliberate student, and males over females (Ben-shakhar & Sinai, 1991).

The gambling set has been found to have little or no relationship to ability (Crocker & Benson, 1976) and to be related to certain personality traits that are irrelevant on ability tests (Cross & Frary, 1977; Ziller, 1957). Examinees with personality scores indicating introversion and low self-esteem tend to omit more items and to omit more items for which they know the answers.

On most tests, examinees can "guess" better than chance (Cross & Frary, 1977; Wood, 1976; Albanese, 1986) because (1) they may have partial information on several items and (2) on many items not all the distracters are plausible. Little and Creaser (1966) asked examinees to indicate whether (a) they guessed, (b) were uncertain of their answers, or, (c) were certain on each item of a test containing three-option questions; the percentages of correct answers were 55, 67, and 93 percent, respectively, for the three categories. If the examinees possessed no partial information and guessed randomly, they would have been expected to have answered correctly only 33 percent rather than 55 percent for items in the "guessed" category. Jackson (1955) similarly found that students correctly answered one-third of the five-option items on which they reported guessing, rather than the one-fifth expected solely from chance.

6.12   CORRECTIVE MEASURES FOR THE GAMBLING SET

The most widely used method to reduce the effects of guessing is the "correction for chance," often erroneously referred to as the "penalty for guessing." The correction-for-chance formula actually corrects for omissions rather than for guessing as such. If the students omit no items, their relative scores (i.e., z-scores or percentile ranks) will be the same, whether or not the formula is applied; in other words the corrected and uncorrected scores will correlate 1.0.

---

[3]The term, "penalty," is misleading; there is a correction, but it does not constitute a penalty (see Section 6.12).

The standard correction formula is

EQUATION 6.1

$$S = R - \frac{W}{A - 1},$$

where

S is the examinee's score corrected for chance,
R is the number of correct (**R**ight) answers for the examinee,
W is the number of **W**rong responses (this does *not* include omitted items, and
A is the number of **A**lternatives (options) per item.

For two-option items, like true-false tests, the correction formula becomes

$$S = R - \frac{W}{2 - 1} = R - W.$$

Standardized tests are frequently composed of four-choice or five-choice items. For the four-option items, the formula is $S = R - (W/3)$; for five-option items, the formula is $S = R - (W/4)$. Obviously, the greater the number of options per item, the less likely it is that one will select the correct answer by chance and, hence, the less the weighting of an incorrect response.[4] Theoretically, negative scores can result if an examinee's "true" knowledge is near 0; the score obtained may (if the examinee marks many items) depart by chance from 0 in either direction.

The formulas that correct for chance success theoretically reduce to zero the expected score of a student who, totally ignorant of the material presented in the test, guesses randomly at all the items. If a test contains 100 true-false items and a student (Bob) guesses an answer to each question, he should, by chance, select the correct answers to 50 items, on the average. Thus, we expect the typical totally uninformed person to receive a score of 50 right and 50 wrong. Bob deserves a final score of zero, which represents his true knowledge of the material. When the 50 wrongs are subtracted from the 50 rights his correct-for-chance score is: $S = R - W = 50 - 50$ or 0. Suppose Bill answers 50 items correctly and *omits* the other 50 items; his expected score will be $S = R - W = 50 - 0 = 50$. Had Bill guessed randomly at the 50 omitted items, he would, on the average, have answered half of them (25) correctly and half of them incorrectly: his "rights score" (R) is 50 known + 25 guessed = 75, and his "wrongs score" (W) is 25, and his corrected-for chance score would therefore be $S = 75 - 25$ or 50—the same score he obtained without any guessing. The possible fallacy in the rationale for this procedure has already been discussed. Because of poor options on some items and the partial information possessed by examinees, they can usually do better than

---

[4]If not all items on a test have the same number of options, each subset of items with the same number of options is treated separately with the appropriate formula. For example, if subtest A of a test is composed of 25 true-false items and subtest B has 30 four-option multiple-choice questions, $S_A = R - W$ is used for the true-false subtest and $S_B = R - W/3$ is used for subtest B. The sum of the two corrected-for-chance scores is the corrected-for-chance score for the entire test ($S = S_A + S_B$).

chance when forced to guess at items that they have omitted (Budescu & Bar-Hillel, 1993; Cross & Frary, 1977; Cureton, 1971; Ebel, 1968; Wiley, Collins & Glass, 1970; Wood, 1976, 1977). Consequently, even when the correction formula is used, the gambler usually obtains a higher score than an equally knowledgeable but less-risk-taking examinee.

One study (Traub, Hambleton & Singh, 1968) reported slightly better results obtained from using a positive rather than a negative correction approach. Even though the formulas yield scores that correlate 1.0, they appear to have different psychological effects on examinees. The following formula was used:

EQUATION 6.2

$$S = R + \frac{O}{A}$$

where S, R, and A are defined as in Equation 6.1, and O is the number of omitted items. This procedure yields scores that lack the logical meaning of the usual procedure; for example, a person who omitted all 100 true-false items on a test would nevertheless receive a score of 50.

The consequences of correction formulas are not consistent across tests, although perhaps a majority of the studies show a negligible decrease in reliability (Frary, Cross & Lowry, 1977; Glass & Wiley, 1964). The evidence on validity is also inconclusive, although the use of corrected scores when all items are not attempted by all examinees is favored (Cross & Frary, 1977; Cureton, 1969; Lord, 1963, 1975; Sax & Collet, 1968).

It should be reemphasized that the correction formula is needed only when some students omit items. When only a few examinees omit a few items, the student ranking will be virtually unchanged whether or not the scores are corrected for *chance*. For psychological reasons, the teacher may wish to return corrected scores to the students even though few items have been omitted. This may be especially advisable with two-option tests, since the poorest students may not realize the extent of their ignorance and may protest if they are given low grades on the basis of uncorrected test scores that to them seem to indicate considerable knowledge (Stanley, 1954). For example, 70 percent correct on 100 two-option items becomes 40 percent after correction for chance, but the student may think that 60 percent of the content is known. The correction formula with true-false and two- and three-option multiple choice test scores more accurately emphasizes the range of knowledge within the group tested, even when omissions are negligible.

If every student tested answers every item, the standard deviation of scores corrected for chance (σ_C) is $\frac{A}{(A-1)}$ times the standard deviation of the uncorrected scores (σ_U).

EQUATION 6.3

$$\sigma_C = \left(\frac{A}{A-1}\right)\sigma_U$$

Equation 6.3 shows that the standard deviation of the distribution of corrected-for-chance scores for a two-option test (with no omissions) will be twice the standard deviation of the distribution of uncorrected (raw) scores; *note:* $\sigma_C = [A/(A-1)]\,\sigma_U = 2\sigma_U$. (See Figure 6–1). On a five-option test with no omissions, the standard deviation of corrected-for-chance scores is 5/4 or 1.25 times the standard deviation of the uncorrected scores ($\sigma_C = 1.25\sigma_U$).

The Educational Testing Service uses the $R - W/3$ or $R - W/4$ formulas to obtain raw scores on the *Preliminary Scholastic Aptitude Test (PSAT), Scholastic Aptitude Test (SAT)*, and *Graduate Record Examination (GRE)*, all of which are composed of four- or five-option multiple-choice items.

Many persons greatly overestimate the influence of chance on objective tests. Unless a test contains very few items, it is virtually impossible to receive a satisfactory score by chance alone. Suppose many students have absolutely no knowledge of the material on a 100-item test on which each item contains two options (*T–F* or two-alternative multiple-choice). The students choose one option for each item entirely by chance. The right-hand distribution, curve 2 of Figure 6–1, shows the distribution of these scores. The average chance score, μ, is 50 (i.e., 50%). The standard deviation of the chance scores, σ, is 5. About two-thirds of the scores group themselves in a rather narrow (50% ± 5%) range on both sides of the mean score of 50 percent. A score above 60 percent ($\mu + 2\sigma$) will occur by chance with the same frequency as a score below 40 percent ($\mu - 2\sigma$)—only about 2 percent of the chance scores will be above 60 percent or below 40 percent (see Figure 6–1). For 98 students in 100, the scores will be below 60 percent correct. The mode chance score is 50, obtained by 8 percent of random guessers. It is virtually impossible to earn a score of 75 percent or more by chance alone—there is less than one chance in 3 million that an examinee

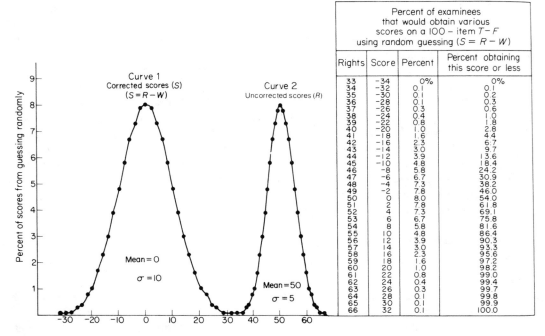

Rights	Score	Percent	Percent obtaining this score or less
33	-34	0%	0%
34	-32	0.1	0.1
35	-30	0.1	0.2
36	-28	0.1	0.3
37	-26	0.3	0.6
38	-24	0.4	1.0
39	-22	0.8	1.8
40	-20	1.0	2.8
41	-18	1.6	4.4
42	-16	2.3	6.7
43	-14	3.0	9.7
44	-12	3.9	13.6
45	-10	4.8	18.4
46	-8	5.8	24.2
47	-6	6.7	30.9
48	-4	7.3	38.2
49	-2	7.8	46.0
50	0	8.0	54.0
51	2	7.8	61.8
52	4	7.3	69.1
53	6	6.7	75.8
54	8	5.8	81.6
55	10	4.8	86.4
56	12	3.9	90.3
57	14	3.0	93.3
58	16	2.3	95.6
59	18	1.6	97.2
60	20	1.0	98.2
61	22	0.8	99.0
62	24	0.4	99.4
63	26	0.3	99.7
64	28	0.1	99.8
65	30	0.1	99.9
66	32	0.1	100.0

Percent of examinees that would obtain various scores on a 100 – item $T-F$ using random guessing ($S = R - W$)

Curve 1 Corrected scores (S) ($S = R - W$)

Curve 2 Uncorrected scores (R)

Percent of scores from guessing randomly

Mean = 0
$\sigma = 10$

Mean = 50
$\sigma = 5$

FIGURE 6–1 Frequency distributions of corrected-for-chance scores ($S = R - W$) (Curve 1) and of number-right scores (Curve 2) resulting from guessing answers to test of 100 two-choice items.

would select the correct answers on 75 or more of the 100 T or F items by chance alone! Only about one examinee in 1000 would score 65 or higher by chance alone.

Notice what happens to the distribution of chance scores when the correction-for-guessing formula (in this case $R - W$) is applied (Curve 1). The mean (μ_C) and mode score become 0. The standard deviation, σ_C, of the corrected-for-chance scores becomes 10 percent (see Equation 6.3). Scores as high as 30 percent are extremely rare. Figure 6–1 graphically depicts the two effects of applying the correction for guessing to chance scores: (1) The average chance score is reduced, and (2) the variability of possible scores is increased.

Although guessing may produce variations among the scores, one should not pay serious attention to students who insist that their high score was due to lucky guessing (unless the test is a short quiz).

In summary, the correction for chance may have some slight advantage over "rights-only" scoring on a standardized test. The correction is especially useful when tests are difficult or speeded, situations in which the speed-versus-accuracy and gambling response sets are operative. However, as Mollenkopf (1960) suggested, it is only fair to inform the examinees that such *a correction is not a penalty* because, as we documented earlier, it usually under-corrects. As Cureton (1971) suggests, if examinees have a hunch, they should respond because hunches are right more frequently than chance. Of course, if examinees have misinformation[5] about the topic, they can receive scores less than chance.

6.13 ELIMINATION SCORING AND ANSWER-UNTIL-CORRECT PROCEDURES

Instead of having examinees select the correct or best answer, examinees can be directed to eliminate all the incorrect options that they can (elimination scoring), or to continue selecting options until the correct alternative is selected (answer-until-correct or self-scoring). Several investigators (Gilman & Ferry, 1972; Hanna, 1975), but not all (e.g., Kane & Maloney, 1978), have found slight gains in reliability. One study (Hanna, 1975) found that a decrease in validity accompanied the use of answer-until-correct scoring. For classroom purposes, these procedures are not worth the extra testing time and special answer forms required (Hakstian & Kansup, 1975; Wood, 1977), but improved computerized test administration may make them worth exploring in the future.

6.14 CONFIDENCE SCORING

Another approach designed to remove the consequences of guessing (first proposed by Soderquist, 1936) asks students to indicate how certain they were of the correctness of their answers. Students received more credit for answers given with confidence than for those of which they were uncertain. The penalty for an incorrect response rated as highly confident was greater than for one rated as uncertain. Soderquist found that confidence scoring yielded slightly higher test reliability than conventional scoring. Interest in Soderquist's approach was

---

[5]For example, a person who thinks that "misspell" is spelled "mispell."

revived by several investigators who found scores had higher test reliability than with conventional scoring (Armstrong & Mooney, 1969; Ebel, 1965a; Friedland & Michael, 1987; Michael, 1968a). The effects of confidence scoring on test validity are much less certain, although the available evidence is disappointing (Diamond, 1975; Friedland & Michael, 1987; Hakstian & Kansup, 1975; Hanna & Owens, 1973; Hopkins, Hakstian & Hopkins, 1973; Koehler, 1971, 1974), especially when test length is defined in terms of testing time, not number of items (confidence weighting requires more testing time per item).

It seems likely that the increase in reliability that results from confidence scoring may be due to its encouraging a reliable response style of gambling or bravado (i.e., examinee rates choices with high confidence). Consequently, the procedure offers no clear advantages at present.[6]

6.15   SOME CONCLUSIONS REGARDING RESPONSE SETS

1. Response styles are reliable. They tend to show consistency from test to test and from item to item, which may allow their effects to contribute to increased test reliability even though validity may be decreased.
2. Knowledge of response sets can be used to improve teacher-constructed tests. For example, the tendency to use too many "true" items can be eliminated in order to increase test validity. Liberal or generous time limits can be established to minimize effects from the speed-versus-accuracy set. Special directions can reduce the role of the gambling set.
3. Response sets, if unchecked, can reduce the validity of test scores. An ability assessment should be as free as possible from personality factors.

6.16   MODE OF ADMINISTRATION

A number of miscellaneous variables associated with the administration of a test have been explored. Several studies have shown that tests administered via television (Burr, 1963; Curtis & Kropp, 1961; Fargo et al., 1967) or overhead projector (Schwarz, 1967) yield results comparable to those obtained on conventionally administered tests, provided that speed is not a factor and other conditions are held constant.[7] Fortunately, advances in computer technology are improving testing prospects for such adaptations. There are several software products that can allow much greater individualization of test content and type of administration.

---

[6]See Stanley and Wang (1970) and Wang and Stanley (1970) for a review of research on other scoring strategies.

[7]Individualized or "tailored" testing, such as Lord's (1971a, 1971b) "flexilevel" testing, in which items of appropriate difficulty are matched with the ability level of the examinee, appears to have promise, especially for low-ability examinees who are continually faced with many guessing/omission decisions. Without computer-assisted testing, the logistic problems are considerable, however (Weiss, 1976; Wood, 1977).

6.17   EXAMINER EFFECTS

One study found only slight effects of a hostile examiner and a congenial examiner on the results obtained from an individual adult intelligence test (Masling, 1959). Under certain conditions, the sex or race of the examiner has resulted in some small differences (Abramson, 1969; Stevenson, 1961). The classroom teacher can be a significant variable in the administration of standardized tests (Hopkins, Lefever & Hopkins, 1967); when teachers administered standardized achievement tests, the grade equivalent of students averaged .2 year higher than when the test administration was controlled via television. Goodwin (1966) also found that classes in which the teacher administered the test averaged .2 grade placement higher than when an outsider administered the tests.

To reduce possible contamination from administration error, some standardized tests offer recorded or video directions that control time and other relevant factors; these efforts have the promise of reducing the effects of errors in test administration. In many instances the validity of scores on *standardized* tests has been seriously eroded by deliberate or inadvertent errors in administration—extending the time limit, giving special instructions about guessing, or even more flagrant violation of the standardized procedures, such as helping examinees with answers. Teachers are primarily instructors, so their attitudes about testing tend to differ considerably from those of measurement professionals. Some have felt compelled to help their students or school score well on standardized tests.

6.18   ADVANCED ANNOUNCEMENT OF TESTING

Little is known about the potential effects of informing students of a forthcoming *standardized* test. A study conducted in Japan showed that the announcement resulted in slightly higher scores (Hashimoto, 1959). Goodwin (1966), however, found no significant difference between groups that received a pre-announcement and groups that did not. If the scores are to be interpreted unambiguously, the procedures used in obtaining test norms should also be followed when the tests are administered in the schools.

6.19   ANSWER SHEET FORMAT

Although many test publishers give the user the option of marking in the test booklet or on a separate answer sheet, the separate answer sheets can cause more difficulty on timed tests, especially for younger and low-ability students.

6.20   SCORING

Unless examinees are given explicit directions and follow them carefully, substantial errors in machine-scored tests can result. Teacher scoring is likely to result in even more errors. Whenever practicable, tests should be machine scored, and they should be administered only after special instructions about marking and erasures.

6.21   DISTURBANCE

One study (Super, Braasch & Shay, 1947) explored the effects of a combination of various disruptions on test performance. A random half of a group of graduate students took a standardized intelligence test under normal conditions. The other random half of the group took the same test, and the following sequence of prearranged events occurred.

> While marking the answer to the third question, one student deliberately broke her pencil point with a loud snap. She made a mild exclamation as she dropped the pencil, slid her chair back with a scraping noise, got up and walked ostentatiously to the examiner to get another pencil.
>
> At the end of the fourth minute, two people walked down the stairs from the fourth floor; they were arguing loudly about a suggested ban of the Communist party. The discussion near the door lasted for about one minute. The examiner had placed himself on the far side of the room so that he would arrive at the door at about the time the two people were ready to walk away.
>
> At the end of ten minutes, a trumpeter played six bars of "Home Sweet Home," faltered, recovered, and then finished the melody. The trumpeter gave the impression that the melody was being played by a novice. The inclusion of musical distractions was not incongruent because music students used nearby rooms for practice.
>
> At the beginning of the test, the examiner set the timer to ring at fifteen instead of twenty minutes. When the bell rang, the examiner picked up the timer, looked at it, looked at his stopwatch and announced, "Go on with the test."

Despite these irregularities, the disrupted group's mean score was not significantly lower than that of the control group. Similar findings with college students have been reported (Ingle & de Amino, 1969). Younger examinees, however, do not possess the powers of concentration necessary to maintain their best performance under such circumstances (Trentham, 1975).

Several factors, such as time of day, physical conditions (lighting, temperature, etc.), and number of tests per day, are essentially unexplored. The safest procedure for administering standardized tests is to approximate norming conditions as closely as possible (although often, unfortunately, many details concerning the norming procedure are not reported in test manuals). These administrative factors are much less important on teacher-made tests because norms are not involved.

6.22   ANSWER CHANGING

Perhaps the most widely disseminated "research" finding is that examinees tend to obtain higher scores if they stay with their first impression and do not change their answers. The actual research on this point speaks with one consistent voice: Answer changes are much more often from "wrong" to "right" than from "right" to "wrong" for all types of examinees, bright or not, test-wise or naive.[8] The "changed-answer" myth should be dispelled once and

---

[8] See Copeland, 1972; Foote & Belinky, 1972; Jacobs, 1972; Lynch & Smith, 1975; Mueller & Shwedel, 1975; Mueller & Wasser, 1977; Pascale, 1974; Prinsell, Ramsey & Ramsey, 1994; Ramos & Stern, 1973; Reiling & Taylor, 1972; Schwarz, McMorris & DeMers, 1991; Smith & Moore, 1976)

for all. Examinees should not stick with their first response when on second thought they definitely prefer a different one. The net consequences from answer changing are usually very small (Mueller & Shwedel, 1975) but are consistent for both factual and more complex items (Smith, White & Coop, 1979).

6.23   CHEATING

> The heart is deceitful above all things. [Jeremiah 19:9]

Cheating on examinations is an extremely widespread and serious cause of test invalidity. In ancient China, civil service examinations were given in individual cubicles to prevent examinees from looking at the test papers of others (Brickman, 1961). Examinees were also searched for notes before they entered the cubicles. The death penalty was imposed on anyone found guilty of cheating. Contemporary attitudes toward cheating are much more tolerant; indeed, Cornehlsen (1965) found that among high school seniors more than one-third of the girls and more than one-half of the boys felt that cheating was justified when success or survival was in jeopardy. Even among graduate students, Zastrow (1970) found a 40 percent incidence of cheating.

The instructor or test administrator and the testing conditions have a great influence on the extent that cheating will occur during an examination (Bushway & Nash, 1977). To protect the innocent, the conditions of test administration must be carefully and continually monitored. In an unpublished study, the authors found less cheating when examinees were required to sit in alternate seats. As might be expected, there is more cheating on unproctored tests (Steininger, Johnson & Kirts, 1964). Many people rationalize cheating behavior by appealing to Aristotle's *ad populum* fallacy: "Everybody's doing it, so it must be OK for me to do it, too." Page (1963) found that candid discussion with students about the immorality of cheating and its effects on students affected their attitudes regarding cheating as well as the amount of cheating behavior in the class. Responsible test administration requires that the opportunities for cheating be reduced as much as possible through conscientious monitoring, seating arrangements, and test design.

SUMMARY

Many irrelevant factors can influence test performance. Test-wiseness can be a substantial factor, especially on poorly constructed tests, and for examinees who are unfamiliar with objective tests. The practice effect is greatest on speeded tests; however, it seldom accounts for more than $.2\sigma$ improvement. Coaching produces small gains in performance (usually less than $.2\sigma$); larger gains may result if the examinee has not had recent contact with the test content. Most effects of practice and coaching are transitory and are no longer evident after a few months.

The response styles of gambling and speed-versus-accuracy can have a major effect on scores on standardized tests, especially on speeded or very difficult tests. Response sets tend to be stable personality characteristics. The correction for chance can be useful when the nature of the correction is carefully explained. Administrative factors usually have only a minor influence on test performance. Standardized instructions and procedures must be followed explicitly if results are to be interpreted in terms of the published norms.

IMPORTANT TERMS AND CONCEPTS

acquiescence
confidence scoring
elimination scoring
positional preference
set to gamble
test sophistication

chance score
correction for guessing
maximum performance
response styles
typical performance

CHAPTER TEST

1. Which one of the following factors that influence test performance is *not* classified as a response style or set?
   a) practice
   b) a tendency to work quickly versus carefully
   c) guessing
   d) acquiescence

2. Among the following factors, which one typically would be expected to *least* influence performance on a standardized cognitive test?
   a) test-wiseness
   b) practice on a parallel form of the test
   c) the gambling response style
   d) the positional-preference response set

3. Which one of the following is *not* an example of test-wise behavior?
   a) using the process of elimination in selecting correct answers
   b) working carefully, double-checking each item before going on to the next item
   c) guessing on all items even when the standard correction-for-change formula is applied, using specific determiners as clues to correct answers

4. Test-retest practice effects on cognitive tests are
   a) greater for inexperienced examinees.
   b) greater on power tests than on speeded tests.
   c) less when the time interval between the tests is short.
   d) usually greater than $.2\sigma$.

5. The effects of coaching on cognitive test performance usually improves subsequent performance
   a) greatly ($.75\sigma$ or more).
   b) quite a bit ($.5\sigma$ to $.75\sigma$).

    c) moderately (.25σ to .5σ).
    d) slightly (.25σ or less).

6. The research on anxiety and test performance suggests that
    a) it depresses cognitive test performance.
    b) it enhances cognitive test performance.
    c) it is negatively correlated with cognitive test performance.
    d) its effects are greater on cognitive tests than on affective tests.

7. The validity of a cognitive test is usually reduced when
    a) it is given as a power test.
    b) test-taking speed is a significant factor in test performance.
    c) all students are allowed to attempt all items.
    d) the correction for chance is employed.

For Questions 8–11, *use the following information:* Alfred attempted only 80 of the 100 items on a *true–false* achievement test; 60 of his answers were correct.

8. What is Alfred's uncorrected raw score?

9. What is Alfred's corrected-for-chance score ($S = R - W$)?

10. If Alfred is a typical examinee and if he had attempted all 100 questions, his uncorrected raw score would probably be
    a) greater than 90.
    b) 90.
    c) 80.
    d) 70.

11. If Alfred had answered 10 of the 20 unattempted items correctly and the other 10 incorrectly, his corrected-for-chance score would have been _____.

12. On a five-option multiple-choice test, what is the appropriate form for the correction-for-chance formula?
    a) $S = R - W$
    b) $S = R - W/2$
    c) $S = R - W/3$
    d) $S = R - W/4$
    e) $S = R - W/5$

13. A test consists of 10 five-option multiple-choice items. If you answered all 10 correctly, what is your corrected-for-chance score?

14. On multiple-choice tests, the standard deviation for corrected-for-chance scores, S, compared to uncorrected scores, R, is
    a) greater.
    b) the same.
    c) less.

15. If no examinee omitted any items and if your score was at the 90th percentile in the uncorrected (R) distribution, in the corrected-for-chance (S) distribution
    a) your percentile rank would not change.
    b) the *T*-score of your performance would change.

    c) your percentile rank score would decrease.

    d) your percentile rank would increase.

16. Elimination scoring usually
    a) increases the test's computed reliability coefficient.
    b) decreases the test's computed reliability coefficient.
    c) increases the test's validity.
    d) decreases the test's validity.

17. Confidence scoring
    a) requires more testing time per item.
    b) tends to increase the test's reliability coefficient.
    c) tends to increase the test's validity.
    d) two of the above
    e) *a, b,* and *c* above

18. Which of these statements is *not* true regarding the effects of response styles on test performance?
    a) They tend to decrease test reliability.
    b) They tend to decrease the validity of tests.
    c) They have greater influence on difficult tests.
    d) They have greater influence on speeded tests.

19. Very young examinees tend to achieve higher raw scores on a standardized achievement test if they
    a) mark in the test booklet.
    b) use a separate answer sheet.

20. Disturbance during a standardized test is likely to affect the test scores of college students less than the scores of younger examinees. (*T* or *F*)

ANSWERS TO CHAPTER TEST

1. a	8. 60	15. a
2. d	9. $S = 60 - 20$ or 40	16. a
3. b	10. d	17. d
4. a	11. $70 - 30 = 40$	18. a
5. d	12. d	19. a
6. c	13. 10	20. True
7. b	14. a	

PART II

The Development of Educational Measure

7

General Principles of Test Construction: Achievement Measures

7.1   INTRODUCTION

There are important reasons why teachers at all levels of education need to become proficient in constructing achievement tests. Tests developed by a teacher without special training, whether essay or objective tests, are usually of poor quality. The research on essay examinations has repeatedly demonstrated this fact, and novice test developers fare even less well with objective tests.

Achievement tests skillfully constructed by teachers can be more valid than some standardized tests. Standardized tests are not focused on the objectives of a particular unit of instruction, whereas teacher-made tests have a more focused and carefully defined domain of content. Standardized tests tend to (1) focus on broad, commonly accepted objectives and (2) cover a wide range of curricular content because they are usually designed to assess a full year or more of instruction.

Periodic assessment is necessary to enable teachers to monitor the progress of individual children and of the class as a whole. Frequent testing provides a more reliable and valid and diagnostic evaluation of student progress than a few major examinations. In this chapter we consider the general principles of constructing achievement tests designed to measure cognitive objectives. The construction and use of essay and objective tests and portfolios are considered in Chapters 8 and 9.

7.2 PLANNING THE TEST

The process of constructing a reliable and valid test is a challenging task. Good tests do not just happen. Indeed, most teacher-made tests are crude measures, thrown together with little care and planning. Test construction is as much of an art as a science, but this "art form" can be dramatically improved with special instruction, systematic practice, and feedback. There are well-established, proven principles of test development that are often unknown or ignored. Constructing a *good* test item is a deliberate process; it demands an understanding of the objectives and content being assessed, how the thinking process of the learner is utilized, the reading and vocabulary level of the examinees, and knowledge of test-taking factors like response styles and test sophistication.

A good test doesn't just happen; careful planning must precede its construction. One must consider the topics and objectives to be measured, the purpose the scores are to serve, and the conditions under which testing will occur. The following general guidelines are useful in developing educational achievement tests:

1. The measure should make provisions for evaluating the important objectives of instruction that are measurable using paper-and-pencil tests.
2. The measure should reflect both the *content* and *process* objectives in proportion to their importance and emphasis in the course.
3. The nature of the test should reflect its purpose (e.g., to assess individual differences or to certify mastery).
4. The test should be appropriate in length and readability level.

Depending on the purpose of the evaluation and the objectives to be measured, the form of the test may vary in length, difficulty, and format: oral, objective, essay, short-answer, open-book, cloze,[1] or take-home.

7.3 INSTRUCTIONAL OBJECTIVES

Provision should be made for evaluating the important cognitive outcomes of instruction that can be directly measured. In Figure 1–1 the interrelationships among three aspects of instructional design were illustrated—objectives, instruction, and evaluation. The objectives should give direction to the evaluation process as well as to the instructional methods and curricular content. The evaluation process seeks to ascertain the degree to which the objectives have been attained, both for the individual students and for the class as a whole. A meta-analysis of 21 controlled studies found that the achievement of students whose teachers use systematic measurement and data-based evaluation procedures is much higher ($.7\sigma$) than that of students whose teachers do not use these procedures (Fuchs & Fuchs, 1986b).

The results of the evaluation provide feedback that can suggest modification of either the objectives or the instruction or both. For example, one study found no significant

---

[1]The Cloze format is considered in Chapter 9.

improvement in listening comprehension during a communications skills course, which was one of the course's important objectives. With careful assessment, a course's unfulfilled "promises" can be discovered. At times, the objectives may be unrealistic; even so, the "unrealism" needs to be demonstrated. For example, some of the objectives of certain educational programs (e.g., bilingual and compensatory educational programs) have been unrealistic—there is a tendency to overstate the case (at times for funding and political reasons) in order to marshal support for special programs. But without realistic objectives and fair evaluations of students' progress, the wheat and the chaff will not be sorted out and continued long-term support for special programs is (and should be) jeopardized.

Some objectives are stated as broad, general, long-range goals. One of the earliest statements of educational objectives is the Yale report of 1830, which emphasized the importance of exercising the mental functions of "reasoning," "imagination," "taste," and "memory" (Ammons, 1969). The "Seven Cardinal Principles of Secondary Education" of 1918 are generally accepted today: good health, command of fundamental processes, worthy home membership, vocational efficiency, good citizenship, worthy use of leisure time, and ethical character. The same can be said of the four objectives of education formulated in 1938 by the Educational Policies Commission of the National Education Association: self-realization, human relationship, economic efficiency, and civic responsibility.

The Educational Policies Commission (1961) stresses "the central role of the rational powers" and devises its own categories:

> The cultivated powers of the free mind have always been basic in achieving freedom. The powers of the free mind are many. In addition to the rational powers, there are those which relate to the aesthetic, the moral, and the religious. There is a unique, central role for the rational powers of an individual, however, for upon them depends his ability to achieve his personal goals and to fulfill his obligations to society. These powers involve the processes of recalling and imagining, classifying and generalizing, comparing and evaluating, analyzing and synthesizing, and deducing and inferring. These processes enable one to apply logic and the available evidence to his ideas, attitudes, and actions, and to pursue better whatever goals he may have. (pp. 4–5)

7.4 SPECIFICITY OF OBJECTIVES

These ultimate educational objectives are obviously important, but they are too general to give clear direction to the design of the curriculum. In addition, they cannot possibly be realized or assessed until long after formal education has been concluded. It is therefore necessary to establish intermediate instructional goals that are logically derived from, and related to, these ultimate objectives.

Probably the most thorough, sensitive, and useful treatment of educational objectives is found in Clark (1972). Clark illustrates that from any *parent* objective many *offspring* objectives can be derived at various levels of specificity. (see Figure 7–1)

Notice that in Figure 7–1 each objective is a subset of all the objectives appearing above it. During the past few decades the emphasis on stating educational objectives in behavioral terms caused educational objectives to be stated at a high level of specificity. But for an objective to be truly behavioral it must be stated at such an atomistic level that the

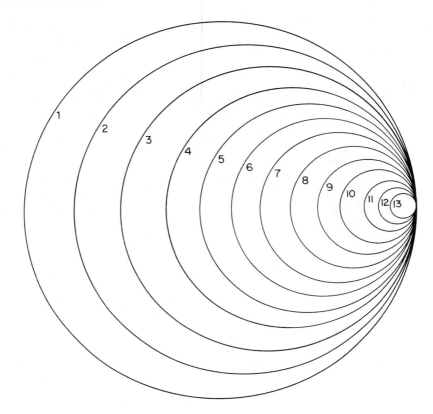

1. The student will be able to achieve personal goals and fulfill his or her obligations to society.
2. The student will be able to demonstrate functional literacy.
3. The student will be able to perform mathematical operations.
4. The student will be able to perform simple addition, subtraction, multiplication, and division operations.
5. The student will be able to perform simple addition operations.
6. The student will be able to add any two single-digit numbers.
7. The student will be able to add 3 and 2.
8. The student will be able to add 3 objects and 2 objects.
9. The student will be able to add 3 apples and 2 apples.
10. The student will be able to add 3 apples and 2 apples when words (not objects) are used.
11. The student will be able to add 3 apples and 2 apples when words are present in writing.
12. The student will be able to add 3 apples and 2 apples 90% of the time, when the problem is posed in written form.
13. The student will be able to add 3 apples and 2 apples 90% of the time when the problem is phrased, "If you had 3 apples and I gave you 2 more, how many would you have?"

FIGURE 7–1   A graphic illustration of the various levels of specificity in statements of educational objectives.

SOURCE: The authors are indebted to Cecil Clark for providing the basis for this example.

number of objectives in any course or unit is overwhelming. In addition, objectives stated at a molecular level are not very functional in that they lose their value as general targets that help keep the instruction on course—the trees get in the way of the forest. Neither extreme, very general or highly atomistic objectives, is very functional. Establishing the proper level of specificity for objectives to give the proper degree of direction to the curriculum and instruction is difficult and is an issue on which there is wide disagreement.

Each school district should have a statement of its educational purposes. Instructional objectives for particular courses and curricular areas are typically available for each content area at every grade level. Most courses of study contain some statement of objectives, but to be functional in giving direction to teaching and evaluation they can neither be sweeping generalities nor fragmented by excessive specificity. The topics to be mastered, or equivalently, the expected *student behaviors* that exemplify the desired objectives should be stated. Such commonly offered objectives as "good citizenship," "an integrated personality," and "functional literacy" have their place but are not very helpful in giving direction to instruction or assessment. Instructional goals need to be stated in more precise and observable form to provide direction to the important tasks of curriculum development and evaluation. A list of specific topics and concepts is often an implicit and functional statement of objectives.

Teachers at all levels of education often instruct and evaluate without giving careful thought to the educational objectives. The objectives are frequently undefined and vague. Without critical, periodic reexamination of objectives, a course is likely to drift off target, become disassociated from its original social relevance, and contribute to the obsolescence in curriculum. Four examples illustrate the point.

- The barbarous, conceptually irrelevant, and quickly forgotten rote procedure for hand computation of square root is still being taught in some middle schools even though the $5 hand calculator has mercifully rendered such instruction obsolete.
- The confusing, imprecise, and time-consuming procedures involving logarithm tables still are a part of the math curriculum in some schools. These should have been put to rest long ago, along with slide rules.
- The use of carbon paper continued to be found in the typing curriculum long after the fact that it had been rendered obsolete by the widespread availability of copy machines.
- What are the objectives of geometry for the *general* student? Unlike algebra, which is used extensively in many college curricula, when was the last time you needed to prove two triangles congruent? (Unlike statistics, geometry adds little to numerical literacy.)

The process of being systematically involved in the process of evaluation clarifies the nature and purposes of the curriculum. Bloom (1961) noted that when teachers participated in the construction of tests in a systematic way, not only were the objectives clarified but also the instruction became more relevant.

Armed with a clear and specific list of content and process objectives, a teacher can develop appropriate procedures for evaluating the instruction and assessing students' progress toward accomplishing the curricular objectives.

7.5   A TAXONOMY OF OBJECTIVES

The publication of the now-classic *Taxonomy of Educational Objectives* (Bloom, 1956, 1984), ("Bloom's Taxonomy," for short) had a powerful influence in the measurement of educational objectives. It provides a framework within which educational objectives can be conceptualized. In the taxonomy instructional objectives are classified into three major domains—*cognitive, affective*, and *psychomotor*. Handbooks have been produced for each of the three domains: cognitive (Bloom, 1956, 1984), affective (Krathwohl et al., 1964), and psychomotor (Harrow,1972; Simpson, 1972).

The cognitive domain (Bloom's taxonomy) includes those objectives that deal with the recall or recognition of learned material and the development of intellectual abilities and skills. The largest proportion of educational objectives falls into the cognitive domain. This domain is the core of most curriculum and test development. The clearest definitions of objectives for the cognitive domain are phrased as descriptions of desired student behavior, that is, in terms of knowledge, understanding, and abilities that can be demonstrated.

The affective domain includes objectives that emphasize interests, attitudes, and values and the development of appreciations. "Objectives in this domain are not stated very precisely; and, in fact, teachers do not appear to be very clear about the learning experiences which are appropriate to these objectives" (Bloom, 1956, p. 7). Chapter 11 deals with the assessment of objectives in this domain. The psychomotor domain is concerned with physical, motor, or manipulative skills. Handwriting and many physical education objectives are examples of skills in the psychomotor domain. The cognitive domain dominates discussions of educational objectives, whereas the affective and psychomotor domains have often been ignored.

Bloom's taxonomy influenced the development of educational curricula and evaluation measures. The taxonomy categorizes behaviors into six hierarchical categories from simple to complex (see Figure 7–2). These six ascending levels are *knowledge, comprehension, application, analysis, synthesis,* and *evaluation.*

The rationale for the hierarchy is based on the assumption that each level is a prerequisite for each subsequent level. For example, attaining an objective in the application category requires (in theory, at least) that certain comprehension goals are achieved, which in turn can be achieved only if certain information in the knowledge category is acquired. *A rather sharp line is suggested in the taxonomy between "knowledge" and the five higher levels*, which involve reasoning and cognitive skills, in addition to knowledge of information. We will discuss and illustrate each of the six levels briefly.

7.6   KNOWLEDGE LEVEL ITEMS

Tasks at the *knowledge* level involve "the recall of specifics and universals, the recall of methods and procedures, or the recall of a pattern, structure, or setting. For measurement purposes, *the recall situation involves little more than bringing to mind the appropriate material . . .* The knowledge objectives emphasize most the psychological processes of *remembering . . .* To use an analogy, if one thinks of the mind as a file, the problem in a knowledge test situation is that of finding in the problem or task the signals, cues, and clues that will most effectively bring out whatever knowledge is filed or stored." People may have various kinds and levels of knowledge,

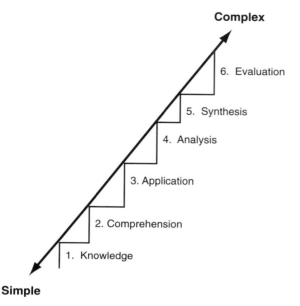

FIGURE 7–2 An illustration of the six hierarchical levels of Bloom's taxonomy.

SOURCE: Adapted from B. S. Bloom, *Taxonomy of Educational Objectives*, in *Handbook I, The Cognitive Domain* (New York: David McKay Company, Inc., 1984.)

from "knowledge of terminology," such as "familiarity with a large number of words in their common range of meanings," to "knowledge of theories and structures," such as "knowledge of a relatively complete formulation of the theory of evolution." (Bloom, 1956, pp. 201–204)

Examples of knowledge-level objectives are the knowledge of specific facts, terminology, dates, persons. Below are two (of many) examples given by Bloom (1956; 1984) and by Hedges (1966) of test items designed to measure an objective in the knowledge category.

1. The Monroe Doctrine was announced about ten years after the
    a) Revolutionary War.
  *b) War of 1812.
    c) Civil War.
    d) Spanish-American War.

Answering this question requires no reasoning, only a simple knowledge of the date 1823 or knowledge that the event occurred after the War of 1812 but before the Civil War.[2]

---

[2]Additional examples of knowledge-level (and higher-level items) can be found in Table 7–2, which classifies the items in the chapter test for Chapter 5.

   2. In physics, the term *acceleration* is defined as
   a) mass/force.
   *b) change in velocity/time.
   c) mass/velocity.
   d) distance/time.
   e) resistance/effort.

Item 2 requires only a knowledge of acceleration in contradistinction to velocity. Item 3 (from Chapter 2) is another example of a knowledge-level item.

   3. Another name for the 50th percentile is
   a) the mean.
   *b) the median.
   c) the mode.
   d) the score that is equal to one-half the maximum score.

7.7   COMPREHENSION AND APPLICATION LEVEL ITEMS

Although it is basic and essential, knowledge is not sufficient for *comprehension*. Translation, interpretation, and extrapolation are common cognitive processes required at this taxonomy level. Comprehension is evidenced by the "care and accuracy with which the communication is paraphrased or rendered from one language or form of communication to another." Some instructional objectives at the comprehension level are

- the ability to understand non-literal statements (metaphors, symbolism, irony, exaggeration);
- skill in translating mathematical verbal material into symbolic statements and vice versa; the ability to grasp the thought of the work as a whole at any desired level of generality; and
- skill in predicting continuation of trends. (Bloom, 1956, pp. 204–205)

Here are three examples of items illustrative of the comprehension level.

   1. Which of the following represents the *best* definition of the term "protoplasm"?
   a) A complex colloidal system made up of water, proteins, and fats.
   b) Anything capable of growth by a regular progressive series of changes into a more complex unit.
   c) A complex mixture of proteins, fats, and carbohydrates, capable of responding to changes in its environment.
   *d) A complex colloidal system of proteins, fats, carbohydrates, inorganic salts, and enzymes manifesting life.

The exercise requires the examinee to judge the *best* of the four definitions, which vary in correctness and completeness. Had choices *a, b,* and *c* been totally incorrect, the item would be functioning only at the knowledge level of Bloom's taxonomy—it would not have required the differentiation between *shades of gray* in correctness and completeness.

   2. List all the verbs in the stem and options of Item 1 above.

The examinee must comprehend what a verb is in order to identify "represents" as the only verb among the 70 words in Item 1.

> **3.** "Milton! thou shouldst be living at this hour: England hath need of thee; she is a fen of stagnant waters." (Wordsworth) The metaphor, "She is a fen of stagnant waters," indicates that Wordsworth felt that England was
>   a) largely swampy land.
>   b) in a state of turmoil and unrest.
> *c) making no progress.
>   d) in a generally corrupt condition.

The correct answer to Item 3 requires the *translation* of one verbal form into another. If this question had been an exercise used directly in instruction, it would represent knowledge rather than comprehension objectives—it would not have the freshness required for an opportunity to represent comprehension.

The third level in Bloom's taxonomy is *application*, which theoretically requires more complexity than comprehension. The application level requires mastering a concept well enough to recognize when and how to use it correctly. Given an unfamiliar problem, the person must select and apply the appropriate concept. "The fact that most of what we learn is intended for application to problem situations in real life is an indication of the importance of application objectives in the curriculum" (Bloom, 1956, p. 122). It has been said that "transferability is the ultimate criterion for demonstrating the mastery of a concept." The effectiveness of a major component of education is dependent on how well the students' skills can be applied to situations that were never directly faced during the learning process.

Three illustrative objectives at the application level are

- the ability to relate principles of civil liberties and civil rights to current events;
- the ability to apply the laws of trigonometry to practical situations; and
- the ability to apply Mendel's laws of inheritance to experimental findings on plant genetic problems.

Two illustrative test items[3] at this level follow.

> **1.** A candy bar was divided among three people. Lorrie had $\frac{1}{3}$ of the bar, Gene had $\frac{1}{2}$; what fraction of the bar was left for Ken?
> *a) $\frac{1}{6}$ b) $\frac{1}{2}$ c) $\frac{2}{3}$ d) $\frac{5}{6}$ e) none of these

This item requires a greater degree of extrapolation and "transfer" from instruction than the related comprehension-level task: $1 - \frac{1}{3} - \frac{1}{2}$

---

[3]Items 1 and 2 were used in the California Assessment Program. Item 1 was answered correctly by 46 percent of sixth-grade students. More than 75 percent of the twelfth-graders also selected the best answer to both items.

2. Below are four sentences expressing the same general thought. Mark the sentence that expresses the thought *most effectively.*
   a) She spoke to me in a very cool manner when we met each other yesterday.
   b) When we met yesterday, I was spoken to in a very cool manner by her.
   c) Her manner was very cool when meeting and speaking to me yesterday.
   *d) Yesterday she treated me coolly.

The examples illustrate that the parroting of textbook definitions and the like is not sufficient to enable the student to answer application questions correctly.

7.8   ANALYSIS, SYNTHESIS, AND EVALUATION LEVEL ITEMS

Analysis is defined by Bloom (1956) as "the breakdown of a communication into its constituent elements or parts such that the relative hierarchy of ideas is made clear and/or the relations between the ideas expressed are made explicit." Typical objectives of this level (Bloom, 1956, p. 146–148) are

- skill in distinguishing facts from hypotheses;
- ability to recognize unstated assumptions; and
- ability to recognize the point of view of bias of a writer in a historical account.

Illustrative analysis items are the following:

1. Analyze the implicit philosophical presupposition in the statement, "If anything exists, it exists in some quantity, and hence is measurable."
2. In 300 words or less, write a summary for Chapter 5 (Test Reliability).

Question 2 asks for a translation of information to a different level of generality.[4]

3. Chlorophyll may be found in many forms that have different characteristics. Two of the most important forms are chlorophyll *a* and *b*. Both types may be involved in photosynthesis, but chlorophyll *b* absorbs more light in blue wavelengths than chlorophyll *a* does. So, it is more efficient in allowing photosynthesis in shady places. The following diagram shows how the plants changed on an abandoned farm in the Midwest during about 150 years. Notice that oak seedlings can grow beneath pine trees, but that pine seedlings are not found under oak trees. Eventually, as a result, the area became a forest of oaks and other hardwoods, with few or no pines.

   Based on the above information, which of the following is a reasonable hypothesis about the chlorophyll in oaks and pines?
   a) Oaks do not need chlorophyll for growth.
   b) Pines contain more chlorophyll *b* than oaks do.
   *c) Oaks contain more chlorophyll *b* than pines do.
   d) Chlorophyll is not necessary for photosynthesis in oaks.

---

[4]In order for Item 2 to be a true analysis item, the chapter summary should not be included in the book; otherwise, only a knowledge or comprehension level might be represented.

Synthesis involves "the putting together of elements and parts to form a whole . . . not clearly there before." Sample instructional objectives at this level are

- skill in writing, using an excellent organization of ideas and statements;
- ability to plan a unit of instruction for a particular teaching situation; and
- ability to formulate a theory of learning applicable to classroom teaching. (Bloom, 1956, pp. 169–172)

Examples of synthesis exercises follow.

1. Add three lines to complete the verse: "I saw old autumn in the misty morn."
2. Write a position paper on closed-shop unionism. For example, should a steelworker be required to join a union in order to be employed? Attend to the following facts in your answer . . .
3. Here are some general findings comparing babies who have colic and those who do not. Formulate a theoretical explanation and at least one testable hypothesis derived from the theory.

Evaluation includes "the making of judgments about the value, for some purpose, of ideas, works, solutions, methods, materials, etc." Examples of this, the highest level of cognitive ability in the taxonomy, are

- the ability to indicate logical fallacies in arguments;
- the ability to evaluate health beliefs critically; and
- skills in recognizing and weighing values involved in alternative courses of action. (Bloom, 1956, pp. 189–192)

The taxonomy levels of analysis, synthesis, and evaluation have been much less valuable for curriculum development and educational evaluation than the knowledge, comprehension, and application levels. There is nothing in the taxonomy per se to suggest that all good tests or evaluation measures will include items from every taxonomy level. The logic of the unitary underlying hierarchical continuum of complexity also is less compelling (Michael, 1968b) above the application level.

7.9 RESEARCH ON THE TAXONOMY HIERARCHY

A summary of the available research on the taxonomy of the cognitive domain generally supports the differentiation of the knowledge level from the other levels and to some extent the separation of the comprehension and application levels (Krathwohl and Payne, 1971). However, support for the hierarchy of the more complex categories—analysis, synthesis, and evaluation—has largely failed to develop (DeLandsheere, 1977). Experience with the taxonomy has demonstrated that it is very difficult to distinguish reliably many application items from items in the higher levels. Several investigators have reported that judges frequently disagree on the taxonomy level represented by items at levels other than the knowledge level. Among the higher categories, agreement is the exception rather than the rule (Fairbrother, 1975; Poole, 1972; Wood, 1977).

The principal contribution of the taxonomy has been its impact on the quality of educational measures. A teacher who has been exposed to the taxonomy, with illustrations of how higher mental processes can be measured (often objectively), can no longer be satisfied with a test that measures only rote learning of isolated facts. Much of the criticism of objective tests has arisen because many are of very low quality and too often emphasize the knowledge level exclusively. Indeed, objective tests lack face validity for many simply because their experience with such tests has been unfortunately limited to knowledge level items.

The *instructional value* that can result from examinations composed of items from the higher taxonomy levels was shown in a study by Hunkins (1969). The experimental group was continually exposed to questions from the higher levels of the taxonomy during the course. The control group encountered fewer questions above the knowledge level during instruction. On the final examination, the experimental group performed significantly better on items that measured higher-level instructional objectives, yet did equally well on the knowledge level questions.

For any course, a description of the particular content, principles, concepts, and skills of the course is needed. These concepts can usually be measured at the knowledge, comprehension, and/or application levels. The higher taxonomy levels more closely approach the broader educational objectives discussed earlier. In questioning students to see whether *comprehension* has actually occurred and *application* can be demonstrated, teachers must avoid using the wording of the textbook and illustrations that have been used directly in instruction or class discussion. Otherwise, the items may assess rote memory, not genuine understanding. Opportunities should be provided in the test to apply the concept to new problems and situations. The teacher must not confuse ends and means. Many years ago a major historical figure in educational measurement, E. F. Lindquist, stated this point well.

> The real ends of instruction are the *lasting* concepts, attitudes, skills, abilities and habits of thought, and the improved judgment or sense of values acquired; the detailed materials of instruction—the specific factual content—are to a large extent only a means toward these ends. (1944, p. 366)

Some curricular areas, such as mathematics and the physical sciences, lend themselves more easily to measurement at higher taxonomy levels (comprehension and above); in other areas such as social studies, considerable ingenuity is often required to develop items at the comprehension and application levels.

7.10   OTHER ITEM CLASSIFICATIONS

Bloom's taxonomy of the cognitive domain is not the only useful scheme available to us, though it is the most extensive attempt thus far. But why bother to use a classification system in constructing an achievement test? The chief reasons are to ensure that the important cognitive objectives are assessed and that items represent higher taxonomy levels—items that involve not only content but related cognitive processing as well.

The "specifications" for the *Scholastic Aptitude Test—Mathematics* (*SAT-M*) illustrate a systematic approach to test construction. They consist of the following seven dimensions, each containing two to six classifications.

1. Content: (a) arithmetic or algebra, (b) geometry, (c) other
2. Context of presentation: (a) unusual, (b) familiar
3. Process for solution: (a) straightforward, (b) novel
4. Type of thinking: (a)computational, (b) numerical judgment, (c) relational thinking, (d) other
5. Characteristics of data: (a) adequate, (b) excessive, (c) insufficient
6. Form of presentation: (a) verbal, (b) tabular or graphic
7. Difficulty (six classifications from "easy" to "hard")

If even a single item of each possible combination were included, the test would contain $3 \times 2 \times 2 \times 4 \times 3 \times 2 \times 6 = 1728$ items. Actually, the *SAT-M* test has less than five percent of 1728 items. Obviously only a sample of combinations can be represented. For example, the specifications for the test might include one question dealing with geometry in an unusual context, requiring a straightforward process for solution, evoking a relational type of thinking, involving excess data, presented in graphic form, and classified as "easy."

How, according to the seven-point scheme just presented, would you classify the following item that has been used on the *SAT*?[5]

In which one of the following ways could 168 pencils be packaged for shipping?
(a) 11 boxes with 18 pencils in each
(b) 14 boxes with 12 pencils in each
(c) 17 boxes with 14 pencils in each
(d) 24 boxes with 12 pencils in each
(e) 28 boxes with 11 pencils in each

One can readily see that there are many ways to classify and evaluate educational objectives and associated test items (Page & Breen, 1973); each has its advantages and disadvantages. A plan is needed, but more elaborate plans like that for the *SAT-M* are too complex to be used extensively for classroom purposes. Such plans are, however, appropriate for research studies and state assessment programs. For classroom assessment purposes, the use of a "table of specifications" (a topic-by-process grid) in which the major content topics (rows) are cross-classified by two (or three) taxonomy levels is a reasonable compromise between completeness and utility. Figure 4–1 contains a table of specifications for a standardized science test. Note the percentages of items for each content and process stratum given below the grid. Table 7–1 illustrates specifications for an examination in this course that covers Chapters 1–5.

Another example is provided in Table 7–2—the mastery test for Chapter 5. Notice that more items are desirable for more complex and more important topics. Note also that top-

---

[5]The item represents category (a) in all classifications except 3.

TABLE 7–1 An Illustration of Table of Specifications of a Content-Process Grid Representing the Test Design for an Achievement Test Covering Chapters 1–5 of this Book

	Taxonomy Level			
Major Content Strata	**Knowledge**	**Application, Comprehension**	**Synthesis, etc.**	**Total**
1. The functions of measurement in education	3	2	0	5 (10%)
2. Basic statistical concepts, central tendency and variability	1	2	2	5 (10%)
3. Norms: types, meaning, interpretation	3	3	4	10 (20%)
4. Validity: content, construction, criterion-related validity and correlation	4	6	5	15 (30%)
5. Reliability: concepts, theory and methods of estimation	4	7	4	15 (30%)
Totals	15 (30%)	20 (40%)	15 (30%)	50

ics are defined at a finer level of specificity than they are in Table 7–1. No distinction between comprehension and application levels was attempted on this test.

7.11 CONTENT AND PROCESS OBJECTIVES

A test should "re-present" the content *and* process objectives in proportion to their importance. A table of specifications ensures that the test has a proper balance of emphases for content validity; the table of specifications guides the test developer like a blueprint guides the building contractor. It is valuable to indicate not only the various topics but also, at least roughly, the relative emphasis to be devoted to each. The test should be a representative sample of the instructional content and objectives. The amount of time devoted to the different phases of the course is usually a rough indication of their relative importance; the content of the test should show similar proportions. The time devoted to a topic can indicate only the *proportion* of test items to be included, it does not dictate the *type* of item evaluation activity (e.g., essay, multiple-choice, or portfolio). The type of exercise will depend on the nature of the content or objective to be measured. The empty cells in Table 7–2 (see Stratum 2) are not unexpected—certain objectives, by their very nature, may fall exclusively into the knowledge category.

Working from a list of instructional objectives or definition of content strata (an implicit representation of objectives), weight each objective or topic in approximate percentage units according to its importance. This ensures that the test content does not overemphasize certain content strata at the expense of others. One may wish to have an equal number of items from each chapter or section of a curriculum guide, or certain areas may

TABLE 7–2   A Table of Specifications for Chapter Test in Chapter 5 (Numerals in Parenthesis Refer to Specific Items on the Test)

Content Strata (Objectives/Topics)	Taxonomy Level		
	Knowledge	Higher	Total
1. Interrelationships between reliability and validity	2 (1, 2)	2 (3, 4)	4 (10%)
2. Knowledge of reliability "vocabulary"	2 (5, 14)	0	2 (5%)
3. Interrelationships among s, s_e, ρ_{xx}	1 (39)	4 (6, 4, 20, 40, 41)	5 (12%)
Understanding of reliability concepts:			
3. Universe scores	0 (7, 23)	2 (5%)	2
4. Standard error of measurement	1 (22)	5 (8–11, 38)	6 (15%)
5. Reliability index and coefficient	1 (13)	2 (15, 16)	3 (7%)
6. Estimating true scores, regression toward mean	0 (18, 19, 21)	3 (7%)	3
7. Effect of length, Spearman-Brown	1 (27)	1 (17)	2 (5%)
8. Split-half	1 (30)	1 (12)	2 (5%)
9. Parallel form, test-retest	2 (24, 25)	0	2 (5%)
10. Internal-consistency (ρ_{KR} and ρ_a)	2 (32, 33)	4 (34–37)	6 (15%)
Totals	14	27	41

deserve more emphasis than others (as in Table 7–1 in which the reliability and validity chapters are more heavily weighted because they are considered more important).

When objectives have been stated at an excessive degree of specificity, their influence in guiding evaluation activity is impeded. For example, notice in Table 7–2 that there are 41 items in a test that covers only a single chapter. Obviously, it will not be possible to give a midterm test on Chapters 1 to 5 at the same level of specificity: 5×40 is 200, too many items for a single test, even for graduate students. Nevertheless, all "parent" or broad objectives need to be represented. Turn to the table of contents of this book, and you will find a topic outline for each of the first five chapters. Obviously several more detailed "offspring" objectives could be generated from each topic. Ideally, at least one question pertaining to the most important concepts at the knowledge and higher taxonomy levels should be included. The testing time is insufficient to have items pertaining to every topic (as a rough rule of thumb, for items above the knowledge level, generally allow about one minute per item). One might be able to include one question per topic for those that represent only information (knowledge level) and additional items above the knowledge level for the more important concepts. Tests on smaller units of study can map the content universe more closely and completely, as indicated in Table 7–2. However, for classroom purposes, is it best to have more frequent testing and feedback on smaller content strata. Examinations at the college level with more mature examinees often must span larger units of instruction (although short quizzes at the beginning of each class session have much to recommend them, even for graduate-level courses).

7.12   TEST ITEMS ARE SAMPLES

It is of fundamental importance to view test items as only a sample from the content universe. The reliability index and the standard error of measurement will indicate how adequately the content universe has been sampled, not objective by objective or topic by topic, but overall. Evaluating how adequately each student has achieved highly detailed behavioral objectives is not feasible—there simply isn't enough time. It may seem paradoxical, but nevertheless is true, that scores on a test can be very good estimates of universe or true scores, yet may not be adequate for diagnostic purposes—for indicating whether an individual student has achieved each specific objective on which the test is based.

An analogy may help clarify this principle. A test given to a nationally representative sample of 1000 students in grade six can estimate with great precision the mean score on that test for the entire population of 5,000,000 sixth-graders. However, just because we have a precise estimate of the national average, it does not follow that we then have highly accurate results for subdivisions of the nation—states, school districts, schools, and so on. The state averages in the larger states, such as California and New York, would each be based on approximately 100 individuals and could be reasonably accurate estimates; but several states have less than 1 percent of the nation's population—obviously, a random sample of 10 students in a given state does not provide a very accurate or stable estimate of that state's average score on the test. It is clearly absurd to subdivide the data into even narrower strata and estimate school district averages on the basis of one or two students.

This situation is an exact parallel to breaking down the total test of a student into detailed strata, each based on very few items. Total scores may be accurate estimates of universe scores, but subtest (part) scores will be accurate only to the extent that they are based on enough items so that the subtest has reliability. A single item simply is not adequate to represent a higher-level objective. *At the very most*, the test described in Table 7–1 would yield only five meaningful scores per examinee, one for each broad content stratum; and even then the estimates of universe scores on content Strata 1 and 2 (Chapters 1 and 2) will be crude, since each is based on only five items. (Class averages, however, can be meaningful even on individual items since several observations are involved.)

Suppose the test described in Table 7–1 is very well constructed and yields the following results.

$$\mu = 80\%, \ \sigma = 14\%, \ \rho_{XX} = .82, \ \sigma_{e\%} = 6.0\%$$

Assuming that the scores are used to evaluate the performance of individual students on each content stratum (broad objective), and that the group's performance is uniform across the five strata, what will be the degree of measurement precision (how closely will observed percent scores estimate the corresponding universe percent scores)?

We can estimate the standard errors of measurement for the five strata (subtests) using Equation 5.8: $\sigma_{e\%} = 43/\sqrt{K}$. For Strata 3, $\sigma_{e\%} = 43/\sqrt{10}$ or 14%. In other words, almost one-third of the students will have percent-correct scores for subtest 1 that differ by more than 14 percent from their true percent-correct score in that content strata. The situation is even worse for content Strata 1 and 2: $\sigma_{e\%} = 43/\sqrt{5}$ or 19. Content Strata 4 and 5 fare better since there are 15 items from each of these strata: $\sigma_{e\%} = 43/\sqrt{15}$ or 11%, but the measurement area is still to great to make accurate inferences about the degree of mastery for an individual student. If the level of reporting was broken down further into even smaller units (as in Table 7–2), the magnitude of measurement error would be even greater.

7.13   DIAGNOSTIC TESTING

The example above illustrates how very difficult the task of diagnostic testing is at the student level. By its very nature, diagnostic testing must break down a content domain into fairly specific strata. Figure 7–3 (after Clark, 1972) illustrates how reading can be broken down into "parent" and "offspring" strata and substrata. Several items at each substratum are needed to compare performance among substrata. It is possible to have a good general (survey) test with 50 or 60 items, but a diagnostic test based on Figure 7–3 would require 160 items even if there were only 5 items per each substratum (of course, a diagnostic test might be limited to a subset of the skills indicated in Figure 7–3). Notice in Figure 4–2 that the number of items per objective (below slash mark in each cell) is usually one or two items for the survey test but usually three for the instructional (more nearly diagnostic) tests. Notice also that the greater the level of specificity at which the objectives are stated, the greater the number of items required to measure each objective.

For educational purposes it is important to emphasize that test data are only one component in student evaluation. Good teachers are continually using *naturalistic* methods of observing, evaluating, and assessing by informal means (e. g., portfolios) the degree to which the class and individual students are achieving instructional objectives. Only recently is the importance of such evaluation methods being recognized (e.g., Gullickson & Hopkins, 1987).[6]

7.14   THE NATURE OF THE TEST

The nature of the test should reflect its purpose. If the purpose of the test is to provide a basis for grouping for selection, it should rank the students in order of overall achievement level. But if its purpose is diagnostic or criterion referenced, it must be designed to reveal specific

---

[6]It is important to distinguish between individual and class assessment. Performance on a single item is based on a single response when $n = 1$ (individual assessment) but on perhaps 25 responses when class assessment is involved. Class assessment involves item analysis techniques treated in Chapter 10.

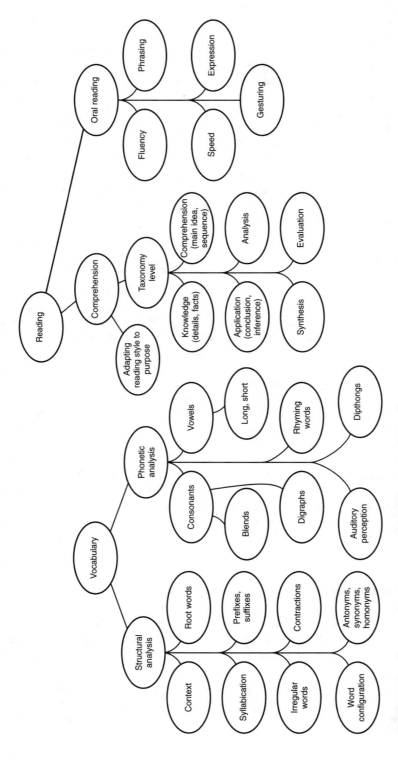

FIGURE 7–3 An example of parent and offspring topics/objectives.

SOURCE: Adapted from D. C. Clark, *Using Instructional Objectives in Teaching* (Glenview, IL: Scott Foresman, 1972), p. 144. Reprinted by permission of the author.

weaknesses in individual achievement. Diagnostic tests tend to cover a limited content domain but in much greater detail than survey achievement tests; they are designed to yield scores on several separate parts. The range of item difficulty and the discrimination indexes of the items are relatively less important in diagnostic tests. This is also true of mastery, criterion-referenced, and minimum-competency tests—diagnostic tests administered to determine whether certain minimum standards of performance have been achieved.

7.15 CRITERION-REFERENCED TESTING

In recent years there has been special interest in the concept of minimum-competency, mastery, and criterion-referenced tests (CRT)—that is, measuring instruments constructed to yield measures that are directly interpretable in terms of "prespecified performance criteria." These tests have the purpose of identifying individuals who have, or have not, acquired certain basal competencies. Differential consequences for instruction, such as remediation, or even high school graduation may result. The rationale underlying behavioral objectives-oriented approaches to education is based largely on CRT.

Criterion-referenced testing is not a new concept (Jaeger, 1988; Glass, 1978c) "It could be argued that teachers have always employed implicit, but nonetheless criterion-referenced, standards in their evaluations of pupils" (Tyler & Wolf, 1974, p. 77).

What Is Mastery? The Problem of Setting a Performance Criterion

There are a few competencies for which complete mastery is possible; for example, everyone should *know* the multiplication table through 10×10 perfectly. Perhaps everyone should be able to identify the major parts of speech of a simple sentence and to write legibly, know the laws pertaining to motor vehicles, tell time, be able to tie shoes, and so on. It is possible on logical grounds to set absolute standards for performance in these areas, for example, to assess whether an examinee has reached the particular level of performance required by the criterion. But is a criterion for mastery of 100 percent realistic? Do you ever make thoughtless mistakes like $8 \times 7 = 42$? Are 100 percent of the words you write legible to others? Do you know all the motor vehicle laws? Do your shoes ever come untied? Even though a 100 percent criterion is logically defensible, in practice the criterion is usually lower, such as 80 percent. But why not 90 percent or 95 percent? This arbitrariness coupled with the arbitrariness in a test's or task's difficulty are impediments to the CRT and mastery learning strategies (Shepard, 1980).

Note that the examples given for CRT almost always represent training or knowledge-level objectives; standards are much more difficult to establish at the higher taxonomy levels—the levels that represent concepts and the more important educational objectives such as reading comprehension or arithmetic problem solving. In certain contexts these standards are not arbitrary, but established on definitive empirical grounds. We discussed earlier the *General Educational Development (GED)* tests, which use the actual achievement of high school graduates to establish the minimum *standard* that must be reached for one to obtain the *GED* high school equivalency certificate. The same principle is used for the Advanced

Placement Tests as a basis for awarding college credit to many high school seniors and accepted in lieu of certain courses at many colleges and universities.

7.16   NORM-REFERENCED VERSUS CRITERION-REFERENCED TESTING

Individual differences are the major emphasis of norm-referenced testing (NRT); but individual differences are not a concern in mastery or criterion-referenced testing (CRT)—if everyone scores 100 percent on the test, so much the better (assuming the test is valid). CRT assessments should reveal what competencies an individual student does and does not possess, not how he or she compares with norms or peers (NRT). A succinct illustration of this distinction is percentile (NRT) versus percentage (CRT) scores. The percentage grades that were used almost universally in schools and colleges until about 1920 (and still common today) represent a primitive type of CRT. Most standardized tests, however, represent NRT. There has been much heated controversy on the pros and cons of CRT and NRT (Ebel, 1972, 1978; Glass, 1978a, 1978b, 1978c; Popham, 1978a, 1978b; Shepard, 1979b, 1979c, 1980).

NRT Misapplied

The CRT movement is in part a reaction to the misuse of psychometric methods (especially reliability theory) that were developed for assessing individual differences in aptitudes and abilities. In measuring aptitudes, the intent is to maximize discrimination (individual differences) among the examinees; other things being equal, the greater the discrimination (variance), the greater the reliability.

In the past, *inadequate attention was given to the standard error of measurement as an indicator of measurement precision for achievement tests.* NRT-oriented persons were often inordinately interested in achievement tests with high reliability coefficients. Items were eliminated or retained for future use solely on the basis of their discrimination and difficulty. Since items that are answered correctly (or incorrectly) by a large percent of the examinees tend to have lower discrimination indexes, they were often eliminated solely on that empirical criterion. If the standard error of measurement of percentage scores (i.e., $\sigma_{e\%}$) had been used as the primary indication of measurement, this abuse might have been reduced.[7] In other words, many achievement test developers lost sight of content validity—that the *items must first and foremost be representative of the domain (content) and process objectives to be assessed, and focused on high reliability as an end in itself.*

Certainly, when there is a difference among students in level of mastery (and there almost is), we want to be able to differentiate between those individuals who have more fully mastered the content universe from those who have less understanding of it. But *discrimi-*

---

[7]Perhaps one reason the standard error of measurement has not been used more was the failure to use percent scores in reporting test results. If raw scores are used, the standard error of measurement increases as test length is increased, even though reliability increases. But if scores are expressed as percent correct, the standard error of measurement ($\sigma_{e\%}$) decreases as test length increases. Percent correct score reporting was prematurely abandoned as an unfortunate and unnecessary side effect of the norm-referenced testing movement (Buros, 1977).

nation per se is not a purpose of teacher-made achievement testing.[8] As illustrated in Chapter 5, theoretically a test may have a small error of measurement even if it has a low reliability coefficient (e.g., if $\rho_{XX} = 0$ and $\sigma = 5\%$, then $\sigma_e = 5\%$). Although a large variance among scores should not be, in and of itself, a goal of classroom achievement testing, *individual differences are a fact of life*, especially whenever we are dealing with concepts rather than with training or knowledge-level objectives. We can be delighted when all first-graders can tie their shoes (and have them remain tied for the entire school day)—that is, when all students achieve this psychomotor objective and individual differences are minimal. But when we are concerned with higher-level cognitive or psychomotor competencies, such as written and oral expression, reading comprehension, arithmetic problem solving, or typing speed, there is no meaningful 100 percent mastery point. Who has 100 percent reading comprehension? If test scores suggest uniformity among typical students in areas like written expression and reading comprehension, the progress of the more able is either being neglected or (more likely) the measuring instrument is like a high-jump stand that goes up to only 4 feet—individual differences beyond that point are there but undetected because the measurement emphasis is geared to a primitive level of mastery (Shepard, 1980).

Several serious problems limit the utility of criterion-referenced tests in most curricular areas. Rarely is there a definitive logical basis for establishing the performance criterion standard. The standard of 70 percent for a passing grade that was common early in this century has been discarded as completely arbitrary by thoughtful educators. Even when a table of specifications is used, it is a simple task to write two sets of items on identical content strata or objectives, one set being composed of very easy items and another of very difficult items. A score of 70 percent on the easy test may reflect extremely poor achievement, whereas a score of 70 percent on the difficult test may represent superior mastery. Consider the following two items, both designed to measure the same sixth-grade science objective.

1. Dark colors absorb heat faster than lighter colors. (True or False)
2. Suppose we have two identical balloons except that one is white and one is black. Both are filled with the same amount of air and are tied so that no air can get in or out. What will happen if both balloons are put in direct sunlight?
   *a) The black balloon will become larger than the white balloon.
   b) The white balloon will become larger than the black balloon.
   c) Both balloons will get smaller.
   d) Both balloons will stay the same size.
   e) Both balloons will burst.

Both items are designed to measure the same concept, yet Item 2 requires much greater understanding than Item 1. Item 2 is in the application taxonomy level, whereas Item 1 is only a knowledge-level question. Obviously, such criteria for mastery as 90 percent of the items on the criterion test are arbitrary, since item difficulty is arbitrary.

---

[8]If an item is marked correctly more often by students with high total scores on a test than by students with low total scores, we say that the item discriminates between high scorers and low scorers or simply that it has discriminating value or power. See Chapter 10 for a treatment of item analysis.

As another illustration, consider the following two questions, which are designed to measure the concept of reliability.

1. If scores on two forms of a test correlate .00, what is the test's reliability coefficient?
   a) 1.0 b) .5 *c) 0.0 d) –.5 e) –1.0
2. Other things being equal, which one of the following will not tend to increase the reliability coefficient computed for a test?
   a) decreasing the number of content strata from 4 to 1
   b) increasing the correlation among items
   *c) increasing the number of examinees
   d) using the split-half rather than the parallel-form method of estimation
   e) giving the test to a more heterogeneous group

This example is deliberately extreme in order to make the following point: Even though both items pertain to the concept of test reliability, most examinees would correctly answer the first question, but many students would not, at this point, be able to select the correct answer to the second question.

What is mastery? How does one logically establish an absolute standard or criterion of mastery? How does one justify a criterion of, say, 80 percent as the cutoff score for mastery of some concept or domain? When does one have a proper understanding? How does one establish a minimum level of competence in reading, spelling, speaking, writing, listening, or even test construction or interpretation?[9] When concepts are complex, we are usually in a continual state of growth in our understanding and never arrive at total mastery (Mills, 1991). Anderson (1970) showed that even the phrasing and format of the items employed in the measurement of a given concept can influence the examinee's performance. Thus, although the concept of mastery testing or criterion-referenced testing has strong logical appeal, at least initially, its practicability for most educational purposes is greatly restricted because of the unavailability of definitive means of establishing performance standards.

An even more dramatic illustration of the problem is given by Glass (1978a). A grade seven state assessment found an average of 86 percent on a *vertical* addition problem but an average of only 46 percent when the same problem was presented with the numbers arranged horizontally. Other studies (Dudycha & Carpenter, 1973; Choppin, 1974) have also found that the difficulty of items can be altered considerably by logically irrelevant format changes.

CRT has considerably more relevance when training and knowledge objectives are involved, for example, in areas such as developmental tasks, driver training, and industrial arts in which a minimal level of satisfactory performance can often be established on logical or empirical grounds.

The rationale for criterion-referenced testing is not new (Airasian & Madaus, 1972; Ebel, 1970b, Glaser, 1994; Thorndike, 1918, p. 18); CRT is a combination of more carefully

---

[9]One large federally funded ($350,000 per year) experimental educational program set a pre-specified criterion performance standard of 80% correct on a CRT to define the point at which the curricular objectives are said to have been achieved. After year 1, when most students failed to achieve the desired criterion, the criterion for mastery was readjusted to 60%; thus, after year 2 it was concluded that 83% of the students achieved the curricular objectives of the project! Obviously, such meaningless "bootstrapping" is not an appropriate use of CRT, but it does illustrate the problem of an arbitrary criterion.

defined objectives used together with pre-specified performance standards. More than a century ago Chadwick (1864) described a "scale book" prepared by the Reverend George Fisher "which contains the numbers assigned to each degree of proficiency in various subjects of examinations." That system was abandoned because examinees' scores were a function of two arbitrary factors—whether the test was easy or difficult and the generosity (or lack of it) of the scorer.

Obviously, a criterion for mastery lacks credibility if it cannot be based on strong logical or empirical grounds. *A criterion for mastery of minimal proficiency can be meaningful if it is empirically based*, and not arbitrary, as with the GED and the college board advanced placement tests. CRT can be justified in carefully developed instructional programs in which a performance criterion (e.g., 90 percent, see Sadler, 1987) has been shown empirically to be necessary in order to progress sequentially through the program in a satisfactory manner. Most classroom testing, however, should not only be geared to determining whether students meet some arbitrary minimum, basal level of achievement but also should assess the individual differences that inevitably are present among the students. CRT should not result in an inordinate preoccupation with slow learners at the expense of average and above-average learners (Shepard, 1976; Madaus & McDonagh, 1979).

The arbitrariness of the criterion in CRT has caused many to abandon the notion of a meaningful pre-specified criterion for mastery[10] and to use instead more appropriate descriptions such as "domain-referenced tests" (Millman, 1974) or "objective-referenced tests." But all good achievement tests should be based on either explicit or implicit objectives or topics in a table of specifications. Except for the pre-specified performance standard in CRT and minimum competency tests, the distinction between them and *appropriately* developed diagnostic tests (or even many survey and teacher-made achievement tests) is not clear-cut. As Wood (1977, p. 262) observed, "In practice the differences between these kinds of tests may be more apparent than real." In practice, domain-referenced and diagnostic tests are more likely to have been developed around a set of stated objectives or table of specifications so that the item content is a better representation of the content universe. But this is just practicing good test development procedures for ensuring content validity. NRT and CRT do differ in the method of reporting results; CRT is apt to employ percent-correct scores, whereas NRT often employs percentiles or standard scores. However, reporting both percent scores and standard scores for classroom tests is more informative than either alone. There has not been enough emphasis on items above the knowledge level in the cognitive taxonomy in all types of classroom achievement tests.

7.17   MINIMUM-COMPETENCY TESTING

In recent years there has been much interest in and controversy about minimum competency testing (MCT) (Winfield, 1987). More than 40 states are actively involved with some aspect of MCT. MCT is a special application of the rationale underlying CRT or mastery testing.

---

[10]It has been suggested (Hambleton, 1978; Popham, 1978a) that CRT has been misdirected. The focus of CRT should be on defining the domain of content and behavior, not a criterion of proficiency.

Students in more than 30 states are now legally obliged to demonstrate "minimum competency" in order to receive a high school diploma. The impetus for MCT came largely from the continuing stream of studies that suggest a decline in academic achievement about two decades ago.

MCT has all the difficulties of CRT in specifying a meaningful criterion. In addition, the consequences to the examinee of failing to achieve the criterion are often quite consequential. But exactly what is minimum competency? Competency in what? For what purpose? The minimum competencies for a lumberjack are far different from those for a clerk. The MCT notion is very appealing until one begins to confront the difficulties in implementing the concept.

In MCT, "survival" skills are often emphasized. But what seems essential apparently is not always so. Consider the two sample items used in the National Assessment of Educational Progress (see Figure 7–4). Defining survival skills is no less difficult than defining minimum competencies (Shepard, 1976). As Burton has observed, "No single skill is so essential that it can be defined as necessary for survival" (1978, p. 271). *If minimum competency standards are to be employed, they should be based on normative data, not arbitrary judgments* (Burton, 1978; Glass, 1978a, 1978b, 1978c; Shepard, 1976). In one state, for example, it was decided that a score of 70 percent was required for passing a MCT, causing nearly 40 percent of the students to fail. Why 70 percent? Why not 60%, 80%, 90%, or 95%? (see Glass, 1978)

The *GED* tests and the *California High School Proficiency Examination* (*CHSPE*), which allows 16- and 17-year-old students who pass such tests to leave school immediately, are based on the normative approach to setting minimal standards. On the *CHSPE*, students must achieve the median of second-semester seniors (Abramowitz & Law, 1978). Empirical normative criteria are much less hazardous than arbitrary standards.

7.18   TEST DEVELOPMENT PLAN

In the development of an educational measure, the following questions must be addressed (Millman & Greene, 1985).

- What is the purpose of the test?
- Who will be taking the test?
- How much time is to be used for the testing?
- How shall the test be administered?
- What will the test cover?
- What sources of content will be used?
- What are the dimensions of the content?
- What is the scope of the domain about which inferences are to be made?
- How many items will represent each of the various content strata?
- Which types of item formats are to be used?
- How many items are available in the item pool, and how many need to be constructed?
- What is the appropriate difficulty and taxonomy level for the items?

A new automobile can be bought for cash for $2,850 or on credit with a down payment of $400 and $80 a month for three years. How much MORE would a person pay by buying on credit rather than by buying the car for cash?

ANSWER

This math exercise was adminis-tered in 1973 to 17-year-olds and adults. The correct response is "$430." 56% at age 17 and 68% of the adults answered correctly.

Below is a sample application blank. Ones like it are used to get information from people who are applying for driver's licenses, credit cards, passports, and other identification cards. Fill out the application below. Do not use your own name. For this application blank, each male should call himself Adam Baker Carson. Each female should call herself Alice Baker Carson. Make up the rest of the information. Be sure to fill in the entire form.

Please PRINT the information requested below

1. _____
    last name   first   middle initial

2. _____
            street address

3. _____
    city or town   county   state   zip code

4. DATE OF BIRTH: _____ 5. SEX: _____
            month   day   year   M or F

6. HT: _____ WT: _____ HAIR: _____ EYES: _____

TODAY'S DATE: _____

This writing exercise was administered in 1969 to ages 9, 13, 17, and adults. To be considered acceptable, all lines had to be filled in and at least the first three had to be printed. 12% at age 9, 26% at age 13, 61% at age 17 and 50% of the adults were able to do this.

FIGURE 7–4 Sample minimum-competency item to measure math and writing skills from the National Assessment Exercises.

SOURCE: "Minimal competency tests," *NAEP Newsletter* (1976), 9.

- How will the items be grouped and sequenced?
- How will the items/test be scored?
- How will the test be evaluated?
- Will an item analysis be performed?
- Will the reliability and measurement error of the test be assessed?

These important questions will occupy our concern and be considered in detail in Chapters 8 to 10.

SUMMARY

General educational goals are not specific enough to give clear direction to curriculum development and evaluation. Instructional objectives need to be explicated. Educational objectives can become dysfunctional if they are stated too atomistically. A carefully prepared topic outline is an implicit expression of certain instructional goals. A table of specifications with a grid of content strata with two taxonomy levels appears to be a functional blueprint for classroom test development.

Bloom's taxonomy differentiates among six levels of cognitive complexity. The first two or three (knowledge, comprehension, and application) are distinct, but the higher levels are not as clearly differentiated. Most teacher-made tests are overloaded with knowledge-level items; tests should have items from higher taxonomy levels as well.

The number of separate subscores to be reported influences the length of a good measuring instrument. Diagnostic, criterion-referenced, and objective-referenced tests need a *minimum* of five or ten items per objective or topic. A good survey test is not usually adequate for detailed diagnostic conclusions pertaining to specific skills and objectives.

The movement toward criterion-referenced, domain-referenced, and objective-referenced tests is, in part, a reaction to inappropriate and undesirable procedures for developing and selecting achievement test items primarily on the statistical characteristics of the items—procedures that are desirable for norm-referenced testing but that can result in sacrificing content validity for increased reliability.

A major problem in CRT and minimum competency testing approaches is the arbitrariness of the criterion. Item difficulty is arbitrary; therefore, the meaning of a criterion such as 80 percent correct is often uncertain. When criteria are established on empirical grounds, the criteria are not arbitrary and therefore can become useful for decision making.

In developing a plan for a test, the following considerations are important: the purpose of the test, the scope of the content of the test, the nature of the examinees, and the conditions under which the test are to be given.

IMPORTANT TERMS AND CONCEPTS

cognitive	content strata	table of specifications
affective	content universe	domain-referenced test
psychomotor	mastery tests	criterion-referenced test
parent objectives	diagnostic tests	minimum competency test
offspring objectives	Bloom's taxonomy	objective-referenced test
behavioral objectives	norm-referenced test	

CHAPTER TEST

1. Which is the broadest, most inclusive term?
   a) educational goals
   b) behavioral objectives
   c) instructional objectives

2. Which is the lowest level of Bloom's taxonomy?
   a) synthesis
   b) application
   c) knowledge
   d) comprehension
   e) analysis

3. Has research supported the contention that all six levels of the taxonomy are clearly distinguishable?

4. Is it desirable to state instructional objectives at extremely specific levels (e.g., "Can add the numbers 9, 5, and 3 when vertically aligned")?

5. If a test is an excellent survey test, can we be certain that it will be useful for appraising the degree to which individual examinees have achieved specific objectives?

6. A major problem with the CRT approach is
   a) its emphasis on item discrimination and difficulty.
   b) the difficulty of developing good test items.
   c) the arbitrariness of the criteria.

7. A practical difficulty with criterion-referenced, objective-referenced, and diagnostic testing is that
   a) it is difficult to develop items to measure behavioral objectives.
   b) several items are needed to assess adequately each objective.
   c) there is much public opposition to these approaches to student assessment.

8. If achievement tests include only those items that have characteristics that are desirable for norm-referenced tests, the net result will be
   a) to sacrifice reliability at the expense of validity.
   b) to sacrifice validity at the expense of reliability.
   c) to sacrifice both reliability and validity for usability.

9. Which level of Bloom's taxonomy is represented by Item 2?

10. Which level of Bloom's taxonomy is represented by Item 9?

ANSWERS TO CHAPTER TEST

1. a
2. c
3. No
4. No

5. No
6. c
7. b

8. b
9. Knowledge
10. Application

8

Constructing and Using Essay Tests

8.1 INTRODUCTION AND BACKGROUND

Some historical background will serve to put current practices in perspective. Measurement and evaluation have played a far more prominent role in human history than is generally recognized. The historical origins of testing and measurement are lost in antiquity. There was an elaborate system of civil service examinations in China several centuries before Christ (DuBois, 1966; Miyazaki, 1976).[1] Testing was a normal part of the education of the ancient Greeks (Chauncey & Dobbin, 1963). The Socratic method involves the skillful interspersing of instruction with oral testing. Some of the earliest records of the use of various testing devices are found in the Bible.

> And the Gileadites took the passages of Jordan before the Ephraimites: and it was so, that when those Ephraimites which were escaped said, Let me go over; that the men of Gilead said unto him, Art thou an Ephraimite? If he said, Nay; then said they unto him, Say now "Shibboleth," and he said "Sibboleth," for he could not frame to pronounce it right. (*Judges* 12:5–6)

The sole test of a man's being a Gileadite was the ability to use the *h* sound in the word *Shibboleth*.

In education, some form of assessment is inevitable; it is inherent in the teaching-learning process. Consider the constant evaluative role of classroom teachers as they attempt to determine the degree of scholastic achievement and growth of students. Measuring devices are indispensable to the teacher, the counselor, the school administrator, the curriculum specialist, and the researcher.

---

[1] It is interesting to note that after a decade of cultural revolution (1966–76), in which systematic examination and marks were virtually eliminated ("They create classes and elitism among the masses"), China reinstituted admissions examinations for universities and other more traditional uses of testing and evaluation of students (Kraft, 1978).

8.2   ORAL EXAMINATIONS

Oral questioning dates back to the beginnings of human language. Four centuries before Christ, Socrates used oral questions to "draw out" his students, as many good teachers do today. Indeed, Christ himself continually used oral questions as stepping-stones to lead his "students" to Truth. But it is important to distinguish between the instructional value of an activity and its appropriateness for general assessment. A spelling bee may be useful as a motivation technique, but as a measurement technique it has serious limitations. Until the availability of inexpensive pencils and paper after the middle of the nineteenth century, oral examinations were standard in American schools. Some countries by law still require oral final examinations (Stanley, 1960). Universities harbor vestiges of this in the form of thesis orals.

A job interview often is nothing more than an oral test that assesses an applicant's cognitive and affective characteristics. From time to time, oral quiz programs appear on radio and television, though the contestants are often chosen in advance for their proficiency on written tests. Not until the second half of the past century did writing instruments largely replace glib or faltering tongues as a basis for educational decisions. Oral examinations were used for every subject except writing.

In the nineteenth century annual public oral tests of teachers were common. Teachers would be assembled in the town hall for the examination and questioned by the superintendent. All teachers who fell below the minimal standard of 75 percent were dismissed. (Who said "minimum-competency teaching" is a new idea?) In a similar vein, "performance contracts" were decreed in England in 1862 (and continued until about 1900); teachers were paid largely according to the results of their students on the annual examinations given by Her Majesty's inspectors (Cureton, 1971).

8.3   WRITTEN TESTS

Important prerequisites for achievement testing via writing were developed early in the nineteenth century, the blackboard in 1809 and the metal pen (replacing the goose quill) in 1828 (Cureton, 1971).

The first important steps toward the scientific use of measurement in education were taken by Horace Mann (1845) more than a century ago. This prominent New England educator, famous for his doctrine of free, compulsory, and universal education, had a remarkable understanding of the importance of examinations and of the limitations of those then in current use. His penetrating analysis of the weaknesses of the oral examination then in vogue and of the superiority of written examinations for classroom purposes can hardly be improved upon today. Mann showed clearly where oral examinations were lacking; he used the concepts that have become the cornerstones of today's theories and are now known as validity and reliability.

Another American educator who understood both the value and the limitations was Emerson E. White, an educational writer and school administrator. He wrote, "It may be stated as a general fact that school instruction and study are never much wider or better than the tests by which they are measured" (1886). In the same volume he enumerated several *special advantages* of the written test:

It is more impartial than the oral test, since it gives all the pupils the same tests and an equal opportunity to meet them; its results are more tangible and reliable; it discloses more accurately the comparative progress of the different pupils, information of value to the teacher; it reveals more clearly defects in teaching and study, and thus assists in their correction; it emphasizes more distinctly the importance of accuracy and fullness in the expression of knowledge . . . it is at least an equal test of the thought-power or intelligence of pupils. (pp. 197–198)

Mann and White realized that the oral test can be unfair, since questions vary greatly in difficulty. Oral testing is also quite inefficient, since only one student can respond at a time. Essay tests have an advantage over oral examinations in that all examinees respond to the same questions. The insights of Mann and White continue to be valid. These pioneers understood the need for good assessment more than many educators do today. Measurement specialists now realize that some of the early enthusiasm for the ordinary essay test was unwarranted, pointing out that some of the limitations of oral tests also hold in some degree for certain written tests.

The improvement of existing tests and other measuring instruments has always lagged far behind theory, and educational practice has been farthest behind of all. Despite the marked superiority of written examinations over oral ones, which Mann pointed out in 1845, in many cases teachers have not moved either to adopt the former or to improve the latter. It is interesting to note, however, that in 1864 an enterprising English schoolmaster, the Reverend George Fisher, proposed the widespread use of objective and standardized measures of academic attainment. Fisher outlined the practice of the new system in his school as follows:

A book, called the "Scale-Book," has been established, which contains the numbers assigned to each degree of proficiency in the various subjects of examination: For instance, if it be required to determine the numerical equivalent corresponding to any specimen of "writing," a comparison is made with various standard specimens, which are arranged in this book in order to merit; the highest being represented by the number 1, and the lowest by 5, and the intermediate values by affixing to these numbers the fractions 1/4, 1/2, or 3/4. So long as these standard specimens are preserved in the institution, so long will constant numerical values for proficiency in "writing" be maintained. And since facsimiles can be multiplied without limit, the same principle might be generally adopted.

The numerical values for "spelling" follow the same order, and are made to depend upon the percentage of mistakes in writing from dictation sentences from works selected for the purpose, examples of which are contained in the "Scale-Book," in order to preserve the same standard of difficulty.

By a similar process, values are assigned for proficiency in mathematics, navigation, Scripture knowledge, grammar, and composition, French, general history, drawing, and practical science, respectively. Questions in each of these subjects are contained in the "Scale-Book," to serve as types, not only of the difficulty, but also of the nature of the question, for the sake of future reference. (Chadwick, 1864)

Apparently, the reverend was too far ahead of his time, since his incisive work seems not to have attracted a widespread audience. As Ayres (1918) expressed it, "Progress in the scientific study of education was not possible until people could be brought to realize that human behavior was susceptible of quantitative study, and until they had statistical methods with which to carry on their investigations."

8.4   SCIENTIFIC PROFICIENCY MEASURES: AN EARLY EXAMPLE

Early in the twentieth century the *Thorndike Handwriting Scale* (E. L. Thorndike, 1910) was published—the first of its kind. It consisted of formal writing samples of children in grades 5 through 8; the samples were arranged in a 15-category scale of increasing quality in essentially the manner suggested 46 years earlier by Fisher (Chadwick, 1864). Figure 8–1 gives

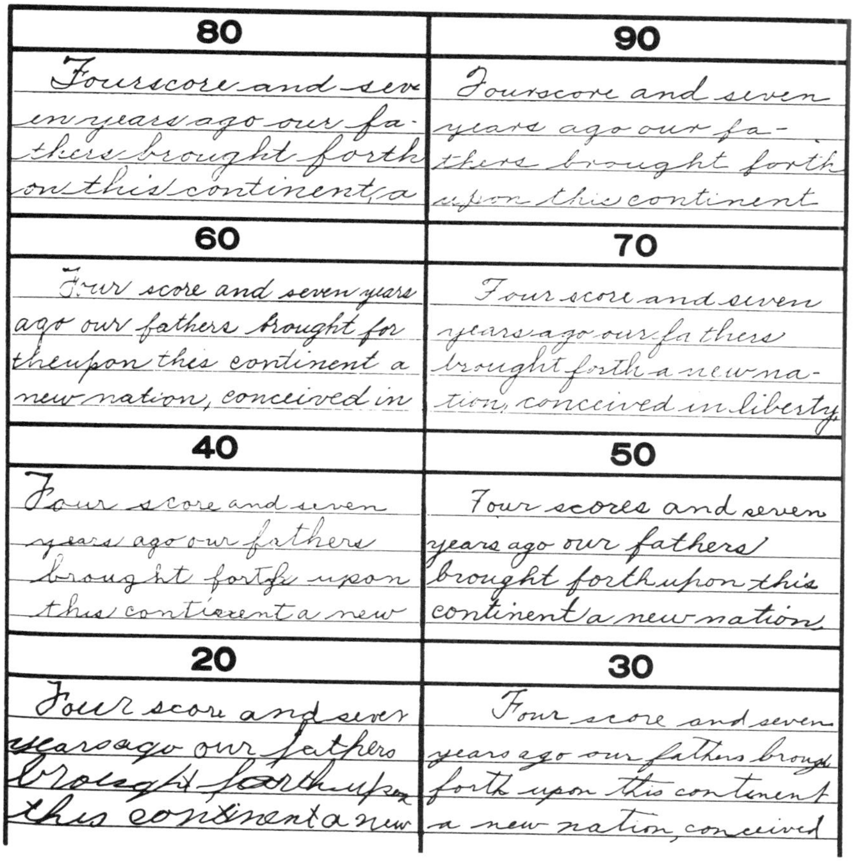

FIGURE 8–1   An abridged version of the Ayres Handwriting Scale.

SOURCE: L. P. Ayers, *Measuring Scale for Handwriting: Gettysburg Edition.* (Iowa City, IA: University of Iowa, Bureau of Educational Research, 1912). Reproduced by permission of the University of Iowa.

an abridged version of the Ayres Handwriting Scale, a refinement of Thorndike's scale. This is an example of "a wheel that was subsequently reinvented" (Lyman, 1978) and is now termed *criterion-referenced measurement* (see Chapter 7). A sample of a person's handwriting can be scaled according to the eight calibration "anchor" points provided. How does a sample of your typical handwriting rate? The median ratings on the Ayres scale for grades 2 to 8 are 38, 42, 46, 50, 54, 58, and 62, respectively.

8.5   ESSAY TESTS AS MEASURES OF ACHIEVEMENT

It is important to distinguish between the two principal uses of essay tests: (1) as an achievement test and (2) as a measure of writing ability. Examples of the first type of use include teacher-made tests in social studies, science, and other curricular areas. The use of essay tests to measure the ability to use effective written communication and other language arts objectives illustrates the second purpose.

Two camps have developed in recent years, one decrying objective testing and the other insisting that most important mental processes, including the composition of essays, can be measured well by objective test items. The anti-objective test group contends that objective tests cannot reflect the quality of an examinee's reasoning; consequently, it is contended that multiple-choice tests discriminate against the bright, discerning student. The empirical research on this issue, however, does not support this position (Chauncey & Hilton, 1965; Jensen, 1980).

Some critics have argued that the objective test can measure only knowledge of facts but that the essay test can measure more complex, higher levels of understanding. Several studies have found that many objective and free-response and essay tests over the same content assess essentially the same factors if allowance is made for measurement error (Bracht & Hopkins, 1970a; Breland & Gaynor, 1979; Coffman, 1971; Godshalk et al., 1966; Horn, 1966; Stafford & Sjogren, 1964; Vernon, 1962; Ward, 1982; Ward, Frederiksen & Carlson, 1980). Of course, the fact that in ordinary use the two kinds of tests do not measure different factors should not be construed to mean that they cannot have unique measurement values *when appropriately developed and scored*. Whether objective or essay, tests used to assess learning are frequently of extremely poor quality. A comparative evaluation of the two types of test was summarized by Chauncey and Dobbin (1963, pp. 79–80):

> Given two examiners fully trained in the arts of achievement testing, one building essay examinations and the other objective tests, the examiner with the essay tests probably can do a better job of estimating a student's present skill in creative writing, but the examiner who builds objective tests can provide more valid and reliable estimates of just about every other kind of school achievement.

Although objective tests are much more commonly used as achievement measures than are essay tests, essay tests are also widely used, especially in secondary schools (Gullickson, 1985). Questions typical of those found on essay examinations at the high school or college level include: "What were the principal political considerations that led to the War Between the States?" "Write an essay of approximately 1000 words about the cinema as an art form." "Distinguish between *connotation* and *denotation*." "Is logic a branch of mathematics, or is mathematics a branch of logic?" "Discuss the relative influence of heredity and environment on the development of verbal intelligence. Support your discussion by citing relevant studies." "Critically evaluate the place of Bloom's taxonomy in the development of classroom achievement measures."

An essay test differs from a short-answer test; in short-answer or simple recall tests a limited and precise set of answers is expected: "List the inert gases," "Give the chemical formula for common sugar," "List the five largest oil-producing states," and so on. Such questions permit a restricted answer expressed in a few words, usually at the knowledge level. True essay questions limit the students' responses much less than short-answer items. The instructor does not merely say, "Write something," but neither is the nature and form of the answer completely specified.

The grading of essay questions, like oral questions, calls for sensitive and thoughtful judgment; unlike objective items, essay questions cannot be graded by untrained clerks. Even if they are graded by experts, the grades will not have much validity if they are graded haphazardly and unsystematically. Even when skilled teachers expend their best efforts in grading them, the reliability of most essay tests is usually quite limited.

For many years major efforts have been made to obtain adequate reliability in grading essay tests, particularly English compositions written by high school students who are applying for entrance to select colleges. Considerable success has been achieved in the use of essay tests as measures of one's ability to write; their virtues as achievement measures in other curricular areas are more modest. Eliminating the use of essay exercises as achievement measures, however, would be a serious educational mistake. *It is important not to confuse the educational value with the evaluation qualities of essays.* The essay exercise has important instructional merits apart from any evaluative weaknesses it possesses. The traditional essay examination has a legitimate place in schools and colleges. In this chapter we consider some of the limitations and advantages of the essay test and offer suggestions that can dramatically increase its reliability and validity. The wise admonition offered more than half a century ago by testing trailblazers Hawkes, Lindquist, and Mann is still true today:

> The intelligent point of view is that which recognizes that whatever advantages either type may have are *specific* advantages in *specific* situations; that while certain purposes may be best served by one type, other purposes are best served by another; and, above all, that the adequacy of either type in any specific situation is much more dependent upon the ingenuity and intelligence with which the test is *used* than upon any *inherent* characteristic or limitation of the type employed. (1936, p. 210)

8.6   LIMITATIONS OF THE ESSAY TEST

As it is ordinarily employed, the essay test has several serious limitations as a measuring instrument. As a measure of achievement (other than writing), it suffers in comparison with most forms of objective tests on the three important criteria for a satisfactory measuring instrument: reliability, validity, and practicability.

8.7 READER UNRELIABILITY

A major problem with essay examinations is the lack of consistency in judgments among competent raters, that is, the lack of scoring consistency (reader reliability). One large study by the Educational Testing Service (1961) had 53 "outstanding representatives" from several fields evaluate 300 essays written by college freshmen. Each rater used a nine-point rating scale to indicate the quality of the essay. *More than one-third (34%) of the essays received all possible ratings*! Another 37 percent received eight ratings, and 23 percent received seven. No essay received fewer than five of the nine possible ratings. Obviously, a highly valid rating must be a function of what is written, not of which person happens to evaluate the response.

In a study (Coffman & Kurfman, 1968) involving the College Board's Advanced Placement Test in American History, it was found that some readers were much more lenient in their grading than others and that this trend was consistent irrespective of whether the scoring was global-holistic or analytical (separate ratings on each of several writing criteria).

Raters differ not only in their standards but also in how they distribute grades of the rating scale employed (Coffman, 1971). Some raters tend to spread scores more widely than others, even though the average scores may be equal. Good papers will receive lower scores and poor papers higher scores than they would from raters who cluster scores more closely around an average value. Thus, the scores of different raters differ in variability as well as central tendency.

One study (Ashburn, 1938) concluded that "the passing or failing of about 40 percent (of students) depends not on what they know or do not know, but on *who* reads the papers" and that "the passing or failing of about 10 percent depends . . . on *when* the papers are read." In another study, the authors found that two sets of grades on the same essay exams read by the same college professors on two different occasions were not highly correlated.

Unfortunately, scorer reliability tends to decrease when one attempts to capitalize on the essay test's unique characteristics—flexibility and freedom of choice (Coffman, 1971). This factor no doubt accounts for the great disparity among the reader reliability coefficients reported in the literature; the correlations between readers range from as low as .32 to as high as .98 (Coffman, 1969, p. 10). It is not difficult to obtain high scorer reliability if essay questions are narrowly focused and carefully structured. For example, "List the four principal causes of the Civil War identified by your textbook" and "Name the countries of South America and the chief export of each" are questions that could present only minor difficulty in scoring reliability. These questions, however, could be cast more efficiently in objective format. Broader, open-ended questions designed to assess more complex concepts in the higher levels of Bloom's taxonomy are precisely the kinds of questions that tend to possess the least scorer reliability. The following essay question would probably have low scorer reliability: Defend or refute the following proposition: 'Liberty can be achieved only by an extension of governmental regulation of competitive business enterprise.' This degree-of-structure factor is probably a principal reason that essay tests in mathematics tend to be more reliable than those in history, which in turn tend to have greater reliability than those in literature (Burton, 1980; Coffman, 1971).

8.8   THE HALO EFFECT

The halo effect is the tendency, when judging one characteristic of a person, to be influenced by another characteristic or by a general impression of the person. For example, in rating intelligence on the basis of observation, psychologists overrated men with introverted personality characteristics. The halo effect can seriously reduce the validity of marks assigned by teachers to essay tests. If Mary is a well-behaved student who loves her teacher and tries very hard to please, these desirable personality and deportment characteristics can (and probably do) influence the teacher's judgment of the quality of Mary's essay test. When essay tests are not read anonymously, the halo effect will seriously confound the results (Chase, 1979a, 1986; Spandel, 1984).

8.9   ITEM-TO-ITEM CARRYOVER EFFECTS

A common contaminant in scoring essay tests is the item-to-item carryover effect, even when the writer is unknown by the rater. Raters acquire an impression of the student's knowledge on the initial item that "colors" their judgment of subsequent items. Bracht (1967) found that the carryover factor had a strong influence on the marks given by college faculty to questions on an essay test. When the responses to each essay question were scored for all students before the next question was marked, the correlation between the marks on the questions was much lower than when the student's response to the first question was allowed to influence the rater's judgment of the response to the second question. Obviously, the response to an essay question should be evaluated on its own merits and should not be influenced by preceding questions on the test.

8.10   TEST-TO-TEST CARRYOVER EFFECTS

It has been observed that the grade assigned to a paper tends to be greatly influenced by the grade given to the immediately preceding paper (Paden, 1986). Stalnaker's (1936) assertion that "a *C* paper may be graded *B* if it is read after an illiterate theme, but if it follows an *A* paper, if such can be found, it seems to be of *D* caliber" (p. 41) may be somewhat overstated but only in degree (Daly & Dickerson-Markman, 1982). Hales and Tokar (1975) found that essays of average quality were rated about 1.5 points higher on a five-point scale when preceded by two poor essays than when preceded by two very good papers. Similar results were found using 25 experienced teachers (Hughes, Keeling & Tuck, 1980), irrespective of whether scoring was analytical or global.

8.11   ORDER EFFECTS

The order in which a paper appears also often influences the score it receives. In several studies (Bracht, 1967; Coffman & Kurfman, 1968; Godshalk et al., 1966), a "slide effect" was observed in the scores awarded by raters. Papers that were read earlier tended to receive higher ratings than those read nearer the end of the sequence. Perhaps readers become weary, and in this physical and mental condition nothing looks quite as good as it otherwise might.

Even when essays are reread by the same teacher, the score a given paper receives is quite often inconsistent. Bracht (1967) found that the first and second scores on a single brief essay question correlated .50 when reread by the same instructor and .47 when read by a different instructor. It is clear that there is considerable intra-rater (within-rater) as well as inter-rater (between-rater) inconsistency.

8.12   LANGUAGE MECHANICS EFFECTS

Investigators have found that teachers are unable to rate essay responses on content alone—they are influenced by errors in spelling, punctuation, and grammar, even when directed to disregard such factors (Chase, 1983; Marshall, 1967; Marshall & Powers, 1969; Scannell & Marshall, 1966). Several investigators (Chase, 1968, 1979a, 1986; Markham, 1976) have found that handwriting quality is related to the scores awarded to essays. Shepherd's (1929) early study showed dramatic differences in the scores received by identical essay responses presented in good and poor handwriting. More recent studies show real but small effects on essay rating for penmanship and general appearance.

Several investigators (Bracht & Hopkins, 1968; Garber, 1967; Klein & Hart, 1968) have found that the length of an answer to an essay question has a substantial relationship (rs of .32 to .56) to the rating assigned (Bracht & Hopkins, 1968) even among students having the same level of mastery of the content. The tendency to be concise or verbose seems to be a response style that has little relationship to the student's level of understanding, and, unfortunately, the tendency to give wordy answers is rewarded by the ratings given to essay tests. Graders seem unconsciously to assume that those who write more, know more, which is not supported by the evidence. Even when grade point average and scholastic aptitude are held constant, the (partial) correlation between the length of the response and the assigned mark is substantial (almost .5). It seems that there is considerable support for the common notion among test-wise students that instructors often assign marks on the basis of the *weight* of student products. It has been suggested that the essay overrates the importance of knowing how to say a thing and saying it in several different ways, and underrates the importance of having something to say.

In an extensive study in England, Pidgeon and Yates (1957, p. 47) concluded that the results of the experiments that we have outlined, however, show that even in ideal conditions, which cannot in practice be contrived—that is, with a faultless system of marking—papers of this kind (essay) do not achieve the level of reliability that is maintained by objective tests, nor do they achieve the same degree of validity.

The essay test also ranks low in usability unless the number of examinees is small. It is inevitable that the scoring of essay tests with professional integrity will be very time-consuming. The additional expenditure of time and energy beyond that needed for objective tests is such a major limitation that the exclusive use of essay tests as an evaluation tool can be justified only as a measure of writing ability. From a practical perspective, one important advantage of the essay test is its high face validity for the layperson and professional alike—written exercises have the appearance of being a rich way to measure higher mental processes and other important educational objectives.

8.13   COMPUTER SCORING

Ellis Page and his associates (Garber, 1967; Page, 1966) have done some interesting work on the incongruous task of grading essays by computer. After studying Table 8–1 you will see that such a feat is not as preposterous as it initially appears; the computer ("Judge C") is indistinguishable from the other four judges.

Strange as it seems, the research has indicated that computer scoring can yield scores that are *superior* to a single judge's rating on each of the following factors: ideas or content, organization, style, mechanics, and creativity (Coffman, 1971.) Although the information used by the computer often lacks face validity and even logical validity (scoring is based on number of words in the essay, average word length, standard deviation of sentence length, number of commas, and so on), there is strong evidence that, when the criterion is the average rating given by several experts, the computer's marks are as valid as those of a typical reader. For the present, the research is more of a graphic illustration of the deficiencies in subjectively scored examinations than a practical teacher's aid for scoring essay tests.

Reader reliability is improved when essay questions are carefully delimited and explicitly framed. Agreements are further increased when the raters are provided with a *model answer* that gives major points or concepts and their corresponding credit allocations.

TABLE 8–1   Which One Is the Computer?

	Judges				
	A	**B**	**C**	**D**	**E**
A		.51	.51	.44	
B	.51		.53	.56	.57
C	.51	.53		.48	.61
D	.44	.56	.48		.49
E	.57	.61	.49	.59	.59

SOURCE: E. B. Page, 'The imminence of grading essays by computer,' *Phi Delta Kappan, 47* (1966), 238–243. Reprinted by permission of the publisher. The intercorrelation matrix generated by the cross-validation of PEG I operates in the following fashion: All "judges" graded the overall quality of a set of 138 essays written by high school students in grades 8–12. One "judge" was a computer, the other four were independent human experts. The correlations in this table show the extent to which each "judge" tended to agree with each other in grading essays. The computer-assigned grades were based upon beta weightings generated from the multiple prediction of human judgments on 138 essays by other students randomly drawn from the same population. Which one, A, B, C, D, or E, is the computer vector?

Much greater reliability can be attained when a set of "representative" essays for anchoring the various categories in grading scale (such as *A-F*) is used (Olson & DiStefano, 1980). Indeed, the subjective judgments of any variable can be greatly improved in reliability, be it judging performance in gymnastics, quality of livestock, or artistic creativity, by having "range finder" prototypes to define (anchor) the various rating categories.

When carefully developed analytical or holistic scoring methods are used along with clearly focused questions, it is possible to achieve high reader reliability. Olson and DiStefano (1980) obtained correlations above .80 with holistic ratings of writing ability when carefully selected prototypical examples anchored the seven-point rating scale. For using essays to assess achievement, or when scored analytically, however, these methods are expensive—they require large amounts of professional time. In an extensive study, Godshalk et al. (1966, pp. 39–40) found that

> If one can include as many as five different topics (of 20–40 minutes each) and have each topic read by five different readers, the reading reliability of the total score may be approximately .92 and the score [test] reliability approximately .84 . . . In contrast, for one topic read by a single reader, the corresponding figures are .40 and .25 respectively.

To achieve satisfactory reliability of essay tests of achievement, several questions, each graded by more than one reader, are desirable.

8.14   ESSAY TEST RELIABILITY

It is significant that most studies on the reliability of essay tests deal with between- or within-rater agreement in marking a particular examination, not with the reliability of the examination itself. Note in the quote from the Godshalk et al. study that the reader reliability for a single topic essay test of 20 to 40 minutes with a single reader was .40, but that test reliability was only .25. Reader unreliability limits test reliability, but it is theoretically possible to have perfect reader reliability (consistency among raters of the same essay) without any test reliability (consistency among ratings for different essays written by the same person).

A few studies have reported on the correlation between two forms of an essay test designed for a particular purpose that were given to the same students and carefully marked by experienced examiners. One study (Coffman, 1971) used this procedure to study tests in 16 subjects taken by 952 eighth-grade students in 11 states. Each paper in the two sets of examinations was marked independently by two experienced teachers. This study made it possible to compare the reliability of the test with agreement in marking the test (reader reliability). The two independent markings of the same papers correlated .62, but the two different sets of examinations independently marked by the same teacher correlated only .43. In a similar study of the New York Regents' Examinations (Coffman, 1971), similar results were obtained. The average agreement of the two independent markings of the same paper was .72, but the average agreement of the two sets of tests marked by the same teacher was only .42. Of course, if each of the two sets was marked by a different teacher, the correlation would be expected to be somewhat lower.

In another study, two independent sets of marks assigned by two "experienced readers of essay examinations" correlated .94 on Form A and .84 on Form B, but the correlation between scores of Forms A and B was only .60, that is, reader reliability was much higher than test reliability. Coffman (1971) found that correlations between two different 45-minute essay questions with two different readers on an advanced-placement test in American history were .3 to .5 (depending on the two questions involved), whereas correlations between readers on the same questions were much higher, .5 to .7. These and other studies (Michael et al., 1980) illustrate an important point: *Agreement among raters marking the same essay test is higher than the true reliability of the test itself*. It is important to have high scorer reliability, but it is more important that the obtained scores are representative of true scores for the content universe being sampled by the examination exercises.

The reliability coefficient of an essay test is the correlation between two different forms of the essay test, scored independently. In simplest form, it is the correlation between Teacher 1's grades for the Form A essays with Teacher 2's grades for the Form B essays of the same students. If two teachers would grade the Form A essays and two other teachers would grade the Form B essays, the reliability would improve. Then for each student the average score would be found on Form A for the two teachers who graded Form A papers and the average score of Form B for the two different teachers who graded the Form B papers. The average scores of the students on Form A would then be correlated with their average scores on Form B. Test reliability is improved when reader reliability is increased.

Notice, however, that a student's average score on the two forms combined would be more reliable than his or her total score on Form A or Form B alone. If ρ_{AB} is the reliability coefficient for either Form A or Form B, then the reliability coefficient of both measures combined, $\rho_{(A+B)}$ can be estimated by the Spearman-Brown formula (Equation 5.6). For example, if $\rho = .50$, then

$$\rho_{(A+B)} = \frac{2\rho_{AB}}{1 + \rho_{AB}} = \frac{2(.50)}{1 + .50} \text{ or } .67.$$

If there were three comparable forms, A, B, and C, each with a reliability coefficient of .50, the reliability of total scores on all three forms combined (A + B + C) would be even higher as estimated by the Spearman-Brown formula (Equation 5.5):

$$\rho_{(A+B+C)} = \frac{3\rho_{AB}}{1 + 2\rho_{AB}} = \frac{3(.50)}{1 + 2(.50)} \text{ or } .75.$$

Therefore, if the number of questions on an essay test were increased, the reliability of scores from that test would increase. If the number of competent readers were increased, an additional increase in reliability would result. It is crucial that the essay questions be prepared carefully so that the ρ_{AB} for Teacher 1 grading Form A with Teacher 2 grading Form B will be as high as possible.

8.15 INDIRECT MEASURES OF WRITING ABILITY

There are two viable approaches to the assessment of writing proficiency (Spandel, 1984). The direct method relies on actual samples of examinees' writing to judge writing ability. The indirect method, having less face validity, relies on objective tests that require the examinee to recognize proper use of effective grammar, sentence construction, organization, and the like. Several studies have observed substantial correlations between scores on both types of measures (especially when allowance is made for the attenuating effects of measurement error). One study (Breland & Gaynor, 1979) found that the correlation of less than .60 between a carefully developed and scored single-question 20-minute essay exercise designed to measure writing ability and an objective test of writing ability (*Test of Standard Written English*, or *TSWE*, a 30-minute test) is increased to more than .70 if three 20-minute essay exercises are used. When both measures were extended to one-hour tests, the correlation was higher (more than .75). In a recent study involving four colleges, Breland (1979) found that writing performance in a course in freshman English was predicted more accurately from an indirect (multiple-choice) writing test (*TSWE*) than from an actual sample of the student's writing.

Many people would be surprised to learn that writing ability can be measured reasonably well with objective writing tests. These tests give narrative passages followed by alternative wordings of various portions, requiring the examinee to make judgments as to how the passages could be improved. The Educational Testing Service developed a one-hour objective measure of English composition skill that yields scores that correlate about .75 with a 140-minute criterion essay test having a reliability of .84. A one-hour *parallel* essay test could not be expected to do appreciably better.[2] Similar results have been found for elementary school students (Hogan & Mishler, 1980).

The *Test of Standard Written English (TSWE)*, a short objective test, is part of the administration of the College Board's *Scholastic Aptitude Tests (SAT)*. There is some indication (Bailey, 1977) that the *SAT* verbal score predicts course grades in English I at least as well as the *TSWE*. The predictive validity coefficients were not high, however, because of the low reliability of the criterion (a grade in a single course, estimated by Etaugh, Etaugh & Hurd, [1972] to be .44 for freshmen). The validity of the *TSWE* for predicting performance in essay tests has been found to be much higher than its validity for predicting a student's grade in a composition course (Osterlund & Cheney, 1978). Other researchers (Hoffman & Ziegler, 1978) have found objective language tests to be an effective and efficient means of identifying college students with deficient writing skills. But the fact that many users will take results more seriously when written compositions are used cannot be dismissed lightly. Face validity is important—the value of medicine may not be realized if the patient does not have faith in it and, hence, does not use it. Another possible beneficial side effect of using essay tests rather than, or in addition to, objective tests of writing is that their use could encourage more curricular emphasis on composition. Writing is often the neglected *R* because of the time-consuming processes of reading and providing diagnostic feedback to students.

---

[2]Using the Spearman-Brown formula (Equation 5.5) to estimate the reliability of the 2.33 hour essay test, the reliability of a one-hour essay test would be expected to be about .70. The observed score would then be expected to correlate with universe scores about $\sqrt{.70} = .84$. The correlation between the observed scores from the one-hour objective examination with universe scores on the essay test is estimated to be .82, employing a "correction for attenuation" in the criterion ($.75 / \sqrt{.84} = .82$).

8.16   THE ESSAY AS A MEASURE OF WRITING ABILITY

Many of the problems in using essay tests as measures of achievement can also contaminate their use as measures of writing or composition ability. The problems of reader and test unreliability, halo effect, penmanship, and item-to-item and test-to-test carryover effects can (and usually do) confound evaluations of students' abilities in written expression.

Questions designed to measure writing ability should not depend on knowledge of facts or prescribed information. Otherwise, a student who writes well but has nothing to say will receive a low rating. Questions oriented toward opinions, short stories, or descriptions of a past event are especially useful. A sample 30-minute essay from a standardized test, the *Primary Essay Tests* (Veal & Biesbrock, 1971), is typical:

> We all do many different things when there is no school. When you are not in school—like in the afternoon or on the weekend or during the summer—what do you like to do best? Tell what you like to do best when there is no school and why it is so much fun.

A second example, used in the *National Assessment of Educational Progress,* is given in Figure 8–2, together with two illustrative responses by 17-year-olds. How would you rate each essay using the categories of "inadequate," "competent," and "excellent"? (If you rated response I as "competent" and response II as "excellent," you agreed with the *NAEP* evaluators.)

When judging writing ability on controversial issues, such as the *NAEP* examples, it is extremely important that the raters do not let their own biases and points of view influence their ratings. Otherwise, the ratings are influenced by personal prejudice and not based exclusively on writing ability.

The purpose of essay exercises dictates how they will be evaluated. A global or holistic rating may be satisfactory for college admission, program evaluation, and quality control purposes, but its effective use in the curriculum requires more diagnostic feedback. "*C*," "average," or "Not bad, Jimmy, but you can do better" do not help students improve their writing skills; they need specific, focused suggestions. Diagnostic statements help students deal with aspects of their writing such as style, organization, length, sentence fragments and run-ons, capitalization, spelling, word choice, sentence structure and length, grammar, appearance, and penmanship (Page, 1958).

8.17   THE DECLINE IN WRITING ABILITY

Along with an achievement decline in most other curricular areas, the *NAEP* writing assessment revealed that the writing performance of middle and high school students declined between 1969 and 1974, rated both holistically and diagnostically (*NAEP,* 1976, p. 7). These findings stimulated interest in more systematic assessments of writing ability at the state and local levels, assessments that are often lacking because of the associated difficulties and costs.

The *NAEP* findings and the public allegations that "most high school graduates can't write" have resulted in the addition of writing tests to the College Board tests.

Task:

_____

Some people believe that a woman's place is in the home. Others do not. Take one side of this issue. Write an essay in which you state your position and defend it.

_____

Response I:

_____

One should not generalize about "a woman's place" because like men, a woman should have the choice of her profession. Being a housewife is like any other full time job which should be chosen by the individual. Keeping women in one profession is like telling all men to do the same job. In this way, our society would not be well rounded or prosper because of the imbalance. Women are human beings like men and should be given the full right of choice.

_____

Response II:

_____

A woman's place is not in the home. Woman (sic) are human beings, it is their God given right to pursue whatever career they desire. Life, liberty and the pursuit of happiness have been mentioned in the Declaration of Independence yet woman (sic) have been denied their rights in this sexist society. Not everyone wants to do the same job or pursue the same goals, must women be limited to a narrowly defined sphere of activity? No, a resounding no! We are people, human beings with as complex mental, emotional, physical needs as men, a fact ignored. We are regarded as the second sex, the incomplete sex, satisfied and made whole only by a family. And it is this false assumption shared by many men and women too, fostered by the society we live in that has destroyed many lives because people were not allowed to express the full range of their Godgiven gifts and creativity.

_____

FIGURE 8–2 A sample question designed to measure writing ability, with two illustrative responses.

SOURCE: National Assessment of Educational Progress, _NAEP Newsletter,_ 10 (1977).

Recent findings (College Entrance Exam Board, 1987, p. v) suggest that the achievement decline has bottomed out, perhaps due in part to the public outcry about the decline and the stimulus provided for the "back to basics" movement.

8.18 ESSAY TESTS IN COLLEGE ADMISSIONS

Until recently, the College Board offered only an unscored writing sample to interested colleges; it did not mark or grade the sample in any way. An essay task is now offered (but only each December) as part of the College Board's English composition test. The essays are scored holistically on a four-point scale by three carefully trained high school and college teachers.

The following description, used by the College Board, illustrates good practice in assessing writing ability. The explicit directions and expectations reduce the influence of test-wiseness on essay tasks.

> The Writing Sample, as its name suggests, is an essay-writing exercise which provides colleges with direct evidence of your competence in written expression. You are given one hour to write an essay on a single assigned topic, and copies of your essay, exactly as written, are sent to your school and to the colleges you specify at the time you write the essay. Here is an example of the kind of topic you will be asked to write on if you are requested by a college to take the Writing Sample:
>
> > "Loyalty is a quality which, in the abstract, we delight to honor. In practice, however, it is something that may vary with circumstances and conditions. There is 'loyalty among thieves,' 'loyalty to an ideal, to country, or to cause.'" Define your concept of loyalty and arrive at a principle regarding its use or abuse.
>
> *DIRECTIONS*: Express your ideas in a well-planned essay of 300 to 500 words, using several paragraphs to organize your discussion. Your point of view should be supported by and illustrated from your own experience, or by appropriate references to your reading, study, or observation. Be specific. You are expected to express your best thought in your best natural manner. After you have written your essay, *underline the sentence which you think comes closest to summarizing your central idea.*

8.19   FIRST-DRAFT VERSUS FINAL-DRAFT SKILLS

The curricular objectives in writing skills are complex. We want students to be able to write clearly, but is it "first-draft" or "final-draft" excellence that should be emphasized? Important writing skills such as those required for reports and business are not first-draft competencies. Some great novelists have stated that their efforts are polished through extensive revision before they achieve any special literary merit. This being the case, we will get closer to our ultimate objectives if, when measuring writing ability, we allow students the opportunity to revise and refine their initial efforts—to correct their punctuation, spelling, and sentence structure. In other words, rewriting and editing skills should not be ignored when assessing writing ability. First-draft writing ability is important, but final-draft writing skills are more important, especially as word processing technology has taken much of the pain out of the editing and retyping process.

8.20   CONTENT VALIDITY OF ESSAY TESTS IN OTHER CURRICULAR AREAS

Since measurement precision is a necessary condition for validity and since reader reliability is a prerequisite for test reliability, the factors that have been considered to limit reliability are also relevant to the validity of essay tests as measures of curricular areas other than writing. But there are additional concerns as well. Since the usual classroom essay examination in history, literature, or other curricular areas has only a few questions, it tends to have limited content validity as an achievement test. The limited subject-matter sampling of the essay test means that a large chance factor (sampling error) is operative in the selection of the questions that appear on the test. Suppose there are a large number of possible questions that might appear on a three-question test. The test might be an essay test in social studies or the three problems that comprise a math or physics test. Suppose you know the answers to only one-half the questions that could conceivably appear on the test. Assuming a random selection of the questions, there is one chance in eight that you will know the answers to all three questions that appear on the test; there is the same probability that the test will contain none of the problems that you can solve. This is a simplistic example because one probably knows something about most of the questions; nevertheless, it illustrates the large role that chance plays when tests consist of only a few questions. If objective tests are very short, they are subject to the same problem. Since short tests are usually less reliable than long ones, the limited sampling—that is, the small number of questions—tends to restrict the reliability of an essay test. Accurate inferences about a population cannot be made by polling only a very small sample; in like manner, an examinee's general level of mastery or understanding of a universe of content cannot be accurately estimated from a very few questions.

A more representative and valid sampling of the content universe can be obtained by increasing the number of questions and reducing the length of the discussion expected on each. In many cases a well-constructed paragraph is a sufficient answer. Few discussions need to exceed one or two pages. In any case, the question should be so worded as to restrict the responses toward the objective that is to be measured. For example, the question "Explain the reasons for the NFL strike in 1987" is too general; it would be improved if it were restricted by the addition of the phrases "to show (1) the grievances of the players, (2) the positions of the owners, (3) related economic factors, (4) the role of the players unions, and (5) the method of striking." Although such suggestions take away some of the "freedom" of the traditional essay examination, they will improve its validity and reliability. They make it less subjective and less susceptible to bluffing by test-wise examinees.

Coffman (1971) reported that a well-constructed 45-minute objective test provided as much information as three 45-minute essay questions, each read by a different reader. The essay scorer is confronted with many irrelevant factors, such as the quality of the spelling, handwriting, and English used, as well as bluffing.

8.21 ADVANTAGES OF ESSAY TESTS AS ACHIEVEMENT MEASURES

Even the most enthusiastic advocate of essay tests would not claim they can compare with objective tests in reliability for classroom testing purposes. The best that can be hoped is that by constructing a long test of several carefully focused questions with sample model answers to anchor rating categories we can make the reliability of essay tests satisfactory, even though it will still be below that of well-developed objective tests. Carefully developed essay exercises require much less time than a carefully developed objective test. The savings in time required to prepare essay tests, however, is more than offset by the extra time required to score them, which is extensive if the scores are to have much validity.

It is apparent that if the use of essay tests is to be justified, it must be for their superior value for certain purposes. What are the unique functions of these tests? If you want novel responses to divergent questions, such as "List in two minutes all the possible uses you can devise for a book," it seems necessary to seek free responses rather than to provide a large number of uses to be checked in some manner. Conversely, if you want to determine whether students can reason ingeniously to arrive at the *best* or *correct* solution, the multiple-choice format can be excellent. As noted earlier, research studies have generally failed to reveal much support for the popular contention that essay and objective tests measure different abilities, in spite of the great face validity of the essay exercise. Coffman, a leading authority on essay testing, has summarized the research on this point (1969, p. 10):

> It seems safe to conclude that the decision to use a particular type of question ought to be made on the basis of efficiency of the type for the particular situation and the skills of the test writer rather than in terms of a supposed uniqueness of the data to be obtained.

In several studies (see Coffman, 1972; Hakstian, 1971), students have reported that the kind of test they anticipate influences the study procedures they use. An opponent of objective tests (La Fave, 1964, p. 171) contended that "when preparing for multiple-choice tests the students probably spend more of their time memorizing facts; when preparing for essay exams, they will spend a considerably higher proportion of their time thinking about relations between facts, and with a problem-solving attitude." Hakstian (1971), in two separate experiments, failed to find that the kind of examination anticipated (essay, objective, or a combination) had bearing on performance on either carefully developed and scored essay tests or objective tests, even though the students reported some differences in their study emphases. More research is needed on this topic, especially for middle and high school students. There is no reason for a teacher not to use a combination of essay and objective questions; this seems to be preferred by a majority of students and teachers (Bracht, 1967; Hensley & Davis, 1952). When the essay exercises can be evaluated fairly, perhaps 20 to 25 percent of the testing time could be allocated to essay tasks in order to reap any accompanying instructional gain.

There has been little empirical research on the kind of examination preferred by students. Bracht (1967) found that only 13 percent of college students preferred essay examinations exclusively; twice that number (26%) preferred entirely objective tests; and most (61%) preferred that the test format be part objective and part essay. Not surprisingly, there was a very high relationship between test preference and the kind of examination on which the student perceived his or her performance to be better. However, it was found that those who preferred essay examinations and those who preferred objective examinations performed equally well on both kinds of tests.

Stanley and Beeman (1956) found that college students from most curricular areas did equally well on the objective and essay portions of a final examination in educational psychology. However, mathematics and science majors performed slightly better on the objective part, whereas English majors did slightly better on the essay portion.

8.22   IMPROVING THE DEVELOPMENT AND USE OF ESSAY TESTS

Although the essay test predates the objective test (in research early in this century, "new-type" test was a synonym for objective tests), far less research has been devoted to free-response testing than to objective testing. Furthermore, much of the research relating to essay tests has been conducted with poor, unimproved versions. However, a study of the meager experimental literature does yield several positive suggestions that, if employed, would substantially increase the validity and reliability of essay examinations.

It is just as important to know *when* to use the essay test as it is to know *how* to use it. It is wise to restrict the use of the essay test to the measurement of those organizing and expressive abilities for which it is best adapted. There seems to be no good reason for employing subjective measurement when objective tests measure the same abilities as validly. Please note, however, that we are dealing with its use for measurement and evaluation purposes. For instructional purposes, it is important for students to be continually required to express their thoughts in writing, irrespective of the measurement limitations of such exercises.

Weidemann (1933, 1941) distinguished among 11 definable types of test items. Arranged in a series from simple to complex, they are (1) what, who, when, which, and where; (2) list; (3) outline; (4) describe; (5) contrast; (6) compare; (7) explain; (8) discuss; (9) develop; (10) summarize; and (11) evaluate. Items of the first two types are in the knowledge level of Bloom's taxonomy; the others are geared to at least the comprehension level.

Essay questions can be divided into many types. The categories devised many years ago by Monroe and Carter (1923) remain appropriate. Several of these categories, together with sample questions from the field of measurement, are given below:

1. *Selective recall—basis given*
   Name three important developments in psychological measurement that occurred during the first decade of the twentieth century.
2. *Evaluation recall—basis given*
   Name the three persons who have had the greatest influence on the development of intelligence testing.
3. *Comparison of two things on a single designated basis*
   Compare essay tests and objective tests from the standpoint of their effect on the study procedures used by the learner.
4. *Comparison of two things, in general*
   Compare standardized and nonstandardized tests in terms of their proper educational uses.
5. *Decision—for or against*
   In your opinion, which are better for educational evaluation, oral or written examinations? (Sometimes this kind of question appears as "What is your favorite *X* and why?" In this case nothing is scorable but the mechanics of composition. Notice that "why" is ambiguous because it may call either for an account of the student's psychological development or for a list of qualities of *X* that have special appeal for him or her. There is no justification for scoring the *opinion*, since it was asked for and given.)
6. *Cause or effect*
   How do you account for the increased popularity of objective tests during the last 50 years?
7. *Explanation of the use or exact meaning of some word, phrase, or statement*
   What is the meaning of *objective* in the preceding question?

8. *Summary of some unit of the textbook or of some article read*
   Summarize in not more than 100 words the advantages and limitations of essay tests. Here is an example of a possible response:

   > The essay test has a long and controversial history, with strong support from some quarters and equally strong criticism from other groups. The essay test has certain distinct advantages and other disadvantages—it can be used properly, but can also be abused; it has its strengths and it has its weaknesses. . . .

   (Notice that in more than 50 words the above response has not revealed any useful information about the question. Any test-wise student could have written such a response without having any specific knowledge regarding the question to be addressed.)

9. *Analysis* (the word itself seldom appears in the question)
   Why are many so-called intellectuals suspicious of standardized tests?

10. *Statement of relationships*
    Why do nearly all essay tests, regardless of the school subject, tend to a considerable extent to be measures of the learner's mastery of English?

11. *Illustrations or examples (the students' own) of principles in science*
    Give two common examples of the Bernoulli effect.

12. *Classification*
    What type of error appears in the following test item? "With what country did the United States fight during World War II?"

13. *Application of rules, laws, or principles to new situations*
    In the light of the United States' experience using examinations in college admissions decisions, what public-relations problem would you expect to arise in developing nations as they begin to use tests in the selection of college students?

14. *Discussion*
    Discuss the role of Sir Francis Galton in the development of the Pearson product-moment coefficient of correlation.

15. *Statement of an author's purpose in the selection or organization of material*
    Why are individual mental tests not treated in greater detail in this book?

16. *Criticism—as to the adequacy, correctness, or relevance of a printed statement, or to a classmate's answer to a question on the lesson*
    Criticize or defend the statement, "The essay test overrates the importance of knowing *how* to say a thing and underrates the importance of having something to say." ("To criticize" assumes a set of standards, given or known.)

17. *Outline*
    Outline the principal steps in the construction of an informal teacher-made test.

18. *Reorganization of facts (a good type of review question to provide training in organization*
    Name five practical suggestions from this book that are particularly applicable in evaluating the subject you teach or plan to teach.

19. *Formulation of new questions—problems and questions raised*
    What are some problems relating to the use of essay tests that require further study?

20. *New methods of procedure*
   Suggest a plan for proving the truth or falsity of the contention that exemption from semester examinations for the ablest students is good policy in high school.
21. *Inferential thinking*
   Is the author of this book likely to use essay tests frequently in measurement classes?

Notice that these examples can distinguish several rather distinct abilities that *can* potentially be measured by carefully prepared and scored essay tests. Most of these same abilities can probably be assessed by creatively developed objective exercises.

Many teachers, especially beginning teachers, believe that the essay test is the easiest kind to construct. *It requires careful thought to construct essay tests of high quality.* Much care and planning must be given to their construction if they are to measure anything but mere memory for factual knowledge. Many of the general principles of testing outlined in Chapters 7 and 9 are as applicable to essay tests as they are to objective tests. The special suggestions of this chapter should help you devise essay questions that assess objectives above the knowledge level of Bloom's taxonomy. Finally, it is quite possible that, in attempting to phrase essay questions so that they can be answered more specifically and scored more objectively, the results may not be as good as those of an objective test. In any case, it is especially important that the test be reviewed by a colleague if possible.

8.23 PREPARING STUDENTS TO TAKE ESSAY TESTS

Several writers have emphasized the importance of *training* students to take examinations of all kinds. This training can be done well by teachers in classrooms. Wider experience and training in preparing for and taking tests of all kinds is likely to increase accuracy of measurement and, therefore, the fairness of scores for the students tested. For essay tests, students should be taught the meanings of the words used in the various types of thought questions. They should be taught that *compare* requires a statement of similarities *and* differences and that the answer to such an item is not complete if it omits either. *Contrast* requires only a statement of differences.

Examinees should be taught to apportion their testing time wisely so as to avoid spending most of it on one or two questions. A thorough and excellent response to one question will almost never receive as much credit as good, but less elaborate, responses to two questions. Students should be cautioned about poor penmanship and the general appearance of their product. They should be aware that teachers apparently cannot ignore spelling and grammatical errors in their grading. They should be told to do their best to respond to every question even if their knowledge is fragmentary. As indicated previously, the length of an essay response tends to have an important relationship to its rated merit. There probably is at least as much test-wiseness in taking an essay test as in taking an objective test. If students are instructed in the *tricks of the trade,* the magnitude of irrelevant effects will be minimized, particularly if the scorers also are acquainted with these factors.

8.24 CONSTRUCTING GOOD ESSAY TESTS

Suggestions for the construction and use of essay examinations include the following items.

1. *Make definite provisions for preparing students for taking essay examinations.* Specific training in preparing for and taking examinations of the kinds commonly encountered is a legitimate objective of instruction. Perhaps the best way is to find or devise good practice tests, administer them, and discuss the results with the students.

2. *Make sure that questions are carefully focused.* The following questions present freedom not only to students but also to graders: "What are the advantages of individualized instruction?" "Discuss collective bargaining." Structure is needed or the student may miss the intent of the question (Coffman, 1971). A common ploy of test-wise students is to appear to have "misunderstood" the intent of the question and to emphasize those aspects with which they are thoroughly familiar.

3. *The content and length of essay questions need to be structured.* Structure can increase the number of questions and reduce the amount of discussion required on each. Such a plan permits a better sampling of the content and, at the same time, allows the responses to be read with greater reliability; both of these increase the validity of the examination.

4. *Have a colleague review and critique the essay questions.* The composer of a question is in a particular frame of reference that often prevents him or her from seeing the intrinsic ambiguity and potential misinterpretations that are readily apparent to another person. In addition, an opinion should be sought about (a) the emphases and breadth of coverage, (b) the appropriateness of difficulty of the questions, and (c) the adequacy of the model answers. The small amount of effort required will reap disproportionately large dividends.

5. *The use of optional questions should ordinarily be avoided, except when one is assessing writing ability where a choice of questions is desirable.* All students should take the same test if their scores are to be compared. On the College Board Advanced Placement Program examination in American history, students write on 3 of 12 possible topics. Even though the questions were devised to be of approximately equal difficulty, the means and standard deviations on the questions vary considerably (Coffman, 1971, pp. 289–291). In studying British students taking an important essay examination in which a choice among five questions was offered, it was found that the more able students tended to choose three of the questions, while the less able students tended to choose the other two (Wiseman & Wrigley, 1958). The question that is easiest to write on may not be the question on which it is easiest to obtain a high score; questions are intrinsically different in difficulty. An examinee's score should not depend on which questions one elects to answer. However, as previously stated, if the intent is to measure writing ability, the tasks should be free of subject matter, since content mastery is incidental to the purpose at hand.

6. *Restrict the use of the essay as an achievement test to those objectives for which it is best.* The testing time required for students to write answers to a representative sample of questions and the time required to obtain satisfactory reader and test reliability are

extensive. Nevertheless, the essay examination remains the preferred method of obtaining evidence of the candidate's ability in some contexts. When it is not clear that an essay test is required for measuring the desired instructional objective, use an objective test.

7. *The use of essay exercises for instructional purposes should not be confused with their measurement merits.* In fact, Pidgeon and Yates (1957, p. 38) reported that students in some primary schools in England that had eliminated essay examinations *because of their weaknesses as evaluation measures* frequently needed remedial instruction in written expression in the secondary schools. It is unlikely that one can learn to write well, one of the 3*R*s, without considerable writing and feedback.

8. *For general achievement testing, several shorter questions are usually preferable to fewer longer questions.* One of the greatest limitations of essay tests is the small number of samples of the content universe they provide. More, shorter tasks have greater reliability than fewer, longer tasks for the same amount of testing time (Coffman, 1972). When a test contains few questions, a significant chance factor is injected. A small gap in a student's knowledge may carry undue weight. This difficulty is also common in math and physical sciences, where tests tend to have few problems or questions. Even though tests in math and the like often have high scorer reliability (objectivity), they may not be an adequate sample of the content universe (i.e., have high reliability or validity) if they contain only a few questions or exercises. This also suggests that frequent short tests will aggregate to a more superior measure than fewer longer tests.

8.25 IMPROVING THE GRADING OF ESSAY TESTS

Strictly speaking, it is more correct to speak of grading or rating essay examinations than it is to speak of scoring them; *grading* is interpreting quality subjectively in terms of a criterion.

All claims regarding the value of the essay test as a measuring instrument are based on the assumption that the test papers can be read accurately. For example, not only must the essay test elicit from more able students responses that are consistently superior, but the teachers marking the papers must be able to *recognize* consistently that the responses are better.

A common procedure for evaluating essay exercises as achievement tests (i.e., not as measures of writing ability) can be taught in 10 minutes. It is noteworthy that the majority of the consistency coefficients of two series of scores made five weeks apart on highly structured essay tests tend to be quite high (above .75) for teachers with 10 minutes of training. Independent scores by experienced readers showed high agreement when the following procedure (given here in a slightly modified and abridged form) was used.

1. Before scoring any papers, review the material in the textbook that covers the questions and also the lecture notes on the subject.
2. Make a list of the main points that should be discussed in every answer. Each of these points must be weighed and assigned a certain value if the scoring is to approach accuracy.

3. Read over a sampling of the papers to obtain a general idea of the quality of answers that may be expected.

4. *Score* one *question through all of the papers before evaluating another question.* There are two outstanding advantages to this procedure. First, the comparison of answers appears to make the ratings more exact and fair. Second, having to keep only one model answer or list of points in mind saves time and improves accuracy.

5. *Read the answer through once and then check it over for factual details.* Attempt to mark every mistake on the paper and write in the correction briefly. As the answer is read, make a mental note of the points that were omitted and the value of each point, so that at the end of the question you have the minimum grade figured. If there is any additional or extra percentage to be given, it is added to the minimum score, and then the value of the question is written in terms of the percent deducted rather than the positive percent. Then, when every question on a paper has been scored, it is a simple matter to add the negative quantities. From this weighted sum one can assign the final grade. The use of illustrative answers for various anchor points is an important calibration activity (see the following section) that decreases the "slide effect" (see Section 8.11) and increases agreement among raters.

6. *More than one reader is always desirable and should be employed when practical.* Two ratings, even if they are made rapidly in order to allow time for rating more papers, are generally preferable to a single rating (Coffman, 1972, p. 7). Three or more are even better.

The importance of the following three essential steps to improve essay testing cannot be overemphasized.

1. Prepare in advance a list of points that are desirable in terms of the objectives of the test.
2. Assign a specific value to each essential part of each answer.
3. Grade one question through all the papers before going on to another question.

8.26 THE USE OF ANCHOR POINTS IN SCORING

The procedure for using anchor points is similar to that used in evaluating handwriting (see Figure 8–1) in relation to illustrated samples along a continuum of proficiency within which there are illustrative examples to "calibrate" the scale at various anchor points. The reader can then judge each essay against these five products rather than a less clearly defined *A-F* scale or some other grading scale. The procedure is as follows:

1. Read quickly through Question 1 on many, if not all, of the papers and sort them into groups: (a) very superior papers, (b) superior papers, (c) average papers, (d) inferior papers, (e) very inferior papers.
2. Reread the papers in each group and select one that is typical of each.
3. Read the papers and compare them to the five anchor point papers. Through the use of + and – markings, a 15-point scale can be developed even though only five anchor points are used.
4. Repeat the procedure for each essay question.

Bear in mind that an equal number of papers in each category is not to be expected. Flanagan (1952) showed that when the ability being measured is normally distributed, the percentages for the five groups are 9, 20, 42, 20, and 9. Therefore, about 10 percent of the papers might be called "very superior" and 10 percent "very inferior." Twenty percent would be "superior" and a like percentage "inferior." The remaining 40 percent are "average." These are rough approximations, of course, depending on the ability level of the particular student group being graded. The assumption of a normal distribution often is not appropriate; the reader should not feel obligated to "normalize" the ratings. For example, perhaps there are few or no papers that are very inferior.

8.27 ANONYMITY

The simple precaution of having the students write their names inconspicuously either on the back or at the end of the paper, rather than at the top of each page, will also decrease the bias with which the paper is graded. When teachers know the handwriting of their students, this problem cannot easily be avoided. If two teachers have common assignments, perhaps they could exchange papers for essay grading if only one reading is feasible. Without anonymity, the halo effect is almost certain to contaminate the essay grades.

8.28 STYLE

Each teacher should adopt a policy regarding what factors should and should not be considered in evaluating a written examination. *Only those factors should be taken into account that afford evidence of the degree to which the student has attained the objectives for that particular course.* Except in English classes, this minimizes the penalties associated with such things as faulty sentence structure, poor paragraphing, bad handwriting, and misspelling of nontechnical words. These factors will be considered only when they affect the clarity of the student's discussion. It is always legitimate to hold the student responsible for the spelling, as well as the meaning, of terms that are part of the curricular objectives, but writing ability should not be what is being measured in most essay tests.

This does not mean that the quality of the written English used in examinations is unimportant and should therefore be disregarded; on the contrary, it is always very important. But it should be considered in determining students' marks in English, not how well they understand physics or economics.

8.29 PROPER USE OF ESSAY EXERCISES

We have stressed repeatedly that, despite the limitations of essay tests, especially as they are ordinarily used in American schools, such tests should be an essential *part* of instructional activities. To a lesser extent, they are useful for measuring and evaluating objectives in most curricular areas. On the other hand, do not avoid using objective testing because of the attacks on such tests that have been published by well-intentioned intellectuals. Such attacks confuse assessment with teaching. The two are related, of course, but have clearly different aims. Compositions, essays, and discussion questions that prove to be poor *tests* may nevertheless be excellent instructional activities. If the teacher goes through an essay carefully and makes constructive remarks, perhaps followed by oral discussion, the student may benefit greatly even if no grade is assigned. If, however, teachers merely mark the paper *A, B,* or the like without comment, the grading may be highly unreliable, and also the students probably will not learn how to improve their skills. It is possible to do both—that is, grade and comment—in which event the comments may be helpful even if the grading is unreliable (Page, 1958).

SUMMARY

Even though essay tests have face validity for students, professionals, and laypersons, alike, as typically used in education they tend to be characterized by moderate scorer reliability and limited test reliability, both of which are essential (but not sufficient) for test validity. Scoring is often contaminated by factors of marginal relevance such as neatness, penmanship, length of response, halo effect, item-to-item carrover effects, and test-wiseness. Essay tests can be scored reliably, but the time costs are substantial.

The quality of essay tests can be improved if questions are carefully structured in content and length and if all students write on the same set of questions. If possible, scoring should be done anonymously. One question should be evaluated on all papers, using prototypical papers to anchor and define the various grading categories, before the next question is graded. More than one rater is highly desirable. Writing essays may be important instructional experiences, apart from their use as evaluation devices.

IMPORTANT TERMS AND CONCEPTS

test-wiseness
test reliability
halo effect
carryover effect

model answer
slide effect
objective tests
bluffing

reader (scorer) reliability
face validity
anchor (calibration)

CHAPTER TEST

1. What is the order in which the following types of tests appear to have been used for the first time in educational evaluation?
   a) Essay, Oral, Multiple-choice
   b) Oral, Multiple-choice, Essay
   c) Multiple-choice, Oral, Essay
   d) Essay, Multiple-choice, Oral
   e) Oral, Essay, Multiple-choice

Questions 2–15. Match the test characteristic with the test format(s) for which it is typical. Answer oral , essay, and/or objective.

2. The scoring of students' responses is quite subjective.

3. The halo effect can easily influence scoring.

4. Students' questions are of unequal difficulty (1 or 2 options).

5. The effect of guessing (not bluffing) is greatest.

6. Bluffing can influence the results.

7. It is difficult to obtain satisfactory test reliability.

8. The potential for measuring originality and creativity is usually rather limited.

9. Evaluations are not contaminated by language fluency.

10. The test is easy to score accurately.

11. The test can measure the ability to solve problems.

12. Scoring is influenced by penmanship.

13. Scoring is influenced by spelling ability.

14. The test requires the most time to develop.

15. The test can be scored quickly.

16. In which one of the following ways are essay tests superior to objective tests?
    a) better samples the universe of content
    b) higher face validity
    c) higher test reliability
    d) less influenced by test-wiseness

17. On essay tests, which of the following two characteristics tends to be higher?
    a) reader (scorer) reliability
    b) test reliability

18. On objective tests, scorer reliability should be approximately
    a) 0.0.
    b) .50.
    c) 1.0.

19. Is it possible to have high test reliability without high scorer reliability?

20. Is it possible to have high reader reliability with low test reliability?

Questions 21–28 pertain to the grading of essay tests.

Select the appropriate option (a-d); options may be used more than once.
    a) Halo effect
    b) Carryover effect
    c) Slide effect
    d) None of these

21. the tendency for tests that are read early to be given higher marks than those read later

22. the tendency for performance on Item 1 to influence the scoring of Item 2

23. the tendency for longer responses to be given higher grades

24. a problem with computer scoring of essay tests
25. the tendency for grades to be influenced by irrelevant characteristics of the examinee
26. can be prevented if questions are graded independently
27. may be prevented if essays are graded anonymously
28. Which two can be reduced if essays are scored in a different order for each question?
29. Which of the following essay tests would probably have the highest reliability?
    a) 500 words on one question
    b) 250 words on each of two questions
    c) 100 words on each of 5 questions
30. Research indicates that teachers tend to evaluate essays mainly for content and are influenced little by errors in grammar, spelling, or punctuation. (*T* or *F*)
31. Research indicates that
    a) more students prefer essay tests than objective tests.
    b) students prefer the type of test on which they think they do best.
    c) students who prefer essay tests do relatively better on such tests than they do on objective tests.
    d) students report that they prepare similarly for both essay and objective tests.
32. Many essay tests measure only at the knowledge level, not at the higher levels of Bloom's taxonomy. (*T* or *F*).
33. An essay question such as "Write a summary of this chapter in 300 words or less" is an example of a question that requires mastery only at the knowledge level in terms of Bloom's taxonomy. (*T* or *F*).
34. If the parallel-form reliability of a two-question essay test is .40, estimate the reliability if Forms A and B are combined into a single four-question test. Recall that
$$\rho_{(A+B)} = \frac{2\rho_{AB}}{1 + \rho_{AB}} .$$
35. If the length of the test in Question 34 is increased to eight questions, estimate its reliability.
36. The authors believe that test-wiseness skills for essay tests should be taught to students (*T* or *F*).

Questions 37–46. Which of the following are generally desirable practices in essay testing? (Yes or No)

37. Provide optional questions.
38. Frame questions to allow examinees maximum freedom in interpretation.
39. Use several shorter questions rather than one or two longer ones.
40. Use essay tests to measure facts.
41. Use model answers in scoring.
42. Grade by sorting into not more than three groups.
43. Reread questions after preliminary sorting.
44. Have more than one reader grade the papers.

45. Keep identity of student in mind while grading the paper.

46. Give extra credit for good penmanship and neatness.

ANSWERS TO CHAPTER TEST

1. e
2. oral and essay
3. oral and essay
4. oral (also essay if the examinee has a choice of questions)
5. objective
6. oral and essay
7. oral and essay
8. objective
9. objective
10. objective
11. oral, essay, and objective
12. essay
13. essay
14. objective
15. objective
16. b
17. a
18. c
19. no
20. yes
21. c
22. b
23. d

24. d
25. a
26. b
27. a
28. b, c
29. c
30. F
31. B
32. T
33. F
34. .57
35. .73
36. T
37. No
38. No
39. Yes
40. No
41. Yes
42. No
43. Yes
44. Yes
45. No
46. No

9

Constructing Objective Tests

9.1   INTRODUCTION

In Chapter 7 we considered general principles for constructing items designed to measure cognitive objectives. In this chapter specific guidelines and procedures for writing achievement items of several types will be developed. This chapter can be one of the most important in the book; if test items are prepared insightfully and skillfully, a more valid evaluation of educational objectives will result, which in turn leads to improved instructional design.

No amount of statistical hocus-pocus will transform poor items into good ones, but techniques such as item analysis (see Chapter 10) are helpful in identifying items that should be eliminated or revised.

9.2   FIXED-RESPONSE ITEMS

In fixed-response items the examinee is offered only a limited number of response options. Fixed-response items include multiple-choice, true-false, and matching questions. Advantages of the fixed-response test include (1) applicability to a wide range of subject matter, (2) objectivity of scoring, and (3) efficiency (wide sampling of the content universe per unit of working time). The most common type of fixed-response item is the multiple-choice question. It is used in most published tests. Here is an example from a social studies test:

1. The House of Representatives has the authority, within limits, to determine who shall become President in case
   a) no candidate receives a majority of the popular votes.
   b) no candidate receives a majority of the electoral votes.
   c) no candidate receives a majority of both the popular and electoral votes.
   d) the elected candidate dies before he can be inaugurated.

Only one of the four options correctly completes the *stem* (the part of the item that precedes the options). The other incorrect options are designed to be attractive to uninformed examinees and are known as *distracters*. For an item to be an effective measure of who does, and does not, deserve credit for the item, distracters must be plausible and tempting to examinees who do not know the correct answer. Indeed, *the single most important skill in constructing good multiple-choice items is the ability to devise plausible, attractive distracters*.

9.3   MULTIPLE-CHOICE ITEMS

Multiple-choice items are sometimes viewed simply as "recognition" items capable of testing only rote facts—to assess only objectives at the knowledge level of Bloom's taxonomy. But they can measure higher taxonomy levels, as was illustrated in Chapter 7. A straightforward arithmetic reasoning item such as "How many minutes will it take you to jog to school if you live one mile from school and jog at a speed of ten miles per hour?" illustrates the application level of Bloom's taxonomy. The question can be asked either with no options being provided or with several options from which the examinee must choose the one correct option. Research indicates that whether or not options are provided, the skills required to answer the above question are at the application level (Traub & Fisher, 1977). The fact that approximately 20 percent of naive examinees may select the correct answer by chance if there are five options does not alter this fact. As was demonstrated earlier (see Section 6.12), chance alone will not allow uninformed examinees to earn extremely high scores even on short multiple-choice tests. For example, on a five-item four-option multiple-choice test, the probability that a naive examinee will obtain a score of 100 percent is less than 1 in 1000 (i.e., $.2^5 = .00032$).

Multiple-choice items typically present two or more options, one of which is correct or definitely better than the others.

9.4   RATIONALE FOR THE MULTIPLE-CHOICE ITEM

Most people assume that multiple-choice tests are popular simply because they are easy to score. Their major virtues, however, are that they can (1) require the examinee to *discriminate* among alternatives that can require a level of mastery that a free-response item may not be able to detect, and (2) remove ambiguity and subjectivity in scoring. The "best-answer" type of multiple-choice item can measure the degree of understanding of abstract concepts. Consider the following item.

2. Which one of the following changes would be expected to *reduce* the test-retest reliability coefficient of a test of 50 items by the greatest amount when no examinee omits any item?
   a) Eliminate the ten items that were answered correctly by all examinees.
   b) Eliminate the ten most difficult items.
   c) Eliminate the ten items that correlated negatively with the total score.
   d) Use the correction-for-chance in scoring.
   e) Base the test-retest correlation only on examinees who scored above the median on the initial test.

If one thoroughly understands the concept of reliability and the factors that influence it, one should be able to determine that option *e* is clearly the *best* answer. Option *a* has virtually no effect on reliability. These ten items serve only to add a constant to all scores. Option *b* would be expected to lower reliability somewhat. Option *c* would be expected to improve reliability. Option *d* would have little effect, because when taking a pure power test, all examinees have enough time to mark all items about which they have some knowledge.

Items like Item 2 can determine whether a concept is mastered or whether the examinee's understanding is incomplete. The item will seem ambiguous to students whose understanding is incomplete—this kind of ambiguity is termed *extrinsic ambiguity*. Extrinsic ambiguity is a desirable characteristic of a test—comprehension and application items should appear ambiguous to those who have a faulty grasp of the concept being tested.

9.5 AMBIGUOUS VERSUS TRICK QUESTIONS

It is important to distinguish between ambiguous and trick questions. Knowledgeable examinees may miss trick questions because they fail to perceive a trivial detail. Consider the following trick question.

> **3.** If you bought 3 candy bars each costing 15 cents, how much change should you get back from $1.00?
> a) $.65   b) .55¢   c) $0.45   d) None of these

Some examinees who have mastered the relevant skills will miss the item because they failed to attend to the decimal point. Other examples of trick questions include trivial misspelling of names or forms and confusing use of negatives. Trick questions are never justified.

9.6 INTRINSIC VERSUS EXTRINSIC AMBIGUITY

Test makers may introduce irrelevant ambiguities by attempting to make too fine a distinction, thus making valid discrimination among options impossible. Such items illustrate *intrinsic ambiguity*, a highly undesirable characteristic. For example, suppose in Item 2 that option *e* was excluded. The knowledgeable student would be at a loss to choose between options *b* and *d*—the item would possess intrinsic ambiguity. Fortunately, intrinsic ambiguity can usually be identified when an item analysis is conducted (see Chapter 10).

In other words, there are two possible types of ambiguity in test items. Ambiguity extrinsic to the item itself is a result of faulty understanding on the part of the examinee. Ambiguity inherent in the item itself (i.e., intrinsic ambiguity) can result from imprecise wording or inadequate framing of the items such that distinctions are asked for that cannot be made validly from the information available even by experts. *Intrinsically* ambiguous items should be revised or eliminated because they reduce the reliability and validity of tests. On the other hand, *extrinsically* ambiguous questions increase reliability and validity—their ambiguity is the fault of the uninformed examinees, not the item.

In attempting to avoid intrinsic ambiguity, test makers sometimes construct multiple-choice items that are so easy that little understanding is needed to identify the correct answer.

Comprehension and application level items are more vulnerable to intrinsic ambiguity because they are more apt to be dealing with concepts and skills rather than facts. Consider the following item:

> **4.** What is the most important characteristic of a test?
> *a) high validity   b) large number of items   c) large number of difficult items

This item is trivial, since it requires only a primitive level of understanding to select the correct answer. Distracters *b* and *c* are not plausible. If an item is to serve its purpose, the distracters must seem plausible to examinees with an inadequate grasp of the concepts being tested . What if two more options—*d*, good norms, and *e*, high reliability—were added to Item 4? The item could then identify examinees with a greater level of mastery, such as an understanding of the difference between validity and reliability. A skillful test constructor must be able to role-play mentally the part of examinees with faulty mastery in order to develop attractive distracters.

9.7   INVERSE MULTIPLE-CHOICE ITEMS

One can also use the multiple-choice item to require the student to select the poorest or least accurate option in a set. Suppose, for example, that on a vocabulary test examinees are asked

> **5.** Which of the following terms is *least* synonymous with the others?
> a) contemplate   b) cogitate   c) comprehend   d) ponder   e) cerebrate

Option *c,* comprehend, has the least semantic overlap with the others and would be identified by examinees who correctly understand the meanings of the various words. Notice how much greater the measurement richness of Item 5 is than the related free-response item: Define contemplate.

Of course, in Item 5 if *comprehend* were replaced by a word such as *disseminate* or *irritate,* the item would function at a more primitive level, since *disseminate* and *irritate* have no semantic overlap with the other terms.

What if the stem of Item 5 were changed to "Which one of the following terms is most similar in meaning to *ruminate*?" The item might be intrinsically ambiguous because there does not appear to be an option that is clearly better than all others.

The multiple-choice item is usually regarded as the most valuable and most generally applicable test form. Years ago the famous measurement trailblazer, E. F. Lindquist, asserted that the multiple-choice item is "definitely superior to all other types" for measuring such educational objectives as "inferential reasoning, reasoned understanding, or sound judgment and discrimination on the part of the pupil." It remains so today. Another leading psychometrician (Cronbach, 1950) demonstrated that multiple-choice items are less vulnerable to response sets than other types of items.

But it is the quality of the items, not the type of item employed, that determines a good test. Some multiple-choice items are so poor that they can be answered correctly by attending to irrelevant clues; others measure only isolated or trivial facts. We emphasize again that *the measurement value of multiple-choice tests depends more on the skillful selection of distracters within items than on any other factor.*

9.8 ILLUSTRATIONS OF MULTIPLE-CHOICE ITEMS[1]

The following items, most of which are taken from various standardized tests, illustrate several different arrangements of multiple-choice tests in a variety of subjects. The multiple-choice test is widely used in all school subjects and on all educational levels for measuring a variety of teaching objectives.

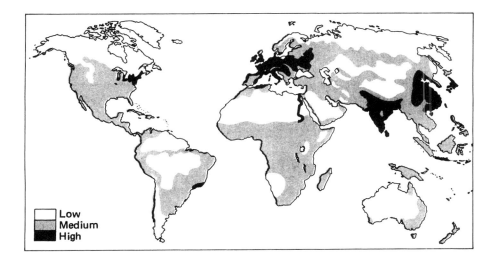

6. The shading on the above map is used to indicate
   a) population density.
   b) percentage of total labor force in agriculture.
   c) per capita income.
   d) death rate per thousand of population.

In many of the multiple-choice questions included in social science tests, an attempt is made to require the student to make use of general knowledge in the interpretation of materials. Thus, this question does not simply ask, "What areas of the world have the highest population densities?" Rather, it presents a novel situation in which the student must infer that, of the choices offered, only population density provides a plausible explanation of the shading on the map.

[1]The first three of the illustrative items that follow are from *Multiple-Choice Questions: A Close Look*. Copyright 1963 by Educational Testing Service. All rights reserved. Reproduced by permission.

7. The graph below represents the political composition from 1922 to 1955 of which of the following?
   a) German Bundestag
   b) French National Assembly
   c) Italian Chamber of Deputies
   d) British House of Commons

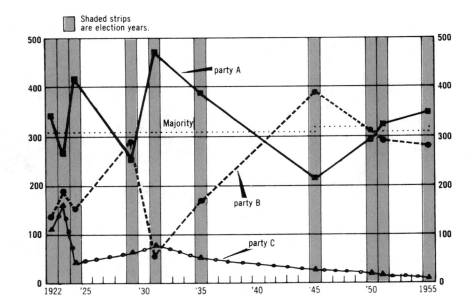

To answer this question correctly, students must be able to do several things. First, they must be able to read the graph. Then, using the information they can infer from it, they must interpret it in the light of their knowledge of European history and government from 1922 to 1955 and draw a conclusion concerning which legislative body may properly be depicted. In such a process it is possible for different students to make use of different information to arrive at the correct answer.

8. One method of obtaining "artificial gravity" in a space station (see figure below) is to have the station rotating about axis AA' as it revolves around Earth. The inhabitants of the space station would call which direction "down"?

a) direction 1   b) direction 2   c) direction 3   d) direction 4

e) any one of the four, depending on speed of rotation

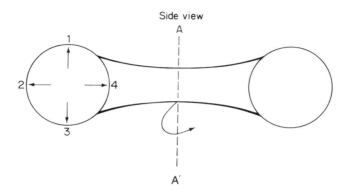

This was part of a set of questions administered to students who were completing a year of high school physics. The question illustrates the kind of response that can be expected of well-trained students of high school age when they are presented with a relatively novel situation based on fundamental concepts from the field of mechanics.

This question requires that the student consider the nature of a possible mechanism for providing a "down" direction in a space station to simulate the gravitational "down" that is so important in our normal activities on Earth. Choice *c* is the direction normally considered "down" in diagrams. Although this direction is not significant in the space station, a sizable number of the poorer physics students chose it. Other students assumed that the "down" direction would be toward the center of rotation of the station, choice *d*. However, objects that are free to move in the space station behave like particles in a centrifuge and "fall" to the outer edge. The direction *b* is the "down" direction in the rotating station. The other choices, *a* and *e,* were not selected by many students.

Sequential Tests of Educational Progress[2]

9. What is the main point of the cartoon below?
  a) Labor-management disputes often lead to violence.
  b) The government is powerless to stop strikes.
  c) Farmers lack a sufficient voice in national politics.
  d) The public often suffers in labor-management conflicts.

"In these disputes, I find myself in an unfortunate position!"

Metropolitan Achievement Tests, Language[3]

> I   We arrived at the bus station early.
> II Everyone wants a seat by a window.

10. An adverb in these sentences is–
  E early   **F** bus   **G** everyone   **H** by

11. A past tense verb in these sentences is–
  A station   **B** wants   **C** the   **D** arrived

The Modern School Achievement Tests, Language Usage[4]

                1. **off**

12. I borrowed a pen 2. **off of** my brother.

                3. **from**

                1. **your**

13. Every student must do 2. **his** best.

                3. **their**

             1. **has got**

14. He 2. **has** his violin with him.

             3. **has gotten**

The Barrett-Ryan Literature Test: Silas Marner[5]

15. ( ) An episode that advances the plot is the—1. murdering of a man. 2. kidnapping of a child. 3. stealing of money. 4. fighting of a duel.

16. ( ) A chief characteristic of the novel is—1. humorous passages. 2. portrayal of character. 3. historical facts. 4. fairy element.

Wesley Test in Political Terms[6]

17. An embargo is

    1. a law of regulation.

    2. a kind of boat.

    3. an explorer.

    4. a foolish adventure.

    5. an embankment.

Unit Scales of Attainment in Foods and Household Management[7]

18. We get the most calories per pound from

    1. proteins.

    2. carbohydrates.

    3. fats.

    4. mineral matter.

    5. vitamins.

---

[4]Published by Teachers College Press.

[5]Published by Kansas State Teachers College, Emporia.

[6]Published by Charles Scribner's Sons, New York.

[7]Published by Educational Test Bureau.

College Board, Foreign-Language Items[8]

19. C'est la fin de l'entracte, et al pièce est très amusante. Vous dites à votre comarade:
 (A) La pièce va commencer tout de suite.
 (B) Qu'allons-nous faire maintenant?
 (C) Allons reprendre nos places.
 (D) Voulez-vous aller fumer une cigarette?

College Board, English Items

DIRECTIONS: The following sentences contain problems in grammar, usage, word choice, and idiom.
    Some sentences are correct.
    No sentence contains more than one error.
        You will find that the error, if any, will be underlined and lettered, and that all other elements of the sentence are correct and cannot be changed.
        If there is an error, select the *one underlined part* that must be changed in order to make the sentence correct, and blacken the corresponding space on your answer sheet.
        If there is no error, mark answer space *E*.

EXAMPLE: He spoke <u>bluntly</u> and <u>angrily</u> to <u>we</u> <u>spectators.</u> <u>No error</u>
           A   B   C   D   E

SAMPLE ANSWER: A   B   C   D   E
                          □   □   ■   □   □

---

20. <u>Had we known</u> of your desire to go with us, we <u>most</u> certainly <u>would of</u> invited you to
             A   B   C
     <u>join</u> our party. <u>No error</u>
        D   E

21. Big Konrad's new helper, though somewhat <u>slighter</u> of build than <u>him,</u> set out <u>to prove that</u>
                                                A   B   C
     skill <u>may</u> compensate for lack of brute strength. <u>No error</u>
           D   E

DIRECTIONS: Each group of sentences in this section is actually a paragraph presented in scrambled order. Each sentence in the group has a place in that paragraph; no sentence is to be left out. You are to read each group of sentences and decide the best order in which to put the sentences so as to form a well-organized paragraph.
        Before trying to answer the questions which follow each group of sentences, jot down the correct order of the sentences in the margin of the test book. Then answer each of the questions by blackening the appropriate space on the answer sheet. Remember that you will receive credit only for answers marked on the answer sheet . . .

---

[8]From *A Description of the College Board Achievement Tests* (Princeton, N.J.: College Entrance Examination Board, 1963).

Sample Paragraph

P. The Empire State Express, loaded with passengers, left new York.

Q. Unlike the businessmen, however, a few reporters on board had been told that this run would be newsworthy and were eagerly waiting for something unusual to occur.

R. At last the big day, May 10, arrived.

S. If some of the important businessmen on board had known what was going to happen, they might have found an excuse to leave the train at Albany.

T. Her secret had been carefully kept.

U. Only a few officials knew that a record was to be tried for.

CORRECT
ORDER
OF
SENTENCES
R
P
T

U
S
Q

Sample Questions

I. Which sentence did you put first?
  (A) P
  (B) R
  (C) S
  (D) T
  (E) U

II. Which sentence did you put after Sentence P?
  (A) Q
  (B) R
  (C) S
  (D) T
  (E) U

Cooperative Test of Social Studies Abilities, Experimental Form Q[9]

DIRECTIONS: The exercises in this part consist of a series of paragraphs each followed by several statements about the paragraph. In the parentheses after each statement, put the number

  1. if the statement is a reasonable interpretation, fully supported by the facts given in the paragraph.
  2. if the statement goes beyond and cannot be proved by the facts given in the paragraph.
  3. if the statement contradicts the facts given in the paragraph.

22. The nineteenth century witnessed a rapid growth in Germany's industrial power. Like England, Germany came to have a fairly satisfactory balance between the amounts of its export and import trade. Heavy exports of coke supplied full cargoes for ships to foreign ports and helped to balance heavy importations of raw materials. The imports especially provided a means of distributing freight rates to the advantage of the German trader competing overseas. By these means Germany was constantly obtaining larger portions of world trade. German wares were carried into every trading realm, and trade meant political as well as commercial power in foreign lands.

---

[9]Originally published by Cooperative Test Division.

4. England was unable to balance the tonnage of her import and export shipments
. . . . .4 (   )

5. By reducing freight rates Germany was constantly gaining a greater percentage of
world trade. . . . . .5 (   )

6. The sale of German wares in every part of the world resulted in added political influence
and commercial growth . . . . .6 (   )

Sequential Tests of Educational Progress (Step), Science[10]

Level 4 (Grades 4–6)

23. SITUATION: Tom wanted to learn which of three types of soil—clay, sand, or loam—would
be best for growing lima beans. he found three flowerpots, put a different type of soil in
each pot, and planted lima beans in each. He placed them side by side on the window sill
and gave each pot the same amount of water.

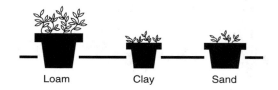

Loam   Clay   Sand

The lima beans grew best in the loam. Why did Mr. Jackson say Tom's experiment
was NOT a good experiment and did not prove that loam was the best soil for plant
growth?
A. The plants in one pot got more sunlight than the plants in the other pots.
B. The amount of soil in each pot was not the same.
C. One pot should have been placed in the dark.
D. Tom should have used three kinds of seeds.

Level 3 (Grades 7–9)

24. SITUATION: Tom planned to become a farmer and his father encouraged this interest by giving Tom a part of the garden to use for studying plant life.

Tom wanted to find out what effect fertilizer has on garden plants. He put some good
soil in two different boxes. To box A he added fertilizer containing a large amount of nitrogen. To box B he added fertilizer containing a large amount of phosphorus. In each box he
planted 12 bean seeds. He watered each box with the same amount of water. One thing
missing from Tom's experiment was a box of soil with
A. both fertilizers added.
B. neither nitrogen nor phosphorus fertilizers added.
C. several kinds of seed planted.
D. no seeds planted.

---

[10]Published by CTB/McGraw-Hill.

The Colorado Needs Assessment Program, Grade 5 Math[11]

25. What is the temperature shown by this thermometer?

  A) 88°
  B) 93°
  C) 96°
  D) 102°
  E) 104°

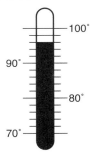

26. If the thermometer shown above is correct, and in Colorado, the season of the year is probably:

  A) spring
  B) summer
  C) fall
  D) winter

27. The time on the clock below is *NOT*

  A) 45 minutes after three.
  B) 15 minutes until 3.
  C) 2:45.
  D) forty-five minutes past two.
  E) quarter until three.

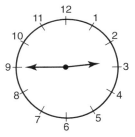

28. Which one of these is the longest period of time?

  A) 600 minutes
  B) 100 hours
  C) 20 days
  D) 2 weeks
  E) 1/2 month

29. If you are calling your grandmother on the phone, and the operator says, "Sixty-five cents, please," which set of coins would *NOT* total 65¢?

  A) 6 dimes, and 1 nickel
  B) 2 quarters, 1 dime, and 1 nickel
  C) 1 quarter, 3 nickels, and 3 dimes
  D) 13 nickels
  E) 3 dimes and 7 nickels

[11]K. D. Hopkins, G. L. Kretke, N. C. Harms, R. M. Gabriel, D. L. Phillips, C. Rodriquez, and M. Averill, *A Technical Report on the Colorado Needs-Assessment Program,* Spring 1973. Boulder: University of Colorado, Laboratory of Educational Research, 1974.

30. Twenty minutes is what part of an hour?
   A) 1/2
   B) 1/3
   C) 1/4
   D) 2/5
   E) 1/5

31. The shaded portions of the diagram below represent what part of the figure?
   A) 1/2
   B) 5/10
   C) 5/9
   D) 5/12
   E) 4/9

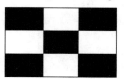

32. Which one of these is the greatest distance?
   A) 1 yard
   B) 5 feet
   C) 1 1/3 yards
   D) 50 inches
   E) 4 1/2 feet

33. The greatest number using the digits 3, 9, 7, 6 only once is:
   A) 3679
   B) 9376
   C) 7963
   D) 9763
   E) 6739

9.9   GENERAL GUIDELINES FOR TEST DEVELOPMENT

The following suggestions are useful in the development of a test. Some of the procedures are not practicable for typical classroom application, but if a test is to be used for research or program evaluation, or other important decisions such as minimum competency, the investment in test development is critical. The bases for some of these suggestions were developed in Chapters 7 and 8 and the earlier parts of this chapter.

   1. *Prepare a table of specifications to guide item development and selection and maximize content validity.* In this way important topics are less likely to be overlooked or underemphasized on the test. Experienced teachers often develop large item pools that can be of great value when used properly. This can be particularly helpful, since developing comprehension and application items is very time-consuming. An additional pool of test items often accompanies textbooks (although, unfortunately, most such items are only at the knowledge level).

   2. *It is usually desirable to include more items in the first draft of the test than will be needed in the final form.* This permits a later culling of inferior items or those not needed to provide proper balance. For each section of the test, perhaps 25 percent or so more items should be prepared than are likely to be required. After some time has elapsed, the test should be reviewed critically. The items should be checked with the original outline to see that the test places the desired emphasis on the various topics. A careful reading of the test at this time will usually reveal some ambiguities and objectionable items. Whenever possible it is wise to have the test reviewed by another person knowledgeable in the subject matter; that person will discover some test items of doubtful importance and others that are not clearly stated. A common and serious error results when items contain *intrinsic ambiguity*—one answer is correct under one interpretation, but from another possible perspective a different answer is correct.

3. *The item should be phrased so that the content rather than the form of the statement will determine the answer.* A common flaw is inclusion of "specific determiners," which provide an irrelevant clue to the correct answer. Specific determiners are especially common in *true-false* items. Statements that contain such words as *always, never, entirely, absolutely*, and *exclusively* are much more likely to be false than to be true. On the other hand, items containing expressions that weaken a statement, such as *may, sometimes, as a rule,* and *in general,* are much more likely to be true. These expressions should be used judiciously, avoiding the exact wording found in the textbook to increase the level of mastery required. Double negatives, needlessly abstruse vocabulary, and complicated sentence structure should be kept at a minimum. Care should also be taken to see that one item does not give away the answer to another.

4. *The difficulty level of the items should be appropriate to the group of examinees.* Lord (1952) has demonstrated that reliability will be at a maximum when item difficulty is approximately midway between chance success and 100 percent. Optimal difficulty for *true-false* items is about 75 percent, for five-option multiple-choice questions about 60 percent, and for completion items approximately 50 percent. But, as stated previously, difficulty is not an end in itself. Tests developed for classroom assessment will ordinarily be easier than tests designed for research purposes where everything rides on a single test. A teacher should not be beguiled into thinking he or she is the world's greatest teacher just because the class average is 95 percent. Perhaps only easy questions were asked, or perhaps instruction was unconsciously or consciously oriented toward the specific test items (i.e., the instructor taught to the test). Difficult items are not necessarily good items. It is simple to ask trivial questions that are difficult. Difficulty is not an end in itself. For classroom achievement tests, the item content should be determined by the *importance* of the subject matter, with questions being asked at a difficulty level appropriate to the group. For example, an adequate diagnostic test or criterion-referenced measure in basic arithmetic for prospective elementary school teachers might yield many nearly perfect scores and still perform its function. It is good practice to have at the beginning of the test a few items that are quite easy. The psychological justification for this is the wholesome effect it has on the morale of the students. Placing difficult items at the beginning may produce needless discouragement, particularly for students of below-average ability.

5. *Before the test is given, it is impossible to estimate the difficulty of the items accurately.* Teacher estimates of difficulty will be only rough approximations. It is usually possible to identify those items that will be at the extremes of the scale; fortunately, this is what is needed most. Although most researchers (e.g., Allison, 1984; Brenner, 1964; Marso, 1970; Sax & Cromack, 1966) have failed to demonstrate that any significant difference results from various item arrangements on power tests, Tollefson (1978) found that highly anxious students obtained higher scores on tests following the easy-to-difficult item order.

The use of the difficulty gradient in item ordering is especially desirable because many teacher-made tests are not pure power tests. The undesirable effects of a speeded test are even more serious if an item difficulty gradient is not employed. If speed is a factor, order becomes significant (Hambleton & Traub, 1974; Sax & Carr, 1962). Even when the order in which the items are arranged is of no psychometric consequence, the easy-to-difficult order has no known disadvantages.

6. *The items should reflect several taxonomy levels.* Items that are similar to the *types* of items used in instruction are quite appropriate for assessment, but when teaching is done with specific items in mind, the items can no longer be viewed as representative samples of the content universe to which we wish to generalize. Hence, success on those items says little about the success students would have on similar items. One of the worst, and most common, defects of teacher-constructed tests is the lack of items beyond the knowledge taxonomy level. Such items tend to be more difficult than relevant knowledge-level items. Instructors too often fail to realize that on very easy tests the few difficult items do nearly all the "work" in assessing individual differences. One study (Sax & Reade, 1964) found that college students who were given difficult tests learned more than students in the same class who took easier tests. Hunkins (1969) also found that when higher taxonomy level questions were used regularly, objectives were mastered at a higher level.

7. *Classroom tests should be power tests, not speed tests.* A test is speeded to the extent that it contains items that are known by some examinees but are not answered because of inadequate time. One of the most common and serious problems results when a test is too long for the time allowed, allowing effects from the speed-versus-accuracy response style (Section 6.7) to contaminate scores. Proficient students are not necessarily fast test takers—the correlation between ability and working rate on the tests has been shown to be low (Hopkins, 1964a; Michael & Michael, 1969). If more than 10 percent or 15 percent of the examinees fail to complete the test in the allotted time, speed is probably a factor for some examinees and the test should be shortened before it is used again. In addition, the scores should be corrected for chance (Section 6.12) to help reduce the disadvantage for the slow test takers. But, if possible, all but the very slowest examinees should be allowed to finish the test. Test-taking speed has been shown to have little relationship to the amount of understanding of the content universe. For fairly short factual items, two items per minute may be reasonable for students above the third grade. For items above the knowledge level, the time allotment should be increased. Younger students and higher taxonomy level items require more time. To prevent disturbance and discipline problems, assigned reading or other work should be required for students who complete the test early. Keep test length such that virtually all students can finish.

8. *The reading level should be relatively easy* (see Section 7.19). Unless your purpose is to measure reading ability itself, use simple vocabulary and sentence structure. This is especially important at the elementary and junior high school levels. For example, in a science or mathematics test, high reading demands of an item may block a knowledgeable student from demonstrating mastery. (Methods of quantifying the reading level [readability] of written material is treated in a later section of this chapter.)

9. *It is often desirable to use more than one type of item.* A test with a variety of item types is less likely to be monotonous, especially with long tests. The requirement that the question types be suited to the material covered may necessitate that a number of item types be used. For classroom tests, these varied objective items are frequently included with one or more essay questions.

10. *All the items of a particular kind should ordinarily be placed together in the test.* Completion, true-false, and multiple-choice items arranged haphazardly can be distracting, especially for younger examinees. The grouping together of similar types of items not only facilitates scoring and evaluation but also enables examinees to take full advantage of the mind set induced by a particular item format.

11. *The directions to the student should be as clear, complete, and concise as possible.* The teacher's aim should be to make the instructions so explicit that the least able examinees in the group are clear about what they are expected to do, even if they may not be able to do it. Examinees should know how and where to mark the items, how much time they have to do so, and the extent to which they should guess. The amount of detail necessary will depend on the age of the students and their experience with that kind of test. In the lower grades the teacher should read the directions aloud while students silently follow the written directions on their test papers. If the form of the test is unfamiliar or complicated, the use of correctly marked samples and practice exercises (or even practice tests) is recommended. Sometimes a chalkboard demonstration is useful. When the examinees become familiar with the various kinds of items, the directions may be abridged greatly.

12. *Before the actual scoring begins, answer keys should be prepared and scoring procedures outlined.* Scoring rules for objective tests are typically one point for each correct response, with no fractional credits allowed. Ordinarily, students will remain in nearly the same rank order regardless of whether the individual items are weighted equally or quite differently (Stanley & Wang, 1970; Wang & Stanley, 1970). Variable credit for items complicates hand scoring but is sometimes needed to allow appropriate weighting of the various topics or content strata when the number of items is not commensurate with their importance or emphasis. In mathematics and other problem-solving tests, some of the scoring procedures will have to evolve as special situations arise. Solutions that are correct in principle but have the wrong answer because of some clerical error or oversight should receive considerable credit; the guiding principle should be to give a score commensurate with the degree of mastery evidence. The availability of optical scanners for test-scoring equipment greatly facilitates the scoring and item analyses of objective tests. Such equipment is currently being used in many universities and in many large schools and school districts. Its availability for secondary teachers should increase greatly within the next few years.

13. *Every reasonable precaution should be taken to ensure excellent testing conditions.* The responses to any test are determined not only by the test itself but can also be influenced by surrounding conditions. It is usually best to administer the test to examinees in the familiar environment of their own classroom. Opportunities to cheat should be minimized by careful supervision; careless proctoring invites abuse and invalid results. Students should be spread out as much as possible, if feasible in a grid consisting of alternate rows and alternate columns so that no examinee has anyone sitting in front, behind, or on either side of him or her. Even with careful planning, however, there may not be enough seats in the room to make that grid possible.

14. *If the test is to be used for program evaluation, research, or important student decisions, it should be field tested with a group of comparable students.* The item analysis (Chapter 10) from the field test will be invaluable for item selection and refinement. An item analysis is desirable for any important test. This allows the reliability of the test to be assessed and provides opportunities to fine-tune and make needed adjustments in scoring due to intrinsically ambiguous items.

9.10 SPECIAL GUIDELINES FOR CONSTRUCTING MULTIPLE-CHOICE ITEMS

Many of the suggestions for constructing good items appear to be just good common sense, but evidently the sense is not all that common, because virtually all teacher-made tests contain violations of these rules (Berg, 1958, 1961; Millman, 1961). These suggestions deal primarily with item form and format. It is presumed that the test constructor has used a table of specifications or some other procedure to ensure content validity and has attended to the need to have higher taxonomy level items.

1. *The stem should ordinarily contain the central problem and all qualifications, including words that would otherwise be repeated in each alternative.* The examinee should not be required to construct the question by consulting the options.

    2. "The study of the price system narrows down to an analysis of these two sets of prices and the interrelationships between them." The two sets of prices referred to are
      a) those for consumption goods and those for capital goods.
      b) those for consumption goods and those for productive services.
      c) those for labor and those for the other productive factors.
      d) those for economic and those for noneconomic goods.

Obviously, the phrase "those for" should have been included in the second sentence of the stem because "those for" occurs as the first two words of every option. If the incomplete stem is used, it must include all the language that is exactly applicable in every option in order to avoid wasting the student's time.

    34. Consumer cooperatives
      a) are to consumers what labor unions are to laborers.
      b) have recently been declared illegal.
      c) originated in the United States and later spread to Europe.
      d) have been criticized as not paying their equitable share of taxes.

Here there are actually four *true-false* questions; each concerns consumer cooperatives, but only one is keyed as true. The stem, "Consumer cooperatives," does not constitute a statement of a central problem. Questions that lend themselves naturally to a *true-false* item form should not be forced into a multiple-choice style.

    2. Each item should be as short as possible, consistent with clarity. Otherwise, valuable testing time is wasted.

    3. *Negatively stated stems must be used with care.* Negatively phrased items tend to be more difficult than those phrased in a positive way (Dudycha & Carpenter, 1973). Negative items can be useful, but it is desirable to group them together and to emphasize the negative words, such as *not, never,* and *least.* Another useful technique is to end the stem with the words "with one exception; select the <u>exception</u>." For example, "Each of the following men *except one* was president of the United States. Which one was *not?*" This helps the examinee to keep the appropriate mental set for the item.

4. *State the problem of the question fully in the stem.* Incomplete stems tend to be more ambiguous and difficult than closed-stem phrasing (Dudycha & Carpenter, 1973).

5. *Ask for the <u>best</u> answer.* Use terms such as *most* and *primary* if more than one answer is at least partially correct. For example, "The one factor generally considered by most historians as being *most* important in causing the United States to enter World War II was . . ."

6. *The omissions in incomplete statements should usually occur toward the end of the stem.* Confusion and excessive rereading of the stem can result if a blank appears near the beginning of the stem. Better yet, rephrase the item as a question whenever possible.

7. *The reading and linguistic difficulty of items should be low.* The incidental vocabulary and phrasing used in items should be kept as simple as possible. Incidental or unnecessarily technical terms should be avoided. Consider this example:

36. Lower animals, in contradistinction to *homosapiens,*
    a) are incapable of any communication.
    b) cannot develop true conditioned responses.
    c) lack adaptive instincts.
    d) do not become objects to themselves.
    e) are independent of the homeostatic principle.

Homosapiens, conditioned responses, and *homeostatic* may be unnecessarily technical for measuring the objective. *Contradistinction* should be replaced by a simpler word.

8. *Whenever possible, arrange the alternatives in a logical order—order of magnitude, temporal sequence, and so on.*

9. *Avoid regular, recurring patterns of correct responses.* Some examinees are likely to detect them.

10. *Distracters must be plausible and attractive if the item is to measure real understanding.* Distracters must be prepared carefully or they will not be functional. Put yourself in the shoes of the examinees and simulate the likely kinds of errors and misunderstandings. After the item has been administered, an item analysis (see Chapter 10) should be performed to determine how well the distracters functioned. Unattractive distracters can be replaced. For example, a teacher of general mathematics in a junior high school might devise the following test item. The various options are designed to reflect different kinds of common errors.

1. What is the circumference (in inches) of a circle with a radius of 5 inches?
    a) $5 \times 3.14 = 15.7$
    b) $10 \times 3.14 = 31.4$
    c) $5^2 \times 3.14 = 78.5$
    d) $10^2 \times 3.14 = 314$
    e) None of the above

Students who confuse circumference with area ($A = \pi r^2$) might choose option *c*. Students who confuse diameter with radius might select option *a;* those who make both errors might choose option *d*.

Of course, not all distracters may or need to function as planned. The item can still do its job even if one of the distracters attracts many students who do not deserve credit. But aim for more than that!

Devising excellent multiple-choice items is a highly creative and challenging process, particularly in the construction of distracters.

11. *To the extent possible, alternatives should be uniform in subject content, form, length, explicitness, and grammatical structure.* In addition, all options should be grammatically consistent with the stem. Inconsistent articles, changes in tense, and the like may introduce intrinsic ambiguity and spoil an otherwise excellent question. An item such as the following gives a strong grammatical clue to the correct option:

38. Lewis and Clark were famous for
   a) inventors.
   b) exploring the Santa Fe trail.
   c) Indians.
   d) the pasteurizing of milk.
   e) the Louisiana Purchase.

The item would be improved by replacing options *a, c, d,* and *e* as follows:

   a) inventing the cotton gin.
   c) exploring the southwestern United States.
   d) devising the pasteurizing process for milk.
   e) exploring the land of the Louisiana Purchase.

The length and degree of technicality of alternatives should ordinarily be fairly uniform. A flagrant violation will illustrate this difficulty.

39. An atom is
   a) an amalgam.
   b) a compound.
   c) a mixture.
   d) a molecule.
   e) the basic "building block" of matter, consisting of a nucleus surrounded by electrons in orbits.

Test-wise students will notice immediately that option *e* is much longer than the other answers. Even without a clear idea of the relationship of atoms to compounds, mixtures, and molecules, they will have little doubt that the correct answer is *e* because it stands out from the others (Chase, 1964). Some experienced item writers occasionally choose to lure students who are test-wise but lack knowledge to a distracter by making it long and elaborate while leaving the correct option short and simple.

The following illustration (Hawkes, Lindquist & Mann, 1936, pp. 146–47) shows how the degree of understanding required can be increased when options are made more homogeneous.

40. Engel's law deals with
   a) the coinage of money.
   b) the inevitableness of socialism.

   c) diminishing returns.
   d) marginal utility.
   e) family expenditures.

41. Engel's law deals with family expenditures for
   a) luxuries. b) food. c) clothing. d) rest. e) necessaries.

42. According to Engel's law, family expenditures for food
   a) increase in accordance with the size of the family.
   b) decrease as income increases.
   c) require a smaller percentage of an increasing income.
   d) rise in proportion to income.
   e) vary with the tastes of families.

To respond correctly to Item 40, the student must know only that Engel's law deals with family expenditures. For Item 41, the student must know that the specific item of expenditure is food. The maximum degree of discrimination, however, is required in answering Item 42, in which more information is given in the stem. Notice that all the options for a given item should have parallel grammatical structure.

   12. *Have three or more options per item unless doing so requires using implausible options.* Three to five alternatives per item are optimal for many situations, but sometimes more options may be available. The format of many separate answer sheets limits the number of options to five. Fewer options may be desirable for examinees in grade 3 or below.

   13. *Use care in the repetition of words or phrases between the stem and the correct answer.* It is legitimate, and even desirable, however, to incorporate such repetition in the incorrect options. Like all rules, this can be overdone. If all distracters are loaded with irrelevant lengthiness, false technicality, and words from the stem, but the correct response stands out because of its quality and simplicity, test-wise students can select the correct answer without much knowledge about the point being tested. The test constructor must be clever and versatile; he or she should be able to "read the students' minds" in advance (and in retrospect, too, from the item analysis) without allowing his or her intentions to be discernible.

   For example, in the following question the word *battle* appears in the stem and in the correct option; thus, it provides a clue for the test-wise examinee.

43. A decisive battle between U.S. soldiers and American Indians was the
   a) battle called "Custer's last stand."
   b) fighting at Yorktown.
   c) War of 1812.
   d) storming of the Alamo.

Notice that option *c,* War of 1812, is poor since it violates rule 11 (grammatical consistency). The stem specifies a single battle, whereas a war usually involves more than one battle. The test-wise student will ignore option *c.* The question might be reworded as follows:

44. A decisive battle between U.S. soldiers and American Indians was the
   a) last stand of Custer.
   b) fighting at Yorktown.
   c) Battle of Gettysburg.
   d) Battle of the Alamo.

   Now the word *Battle* appears in two incorrect options but not in the correct option, so it may distract test-wise students who do not know the correct answer.

14. *Avoid textbook wording or stereotyped phraseology* (except perhaps in distracters, as discussed earlier). The comprehension and application taxonomy levels require that the question be posed in a fresh context; otherwise, the correct answer can be selected by thoughtless parroting of the textbook.

15. *Avoid items that reveal the answer to another item.* One item should not help the test-wise student detect the answer to another. The items that form the test should be reviewed carefully. When possible, it is helpful to have a competent person review the entire test for overlapping items, grammatical inconsistency, misspellings, and other flaws.

16. *Ordinarily, distracters should not overlap, subsume, or be synonymous with one another.* Consider the following item:

> **45.** A substance that in its pure form is a good conductor of electricity is
> a) water.   b) silver.   c) H_2S.   d) H_2O.

Since there is only one correct answer, the alert student can eliminate options *a* and *d* immediately. The chances of getting undeserved credit for the item are greatly increased.

17. *Avoid specific determiners* such as *always* and *never*, except perhaps to tempt test-wise examinees who know that few things are always true or never true. This requires that a word that is usually a specific determiner be employed in a nondetermining way part of the time. Options containing *always* should be true about as often as they are false, so that test-wise examinees cannot reject them automatically. Words that are usually specific determiners can be used to increase validity if used judiciously. For example:

> **46.** If two parallel forms of a test, each with $r_{xx} = .5$, are combined into a single test,
> a) the reliability coefficient will always increase.
> b) the mean percent score will probably change considerably.
> c) the test will be too long to be very functional.
> d) its validity coefficient will be approximately doubled.

Notice that the correct answer contains *always,* which ordinarily denotes a distracter. Also, the qualifiers *probably* and *approximately* are included in distracters *b* and *d* to make them more attractive to unprepared examinees.

18. *Avoid arranging items in the order in which they were presented in the textbook.* This is especially important for tests on spelling and multiplication facts and other learning tasks in which serial learning is possible. Although test scores are sometimes slightly higher when items are arranged in the order in which they were learned (Marso, 1970; Norman, 1954), the logical validity of the test is reduced.

19. *Do not include so many items in the test that it becomes a speed rather than a power test.* Thought-provoking and problem-solving items can be time-consuming; items that measure rote knowledge can be answered quickly. If an instructor realizes that too many items have been included in the test for the time allowed, probably the class should be informed that a specified number of the later items will not be scored. Allowing speed of response to be a significant factor influencing test results is a serious threat to the test's validity. Many able students are not speedy test takers.

20. None of these *may be a useful last option for correct-answer items* (Williamson & Hopkins, 1967), *although its use tends to make items somewhat more difficult* (Choppin,

1974). Avoid using it when the keyed response is merely the *best* answer among the responses given, rather than the wholly correct or best possible answer. The option saves the test maker's time, since it can be used repeatedly. What answer would you mark for the following item?

47. Which word is spelled correctly?

   a) occurrence   b) desireable   c) mispelled   d) vacuum   e) none of the above

If you selected option *e,* give yourself a gold star. Notice how much more knowledge was required than would be the case if you had to identify only one correctly spelled word. The *none of these* option can introduce intrinsic ambiguity if it is not used carefully. What if option *d* were changed to *judgment*? Since this spelling of *judgment* is given as an acceptable spelling in most dictionaries, the item would be intrinsically ambiguous.

Also, make sure that *none of these* is sometimes the correct response. It is used rather infrequently by professional item writers, except on mathematics, spelling, and grammar tests for which correct-answer rather than best-answer options are typical.

   21. All of the above *or* more than one of the above *options may sometimes be useful.*

   48. If *h, k, m,* and *n* are positive numbers, *k* is greater than *m*, and *n* is greater than *h*, which of the following *can* be true?

   1. $n + h = k + m$
   2. $k + h = n + m$
   3. $k + n = m + h$

   a) 2   b) 1 and 2   c) 3   d) all of the above

Notice that the three equations could be combined in eight ways, producing eight possible options. The eight alternatives for each such item would yield a slight gain over just five, since the probability of getting the answer correct by chance would be reduced from one-fifth to one-eighth. A better possibility would be to recast statements 1, 2, and 3 as *T-F* items, following the common stem.

   22. *Paragraph each option*, unless all the options are so brief that they easily fit on a single line. This reduces the time and effort needed to locate the correct answer and the chances of incorrectly reading or mis-marking an answer.

   23. *Use numerals for items and letters for options.*

   24. *Punctuate the options correctly.* If the stem of the item is an incomplete statement, each option is a possible completion of the statement. Therefore, each option should begin with a lowercase letter and be followed by a terminal mark of punctuation (period, question mark, exclamation point). If the stem is a direct question and each option is a sentence that might possibly answer it, begin each option with a capital letter and follow it with a terminal mark of punctuation. If the stem is a question but the options are words or phrases and not complete sentences, begin each option with a lowercase letter but do not put any mark of punctuation at its end.

   25. *Note:* There are exceptions to even the best guidelines. But careful consideration of these 24 suggestions should help you construct better multiple-choice items. There is no substitute for practice. Practice is invaluable, especially when it is accompanied by the critical reactions of examinees and a measurement specialist as well as an item analysis.

9.11   TRUE-FALSE AND TWO-OPTION ITEMS

If you're smart, you can pass a true or false test without being smart. (Linus in "Peanuts")

The *true-false test*, a form that is very popular with classroom teachers, has been the object of more criticism than any other form of objective test. Ebel (1970, 1971) has demonstrated that much of the criticism is undeserved and that true-false items are not limited to measuring at the knowledge level of Bloom's taxonomy. Although multiple-choice items tend to be more reliable and valid than true-false items, *T-F* tests can contain at least 50 percent more items in the same amount of testing time (Frisbie, 1973). Well-constructed *T-F* tests can compare favorably with multiple-choice tests when using testing time rather than number of items is the basis for comparison (Frisbee, 1973; Ebel, 1971; Irvin, Halpern & Landman, 1980).

The negative-suggestion effect of the true-false item (i.e., the presumably undesirable effect of incorrect statements on students) and the guessing factor are often pointed to as its greatest limitations. The correction formula may provide a fairly satisfactory adjustment for the effect of guessing.

The danger of negative suggestion when students read statements that are false has been overstated, but it may not be wise to use true-false tests as pretests when misinformation might be learned or with young children, who may be more susceptible to misinformation. In such cases it is better to avoid the true-false format; instead of a declarative statement, use a question that can be answered by the two options *yes* or *no*.

Several modifications of the true-false test have been proposed, such as having students cross out the part of the statement that is in error. Some researchers (Curtis, Darling & Sherman, 1943; Wright, 1944) have found that having students correct the wrong statements can increase the reliability of the test. These suggestions add to the labor of scoring, however, and have not been widely accepted. The most obvious ways to improve the true-false test are to *prepare it more carefully and make the test longer*. An important and often unrecognized advantage of the true-false test is that more items can be included in the same testing time. To achieve satisfactory reliability, however, more true-false items are required than would ordinarily be necessary with multiple-choice tests.

The low regard that many test experts have for true-false items is reflected in their absence from most recent standardized achievement tests. Although this type of item has been overused by classroom teachers, it does have a legitimate use in achievement tests. In some situations it is difficult or impossible to construct more than two plausible responses for a multiple-choice item in which one alternative is correct and the other incorrect. Common examples include the case forms of pronouns (such as *who* versus *whom*); correct use of singular and plural verbs; confusion of the past tense and past participle; the use of *sit* and *set*, *lay* and *lie*; and many others. Since true-false items are particularly susceptible to intrinsic ambiguity, it is often preferable to reword declarative statements into questions that can be answered *yes* or *no*. Better yet, recast the item into a multiple-choice format with two or more options. For example, instead of

49. Columbus discovered America in 1492. (*T* or *F*)

use one of the following options.

50. Columbus discovered America in the year _____.
   a) 492   b) 1482   c) 1492   d) 1692   e) none of these

51.–52. _____ discovered America in the year _____.
   a) Columbus   a) 492
   b) Cortez   b) 1482
   c) Sir Francis Drake c) 1492
   d) Magellan   d) 1692
   e) Napoleon   e) 1942

53.–55. _____ discovered _____ in _____.
   a) Columbus   a) Africa   a) 492
   b) Cortez   b) Alaska   b) 1482
   c) Sir Francis Drake c) America   c) 1492
   d) Magellan   d) Australia d) 1692
   e) Napoleon   e) Toledo   e) 1942

Of course, care is needed to ensure that only one of the 125 possible response patterns is correct.

9.12   SUGGESTIONS FOR CONSTRUCTING TRUE-FALSE ITEMS

The true-false test is generally thought to be one of the easiest to prepare. This ease is more apparent than real. Unusual care must be exercised in wording true-false statements and questions so that the *content* rather than the *form* of the statement determines the response. The test maker's aim should be to phrase the statement so that no unwarranted clues are provided, without needlessly obscuring the meaning. With practice and care, one can attain this balance. The following suggestions may be helpful in constructing true-false tests. Many of the suggestions for constructing multiple-choice tests are also applicable.

1. *Avoid using specific determiners as clues.* It has been found that strongly worded statements are more likely to be false than true but that moderately worded statements are more likely to be true than false. (As a wit once said, "Every generalization, including this one, is false.") Strongly worded statements often contain *all, always, never, no, none,* or *nothing.* Moderately worded statements often contain qualifying words such as *many, some, sometimes, often, frequently, generally,* and *as a rule.* If one carefully balances the number of true and false statements containing such expressions, these words cease to be specific determiners that decrease the validity of an item. For example,

> **56.** For a given set of test data, the reliability coefficient yielded by Kuder-Richardson formula 21 can never exceed that yielded by K-R formula 20. (*T* or *F*)

Test-wise examinees who lack knowledge will tend to answer *false* because of the apparent specific determiner *never.* In other words, because of test-wiseness, fewer ignorant students will select the correct answer. Along the same lines, many ignorant examinees will select *true* to the following item because of the qualifier *usually.*

57. Kuder-Richardson 21 reliability estimates are usually larger than K-R 20 reliability estimates. (*T* or *F*)

2. *Avoid a disproportionate number of either true or false statements.* Several studies have shown that false *T-F* items tend to be slightly more valid than true *T-F* items because many examinees who do not know the correct answer tend to have an acquiescence response style and mark *true* (Cronbach, 1942). Therefore, it is sometimes suggested that a test should contain more false statements than true ones; Ebel (1965b) suggested that perhaps 60 percent of the items should be false. If this is overdone, however, the validity of the false statements will probably decrease because the word will get out to select *false* when in doubt.

3. *Avoid the exact wording of the textbook.* Lifting true statements directly from the textbook or making true statements false by changing a single word or expression emphasizes rote memory rather than understanding.

4. *Avoid trick statements.* These are usually statements that appear to be true but are really false because of the petty insertion of some inconspicuous word, phrase, or letter. For example,

58. "The Raven" was written by Edgar Allen Poe. [Notice the misspelling of *Allan.*]
59. The Battle of Hastings was fought in 1066 BC. [Notice "BC."]

A better approach would be

60. "The Raven" was written by Henry Wadsworth Longfellow.
61. What famous battle was fought in 1066 AD?
   a) Battle of Bull Run
   b) Battle of Hastings
   c) Battle of Rome
   d) Battle of Waterloo

5. *Limit each statement to the exact point to be tested.* Do not use two or more stimuli to elicit one response, as in the following partly true, partly false statement.

62. "Poe wrote *The Gold Bug* and *The Scarlet Letter.*"

6. *Avoid excess use of negative words and phrases.* Such statements introduce intrinsic ambiguity. Knowledgeable students may select the incorrect option because of semantic confusion. An extreme example will graphically illustrate this point:

62. On true-false tests negative phrases should not be disallowed. (*T* or *F*)

7. *Avoid ambiguous words and statements.* With one interpretation certain statements can be true, and with another equally plausible interpretation they can be false. It is impossible to tell what is being measured by intrinsically ambiguous statements that have more than one legitimate interpretation. The statement "The Aztecs were a less advanced people" is true if they are compared with Europeans of the same period, but false if they are compared with American Indians of that time. The true-false item "Ambiguity is a desirable characteristic of a classroom test" is itself intrinsically ambiguous and is undesirable as a test item since *ambiguity* can refer to either extrinsic (desirable) or intrinsic (undesirable) ambiguity.

8. *Avoid complex vocabulary and unnecessarily complex sentence structure.* Use simple and concise language. The level of the examinees must be considered in the wording of items. A statement is badly worded if examinees understand the point involved but miss the item because of the language employed. Consider this flagrant violation.

63. It is considered good practice to use recondite expressions in true-false items. (*T* or *F*)

9. *Require the simplest possible method of indicating the response.* When separate answer sheets are not used, let the examinee circle *T* or *F* or *yes* or *no* or underline the correct response.

10. *Use true-false items only for points that lend themselves unambiguously to this kind of item.* Rarely should a major test be composed exclusively of true-false items.

9.13   MATCHING EXERCISES

A *matching exercise* typically consists of two columns; each stem in the first column is to be paired with an alternative in the second column. Matching exercises that provide more responses than stems are frequently used because they reduce the examinee's chances of guessing successfully. Sometimes the stems in the first column are incomplete sentences, each requiring a word or phrase from the second column for its completion. The matching exercise is useful for measuring terminology, knowledge of facts, geography, charts, and diagrams. Matching questions usually measure only knowledge level objectives.

Many types of learning involve the association of two things in the learner's mind. Common examples are events and dates, events and persons, events and places, terms and definitions, foreign words and English equivalents, laws and illustrations, rules and examples, authors and their works, and tools and their use. The matching exercise is very convenient for measuring such associations.

Matching items are particularly well adapted to testing in *who, what, where,* and *when* situations. Their principal limitations are as follows:

1. Matching items are not well adapted to the measurement of understanding, as distinguished from mere memory—it is difficult to design a matching exercise that will measure higher taxonomy levels of understanding, such as the ability to interpret complex relationships.
2. With the possible exception of the true-false test, the matching exercise is the item form that is most likely to include irrelevant clues to the correct response.
3. If they are not skillfully constructed, matching items can be time-consuming and inefficient.

The illustrations and suggestions in Section 9.14 are designed to overcome the last two of these limitations.

9.14   ILLUSTRATIONS OF MATCHING EXERCISES

Because matching exercises often have too many options (more than five) for many standard answer sheets, they appear infrequently in current published tests. However, they are still common in teacher-made tests. The following example is a *square,* 10-by-10, matching exercise from a social studies quiz in which we can "learn by undoing."

_____	1. The country that aided Columbus with money and ships	a) St. Augustine
_____	2. The oldest town in the United States	b) Boston
_____	3. A famous Quaker	c) Cartier
_____	4. The first English settlement in America	d) Thomas Hooker
_____	5. "City of Brotherly Love"	e) Jamestown
_____	6. A city in Massachusetts	f) Magellan
_____	7. First French explorer in America	g) William Penn
_____	8. He founded Connecticut.	h) Philadelphia
_____	9. They landed at Plymouth Rock.	i) Pilgrims
_____	10. His ship sailed around the world.	j) Spain

The material in this set is too heterogeneous for a single matching exercise. Four of the options are names of cities, four are names of persons, one is the name of a country, and one is a plural noun. How much do students have to know about early U.S. history to figure out the correct answers? For Item 1, they have only to recognize that Spain is the only country in the list of alternatives. The choice for Item 2 lies among *a, b, g,* and *j.* For Item 3, they are likely to reject "Cartier" and "Magellan" as not sounding "Quakerish," leaving just *c,* William Penn, and *d,* Thomas Hooker. Item 4 uses the same four options as Item 2, and perhaps "St. Augustine" does not sound like an English name. Item 5 has a nonhistorical ring that is out of context with the other nine items. Item 6 is the fourth and last of the "city" items; it is automatically answerable if one has surmised the correct answers to items 2, 4, and 5. In effect, the "city" questions constitute a 4-by-4 matching exercise that might have better been presented as such, instead of being buried in the 10-by-10 format, which takes more testing time and favors the test-wise.

"Persons" also constitutes an embedded 4-by-4 matching exercise. Item 7 contains the giveaway "French," which points to Cartier, the only French-sounding name among the four. Ignorant but shrewd students will probably choose the answer to Item 8 between options *c* and *f,* because it seems unlikely that Connecticut was founded by a person with a name like Cartier or Magellan. (True, this is a hazardous procedure and requires a little knowledge, but it is the stuff of which test-wiseness is made—the ability to increase the odds of getting credit by using test-taking skills.) Item 9 is ridiculous, for the *They* who landed at Plymouth Rock *must* be the only plural word among the ten alternatives. By the time the average student comes to Item 10, the fourth person in the list of ten items (it may not have been saved for last), he or she probably feels that cunning is more important than knowledge in getting through this maze. Far better exercises could have been prepared to cover the material.

This ten-item matching exercise appeared in a forty-item social studies test along with ten three-option multiple-choice items, ten true-false items, and ten completion items. It was administered to thirty-three students who had just completed a unit on instruction on U.S. colonial history. The four teachers who constructed the test claimed that the objectives for the social studies course were to (1) help students understand how America developed into a great nation, (2) teach the children the pertinent facts about the discovery and colonization of our country, and (3) intensify student interest in the workings of democracy. The matching exercise obviously emphasized the second objective.

The results of the item analysis based on the thirty-three students tested are interesting. First, the papers were graded for all forty items. They were then arranged according to total score, from the highest to the lowest (thirty-third). Then the highest 27 percent (nine tests) and the lowest 27 percent (also nine tests) were compared for responses to each item. The most discriminating item was number 9, "They landed at Plymouth Rock," which we have already decided could be answered solely from the correspondence of the *They* to the plural *Pilgrims* because these were the only plurals among either the items or the alternatives. The nine top-scoring students on the entire test all marked this item correctly, while the nine lowest-scoring students all marked it incorrectly! It may be that this is the central theme of the unit and that the ablest students would have gotten it right even without the specific determiner. However, it is uncomfortable to suspect that the primary determinant of score on the test *might* be verbal ability, reading ability, or test sophistication, not specific knowledge of the topic studied.

The least discriminating of the ten matching items was number 2, "The oldest town in the United States." Only one of the nine in the low group and three of the nine in the high group answered it correctly. The most difficult item on the entire test was number 6, "City of Brotherly Love," which was missed by all nine in the low group and by six in the high group. By looking at the actual options marked, a teacher can to some extent "read the students' minds" to give direction for remedial teaching. With just a little direction and practice, the four teachers could devise items that are less vulnerable to the faults we noted.

The following is another type of matching exercise; it was devised as part of a ninety-three-item test for a grade 9 English class of 36 students.

<u>She</u> and <u>Margaret</u> <u>have</u> <u>probably</u> <u>gone</u> to the <u>little</u> <u>grocery</u> store <u>around</u> the corner.

Match the following words with the part of speech it has in the above sentence.

_____	1. She	A.	noun
_____	2. Margaret	B.	pronoun
_____	3. have gone	C.	verb
_____	4. probably	D.	adjective
_____	5. little	E.	adverb
_____	6. grocery	F.	preposition
_____	7. around		

This is a 7-by-6 matching exercise. Any number of items could be used with the six alternatives. Items 3 and 6 were the most discriminating of the seven shown here, and Item 2 was the least discriminating. All items appeared to measure the desired behavior. The most difficult of the seven items was number 6, which was missed by 11 of the 12 lowest scorers but by only one of the 12 highest scorers.

A little knowledge can be a dangerous thing, and misapplication of knowledge can sometimes be detected from the item analysis. Consider the following item:

"No one but (A. he) (B. him) came to the meeting."

Five of the lowest-scoring group chose *he* and missed the item, but nine of the 12 highest-scoring group missed it. Apparently, the more able students know that "but" is usually a conjunction and concluded that this is a compound sentence in which "he" is the subject of the verb "came." The lowest-scoring students, not knowing much about parts of speech, may have based their answer on the sound of the sentence. They were probably used to saying, "This is him," and *him* sounded right in the test sentence. To check this hypothesis, high and low scorers could be questioned about their reasons for marking *A* or *B,* or administered the item "This is (A. he) (B. him)."

Consider three other examples of matching exercises (Stecklein, 1955). The first goes readily with six-option printed answer sheets when options are lettered.

DIRECTIONS: Famous inventions are listed in the left-hand column below. In the right-hand column are names of famous inventors. Place the letter corresponding to the inventor in the space before the invention for which he is famous.

Inventions	*Inventors*
_____ 1. Steam boat	a) Alexander Bell
_____ 2. Cotton gin	b) George Washington Carver
_____ 3. Sewing machine	c) Robert Fulton
_____ 4. Reaper	d) Elias Howe
	e) Cyrus McCormick
	f) Eli Whitney

DIRECTIONS: Quotations from poetry written during the Romantic Period are listed below. You are to indicate the author of each of the quotations by selecting the letter corresponding to the name of its author.

_____ 1. Hail to thee, blithe Spirit!
    Bird thou never wert,
    That from Heaven, or near it,
    Pourest thy full heart in profuse
    Strains of unpremeditated art.

_____ 2. She walks in beauty, like the night
    of cloudless climes and starry skies;
    And all that's best of dark and bright
    meet in her aspect and her eyes.

_____ 3. My heart leaps up when I behold
    a rainbow in the sky;
    So was it when my life began;
    So is it now I am a man;
    So be it when I shall grow old,
    or let me die!

_____ 4. A thing of beauty is a joy forever:
    Its loveliness increases; it will never
    Pass into nothingness; but still will keep
    A bower quiet for us, and a sleep
    Full of sweet dreams, and health,
    and quiet breathing.

a) Robert Burns
b) Lord Byron
c) Samuel Taylor Coleridge
d) John Keats
e) Percy Bysshe Shelley
f) Alfred Lord Tennyson
g) William Wordsworth

DIRECTIONS: Three lists are presented below. Famous English authors of plays are listed in the column farthest to the right, names of well-known plays are listed in the center column, and in the column farthest to the left are names of characters in some of these plays. You are to look at the name of the character listed, decide in which play this character appears, and identify the author of this play. Indicate your answers as follows: place the small alphabet letter corresponding to the play in which the character appears in the first space before the name of the character and place the capital alphabet letter corresponding to the author of this play in the second space before the name of the character. Note that there are more names of plays and authors than there are names of characters, so not all answers will be used.

___ ___ 1) Mildred Tresham	a) The Silver Box	A) John Millington Synge
___ ___ 2) Ralph Rackstraw	b) Riders to the Sea	B) Clemence Dane
___ ___ 3) Algernon Moncrieff	c) Easy Virtue	C) Robert Browning
___ ___ 4) Elizabeth Saunders	d) H. M. S. Pinafore	D) W. Somerset Maugham
___ ___ 5) Marion Whittaker	e) A Bill of Divorcement	E) Henry Arthur Jones
___ ___ 6) Bartley	f) A Blot on the Scutcheon	F) Noel Coward
___ ___ 7) Montague	g) Our Betters	G) Oscar Wilde
___ ___ 8) Lushington	h) The Masqueraders	H) W. S. Gilbert
	i) The Importance of Being Earnest	I) John Galsworthy

9.15 SUGGESTIONS FOR CONSTRUCTING MATCHING EXERCISES

In addition to the suggestions for constructing multiple-choice and true-false items, certain recommendations pertain especially to matching exercises.

1. *Include only homogeneous material in each matching exercise.* Do not mix such dissimilar responses as persons and places in a single exercise. The Colonial America exercise in Section 9.14 demonstrates why such heterogeneity is undesirable.

2. *Check each exercise carefully for unwarranted clues to matching pairs.* For each item, ask yourself the following question: What is the least amount of information that must be known to select the right response?

3. *Be sure that the students fully understand the rationale for the matching.* May an option be used for more than one item? May the desired response to a given item consist of more than one option? (This is usually an undesirable practice.) Communicate your exact intent to the students.

4. *Place items on the left and number them; place options on the right and designate them by letters.* Item numbers should run consecutively throughout the test, but option letters should begin anew with each matching exercise.

5. *Arrange items and options in a systematic order.* If the list consists of numerals or dates, arrange then in order. Option words may be alphabetized to make it easier for the student to locate the desired response.

6. *Place all the items and options for a matching exercise on a single page*, if possible. Turning the page back and forth in search of desired responses is confusing and time-consuming.

7. *Limit a matching exercise to not more than ten to fifteen items.* Longer lists tend to be too heterogeneous and afford clues for the test-wise; they also require more time per item. If testing time is limited, they can be influenced by clerical speed and accuracy.

9.16   SHORT-ANSWER ITEMS

The *short-answer test* is an objective test in which each item is in the form of a direct question, a stimulus word or phrase, a specific direction, a specific problem, or an incomplete statement or question. The response must be *supplied* by the examinee rather than merely *identified* from a list of suggested answers supplied by the teacher. This kind of test differs from the essay examination primarily in the degree of structure imposed on the examinees and the length of the response. The typical answer to the free-response item is short, usually requiring a single word, number, or phrase. Thus, it is sometimes called a short-answer objective item. For example: "In psychometrics, *consistency* is synonymous with _____."

The short-answer test has the obvious advantage of familiarity and *naturalness*. It can eliminate guessing almost completely because the student does not choose among a number of possible options. The short-answer test is particularly valuable for mathematics and the physical sciences because the stimulus appears in the form of a problem requiring computation. It also has wide application to test situations when it is presented in the form of maps, charts, and diagrams for which the student is required to supply, in spaces provided, the names of parts keyed by numbers or letters. The short-answer test may have some advantage over a fixed-response item test by increasing long-term retention (Gay, 1980).

A limitation of the short-answer test is that it encourages the measurement of highly specific facts and isolated bits of information. This problem is avoidable if the item writer is ingenious. Also, the scoring must be done by hand and is not always entirely objective. For example, which of the following answers to the item "Who developed the 1916 Stanford-Binet Intelligence Scale?" is correct: Lewis M. Terman, L. Madison Terman, Lewis Terman, L. M. Terman, Louis Terman, Tarman, Termen, or Tarmen? Probably most teachers will consider any of the first three answers fully correct. Some would penalize the last four for inaccurate spelling, even though the student's intent is clear.

Striking illustrations of scorer unreliability on apparently objective content have been documented. One classic study analyzed facsimiles of the same geometry paper marked independently by 116 high school mathematics teachers (Starch & Elliott, 1912). The grades given ranged from a low of 28 percent to a high of 92. These differences resulted from partial credit for answers containing certain types of errors, such as clerical or computation errors, spelling errors, and the like. These limitations need not be serious when tests are carefully prepared and are scored with the curricular objectives of geometry clearly in mind.

9.17 ILLUSTRATIONS OF SHORT-ANSWER ITEMS

The following are a few sample short-answer test items taken from published tests.[3]

Stone Reasoning Tests in Arithmetic[4]

1. James had 5 cents. He earned 13 cents more and then bought a top for 10 cents. How much money did he have left?
2. How many oranges can I buy for 35 cents when oranges cost 7 cents each?

Stones-Harry High School Achievement Test, Part II[5]

1. What instrument was designed to draw a circle?
2. Write in figures: one thousand seven and four hundredths.

Cooperative General Mathematics Tests for College Students[6]

1. Eight is what percent of 64?
2. Write an expression that exceeds m by X.
3. Solve the following formula for h: $V = Bh^3$

Iowa Placement Examinations, Chemistry-Training[7]

1. The atomic weight of K is 39; of Cl, 35.5; of O, 16. What is the molecular weight of $KClO_3$?
2. If 7 gm. of iron unite with 4 gm. of sulphur, how many gm. of iron sulphide will be produced?

Tests on Everyday Problems in Science, Unit XII[8]

1. What is the pressure in pounds of ordinary air per square inch at sea level?

---

[3]In the examples of various test items, an effort was made to illustrate a wide variety of formats as well as subject matter and grade level. It is recognized that they are not all of equal merit. Some of the tests referred are out of print but are needed as illustrations because recent published tests are primarily of the multiple-choice variety.

[4]Published by Teachers College Press.

[5]Published by Harcourt Brace Jovanovich.

[6]Published by Cooperative Test Division, Educational Testing Service, Princeton, N.J.

[7]Published by Extension Division, State University of Iowa.

[8]Published by Scott, Foresman.

[9]Published by Houghton Mifflin.

Figures, illustrations, and graphs are often useful test stimuli in social studies, science, and mathematics.

Exercise Adapted from the Test of Academic Progress[9]

DIRECTIONS: In the sketch below give the names of the chambers of the heart.

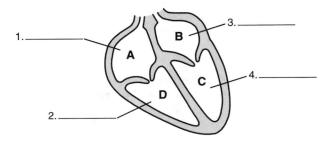

1. Using the letters to represent the chambers in the figure above, in what order does the blood circulate through the chambers, lungs, and body?

The item could be recast into a fixed-response format but in the short-answer format 24 different options are implicit.

76. Name the three parts of the body of an insect.

9.18 COMPLETION ITEMS

The *completion item*, a special form of the short-answer item, may be defined as a sentence in which certain important words or phrases have been omitted, with blanks inserted for the student to fill in. The sentence may contain one or more blanks. The sentences in the test may be disconnected, or they may be organized into a paragraph. Each blank is usually worth one point.

Completion tests have wide applicability. But unless they are prepared with extreme care, they are likely to measure rote memory rather than understanding. Although these limitations cannot be eliminated entirely, they can be greatly reduced, as in the following illustrations in Section 9.19.

9.19 ILLUSTRATIONS OF COMPLETION ITEMS

Test of Everyday Problems in Science, Unit XI[10]

77. A pry-pole is an example of a machine called the _____.
78. A screw is an example of a machine called the _____.

---

[10]Published by Scott, Foresman.

Gregory Tests in American History[11]

79. The name of the man who headed the first expedition to circumnavigate the globe was
_____.

80. In the year _____, the "Old Liberty Bell" rang out the decision of Congress to be free from England.

Cooperative English Test, Series 1[12]

81. Write on the lines to the right the contractions—shortened form to represent how the words are naturally spoken—for the seven groups of words underlined in the following sentences. For instance, for *do not*, you would write "don't." You need not copy the sentence, but only provide the seven contractions.

_____ I have read his story,

_____ but I cannot believe

_____ that he will get a passing grade on it,

_____ for it is not well written

_____ and has not a clear-cut plot.

_____ The characters are not at all

_____ interesting; they are not even human.

9.20 SUGGESTIONS FOR CONSTRUCTING SHORT-ANSWER ITEMS

The free-response item is one of the most familiar and one of the easiest to prepare. Except in mathematics and science and other problem-solving contexts, the main challenge is to phrase the items so that they require responses above the knowledge or rote memory level.

1. The direct-question form is often preferable to the statement form. It is more natural for the student and is often easier to phrase.
For example:

82. While it circles the sun once, the earth rotates on its axis _____ times.

A better approach would be

83. How many times does the earth rotate on its axis while it circles the sun once? _____

2. The questions should be worded so that the response required is as brief as possible. This will facilitate objectivity in scoring.

3. Avoid using textbook wording in phrasing items. Fresh phrasing will reduce the possibility of correct responses that represent mere meaningless verbal associations; it also will encourage students to think as they are reading and studying the book.

4. The questions should be structured to minimize ambiguity in the correct response; avoid indefinite statements. This standard is difficult to achieve because students are ingenious in reading into questions interpretations that the teacher never intended. When challenged on a history test to "name two ancient sports," one resourceful student answered,

---

[11]Published by C. A. Gregory Company.
[12]Published by Cooperative Test Division, Educational Testing Service, Princeton, N.J.

"Anthony and Cleopatra." This possibility would not have arisen if the question had taken the form, "What were two popular athletic contests in ancient Greece?" When there is clearly more than one legitimate interpretation of a question, all acceptable replies should be included on the scoring key. Extra care in wording the questions will prevent much of this ambiguity. Care is needed to prevent "frozen subjectivity" in scoring, that is, not giving credit for an equally satisfactory answer just because it is not the keyed answer. If, for example, the answer appears as "2 feet 4 inches," "28 inches" should ordinarily receive full credit. Even "28" without the unit specified should probably receive partial credit.

If they are developed carefully, short-answer questions can measure levels of understanding beyond the knowledge level of Bloom's taxonomy. For example, consider these completion items:

84. What is the taxonomy level represented by Item 76?   (knowledge)
85. . . . and by Item 77?   (comprehension)

5. *Omit key words and phrases, rather than trivial details.* If this is not done, the response may be as obvious as the *first* of the following examples or as unnecessarily difficult as the *second.*

86. Abraham Lincoln was born February ___, 1809.
87. Abraham Lincoln was born in _____ County, Kentucky.

6. *Avoid overly mutilated statements.* If too many key words are left out, it is impossible to know what meaning was intended. In its present form, it is impossible to tell what the statement in the following example refers to.

For example:

The (88) is obtained by dividing the (89) by the (90).
88. _____   89. _____   90. _____

A better approach would be

The ratio IQ is obtained by dividing the (91) by the (92).
91. _____   92. _____

7. *Avoid grammatical and other clues to the correct answer.*
For example:

93. The authors of the first verbal intelligence test were _____.

A better approach would be

94. The first verbal intelligence test was prepared by _____.

An even better approach

95. Who prepared the first verbal intelligence test? _____

Whenever the indefinite article is required before a blank, write it in the form *a(n)* so that the examinee must decide whether the correct answer begins with a consonant sound or with a vowel sound.

For example:

96. An elementary particle consisting of a charge of negative electricity is called an _____.

A better approach would be

97. An elementary particle consisting of a charge of negative electricity is called a(n) _____.

Clearly, such words as *proton, coulomb, molecule, quark,* and *meson* could not be used in the first statement. The second statement does not contain this specific determiner.

The blanks should be made uniform in length. If the blanks vary in length, the student has a clue to the length of the correct answer. Even more of a clue is afforded by using a dot or a dash for each letter in the correct word.

8. *Prepare a scoring key that contains all anticipated acceptable answers.* Although it is desirable to have only one *correct* answer for each blank, it is not always possible.

The completion item usually is less than fully satisfactory for measuring objectives above the knowledge level, except in the case of problem-solving exercises. Disillusioned writers of completion items may wish to try recasting them into multiple-choice form.

Scoring free-response completion items usually requires expert judgment because decisions about the correctness of various answers must be made by the scorer.

9.21   CLOZE TESTS

The *cloze test* is a relatively recent and promising adaptation and extension of the completion test. Invented in 1897, by Ebbinghaus, it is sometimes referred to as the Ebbinghaus completion method (Buros, 1978). It was presented by Taylor[13] (1953) as a way to measure readability (reading difficulty); later, Taylor (1956) suggested that it could also measure reading comprehension. It is now recognized as having much broader applicability. Cloze tests have had promising validity and reliability results in foreign-language assessment (Aitken, 1977; Jonz, 1976) and in a variety of other fields (Anderson, 1974; Bormuth, 1967, 1969; Buros, 1978; Panackal & Heft, 1978).[14]

Representative samples (often selections totaling approximately 250 words) of the subject matter are selected and every fifth word is deleted. The examinee must have enough understanding of the content to supply the missing information from the fragments provided. One cannot ordinarily supply many of the "correct" words if understanding is lacking. For example, imagine the difficulty a fourth-grader would have with a typical paragraph from the *Encyclopaedia Britannica*. An understanding of the general domain and knowledge of the vocabulary at the level at which the selection is written are required to respond successfully to a cloze selection.

A variation of the cloze technique that is probably better for achievement test use (except perhaps on tests designed to measure reading comprehension) is to delete *key* words

---

[13]The term *cloze* was coined by Taylor (1953); its relation to the phrase "reading closure" is evident. *Cloze* refers to an activity in which an examinee fills in a blank. A *modified cloze format* requires the examinee to select the correct words from a set of choices (Pearson & Johnson, 1978).

[14]Critical reviews of the cloze procedure by J. C. Anderson, W. B. Elley, and W. L. Smith and references to 400 related articles and studies can be found in Buros, 1978.

rather than every fifth word. The following example pertains to test reliability. (Answers are given at the bottom of the page.[15])

> When a test is administered to an (1) , a score is (2) . If the examinee had been (3) on some other test or (4) , the exact same (5) probably would not have been earned. The (6) that would be earned, on the average, if the (7) had been tested at various times under the same (8) conditions is called his or her (9) or (10) score. Although we can never actually (11) universe scores, we can be aware of the discrepancy between (12) scores (which we know) and (13) scores (which we do not know). This difference, the (14) score minus the true (15) , is called error of (16) . The (17) deviation of the (18) of measurement is the standard error of (19) (σ_e). About (20) thirds of the examinees will have obtained (21) that are within (22) σ_e of their (23) scores. Only about one person in twenty will obtain a score that (24) from his or her universe score by as much as (25) .

An important advantage of the cloze approach is the simplicity of test development. A teacher can select a representative set of paragraphs from the topics and chapters to be assessed. One can expect a power test to result if there are no more than three to five blanks per minute of testing time.

A practical disadvantage of the cloze approach, as with other short-answer items, is that the scoring has imperfect objectivity and requires more time than the scoring of multiple-choice tests. These can be overcome by utilizing a fixed-response format, which may actually improve reliability and validity (Panackal & Heft, 1978). Cloze selections are usually longer than a single sentence, often running to as many as 250 words (as will be illustrated in the summary of this chapter).

The modified cloze technique is illustrated in the following items, which are used in the *Colorado Needs Assessment,* Grade 5 Reading.

> *Select the word that fits best in each of the blanks of the sentences below:*[16]
>
> Hares belong to the same (77) as rabbits. Hares, however, are usually larger (78) rabbits. Unlike rabbits, however, their young are (79) with fur and their eyes open.
>
> 77. A) color   *B) family   C) animals
>
> 78. A) size   B) important   *C) than
>
> 79. *A) born   B) naked   C) grown
>
> In a cave in the mountain, two tiny spotted (80) were born. They were baby cougars. One day they would be the (81) hunters in the mountains. But now they were small and (82) .
>
> 80. *A) kittens   B) gnats   C) ducklings
>
> 81. *A) fiercest   B) funniest   C) hungriest
>
> 82. A) strong   B) cold   *C) helpless

---

[15]Answers to cloze exercise: 1. examinee; 2. obtained, earned; 3. tested, assessed; 4. occasion, time; 5. score; 6. score; 7. person, examinee; 8. testing; 9, 10. true, universe; 11. know, obtain; 12. obtained; 13. true, universe; 14. obtained; 15. score; 16. measurement; 17. standard; 18. errors; 19. measurement; 20. two-; 21. scores; 22. one; 23. true, universe; 24. deviates, varies; 25. $2\sigma_e$.

[16]Correct answer is denoted by *.

9.22   SUMMARY REMARKS

Test-item writing is both a skill and an art; it is assisted by the statistical procedures of item analysis (Chapter 10) and by the evaluative reactions of examinees and people who are knowledgeable in the subject matter and in measurement procedures. As automation becomes more available as an aid in scoring tests, obtaining frequency distributions, item analysis, and determining reliability coefficients and standard errors of measurement, it is important that the heart of the test—its items and exercises—not be neglected by test publishers or teachers. Undue emphasis on mechanical and statistical procedures can lead to undesirable consequences. Too great a preoccupation with indexes of item discrimination, for example, may result in neglect of the item's content validity and its motivational and communication properties. A paragraph in a science test should be acceptable to a subject matter expert, well written, and thought-provoking to the student. An item may discriminate well between high and low scores on a test as a whole and still measure trivia. This situation usually arises when items are not scrutinized for content validity or when a table of specifications is not used in framing the test. Mastery of measurement concepts is necessary but not sufficient; knowledge of subject matter, sufficient time, and creativity are essential, too. If possible, the items should be thoroughly reviewed by other well-qualified people. Items should be edited, revised, or deleted on the basis of these reviews. This will help compensate for the inevitable limitations of any one person. Further editing for future use results from a detailed item analysis, an important step that is frequently omitted.

In the future, classroom testing may be largely computerized. There are a few experimental situations in which a teacher chooses, from a large pool of items, those that are relevant for the forthcoming test. The computer assembles and numbers the items and even produces a Ditto or mimeograph master. Considerable experimental work is being done in this area of "tailored," "adaptive," or "computer-assisted individualized" testing, in which an examinee's response to a preliminary set of items is used to select an appropriate set of items to follow (Lord, 1976).

For some time, however, test items and exercises will probably be devised mainly by humans in the current painstaking manner. Therefore, teachers must learn the art of test making, or inferior evaluation measures will result. We have presented the *ABC*s of test construction. With practice and further study, you should be able to prepare excellent tests well worth the effort required!

IMPORTANT TERMS AND CONCEPTS

option	multiple-choice items	specific determiner
distracter	matching exercise	power test
free-response items	cloze technique	speed test
completion items	test-wiseness	"best-answer" items
short-answer items	extrinsic ambiguity	tailored testing
recall items	intrinsic ambiguity	stem
fixed-response items		

CHAPTER SUMMARY AND TEST

For this chapter we will use a cloze test as the chapter summary. Each blank should be filled with a single word. We have supplied the more obvious correct answers. (Other synonymous responses should also be credited.)

The most important characteristic of a test _(1)_ is content _(2)_ —does the item _(3)_ the content and _(4)_ of the domain being _(5)_? The process for item _(6)_ should be preceded by a carefully prepared test blueprint or _(7)_ (see Chapter 7) to ensure _(8)_ validity.

Each kind of _(9)_ has unique advantages and _(10)_. True-false items can be _(11)_ quickly and require less examinee _(12)_ than most other item _(13)_, but they usually _(14)_ to measure more complex _(15)_. If not prepared carefully, they often are intrinsically _(16)_.

An item is intrinsically _(17)_ when people with a thorough _(18)_ of the domain do not _(19)_ on which option is the best _(20)_; it results from a fault in the _(21)_. _(22)_ ambiguity results from an examinee's _(23)_ understanding of the _(24)_; it is a fault of the _(25)_.

Multiple-choice items have the _(26)_ flexibility and potential for measuring _(27)_. The essential ingredient in their effective _(28)_ is the preparation of attractive _(29)_. This is also a great practical _(30)_, because constructing _(31)_ alternatives requires a high level of skill that is developed only with time and _(32)_.

Matching and short-answer items can measure _(33)_ in an economical manner, although they do not readily lend themselves to measuring comprehension and other _(34)_ level objectives (except in mathematics and other problem-solving contexts).

The most important guidelines for item construction may be summarized as follows:

1. Except for measuring rate of responding itself, tests should be _(35)_, not speed measures. Test-taking speed is a response _(36)_ that is not highly _(37)_ with proficiency.
2. The reading level of tests should be kept _(38)_. The poor reader should be _(39)_ to demonstrate what he or she can _(40)_ in other curricular areas without encountering unnecessary _(41)_ of complex but irrelevant vocabulary and linguistics. Complex, negative, and textbook phrasing should be _(42)_. Direct questions are often _(43)_ to declarative statements.
3. Incorrect response options must be _(44)_ to examinees who lack sufficient knowledge and understanding. Skillful test development _(45)_ the odds of selecting the _(46)_

answer on the basis of (47) alone. Options should be (48) , homogeneous, and (49) consistent. "Best-answer" items are often superior to (50) items in measuring understanding at the higher levels of Bloom's (51) .

ANSWERS TO CHAPTER TEST

1. item, exercise
2. validity
3. represent, sample
4. goals, aims, purposes, objectives
5. assessed, measured, evaluated
6. construction, development, writing
7. set of specifications
8. content
9. item, test, exercise
10. disadvantages, limitations, drawbacks
11. constructed, developed, built
12. time
13. types
14. fail
15. concepts, objectives
16. ambiguous
17. ambiguous
18. comprehension, knowledge, understanding

19. agree
20. answer, response
21. item, exercise, test
22. Extrinsic
23. inadequate, insufficient
24. domain, content, universe, objectives
25. examinee, person, student
26. greatest
27. understanding, concepts
28. use, utilization, usage
29. distracters, alternatives, decoys, incorrect options, foils
30. drawback, obstacle, challenge, disadvantage
31. plausible, attractive
32. effort, work, practice
33. knowledge, facts, details, information

34. higher
35. power
36. style, set
37. correlated, associated
38. low, easy, simple
39. allowed, able
40. do, accomplish
41. hurdles, obstacles
42. avoided, minimal, minimized
43. preferable, superior
44. attractive, plausible
45. reduces, decreases, minimizes
46. best, correct, right
47. test-wiseness, test sophistication, guessing
48. plausible, attractive
49. grammatically, logically
50. correct-answer
51. taxonomy

10

Item Analysis for Classroom Tests

10.1   INTRODUCTION

If the procedures for test development outlined in Chapters 7, 8, and 9 are followed, the most important quality of test—*content validity*—will be achieved. This is the sine qua non for any good test of test item. Logical relevance is the principal criterion for test validity. An item analysis is needed to confirm that the items on a test are functioning in the desired manner. It is not uncommon for an item to appear satisfactory to the instructor, yet be found by the item analysis to be intrinsically ambiguous and to elicit an undesired response pattern from students (Coffman, 1969, p. 14). The chief purposes of an item analysis, therefore, are to determine the *difficulty* and *discrimination* of each item.

When a test is subjected to item analysis, important insights into the students' thinking and understanding of the content being assessed are found. The empirical feedback from item analysis almost certainly will improve an instructor's skills in test construction to a degree that is not otherwise possible (Ebel, 1965b, p. 346). Blessum (1969, p. 5) reported that item analysis feedback to university faculty "resulted in an improvement not only in the quality and fairness of each individual examination, but also in the technical and educational quality of successive tests."

An item analysis can reveal unsuspected defects of specific items, *and* the class's performance on the individual items is useful formative evaluation feedback to the instructor. The feedback on individual items can help the instructor to identify points or concepts that are in need of review and further instruction. The response of one student to a constructed-response item can help identify misunderstandings, and the aggregated responses of a group of students can be useful in the subsequent instructional designs.[1]

---

[1]For example, the author's instruction design always includes a written weekly quiz. This week's statistics quiz revealed that the instruction design to distinguish between the sampling error in a statistic and the bias in that statistic was not successful. This distinction then is the initial topic for the next class session.

The item analysis can identify items that need to be eliminated because of intrinsic ambiguity. An item analysis also produces an estimate of the measurement precision of the test—reliability and standard error of measurement.

To minimize response-style effects on teacher-made tests, each examinee should be strongly encouraged to answer every item. The time allowed should be such that adequate time is available for nearly everyone to attempt every item.[2] The items generally should be grouped by topic or instructional sequence, with the initial items being easier, although this is critical only on speeded tests. Although *an item analysis of a test is not nearly as important as the need for careful planning, constructing, and editing of the test's items,* it can be a valuable activity that can enhance the test's reliability and validity. Students appreciate an instructor who makes the effort to increase the fairness of classroom tests.

10.2   INFORMATION YIELDED BY AN ITEM ANALYSIS

An item analysis provides information regarding the difficulty (the percent of the group tested that answered the question correctly) and the discrimination (how well the item distinguishes between the more knowledgeable and the less knowledgeable students) of the items on the test. These two item characteristics are not closely related. If all students mark an item incorrectly, then the item has no discriminating power within the group—it does not assess individual differences. But on classroom tests, all items need not discriminate. Perhaps all the students have mastered the objective, for example, telling time. Items on classroom or mastery tests need not discriminate in order to serve their purpose. If all students respond correctly to the item, so much the better. But total mastery is a realistic expectation only for "training" or knowledge-level objectives. For items above the knowledge level of Bloom's taxonomy—items that are assessing concepts—individual differences among examinees are expected. If the mean on a test is greater than 90 percent, it is unlikely to have many good items above the knowledge level of Bloom's taxonomy. Instructors must be aware of the fact that class averages can be expected to be lower on tests composed of items that cannot be answered by rote knowledge but require reasoning and application. For example, a score of 80 percent on a set of items that require problem solving or novel applications of concepts can represent excellent achievement that deserve the highest mark.

10.3   PROCEDURES FOR AN ITEM ANALYSIS

All tests developed for purposes of research and evaluation projects should be carefully developed and item analyzed, but item analysis procedures are practicable only when a computerized item analysis program is available. Fortunately, in recent years, inexpensive[3] item analysis programs have become available for personal computers and can be available to classroom teachers, especially if they have access to a scanner for data entry.

---

[2]This is not necessarily the same as allowing examinees all the time they want. Some examinees will take inordinate time in inconsequential review and checking.

[3]Perhaps the best is the inexpensive LERTAP program (e-mail address: nelson@educ.curtin.edu.au).

For pedagogical purposes we will approach the procedures of item analysis intuitively, as if it were done by hand. The extension to the use of more statistically-oriented analyses is straightforward once the basic concepts are in place.

10.4   THE STEPS OF AN ITEM ANALYSIS

After the test has been given, the test must be scored. Because test directions usually require the examinee to answer all items, omissions should be few. Each student's raw score will be the number of errors (wrong or omitted items) subtracted from the number of items in the test. In school settings, the raw scores are usually converted to percent-correct scores for reporting purposes.

1. Order the N papers by score, placing the one with the highest score on top and continuing sequentially until the one with the lowest score is on the bottom.
2. Take the highest third of the tests; this is the "high" group. If N is 24, there will be $n = 8$ students in the high group.
3. Take the lowest third of the tests; this is the "low" group.
4. Determine the proportion in the high group (p_H) answering a particular item correctly by dividing the number of correct answers for the high group by n; that is

$$p_H = \frac{(\text{number of correct responses to the item})}{n}.$$

5. Determine the proportion in the low group (p_L) answering a particular item correctly by dividing the number of correct answers for the low group by n:

$$p_L = \frac{(\text{number of correct responses to the item})}{n}.$$

6. To obtain an estimated item difficulty index, p (that is, the proportion of the total group that answered the item correctly), average p_H and p_L:

$$p = \frac{(p_H + p_L)}{2}.$$

7. To obtain a measure of item discrimination[4] (i.e., how well this item distinguishes between the students who understand the content universe of the test well and those who do not), subtract p_L from p_H:

$$D = p_H - p_L.$$

---

[4]A standard index of item discrimination is the coefficient of correlation of the examinees' scores on an item with their total scores on the *rest* of the test. The differences in results from using D versus any of the other various measures of item discrimination are "extremely small or nonexistent" (Beuchert & Mendoza, 1979, p. 116).

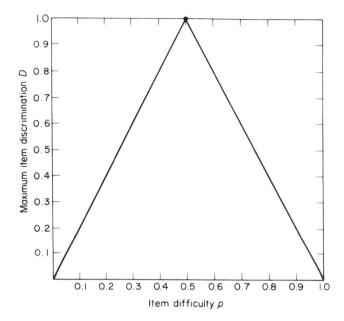

FIGURE 10–1 The relationship between item difficulty and corresponding maximum item discrimination.

The item discrimination indices from an item analysis generally agree with independent subjective evaluations of item quality (Pyrczak, 1973). Items that yield a discrimination index of .30 or more are relatively good in distinguishing between knowledgeable and less knowledgeable examinees. Those with *D*-values below .1 are relatively low in discrimination. Items that were miskeyed or are intrinsically ambiguous[5] will tend to have very low or negative *D*-values; for these items other options often have higher *D*-values than the keyed option.

10.5 ITEM DIFFICULTY AND ITEM DISCRIMINATION

The relationship between item difficulty and *maximum* item discrimination is illustrated in Figure 10–1. The maximum measurement of individual differences by an item is at a maximum when the item difficulty level is .5, that is, when only one-half of the examinees are able to answer the item correctly. Figure 10–1 also shows that there is little opportunity for

---

[5]The reason for the intrinsic ambiguity may not be readily apparent to the author of the test, but can usually be ascertained by interviewing some high-scoring examinees who did not select the keyed option. If the distinction between the best and next-best options is too fine for the knowledgeable students to discern, items should be double-keyed. Of course, no item should be double-keyed if there is no logical justification in terms of the concept being measured.

an item to assess individual differences if the item is very easy or extremely difficult. Note in Figure 10–1 that items that are neither extremely difficult nor very easy (for example, item difficulty between .25 and .75) have the *potential* for very high discrimination ($D \geq .5$).

Of course, just because the difficulty level for an item allows for item discrimination, it does not ensure that the item will function well. The crucial test for an item is whether those who best understand the domain of content (the high scorers on the total test) agree with the keyed answer on the item to a greater extent than those who know least about the subject (the low scorers on the total test). This is the information conveyed by the D-value for the item. The relationship between item difficulty and observed D-values for a carefully developed multiple-choice test of 120 items is shown in Figure 10–2. The median D-values for the 18 difficult items ($p \leq .25$) and the 23 easy items ($p \geq .75$) are only .10 and .20, respectively, whereas the median D-values for moderately difficult items (ps of .45 to .70) is .36. Notice also that four items on this test actually reduced the test's reliability (i.e., they

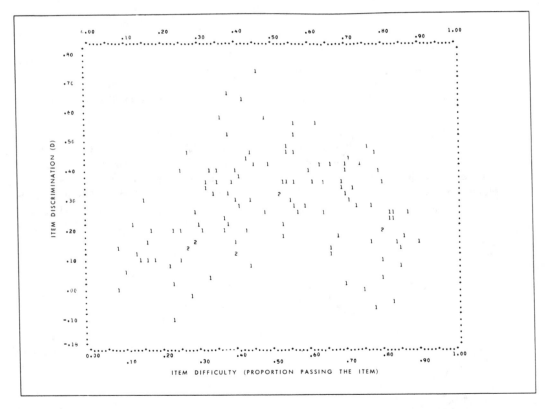

FIGURE 10–2 The relationship between item difficulty and item discrimination for 120 items.

SOURCE: Based on data given by M. D. Engelhart, "A comparison of several item discrimination indices," *Journal of Educational Measurement*, 2 (1965), 69–76. The author is grateful to Richard C. Bennet for providing Figure 10–2.

have negative D-values). On subsequent versions of the test, these items should be revised or eliminated.

If the average D-value, $\overline{D}$, on a test is .2, then the mean total score of the high group is .2, or 20 percent greater than the mean for the low group. In other words, the mean of the high group, μ_H, exceeds the mean of the low group, μ_L, by $.2k$ items, where k is the number of items on a test. For example, on a 50-item test ($k = 50$), if $\overline{D}$ is .2 and the high group's mean is 80 percent, the low group's mean will be 60 percent (i.e., 20 percent below that of the high group).

10.6 ITEM DISCRIMINATION AND TEST RELIABILITY

Lower D-values are associated with lower test reliability. The direct relationship between item discrimination values and a test's internal consistency reliability (ρ_{KR21}) is illustrated in Figure 10–3, which depicts the relationship between the mean D-value ($\overline{D}$) and the corresponding ρ_{KR21} coefficients for tests of 80 percent difficulty (i.e., mean $p = .8$) and various test lengths. For example, if $\overline{D} = .3$, the estimated values of ρ_{KR21} are .0, .6, .8, and .9 for tests of 10, 25, 50, and 100 items, respectively. Or, read differently, a ρ_{KR21} reliability coefficient of .7 requires 100 items when $\overline{D} = .18$, 50 items when $\overline{D} = .25$, 25 items when $\overline{D} = .35$, but only 10 items when $\overline{D} = .52$.

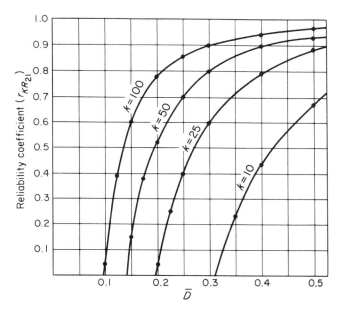

FIGURE 10–3 The relationship between the average D-value, $\overline{D}$, and Kuder-Richardson formula 21 reliability estimates for tests with a mean difficulty of 80 percent ($\bar{p} = .8$) with 10, 25, 50, and 100 items.

Each item on the test also contributes to the total test score, which is the basis for determining the "high" and "low" groups. If the test is very short, the "overlap" of the individual items with the total test score results in inflated item discrimination indices. The fewer the number of items on the test, the greater the proportion each item contributes to the total score. This factor becomes serious, however, only on very short tests.

The following guidelines for interpreting item discrimination index values for classroom tests are relevant only for describing the contribution of an item to a test's reliability, that is, the item's sensitivity to measuring individual differences. As noted in the guidelines, items with zero or negative D-values may have been miskeyed inadvertently or be intrinsically ambiguous. However, if the number of examinees is small, negative values may represent chance fluctuations (sampling error). Sometimes in small classes, all examinees simply are ignorant or misinformed about the content measured by the item. The evaluations in the table are relevant only for the ability of the item to measure individual differences and when the number of examinees is at least 30. Criterion-referenced or mastery items often are included in classroom tests for diagnostic or certification purposes and should be retained even if they are answered correctly by almost all students and contribute little or nothing to the measurement of individual differences among the examinees or to the test's reliability coefficient.

Index of Discrimination	*Item Discrimination Evaluation*
.40 and up	Excellent discrimination
.30 to .39	Good discrimination
.10 to .29	Fair discrimination
.01 to .10	Poor discrimination
Negative	Item may be miskeyed or intrinsically ambiguous

Computerized item analysis programs do not ordinarily express item discrimination using the D-index but by the correlation of the item with the total score on the test. Fortunately, these correlations differ little in value from Ds (Hopkins, Stanley & Hopkins, 1990, p. 280), thus the r for an item can be interpreted similarly to the D for that item.

10.7   AN ILLUSTRATIVE ANALYSIS

The four illustrative test items to be discussed were selected from a test that had been given to an introductory measurement class of 30 students. The results of the item analysis are given in Figure 10–4 for items 1, 2, 3, and 4 selected to illustrate various outcomes from an item analysis.

Item 1 functioned well from a measurement perspective; it also provided diagnostic feedback to the instructor by indicating a misconception that needed to be clarified for the

Item Number		Number of Correct Responses for Groups (n = 8)	Proportion of Correct Responses	Item Discrimination $D = p_H - p_L$	Item Difficulty $p = \dfrac{p_H + p_L}{2}$
1	H	7	$p_H = 7/8 = .88$	$(.88 - .38) = .5$	$\dfrac{.88 + .38}{2} = .63$
	L	3	$p_L = 3/8 = .38$		
2	H	8	$p_H = 1.00$	$D = .25$	
	L	6	$p_L = .75$		$p = .88$
3	H	4	$p_H = .5$	$D = .0$	
	L	4	$p_L = .5$		$p = .5$
4	H	2	$p_H = .25$	$D = -.50$	
	L	6	$p_L = .75$		$p = .50$

FIGURE 10–4   Item analysis data for four items

37 percent of students ($p = .63$) who answered the item incorrectly. Item 2 was quite easy ($p = .88$) and contributed modestly to the test's reliability ($D = .25$). Item 3 was in the optimal difficulty range but failed to discriminate; it may be intrinsically ambiguous. It needs to be eliminated or revised. Item 4 is probably miskeyed or, at least, is seriously intrinsically ambiguous. The examinees appear to be in a different mental set than the instructor. The item appears to have good measurement potential (note the large D-value) but should be either double-keyed or excluded from the present examination. In its present form, Item 4 actually lowers test reliability and, no doubt, validity as well. Items like this are frequently found on classroom tests; such items are miskeyed or at least are intrinsically ambiguous. Such items typically remain unidentified unless an item analysis is performed.

For objective items with three or more options, a further analysis is needed to identify the options that are creating the difficulty. Computerized item analysis programs provide this kind of information to the test developer.

Distribution of Responses to Item 3 for High-Scoring (H) and Low-Scoring (L) Examinees

Item	Group	Option					D	p
		A	B*	C	D	Omit		
	H	0	4	3	0	1		
3	L	0	4	0	4	0	.00	.50

*Keyed correct answer.

Suppose there were four options to Item 3. Consider the following distribution:

Option C deserves scrutiny. It is likely that the distinction between options B and C is ambiguous; perhaps the distinction has not received adequate instructional emphasis. A study of the items may reveal that both B and C are reasonable and, hence, should be credited as correct. Distracter A probably should be changed or revised for future use, since it was nonfunctional. Option D seems to be an excellent distracter.

Ordinarily, poorly functioning items can be revised by improving the distracters. Some items, such as those for mathematics and science, are much easier to develop than are others, such as those for social studies and literature.

Item 4 appears to have been miskeyed, or perhaps the abler students are misinformed (sometimes partial information is misinformation). Only a study of the content of the item can diagnose the reason for its failure.

Distribution of Responses to Item 4 for High-Scoring (H) and Low-Scoring (L) Examinees

Item	Group	Option					D	p
		A	B	C	D*	Omit		
	H	0	5	1	2	0		
4	L	1	1	0	6	0	–.00	.50

*Keyed correct answer.

Of course, one would not give credit for an incorrect answer such as might be found on an arithmetic test. When the item analysis "faults" an item, the source of the intrinsic ambiguity can usually be identified, particularly if it is discussed with the class. When the number of examinees is small, one will often obtain peculiar results owing to sampling fluctuations.

10.8 OTHER EXAMPLES

The following item was developed by Educational Testing Service and administered to 370 students:

In the following questions you are asked to make inferences from the data that are given on the map of the imaginary country, Serendip. *The answers in most instances must be probabilities rather than certainties.* The relative size of towns and cities is not shown. To assist you in the location of the places mentioned in the questions, the map is divided into squares lettered vertically from A to E and numbered horizontally from 1 to 5.

5. Which one of the following cities would be the best location for a steel mill?
(A) Li (3A)   (B) Um (3B)   (C) Cot (3D)   (D) Dube (4B)

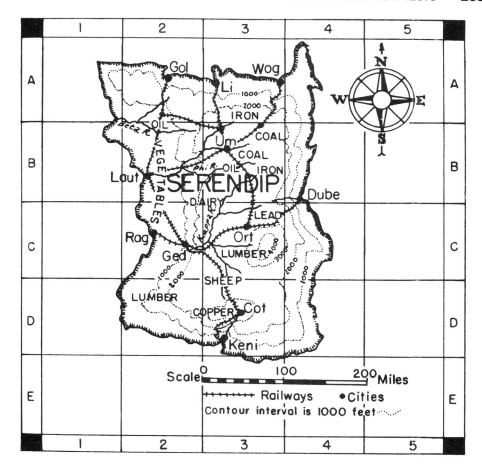

The question requires knowledge of the natural resources used in producing steel and awareness of the importance of transportation facilities in bringing these resources together. It was part of a social studies test given to high school seniors.

Students who know that iron is the basic raw material of steel and that coal commonly provides the necessary source of heat would proceed to locate deposits of these resources in relation to the cities listed in the question. They would be able to eliminate *Cot* immediately, since there is no iron or coal in its vicinity, although it might be an attractive choice to students who mistakenly think that copper is a basic ingredient of steel. Both *Li* and *Dube* are located reasonably near supplies of iron and therefore might be attractive choices. *Um,* however, is the more clearly *correct* response because not only are deposits of iron and coal nearby, but they are more readily transportable by direct railroad routes.

Item analysis data for the 370 students are as follows:

Examinee Response to Item 5

		Option					D	p
Item	**Group**	Li A	Um B*	Cot C	Dube D	Omit		
5	H	2	84 $p_H = .84^a$	1	6	7	.44	.62
	L	10	40 $p_L = .40^a$	4	9	37		

*Keyed correct answer.

Although the item was rather difficult for the group (it was answered correctly by only 62 percent [$p = .62$] of the examinees), it did discriminate well ($D = .44$). However, some of the discrimination resulted from the fact that 37 percent of the "low" group did not attempt the item. Distracters A, C, and D functioned only slightly but in the right direction. Additional study of the test on which this item appeared revealed that all 7 omits in the "high" group and 29 of the 37 omits in the "low" group were from students who ran out of time before they had a chance to attempt the item (which appeared near the end of the test). The analysis of this item suggests that there may be a substantial speed element in the test; hence, many examinees with low total scores may not have low map-reading ability but are slow workers who did not have time to respond to many items that they would have been able to answer correctly.

The following item is taken from a writing test[6] administered to 250 college-bound high school students.

In the following question you are given a complete sentence to be rephrased according to the directions which follow it. You should rephrase the sentence mentally to save time, although you may make notes in your test book if you wish.

Below the sentence and its directions are listed words or phrases that may occur in your revised sentence. When you have thought out a good sentence, find in the choices A to E the word or entire phrase that is included in your revised sentence. The word or phrase you choose should be the most accurate and most nearly complete of all the choices given.

Although the directions may require you to change the relationship between parts of the sentence or to make slight changes in meaning in other ways, *make only those changes that the directions require*; that is, keep the meaning the same, or as nearly the same as the directions permit. If you think that more than one good sentence can be made according to the directions, select the sentence that is most exact, effective, and natural in phrasing and construction.

---

[6]From *Multiple-Choice Questions: A Close Look*. Educational Testing Service. All rights reserved. Reproduced by permission.

<u>Sentence</u>: **John, shy as he was of girls, still managed to marry one of the most desirable of them.**
<u>Directions</u> Substitute <u>John's shyness</u> for <u>John, shy.</u>
Your rewritten sentence will contain which of the following?
    (A) him being married to
    (B) himself married to
    (C) him from marrying
    (D) was himself married to
    (E) him to have married

In order to select choice *A,* a sentence like "John's shyness with girls did not stop him being married to the most desirable of them" would have to be used. To make this sentence correct, formal written English demands that the word "being" be preceded by the possessive pronoun "his." Choice *B* presents a sentence similar to "Despite John's shyness with girls, he managed to get himself married to one of the most desirable of them." This sentence is wordy and inappropriate in tone (for formal English). Choice *C,* however, yields a sentence on the order of "John's shyness with girls did not prevent him from marrying one of the most desirable of them." This retains the meaning of the original sentence and contains no errors in grammar; it is the correct answer. The fourth choice might lead to "John's shyness with girls did not keep him single; he was himself married to one of the most desirable of them." This sentence changes the meaning of the original sentence, and it is, at the same time, ambiguous in its own meaning. "John's shyness with girls was not a reason for him to have married the most desirable of them," an attempt to use the fifth choice, results in a complete change of meaning. It is therefore unacceptable, even though it is grammatically correct.

Examinee Response to Item 6

Item	Group	A	B	C*	D	E	Omit	D	p
6	H	3	0	**61** $p_H = .90$[a]	1	3	0	.58	.75
	L	5	11	**17** $p_L = .40$[a]	14	15	6		

*Keyed option.
[a]$N = 250$, $n = 68$.

The analysis reveals that few of the able students had difficulty with this item, whereas the "low" group had extreme difficulty. Distracters *B, D,* and *E* appear excellent.

More elaborate item analysis, such as the one shown in Table 10–1, are facilitated when a computer is available. The *p*-values in Table 10–1 are estimates of the item-test (biserial) correlation; they convey the same information as the *D*-values and correlate very highly with them (Bridgman, 1964).

The first column, "Item Number," refers to the number of each question on an 84-question multiple-choice test. Each question includes four possible alternatives; the double column

TABLE 10–1   Item Analysis of a Final Examination[a]

Item Number	A		B		C		D		Total			
	High	Low	High	Low	High	Low	High	Low	Key	p	r	D
1	01	03	13	17	**85**	**79**	02	02	C	.82	.09	.06
2	**34**	**36**	03	09	55	40	08	15	A	.35	−.02	−.02
3	00	07	01	07	01	05	**98**	**81**	D	.89	.45	.17
4	03	04	**83**	**59**	13	30	01	07	B	.71	.29	.24
5	03	01	17	34	**10**	**04**	69	61	C	.07	.19	.06
6	**79**	**61**	19	31	01	05	01	04	A	.70	.21	.18
7	13	20	**73**	**49**	01	04	14	27	B	.61	.25	.24
8	05	08	01	11	04	43	**89**	**35**	D	.62	.57	.54
9	73	81	**07**	**05**	17	05	03	09	B	.06	.07	.02
10	01	15	**76**	**44**	21	31	02	10	B	.60	.34	.32
.												
.												
.												
81	03	11	66	39	**05**	**13**	24	37	C	.09	−.21	−.08
82	**81**	**39**	01	16	11	27	07	15	A	.60	.44	.42
83	04	26	01	13	03	13	**92**	**44**	D	.68	.56	.48
84	00	07	**71**	**33**	13	31	15	25	B	.52	.38	.38

SOURCE: H. Grobman, *AERA Monograph Series in Curriculum Evaluation*, no. 2, *Evaluation activities of curriculum projects* (Chicago: Rand McNally, 1968). Reprinted by permission of the publisher.
[a]"High" group consists of the top 27 percent of the students in the sample on total test score. "Low" group consists of the bottom 27 percent of the students in the sample on total test score.

labeled *A, B, C,* and *D* across the top of the table refer to the number of students selecting that option for each question. Thus, the column labeled *A* refers to those students who selected alternative *A* for a given question, and similarly for *B, C,* and *D.*

Under each option (*A, B, C, D*) are two sub-columns, "High" and "Low." "High" refers to those students whose total scores on the test were the highest of all students taking the test. "Low" refers to the students in the low group. Thus, for item 1, the overwhelming majority of both good and poor students (categorized on the basis of overall success on the test) selected answer *C*; 85 percent of the high scorers and 79 percent of the low scorers chose it.

Under the "Total" heading at the far right of the table, the column labeled "Key" indicates the answer that was considered best by the test writers (also given in boldface type). The column labeled "*p*" indicates the proportion of all students taking the test who selected the correct answer. For question 1, 82 percent of the examinees selected option *C,* the correct answer. Thus, question 1 was very easy for these students.

The next column, "*r,*" is the biserial correlation. This is a way of stating statistically the extent to which a question discriminates between the high-scoring students and the low-scoring students on the total test. Thus, for question 1, an *r* of .09 (*D* = .06) indicates that this question did not effectively discriminate between these two groups of students. (Note that $D = .06 = .85-.79$; D and r convey essentially the same information.) Question 83, with an r of .56 ($D = .48$), was effective in discriminating between good and poor students. Item 81 discriminated negatively. This means that the correct answer was selected more often by the poorer students than by the better students. A majority of the good students selected option B rather than the keyed correct answer, C. This is an indication of some kind of trouble either with the item or with the curriculum. The problem may be that the question was keyed incorrectly, that is, that the correct answer is B rather than C. Or the question may be intrinsically ambiguous. It may have two correct or equally defensible answers. Another possibility is that some of the abler students in the class may be *mis*informed.

10.9   ITEM ANALYSIS IN LARGE SCALE ASSESSMENTS

The following table presents item analysis data for a science question that was administered to approximately 500 representative 6th and 11th grade students in Colorado. Note that the correlation of each distracter with the total score is given in addition to the item discrimination index for the correct answer. The rs are used in exactly the same way as Ds.

7. Which one of these things would happen if you filled a balloon with air and put it in the refrigerator for a while?

	6th Grade (N = 451)		11th Grade (N = 469)	
	p	r	p	r
a) The air in the balloon would freeze.	.05	−.11	.01	−.02
b) The balloon would get larger.	.14	−.03	.12	−.06
c) The air in the balloon would get warmer.	.04	−.11	.02	−.15
d) The balloon would get smaller.*	**.38**	**.30**	**.61**	**.46**
e) The balloon would burst.	.21	−.17	.21	−.27
OMITS (students who left item blank)	.18	−.31	.03	−.40

Note that only 38 percent of the sixth-graders selected the correct answer, whereas 61 percent of the eleventh-graders answered the question correctly. The item discriminated well at grade 6 ($r = .30$), but even better at grade 11 ($r = .46$). The negative rs for distracters are desirable; they indicate that poorer students selected the distracters more often than better students. Note that distracter a was not attractive—only 5 percent and 1 percent of the students selected this option. Note also that e was the most effective distracter at both grade levels. Not only was it most attractive (39 percent and 21 percent), but also it was highest in discrimination. The expected pattern is negative rs for distracters and positive rs for the correct option. At grade 11, 3 percent of the examinees did not answer the question. These examinees probably omitted other questions as well, which helps explain the r of −.40. As expected, students who tend to omit items tend to have lower test scores, especially when there is no correction for chance (see Section 6.12).

10.10   ITEM ANALYSIS WITH AN EXTERNAL CRITERION

When one is developing a test that is going to be used for program evaluation, research, or district-level or state assessment, an external criterion can sometimes be used to evaluate the validity of the items. This procedure is rarely useful for classroom test development.

A useful external criterion for achievement tests is independent teacher ratings of students' proficiency levels. In the development of items for the *Colorado State Assessment,* before the tests were administered, classroom teachers were asked to rate the reading ability of their students on a five-point scale. These ratings served as an external criterion with which the responses to the reading items could be correlated. As a group, good readers, as defined by teachers' ratings, should perform better than average or poor readers on all items that are validly measuring reading ability. The correlation of the item with the criterion is a validity index (r_{ext}) for the item. The validity index of an item is a stronger indication of quality than the item discrimination index (r)—the latter pertains directly to reliability and only indirectly (and logically) to validity, whereas the correlation of an item with an external criterion is a direct indication of validity.

The results for two items on a test with an external criterion are shown here; the first item (item number 69) is from a reading comprehension test. Only 67 percent ($p = .67$) of the fifth-grade students were able to make the proper inference from the passage. Notice that those who selected the correct answer, *a,* also had higher total scores on the reading test ($r = .42$); they were also rated by their teachers as better readers than those who selected the incorrect option ($r_{ext} = .23$). Item 69 appears to be an excellent item for measuring reading comprehension.

Read this paragraph from the book Tom Sawyer:

> **About noon the next day the boys arrived at the dead tree; they had come for their tools. Tom was impatient to go to the haunted house; Huck was measurably so, also—but suddenly said, "Looky here, Tom, do you know what day it is?"**
> In the paragraph above we learn that:

69. Tom wanted to go to the haunted house. a) Yes b) No

Option	p	r	r_{ext}
a) Yes	**.67**	**.42**	**.23**
b) No	.28	−.23	−.15
OMITS	.05	−.43	−.19

Illustrative data for an item (no. 86) on a fifth-grade math test are given below. The external criterion was teacher ratings of students' math competence. Notice the correspondence between the item discrimination (r) and item validity (r_{ext}) indices. Does it surprise you that only about two out of three fifth-grade students can discriminate correctly between these response alternatives? What do you think would have happened if "3 inches" had been included as an option?

86. About how long is the line drawn below?

	a) 1 inch	**b) 2 inches***	c) 4 inches	d) 1 foot	e) 1 centimeter	OMITS
p	.07	**.67**	.18	.04	.04	.01
r	−.11	**.23**	−.13	−.10	−.23	−.38
r_{ext}	.09	**.26**	−.15	−.10	−.15	−.03

Notice that there is good agreement between the item discrimination rs and the item validity r_{ext}s.

Several other types of external criteria can be used for certain test validation purposes. The *contrasting groups method* selects two groups that should differ on the measured variable; the performance of the two groups is compared on each item. For example, on the *Strong-Campbell Interest Inventory* only those items that discriminate between engineers and non-engineers are employed on the engineer scale. One personality inventory eliminated items on which hospitalized mental patients did not differ from nonhospitalized persons.

A scale designed to identify potential school dropouts might administer a pool of items to two groups of persons of high school age who have, and have not, dropped out of school. Items on which the two groups differ have promise as items for identifying potential dropouts.

SUMMARY

The principal purposes of an item analysis are to determine the difficulty and discrimination of each item. Items of moderate difficulty have the *potential* for good item discrimination. The theoretical maximum item discrimination D-value (1.0) is possible only when item difficulty is .5. The standard deviation and reliability of a test may be estimated from the mean item discrimination and number of items.

An item analysis—comparing the performance on each item of the most and least successful examinees on the total test—will identify items that are nonfunctional, intrinsically ambiguous, or miskeyed, so they can be revised or thrown out. Usually, this procedure will improve the reliability and often the validity of a particular test, and the experience of studying the students' responses diagnostically will help the instructor both in teaching and in subsequent test construction.

A chain of relationships exists between certain item and test characteristics. Item difficulty affects possible item discrimination, which in turn directly determines the variability and internal consistency reliability of the test scores. An external criterion (e.g., independent teacher ratings) can be useful in test development for validating items.

For mastery and criterion-referenced testing, high p-values (easy items) and low D-values are acceptable. Indeed, for them $p = 1.0$ (and, hence, $D = 0$ and $r = 0$) may be the goal. Values of p of 1.0 are unlikely for good items if the item represents any level other than the knowledge level of Bloom's taxonomy.

IMPORTANT TERMS AND CONCEPTS

item analysis	item validity
intrinsic ambiguity	item difficulty (p)
item discrimination (D or r)	external criterion

CHAPTER TEST

1. The most important characteristic of an achievement test item is its
   a) item difficulty, p, of 0.5–0.8.
   b) item discrimination, D, of 0.35 or above.
   c) perfect objectivity (scorer agreement).
   d) content validity.
   e) test-retest reliability.

2. The rationale underlying the use of item discrimination indices as a *basis for judging item quality* is that
   a) item evaluations should be scientific and objective.
   b) as a group, high-scoring examinees know more than low-scoring examinees on all items in the content universe.
   c) high item discrimination indices are impossible with extremely easy or difficult items.

Match the following symbols with the verbal definitions in Questions 3–5.
   a) p_H b) p_L c) p d) $\bar{p}$ e) D

3. The proportion of correct answers in the high-scoring group

4. A symbol for the difficulty of an item

5. The average p-value on the test

6. The item discrimination index, D, is
   a) equal to $\dfrac{(p_H + p_L)}{2}$.
   b) the difference between the proportion of correct responses in the high and low groups.
   c) the average of the percent of correct answers in the high and low groups.
   d) More than one of the above

7. The largest possible value of D is   a) 0.0. b) 0.5. c) 1.0.

8. The maximum value of D occurs when
   a) $p = .05$.
   b) $p = .25$.
   c) $p = .50$.
   d) $p = .75$.
   e) $p = 1.0$

9. The empirical relationship between p and D (see Figure 10–2) is
   a) very high and linear.
   b) moderately high and linear.
   c) very high and curvilinear.
   d) moderately high and curvilinear.

Items 10–13. On a test of 50 items with $\mu = 35$ and $\bar{D} = .25$:

10. The mean percent-correct score was ___.

11. The average score in the high group was ___ percent more than in the low group.

12. Is this test is too easy to assess accurately student differences in mastery level?

13. If rs (rather than Ds) were used to evaluate items, there would be substantial agreement in the items judged to be good and poor.

14. Use Figure 10–3 and estimate the reliability coefficient (ρ_{KR21}) for 25-, 50-, and 100-item tests having a mean score of 80 percent when the mean item discrimination index, $\bar{D}$, is = .30.

Questions 15–16 are based on the item analysis in Table 10–1 (p. 266).

15. Which item is the easiest?

16. Which item is the most difficult?

Questions 17–24: For each of these items in Table 10–1 (p. 266) indicate whether the item analysis suggests possible intrinsic ambiguity. When the answer is *yes,* indicate the option that contributes to the ambiguity (and hence may need to be double-keyed).

17. item 1

18. item 2

19. item 3

20. item 4

21. item 5

22. item 9

23. item 10

24. item 81

25. With respect to Table 10–1, the reliability of the test would increase most if which two items were deleted or double-keyed?

26. If all examinees answer an item correctly, the item could still be serving a significant educational function. *(T or F)*

27. Which one of the following requires an external criterion?
a) item discrimination index
b) item difficulty index
c) item validity index

28. The keyed option of an item that has a negative D was
a) selected more often by poorer students.
b) selected less often by poorer students.
c) selected more often by better students.
d) More than one of the above

29. Which one of the following examples does *not* employ an external criterion for evaluating items on a reading test?
a) The performance of students in, and not in, remedial reading is compared on each item.
b) Performance on each item is correlated with teacher ratings of reading proficiency.
c) Performance on each item is correlated with semester marks in reading.
d) Performance on items is correlated with total score on the test.

30. An external criterion is *least* useful for
  a) the development of a standardized science test.
  b) the development of a classroom achievement test.
  c) the development of a social-maturity inventory.

ANSWERS TO CHAPTER TEST

1. d	11. 25%	21. No
2. b	12. No	22. Yes, c
3. a	13. Yes	23. No
4. c	14. .60, .80, .90	24. Yes, b
5. d	15. 3, $p = .89$	25. 2, 81
6. b	16. 9. $p = .06$	26. T
7. c	17. No	27. c
8. c	18. Yes, c	28. a
9. d	19. No	29. d
10. 70%	20. No	30. b

11

The Assessment of Affective Variables

11.1 INTRODUCTION

Cognitive tests assess *maximum* or *optimum* performance (what a person *can* do); affective measures attempt to reflect *typical* performance (what a person usually *does* or *feels*). The objectives for all courses include attitudes, appreciation, and interests, as well as knowledge and proficiencies. Common affective objectives in education include such phrases as "a positive self-concept," "an enjoyment of literature," "an interest in science," and "an acceptance of persons from different cultural and social backgrounds." Many of these aims are assumed to follow naturally from the attainment of cognitive objectives. "Human feelings are important both as means and ends in education" (Tyler, 1973, p. 2). In spite of the lack of explicit formulation, nearly all cognitive objectives have an affective component. (Probably the converse also holds—nearly all affective objectives have a cognitive component.) If students are taught to read but then read only when required to, the educational experience has failed to achieve an extremely important affective educational objective.

Although much attention is given to the assessment of cognitive objectives, rarely is any *systematic* effort directed toward the evaluation of affective educational objectives. Studies have found that teachers are not good predictors of the affective responses of their students. For example, a course on the psychology of the adult had little effect on the attitudes of graduate students toward other people, even though such an outcome had frequently been taken for granted. Another study found that a special unit of instruction designed to improve students attitudes toward a minority group did not affect students' stereotypes of the minority group, even though this was the major goal of the unit (Schon, Hopkins & Vojir, 1980). This chapter is concerned with the development and use of affective measures and certain other noncognitive variables.

11.2 THE AFFECTIVE TAXONOMY OF EDUCATIONAL OBJECTIVES

Since the taxonomy of cognitive objectives had an extraordinary impact on cognitive measures in education, an affective taxonomy was devised to stimulate and systematize the assessment of objectives in the affective domain.

> The taxonomy, like the periodic table of elements or a check-off shopping list, provides the panorama of objectives. Comparing the range of the present curriculum with the range of possible outcomes may suggest additional goals that might be explored. (Krathwohl, 1965, p. 89)

The degree of *internalization* is proposed as the unifying hierarchical factor underlying the affective taxonomy. Various affective concepts are defined in relation to the internalization hierarchy, as shown in Figure 11–1. The shallowest degree of internalization of feeling is represented by *awareness*; the deepest is represented by *characterization*. Recall that assessment at the higher levels of the cognitive taxonomy is quite difficult to achieve in practice; measuring character and values often poses even greater problems. The affec-

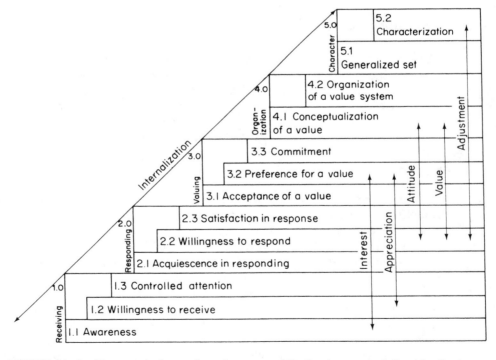

FIGURE 11–1 The range of meaning of common affective terms as defined by the taxonomy of affective educational objectives.

SOURCE: Adapted from D. R. Krathwohl et al., *Taxonomy of educational objectives: Handbook II, Affective domain* (New York: David McKay, 1964), p. 37.

tive taxonomy has not had the impact on education that the cognitive taxonomy has had. This is due, in part, to the unique assessment problems associated with affective measurement, but the basic impediment in the process is probably ever-present inertia—things at rest remain at rest unless acted upon by some external force. We hope this book may stimulate attempts to assess affective educational objectives in addition to the conventional cognitive outcomes. Krathwohl's taxonomy can be a useful general framework to help organize such assessments.

11.3   COGNITIVE VERSUS AFFECTIVE APPRAISAL

"Who was the third President of the United States?"

If you respond, "Thomas Jefferson," your answer is correct.

"Do you enjoy doing math?"

Unlike the first question, this item does not have a correct answer that can be designated in advance, because for matters of personal preference the correct (true) answer is not the same for everyone. Rather than offering a crude *yes–no* response option, the question could be rephrased so that different degrees of preference or liking can be assessed:

"How well do you like to study math?"
1) Loathe it.   2) Dislike it.   3) Indifferent.   4) Like it   5) Love it.

The five response categories could then be scored 1, 2, 3, 4, or 5.

Another kind of question combines both a knowledge aspect and an affective component. If you ask a student

"Have you read any book just for fun this semester?"

the desired response (*yes*) may be correct or incorrect. The student either did or did not read such a book, but it may be difficult to verify the validity of the statement. The correct answer may not be the ideal answer. *The correct answer to an affective question depends on the person queried; the correct answer to a cognitive question is the same for all respondents.* Note in this example that the implicit affective objective (enjoyment of reading) is inferred from a behavior.

Attitude scales are the most widely employed means of assessing affective objectives, however, many other means are used that involve self-reports or reports by others, such as naturalistic observation, anecdotal records, questionnaires, sociometric techniques, interviews, and letters of recommendation. Certain measurement problems are common in all such measures. *Situational factors,* such as the "set" given to the examinees by the instructions, the social-desirability response, and whether the examinee's response is anonymous (or confidential), have a very substantial influence on the results of affective measures—far more than they do for ability measures.

11.4   THURSTONE ATTITUDE SCALES

Ever since the ground breaking studies by Thurstone at the University of Chicago in the 1930s, scales have been devised to assess people's attitudes toward a multitude of objects and situations ranging from war to God. Thurstone-type scales have been used to measure innumerable attitudes, for example, to determine the level of employee morale, the effects of movies on attitudes toward crime and toward ethnic groups, the effects of social science courses on students' attitudes, and the effects of propaganda on attitudes. Most attitude scales have been developed to answer specific research questions and are not standardized and have either poor norms or no norms at all.

Thurstone showed how attitude scales could be constructed for any specified topic and how to develop items that reveal various degrees of feeling toward the topic or situation. The attitude-toward-movies scale is presented in Figure 11–2. We suggest that you take this inventory by responding to the items according to the directions at the top of the figure. After you have completed the scale, determine your score by finding the median scale value (given in parentheses) of all the statements with which you agreed.

What does your score on the *Attitude toward Movies* scale mean? How did Thurstone arrive at the item intensity values? The scale of intensities is considered to run from 0 to 6. The higher your score, the more favorable your attitude toward movies; the lower the score, the less favorable. It would be interesting to tabulate the anonymous scores of the members of your class (perhaps separately by gender). You can describe your class using the absolute meaning of the mean intensity scores. Is the median of the scores in your class approximately $\frac{(0 + 6)}{2} = 3.0$? How far above or below the median for your class are you?

Thurstone-type attitude scales are developed by giving several hundred persons (*judges*) a large number of statements about a topic. Each judge sorts each statement into one of several categories (six in the development of the movie attitude scale) that range from "extremely favorable" through "neutral" to "extremely unfavorable." Each statement is written on a separate slip of paper. Each judge is asked to rate the intensity of each statement (not the extent to which he or she agrees with it). This sorting procedure has been described as the method of "equal-appearing intervals," although the judges are not told that the intervals between categories are equal. Those statements on which there is a consensus among the judges on the intensity ratings are used as a criterion for selecting items for the final scale. A Thurstone attitude scale usually consists of 20 to 45 statements that are spread evenly over the various values of the intensity scale in order to differentiate among the levels of "favorableness." The intensity scale value of a given statement is the average category of the distribution of the judgments assigned to that statement by the original group of judges (for example, compare items 4 and 27). The order of these statements is randomized on the final printed form. The examinee is asked to mark those statements with which the examinee agrees; the examinee's score is the median intensity of these statements.

Thurstone attitude scales can be constructed for measuring attitudes toward any subject—classical music, collective bargaining, bilingual education, affirmative action, born-again Christians, and so forth. It should be evident that considerable time and effort are required in the development of Thurstone scales, factors that limit their applicability. Thurstone scales are, however, available on a large number of topics. Several extremely use-

ATTITUDE TOWARD MOVIES

This is a study of attitudes toward the movies. You will find a number of statements expressing different attitudes toward the movies.

√ Put a check mark if you agree with the statement.

X Put a cross if you disagree with the statement.

If you simply cannot decide about a statement, mark it with a question mark.

This is not an examination. There are no right or wrong answers to these statements. This is simply an appraisal of people's attitudes toward the movies. Please indicate your own attitude by a check mark (√) when you agree and by a cross (X) when you disagree.

LIST OF OPINIONS IN THE SCALE

1. (1, 5) The movies occupy time that should be spent in more wholesome recreation.
2. (1, 3) I am tired of the movies; I have seen too many poor ones.
3. (4, 5) The movies are the best civilizing device ever developed.
4. (0, 2) Movies are the most important cause of crime.
5. (2, 7) Movies are all right but a few of them give the rest a bad name.
6. (2, 6) I like to see movies once in a while but they do disappoint you sometimes.
7. (2, 9) I think movies are fairly interesting.
8. (2, 7) Movies are just a harmless pastime.
9. (1, 7) The movies to me are just a way to kill time.
10. (4, 0) The influence of the movies is decidedly for good.
11. (3, 9) The movies are good, clean entertainment.
12. (3, 9) Movies increase one's appreciation of beauty.
13. (1, 7) I'd never miss the movies if we didn't have them.
14. (2, 4) Sometimes I feel that the movies are desirable and sometimes I doubt it.
15. (0, 0) It is a sin to go to the movies.
16. (4, 3) There would be very little progress without the movies.
17. (4, 3) The movies are the most vital form of art today.
18. (3, 6) A movie is the best entertainment that can be obtained cheaply.
19. (3, 4) A movie once in a while is a good thing for everybody.
20. (3, 4) The movies are one of the few things I can enjoy by myself.
21. (1, 3) Going to the movies is a foolish way to spend your money.
22. (1, 1) Moving pictures bore me.
23. (0, 6) As they now exist movies are wholly bad for children.
24. (0, 6) Such a pernicious influence as the movies is bound to weaken the moral fiber of those who attend.
25. (0, 3) As a protest against movies we should pledge ourselves never to attend them.
26. (0, 1) The movies are the most important single influence for evil.
27. (4, 7) The movies are the most powerful influence for good in American life.
28. (2, 3) I would go to the movies more often if I were sure of finding something good.
29. (4, 1) If I had my choice of anything I wanted to do, I would go to the movies.
30. (2, 2) The pleasure people get from the movies just about balances the harm they do.
31. (2, 0) I don't find much that is educational in the current films.
32. (1, 9) The information that you obtain from the movies is of little value.
33. (1, 0) Movies are a bad habit.
34. (3, 3) I like the movies as they are because I go to be entertained, not educated.
35. (3, 1) On the whole the movies are pretty decent.
36. (0, 8) The movies are undermining respect for authority.
37. (2, 7) I like to see other people enjoy the movies whether I enjoy them myself or not.
38. (0, 3) The movies are to blame for the prevalence of sex offenses.
39. (4, 4) The movie is one of the great educational institutions for common people.
40. (0, 8) Young people are learning to smoke, drink, and pet from the movies.

The person who has the larger score is more favorably inclined toward the movies than the person with a lower score.

In scoring the attitude scale, we cannot conclude that one score is better or worse than another; we can only say that one person's attitude toward the movies is more or less favorable than another person's. It is purely arbitrary that attitudes unfavorable to the movies have lower scale values than favorable attitudes.

Any individual's attitude is measured by the average or mean scale value of all the statements he checks.

For the purpose of comparing groups, the distributions of attitude in each group can be plotted, and it can then be said whether and how much one group is more favorable to the movies than another group.

FIGURE 11–2   An attitude-toward-movies scale.

SOURCE: L. L. Thurstone, *The measurement of values* (Chicago: University of Chicago Press, 1959), pp. 285–86. Reprinted by permission of The University of Chicago Press.

ful collections of attitude scales and discussions on many topics have been assembled. These are found, along with descriptive annotations, in Appendix A.

11.5 LIKERT SCALES

There are many types of measures for obtaining information regarding affective variables. Perhaps the most widely used technique for attitude measurement is the *Likert scale*, on which a statement is followed by the five-category response continuum:

Strongly Agree, Agree, Undecided, Disagree, Strongly Disagree.

The examinee selects the response that best describes his or her reaction to each statement; the response categories are weighted from 1 to 5 and averaged for all the items.

For younger examinees (for example, students in elementary school), using only three response categories (e.g., Agree, Uncertain, Disagree) is common. More than five categories are occasionally used, although the additional categories are usually not worth the extra frustration they create for examinees as they try, for example, to choose between "Very Strongly Agree" and "Strongly Agree."

The *Education Scale* shown in Figure 11–3, is an example of a Likert scale. (To conserve space, the response options are given only for item 1.) Test-retest and split-half reliability estimates of 0.80 or above are commonly reported for this scale. Many other examples of attitude scales can be found in resource compendia in Appendix A (such as Shaw and Wright's, 1967, *Scales for the Measurement of Attitudes*).

Likert scales are very flexible and can be constructed more easily than most other types of attitude scales. To generate items, it is often helpful to role play and put yourself in the shoes of a typical examinee to construct statements that typify positive and negative attitudes. Ordinarily, the items are a mixture of statements that represent positive and negative attitudes; this reduces an examinee's tendency to respond perfunctorily. However, statements should not be changed so that they are artificially negative, such as by the addition of *not* or *un-* (Schriesheim & Hill, 1981). As in cognitive assessment, the use of simple language and vocabulary is important. Since the intent of the assessment is affective, not cognitive, items can be read to the examinee if the examinee has a reading problem.

11.6 RATING SCALES

Rating scales are not fundamentally different from Likert scales. Whereas Likert scales use a standard set of response options that represent varying degrees of agreement, rating scales use descriptive terms (for example, "like" to "dislike," or "like me" to "not like me") that pertain to each particular question.

An example of a rating scale is the *Personality Record* (Figure 11–4) that is used by high schools to send information on noncognitive variables that is of interest to colleges. A teacher or counselor evaluates a student on eight factors; each of the eight represents an important student characteristic and educational objective. Such ratings can be made quickly. If the ratings

THE EDUCATION SCALE

READ EACH ITEM CAREFULLY AND UNDERLINE QUICKLY THE PHRASE WHICH BEST EXPRESSES YOUR FEELING ABOUT THE STATEMENT. Wherever possible, let your own personal experience determine your answer. Do not spend much time on any item. If in doubt, underline the phrase which seems most nearly to express your present feeling about the statement. WORK RAPIDLY. Be sure to answer every item.

*1 A man can learn more by working four years than by going to high school.
    Strongly Agree Agree Undecided Disagree Strongly Disagree
2 The more education a person has the better he is able to enjoy life.
3 Education helps a person to use his leisure time to better advantage.
4 A good education is a great comfort to a man out of work.
*5 Only subjects like reading, writing, and arithmetic should be taught at public expense.
*6 Education is no help in getting a job today.
*7 Most young people are getting too much education.
8 A high school education is worth all the time and effort it requires.
9 Our schools encourage an individual to think for himself.
*10 There are too many fads and frills in modern education.
*11 Education only makes a person discontented.
*12 School training is of little help in meeting the problems of real life.
13 Education tends to make an individual less conceited.
14 Solution of the world's problems will come through education.
*15 High school courses are too impractical.
*16 A man is foolish to keep going to school if he can get a job.
17 Savings spent on education are wisely invested.
18 An educated man can advance more rapidly in business and industry.
*19 Parents should not be compelled to send their children to school.
20 Education is more valuable than most people think.
21 A high school education makes a man a better citizen.
*22 Public money spent on education during the past few years could have been used more wisely for other purposes.

*These are negative items, agreement with which is considered to reflect an unfavorable attitude. Their weights must be reversed for purposes of scoring. The same response alternatives are used with all items.

FIGURE 11–3 An example of a Likert scale.

SOURCE: E. A. Rundquist and R. F. Sletto, *Personality in the depression* (Minneapolis: University of Minnesota Press, 1936). Reprinted by permission of the publisher. Copyright 1936 by the University of Minnesota Press.

are consistent among raters, one becomes more confident that the ratings reflect a generalized trait or traits and are not merely a function of the idiosyncrasies of a particular rater. The use of rating scales is common in reporting students' progress in noncognitive objectives, especially in elementary and middle schools.

Noncognitive objectives are also assessed when students evaluate teachers and courses. Rating scales are used at most colleges and universities to help evaluate instruction and instructors. Unfortunately, the use of anonymous student ratings of instruction below the college level is very limited. Such feedback has great potential for the improvement of

Personality Record (Confidential)
(REVISED)

Last Name .... First Name .... Middle Name ....

Room .... Grade ....

School .... Town or City .... State ....

PERSONAL CHARACTERISTICS OF ....

The following characterizations are descriptions of behavior. It is recommended that where possible the judgments of a number of the pupil's present teachers be indicated by the use of the following method or by checks:

Example: MOTIVATION

Purposeless	Vacillating	Usually purposeful	Effectively motivated	Highly motivated
	1 √	M (5) √√√√		2 √√

M (5) indicates the most common or modal behavior of the pupil as shown by the agreement of five of the eight teachers reporting. The location of the numerals to the left and right indicates that one teacher considers the pupil vacillating and that two teachers consider him highly motivated. If preferred, the subject fields or other areas of relationship with the pupil may be used to replace the numerals.

1. MOTIVATION Purposeless	Vacillating	Usually purposeful	Effectively motivated	Highly motivated
2. INDUSTRY Seldom works even under pressure	Needs constant pressure	Needs occasional prodding	Prepares assigned work regularly	Seeks additional work
3. INITIATIVE Merely conforms	Seldom initiates	Frequently initiates	Consistently self-reliant	Actively creative
4. INFLUENCE AND LEADERSHIP Negative	Co-operative but retiring	Sometimes in minor affairs	Contributing in important affairs	Judgment respected—makes things go
5. CONCERN FOR OTHERS Indifferent	Self-centered	Somewhat socialy concerned	Generally concerned	Deeply and actively concerned
6. RESPONSIBILITY Unreliable	Somewhat dependable	Usually dependable	Conscientious	Assumes much responsibility
7. INTEGRITY Not dependable	Questionable at times	Generally honest	Reliable, dependable	Consistently trustworthy
8. EMOTIONAL STABILITY Hyperemotional / Apathetic	Excitable / Unresponsive	Usually well-balanced	Well-balanced	Exceptionally stable

FIGURE 11–4 An illustrative rating scale: the Personality Record.

SOURCE: Prepared by a joint committee representing high schools and colleges. Copyright © 1958, National Association of Secondary School Principals of the NEA. Reproduced by permission.

instruction and should become standard practice. Unlike cognitive assessment, many variables can be measured in a very brief period of time. Of course, since it is human nature to act in one's own self-interest, students cannot be expected to place themselves at risk in giving negative feedback, and the feedback has logical (construct) validity only if the measures are administered under conditions that encourage response integrity, the most important of which is anonymity. The results can have diagnostic and remedial value for the teacher, as well as potential value in teacher evaluation, which historically in public education has been done perfunctorily. Research suggests that when teachers provide opportunity for such simple, straightforward, and systematic student feedback, the quality of instruction improves (Gage, Runkel & Chatterjee, 1960). *The Faculty Course Questionnaire*, developed and used at the University of Colorado, is shown in Figure 11–5. Note that there are 12 common questions and space for optional questions that an instructor may wish to add. On the reverse side, students respond in writing to three additional items: (1) the *most* effective aspects of this course were . . . , (2) the *least* effective aspects of the course were . . . , and (3) the *best* ways to improve this course would be to . . .

Research has also shown that student ratings of teachers tend to be reliable (Morrow, 1977; Smith, 1979), to have only moderate relationship to student grades and to the difficulty of a course, and to be higher for more experienced teachers (Driscoll & Goodwin, 1979). Empirical studies also tend to corroborate the validity of student ratings of teaching effectiveness (Marsh, 1977; Kulik & McKeachie, 1975; Aleamoni, 1978; Rotem & Glasman, 1979). Student evaluations (obtained under conditions designed to encourage integrity in the ratings) are a necessary component in any comprehensive program for evaluating instruction and teachers (Millman, 1981a).

If public schools would begin to take the evaluation of teachers more seriously and act in deed and word that their principal purpose is to act in students' interest, public trust in education could begin to be restored. Too often principals have given gratuitous and overly-generous evaluations of teachers to avoid conflict with an incompetent teacher. In addition, their judgments are often based on inadequate or irrelevant criteria.

Colleges and universities have made substantial improvement in the evaluation of instruction in recent decades, although it is unrealistic to expect any system of personnel evaluation to be completely fair and valid. There are many major political and interpersonal forces that mitigate against procedures that have validity. Nevertheless, actions based on the welfare of students is the real test of the professionalism of administrators in facing this challenge.

Teacher evaluations should serve two functions: (1) diagnosis—the identification of areas in need of improvement, and (2) sorting out instructors who, for whatever reasons, lack the ability to become good teachers. Certain factors can be readily remediated, others (for example, psychological problems) cannot. Of course much of what is said about evaluating teaching can also be said about evaluating administrators as well.

An example of a rating scale carefully developed for classroom observation by Ryans (1960) in an extensive study of teacher characteristics is presented in Figure 11–6. (Note the use of bipolar adjectives; the same technique is employed on the semantic differential scales described in the next section.) With trained raters, inter-observer agreement can be quite high (ρ_{XX}s of .8 and above).

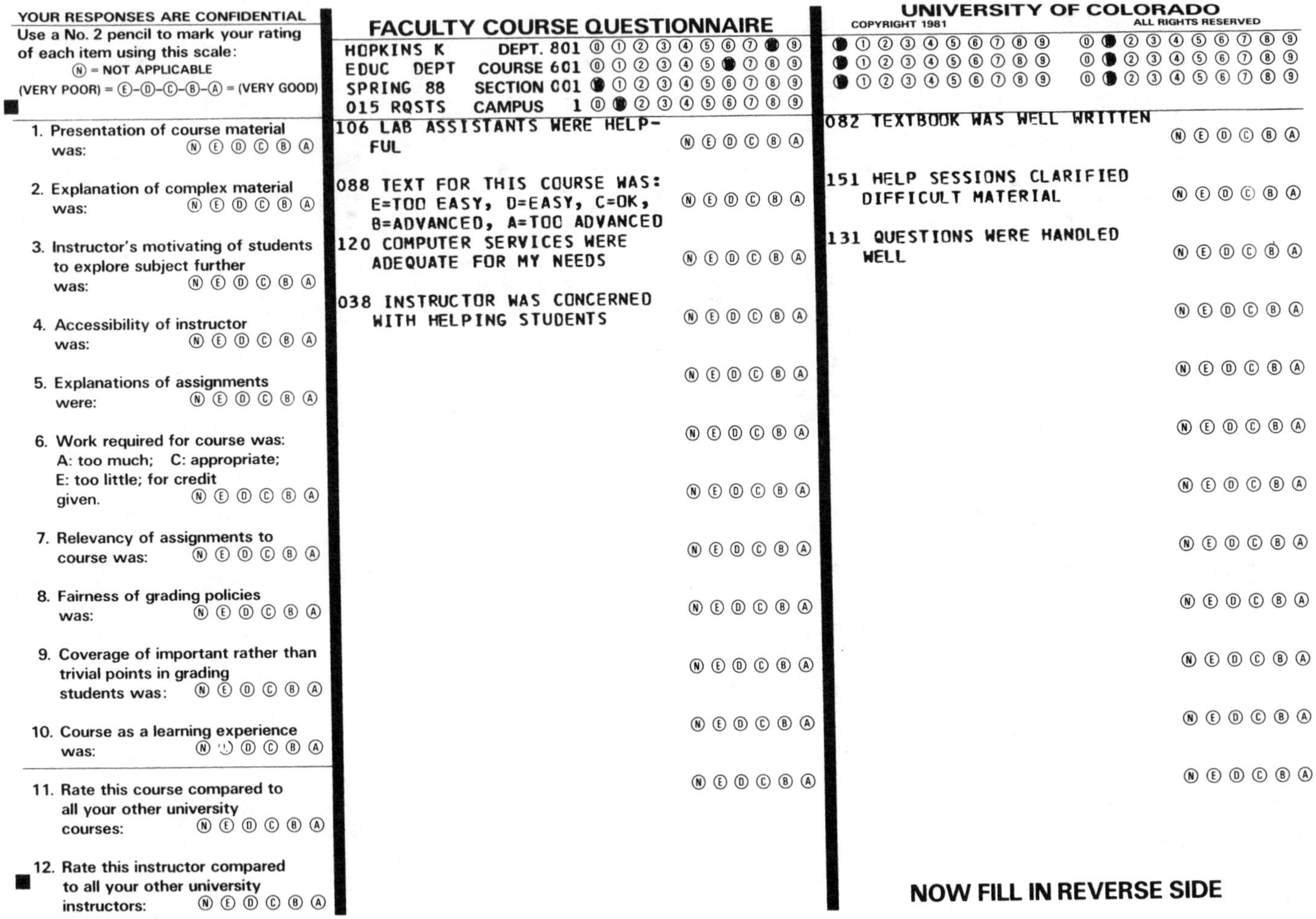

FACULTY COURSE QUESTIONNAIRE

UNIVERSITY OF COLORADO
COPYRIGHT 1981   ALL RIGHTS RESERVED

HOPKINS K   DEPT. 801
EDUC DEPT   COURSE 601
SPRING 88   SECTION C01
015 RQSTS   CAMPUS 1

YOUR RESPONSES ARE CONFIDENTIAL
Use a No. 2 pencil to mark your rating of each item using this scale:
(N) = NOT APPLICABLE
(VERY POOR) = (E)–(D)–(C)–(B)–(A) = (VERY GOOD)

1. Presentation of course material was:

106 LAB ASSISTANTS WERE HELP-FUL

2. Explanation of complex material was:

088 TEXT FOR THIS COURSE WAS:
E=TOO EASY, D=EASY, C=OK, B=ADVANCED, A=TOO ADVANCED

3. Instructor's motivating of students to explore subject further was:

120 COMPUTER SERVICES WERE ADEQUATE FOR MY NEEDS

4. Accessibility of instructor was:

038 INSTRUCTOR WAS CONCERNED WITH HELPING STUDENTS

082 TEXTBOOK WAS WELL WRITTEN

5. Explanations of assignments were:

151 HELP SESSIONS CLARIFIED DIFFICULT MATERIAL

6. Work required for course was:
A: too much;   C: appropriate;
E: too little; for credit given.

131 QUESTIONS WERE HANDLED WELL

7. Relevancy of assignments to course was:

8. Fairness of grading policies was:

9. Coverage of important rather than trivial points in grading students was:

10. Course as a learning experience was:

11. Rate this course compared to all your other university courses:

12. Rate this instructor compared to all your other university instructors:

NOW FILL IN REVERSE SIDE

FIGURE 11–5   An example of a course evaluation inventory designed for colleges and universities.

SOURCE: Copyright © 1981, University of Colorado. Reproduced by permission.

CLASSROOM OBSERVATION RECORD

TEACHER CHARACTERISTICS STUDY

Teacher _____ No. _____ Sex _____ Class or Subject _____ Date ____

City _____ School _____ Time _____ Observer _____

Pupil Behavior									Remarks:
1. Apathetic	1	2	3	4	5	6	7	N	Alert
2. Obstructive	1	2	3	4	5	6	7	N	Responsible
3. Uncertain	1	2	3	4	5	6	7	N	Confident
4. Dependent	1	2	3	4	5	6	7	N	Initiating
Teacher Behavior									
5. Partial	1	2	3	4	5	6	7	N	Fair
6. Autocratic	1	2	3	4	5	6	7	N	Democratic
7. Aloof	1	2	3	4	5	6	7	N	Responsive
8. Restricted	1	2	3	4	5	6	7	N	Understanding
9. Harsh	1	2	3	4	5	6	7	N	Kindly
10. Dull	1	2	3	4	5	6	7	N	Stimulating
11. Stereotyped	1	2	3	4	5	6	7	N	Original
12. Apathetic	1	2	3	4	5	6	7	N	Alert
13. Unimpressive	1	2	3	4	5	6	7	N	Attractive
14. Evading	1	2	3	4	5	6	7	N	Responsible
15. Erratic	1	2	3	4	5	6	7	N	Steady
16. Excitable	1	2	3	4	5	6	7	N	Poised
17. Uncertain	1	2	3	4	5	6	7	N	Confident
18. Disorganized	1	2	3	4	5	6	7	N	Systematic
19. Inflexible	1	2	3	4	5	6	7	N	Adaptable
20. Pessimistic	1	2	3	4	5	6	7	N	Optimistic
21. Immature	1	2	3	4	5	6	7	N	Integrated
22. Narrow	1	2	3	4	5	6	7	N	Broad

FIGURE 11–6   A rating scale employed by classroom observers.

SOURCE: D. G. Ryans, *Characteristics of teachers* (Washington, D.C.: American Council on Education, 1960), p. 86. Reprinted by permission of the author and publisher.

Pictorial response scales are sometimes more effective for assessing attitudes, especially for children. Figure 11–7 illustrates a three-rating scale that uses a pictorial response continuum. The stimuli could be math, kids at school, teachers, gymnastics, spinach, career day, or whatever.

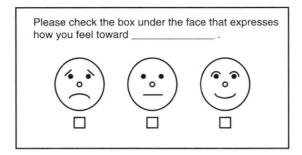

FIGURE 11–7   A pictorial response format for assessing attitudes.

11.7   SEMANTIC DIFFERENTIAL SCALES

Another useful technique for measuring psychological meaning is the *semantic differential*, a type of scale originally developed by Osgood (Osgood, Suci & Tannenbaum, 1957). In its orthodox use, concepts are measured and portrayed in three dimensions of meaning—a three-dimensional *semantic space*. The dimensions are *evaluation* (good-bad), *potency* (strong-weak), and *activity* (fast-slow). Sample directions for the semantic differential are given in Figure 11–8. Each of several concepts (e.g., "teachers" in Figure 11–9) is followed by a set of 3 to 15 bipolar adjectives. Each dimension to be measured typically uses at least three separate *scales* that have been empirically shown to be relatively pure measures of that dimension. The *scores* on the bipolar scales for each of the three dimensions are averaged for each concept. The concepts can then be plotted in the three-dimensional semantic space along the three axes of evaluation, potency, and activity.

The semantic differential format is illustrated in Figure 11–9, in which a student has recorded a judgment on each of the nine (*a–i*) seven-point scales. Such responses are usually scored by converting the positions of the check marks into ratings (1–7) in a consistent "low-to-high" direction. For example, the three items for the most important factor, evaluation, are *b*, *e*, and *h*. On these, the leftmost position of scale *b* (*good–bad*) receives a rating of 7, but the rightmost position in scale *e* has the rating of 7. The measurements on these three evaluation items (*b*, *e*, and *h*) in Figure 11–9 are 6, 7, and 5, respectively, which are averaged: $\frac{(6 + 7 + 5)}{3} = 6$ to represent the evaluation dimension. The procedure is repeated to obtain the mean of the activity scales (*a*, *c*, and *i*), that is, $\frac{(4 + 3 + 5)}{3} = 4$, and the mean of the potency scales (*d*, *f*, and *g*), that is, $\frac{(4 + 5 + 5)}{3} = 4.67$.

In actual practice, the major educational concern is with the *value* held by a person for a concept or procedure—whether it is liked, is interesting, and is considered to be useful, valuable, and important. Consequently, most current educational applications of the semantic differential have deviated from the orthodox three-dimensional approach and concentrated solely on the evaluation factor. Scales that have intrinsic relevance for the concept in question are used whether or not they are pure measures of a given dimension (e.g.,

SEMANTIC DIFFERENTIAL INSTRUCTIONS

On the following pages there is either a word or an expression in capitalized letters followed by pairs of opposite words underneath the capitalized word or sentence. Between each of the pairs of opposites there are 7 dashes. You are to place a check mark on one of the 7 positions that are between the two opposite words. The check mark should indicate how you feel about the word or concept. Look at the examples below:

EXAMPLE 1:   EDUCATION

Good	✔:___:___:___:___:___:___	Bad
Slow	___:✔:___:___:___:___:___	Fast
Cruel	___:___:✔:___:___:___:___	Kind

In this example EDUCATION is the concept being assessed and the pairs of opposites are Good - Bad, Slow - Fast, and Cruel - Kind. If EDUCATION seemed to you to mean something very Good, you would make a check in position 1 of the Good - Bad scale. If EDUCATION seemed to you to mean something Slow, then you would place your check mark in position 2 of the Slow - Fast scale. And if you feel that EDUCATION means something which is neither Cruel nor Kind, then you would put your check mark in position 4.

In the following example a check has been placed to illustrate how someone would place his check marks if he thought that TEACHERS were very Bad, very Fast, and very Cruel:

EXAMPLE 2:   TEACHERS

Good	___:___:___:___:___:___:✔	Bad
Slow	___:___:___:___:___:___:✔	Fast
Cruel	✔:___:___:___:___:___:___	Kind

On the following pages, place your check marks rapidly. What is wanted is your first impression. This is not a test; the "right" answer is the one that is true for you. Be sure to make only one check mark for each pair of words. Do not skip any pairs of words or pages.

FIGURE 11–8   Sample semantic differential items and directions.

interesting-dull, useful-useless). The same very efficient format is used, but the semantic space notion is ignored. The individual items are typically interpreted directly, without averaging.

Virtually any relevant concept, activity, or person can be studied using the semantic differential technique: geometry, reading, school, the ideal teacher, me, most kids, basketball, cheating on tests, and so on. When the integrity of the information is protected, the semantic differential approach can yield much valuable information. Very little reading and testing time are required. The semantic differential has been found to yield reasonably reliable information at levels as low as grade two, but the reliability is greater with older students. The

TEACHERS

a.	fast				✔				slow
b.	good	✔							bad
c.	passive			✔					active
d.	small				✔				large
e.	worthless							✔	valuable
f.	strong			✔					weak
g.	light					✔			heavy
h.	helpful	✔							not helpful
i.	moving			✔					still

FIGURE 11–9 Responses of one student regarding the concept "teachers," using the semantic differential technique.

semantic differential measurement technique has been useful for measuring attitudes in a wide spectrum of applications in many fields. Its chief advantage over Likert scales is ease of construction and administration. Its disadvantages are its lack of flexibility and its greater ambiguity in interpretation—it is easier to interpret responses to direct statements.

11.8 SELF-REPORT INVENTORIES

Self-report inventories typically consist of structured questions or statements to which the respondent answers *yes* or *no* or *yes, ?,* or *no.* Self-report inventories are not fundamentally different from Likert or rating scales. Indeed, the items on self-report inventories often use Likert or rating scale formats. Illustrative items, along with the domain they represent, are the following:

1. I usually wait to the "last minute" before doing my homework. (*study habits*)
2. Most teachers care about me as a person. (*attitude toward teachers*)
3. Most kids at this school are unfriendly. (*attitude toward peers*)
4. I feel guilty because I'm so dumb. (*learner self-concept*)

Table 11–1 gives sample items from a self-report inventory, the Student Attitude Inventory (Hopkins & Kretke, 1983), together with results from its use as part of a school district's testing program.[1] The percentages of students responding *yes* are given for two grade lev-

[1]Items in this inventory are similar to those on the Survey of School Attitudes published by Harcourt Brace Jovanovich in 1975. Other measures of school climate are considered in Chapter 15.

TABLE 11–1   Illustrative Items from the School Attitude Inventory

Items Pertaining to Attitudes Toward School and Teachers	Grade	% Last Year[a]	% This Year	Change
22. Do most of your teachers care about what happens to you as a person?	5	70	69	**–1**
	11	53	55	+2
23. Do you feel that you are really a part of your school?	5	67	69	+2
	11	55	55	0
32. Is there a teacher in your school you would go talk to if you were worried about something?	5	64	65	+1
	11	52	52	0
36. Are most teachers friendly?	5	85	87	+2
	11	77	78	+1
37. Are most teachers helpful?	5	86	86	0
	11	72	71	**–1**
38. Do you think kids should have to go to school even if they don't want to?	5	73	74	+1
	11	54	56	+2
39. Is going to school important for a happy life?	5	84	85	+1
	11	56	59	+3
41. Do you often use things you learn in school outside of school?	5	79	78	**–1**
	11	75	77	+2
42. Do you think that most people who drop out of school before graduation will be sorry someday?	5	85	87	+2
	11	80	81	+1

Items Pertaining to Educational Aspirations

	Grade	% Last Year[a]	% This Year	Change
27. Do you plan to finish high school?	5	92	93	+1
	11	97	97	0
28. Do you plan to go to college?	5	81	83	+2
	11	72	71	**–1**

SOURCE: K. D. Hopkins, G. Kretke, and M. Averill, *District testing report* (Boulder, CO: Boulder Valley School District, 1983, 1984).

[a]Percent responding *Yes*

els (5 and 11) for two consecutive years. Note that, at grade 11, means are much less positive than at grade 5 and that there was little change in means between last year and this year.

Notice that the data in Table 11–1 are aggregated—they are reported for all students in the school district. Findings could also be useful if reported at the school or classroom level. Research indicates that teachers and administrators are not good judges of students' attitudes toward school. For example, most teachers would be surprised to learn that the most-liked subject is math but that is what surveys using the *Student Attitude Inventory* (Hopkins & Kretke, 1983) have found repeatedly. Students' aggregated descriptions will have considerable validity when the students respond anonymously and are properly motivated.

Self-report inventories can also be used in the area of study habits and skills. Academic aptitude is of little benefit if it is not nurtured and exercised. Any teacher can point to students who have untapped potential—potential that is wasted because of poor study habits and motivation. In spite of their obvious importance, little *systematic* effort is made in the curriculum to assess, teach, or develop good study skills and habits. When these survival skills are lacking, underachievement is inevitable. Research indicates that these survival skills should not taken for granted and that they can be learned when given special instruction.

A few published study habit inventories are available. One of the most widely used is the *Survey of Study Habits and Attitudes* (SSHA).[2] The SSHA includes four subtests: (1) Delay Avoidance (e.g., "Daydreaming distracts my attention while I am studying"), (2) Work Methods (e.g., "My teachers criticize my work for being poorly planned or hurriedly written"), (3) Teacher Approval (e.g., "My teachers make their subjects interesting and meaningful to me"), and (4) Educational Acceptance (e.g., "I feel that I would study harder if I were given more freedom to choose subjects I like"). The items have been shown to have validity for predicting grades and teachers' ratings when examinees are motivated to respond truthfully.

11.9   SELF-CONCEPT

As a man thinketh in his heart, so is he. *Proverbs* 23:7

Public opinion is a weak tyrant compared with our own private opinion. What a man thinks of himself, that it is which determines . . . his fate. (Thoreau, *Walden*, 1854)

In recent decades there has been much interest in the measurement of self-concept. One of the most widely used self-esteem inventories (Coopersmith, 1967) that has been employed successfully in the upper elementary grades and above, as well as with adults, is given in Figure 11–10. Several studies have produced results that are in exact contradiction to current stereotypes, with more positive concepts being reported by blacks than by whites and by students of lower socioeconomic status than by members of the middle class.

11.10   Q-SORT TECHNIQUE

A procedure by which one can assess attitudes, interests, and other affective variables is the *Q-sort technique*, originally developed by Stephenson (1953). An individual is given a set of cards containing statements, traits, pictures, or whatever; they are then sorted into piles according to their relative standing along a single dimension. The continuum can take many forms: "most like me" to "least like me," "most important to least important," "best to worst," and so forth. The number of cards allowed in each pile is usually predetermined to approximate a normal frequency distribution.

The respondents may describe themselves, a course, their interests, their school principal, and so on. The Q-sort technique has been widely used in counseling studies in which

---

[2]Published by the Psychological Corporation. Form H is for grades 7–12; Form C is for high school seniors and college students.

SELF-ESTEEM INVENTORY

Items are answered either "like me" or "unlike me." The high esteem response is indicated in parentheses after each item.

1. I often wish I were someone else. (Unlike me)

2. I find it very hard to talk in front of a group. (Unlike me)

3. There are lots of things about myself I'd change if I could. (Unlike me)

4. I can make up my mind without too much trouble. (Like me)

5. I'm a lot of fun to be with. (Like me)

6. I get upset easily at home. (Unlike me)

7. It takes me a long time to get used to anything new. (Unlike me)

8. I'm popular with people my own age. (Like me)

9. My family expects too much of me. (Unlike me)

10. My family usually considers my feelings. (Like me)

11. I give in very easily. (Unlike me)

12. It's pretty tough to be me. (Unlike me)

13. Things are all mixed up in my life. (Unlike me)

14. Other people usually follow my ideas. (Like me)

15. I have a low opinion of myself. (Unlike me)

16. There are many times when I'd like to leave home. (Unlike me)

17. I often feel upset about the work that I do. (Unlike me)

18. I'm not as nice looking as most people. (Unlike me)

19. If I have something to say, I usually say it. (Like me)

20. My family understands me. (Like me)

21. Most people are better liked than I am. (Unlike me)

22. I usually feel as if my family is pushing me. (Unlike me)

23. I often get discouraged at what I am doing. (Unlike me)

24. Things usually don't bother me. (Like me)

FIGURE 11–10   The Coopersmith self-esteem inventory.

SOURCE: Copyright 1967 by W. H. Freeman and Company. Reproduced by permission of Stanley Coopersmith.

an individual describes himself or herself with one Q-sort and re-sorts the cards to describe his or her ideal self. The sorted piles can then be correlated with other methods of assessing attitude. The content of the Q-sort can be tailor-made to the immediate particular purpose. There are a few standard Q-sorts, the most common of which is the California Q-sort set. One hundred descriptive statements are sorted into nine categories ranging from "extremely characteristic" to "extremely uncharacteristic" of the examinee. A special feature of this Q-sort set is a description of optimal adjustment, which is based on the judgments of nine clinical psychologists. This and other examples can be found in Block (1961).

The major use of the Q-sort technique has been in counseling and psychotherapy. For example, a Q-sort by teachers has been used to ascertain whether the behavior of students undergoing counseling was improving more than that of students who were not receiving any treatment (Oldridge, 1963). The potential applicability of the Q-sort technique is very broad. Armitage (1967) used the Q-sort technique to compare the values attached to certain social studies objectives by *experts* and classroom teachers. Sheldon and Sorenson (1960) used the technique to study changes in the educational philosophy of prospective teachers during their student teaching.

The difficulty and time required for administering and scoring the Q-sort, and its focus on a single dimension, reduce its usability for general assessment purposes in comparison to that of the Likert and semantic differential approaches.

11.11 QUESTIONNAIRES

Sets of questions are frequently used in educational surveys. Questionnaires are usually mimeographed or printed and sent through the mail or administered to "captive" audiences such as groups of students or teachers. The questions may be of any kind that we have discussed in this book. They may begin with background biographical data, such as sex, date of birth, and number of years of school completed. The subsequent questions may be factual ("How many students are enrolled in your classes?" "Which subject do you teach?"), or the instrument may include Likert-type items or a rating scale. One might, for instance, have *The Education Scale* (Figure 11–3) filled out and returned. More likely, however, one would select and revise items from previously used inventories (see Appendix A) or construct questions for the particular purpose at hand.

Questionnaires have all the usual limitations of self-report devices plus some special problems of their own. If they are mailed to individuals to be filled out at whatever time and under whatever circumstances happen to prevail in the home or office of the recipient, the results may vary greatly from one individual to another, depending on the time and care the respondent chooses or is able to give. Typically, some returned questionnaires are completed carelessly and incompletely, especially if respondents are not properly motivated to give the time and care required. Other questionnaires will not be returned unless reminders are sent—the typical return rate is less than 50 percent. Despite the best efforts, unless the investigator administers the questionnaire to a captive group, there are always many persons who will not return the questionnaire. These nonrespondents typically bias findings and weaken generalizations to be made from the survey, more or less, depending on their proportion of the total group. Most surveys gratuitously assume that the respondents are a representative sample of the population being surveyed, which is rarely the case.

Suppose, for example, that we sent out a double postal card to every teacher in your state and asked, "In your opinion, which are better measures of most educational objectives—essay tests or objective tests?" If in two weeks half of the cards have been returned, we would not be in a good position to tabulate and report our results because we would not know if both groups are equally likely to respond—those who favor essay tests and those who prefer objective tests. We could *assume* that a representative sample of the teachers has responded, but careful readers of our report might not be willing to permit us that assumption without further justification. In mail surveys it is essential to build at least one or two follow-ups into a study plan in order to reduce nonrespondents to as small a percentage as possible. If the initial respondents are compared with the follow-up group(s), one can sometimes get clues as to how the nonrespondents might have answered; that is, the direction of the bias in the sample may be assessed. If the percents answering "essay" are 30 percent, 40 percent, and 45 percent for the initial group and the first and second follow-up groups, respectively, we can be reasonably confident that the nonrespondents would be more sympathetic to essay tests than the total group of respondents.

Even with 100 percent returns, however, we would still need to qualify our conclusions. Our results represent what respondents report feeling, not necessarily how they actually feel. Careless errors, fallible memories, and willful deceptions can distort findings to some extent. The problems are much greater when the questionnaire includes sensitive attitudinal questions, or when respondents perceive it to be in their best interest to give a certain answer even if it is not accurate.

Before you attempt to conduct a questionnaire study, additional reading and study pertaining to procedures for administration and development are recommended.

11.12 ADJECTIVE CHECKLISTS

Adjective checklists are easy to develop and easy to administer and score. One role-plays, thinking of all the relevant descriptors possible of what is to be rated. If used to assess self-concept, the adjectives that are to be checked or left blank might include

fair ___, well-liked ___, dependable ___, selfish ___, creative ___, stupid ___, worthless ___,

and so on. Individuals or groups can thus be profiled and studied.

11.13 INTERVIEWS

Although not always recognized as such, the interview is one of the most widely used assessment techniques. What are the purposes of an interview? It is used to assess a wide variety of variables—affective, psychomotor, and cognitive. A few highly select colleges and most medical schools use interviews as a part of their selection process and also, sometimes, to recruit the most desired students.

Interviews vary in quality as much as interviewers do. Indeed, it is the interviewer who is the yardstick in this assessment procedure. Unplanned and completely unstructured interviews by naive interviewers have few measurement virtues. Unplanned interviews tend to use up the available time on a few limited topics. Typically, "time runs out" before many important areas have been discussed. The interview has resembled a social exchange more than a procedure for assessing variables that have relevance and predictive validity for the criteria in question.

Untrained interviewers often become too active in the interviewing process and "shape" the interviewee's responses. As in other situations involving human interaction, the *actors* are continually *reading* each other—searching for responses that will be reinforced by the other partner. Especially in contexts in which the interviewer has something the interviewee wants (i.e., controls the reinforcers), as in job or school interview situations, the interviewee is likely to respond to the perceived demand characteristics of the situation. Interviewees are typically in the "set" to supply information that the interviewer wants to hear, rather than the "whole truth and nothing but the truth." The skillful interviewer provides few clues to the *right* answers, although the social-desirability set suggests the *right* answers to many questions. "Do you enjoy your work?" "Tell me about your study habits." "Do you have kids?" "Why did you leave your last job?"

The use of the interview as a data-gathering technique in survey research has fewer problems than does its use in making a decision about the interviewee. In research and evaluation projects, there is usually less need for the interviewee to "put his or her best foot forward." But even here the social-desirability response set can contaminate findings unless this incentive is not skillfully disarmed by a competent interviewer and a high level of rapport. In one study the attitudes of a random half of the interviewees were questioned orally and the other half responded anonymously in writing. Those who were questioned orally were much more favorable to the proposition, yet the proportion obtained from those who responded anonymously was much closer to the actual proportion in the referendum. Other studies have shown that interviewees tend to exaggerate their voting frequency, the number possessing library cards, their giving to charity, and other socially desirable behaviors. Interviewers can sometimes insert a few questions designed to assess the social-desirability response tendency (see Section 11.15) and thereby help evaluate the validity of respondents' answers.

Many studies have shown that the personality and other characteristics of the interviewer can have a profound influence on the responses he or she elicits from interviewees. The more the interview is structured, the less the interviewer becomes a factor in determining the responses.

The interview is very much overrated as an assessment procedure. Meehl's classic *Clinical versus Statistical Prediction* (1954) found that the simple statistical use of one or two test scores was generally better in predicting or revealing a person's status than judgments made by trained and experienced people via interviews and other informal observational techniques. The popularity of the interview is based more on its face validity than on its demonstrated validity as a method of appraising people. One may ask, "If the interview is such a good method of appraisal, why are there so many poor teachers (and other workers) employed in positions for which they lack the necessary attitudes and skills for effective performance?" The validity of interview "data" is highly dependent on the skill of the interviewer, which means in part that the interview will be planned and, to some degree, structured. In essence, the skillful interview is a special instance of systematic observation of a person in a situation in which the interview is providing the stimuli.

Potential users of interviews should consult more comprehensive treatments of the topic, such as those of Selltiz, Wrightsman, and Cook (1981) and of Kerlinger (1986).

11.14 PROBLEMS OF AFFECTIVE MEASUREMENT

There are four basic types of problems in measuring attitudes and other affective variables: *fakability*, *self-deception*, *semantic problems*, and *criterion inadequacy*.

> During an interview for a summer position in a music store Carol's reported liking for classical music may differ greatly from what she would convey to a close friend. But it is very unlikely that her score on an "ability" test of music knowledge would be affected much by her desire for employment. For the manager of the music store to learn the true extent of her knowledge, it is only necessary that Carol take a music knowledge test. Motivation and inducements cannot compensate for any lack of knowledge she may have.

Ability tests are keyed a priori; it is not possible to fake a high (or good) score (although, of course, one could fake a low score, but then why would one do that?). On affective measures one can usually fake a high or a low score: Carol could tell the music store owner that she prefers classical music and tell her friends that she prefers rock, when country music is actually her favorite. Properly constructed and administered ability tests yield measures of performance that have validity; self-report affective measures may only reflect the desire to conform to the special situation, as perceived by the examinee, because such devices do not lend themselves to direct scoring of the right answers. Liking spinach may be *right* for one person and *wrong* for another, but the correct spelling of *grandiose* is independent of the context in which the word appears.

All affective self-report measures are fakable to some degree, especially by the test-wise opportunist; therefore, *if the assessment is to be valid, it must be obtained in such a way to minimize any incentive to be untruthful*. Anonymity is an important ingredient in valid attitude assessment in any situation in which the subject may be rewarded for, or embarrassed by, or publicly accountable for certain responses. Anonymity ordinarily precludes the use of the information for clinical purposes, but it can still yield feedback that is invaluable in assessing and comparing groups, such as an aid to the teacher in assessing the degree to which various affective educational objectives have been achieved by the class. Program and course evaluation measures are typically administered so that the respondent is free from self-jeopardy.

When the identity of the subject is necessary, an honest sharing of one's values, attitudes, interests, and feelings can be expected only when a deep level of rapport and trust has been established between the individual and the users of the information. This was graphically illustrated in a study in which a group of industrial workers filled out identical health questionnaires under two conditions. One questionnaire was returned to the company medical department as a preliminary to a medical examination. The other was mailed directly to a research group at a university. Far more symptoms were indicated on the research questionnaire than on the company's, even though an honest report on the latter might facilitate the obtaining of medical help.

11.15 THE SOCIAL-DESIRABILITY RESPONSE STYLE

Unless examinees are properly motivated and are given instructions that elicit integrity in responding, many examinees have a tendency to give a socially desirable impression on self-report inventories; this is sometimes referred to as the "facade" effect. It is a truism that most people tend to act in their own perceived best interest to the extent that their personal integrity will allow. When it is to one's advantage to "fake bad," a negative facade effect can be expected. A draftee who wants a medical discharge may report a staggering array of physical and psychological symptoms.

The giving of socially desirable responses on a self-report inventory does not always indicate deliberate deception by the respondent but, rather, may be an unconscious tendency to put up a good front. Affective measures can be falsified to some degree no matter how they are constructed, although faking can be greatly reduced by the instructions and context of the information being requested.

Edwards (1957) developed a special social-desirability (SD) scale that can be embedded in other scales on an inventory in order to assess the magnitude of the effect of the social-desirability factor on the affective measures. For items on the SD scale, the true answer is almost always different from the *good* (socially desirable) answer. The scale is of value in investigating the extent that the facade effect contaminates scores on some other measure. If scores on the SD scale correlate highly with scores on another measure, the validity of the measure is highly suspect.

In the following items from a social-desirability scale designed for children (Crandall, Crandall & Katkovsky, 1965), note that the correct answer is usually socially undesirable:

"I am always respectful of older people."
"I sometimes feel angry when I don't get my way."
"When I make a mistake, I always admit I am wrong."
"I always wash my hands before every meal."

How would you respond to the following ten items, which are taken from the *Marlowe-Crowne Social-Desirability Scale* (Crowne & Marlowe, 1964)?

1. Before voting I thoroughly investigate the qualifications of all the candidates. (*T*)
2. I never hesitate to go out of my way to help someone in trouble. (*T*)
3. I like to gossip at times. (*F*)
4. There have been occasions when I took advantage of someone. (*F*)
5. I always try to practice what I preach. (*T*)
6. I sometimes try to get even rather than forgive and forget. (*F*)
7. When I don't know something I don't at all mind admitting it. (*T*)
8. I am always courteous, even to people who are disagreeable. (*T*)
9. There have been times when I was quite jealous of the good fortune of others. (*F*)
10. I have never deliberately said something that hurt someone's feelings. (*T*)

If the correct answer in your case agreed with the key (the socially desirable answer) on more than two or three of the questions, you are either a very unusual person or you are evidencing the SD response style. Notice, too, how much easier it is to respond privately to these items than it would be if others would have access to your answers. Consider the difference between the responses to these ten items versus the answers that might be given if the examinee needed a job and these questions were part of the application procedure.

Social-desirability items, also called response integrity items (Hopkins, 1986), have been implanted in surveys of students' school attitudes to determine whether the more positive school attitudes reported by elementary school students were partly attributable to a greater set to give SD responses (Hopkins & Kretke, 1983). When responding anonymously, only 7 percent to 8 percent of the elementary school students gave the SD response.

SD items often have to be adapted to the content being assessed. The following are sample SD items that were embedded in a scale designed to measure attitudes toward an ethnic minority:

"I'm always courteous to Mexican American students even when they are rude."
"All Mexican American kids are easy to like."

A recent study (Montei, 1996) found that a scale measuring attitudes toward diversity did not correlate with the social desirability response style, which significantly enhances the construct validity of the scale. Another study (Schon, Hopkins, and Vojir, 1980) investigated the question of whether a specially designed curriculum improved students' attitudes toward Mexican Americans. In such a study, the experimental group (which received the special curriculum) might be expected to be "helpful" and acquiesce to the perceived "demand characteristic" of the situation and, hence, report better attitudes than the untreated control group, even if their attitudes were unaffected. This is particularly true if students do not respond anonymously. But if the experimental and control groups do not differ on the SD items but differ on the "real" attitude items, the difference has much more credibility (Hopkins, 1986).

The *forced-choice* item format can sometimes reduce the influence of the social-desirability set. Items of this type require the respondent to discriminate between two or more alternatives that, ideally, are equally acceptable. A sample forced-choice item follows. Items of this kind attempt to minimize the SD response set by making each choice equally attractive or unattractive.

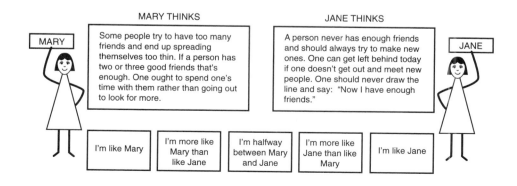

The forced-choice procedure is widely used on published affective measures (see Chapter 15).

The forced choice can be among more than two alternatives. On the *Kuder Vocational Preference Record*, for example, the examinee is asked to select one of three activities that he or she likes most and least among, for example, collecting autographs, collecting coins, and collecting butterflies.

Forced-choice measures are much more difficult to develop and interpret than most other types of scales. The forced-choice procedure is more useful on standardized affective measures; it is less useful for assessing affective outcomes because of the difficulties in the interpretation of the results.

11.16 SELF-DECEPTION

A common adjustment phenomenon in human behavior is the tendency to want to like what we see when we look at ourselves. Human defense mechanisms cushion failures, minimize faults, and maximize virtues so that we maintain a sense of personal worth (which, as a consequence, is usually distorted to varying degrees). When one is asked questions about oneself, the validity of the responses is vulnerable to the distortions of self-deception. This "blurring" can become a major threat to the validity of self-report measures: People who have the greatest personality problems are those who are the least able to give an accurate self-description. Their "honest" answers to personal questions will probably reflect any delusions they have. The validity of their responses is, of course, another matter.

Other than for purposes of school counseling and guidance and psychological case studies, there is rarely a need for assessment of matters that are so sensitive that self-deception becomes a serious problem. There is little need for self-deceit on attitudes and interests toward educational experiences. Teachers and others with "a little learning" should resist any temptation to play junior psychiatrist by probing into private matters. Comparing the anonymous responses of *groups* of persons when evaluating teachers or programs is quite a different matter from questions of a very personal nature.

11.17 SEMANTIC PROBLEMS

On cognitive measures, the response options to an item are usually categorically different, and only one of them is correct. On affective measures, however, the responses usually represent differences in degree. Consequently, words like *often, seldom, frequently, usually,* and *sometimes* are required (for example, see the "Mary versus Jane" forced-choice item in Section 11.15.) Unfortunately, there is considerable variation in the explicit meanings that people attach to such words. When students were asked what percentage frequency of a particular response would correspond to what they "frequently" did, one-fourth of them applied "frequently" only to events occurring at least 80 percent of the time, while another one-fourth indicated that "frequently" could mean a frequency below 40 percent of the time. Similar semantic difficulties occur with other types of terms and expressions. A question such as "Do you find reading interesting?" seems straightforward, but how interesting is "interesting"? Consider, "Do you make friends easily?" How easy is "easily"? Also, is a friend a casual acquaintance or a very intimate associate? The validity of self-report information is reduced to the extent that the descriptive terms employed do not have uniform meaning across individuals.

11.18   CRITERION INADEQUACY

Definitive criteria against which the validity of the self-report information can be checked are usually either impossible or very difficult to obtain. How is a test of emotional stability or adjustment validated? There is no definitive criterion that will unequivocally demonstrate the test's validity. Only after many varied and extensive studies would it be possible to establish scientifically the construct validity of tests of this kind. Consequently, one must interpret cautiously the results of published and unpublished affective measures, since only fragmentary data with relevance for validity are available. Only rarely are some direct or indirect validity data available such as one study by Shortland and Berger (1970), which found that examinees who reported a high personal value for honesty, helpfulness, and salvation returned the pencils that were loaned to them significantly more frequently than those who reported lower values on these scales.

One is on safer ground when one is measuring attitudes and interests rather than personality and psychological adjustment. On attitude and interest measures there is usually less incentive to distort the truth. If the nature of questions is not emotionally self-jeopardizing, the responses have more logical validity and an interpretation can be made with more confidence.

11.19   NATURALISTIC OBSERVATION AND UNOBTRUSIVE MEASURES

In recent years an increasing emphasis is being given to naturalistic research and methods (Keeves, 1988). Naturalistic research utilizes *disciplined* observation as its principal method of obtaining information. Disciplined observation differs from casual observation in that it is planned and deliberate, with increased sensitization on the part of the observer. Naturalistic observation has been used primarily in cultural anthropology and for case studies but is now becoming common in educational inquiry as well. The observer attempts to be as unobtrusive as possible, being careful to observe, describe, and record what is being studied, rather than confirm preconceived notions, stereotypes, and prejudices (i.e., avoid the self-fulfilling prophecy effect). The naturalistic researcher makes extensive use of "unobtrusive measures"—measures that occur naturally without a special assessment. Examples of unobtrusive measures include tardiness, daydreaming, bringing no lunch or lunch money, books checked out from the school library, hair-combing, sleepiness, and the like.

In a very real sense, outstanding teachers are usually sensitive naturalistic observers, even though they may not be consciously aware of the fact. This is especially true at the elementary school level; there the culture of the classroom is much more stable than it is at the secondary level, where students tend to change teachers each hour. Teachers can obtain a wealth of useful and valid information by periodically putting on their naturalistic researcher *hat.* Naturalistic observation is especially useful for students who are experiencing cognitive or emotional disability. An observational diary is useful for documenting the observation. It prevents the present from unduly influencing and changing perceptions from the past. Even if the observations are not recorded, it is critical for teachers to shift into naturalistic research mode to obtain a bird's-eye view of what is actually taking place in their class, who appears to be having difficulty, who appears to be bored, who never volunteers an answer, who appears sad, and so on. Unless teachers discipline themselves to think and observe like disciplined naturalistic inquirers, a very useful and rich data base may go unnoticed. Naturalistic observations often lead to interviews with students, parents, and other teachers and students to gain additional understanding.

11.20 INVASION OF PRIVACY

In the measurement of attitudes, values, personality, and interests, it is important to avoid the invasion of an individual's privacy. The irresponsible use of certain tests and items has resulted in the need for ethical guidelines. Thorndike and Hagen (1977) offer the following relevant questions to be posed in this regard:

1. *For whose benefit will the information be used?* The information should result in some potential personal and/or social good without undue risk of psychological or physical harm to the individual.
2. *How personal and relevant is the information?* The measures should have established validity if they are to be used in any important decisions.[3] Emotional stability is far more crucial in a pilot than in a janitor. In the past many employers have used personality tests with some "face" validity but little or no criterion-related validity. Topics so personal that questions pertaining to them are often considered to be an invasion of privacy include sexual habits (87%), finances (66%), political beliefs (64%), description of spouse's personality (59%), and family background (49%). Cognitive attributes are rarely "personal"—only 9 percent of the respondents considered IQ to be an invasion of privacy. Obviously, the content and purpose of the query are critical factors in whether the information is "personal" or not. When the respondent's anonymity is protected, many questions can be asked that would otherwise be too personal, threatening, or self-incriminating.
3. *Has "informed consent" been granted?* Has the respondent been told what information will be collected and for what purpose? Does the person understand that he or she may decline to participate? Is the person competent to decide on the appropriateness of participation? Informed consent is required in most medical and psychological research, although the legal provision of *in loco parentis* allows responsible educators to make many decisions for school-related testing of students under their authority if the information sought can be justified as consistent with the mission of the school.

---

[3]The Equal Employment Opportunities Commission (EEOC) is the federal watchdog that has been created to promote fairness in employee selection. Employers must be able to demonstrate the criterion-related validity of measures used in their selection process.

SUMMARY

The appraisal of feelings, interests, and attitudes has been neglected in public education, even though affective objectives are implicit (if not explicit) in virtually every educational endeavor. Several techniques have been devised for measuring affect. Common examples are Thurstone, Likert, rating, and semantic differential scales, adjective checklists, and the Q-sort technique. Thurstone attitude scales are time-consuming to construct; a number of them are available (although the intensity values are usually somewhat outdated). Likert scales are flexible and easily constructed. They use a uniform response continuum ("strongly agree" to "strongly disagree") for the responses. Rating scales are easily constructed and have wide applicability. The semantic differential is a special type of rating scale that requires very little response and administration time. The Q-sort technique, although difficult to administer, facilitates assessment of the degree of relationship between persons or within the same person. Its greatest application has been in personality research, although there are many rich, untapped areas in which it might be used. The interview can be used to assess affective and other variables. Its validity is dependent on the skill of the interviewer. It is highly vulnerable to the social-desirability response set.

Unique assessment problems are encountered in the affective domain: The measures are fakable, vulnerable to self-deception, and usually lacking in definitive external criteria. Forced-choice items and the use of social-desirability scales can help improve the validity of many self-report affective measures. Semantic problems exert great influence on responses to items that reflect differences in degree rather than having a correct answer. Anonymity and special instructions to encourage response integrity are usually required for valid affective measurement.

Naturalistic observation is a useful method of obtaining information concerning a school, class, learning environment, or student.

IMPORTANT TERMS AND CONCEPTS

affective	semantic differential	forced-choice items
self-deception	self-report inventory	affective taxonomy
internalization	questionnaire	semantic problems
Thurstone scale	structured interview	criterion inadequacy
rating scale	Likert scale	fakability
social desirability	naturalistic observation	unobtrusive measure

CHAPTER TEST

1. Which of these terms do *not* belong in the affective domain?
   a) knowledge   b) cognitive   c) attitudes   d) values
   e) interests   f) abilities   g) aptitudes   h) appreciations

2. Which one of these represents the lowest degree of internalization in the affective domain according to the Krathwohl taxonomy?

   a) awareness b) characterization c) acceptance d) commitment

Use the following response options for Questions 3–6:

   a) Likert scale
   b) Thurstone scale
   c) rating scale
   d) semantic differential
   e) Q-sort

3. Which one of these types of attitude measures requires the most time and effort to develop?

4. Which one of the measurement techniques uses the strongly disagree-to-strongly agree response continuum?

5. In which one does each item carry a designated and *variable* weight that is used to determine an examinee's total score?

6. Which one is often used to obtain a correlation between the ideal and the actual?

7. Which one of the following is the chief limitation in the use of mailed questionnaires for assessing attitudes?

   a) Attitudes cannot be validly measured.
   b) The number of respondents is usually small.
   c) Some respondents do not answer truthfully or accurately.
   d) Attitudes cannot be measured reliably.

8. The tendency of some examinees to give the ideal answer even when it is not accurate is termed

   a) the acquiescence response style.
   b) the gambling response style.
   c) the speed-versus-accuracy response style.
   d) the social-desirability response style.
   e) the impulse response set.

9. Items that are designed to measure the social desirability response style are those

   a) for which the true answer is socially desirable.
   b) for which the truthful answer is socially undesirable.
   c) designed to measure popularity.
   d) designed to measure desire for social acceptance.

10. Which one of the following is *not* an example of an item that could be used to detect the social desirability set?

    a) I have never intensely disliked anyone.
    b) On occasion I have had doubts about my ability to succeed in life.
    c) I've never met a person I didn't like.
    d) I never resented being asked to return a favor.
    e) I sometimes regret something I've said or done.
    f) none of these

11. If you answered "true" to statements *a, c,* and *d* in Question 10,
    a) you are a liar.
    b) you have deceived yourself.
    c) you lack insight into yourself.
    d) you need psychotherapy.
    e) you're pulling my leg.
    f) one or more of the above

Self-report measures of attitudes and values have four basic drawbacks from the standpoint of validity. Match the following statements (Questions 12–16) with the problem indicated.

    a) fakability
    b) self-deception
    c) semantics
    d) inadequate criterion

12. The meanings attached to words such as *seldom, often, frequently, usually,* and *rarely* are not constant from one person to another.

13. Can you define the behavior of a person with perfect emotional stability?

14. "I'm not lying. I am the Messiah."

15. "I knew they would not hire me if they knew I hated kids, so I played games with them on their little test."

16. "I don't care what all my classmates say. I am the most popular girl in the class."

17. Compared with skillful interviewers, unskilled interviewers are more likely to
    a) participate more actively in the interview—do more talking and less listening.
    b) sample a broader domain of variables.
    c) withhold the "desired answers" to questions from the interviewee.
    d) minimize the social-desirability response set.
    e) establish a high level of credibility and rapport with the interviewee.

Use Table 11–1 in responding T *or* F *to Questions 18–20.*

18. If they responded honestly, students in grade 11 feel that only about one teacher in two cares about what happens to them as people (item 22 in Table 11–1).

19. Student attitudes appear to have changed little between "Last Year" and "This Year."

20. Eleventh-graders report less positive attitudes toward school and teachers than do fifth graders.

ANSWERS TO CHAPTER TEST

1. a, b, f, g	8. d	15. a
2. a	9. b	16. b
3. b	10. f	17. a
4. a	11. f	18. T
5. b	12. c	19. T
6. e	13. d	20. T
7. c	14. b	

12

Grading and Reporting

12.1   INTRODUCTION

The philosopher Michael Scriven (1970, p. 114) has written

> Like so many other everyday practices, grading has often seemed too humble to merit the attention of high-powered test and measurement people. My feeling is that it is far more important and in more need of help than anything else they work on.

"Assigning grades to students is undoubtedly one of the most distasteful aspects of teaching. If pushed, most teachers will state that the assignment of grades is, at best, a necessary evil that has little to do with the task of teaching," (Terwilliger, 1971). The failure to recognize that evaluation is an integral part of the educational process is common even among teachers.

The process of measurement is one aspect of evaluation. At regular intervals feedback regarding the quality of students' progress should be conveyed to them and their parents. Converting scores and performance into grades is at best a rather arbitrary process. This is further complicated by interpersonal and public relations problems associated with this type of communication. Frequently, these difficulties produce double-talking teachers and confused students and parents.

The translation of performance information into meaningful judgments of quality and progress has been a hotly debated topic for many decades. Prior to the use of objective tests, marking and grading were usually synonymous, and the validity of the teacher's judgment was rarely questioned. Almost a century ago, the classic studies of Johnson (1911) and Starch and Elliot (1912, 1913) revealed the gross subjectivity of teacher-assigned marks, even in such objective subjects as geometry; their research initiating a series of controversial innovations in marking that continue to this day. In the 1960s, emotional pleas for the abolition of grades were common (Anderson, 1966; Glasser, 1969; Holt, 1968). Such proposals are at least 60 years old (Dadourian, 1925). In China's "cultural revolution," initiated in 1966, grading was greatly de-emphasized to help create a "classless society." But after that chaotic period, the pendulum began swinging back to "the basics" (Kraft, 1978). In the United States, both faculty and students believe grading serves several necessary and useful purposes (Buckley, 1987; Chase, 1979b).

The extreme diversity of reporting systems and reporting forms reflects the general confusion and difficulties in arriving at a satisfactory feedback system. All methods have problems, but this should not deter efforts to minimize the difficulties.

12.2 OBJECTIONS TO GRADES

Opposition to grading students generally rests on one or more of the following claims. These allegations have been carefully evaluated by Thorndike (1969) and Ebel (1974); the following summary is based on their cogent observations.

1. "Marks are inaccurate and not comparable across instructors, departments, or schools." There is some truth in this allegation. Personality factors, good behavior, promptness, and other factors do influence grades. For example, on the average, girls get higher grades than boys of equal ability and achievement (Caldwell & Hartnett, 1967).

The average GPA at most colleges is approximately the same regardless of the ability level of its students—whether the mean ability of the students is nationally at the 95th percentile or the 5th. There is a latent sliding curve that moves to adapt to the particular group being evaluated. Teachers' evaluations can never be totally free of subjectivity. The teacher who gives more *F*s is the same teacher who would more frequently describe students' performance as "unsatisfactory," "inferior," "below acceptable standards," and so on, if verbal evaluations were substituted for letter grades. It is naive to assume that a change in symbols from letters to words, percentages, or any other simple substitute would remedy the defects of the conventional system. Indeed, some studies have found less consistent interpretations of information when communicated in verbal form than when it was in numerical form. It is easy to identify imperfections in grading, but it is difficult to propose a satisfactory alternative. This is not to say, however, that the validity of the practices and procedures cannot be improved substantially.

2. *"Marks focus on false and inappropriate objectives and have little relationship to important educational objectives."* This criticism is really directed toward the assessment procedures employed by teachers rather than toward the use of grades. The evaluation procedures employed by many instructors are deplorable, but there is little reason to believe that some other method of *describing* student performance would improve the quality of the evidence on which student evaluations are based. This book has failed in its purpose if the assessment procedures teachers employ are not more valid as a consequence of having studied it. The remedy implied in the criticism is not to eliminate formal reporting procedures but to improve the assessment procedures.

3. *"Marks have limited value as a medium of communication between teachers, students, and parents."* This allegation is certainly true. To imply that this point justifies the abolition of marks, however, is illogical. It should be made clear to students and parents that marks reflect only certain educational factors, primarily cognitive achievement as measured by written tests. Reporting on academic performance of this kind should be only part of the communication system. The school should employ other means as well for communicating students' performance such as written comments and parent-teacher conferences.

4. *"Marks are responsible for a variety of detrimental side effects such as anxiety, dishonesty, hostility, and poor mental health; they produce negative attitudes resulting from chronic failure, encourage undesirable value patterns (striving for grades rather than learning), are incompatible with democracy, and so on."* An early critique of grading (Glaser, 1963) stated that "the school practice that most produces failure in students is grading" (p. 59) and "grades are also bad because they encourage cheating" (p. 64). The first contention is like claiming that "thermometers produce bad weather"; the second is like saying, "Money is bad because it encourages stealing." There is nothing wrong with encouraging students to work for high marks if the marks are valid measures of achievement. When properly given, high grades report success in learning and low grades identify a problem that needs attention.

It is most unfortunate that some students do not read well or have trouble learning math, but it is erroneous to assume that the cognitive or affective consequences are results of employing letter grades to summarize student performance. Although students are not graded on physical attractiveness, certain unfortunate side effects often accompany peer reactions to social unattractiveness. Poor athletic ability may affect a child's self-concept adversely, but teacher-given marks are not responsible. All first-grade children are aware of whether their reading group is high, average, or low, and even which students in the group read better or less well than they; the child knows these facts whether or not marks are assigned. The problem is not marks; it is the perception of inferior performance or failure and the consequences of that perception.

The best creative educational efforts should be directed toward finding methods by which every student can learn effectively. In any group and on any trait there will always be comparisons among members of the group. The lowest-achieving student in an honors class of gifted students is vulnerable to the same detrimental side effects of failure that have been attributed to marks—even if the student receives a good mark and would be near the top of a typical class. Avoiding all of the negative attitudinal side effects is impossible; a sterile environment would not prepare individuals for the real world. Individualization, and isolation, of instruction can minimize comparisons among learners but cannot prevent them entirely. We are misled if we assume that marks in and of themselves are the culprit. In the final analysis, a mark is a judgment of an instructor of the extent to which educational objectives have been attained by a student; it can provide both information and incentive. Unfortunately, some students and parents exaggerate the importance of grades and view them as a measure of their worth; a few others do not give them the importance that they deserve. Any person is destined for emotional difficulties if their worth is determined by their cognitive or psychomotor performance or by other physical characteristics.

It is interesting to note that the educational values of teachers have been shown to distort their perceptions of students' satisfaction with school. One study found that a teacher's estimate of a student's satisfaction was more closely related to the student's academic record than to the student's own rating of satisfaction! The study found little relationship between scholastic performance and the student's rating of satisfaction. Sooner or later, most of us come to grips with our strengths and weaknesses and adjust to them, at least to some degree.

The problems with grades are many, but to assert that imperfect information and feedback is worse than none at all is to argue for ignorance. Moynihan (1971, p. 4) observed that

> One of the achievements of democracy, although it seems not much regarded as such today, is the system of grading and sorting individuals so that young persons of talent born to modest or lowly circumstances can be recognized for their worth. (Similarly, it provides a means for young persons of social status to demonstrate that they have inherited brains as well as money, as it were.) I have not the least doubt that this system is crude, that it is often cruel, and that it measures only a limited number of things. Yet it measures valid things, by and large. To do away with such systems of accreditation may seem like an egalitarian act, but in fact it would be just the opposite. We would be back to a world in which social connections and privilege count for much more than any of us, I believe, would like. If what you know doesn't count, in the competitions of life, who you know will determine the outcomes.

Surprisingly, and unfortunately, it is a little known fact that among the 20 percent of students with the highest academic achievement, half are from lower-SES homes. Without grades there would be more able students from lower socioeconomic backgrounds whose college aptitude would go unnoticed.

12.3   TESTING AND GRADING

Consider the process of assigning a grade to a test or assignment. Sometimes the grade is given directly, as when an English teacher judges that this is an *A* theme and that is a *C* theme. In the teacher's mind some sort of evaluative process has occurred, a process moderated by the teacher's criteria and standards of grading. The teacher is accustomed to giving certain proportions of students grades of *A, B,* and so on. The teacher may have higher or lower standards when compared with other teachers of the same course. The teacher's marks will fluctuate to some extent from time to time, but year after year the grades given probably tend to be higher or lower than those of certain other teachers of the same course.

Often graders give a paper a total point score, which is also a percentage mark, as when each of four questions on an essay test is worth up to 25 points. These percentages are used either directly or in the assignment of letter grades (e.g., $70 - 79 = C$, $80 - 89 = B$, $90 - 100 = A$). Since the difficulty of a test depends on the questions that happen to be used, subjective marking usually causes the grader to mark more difficult tests more leniently than easier tests in order to make the distribution of grades come out *right*. For example, if percentages are running low, an instructor is more prone to give partial credit. If scores are running too high, only near-perfect answers can be credited and all the others may be counted wrong. If all this adjusting of scoring methods results in a distribution of grades that is different from that desired, the teacher can make the next test easier or harder or adjust the "standards" in order to bring the average grade up or down.

Changing standards so that the percentage grades are in line with the letter grades can be confusing to students and is unnecessary. If raw scores on the test are converted to percentages (to remove the arbitrariness of the number of items or maximum score on the test), teachers can then make the conversion of percentage scores into grades according to their best professional judgment. The rigid adherence to the conventional percentages (for example, *A* for 90% and above) can discourage teachers from including many challenging items from the higher taxonomy levels and, hence, do an educational disservice both in terms of instruction and evaluation.

No one has ever been able to devise an effective strategy to change instructors whose distributions of grades are out of line, but sometimes a discussion of grading practices and rationale, together with consideration of the distribution of grades assigned by various teachers, can be helpful. It is difficult, if not impossible, however, to change the grading of the teacher who argues that his or her lenient grading is indicative of good teaching. (Grading differences among instructors at the college level are probably even greater than they are in high schools and elementary schools.)

12.4 MARKS AND CRITERION-REFERENCED MEASURES

Individual differences among students are inevitable, regardless of the type of instruction or evaluation measures employed. Even with individualized, mastery learning approaches, students will differ in rate and degree of mastery. The notion that criterion-referenced testing will avoid problems of marking seems to be based on quite unrealistic expectations of uniform achievements in learning by all students. Programs of mastery learning cannot abolish individual differences in ability, interest, and determination. Students will continue to have strengths and weaknesses irrespective of the instructional strategies employed, and these should be diagnosed and communicated to the students and their parents.

12.5 GRADING ON THE CURVE

A few schools and departments have set limits on the percent of students who can receive various grades (e.g., not more than 10 percent *F*s in general mathematics at the end of the year) that all teachers are urged or even required to follow. Such prescriptions are of limited value, since the abilities of students, even in different sections of the same course, can vary considerably. It would be unfair to require the same distribution of grades in both honors mathematics and regular mathematics. A common and often valid complaint against accelerated or honors classes is that the grades of many students in these special classes often suffer. Teachers in honors courses should not confuse difficulty of the course with difficulty in grading; teachers should resist the temptation to grade the course as if it were a college course. The grading in such courses should correspond to what the students would obtain if there were no honors section. Unrealistically high requirements for grades in honors courses is such a common problem that many schools have changed the definition of grade points in such courses (e.g., from *A* = 4 to *A* = 5) so that students are not placed at a disadvantage in admission decisions for selective colleges. This change creates new evaluation problems.

The rationale for grading on the normal curve was suggested almost a century ago ago (Meyer, 1908) after a professor at the University of Missouri flunked his whole class! Many studies have documented that grading standards vary considerably among departments and instructors. Grading on the normal curve became a popular "solution." The most common method (Cureton, 1971) uses 1.5 or more standard deviations (1.5σ) above the average score ($z \geq 1.5$) for As (about 7%), $.5\sigma$ to 1.5σ for Bs (about 24%), $-.5\sigma$ to $.5\sigma$ for Cs (about 38%), $-.5\sigma$ to -1.5σ for Ds (about 24%), and below -1.5σ for Fs (about 7%).

Stripped of its unnecessary complexities, this grading on the curve simply amounts to determining in advance approximately what percentage of the class can be expected to get As, Bs, and so on. Some amusing and revealing tales are told about how this procedure can miss the mark. On the first day of class, a professor of Latin informed the seven students taking his advanced course that he had learned about grading on the curve the previous summer and would use it in the class. As a result, it was certain that one of the seven students would fail the course. As the students left at the close of the class, the least able student muttered to the other six, "I'm sure to be the one who fails, so I'm dropping the course right now." "But you can't do that," the others exclaimed, "because then one of us would fail." So the six pooled their money and paid the predestined failure to stay in the course and absorb the failing grade.

Another story is similar. During the first few years after World War II, the wives of veterans who were studying at a certain large state university enrolled for the more difficult courses in sufficient numbers to absorb all the failing grades themselves. They simply did little or no work and received Fs and Ds, while their husbands got grades of C or better with only moderate effort.

Actually, grading on the curve fixes the percent of As or Fs only if the distribution of scores is perfectly normal in shape. If scores are positively skewed, all scores could fall above the point, -1.5σ below the mean (i.e., $z > -1.5$); hence, it is not inevitable that some students will receive a grade of F even when the above method is employed.

Grading on the curve may be justifiable for, say, the 400 persons enrolled for a required freshman course in psychology. Even then, however, the instructor should have some discretion to weigh the balance of course work, the students' effort that semester, and other considerations in determining the final grades.

12.6 NARRATIVE REPORTS

Narrative reports can be very useful, especially at the elementary school level. Indeed, a strong case can be made for the exclusive use of narrative reports for the primary grades if teachers will take the time to complete a structured report form (see, for example, Figure 12–1) carefully. Such reports should include statements about effort, attitude, and behavior, as well as achievement. Narrative descriptions also reduce the impact of comparisons among students by parents and by the students themselves. They give the teacher a better opportunity to bring important matters to the parents' attention. At the upper elementary grades, narrative comments can also be a useful supplement to grades by bringing to light matters that can help parents better understand their child's progress. Research finds that parents want report cards with grades but can understand the merits of narrative reporting during the primary grades if a reasonable rationale is provided.

Narrative reports are especially useful for children receiving special education. It is probably counterproductive to use grades with children with learning disabilities prior to high school. Reporting of their achievement status and progress is important, but valid letter grades are less useful vehicles of communication for them than descriptions expressed in words.

Narrative reports are less promising at the secondary level, where the teacher has many times more students and knows them less well. The reporting task, if taken seriously, could be so onerous that it would certainly encourage perfunctory reporting.

Many report forms currently in use at the elementary school level give the teacher an opportunity to make special comments in addition to the formal marks. The usefulness of narrative reports (and skills checklists) in elementary schools is strongly supported by teachers, principals, and parents (Buckley, 1987).

12.7 PARENT CONFERENCES

Several substitutes for marking have been proposed. Most of them have created additional problems. Parent-teacher and/or teacher-student conferences have been suggested as a replacement for marks. Conferences have been wisely and, in general, effectively used to *supplement* conventional report cards on the elementary school level, especially if portfolios of the student's work is included. The major disadvantages are the scheduling problems (especially for employed parents) and the time required for conferences. In addition, teachers need some counseling skills; such skills are particularly vital when students are performing below parental expectations. Time and scheduling problems often preclude individual conferences at the junior and senior high school levels where departmentalized programs are typical. Some departmentalization and specialization are common even in elementary schools.

It is unfortunate that school-to-home communication often takes place only after unsatisfactory progress. Many secondary schools pass out "sad news" slips to alert the student and their parents of a problem early enough that corrective efforts can be attempted before a grade is assigned. To offset this, some schools now have a practice of including "glad slips."

Most schools maintain a cumulative record (cum folder) of standardized test scores and other information for each student; this record can be useful in parent-teacher conferences. One drawback of most parent conferences is that there is no systematic record of the exchange. A parent-teacher conference report form like that shown in Figure 12–1 can overcome this deficiency. The form illustrates that a parent conference has much in common with a structured interview: Without guidelines, important gaps will result. It is a checklist in triplicate, with one copy each for the teacher, the parent, and the *cum folder*.

It is also important to report standardized test results to students and their parents. Much valuable information that is of interest to parents and students lies buried in files. These results complement grades and teacher evaluations and assist in giving a more complete picture of the student's performance and progress. Reporting to parents has its risks and must be done skillfully and carefully. But we are convinced that it should be done. Schools have sometimes avoided this responsibility by contending that "parents will misinterpret scores." This statement, however, says more about deficiencies in the teachers than about deficiencies in parents. Many standardized achievement tests provide special inter-

Parent-Teacher Conference Report   Teacher _____

Student _____   Name of parent _____

Date _____

ACADEMIC

  Reading _____

  Math _____

  English _____

  Social studies _____

  Science _____

  P. E. _____

  Music _____

  Art _____

PHYSICAL

  General Health _____

  Vision/Hearing _____

  Attendance _____

  Health habits (eating, sleeping,
    grooming) _____

  _____

  Special needs _____

  _____

  _____

SOCIAL/EMOTIONAL

  Peer relationships _____

  Teacher/student _____

  Parent/child _____

  Special needs _____

  _____

  _____

WORK HABITS

  Attentiveness _____

  Effort _____

  Leadership _____

  Neatness _____

  Use of time _____

  Work style _____

  Interests _____

  Special needs _____

  _____

  _____

  _____

Teacher comments (parental attitudes, effectiveness of conference, suggestions, etc.)

_____

_____

_____

FIGURE 12–1   A sample parent-teacher conference report form.

pretive report forms for parents (see Section 14.11) that can be very helpful in communicating test results.

    The following guidelines for effective parent conferences are abridged from suggestions from several sources.

Dos of Parent Conferences

1. Review the student's cumulative record prior to the conference.
2. Assemble samples of the student's work. Point out that every child has strengths as well as weaknesses. It is hoped that information about our strengths will encourage us in these areas. Feedback about our weaknesses is necessary diagnostic information that can be a springboard for improvement.
3. Use a structured outline like the one in Figure 12–1 to guide the conference.
4. List questions to ask parents and anticipate parents' questions.
5. Be professional and maintain a positive attitude.
6. Be willing to listen; be understanding; encourage two-way communication.
7. Be honest; begin by describing the student's strengths.
8. Accept some of the responsibility for problems.
9. Conclude the conference with an overall summary.
10. Keep a concise written record of the conference, listing problems and suggestions, with a copy for the parents.

Don'ts of Parent Conferences

1. Don't blame parents or put them on the defensive; never argue.
2. Don't make derogatory comments about other teachers, other students, or the school.
3. Don't play amateur psychiatrist.
4. Don't discuss the conference with others, except other school personnel directly involved with the student.
5. Don't do all the talking; skillful professionals are good listeners. Don't be uncomfortable with periods of silence.

12.8   PORTFOLIOS

There is a healthy trend in education to base student evaluations on more authentic, performance-based indicators and to systematically collect these in an organized way into a portfolio that represents the students' work and capabilities. This provides a broad framework for evaluating students and assigning grades. The nature of the portfolio will differ markedly by subject-matter and grade level. Several states have adopted the portfolio approach as a component in state assessments, even though "performance assessment is not ready to implement on a large-scale basis" (Burger & Burger, 1994, p. 14).

Portfolio approaches are usually linked to projects in which the student is a major decision maker, to encourage individual initiative, interest, and creativity. The evaluation rationale places more emphasis on the products contained in the portfolio and less emphasis on traditional paper-and-pencil tests.

As with most new movements, there are enthusiastic and overenthusiastic proponents of the use of portfolios in student assessment. Some want to throw out all uniform tests and allow the student evaluations to be more phenomenological and idiosyncratic, without realizing the major problem of the portfolio approach as a "stand-alone" method of student assessment. As Moss (1994, p. 6) has observed,

Less standardized forms of assessment, such as performance assessments, present serious problems for reliability, in terms of generalizability across readers and tasks as well as across other facets of measurement . . . In the case of portfolios, where the tasks may vary substantially from student to student and where multiple tasks may be evaluated simultaneously, inter-reader reliability may drop below acceptable levels for consequential decisions about individuals.

What is very evident from the research on portfolios is this—they are a useful complement to traditional means of student evaluation but should never supplant tests and other standard assessment approaches. The number of tasks within the portfolio needs to be large, with two or more independent judges of the quality of each if the resulting evaluations are to be reliable and valid (Linn and Burton,1994). In other words, as typically employed, if the portfolio is used exclusively, or even predominately, as the basis for student evaluations, these evaluations will depend greatly on who is doing the judging and not just on the quality of what is being judged (Koretz, Stecher, Klein, and McCaffrey, 1994). The evaluation problems are not unlike those associated with a science fair—the extent to which the student is uniquely responsible for the quality of a task is usually uncertain.

The use of portfolios has great potential for enriching education and student assessment but should not be viewed as an alternative to traditional tests and examinations. Students still need to demonstrate proficiency on uniform tasks designed to be a representative sample of the objectives of a course of study. One may have wonderful tasks in a science portfolio (collections of rocks, leaves, insects, experiments) but have great gaps in understanding about major laws of physics, genetics, and so on.

12.9   OTHER ALTERNATIVES

Student self-evaluation has been tried, but experimental results have not been very encouraging. Self-ratings of proficiency have been found to be consistently higher than corresponding peer ratings. However, some elementary school teachers have used self-evaluations as a starting point for conferences with students or their parents about grades. Page (1960) suggested that marks be given by someone other than the teacher; he contends that marking "kills the enjoyment of the class." But if the teacher is competent, who is in a better position to evaluate performance? The suggestion may have some merit, but the reassignment of the responsibility for grading is probably not generally realistic. A skillful instructor can communicate to the student that they are partners in a common endeavor and at the same time assign valid grades. As with so many other things, how something is done is often more critical than what is done.

The usefulness of the various substitutes must be evaluated from a realistic perspective. Teachers can hardly be expected to be enthusiastic about any alternative that adds to their already demanding duties. Checklists are frequently used in addition to academic grades in elementary schools and have been found to be a useful adjunct to marks (Buckley, 1987).

Roelfs (1955), studying the marking trend from 1925–1953, found a decided shift toward letter grades. The National Education Association's national survey (1967) of over 600 school systems found letter or numerical grades used in 80 percent of public schools, except in first grade (73 percent) and kindergarten (17 percent). A survey of elementary school teachers in 1987 found that the *A–F* grading system was used by 81 percent of the teachers. The teachers (as well as parents) preferred the conventional five-point *A–F* system to three-point (e.g., *O–S–U*) schemes. It is apparent that, despite the continuing controversy over marking, the measurement and reporting of student achievement are necessary, and no substantially better or more scientific means of doing so is on the horizon (Buckley, 1987; Ebel, 1970b; Englehart, 1964). The validity of the information on which marks are based and, hence, of marks themselves can be increased substantially, however, by improved assessment methods, considered in Chapters 7 to 11.

12.10   THE MEANING OF MARKS

In assigning quarter, semester, and year-end grades for a course, many instructors consider not only achievement as measured by tests but also more subjectively evaluated characteristics, such as effort, punctuality, behavior, and neatness of written work. Usually these noncognitive aspects get much more weight in elementary school than in high school. Often, children who are "working up to capacity" may obtain an excellent mark, even though they are not high achievers, while those who do not seem to be expending "enough" effort receive lower grades despite better achievement. This system is confusing to students and parents, especially when a child moves from elementary to junior high school and his or her grades change sharply because the bases for them have changed.

One does not average oranges and bicycles; it is also wise to *keep marks for achievement separate from ratings of study habits and attitudes*. Achievement can be judged from classroom tests and assessments, oral and written work in class, and standardized tests. The meaning of marks is obscured when other aspects of a student's behavior are determiners of marks. Most parents want to know how well their children are doing, how much industry and effort they are giving to the subject, how regular their attendance has been, and so on. Noncognitive factors that are important should be evaluated and reported separately. If both student and parents have an accurate picture of the student's total performance and behavior, they are in a better position to work cooperatively with the schools in developing appropriate educational goals.

12.11   THE CRITERION OF QUALITY

There are several questions pertaining to the criterion to which achievement is referenced: Should it be performed in relation to an absolute standard, student aptitude, individual student growth, or the student's peer group?

Achievement in Relation to an Absolute Standard

In the past, a simplistic absolute standard percentage was often employed, and marks were considered to represent a percentage of complete or perfect mastery. Criterion-referenced measurement is a modern version of this practice. Close scrutiny reveals the "absolute standard" to be quite arbitrary. A lenient teacher can give an easy test in which all students will score 90 percent or higher. An excellent teacher can administer a more valid and reliable test and have a class average of 60 percent. Test difficulty is a matter of item construction; it is far from being an absolute standard. On nonobjective evaluations the standard "is in the eye of the beholder"—in this instance, the grader. Under scrutiny, the absolute standard is usually found to be based on some version of normative performance, as indeed it should be. But this fact is often lost in the heat of rhetoric (e.g., "Kids should be measured against performance standards, not against each other"). The notion of complete mastery of a subject such as English, literature, mathematics, handwriting, or social studies is illusory and should be so identified to prevent erroneous interpretations of performance. Our measurement technology is inadequate to provide grading on a meaningful absolute standard. The most meaningful standard is the normative performance of similar previous students.

Achievement in Relation to Aptitude

Teachers have little valid basis for estimating aptitude (potential) apart from performance and achievement, except via standardized aptitude and intelligence tests. Different school subjects require a somewhat different set of aptitudes. The technical difficulties in interpreting differences between achievement and aptitude are very complex even when standardized achievement and aptitude tests are employed (Thorndike, 1963a; Green, 1974). Since the more specific course-related objectives are not assessed by standardized achievement tests, they should not be used as an exclusive or even the principal basis for assigning marks. Achievement in relation to aptitude is an untenable basis for marking, despite the obvious appeal the idea has for many educators.

Individual Student Growth

The problems of assessing improvement or progress are even more difficult than those associated with contrasting achievement with aptitude (Cronbach & Furby, 1970; Harris, 1963). Even with highly refined instruments, gain or growth scores are usually not very reliable. When the procedure is attempted on the informal, unsystematic basis available to the teacher, such scores are almost certain to have little validity. Also, if grading were based on growth on standardized tests, it would not take long for "the word" to get out and students would "sandbag" on the pretest.

Achievement in Relation to Peer Achievement

Most marking is a derivative of this model. A child who reads well in the first grade is usually an inferior reader compared with fifth-graders. The teacher evaluates the child's performance on what can reasonably be expected from a representative group of students of the same age. This "phantom" representative group usually turns out to be an imprecise, internal standard developed through the teacher's observations and experience. In most cases the major determiner of the assigned marks is the teacher's perception of the students' performance in relation to that of other students in the present class and perhaps recent classes.

This "internal standardization" or adaptation was demonstrated by Aiken (1963) and Baird and Feister (1972), who found that despite substantial changes in the abilities of entering college freshmen, there was no real change in the distribution of assigned marks.

In spite of the lack of a clearly and objectively defined reference group, marks have considerable meaning. This is evidenced by the predictive validity they have for subsequent academic performance. Hicklin (1962) found a correlation of .73 between marks at grade 9 and grade 12. One study found that the year-to-year consistency of grades in college was in the .50 to .70 range; the consistency was found to be less (approximately .40) in graduate school, as might be expected because of the restriction in the range of ability (see Etaugh, Etaugh & Hurd, 1972 pp. 1102–1104). Nell (1963) found that grades in a subject correlated .64 to .81 with performance on the respective subtest of a standardized achievement test battery. High school grades are even better predictors of college grades than standardized intelligence and achievement tests (see, e.g., Hills, 1971; Richards & Lutz, 1968), although their predictive validity has been reduced by grade inflation. In a study by the American College Testing Program (Hoyt & Munday, 1966) of over 100,000 students, the correlation with freshman grades was .58 and .55 for high school marks and composite standardized test scores, respectively. (When both were used, the correlation increased to .65).

It is true that (1) grading standards differ among teachers, (2) grades tend to be scaled within a class regardless of differences in the students' aptitude levels, (3) grades are often contaminated by student deportment, (4) grades often represent crude efforts to mark in relation to aptitude or progress or in relation to an absolute standard, and (5) the anchor points for grades drift with the prevailing winds of fashion. For example, the mean GPA for high school seniors taking the *ACT* increased from 2.6 to almost 3.0 between 1970 and 1980 but has now dropped slightly to 2.9. There was a similar pattern of findings for college students. In spite of their imperfections, grades continue to have considerable meaning and predictive validity (Schoenfeldt & Brush, 1975).

12.12 A BETTER PROPOSAL?

If a within-class ranking method were employed, grade inflation would be impossible. This rank in class is essentially the method of reporting success in many law schools. Many colleges convert high school GPA to percentile rank in the graduating class to reduce differences in grading leniency among schools. But ranking has its problems, too. The 70th percentile in some classes would be equivalent to the 40th percentile in others. Most certainly, the use of both would be an improvement over the use of either separately. A high school or college instructor would send in two performance indicators: the conventional grade, but also the rank in class (which could be converted to a normalized *T*-score or percentile rank to offset the problems associated with different class sizes). If we know that an applicant to graduate school had a GPA of 3.1 but a mean *T*-score of rank in class of 40, we would know the applicant was a below-average student at that institution—indeed, in the bottom 20 percent of the class! The use of both conventional "absolute" marks and relative standing could be especially valuable at the secondary and college levels.

12.13 ASSIGNING MARKS AND WEIGHTING COMPONENTS

In arriving at an overall evaluation of student performance, some method must be used to pool the various kinds of information on which the mark is based. The results from tests, homework, and other assignments must be combined in some way. If points on all components are summed, and each component is transformed to have the same standard deviation, each will contribute proportionally to the composite score. Or, equivalently, if each ingredient were converted into a standard score (say, a T-score) and the scores were totaled for each student, each factor would be weighted according to its actual contribution to the composite.

Intuitively, it seems as if the maximum possible score on a factor would reflect its influence on the final ordering of the students, but such is not the case as far as position in the composite distribution is concerned. Consider a science project with 100 possible points. Suppose that each child worked diligently and received 100 points. When these points are added to all the other information on which the grade is to be based, what effect does the project have on the distribution? Every score is increased by 100 points, so the relative standing of each student is unchanged. The mean would be increased by 100 points, but the standard score for any student on the composite would be unaffected. When scores from various tests, projects, and so on are combined into a total score, each measure contributes to the composite distribution in direct proportion to its standard deviation and to its correlation with the other measures. (see Stanley & Wang, 1970; Wang & Stanley, 1970).

Consider the following data for four components, each of which has a maximum point value of 100:

	Essay	Objective Test	Project	Homework
μ	70	70	70	70
σ	20	10	10	5

If the teacher simply sums each student's points to arrive at a total score on which a final grade will be based, the essay test would tend to have more influence than the other three factors combined, even though each of the four factors might carry an identical number of maximum credits.

When scores are to be totaled, the standard deviations need to be at least approximately in proportion to the desired weights. Fortunately, this can easily be controlled. Recall from Chapter 3 that if every score in a distribution is multiplied by 2, the standard deviation likewise is doubled. If, in this example, you want each factor to be weighted equally, you will multiply the project scores by 2, the objective test by 2, and the homework by 4. Then the standard deviation of the scores on each component will be 20. Or, equivalently, convert all components into T-scores. In actual practice, this is too much trouble for busy teachers (unless they have access to microcomputers and spreadsheets). But simply being aware of the issue will help you score various projects and assignments that are evaluated subjectively. If the standard deviation on the objective portion of a test is 10 and you desire to weight the essay portion equally, you should scale your scoring of the essays so that the middle two-thirds will fall within roughly a 20-point range, with a total range of about 40 to 60 points (4σ to 6σ).

If each component is converted into a mark before the information is combined, the task of arriving at a final mark is much simpler. Unfortunately, the reliability is decreased somewhat because not all the information is used. For instance, students who receive the highest and lowest *B*s on a test are treated equally in this plan. If there are several components to be combined, this loss is not serious. If pluses and minuses are used for *A* through *D*, the loss will be much less (i.e., there are 13 rather than 5 possible grading categories).

In most instances numerical summation of scores is unnecessary. The teacher can look over the marks of the components and weight them subjectively. Ordinarily, one should give some consideration to improvement, especially on the final examination (if it is comprehensive, as it should be). A sequence of grades like *A, B, C* should be viewed differently from a pattern like *C, B, A* even if the composite scores are equal. The teacher must remember that the final grade in the course should reflect the *extent* to which the student has mastered the course objectives, not *when* they were mastered. Performance on early tests and assignments should usually be weighted less heavily than more current (and inclusive) indicators of terminal mastery level.

12.14 HOMEWORK AND MARKING

Ordinarily, homework should not have much influence on students' marks, unless they do not do the assignments. Homework should be viewed primarily as an instructional activity, not an activity that has direct implications for evaluation. Students should be able to get help on their homework assignments, but such help also means that the resulting product is not a good indicator of the student's mastery. If homework carries substantial evaluation credit, some students will become too concerned about having the correct answers, and their success on the assignments may reflect the ability to use resources such as parents and other students rather than mastery of the material.

12.15 NUMBER OF CATEGORIES

The common percentage system of marks has 101 possible categories (0–100). This system still prevails in many countries and in about one-sixth of American high schools (Pinchak & Breland, 1974) and one-eighth of elementary schools (Buckley, 1987). The most common marking system in American schools utilizes 5 categories (*A, B, C, D, F*), which are expanded to 13 categories if pluses and minuses are used (+ and – are not used with *F*). Some educators favor a two-category pass-fail (*P–F*) system—that is, a credit–no credit system. Philosophical and technical measurement issues must be considered in deciding the best number of classifications.

In the late 1960s and early 1970s, colleges and universities began to give students the option of taking a limited number of courses outside their major and minor fields using the pass-fail system. This system is designed to encourage students to broaden their education by exposing themselves to other fields without jeopardizing their academic record. Such a program has logical appeal for increasing the breadth of academic experience, although one study (Warren, 1975) found that this does not, in fact, happen. As a grading strategy, the system has major defects. Princeton students reported that they tended to study less and learn less in pass-fail courses than they did in conventionally evaluated courses. The results have been similar at other institutions.

Ebel (1965b, p. 423) showed that even when the composite on which the marking was based had a reliability of .95, the reliability of the resulting *marks* using a two-category system would be only .63. If 5 categories were used, the reliability of the corresponding *marks* would be .85; if 15 categories (say, *A, B, C, D, F,* with + and –) were used, the reliability would be .94. With fewer categories, one loses all the information that is pertinent to individual differences within category. The severity of any misclassification is much greater as the number of categories is reduced. It is not serious when a student who deserves a *B* receives a *B–*, but it may be critical when a student who deserves a *P* receives an *F,* or vice versa. Reducing the number of categories to two or three clearly compounds the problem of the unreliability of marks.

It is unlikely that a widespread move away from the five-category system will occur in the near future, even though the reliability of the marks could be increased with more categories. The two-mark system—"absolute" (e.g., letter grade) and relative (e.g., percentile rank or *T*-score in class) described in this section—has advantages but is practical only with computerized reporting systems. These proposals will probably languish, along with many other attempts to reform marking, until enough momentum is generated for a fundamental reform in the marking systems.

Most elementary school report cards consist of both grades and checklist items; some also contain achievement test scores. The trend is toward keeping parents better informed, but, as stated earlier, it is important to separate achievement assessment from effort, neatness, citizenship, attendance, and the like. Parents need to be informed about several areas: How is my child achieving in each subject (i.e., cognitive attainments), and how is my child faring in affective and social areas? Is he or she using time constructively? Completing assignments on time? Does the child demonstrate good work habits and attitudes?

No single report card is without imperfections. Each school system must work out its own reporting system and have written district guidelines for the teachers. In many schools computer facilities have simplified and automated reporting procedures. Figure 12–2 illustrates an informative report card at the secondary school level. Some explanatory information is given to the parent on the reverse side of the card. The card gives marks for each subject, associated final-examination grades, citizenship and attitude ratings, and attendance data for each quarter and semester. The student's GPA is given for the current grading period (3.50), along with the cumulative GPA (3.42).

12.16 SUGGESTIONS FOR IMPROVING MARKING AND REPORTING

After ten years of experimenting with a number of ways to improve marking and reporting practices, Wrinkle (1956), a school principal, listed 22 generalizations that seemed to him to summarize what he and his staff had learned. These suggestions are integrated with those of Gronlund (1974) and listed here. They should give direction for developing an adequate, yet functional, marking and reporting system.

BOULDER VALLEY SCHOOL DISTRICT RE-2

SCHOOL	GRADUATION CREDITS	SCHOOL YEAR	HOME ROOM	STUDENT NUMBER	1ST PERIOD		2ND PERIOD		3RD PERIOD		4TH PERIOD		
					DAYS A	TT	DAYS A	TT	DAYS A	TT	DAYS A	TT	
CENTENNIAL JR. HIGH		79-80	203	258000	2		1						

TO THE PARENTS OF	CLASS	SUBJECT	1ST QTR		2ND QTR		SEMESTER 1		3RD QTR		4TH QTR		SEMESTER 2		TEACHER
			SUBJ	C	SUBJ	C	EXAM	GRADE	SUBJ	C	SUBJ	C	EXAM	GRADE	
	8	ENGLISH	A	1	A	1	A-	A							TONSO
HIRTER NANCY L		GEOGRAPHY	B+	2	A-	2	A-	A							CLEMENTS
2530 GLENWOOD		LIFE SCIENCE	C+	2	C	2	C+	C							MACY
BOULDER, COLORADO 80302		BASIC MATH	A-	2	A	2	C	B							GODDEN
		SPANISH LAB	A	2	A-	2		A							TERRELL
		ART	B	2	A	1		A							RICHARDSN
		ORCHESTRA	B	2	B+	2		B							FORD
		GIRLS P E	A	2	A	1		A							HOBSON

(S) SUBJECT   (C) SCHOOL CITIZENSHIP AND CLASS ATTITUDE

A -SUPERIOR
B -VERY GOOD
C -AVERAGE
D -BELOW AVERAGE
F -FAILING
I -INCOMPLETE
S -SATISFACTORY

1 -OUTSTANDING
2 -SATISFACTORY
3 -UNSATISFACTORY
4 -CONFERENCE REQUESTED

GRADE POINT AVERAGE	
ACCUM	CURRENT
3.42	3.50

SCHOLARSHIP GRADE is an evaluation of the student's achievement and progress in the subject.
CLASS ATTITUDE is an evaluation of the student's RESPECT for authority, property, fellow student and his DEMONSTRATION of self-motivation, responsibility of self and others, cooperation, sportsmanship, punctuality, dependability, honesty, leadership and service.

FIGURE 12-2 A sample report card of an eighth-grade student.

The marking and reporting system should be carefully planned and guided by stated objectives, such as school-related motivation; student, parent, and teacher understanding; and home-school cooperation.

The reporting system and forms should be developed by students, parents, teachers, and administrators, usually with the aid of a technical expert. This is best done at the district (not school) level to avoid unnecessary and expensive duplication of effort.

Informal teacher-student reporting and direct communication should be an ongoing process. Student-teacher conferences should not be a last resort but should be encouraged as a normal part of the reporting system.

Parent-teacher conferences can be very effective. Released time for teachers is often necessary for this activity to be practicable. It is very difficult to make parent conferences practical for every student at the secondary school level, but conferences are especially desirable for students whose academic performance begins to decline. Report forms for parent conferences, with copies for each party, are desirable.

The reporting system should include feedback on school behavior, attitudes, work habits, and attendance, as well as describe performance in school subjects.

Marks (supplemented with explanatory teacher comments) and parent conferences are necessary to fully describe performance, at least at the upper elementary and secondary school levels. Reporting systems in the primary grades can be less standardized, with greater reliance on parent conferences. Some parents need time to adjust to the reality of their child's abilities.

Failing marks are rarely justified or needed in the primary or even upper elementary grades.

SUMMARY

Reports of academic achievement, attitudes, and behavior are desirable and necessary in education; marks in some form will continue to be needed.

Marks are a means of feedback to students and to their parents; they should be as valid and accurate as possible. Critics of grading have failed to supply superior alternatives. Although marks have several major defects, they have considerable meaning, reliability, and validity for predicting subsequent academic performance.

The meaning of marks can be greatly improved if the basis on which they are to be assigned is clearly defined. Great difficulties arise when one attempts to evaluate achievement in relation to aptitude or to evaluate on the basis of improvement. Marks using a standard based on previous normative performance are more defensible than an illusionary absolute standard.

Marks should reflect demonstrated achievement. Other important facets, such as student attitude, effort, and citizenship, should be evaluated and reported independently.

When components are summed into total scores, one needs to be aware that the actual weighting of factors corresponds to the relative size of the standard deviations of the components. Less arithmetic methods of aggregation are usually preferable.

Even when composite scores have very high reliability, the reliability of assigned *marks* decreases (and the severity of errors increases) as the number of categories in the marking system is reduced. The traditional *A–F* marks with pluses and minuses have an adequate number of categories to describe performance accurately.

Marks should be supplemented with written comments and other means of communication among teacher, student, and parent.

CHAPTER TEST

1. Which one of the following three methods of reporting test scores is *least* informative?
   a) raw scores
   b) raw scores converted into percent-correct scores
   c) raw scores converted into percentile ranks

2. Grading on the normal curve, if adhered to rigidly, would *not* keep the mean GPA constant
   a) from class to class.
   c) from grade to grade.
   b) from year to year.
   d) for boys and girls.

3. According to the authors, grading on the normal curve is the best method for assigning school marks. (*T* or *F*)

4. Which of the following statements about marks is(are) correct? Marks
   a) are not exactly comparable across instructors.
   b) have little predictive validity.
   c) do not reflect important educational objectives.
   d) are undesirable because they encourage cheating.
   e) are incompatible with democratic ideals.

5. Thom and Anna each scored 60 percent on a physics test. We know that both
   a) are academically dull.
   b) obtained an *F* on the test.
   c) experienced a sense of failure associated with the test.
   d) were emotionally harmed by the test experience.
   e) None of the above

6. Parent-teacher conferences are *not*
   a) a useful method of school-home communication.
   b) at all like a two-way interview.
   c) a good way to inform parents about a student's behavior at school.
   d) a quick and easy reporting method.
   e) a good supplement to a standard reporting form.

7. Which one of the following is a recommended practice for parent conferences?
   a) Deal with only a single aspect of a child's school behavior.
   b) Delve deeply into a child's emotional relationship with his or her parents.
   c) Review the student's "cum folder" prior to the conference.
   d) Place the responsibility for any difficulty squarely in the home.
   e) Cover all aspects of the child's performance before allowing the parent to respond.

8. Which one of the following is the most reasonable basis for assigning grades?
   a) a true, absolute standard of performance, growth and improvement
   b) achievement in relation to aptitude
   c) effort
   d) achievement in relation to that of a representative peer group

9. If total, cumulative scores in a class are based on a test, an oral report, and a project, and if each is worth a maximum of 100 points, scores on which one of the following will contribute most to the variability of the total scores?

	Test	Oral Report	Portfolio
μ	80	90	85
σ	5	5	10

   a) test b) oral report c) project d) all will correlate equally

10. According to the author, homework should be weighted heavily in assigning marks. *(T or F)*

11. In addition to academic performance, it is desirable that report cards include information pertaining to
    a) class attitude.
    b) attendance.
    c) study habits.
    d) Two of the above
    e) Three of the above (a, b, and c)

ANSWERS TO CHAPTER TEST

1. a	5. e	9. c
2. d	6. d	10. F
3. F	7. c	11. e
4. only a	8. d	

PART III

Standardized Measures

13

Measuring Scholastic Aptitude

13.1 INTRODUCTION

The first documented instance of the measurement of individual differences in behavior occurred fortuitously in 1796, when astronomers at Greenwich Observatory were found to differ in the speed with which they could respond to visual stimuli using telescopes. Four decades later, in 1838, a French physician named Esquirol used various physical and psychological measures in an attempt to assess different degrees of feeblemindedness. He found that language usage was the single best indicator of mental level. Unfortunately, Esquirol's work did not have a wide impact and not until a half century later was the importance of verbal ability as a measure of "intelligence" recognized. The use of the term "intelligence" for these abilities is unfortunate—it is too inclusive. Only a limited portion of the domain of intelligence is represented in these measures. The terms *scholastic aptitude* and *academic aptitude* are much more descriptive and appropriate, since these measures are oriented primarily toward school learning. In recent years, several "intelligence" tests have been renamed to correct this unwarranted and grandiose label.

13.2 THE SEARCH FOR A VALID MEASURE OF INTELLIGENCE

Individual differences in such mental abilities as comprehension, problem solving, and analytic thinking—qualities that are usually grouped under the heading of intelligence—were recognized long before the discipline of psychology began in the late 1800s. Terms like *idiot, imbecile, genius, bright*, and *dull* (but not moron) have a long history in our language.

Psychology's genuine contribution to the study of cognitive abilities has been that of clarifying the nature of cognitive aptitudes and in devising measures of these abilities. One of the most esteemed psychologists of the 20th century, Lee Cronbach (1970, p. 197) observed, "Despite occasional overenthusiasm and misconceptions, . . . the general mental

323

test stands today as the most important technical contribution psychology has made to the practical guidance of human affairs."

13.3   GALTON AND THE STUDY OF HUMAN DIFFERENCES

Coincident with the beginnings of experimental psychology through the influence of Wundt and his laboratory in Leipzig in 1879, a different empirical tradition developed in England, spearheaded by Sir Francis Galton (1822–1911). Wundt and his colleagues were interested in finding universal psychological processes and had little interest in the differences among subjects. On the other hand, Galton was particularly interested in differences among persons. Galton's work was the beginning of the study of *individual differences*, which led to the development of the science of psychometrics which led to fundamental improvements in educational and psychological testing. From his laboratory of anthropometry, established in London in 1884, Galton studied topics such as word association, mental imagery, and the genetic basis of physical characteristics. To facilitate his research, Galton invented several statistical devices, including the scatterplot—a graphic method for depicting the degree of relationship between two variables such as aptitude and achievement (for example, Figures 4.6–4.8 in Chapter 4). As later refined by Galton's colleague, the statistician Karl Pearson, the degree of relationship evidenced in a scatterplot led to the ubiquitous *coefficient of correlation* (Chapter 4) that has been used extensively in all social and behavioral sciences.

Galton also devised the earliest mental tests. He studied individual performance differences on tests of reaction time, memory, and sensory acuity. Galton has been credited as the person who was primarily responsible for launching the testing movement (Anastasi, 1988, p. 8). Galton's practice of using rather simple "sensory" and "psychomotor" tasks as indicators of intellectual ability was continued by James McKeen Cattell, one of the earliest and best known American psychologists. Cattell was a product of Wundt's experimental psychology laboratory at the University of Leipzig and did his doctoral thesis on individual differences in reaction time. His interest in individual differences was reinforced by contact with Galton at Cambridge in 1888. In 1890 Cattell coined the term *mental test* in describing a battery of tests with which he attempted to measure the intelligence of college students at the University of Pennsylvania. Cattell and many of his contemporaries regarded simpler mental and psychomotor processes, such as speed of tapping, reaction time, judgment of time intervals, and keenness of vision and hearing, as indications of intelligence. But because he directed his efforts away from measures of more complex mental and verbal processes, his efforts were doomed to failure.

At the turn of the century, Seashore (1899) found virtually no relationship between teachers' estimates of general mental ability and children's ability to judge time intervals, estimate length of lines, and discriminate loudness and pitch. Shortly thereafter, Bagley (1900) reported that simple motor abilities such as hand strength, trilling a telegraph key, and reaction time had virtually no relation to a child's actual class standing or to a teacher's judgment of that child. Wissler (1901) was the first to apply Pearson's correlation to test scores. Using Cattell's tests with college students, Wissler found no significant relationship between the tests and college marks (rs of between $-.09$ and $.16$), and little relationship among the tests themselves. Consequently, the attempt to measure cognitive aptitudes with such tests was all but abandoned because the empirical findings were inconsistent with the theoretical expectation of a measure of intelligence—that is, Cattell's tests lacked construct validity (see Section 4.8).

13.4 BINET'S BREAKTHROUGH

In France, incisive work was being done by a French physician-psychologist named Alfred Binet (1857–1911), often called the father of modern intelligence testing. As early as 1896 Binet had published a proposal for a series of tests designed to measure children's intellectual capacity. Binet believed that a measure of intelligence must include a range of performances that are normally regarded as intelligent behavior. The test should comprise a series of tasks requiring the ability to reason, make sound judgments, recognize familiar objects, and understand commands; that is, it should call for a variety of mental skills. A child's intelligence was to be represented by a summation of his or her scores on the separate cognitive tasks. For Binet, intelligence was a phenomenon requiring many different abilities.

In 1904 Binet was commissioned by the French minister of public instruction to extend his investigations to determining workable methods of identifying mentally retarded children so that they might be given special schooling. He tried, but then rejected, sensory discrimination tasks, size of cranium, handwriting analysis, responses to inkblots, and several other measures. Binet's findings appeared in three classic papers, published in 1905 (see Binet & Simon, 1916), in which Binet presented a number of tasks that he had found useful. These were arranged in order of difficulty and then "normed" on a group of typical children at each age level from 3 to 11. By comparing an individual child's performance with the age of children who typically performed likewise, Binet was able to get an indication of the subject's intellectual development—that is, a child's *mental age* was determined by referring his or her performance to the chronological age at which the average child successfully completed the same tasks.

13.5 THE STANFORD-BINET SCALE

Binet's method of assessing intelligence met with some criticism but much acclaim. By 1916 his scales had been translated into seven languages and were used in at least twelve countries (Binet & Simon, 1916). In 1911 Kuhlmann published a revision of the Binet scale. He made the unwise decision to extend the scale downward to the age of three months, much below Binet's three-year limit. It remained for psychologist Lewis M. Terman of Stanford University to make the first thorough revision of the Binet scale. Terman carefully adapted and standardized the scale for use with average, as well as mentally limited children. Notice how the following sample items require reasoning and problem solving.

- In what way are a knife blade, a penny, and a piece of wire alike?
- What is the difference between laziness and idleness?
- If you lost a purse in a field, how would you go about trying to find it?

- I planted a tree that was 8 in. tall. At the end of the first year it was 18 in. tall; and at the end of the third year it was 27 in. tall. How tall do you think it would be at the end of the fourth year?

Terman's scale, known as the *Stanford-Binet Intelligence Scale*, appeared in 1916 with a comprehensive manual, *The Measurement of Intelligence*. In 1937 and 1960 two further revisions of the Stanford-Binet appeared; the latter was renormed in 1972 (Terman & Merrill, 1937, 1960, 1972). The current and fourth edition of the Stanford-Binet appeared in 1986 (Thorndike et al., 1986). Like previous editions, the latest edition is designed to assess persons from age two to adult, but it departs markedly from previous editions in design. Items are now grouped into subtests rather than by age levels; these 15 subtests are further nested within four cognitive areas, as in the following outline:

    I. *Verbal Reasoning*
          1. Vocabulary
          2. Comprehension
          3. Absurdities
          4. Verbal Relations

    II. *Quantitative Reasoning*
          5. Quantitative
          6. Number Series
          7. Equation Building

    III. *Abstract/Visual Reasoning*
          8. Pattern Analysis
          9. Copying
          10. Matrices
          11. Paper Folding and Cutting

    IV. *Short-Term Memory*
          12. Bead Memory
          13. Memory for Sentences
          14. Memory for Digits
          15. Memory for Objects

Whereas earlier versions of the Stanford-Binet emphasized a single score to represent general intelligence, the current version gives normalized[1] standard scores with a mean of 50 and a standard deviation of 8 for each of the 15 subtests. *Standard Age Scores* (*SAS*) are obtained for each of the four cognitive areas and the composite, but these normalized stan-

---

[1]To *normalize*, scores are first converted into percentiles, then the percentiles are converted to the standard score that is associated with that percentile in a normal distribution. Consequently, the resulting distribution of standard scores more closely approximates a perfect normal distribution as a consequence of the normalization (see Section 6.12 in Glass & Hopkins, 1996).

dard scores use a mean of 100 and a standard deviation of 16. Although the fourth edition no longer uses the term IQ to describe performance, the metric for the four areas and the composite have the same statistical meaning as deviation IQ scores. The new organization and reporting scheme makes the Stanford-Binet similar in format to the popular Wechsler scales and may increase its clinical and diagnostic value. The Stanford-Binet has remained a standard among individually administered cognitive ability scales for more than half a century, although the extent to which the extensive body of evidence that accumulated over the years to support its construct validity generalizes to the current edition is uncertain.

13.6   PERFORMANCE AND GROUP TESTS

The original Stanford-Binet had two disadvantages that limited its usefulness: (1) It was highly *verbal*, and (2) it was an *individual* test; that is, only one person can be tested at a time. In addition, extensive training is required for valid administration and scoring.

Obviously the Stanford-Binet was unsatisfactory for deaf children; this difficulty was reduced by developing a series of manipulation or performance tasks (used only at the preschool levels of the Stanford-Binet). The form board (a type of jigsaw puzzle), block design (assembling blocks to copy designs), and other nonlanguage tasks appeared in 1917 as the *Pintner-Paterson Performance Scale,* the first nonverbal measure of cognitive aptitude.

As the United States entered World War I, it faced the necessity of training a large citizen army with too few commissioned and noncommissioned officers. In this emergency the American Psychological Association offered its services to the War Department. Since the Binet-type individual intelligence tests were not only unsuitable for recruits who did not speak English, an individual test was not practicable with a large number of examinees. To deal with this problem, the *Army Alpha*, the first *group* intelligence test, was designed. Thus, the second problem of the early tests, their "one-at-a-time" limitation, had been solved. Group tests can be administered to a large number of people at one time and can be scored objectively without specialized training. Figure 13–1 is a sample page from the *Army Alpha*. Notice that the verbal analogy items require reasoning, even though the vocabulary is relatively simple. The analogy item format continues to be widely used today.

Group tests of verbal and scholastic aptitude have become important working tools for psychologists and educators. For example, if two sixth graders are reading at the fourth grade level, but one scores 90 and the other 120 on an intelligence test, the difference in the educational diagnosis and appropriate intervention plan is obvious.

13.7   NONVERBAL TESTS

Group tests of the *Army Alpha* type were generally even more verbal than the Stanford-Binet. The early performance scales such as the Pintner-Paterson were nonverbal, but they required individual administration. The *Army Beta*, designed for illiterate and non-English-speaking recruits in 1917, was the first test to combine the group and performance ideas. Figure 13–2 shows the picture-completion portion of the *Army Beta*; the examinee must

TEST 7

SAMPLES
{
sky—blue::grass—**table <u>green</u> warm big**

fish—swims::man—**paper time <u>walks</u> girl**

day—night::white—**red <u>black</u> clear pure**
}

In each of the lines below, the first two words are related to each other in some way. What you are to do in each line is to see what the relation is between the first two words, and underline the word in heavy type that is related in the same way to the third word. Begin with No. 1 and mark as many sets as you can before time is called.

1. finger—hand::toe—**box foot doll coat** 1
2. sit—chair::sleep—**book tree bed see** 2
3. skirts—girl::trousers—**boy hat vest coat** 3
4. December—Christmas::November—**month Thanksgiving December early** 4
5. above—top::below—**above bottom sea hang** 5
6. spoon—soup::fork—**knife plate cup meat** 6
7. bird—song::man—**speech woman boy work** 7
8. corn—horse::bread—**daily flour man butter** 8
9. sweet—sugar::sour—**sweet bread man vinegar** 9
10. devil—bad::angel—**Gabriel good face heaven** 10
11. Edison—phonograph::Columbus—**American Washington Spain Ohio** 11
12. cannon—rifle::big—**bullet gun army little** 12
13. engineer—engine::driver—**harness horse passenger man** 13
14. wolf—sheep::cat—**fur kitten dog mouse** 14
15. officer—private::command—**army general obey regiment** 15
16. hunter—gun::fisherman—**fish net bold wet** 16
17. cold—heat::ice—**steam cream frost refrigerator** 17
18. uncle—nephew::aunt—**brother sister niece cousin** 18
19. framework—house::skeleton—**bones skull grace body** 19
20. breeze—cyclone::shower—**bath cloudburst winter spring** 20
21. pitcher—milk::vase—**flowers pitcher table pottery** 21
22. blonde—brunette::light—**house electricity dark girl** 22
23. abundant—cheap::scarce—**costly plentiful common gold** 23
24. polite—impolite::pleasant—**agreeable disagreeable man face** 24
25. mayor—city::general—**private navy army soldier** 25
26. succeed—fail::praise—**lose friend God blame** 26
27. people—house::bees—**thrive sting hive thick** 27
28. peace—happiness::war—**grief fight battle Eurpoe** 28
29. a—b::c—**e b d letter** 29
30. darkness—stillness::light—**moonlight sound sun window** 30
31. complex—simple::hard—**brittle money easy work** 31
32. music—noise::harmonious—**hear accord violin discordant** 32
33. truth—gentleman::lie—**rascal live give falsehood** 33
34. blow—anger::caress—**woman kiss child love** 34
35. square—cube::circle—**line round square sphere** 35
36. mountain—valley::genius—**idiot write think brain** 36
37. clock—time::thermometer—**cold weather temperature mercury** 37
38. fear—anticipation::regret—**vain memory express resist** 38
39. hope—cheer::despair—**grave repair death depression** 39
40. dismal—dark::cheerful—**laugh bright house gloomy** 40

FIGURE 13–1 Test 7 from the Army Alpha.

SOURCE: Reproduced by permission of the National Academy of Sciences.

TEST 6

FIGURE 13–2 Test 6 from the *Army Beta*.

SOURCE: Reproduced by permission of the National Academy of Sciences.

identify "what's missing" from each picture. Similar items are found on the Stanford-Binet and Wechsler scales.

The *Army Alpha* and *Army Beta* proved quite useful (in spite of the fact that findings were used by some to make fallacious racial comparisons—a fault of users rather than the tests themselves). Following World War I, a large number of group "intelligence" tests generally similar in content to the *Army Alpha* and *Army Beta* were developed. These tests became widely used in schools and for personnel selection.

13.8   CHANGING VIEWS OF INTELLIGENCE TESTING

Unfortunately, there has been considerable misuse of IQ scores. Too often IQ was viewed as a pure measure of intellectual potential, fixed at the moment of conception. Misinterpretation of the meaning of an IQ score was widespread because most users had little or no training in testing or the psychology of intelligence.

Several decades of research and experience with cognitive tests have resulted in a more realistic perspective on the meaning of scores on group intelligence or scholastic aptitude tests. It is generally agreed, for example, that verbal, numerical, and reasoning abilities are the major determinants of scores. These abilities are certainly dependent on past learning experiences, though they are influenced less by one's environment than are tests of school-related achievement. The value of the tests has been demonstrated by their success in predicting academic performance and success in various majors and occupations. The misuse and misinterpretation of IQ scores led to the unpopularity of the IQ concept. Many tests, like the Stanford-Binet, have replaced *IQ* with a more socially accurate and palatable term such as *SAS* (Standard Age Score).

13.9   TESTS DESIGNED FOR ADMISSIONS DECISIONS

There are several cognitive tests that yield separate scores for scholastic abilities. These tests are similar to group tests of "intelligence" and "mental ability" tests, but their content universe is restricted, focusing on items that are related to school learning. *The principal function of admissions tests is to forecast future academic performance; their usefulness depends on their criterion-related validities—they do not claim to be intelligence tests.* Although they are broader in scope than standardized achievement tests, they measure students' ability to recognize, understand, and manipulate verbal and mathematical symbols, as well as reading comprehension.

The College Board's *Scholastic Aptitude Test* (*SAT*) is a widely used examination of the verbal-quantitative abilities type. Four item types are used on the verbal portion: antonyms, verbal analogies (e.g., circle : sphere :: square : cube), sentence completion, and reading comprehension. The items on the mathematics portion draw upon elementary arithmetic, algebra, and geometry. Most require quantitative reasoning, rather than just computation.

The *American College Testing Program* (*ACT*) has become a popular alternative to the *SAT* over the past two decades; both are widely used by colleges as part of their selection process for incoming students. The four *ACT* tests (English Usage, Mathematics Usage, Social Studies Reading, and Natural Sciences Reading) are general achievement and reading comprehension tests. The *ACT* also provides the college with a comprehensive picture of a student's interests and vocational goals. Figure 13–3 is a sample *ACT* student profile report.

The *Graduate Records Examinations* (*GRE*) have the same purpose as the *SAT* but are directed to graduate school admissions decisions. The three General Tests (formerly called Aptitude Tests) are Verbal, Quantitative, and Analytic. There are also subject-specific tests (formerly called Advanced Tests) for most college majors (see Figure 4–10). The *SAT, ACT,* and *GRE* have all been found to have validity for predicting academic criteria when the effects of range restriction (Section 4.17) and measurement error in the criterion (Section

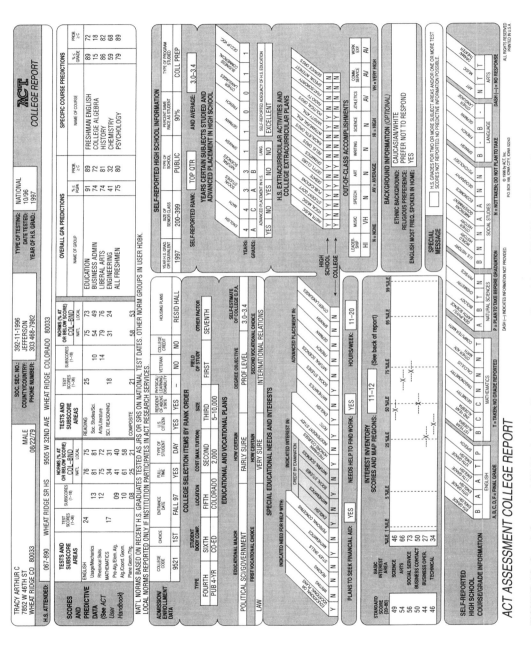

FIGURE 13–3 A Sample ACT Student Profile.

Copyright © 1996 by ACT, Inc. Reproduced by permission.

4.16) are taken into account (Aiken, 1985; Breland, 1979; Conrad et al., 1977; Donlon, 1984; ETS, 1980a; Kifer, 1985; Vecchio & Costin, 1977; see also Figure 4–11 and Section 4.17).

The College Board's Validity Study Service has conducted more than 2000 studies in almost 700 colleges; the mean validity coefficient for freshman GPA for the *SAT* was .42. The mean validity coefficient for academic performance in high school was slightly higher, .48. When both predictors were combined, the validity coefficient rose to .55. These validity coefficients are reduced considerably by the range restriction that results from their use in admissions decisions (see Section 4.11). In unselective colleges where the effect of range restriction is less, the predictive validity coefficients were .57, .55, and .65 for the *SAT*, high school record, and using both, respectively.

13.10 THE NATURE OF INTELLIGENCE

The Binet scales and their descendants are perhaps the most publicized accomplishments of psychology. The term *IQ*, though often misunderstood, is a household word. The practical success of the "IQ test," placing individuals along a spectrum of scholastic aptitude from dull to bright and in its relationship to school and occupational success, has overshadowed the uncertainty about what the test was measuring in an exact, psychological sense. Binet continually revised his views of the nature of intelligence as determined by his test; he finally characterized intelligence as *inventiveness* dependent on *comprehension* and marked by *purposefulness* and corrective *judgment* (Binet, 1911). His efforts to define these abilities more exactly or to indicate the specific test behavior that demonstrated them were cut short by his untimely death in 1911.

The *Journal of Educational Psychology* published a series of articles by 14 prominent psychologists, each of whom presented a conception of the nature of "intelligence." Although there was some agreement, it was startling and undeniable that 14 clearly different conceptions of intelligence emerged. Some of the participants stressed the adaptive nature of intelligence; others saw it as the ability to learn, the ability to think abstractly, or the degree of past learning. This confusion prompted later researchers to propose that since the only intelligence one can discuss objectively is the intelligence that is measured, one should define intelligence as "that which an intelligence test measures" (Peak & Boring, 1926). This "operational definition" has been a favorite among psychometricians who are wary of theoretical disputes but very impressed with the widespread utility of intelligence tests, but it fails to confront the more fundamental question of the nature of intelligence.

13.11 WECHSLER INTELLIGENCE TESTS

Shortly before World War II, a clinical psychologist, David Wechsler, developed an individual intelligence examination especially for adults; Wechsler's test included a verbal and a performance measure of intelligence. First published in 1939, revised in 1955 as the *Wechsler Adult Intelligence Scale* (*WAIS*), and revised again in 1981 as the *Wechsler Adult Intelligence Scale*—Revised (*WAIS-R*), this test consists of 11 different subtests. In 1949 the test was adapted for use with children and named the *Wechsler Intelligence* Scale for Children (*WISC*). Revised in 1974 (the *WISC-R*), and again in 1991 (the *WISC-III*), it has become the most widely used individual intelligence test for testing at ages 6 to 16. A noteworthy feature of the *WISC-III* was the development and simultaneous norming of a standardized achievement measure, the *Wechsler Individual Achievement Test* (*WAIT*); the *WAIT* includes tests of reading and math. The companion achievement measure is an important aid in assessing aptitude-achievement discrepancies in children.

In 1967 the scale was further extended downward (and named the *Wechsler Preschool and Primary Scale of Intelligence, (WPPSI)* to allow testing of children in the 4- to 6.5-year age range. The most recent revision of the *WPPSI* (*WPPSI-R*) is designed for children ages 3 to 7.

The verbal subtests for the Wechsler tests (with only minor variations among the *WAIS, WISC,* and *WPPSI*) are Information ("Which month has one extra day during leap year?"); Similarities ("In what way are liberty and justice alike?"); Arithmetic ("A workman earned $36; he was paid $4 an hour. How many hours did he work?"); Vocabulary ("What does *compel* mean?"); Comprehension ("Why should a promise be kept?"); and Digit Span (repeating a sequence of digits, such as 3-8-9-1-7-4 forwards or backwards). The nonverbal part is dependent mainly on performance or manipulative and visualization skills: Picture Completion ("What is missing in this picture?"); Picture Arrangement (placing cartoon pictures in a correct time sequence); Block Design (reproducing a given design using colored blocks); Object Assembly (puzzles of common objects); Coding or Digit Symbol (converting numerals into a different set of symbols); and Mazes. Performance on each subtest is expressed using a standard score with a mean of 10 and a standard deviation of 3 (see Figure 3–1).

In the design of the Wechsler tests it was deemed important to determine an individual's *profile* of abilities. The use of the individual subtest profiles for diagnostic purposes when subtests are only moderately reliable is hazardous at best (Hopkins, 1964b). *The Verbal IQ, Performance IQ, and Full Scale IQ yielded by the Wechsler scales are standard scores with a mean of 100 and a standard deviation of 15; these scales are much more reliable and useful than are the scores from the ten or so subtests.*

13.12 THE KAUFMAN ASSESSMENT BATTERY FOR CHILDREN (K-ABC)

The *K-ABC* is a relatively new individual test of intelligence and achievement designed for children 2.5 through 12.5 years of age. It is being marketed aggressively as if it were a worthy successor of the Wechsler and Stanford-Binet tests (e.g., "The first major advance in intelligence testing in over a generation"). The *K-ABC* is composed of 16 subtests grouped into three cognitive areas of functioning: Sequential Processing (Hand Movements, Number Recall, and Word Order); Simultaneous Processing (Magic Window, Face Recognition, Gestalt Closure, Triangles, Matrix Analogies, Spatial Memory, and Photo Series); and Achievement (Expressive Vocabulary, Faces and Places, Arithmetic, Riddles, Reading/Decoding, and Reading/Understanding). In addition, the Sequential Processing Scale and the Simultaneous Scale are combined to form a fourth global scale, the Mental Processing Composite, which is analogous to a total IQ score. A fifth scale, Nonverbal, is formed from two of the sequential processing subtests and four of the simultaneous processing subtests. The authors view the Mental Processing scales as measures of Cattell's fluid intelligence.

Unfortunately, the standardization and norms for the *K-ABC* leave much to be desired (Hopkins & Hodge, 1984). Thirty-four sites representing 24 states were used in the selection of the sample; exactly how these sites were selected is not stated in the manual. One is left with the impression that neither the sites nor the school districts were selected using random or stratified-random sampling procedures. What is certain is that the sample on which the norms are based is not representative; what is uncertain is whether the particular biases are consequential or negligible. The scales used for reporting the examinee's results are patterned after the Wechsler: the subtests use a mean of 10 and a standard deviation of 3. Although the five global scales formed by various combinations of the subtests have a mean of 100 and a standard deviation of 15, they are termed *K-ABC* standard scores, rather than IQ scores. "Sociocultural" percentile ranks are offered based on three levels of parents' education (below 12, 12, or above 12 years of schooling) and two ethnic groups (black/white). These percentile ranks appear to be quite crude. It is difficult to place much confidence in these, given the uncertainty in the representativeness of the norming sample (Mehrens & Lehmann, 1984).

Concurrent validity coefficients are given between the *K-ABC* and the Wechsler tests for various groups. A coefficient of .70 was reported between the Mental Processing Composite and *WISC-R* total score for 182 normal students. The corresponding value with the Stanford-Binet for 121 normals was .61; these appear to be somewhat less than what one typically finds between the Wechsler and Stanford-Binet scores. The Achievement global scale presents some difficulties as far as content validity is concerned. It is achievement in a very generic sense. It may suffice as a general, global estimate, but it is apparent that there was no careful planning for content validity. It would appear difficult to make specific remedial or curricular recommendations on the basis of these six subtests. The fact that the manual gives Grade Equivalent scores for only three of the Achievement subtests illustrates the problems with curricular validity.

In short, the *K-ABC* is an attractively produced and vigorously marketed individual test of mental ability. It is obviously intended to compete with other individual tests of intelligence such as the Wechsler and the Stanford-Binet. It appears somewhat easier to administer and more objective to score. There are serious questions, however, regarding the representativeness of the normative samples, especially when they are broken down into two ethnic groups, three levels of parental education, and age. The Achievement scale does not correspond closely to most other standardized achievement tests since some of the subtests are not highly related to the curriculum. Reliability coefficients appear to be comparable to those for the Wechsler tests. Profiles must be interpreted cautiously because the reliability of the difference scores is not high (as is also the case with the Wechsler subtests). The heavy reliance on a particular theory restricts the range of cognitive abilities that are assessed compared to the more inclusive set of abilities measured by the Wechsler and Stanford-Binet tests. Indeed, this seems to impoverish the content and construct validity of the *K-ABC* (in comparison to that of the Wechsler and Stanford-Binet) without enriching its clinical value and educational usefulness (Anastasi, 1985a: Page, 1985).

13.13 OTHER VIEWS OF INTELLIGENCE

There are many different conceptions of intelligence (Sternberg, 1982). Louis Thurstone, a major figure in psychometrics, characterized intelligence as a series of distinct abilities. According to Thurstone, an ability is isolated by giving mental tests to a great number of people and then determining, through a mathematical process known as factor analysis, the smallest number of abilities necessary to explain the correlations among the tests; factor analysis is a statistical procedure that finds the minimum number of abilities (factors) necessary to explain the correlations among the tests. In his pioneering studies, Thurstone isolated six "factors" that accounted for most of the score similarity of 56 different tests given to a group of college students. These were verbal (V), number (N), spatial (S), word fluency (W), memory (M), and reasoning (R). Out of this research came the first of the "multi-aptitude" test batteries, the *Primary Mental Abilities Tests*. Later investigations showed, however, that the number of factors isolated depended considerably on the educational and environmental backgrounds of the subjects tested and on the number and types of tests used in the factor analysis. It was even shown that Thurstone's so-called primary mental abilities correlated positively with each other, which suggests the presence of a still more basic and general (second-order) mental factor, as had long been argued by the British psychologist Charles Spearman (1927).

Recent thinking among factor analysts about the nature of human intelligence has led to two slightly different ideas. One is represented by Spearman's British tradition of investigation, exemplified by Philip Vernon's (1950) structure of human abilities, in which human mental abilities are arranged in a hierarchy with a broad general factor (*g*) and split into two major "group" factors, one distinguished by verbal and educational abilities (*v:ed*) and the other by practical or performance abilities (*k:m*). Each of these major group factors is then differentiated into more specific factors like Thurstone's verbal, number, and space. These finally break down into factors found in specific types of tests. (See Figure 13–4.) Thus, any mental performance can be described as involving percentages of *g, v:ed*, verbal, and others until all the factors needed to account for the performance have been determined.

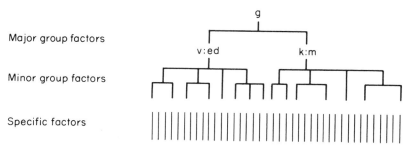

FIGURE 13–4 Diagram illustrating hierarchical structure of human abilities.

SOURCE: Adapted from P. E. Vernon, *The structure of human abilities* (New York: John Wiley, 1950), p. 22. Reprinted by permission of the publisher.

The scheme of Raymond Cattell and John Horn has some similarity to Vernon's structure (Horn & Cattell, 1966). Cattell distinguishes between *fluid* and *crystallized* intelligence. Crystallized intelligence is largely a function of environment and is much like the *v:ed* abilities. Fluid intelligence is presumed to reflect the genetic aspect of intelligence and be more clearly involved in nonlanguage tasks that are less related to background or previous experience.

A two-level theory of mental ability was advocated by Jensen (1968, 1973a, 1973b). Level I consists of associative learning ability, which is represented in rote learning and rote memory. Level II consists of the higher mental processes of conceptualization, reasoning, and problem solving.

Another view of mental organization grows from the Thurstonian tradition of investigation. Its chief advocate is J. P. Guilford (1967, 1968), who devised a theoretical structure-of-intellect (*SI*) model in which he classifies all mental abilities in three dimensions. The first is defined by the kinds of test content confronting the individual—Figural, Symbolic, Semantic, or Behavioral. The second is defined by the types of mental "operations" necessary to deal with the various content forms—Cognition, Memorization, Convergent Thinking, Divergent Thinking, and Evaluation. The last dimension deals with the outcomes or "products" yielded by the various mental operations applied to the various content forms. There are six products: Units of Information, Classes of Units, Relations between Units, Systems of Information, Transformations, and Implications. With four kinds of content, five kinds of operations, and six kinds of products involved in mental performance, Guilford postulated 120 ($4 \times 5 \times 6$) distinct mental abilities in the *SI* model. Guilford's *SI* model purports to be sufficiently inclusive to allow for creativity (divergent thinking) and social intelligence (Hoepfner & O'Sullivan, 1968; O'Sullivan & Guilford, 1975). Guilford reports that more than ninety of these abilities have been isolated, but Horn and Knapp (1973) and others have questioned his results.

Several authorities have expressed pessimism about the predictive validity of *SI* tests (Hunt, 1961; McNemar, 1964; Vernon, 1964). Many of the abilities seem to have little practical relevance. Holly and Michael (1972, 1973), however, found that certain of the *SI* tests combined had validity at least equal to that of traditional standardized tests for predicting academic performance in high school mathematics.

Perhaps the most important application of factor analytic studies of mental abilities has been the increasing use of "multi-aptitude" test batteries in educational and vocational guidance (see Section 13.23). These batteries are composed of a series of individual tests built around the findings of factor analysis; to a certain degree, each of the general battery's subtests assesses a specific ability. One such battery is the *Differential Aptitude Test* (*DAT*) for use with high school students. The *DAT*'s seven subtests measure Verbal Reasoning, Numerical Ability, Abstract Reasoning, Space Relations, Mechanical Reasoning, Clerical Speed and Accuracy, and Language Usage. Although the *DAT* subtests are not intended to be *pure* measures of single *factors*, they provide a profile of an individual's mental strengths and weaknesses that is designed to be more specific, descriptive, and meaningful than an omnibus test of "general mental ability." In addition to the great *descriptive* value of such a test, *prediction* of success or failure in a variety of academic or occupational endeavors can be achieved by isolating the important abilities that are specifically required (see Section 13.23). This can be done via a statistical procedure known as multiple regression analysis (Glass & Hopkins, 1996).

From the preceding discussion it is evident that there are many different ways of conceptualizing intelligence, the nature of intelligence is exceedingly complex and multifaceted, most cognitive abilities are significantly interrelated, and the "final word" on the nature of intelligence is nowhere in sight.

13.14 INFANT INTELLIGENCE SCALES

Research findings have revealed that results from infant "intelligence" tests have little predictive validity during the first two years of life. A child's intellectual status at age six can be predicted much better from his or her parents' education than from an intelligence test or any other measure taken at two years of age or younger (Bayley, 1955). In fact, infant tests have been shown to have virtually no predictive value below 20 months of age (Escalona & Moriarty, 1961; Lewis & McGurk, 1972).

The lack of relationship between IQs (or DQs—development quotients) from infant tests and later scores probably occurs because the tests are measuring in different domains. The infant scales must rely primarily on psychomotor responses (e.g., puzzles) because of the limited verbal facility of very young children. Yet abstract thinking is best reflected in language. One of the primary uses of infant scales is in the placement of children for adoption. Intelligence tests should be recognized for what they are—measures that have very limited validity below age two. Knowledge of parents' education, occupational level, or IQ scores is more useful in predicting a young child's later academic success than are IQs from tests that require little abstract thinking.

At about age two, the cognitive development of the child is such that a very crude assessment of scholastic aptitude can be made. IQ scores at 24 months correlate about .4 with IQ scores two years later, .3 with IQ scores at age six, and only .2 or less with adult IQs. The validity of individual intelligence test results is much greater by the time a child is four or five years of age (Sternberg, 1982, p. 959).

13.15 INTELLIGENCE GROWTH CURVES

Many studies have been conducted to ascertain the sequence and termination of intellectual growth. Figure 13–5 is based on cross-sectional data from Wechsler's first (1939) intelligence test and is widely reproduced in psychological textbooks. The basic flaw in the data results from their *cross-sectional* nature, that is, the use of a different sample of persons at each age level: Consequently, variables (other than age) on which they differ, such as formal educational attainment, confound the findings. In the test revisions and restandardizations of the Wechsler scale, the intellectual decline with age was much less marked than that shown by the original Wechsler data given in Figure 13–5. This supports the hypothesis that a substantial portion of the decline in Figure 13–5 is *not* a decline; it simply reflects in large measure the educational differential and, to some extent, differences in test-taking speed among the age groups. In several studies (Owens, 1953, 1966), no loss occurred on verbal

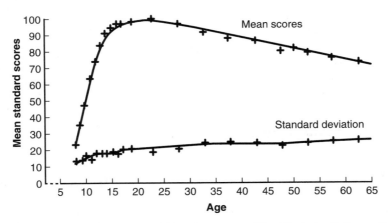

FIGURE 13–5   Changes in full-scale scores of the Wechsler-Bellevue Form I, ages 7–65.

SOURCE: David Wechsler, *The measurement and appraisal of adult intelligence,* 4th ed. (Baltimore: Williams & Wilkins, 1958), p. 31. Reprinted by permission of the author. Copyright © 1958 by David Wechsler.

measures, when education was controlled, until 60 or more years of age. *Longitudinal* studies (following the same persons over a long period of time) often show improvement with age, especially for college graduates and other persons who remain intellectually active (Anastasi, 1988). Measures that require psychomotor responses, visual perception, or an element of speed show considerable decline over the 18- to 70-age span even with education controlled, but the difference is less than when the education factor is ignored.

Various intellectual functions seem to have different developmental patterns. Thurstone (1955), using cross-sectional data from the *Primary Mental Abilities Tests*, reported that 80 percent of adult-level perceptual-speed ability was reached by age 12; for spatial abilities, the 80 percent point occurred at age 14; for verbal meaning, at age 18, but not until age 20 for verbal fluency.

Most studies show a marked tendency for performance on intelligence tests to begin to level off at age 13 or 14. Generally, performance increases little after age 16, although there may be some slight increase until about age 20. The maximum performance on the *Wechsler Adult Intelligence Scale* is not reached until age 25. This increase probably reflects the effects of continued education and learning rather than an increase in the capacity to learn.

13.16   THE RELIABILITY OF INTELLIGENCE TESTS

The reliability coefficient of a test reflects the amount of measurement error in the scores (see Chapter 5). *Reliability is a necessary but not sufficient condition for validity.* A reliability coefficient quantifies the degree of agreement (consistency) between two independent estimates from parallel forms. The reliability of *most* tests of scholastic aptitude or intelligence is satisfactory for individual use, but there are many exceptions. Reliability estimates

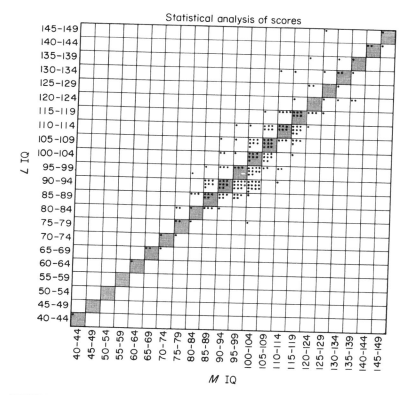

FIGURE 13–6 IQ scores on two forms of the Stanford-Binet obtained by seven-year-old children.

SOURCE: L. M. Terman and M. A. Merrill, *Measuring intelligence* (Boston: Houghton Mifflin Company, 1960), p. 11. Reproduced by permission of the publisher, Houghton Mifflin Company.

for the best tests available, determined by internal consistency methods (Section 5.16) or by retesting with an alternate form often exceed .90. Standard errors of measurement (see Section 5.5) of 3 to 7 IQ points exist, however, even with reliability coefficients in the .80 to .95 range. The relationship between IQ scores on parallel forms L and M of the Stanford-Binet, shown in Figure 13–6, graphically illustrates the degree of reliability in IQ scores.

13.17 THE RATIO IQ

The "intelligence quotient" was originally the *ratio* of mental age (*MA*) to chronological age (*CA*), multiplied by 100 to remove the decimal point (Equation 13.1). The examinee's mental age (*MA*) on the test is the age at which his or her score is the average score. For example suppose Maria, age 10, correctly answers 38 items on a test, and 38 is the average score for children at 12.5 years of age, Maria's *MA* is then 12.5; Maria's IQ score is computed to be 125:

EQUATION 13.1

$$IQ = 100\left(\frac{MA}{CA}\right)$$

$$\text{For Maria}: \quad IQ = 100 \times \left(\frac{12.5}{10}\right) \text{ or } 125.$$

With the ratio IQ the standard deviation of the IQs varied considerably from one age to another. Although a σ of 16 was a "typical" value on intelligence tests, the values varied substantially from test to test, even within well-developed tests. Figure 13–7 shows the wide variation in σs across ages for the two forms of the 1937 Stanford-Binet. This factor would cause considerable fluctuation in IQ scores even if IQs correlated perfectly ($r = 1.0$) from one year to the next! For example, as shown in Figure 13–7, a child who consistently remained at the 98th percentile in intelligence would receive ratio IQ scores of 141, 125, and 140 at ages 2.5, 6, and 12, respectively—if the child's performance was completely constant relative to that of his or her age peers and the tests correlated perfectly. Users of ratio IQs were rarely aware of this "technicality"; hence, many interpretive errors resulted, particularly in the area of *change* in intellectual status. For example, IQs below 70 are often considered to represent mental retardation. However, by this criterion the percentage of "mental retardation" (on form L) would be only 1 percent at age 6, but 7 percent at age 12 because of the differences in the values of σ.

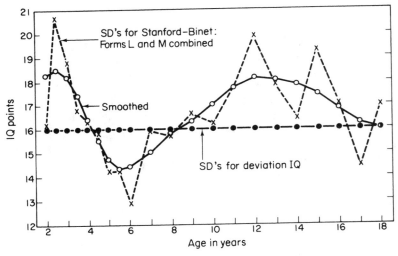

FIGURE 13–7   Fluctuations in the size of standard deviations of conventional (ratio) IQs at different age levels.

SOURCE: S. R. Pinneau, "Conventional and deviation IQs for the Stanford-Binet," *Testing Today*, no. 4 (Boston: Houghton Mifflin, n.d.).

The *ratio* IQ (Equation 13.1) was popular until about 1960. Since then, it has been largely replaced by the *deviation* IQ, a type of standard score based on one's age peers (see Figure 3-1).

13.18 THE DEVIATION IQ

The deviation IQ concept was introduced so that the σs would have a constant value at each age (which would eliminate the aberrant variability of the ratio IQ that is evident in Figure 13–8). The deviation IQ is simply a kind of standard score with a mean of 100 and a constant value for the standard deviation (usually 15 or 16) irrespective of age. A constant σ value of 16 deviation IQ points is illustrated in Figure 13–8. A given deviation IQ value represents the same relative degree of cognitive performance for all age levels; there is no vacillation in IQs resulting from scaling artifacts that accompany the use of the ratio IQs (see Figure 3-1).

For a proper interpretation of results from a scholastic aptitude test, the user must know whether the test employs a ratio or deviation IQ and, if a ratio is used, the value of σ for each age level. The ratio IQ continues to be employed for a few tests, although this practice should soon become a rarity.

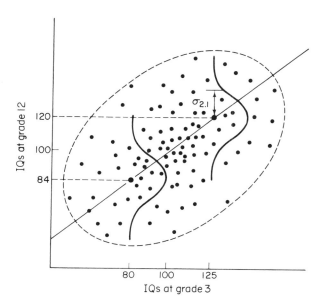

FIGURE 13–8   The relationship ($r = .8$) between deviation IQ scores obtained on the Stanford-Binet (at grades 3 and 12). The distributions of grade 12 IQ scores obtained by examinees who received scores of 80 and 125 at grade 3 are specifically illustrated.

SOURCE: Based on data from B. S. Bloom, *Stability and Change in Human Characteristics* (New York: John Wiley, 1964), p. 56.

13.19 IQ CONSTANCY: COMMON VARIANCE VERSUS SCORE STABILITY

A test must have constant means and standard deviations for each age level if IQ scores are to be stable. Thus, the use of deviation IQs is necessary but not sufficient to obtain a high degree of stability in IQ scores. Correlation coefficients do not necessarily depict score stability. For example, one study (Hopkins & McGuire, 1966) found that two intelligence tests correlated very highly ($r = .86$), although the means for the two tests differed by 8.5 points; in addition, the two standard deviations differed substantially (16.0 versus 22.7). The high correlation (when corrected for attenuation, $r = .94)^2$ indicates that the tests were measuring essentially the same cognitive factors, yet the two tests assigned quite different IQ scores to the same relative level of performance.

The vast majority of studies of IQ constancy have used only the Stanford-Binet test. The constancy is represented by a correlation coefficient, r (r is the value for the sample, ρ is the population coefficient, (see Section 4.9), but the coefficient does not directly and explicitly quantify change in IQ scores.

The formula for a correlation coefficient can be written as follows:

EQUATION 13.2

$$r_{12} = \frac{\Sigma z_1 z}{n}$$

Equation 13.2 shows that a correlation coefficient is the average of the products of the z-scores for the two variables. Thus at times 1 and 2, the correlation coefficient between IQ scores is *blind* to differences resulting from differences in means or standard deviations between the two tests. Theoretically, two intelligence tests *could* correlate 1.0, yet one could have a mean of 100 and the other a mean of 130! When deviation IQs are used, the IQ stability coefficients are more meaningful, since the means and σs are the same at every age level—assuming, of course, that the examinees in the standardization group are representative.

---

[2]The correction for attenuation is a statistical procedure for estimating the correlation between "true" scores on two measures—that is, what the correlation between them would be if all measurement error is removed from both tests (see Muchinsky, 1996). It is useful for estimating the extent to which two tests measure the same or different factors, after allowance (compensation) has been made for errors of measurement. The formula is:

$$r'_{12} = \frac{r_{12}}{\sqrt{r_{11}r_{22}}},$$

where r'_{12} estimates the correlation between true scores on measures 1 and 2, r_{12} is the observed correlation between measures 1 and 2, and r_{11} and r_{22} are the reliability coefficients of measures 1 and 2, respectively.

In the example noted above, $r_{12} = .861$, $r_{11} = .895$, and $r_{22} = .847$; hence, $r'_{12} = 0.989$. For further information, see Linn (1988) or Lord and Novick (1968).

Figure 13–8 graphically illustrates the meaning of such coefficients. It depicts the relationship, $r = .8$, of Stanford-Binet deviation IQs at grade 3 with corresponding IQ scores at grade 12. The coefficient of .8 indicates that the IQ predicted for an examinee at grade 12 will be only eight-tenths (.8) as far from the mean as his or her IQ score at grade 3. As shown in Figure 13–8, students who scored 125 in grade 3 tended on the average to score 120 (.8 × 25 = 20) in grade 12. Those examinees who received IQ scores of 80 in grade 3 tended to be only 80 percent as far from the mean (.8 × –20 = –16) at grade 12 and, hence, to have an average IQ of 84.[3]

The accuracy of these predictions is reflected by the standard error of estimate ($\sigma_{2.1}$), which is the standard deviation of actual scores on the criterion about their predicted scores:

EQUATION 13.3

$$\sigma_{2.1} = \sigma_2 \sqrt{1 - \rho_{12}^2}$$

In the Stanford-Binet example (Figure 13–8), where $\sigma = 16$;

$$\sigma_{2.1} = 16\sqrt{1 - .8^2} = 16\sqrt{.36} \text{ or } 9.6, \text{ about 10 points.}$$

The standard error of estimate of 10 points indicates that even with a substantial degree of stability ($r = .8$), there is still considerable fluctuation in individual scores. The $\sigma_{2.1}$ value of 10 indicates that about one-third of the examinees depicted in Figure 13–8 will have IQs that differ from their *predicted* IQ scores at grade 12 by ten or more points. A .95 confidence interval (Section 4.9) for a student's grade 12 IQ, predicted from the score at grade 3, is the predicted IQ at grade 12 $\pm 2\sigma_{2.1}$—in other words, it would span a range of more than 40 points! Clearly, a high stability coefficient still allows considerable variation in individual performance. This fact is further illustrated in Figure 13–9, which shows the plot of the actual IQ scores obtained by 354 pupils at grades 5 and 7 on the *California Test of Mental Maturity* (*CTMM*). Even though the scores over the two-year period are rather stable ($r = .829$), notice that although the grade 7 mean (99.7) differed little from the grade 5 mean (99.0), of the nine students who received "average" IQ scores of 99 at grade 5, one scored 114 at grade 7 and another scored 86, but the grade 7 mean (99.7) differed little from the grade 5 mean (99.0).

As pointed out earlier, almost all studies of IQ constancy have been done with individual intelligence tests (usually the Stanford-Binet); only a few have employed group tests. Yet individual tests are administered to only a very small percentage of students. Figure 13–10 illustrates the typical findings on IQ stabilities with an individual verbal test (the Stanford-Binet), along with corresponding information on *group* verbal and nonverbal intelligence tests. It is evident that IQ scores from individually administered verbal tests are much more stable at younger ages than those from group tests. Whereas IQ scores on indi-

---

[3]If the means or standard deviations are not constant at both ages, the prediction must allow for this by converting the grade 3 IQ score to a z-score (z_1) and multiplying z_1 by r_{12} to obtain the predicted z-score (z_2') at grade 12—that is, $z_2' = r_{12}z_1$; z_2' is then converted to the relevant units by multiplying z_2' by the σ of the predicted variable and adding this value to the mean of the predicted variable: $X_2' = \sigma_2 z_2' + \mu_2$.

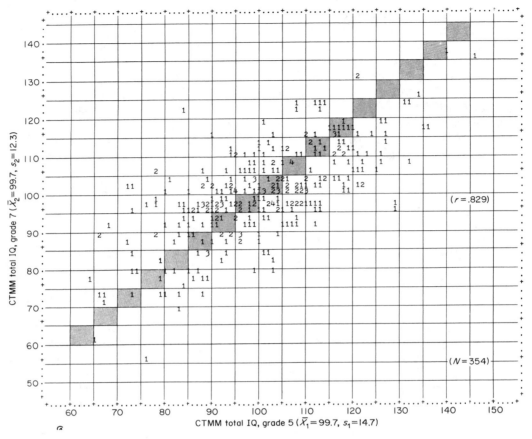

FIGURE 13–9 Scatterplot of IQ scores at grades 5 and 7 for 354 pupils.

SOURCE: Based on data from K. D. Hopkins and M. Bibelheimer, Five-year stability IQs from language and nonlanguage group tests. *Child Development, 42* (1971), 645–649.

vidual verbal tests at age six correlate about .7 with corresponding IQs at maturity, scores on *group* intelligence tests do not reflect the same degree of stability until two to three and five to six years later for verbal and nonverbal tests, respectively.

One study (Hopkins and Bracht, 1971, 1975) studied IQ constancy and change with group intelligence tests by following a large sample of students in grade 1 through elementary, junior high, and high school. Figure 13–11 shows the stability coefficients for verbal and nonverbal IQs. Each line in the figure depicts the correlation of the IQ scores from an initial grade level with scores obtained at subsequent grade levels. For example, the grade 1 verbal IQ (see bottom solid line in Figure 13–11) correlated .51 with grade 2 verbal IQs and .52, .50, .44, and .50 with IQs obtained in grades 4, 7, 9, and 11, respectively. Notice that IQs obtained for students in the primary grades have rather low correlations with their IQ scores in subsequent grades (grade 1 IQs are not even highly related to IQs obtained one

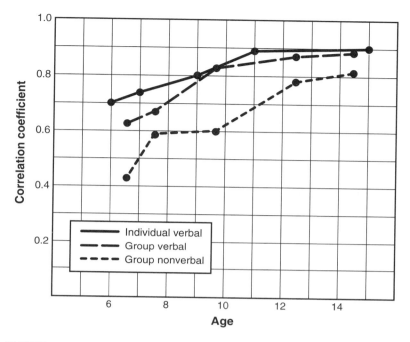

FIGURE 13–10 Correlation coefficients between IQ scores at maturity (age 17, corrected to a common terminal variability) for individual verbal, group verbal, and group nonverbal intelligence tests.

SOURCE: B. S. Bloom. (1956) The 1955 normative study of the tests of general educational development. *School Review, 64*, 110–124.

year later). Verbal IQs at grade 4 have considerable stability, correlating .81, .79, and .77 with IQs in grades 7, 9, and 11, respectively. Figure 13–11 illustrates that nonverbal IQs fluctuated significantly more than verbal IQs and did not show much stability until grade 7. The pattern of results reported in Figure 13–11 is consistent with the results of other groups using different tests (Hopkins & Bibelheimer, 1971; Magnusson & Backteman, 1978; Tyler, 1958). When verbal and nonverbal IQs are combined into a total IQ score, its stability closely parallels that shown for verbal IQ (stability coefficients average only about .03 higher than the verbal IQs).

The stability of IQ scores expressed directly in IQ units is more directly interpretable than stability coefficients. One study (Hopkins and Bracht, 1971) found that the *mean absolute change* (+ or –) in total IQ scores from grade 1 to any grade thereafter was 10 to 12 points. The average absolute difference in grade 2 IQs and IQs from subsequent grades was 9 to 10 points; grade 4 IQs differ 7 to 9 points from subsequent IQs, on the average. The mean difference between IQ scores at grades 7, 9, and 11 was 5 to 6 points. It is important to note that these are *mean absolute* differences; such differences include both increases and decreases. Recall that the changes are least at the mean and are expected to be progressively greater as scores deviate from the mean. The changes are usually greater when the IQs are

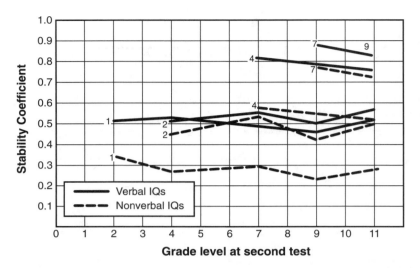

FIGURE 13–11 Graphic representation of stability coefficients for verbal and nonverbal IQs (CTMM used at grades 1, 2, and 4; Lorge-Thorndike at grades 7, 9, 11.) Grade level of initial testing precedes each line.

SOURCE: K. D. Hopkins and G. H. Bracht. (1975) Ten-year stability of verbal and nonverbal IQ scores. *American Educational Research Journal, 12,* 469–477.

obtained on different tests (e.g., Stanford-Binet versus WISC) than when a different level of the same series is repeated. Some tests consistently yielded IQs 5 to 7 points higher than those yielded by others, showing that degree of IQ change will be even greater across different tests than within the same test.

The standard errors of estimate (standard deviation of obtained IQ scores from the most probable IQ score, predicted from a prior test, see Figure 13–11) were as follows:

1. 12 to 17 points using grade 1 or grade 2 scores as predictors
2. 9 to 12 points using grade 4 scores as predictors
3. 7 to 8 points using grade 7 scores to predict scores in grades 9 and 11
4. 7 points in predicting grade 11 IQs from grade 9 IQs

Several conclusions can be drawn regarding IQ consistency:

1. The stability of IQs from individual verbal tests is fairly high as early as age five (Sternberg, 1982). Infant tests have virtually no validity as predictors of later IQ scores.
2. The stability of IQs from group tests is much less than that of IQs from individual verbal tests until at least 10 to 12 years of age but becomes comparable thereafter. Accurate long-term predictions cannot be made from group intelligence tests given during the primary grades. IQs from nonverbal group tests tend to be less stable than those from verbal group tests, perhaps because the former measures *general* intelligence less well than the latter.

3. Even when there is a high degree of overall stability, the scores of a few individuals will change greatly.

4. Each test varies somewhat in the cognitive abilities that are tapped. An IQ score should always be interpreted in terms of the test on which it was obtained.

5. Various intelligence tests differ considerably in IQ stability. For the *Primary Mental Abilities Tests*, which yield Verbal, Numerical, Spatial, Reasoning, and Word Fluency scores, much less long-term stability is reflected in the Spatial and Word Fluency abilities than in other areas.

6. IQ changes are greater when the type of intelligence test used is varied. IQ differences are especially great when the type of test given (verbal versus nonverbal) is varied. The correlation between verbal and nonverbal IQs from group tests at most grade levels correlates only .4 to .6.

These conclusions indicate that *great care must be taken in interpreting IQs*, especially from group tests, which are the only ones available for the great majority of students. Scores from group tests given during the primary grades should be viewed only as general indicators of *present* intellectual status. The findings suggest that there are dangers in disseminating IQ scores to students and parents, who may interpret results with much less tolerance for error and change than is required for a proper evaluation. Certainly, no one has more right to knowledge of a child's abilities than his or her parents, but the information should be given in terms that are meaningful to parents. Perhaps percentile ranks would be more meaningful than IQ scores in this context. Fortunately, many test publishers now provide report forms that interpret a student's performance in terms that both student and parents can understand (see Figures 13–3, 14–8, and 15–1).

Many parents are unaware that intelligence tests tend to measure primarily scholastic aptitude and that many other cognitive abilities that can be legitimately considered to reflect intelligence and special abilities are untapped. For example, studies have found that measures of social intelligence correlated only .3-.4 with scores from conventional intelligence tests.

13.20 THE RELATIONSHIP BETWEEN IQ AND SCHOLASTIC ACHIEVEMENT

The data in Table 13–1 show the relationship between IQs from a widely used group verbal and nonverbal intelligence test and various areas of academic achievement as measured by a popular battery of standardized achievement tests. At each grade level, the correlation coefficient is based on a very large sample of students from a nationally representative sample. The results illustrate that there is a substantial relationship between achievement in various subject matter areas and measured intelligence. Notice that the degree of relationship tends to increase with grade level. The nonverbal scores tend to have a lower relationship in every achievement area than the verbal and quantitative scores, but, as would be expected, the difference is smaller in areas that are less verbal.

Most authorities feel that current intelligence tests are more aptly described as scholastic aptitude tests because they are so highly related to academic performance, although present use suggests that the term *intelligence test* (for example, the Wechsler tests) is going to

TABLE 13–1 The Relationship Between Verbal, Quantitative, and Nonverbal IQ[4] Scores and Standardized Achievement Tests

Test[5]	Listening	Reading	Language	Math	Social Studies	Science	Composite
Verbal—1	.66	.55	.69	.65	.65	.62	.75
2	.55	.68	.72	.63	.64	.58	.78
3	.69	.76	.71	.71	.71	.68	.81
4		.80	.76	.76	.74	.74	.86
5		.81	.76	.76	.75	.73	.86
6		.82	.78	.76	.76	.73	.87
7		.84	.78	.76	.77	.76	.87
8		.84	.76	.74	.76	.76	.86
9		.85	.75	.72	.76	.75	.85
10		.85	.76	.71	.75	.75	.85
11		.84	.75	.69	.76	.75	.84
12		.81	.71	.67	.73	.75	.83
Quantitative-1	.60	.58	.69	.74	.56	.55	.74
2	.60	.65	.70	.73	.55	.52	.76
3		.62	.65	.73	.59	.58	.72
4		.65	.71	.81	.62	.63	.78
5		.65	.71	.83	.62	.63	.78
6		.67	.73	.83	.65	.64	.80
7		.68	.72	.84	.67	.66	.81
8		.66	.71	.83	.67	.67	.80
9		.71	.70	.83	.70	.71	.82
10		.70	.69	.81	.69	.71	.80
11		.67	.65	.80	.68	.69	.79
12		.67	.65	.81	.66	.71	.79
NonVerbal—1	.51	.51	.60	.61	.45	.45	.63
2	.48	.55	.60	.62	.43	.43	.64
3		.58	.56	.67	.56	.57	.69
4		.61	.61	.71	.60	.62	.73
5		.60	.60	.73	.59	.62	.73
6		.62	.62	.74	.61	.63	.74
7		.62	.64	.75	.63	.65	.75
8		.60	.62	.72	.62	.64	.73
9		.65	.65	.72	.66	.68	.75
10		.64	.63	.73	.64	.69	.75
11		.61	.60	.71	.65	.67	.73
12		.60	.56	.70	.61	.67	.72

[4]From the *Cognitive Abilities Test* (Thorndike & Hagen, 1997) that reports "Standard Age Scores" rather than the classical term, "IQ scores," but the meaning is the same ($\mu = 100$, $\sigma = 15$). For grades 1–8, data are from the *Iowa Tests of Basic Skills* (ITBS); high school data are from the *Tests of Achievement and Proficiency*(TAP).

[5]*ITBS*: Reading = Vocabulary + Comprehension;

Language = Spelling + Capitalization + Punctuation + Usage and Expression;

Math = Concepts and Estimation + Problem Solving and Data Interpretation + Computation; Composite = aggregate of all tests.

TAP: Reading = Vocabulary + Comprehension;

Language = Written Expression;

Math = Concepts and Problem Solving + Computation;

Composite = aggregate of all tests

be with us for some time. This reservation is based not on the opinion that intelligence tests do not reflect intelligence but instead on the belief that there are other kinds of intelligence not reflected in current tests; the term *intelligence* is too inclusive. It should be clear that intelligence tests reflect abilities very important and relevant to educational performance. In spite of the not uncommon statement that intelligence tests do not predict ability to learn, the evidence that they do continues to accumulate. Only when the learning tasks are of a primitive, rote type, such as paired-associates tasks, do IQ scores have little relationship with learning behavior. For complex tasks, intelligence tests are substantially related to learning speed and ease (Estes, 1982).

13.21 CONSTRUCT VALIDITY

The critical evidence for the validity of intelligence tests lies in the realm of the construct validity. In Chapter 4 (Section 4.18) we used intelligence tests to illustrate this concept of construct validity. In a very real sense every bit of information one obtains about a test has implications for construct validity; that is, the data respond to the question "Is the information congruent with theoretical expectations?" IQ constancy has important implications for the construct validity of a given intelligence test. The validity of IQs from infant intelligence tests is rejected because they possess so little consistency with later cognitive performance.

Other early intelligence measures (phrenology and psychomotor measures) came to be shown to be invalid because they did not correlate with achievement in an academic environment.

The nature-nurture studies on measured intelligence have an important bearing on the construct validity of IQ scores. If there were no relationship between the IQs of siblings when they are reared apart and a very high relationship between their IQs when they are reared together, we would either revise the theory of intelligence (the proposition that genetic factors play a significant role would have to be eliminated) or reject the validity of the measurements. Either an ingredient in the theory is invalid or else the measurement of the construct must lack validity.

Contrary to indications in much of the popular literature, genetic factors have a substantial relationship to IQ scores (Jensen, 1981; McAskie & Clarke, 1976; Scarr & Carter-Saltzman, 1982; Sternberg, 1982). Of course, correlation does not necessarily mean causation; much heat and little light has been generated over the nature-nurture issue in intelligence. The question is exceedingly complex, especially as applied to racial differences (Kempthorne, 1978). Table 13–2 presents the median correlation between IQ scores for varying degrees of genetic similarity. The correlations are generally consistent with theoretical expectations. The correlation between IQ scores of unrelated people reared together is only about .20, but the IQ scores of identical (monozygotic) twins reared apart correlate highly ($r = .75$). In typical environments in the United States and England, genetic factors bear a much stronger relationship to IQ than environmental factors do (Pezzullo et al., 1972; Scarr & Carter-Saltzman, 1982). Of course, for certain individuals or subgroups the environment may have dramatic effects on IQ—as with, for example, brain damage at birth, metabolic types of mental retardation, or extreme environmental deprivation. Although

TABLE 13–2 Correlations between IQ Scores and Academic Achievement Measures for Persons of Various Degrees of Genetic and Environmental Similarity[6]

	IQ scores	Academic Achievement
Identical twins, reared together	.90	.95
Identical twins, reared apart	.70	.50
Fraternal twins	.55	.85
Siblings, reared together	.50	.80
Siblings, reared apart	.40	.50
Parent and child, child reared with parent	.50	
Adopted child with genetic parent	.40	
Genetically unrelated siblings reared together	.25	.50
Parent and adopted child	.25	
Grandparent and child	.25	
First cousins	.25	

SOURCES: Data from C. Jencks, *Inequality: A reassessment of the effect of family and schooling in America* (New York: Basic Books, 1972); B. Rimland and H. Munsinger, (1977) "Burt's IQ data," *Science, 195,* 248; A. R. Jensen, (1968) "Social class, race, and genetics: Implications for education," *American Educational Research Journal, 5,* 1–42; and S. A. Scarr and L. Carter-Saltzman, "Genetics and intelligence," in *Handbook of human intelligence*, ed. R. J. Sternberg (Cambridge: Cambridge University Press, 1982), Chap. 13.

genetic factors are strongly related to academic achievement, that relationship is less than with intelligence tests (Jensen, 1968). The achievement scores of unrelated persons reared together are substantially correlated, and *it is achievement, not intelligence per se, that is socially important.* The environment tends to have more influence on a student's academic performance than on his or her IQ score. For example, the achievement correlation of identical twins reared apart was .68, whereas that of siblings reared together was much higher, .81 (Jensen, 1968).

It is evident that genetic factors have a strong relationship to IQ scores. As evident in Table 13–2, the relationship of genetic factors with academic achievement is much less. Conversely, the environment has a much stronger relationship with children's academic achievement than with performance on measures of intelligence. For example, note that an adopted child's IQ score correlates more highly with the genetic parent than with the nurturing parent. Note also, however, that the academic achievement of siblings and fraternal twins reared together is more highly correlated than for identical twins reared apart. In addition, although there is a small relationship (.25) between IQ scores among genetically unrelated persons reared together, there is a substantial relationship (.5) between their academic achievement.

---

[6]The values (rounded) in the table do not include the controversial data of Sir Cyril Burt. Most of the correlations are based on individual intelligence tests, especially the Stanford-Binet.

13.22 INTELLIGENCE AND OCCUPATIONAL LEVEL

The relationship of measured intelligence to occupational level is illustrated in Figure 13–12. These data are based on the testing of approximately 90,000 Caucasian recruits during World War II using a group intelligence test, *the Army General Classification Test* (AGCT). The median *AGCT* scores for several different occupations were converted to corresponding IQ equivalents ($\mu = 100$, $\sigma = 16$) in Figure 13–12. The variability within each occupation (see last line of Figure 13–12) is shown by the bars that extend from the 25th to the 75th percentile in IQ units and the lines that extend from the 10th to the 90th percentile.

Two very important generalizations are apparent from the data given in Figure 13–12. First, *there is a substantial relationship between* average *mental ability and various occupations*. The median IQ for the higher occupational groups is substantially higher than that for the lower occupational groups. Note that we are talking about *measured intelligence*; the variation in amount of education probably magnifies the observed differences; which is no doubt greater than the true differences in intellectual aptitude.[7]

MY APTITUDE TESTS SHOWED I'D MAKE A
GOOD EXECUTIVE, BUT MY I.Q. TESTS SHOWED
I'D BE SMART ENOUGH NOT TO BECOME ONE.

NCME Measurement News, 19 (1976), 2.
Reprinted by permission.

---

[7]Since a greater proportion of today's students are remaining in school longer, the measured differences among the means of the various occupational groups today may be considerably less.

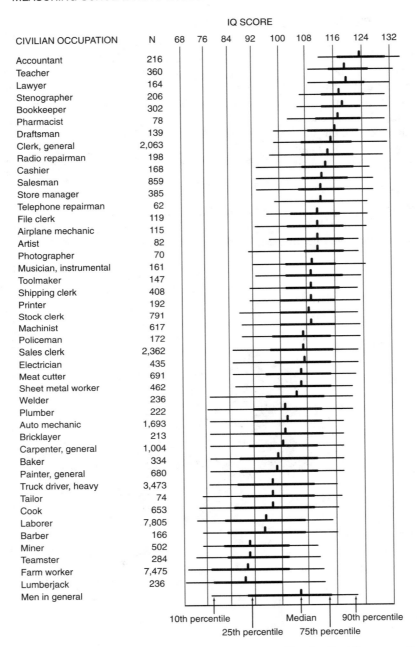

FIGURE 13–12 Scores on the Army General Classification Test for occupational groups converted into deviation IQ equivalents.

SOURCE: Based on data from N. Stewart. AGCT scores of army personnel grouped by occupation. *Occupations, 26* (1947), 5–41.

Second, *there is a wide range of mental ability within each occupation.* The correlation between an individual's occupational level and corresponding IQ score is much lower than commonly assumed, .3 or less (White, 1982, ETS, 1980; Jensen, 1980, pp. 43–44). The correlation between occupational level and educational level tends to be higher. Although the accountants' median IQ score was 123, 25 percent of the accountants scored below 117.

Notice that the variability within the occupational groups tends to decrease as socioeconomic level of the position increases. There are many bright people in "blue collar" occupations, but there are few persons of limited cognitive aptitude in professions that require high mental ability. Note, for example, that one-fourth of the lumberjacks scored above a score of 100, even though as a group they had the lowest average.[8]

13.23 MULTIPLE-APTITUDE BATTERIES

Although tests that yield a total score and/or separate verbal and nonverbal scores account for the most of cognitive aptitude assessment in school testing programs, an increasing use is being made of tests that yield a profile of different aptitudes, especially in vocational guidance. The most popular test battery of this type is the *Differential Aptitude Test* (DAT), which yields separate scores on eight somewhat independent aptitudes or abilities: Verbal Reasoning, Numerical Ability, Abstract Reasoning, (i.e., nonverbal) Clerical Speed and Accuracy, Mechanical Reasoning, Spelling, Space Relations, and Language Usage.

The basic rationale underlying these tests is that various academic and occupational pursuits require different patterns of aptitude and, hence, a decision in which a profile of aptitudes is available should be more appropriate than a decision based on a single "omnibus" score. This assumption has been strongly contested. Nevertheless, the various aptitude tests do correlate with various academic and occupational criteria. Some of the differences are counterintuitive; for example, girls who entered clerical work tended to have less clerical ability than the girls who became teachers. High school students who subsequently graduated from college were superior to those students who did not pursue further education on all tests, but especially on those assessing verbal and mathematical reasoning. However, there were substantial numbers of high-ability students who did not attend college.

The separate subtest scores can have substantial validity for differential occupational pursuits as illustrated in the expectancy table in Table 13–3 (see Section 4.14), which shows the relationship between the *DAT* Space Relations Test scores obtained at the beginning of the term and final grades in a watch repair training program. Note that 67 percent of those with very high *DAT* scores (80 or above) received *A*s and none obtained a grade of less than *B,* whereas no student with a *DAT* score below 60 received an *A* and many got *D*s and *F*s.

Multiple-aptitude tests can provide important information for career planning; however, their superiority over general scholastic aptitude tests for predicting differential *academic* success is small at best. The great commonality among the abilities required to

---

[8]An entire issue of the *Journal of Vocational Behavior* is devoted to the topic of The *g* Factor in employment (Gottfredson, 1986).

TABLE 13–3 An expectancy table illustrating the predictive validity of the *DAT* space relations test for forecasting end-of-course grades for 111 students in the American Institute of Specialized Watch Repair ($r = 0.69$).

	0	20	40	60	80	100
A				21%	67%	
B	9%	14%	40%	58%	33%	
C	33%	29%	40%	21%		
D	25%	36%	18%			
E	33%	21%	2%			
	$n = 12$	$n = 14$	$n = 43$	$n = 33$	$n = 9$	

Grade in watch repair (vertical axis, A–E)

*Raw score on **DAT** space relations test*

succeed in most academic subjects is no doubt a major factor that prevents multiple-aptitude tests from excelling over the omnibus tests in predicting academic success. Over many school subjects and job areas, general intelligence (*g*) is usually the best single predictor of success (Gottfredson, 1986).

13.24 CULTURAL INFLUENCE ON TEST SCORES

An examinee's test score reflects all the experiences the individual has had from conception to time of testing, including the effects of the particular genes he or she has inherited. As documented in Table 13–2, genetic potential interacts with environmental stimulation (or lack of it) to produce a person who scores high, average, or low on a particular test at a particular time. A child of five or even much younger has been exposed to so many strong environmental influences that his or her scores on intelligence tests are almost certainly different to some degree from what they would have been had that child been reared in a different environment (including nutrition and medical care).

"Culture-free" tests are culture-free in name only—there are no tests that measure potential or aptitude directly. Intelligence—unlike height and weight, but like all psychological constructs—must be measured indirectly; it must be inferred from intelligent behavior, past and present.

Since environment-free and culture-free tests cannot be devised, there have been many attempts to develop culture-*fair* tests. Obviously, it is unfair to judge Jim's verbal aptitude solely from his vocabulary when both of his parents are school dropouts whereas Jack's parents are college graduates. Intelligence tests would have more validity if test content sampled equally the background of all people. Test developers strive, with varying degrees of success, to select tasks that will be equally familiar (or equally unfamiliar) to all examinees. This goal is never achieved perfectly but is more closely approximated on some tests than many test critics realize. Anti-testing crusaders typically single out and attack a few bad items as if those items were representative (e.g., Hoffman, 1962, 1967a, 1967b) and try to "toss out the baby with the bath water."

Contrary to popular opinion, the correlation among students' socioeconomic status (SES) and academic ability is not high (rs are typically .3 or less unless confounded with racial factors (see Coleman et al., 1966; White, 1982; Jensen, 1980, p. 43). Note, for example, the great variability *within* the various occupations in Figure 13–12. (Occupation and education are the major ingredients of SES; see Section 15.31). Although there is a positive correlation between SES and IQ, because of their greater number, more examinees who score in the upper 25 percent on intelligence tests (i.e., IQs above 110) come from working-class homes than from the upper and upper-middle classes combined (Havighurst and Neugarten, 1975)!

You probably know parents who have devoted themselves to giving their children every educational advantage by providing an intellectually enriched environment—educational toys from the crib on, daily reading to the children at the earliest possible age, books and weekly trips to the library, problem-solving puzzles, achievement-oriented preschools, and reward systems tailored to "shape" academic interests and achievements. But many children from this type of experiential background do not become exceptional students—indeed, many are mediocre learners. Obviously, a propitious environment is only one of the important ingredients of superior academic achievement.

Despite its desirability, attempts to produce an intelligence test in which "culturally disadvantaged" people perform as well as those from enriched backgrounds have been largely unsuccessful. A long major study at the University of Chicago resulted in a specially designed "culturally fair" test, the *Davis-Eells Test of General Intelligence*; the test, however, did not reduce the differences among the means of the socioeconomic groups—the differences were of the same order of magnitude as those found with conventional intelligence tests. Later results with other tests have been similar (Cleary & Hilton, 1968).

Mercer (1977) has proposed a *System of Multicultural Pluralistic Assessment (SOMPA)* that, in effect, uses two sets of norms in assessing each examinee: the national norm group and a comparison group that is similar to the examinee in social and cultural background. The child's "learning potential" is a standard score based on performance in relation to that of other children from the same socio-cultural and ethnic background. This procedure is based on the tenuous assumption that all differences among social and ethnic groups are the result of unequal environments. Hilliard (National Institute of Education, 1979) has concluded that *SOMPA* "appears to have all the weaknesses of the old tests, plus a whole host of new weaknesses all its own, not the least of which is the absence of any construct validity." The *SOMPA* may be an overreaction to deficiencies in current intelligence tests (see Gordon, 1975).

Bear in mind that many very high-scoring individuals emerge from impoverished environments. In addition, the variability of IQ scores among siblings is quite large ($\sigma = 12$). Clearly, environment is a factor, but not the only factor, that affects performance on scholastic aptitude tests.[9] Note in Table 13–2 that the IQs of genetically unrelated children are only slightly correlated with the IQs of their foster parents; the IQs of adopted children are more closely related to those of their genetic parents ($r = .4$) than to their adopted parents ($r = .25$, see Table 13–2)). Table 13–2 documented that among Caucasians in America and Great Britain, measured academic aptitude is rather strongly, but by no means completely, a function of heredity. Research on the heritability of intelligence within an African American population is very limited.

As a group, the culturally disadvantaged tend to score lower on measures of academic aptitude; they also tend to make poorer grades. This is not surprising, because most of the abilities needed to score well on such tests are also required if a student is to do well in class. Many studies (Hills & Stanley, 1970; Kendrick & Thomas, 1970; Stanley, 1971a; Stanley & Porter, 1967; Thomas & Stanley, 1969; Wilson, 1978) have shown that scores on academic aptitude tests predict the college grades of blacks at least as well as they predict those of whites. More often than not, the *SAT* has been found to overpredict the college GPA of African Americans (Breland, 1978) and Mexican Americans (Goldman & Richards, 1974). Whereas high school grades predict college GPA somewhat better than scholastic ability tests among Caucasians, the pattern appears to be reversed for African Americans (Thomas & Stanley, 1969).

It is theoretically possible to construct tests that do not discriminate among socioeconomic classes but do predict academic achievement well; however, the many rather fruitless efforts thus far make this seem unlikely unless a fundamentally different method of measuring academic aptitude is discovered.[10]

The U.S. Employment Service has taken steps to improve the assessment of culturally disadvantaged applicants—experimenting with novel tests, improved test orientation and practice, development of nonreading forms of existing tests, and so on (Jurgensen, 1966). In 1980 the U.S. Supreme Court ruled in the Bakke case that it is unconstitutional to base selection decisions on racial quotas.[11]

---

[9]The reader may have read reports of a widely disseminated study by Rosenthal and Jacobson (1968) in which experimenter-induced teacher expectancies are purported to have resulted in significant gains in IQ scores in certain students. The interested reader should consult critical reviews of the study (Snow, 1969; Thorndike, 1968), which raise some serious questions regarding its validity. Attempts to generate a related effect have not been successful (Cooper, 1979; Dusek, 1975; Fleming & Anttonen, 1970; Gozali & Meyer, 1970; Haberman, 1970; Jose & Cody, 1971; Mendels & Flanders, 1973; Wineburg, 1987). The large increases in IQ scores in the "Milwaukee miracle" are also highly suspect as artifactual (see Page, 1972).

[10]The research on using brain waves to estimate intelligence is not promising (Fischer et al., 1978).

[11]Allan Bakke is a Caucasian who was denied admission to the medical school at the University of California at Davis even though his GPA and scores on the admissions test were higher than those of minority students who were admitted. The medical school had set aside 16 of the 100 openings for minorities. Bakke sued the university; the California State Supreme Court ruled in favor of Bakke because his rejection had been racially discriminatory. The U.S. Supreme Court (in a 5 to 4 decision) ruled the medical school had violated the "equal protection" clause of the Constitution because Bakke's rejection was based on a racial quota. The Court did uphold the "affirmative action" principle, indicating that race might legitimately be one element in assessing students for admission, provided that racial quotas are not used. The debate involves fundamental philosophic positions and value judgments in the weighing of one social good against another, as the growing insistence on group rights runs head-on into the traditional democratic belief in equality of individual opportunity. These questions of values and social policy and justice cannot be answered by scientists (Jensen, 1980).

Tests are not enemies of the culturally disadvantaged. "To conceal the effects of cultural disadvantages by rejecting tests or by trying to devise tests that are insensitive to such effects can only retard progress toward a genuine solution of social problems" (Anastasi, 1988, p. 66). Tests can provide a safeguard against favoritism and arbitrary and capricious decisions when social stereotypes and prejudice could otherwise distort interpersonal evaluations and decisions. In "Guidelines for Testing Minority Group Children," Fishman and colleagues (1964, p. 139) commented, "Without the intervention of standardized tests, many such [bright, non-conforming, and culturally handicapped] children would be stigmatized by the adverse subjective ratings of teachers who tend to reward conformist behavior of middle-class character."

The National Council on Measurement in Education, in its official statement on admissions testing (NCME, 1980, p. 5), stated, "Although some interpret group differences in performance as bias in a test, it is now recognized among measurement experts that the mere existence of such group differences in performance is not evidence of bias . . . Few people suggest that differentials in school-related performance could disappear if there were no tests."

Tests should be used as an aid in understanding students. No responsible person should fail to take a student's background into consideration in interpreting a test score. The fact that undernourished children weigh less than those who are well fed hardly builds a case for banning scales. In the same vein, Clifford, a black educator, stated that to disparage tests for revealing inequalities is as erroneous as for the residents of Bismarck, North Dakota, to condemn the use of thermometers as biased because when it was $-11°$ in North Dakota it was $73°$ in Miami, Florida (Clifford & Fishman, 1963, p. 87).

The following summary is offered (Loehlin, Lindzey, and Spuhler; 1975, p. 239): Observed mean differences on intelligence-ability tests probably reflect a combination of both (1) inadequacies in the tests and differential environmental conditions, and (2) genetic differences among the groups. The relative weights of these two factors will differ on different tests and with different groups, but regardless of the relative importance of these factors, it seems clear that the differences among individuals *within* racial-ethnic (and SES) groups are much greater than the average differences *between* such groups.

Several conclusions regarding performance on scholastic aptitude tests as related to SES and race can be stated:

1. There are no direct, pure measures of intellectual aptitude; hence, comparisons of native intelligence or the like are equivocal. Whether there are, or are not, differences among different ethnic and racial groups cannot be definitively established or refuted on the basis of current research evidence. Scores on scholastic aptitude tests represent the examinee's current level of functioning.

2. An enriched environment enhances performance, but a superior environment, compared with an average environment, is not sufficient to produce a bright child. The effects at the other end of the environmental spectrum are greater. An extremely poor environment (lack of school attendance, deaf parents, and the like) can substantially depress intellectual performance.

3. Any responsible interpretation of scholastic aptitude or intelligence tests must take the social and ethnic background of the examinee into account.

4. Scholastic aptitude measures do not generally under-predict the academic achievement of members of ethnic and social minorities. Similar results have been obtained in certain employment and military settings.
5. Many of the issues pertaining to the appropriate use of scholastic aptitude tests are inextricably mixed with political and social values and orientations and, as such, do not readily lend themselves to resolution by means of scientific research.

Table 13–4 (adapted from Sternberg, 1996) summarizes many of the myths and countermyths about intelligence.

13.25 ASSESSING CREATIVITY

In his presidential address to the American Psychological Association, Guilford (1950) documented the dearth of attention that psychologists were giving to the study of creativity. His address stimulated interest in the topic and, subsequently, considerable research effort has been directed toward the definition and assessment of creativity.

Creative thinking is in the Divergent operation of Guilford's model of intelligence. He and others have attempted to develop tests of creativity, of which the most common are the *Torrance Tests of Creative Thinking* and the *Wallach and Kogan Creativity Test*. Both tests include verbal and visual sections. In these tests examinees are asked how many different uses they can think of for a brick or a tin can and such questions as "What would happen if birds could speak the language of man?" "What might be about to happen in the picture above?" "Make up a story to fit the title *The Lion That Won't Roar*" "Just suppose that no one ever has to go to school anymore; what would happen?" "Name all the round things you can think of." "Name all the ways a potato and a carrot are alike." Illustrative Torrance items are given in Figure 13–13. Responses are scored by trained scorers according to three criteria: originality, fluency (number of responses), and flexibility (number of different categories of responses).

The creativity tests developed to date have yet to demonstrate their practical value; their predictive validity tends to be low (Anastasi, 1988). The tests tend to be too unreliable for individual use (test-retest reliability tends to be in the .45 to .75 range, with a median value of perhaps .65). In addition, many creativity tests do not correlate highly with each other. Thorndike (1963b) showed that tests of creativity correlate as highly with conventional "convergent" intelligence measures as they do with other "divergent" tests. Performance on creativity measures has much less stability over time than performance on intelligence tests.

Continued research efforts may refine or develop creativity measures so that they have practical utility, but at present they must be viewed as bold attempts rather than successes in creativity assessment. The current status of instruments for assessing creativity is less than satisfactory. Evidence for the validity and reliability of creativity measures fails so far to promote much confidence in their use in assessing specific components of creativity. In her review of creativity tests, Crockenberg (1972, p. 40) wrote, "Therefore, while it may be eminently reasonable to study the processes that appear to be involved in creativity production, it is conceptually unjustifiable to call these tests 'tests of creativity'." The same can be said today. It is becoming increasingly evident that creativity is domain-specific and represents a combination of cognitive and personality factors.

TABLE 13–4   Facts and Fictions about Intelligence

Myth 1: Intelligence (or IQ) is a single trait.
Countermyth 1: Every trait is Intelligence.
Fact 1: Intelligence is multidimensional but measurable, although the measures are imperfect.

Myth 2. The social order is a natural outcome of intelligence.
Countermyth 2: Tests are the dominant determiner of social and economic outcomes.
Fact 2: The social order is partially, but not exclusively, determined by intelligence and test results.

Myth 3: Intelligence cannot be taught to any meaningful degree.
Countermyth 3: We can, from environmental enrichment, affect great increases in IQ scores.
Fact 3: We can increase intelligent behavior in at least some meaningful degree but cannot today effect radical changes.

Myth 4: IQ tests measure virtually all that's important for academic and job success.
Countermyth 4: IQ tests measure virtually nothing that's important for academic and job success.
Fact 4: IQ tests measure skills that are of moderate importance in academic and job success.

Myth 5: We are using tests too little, losing valuable talent and information.
Countermyth 5: We're overusing tests, they're evil and should be abolished.
Fact 5: Tests as tools, when properly interpreted, can serve useful functions and reduce favoritism; but often they are not properly used or interpreted.

Myth 6: We as a society are getting stupider because of the dysgenic effects of stupid superbreeders.
Countermyth 6: We have no reason at all to fear any decline in intellectual abilities among successive generations.
Fact 6: We have some reason to fear loss of intellectual abilities in future generations.

Myth 7. Intelligence is all inherited.
Countermyth 7: Intelligence is essentially attributable to environment.
Fact 7: Intelligence involves substantial heritable and environmental components.

Myth 8: There are racial and sexual differences in cognitive aptitudes.
Countermyth 8: There are no sexual or racial differences in cognitive aptitudes.
Fact 8: Research cannot establish with certainty whether there are differences in sexual or racial cognitive aptitudes, but there are performance differences.

Myth 9: We should write off stupid people.
Countermyth 9: There are no stupid people.
Fact 9: We should not judge the worth of persons by their IQ score.

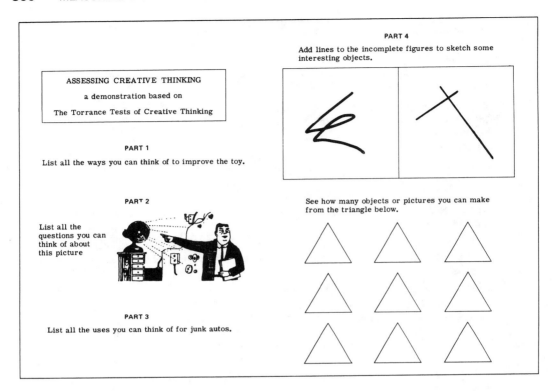

FIGURE 13–13   Illustrative items for a creativity test.

SOURCE: Reproduced by permission of the Personnel Press, Inc., Princeton, N.J., a division of Ginn and Company.

13.26   USING TESTS TO IDENTIFY AND HELP GIFTED CHILDREN[12]

Intellectually gifted children are often defined as those with Stanford-Binet or Wechsler IQs of at least 130, the top 2 or 3 percent of their age group. Usually, however, there is much subjectivity in the identification of youths to be labeled "gifted." Substantial representation of various gender, racial, and ethnic groups is often sought via various ratings by teachers, parents, fellow students, and even the individual herself or himself. Where accelerated growth in certain subject matter areas, such as mathematics, is a major goal of the program, it is crucial to identify those students who will benefit from that type of educational environment and enrichment.

For example, the *Study of Mathematically Precocious Youth* (*SMPY*) at Johns Hopkins University started in 1971 to find "youths who reason exceptionally well mathemati-

---

[12]The material in this section is adapted from Stanley (1984). (See also Stanley, 1980).

cally." This was defined as scoring at least 500 on the mathematical part of the *College Board Scholastic Aptitude Test* (*SAT-M*) before age 13. The *SAT* is intended mainly for college-bound high school seniors whose average score on this instrument at present is somewhat less than 500. Thus, when a seventh-grader scores 500 or more, his or her mathematical reasoning ability is very advanced. Stanley and Benbow (1986) estimate that such a person is in the top 1 percent of 12-year-olds with respect to potential for rapid mastery of mathematics and related subjects such as computer science, physics, and chemistry. Special, supplemental educational opportunities can be created for persons with this level of aptitude. Thereby, they can be helped to avoid the frustration and boredom that subject matter, when paced too slowly, can cause. Out-of-level testing (see Section 14.14) is especially useful in this context.

A similar approach via *SAT-Verbal*, to identify youths who reason exceptionally well verbally, grew out of *SMPY*'s work. In 1979 the Center for the Advancement of Academically Talented Youth (CTY) was founded at Johns Hopkins University to conduct talent searches among seventh-graders in the East. Shortly thereafter, the Talent Identification Program (TIP) was established at various universities across the nation. By 1988, each year some 120,000 seventh- and eighth-grade students in the United States took all three parts of the *SAT:* mathematical, verbal, and *Test of Standard Written English* (*TSWE*). Seventh-graders in every state had a talent search via *SAT* available, and there were many special academic programs for those who scored high on *SAT-M* and/or *SAT-V*.

If only *one* test were to be used to identify intellectually talented youth during kindergarten through elementary school, probably a well-administered individual scholastic aptitude test, such as the Stanford-Binet or Wechsler, would be best. Administering individual intelligence tests, however, requires much time and a highly trained examiner to test each examinee and score and interpret the responses. However, requiring individual testing as the chief or only way to qualify for a gifted-child program is probably undesirable.

Whereas achievement scores or IQs from general intelligence tests (both individual and group) can be helpful from kindergarten through junior high school, testing for multiple aptitudes at various ages seems essential. Also, this is a more democratic procedure. For example, a third-grader who cannot qualify for a gifted-child program via the Stanford-Binet might do so if administered the Raven Progressive Matrices Test, which involves nonverbal reasoning ability. Alternatively, scores on achievement test batteries should be inspected carefully to determine whether they suggest that a suitably bright person has been overlooked in the formal identification process.

As the student grows older, or if the youngster is highly precocious, a standardized aptitude test battery such as the *Differential Aptitude Test* (*DAT*) (see Section 13.23) may provide a basis for discovering the combination of aptitudes on which the individual excels. As noted earlier, the *DAT* yields eight scores but no total score. It might be administered in the middle of the sixth or seventh grade to all persons who had scored in the top 10 percent of their age or grade level on a battery of achievement tests. This illustrates a fundamental concept of seeking talent: Administer tests that are sufficiently difficult to challenge the bright youth, usually those designed for typical students in higher grades.

One could go further and retest persons qualifying in any aptitude with a more difficult test. For example, those scoring at the 95th percentile or higher on certain *DAT* tests might take the *College Board Scholastic Aptitude Tests* in a regular national testing.

One primary reason for identifying intellectually talented children is to provide them with a better education. It will take considerable ingenuity on the part of coordinators of special educational experiences for the intellectually talented (preferable to the more common term "teachers of the gifted") to provide educational opportunities concordant with their special talents. Focusing on specific aptitudes, rather than general mental ability, usually symbolized by an IQ, makes this search for a match between talent and relevant educational experiences more promising. Often in the regular classroom, the math-talented youth is given some "busy work" or something else to do while she or he remains bored and frustrated in the age-in-grade mathematics course. Likewise, the high IQ child whose verbal reasoning ability greatly exceeds his or her mathematical aptitude may feel lost in a fast-paced, advanced mathematics course thought to be excellent for all children who are gifted.

Nine precautions may be helpful in using tests to identify gifted youth in order to better meet their educational needs.

1. Identifying intellectually talented youths before age seven or so is more difficult and less valid than at later ages, but one does need to get started early on a properly tentative basis.

2. IQ is based upon a composite of various abilities. Two students may have exactly the same IQ, on the same test, administered by the same tester, and yet be quite different in, say, mathematical reasoning ability and in verbal reasoning ability. Student A might have a math IQ of 175 versus a math IQ of 125 for student B, whereas the discrepancy between their abilities in verbal reasoning might be reversed. Student A would have a decided advantage over student B in courses requiring intricate mathematical reasoning, but the situation would be reversed for topics requiring advanced verbal reasoning. Therefore: *Don't group for instruction on the basis of IQ alone.* Instead, use special ability scores relevant to the subject being studied.

3. Be sure the test is sufficiently difficult to challenge the person being tested. For example, if a child already known to be bright is only a few months younger than the minimum age for which *WISC-III* is recommended, don't test her or him with *WPPSI-R*. SMPY has had great success administering the *SAT* to 12-year-olds in the upper 3 percent ability range, even though that difficult test is designed mainly for 17- or 18-year-old high school juniors and seniors applying to selective colleges and universities. A seven-year-old has scored 670 on *SAT-M* and an eight-year-old 760!

4. Feed the intellectually talented youth's specific academic hunger directly. For example, if she or he reasons exceptionally well mathematically, allow the student to forge ahead more rapidly in the mathematics sequences along with related subjects such as physics, computer science, and chemistry. Don't impose a favorite "enrichment" subject on a student rather than appropriate subjects, assuming your preferences will meet the student's needs equally as well.

5. Recognize *degrees* of intellectual talent. For instance, some students will require only a little acceleration in the mathematics sequence, such as being allowed to take first-year algebra a year early, whereas a few others will be delving into calculus before the age of ten. Therefore, don't think that moving ahead one year in a subject is enough for everyone, however highly math-apt they might be.

6. Avoid talking about a student's age mates as his or her peers, except in a political or social sense. One's *intellectual* peers are those individuals on one's own intellectual level. The mental age of a high IQ student exceeds that person's chronological age. Using an adjective before the word "peer" is probably good strategy, as in "athletic peer," "social peer," or "musical peer," if one wishes to use the word "peer" at all in such contexts.

7. There is no upper limit to the potential ability or precocity of a child. It is not true that after an IQ of 120 or so extra points don't matter, except in the unfortunate sense that the academic work being presented may be too little a challenge to warrant much effort from the student. It is not uncommon to see typical participants of a three-week residential summer program for the mathematically gifted learn two years of mathematics in just those three weeks! Extremely able students 11 to 15 years old can learn biology, chemistry, or physics, with laboratory, better in three intensive summer weeks than most students do in an entire school year devoted to the subject.

8. "Curricular flexibility" and "appropriate articulation" are key concepts in providing simple, straightforward, cost-effective ways to help specially talented youths forge ahead faster and better. Use what is available rather than building up expensive, politically vulnerable special programs. For example, the best way to "enrich" algebra I for students who already know the content is probably to help them get smoothly into the best available algebra II class.

9. Diagnostic testing, followed by prescribed instruction, can be very useful. Ascertain what the talented students do not yet know about the subject and help them learn the unknown specifically, without having to repeat the parts she or he already knows. Concentrating on the top 10 percent itself can be highly effective with youths already so advanced in the subject that they have mastered most of the material before the class begins.

The goal of a truly democratic education is to provide the type of educational opportunities and environments that allow each student to develop and make the fullest use of her or his unique aptitudes.

SUMMARY

Intelligence measurement became successful shortly after 1900, when Binet employed verbal and abstract reasoning items. There continue to be several theories of intelligence, although it is measured principally by the use of rather heterogeneous collections of verbal or nonverbal items.

The construct validity data for intelligence tests include (1) age differentiation, (2) the considerable stability of IQ scores, (3) the substantial relationship of IQ scores with academic achievement and occupational levels, (4) the substantial relationship of genetic factors with measured intelligence, and (5) the logical content validity of the test items—do they require reasoning, conceptualization, higher-level thought processes, and so forth?

Several conclusions regarding the measurement of scholastic aptitude can be stated.

1. Intelligence tests are best viewed as scholastic aptitude tests; they are heavily oriented toward academic criteria. They tap only a subset, albeit an important one, of the domain of what may be regarded as intelligence.
2. Infant intelligence tests have almost no predictive validity. Estimates obtained from individual tests at about age five have much more validity.
3. Scholastic aptitude (general intelligence) continues to develop until about age 16 to 18.
4. Deviation IQ scores are superior to ratio IQ scores because, unlike ratio IQs, their meaning is not blurred by fluctuations in standard deviations across various age levels. Because of the widespread misunderstanding of the IQ, many tests are discontinuing its use. Percentile ranks are less likely to be misinterpreted.
5. A high correlation between intelligence tests indicates that they are measuring common abilities but does not necessarily mean that the tests yield similar IQ scores.
6. High stability coefficients on intelligence tests represent the general consistency in scores, although the scores of some individuals may change dramatically. The degree of stability decreases as the time interval increases and increases with age until maturity.
7. Individual verbal intelligence tests tend to have greater IQ stability than group verbal tests.
8. IQ scores from verbal tests tend to have more stability than scores from nonverbal tests.
9. Intelligence test scores have a substantial relationship to academic achievement. The relationship tends to increase with grade level and is greater for verbal than for nonverbal tests.
10. There are no truly culture-free or culture-fair tests. Performance and nonverbal tests contain content that is less related to the environment of particular cultures and social classes.
11. Multiple-aptitude tests are widely used in vocational guidance. They are less exclusively academically oriented than general verbal intelligence tests.
12. Available creativity tests should not be viewed as valid measures of creativity.

IMPORTANT TERMS AND CONCEPTS

academic aptitude
achievement test
cognitive abilities
creativity
culture free
intelligence quotient (IQ)

mental age
scholastic aptitude
standardized test
Stanford-Binet Scale
Wechsler Adult Intelligence Scale (WAIS)
Wechsler Intelligence Scale for Children (WISC)

CHAPTER TEST

1. Intelligence tests are best viewed as
   a) measures of innate cognitive potential.
   b) reading tests.
   c) academic achievement tests.
   d) scholastic aptitude tests.

2. Which one of the following types of early intelligence test items was *not* discarded because of lack of construct validity?
   a) reaction time
   b) picture completion
   c) size of cranium
   d) sensory discrimination

3. Which type of mental ability test was developed *first*?
   a) individual verbal
   b) group verbal
   c) individual performance
   d) group nonverbal

4. Which type of mental ability test ordinarily is not used by colleges for selection purposes?
   a) *GRE*   b) *SAT*   c) *ACT*   d) *WAIS*

5. If IQ scores are used, which type is preferable?
   a) deviation IQs   b) ratio IQs

6. The value of σ is constant at all age levels with
   a) deviation IQs.   b) ratio IQs.

7. On most tests that yield IQ scores, the value of σ is approximately
   a) 9–10.   b) 12–13.   c) 15–16.   d) 18–20.

8. For the major individual intelligence tests, the standard error of measurement, σ_e, in IQ units, is closest to which of the following values for the more typical examinees?
   a) 1 point   b) 3 points   c) 5 points   d) 15 points

9. On the *Stanford-Binet*, σ_e is *least* for (see Figure 13–6)
   a) low IQ values.   b) average IQ values.   c) high IQ values.

10. If the correlation between Forms 1 and 2 of the *ABC* IQ test (parallel-form reliability) is .91 and $\sigma = 16$, what is the value (rounded) of the standard error of measurement $(s_e = s\sqrt{1 - r_{11}})$?
    a) 3   b) 4   c) 5   d) 6   e) none of these

11. If $\rho_{12} = 1.0$, which one of the following could *not* possibly be true?
    a) mean of test 1 = 100, mean of test 2 = 110
    b) $\sigma_1 = 12, \sigma_2 = 15$
    c) $\sigma_{2.1} = 5.0$
    d) for variable 1, $\sigma_e = 0.0$

12. Which of the regression-toward-the-mean tendencies is/are evident in Figure 13–9?
    a) Low scorers at grade 5 tend to obtain higher IQ scores at grade 7.
    b) High scorers at grade 5 tend to obtain higher IQ scores at grade 7.
    c) Average scorers at grade 5 tend to obtain higher IQ scores at grade 7.
    d) Two of the above are evident.
    e) Three of the above (i.e., a, b, and c) are evident.

13. The validity of IQ scores from infant intelligence tests for predicting later IQ scores is
    a) almost zero. b) moderately high. c) very high.

14. In Figure 13–8, is $\sigma_{2.1}$ another name for the standard error of measurement?

15. IQ scores on which type of test have the *greatest* degree of stability over several years?
    a) individual verbal tests
    b) group verbal tests
    c) group nonverbal tests

16. IQ scores on which type of test have the *least* degree of stability over several years?
    a) individual verbal tests   b) group verbal tests   c) group nonverbal tests

17. Which one of the following methods of reporting results of scholastic aptitude tests to students and parents is generally preferable?
    a) percentile ranks   b) deviation IQs   c) ratio IQs   d) mental ages

18. The correlation between IQ scores and achievement is greater
    a) in high school than in grades 4–6.
    b) in grade 1 than in grade 6.
    c) in math than in reading.
    d) for nonverbal than for verbal.

19. Among Caucasians, the IQs of which of the following correlate the *lowest*?
    a) identical twins, reared apart
    b) siblings, reared together
    c) fraternal twins, reared together
    d) genetically unrelated children, reared together
    e) fraternal twins, reared apart

20. Among Caucasians, the IQs of which of the following correlate the *highest*?
    a) identical twins, reared apart
    b) siblings, reared together
    c) fraternal twins, reared together
    d) genetically unrelated children, reared together
    e) fraternal twins, reared apart

21. Which one of the following is certainly true of standardized intelligence tests?
    a) They are direct measures of scholastic aptitude.
    b) They reflect only environmental effects.
    c) All races and ethnic groups would have exactly the same mean on all aptitude measures if environmental differences were removed.
    d) They correlate highly with SES.
    e) They are influenced by both hereditary and environmental factors.

22. Which one of the following statements pertaining to IQ and occupation is *not* correct? (see Figure 13–12)

a) The mean IQ score of blue-collar workers is less than that of white-collar workers.

b) The mean IQ of individuals in several blue-collar occupations is above 100.

c) There are very bright individuals in all occupations.

d) There is great variability within all occupations.

e) The variability within high SES occupations is greater than within lower SES occupations.

23. Using Figure 13–15, if Lola scored 50 on the *DAT* Space Relations Test, estimate the probability that she will receive a *B* or better in watch repair.

a) 1.0   b) .60   c) .40   d) .20   e) .00

24. The demonstrated validity of current creativity tests is

a) very strong.   b) moderately strong.   c) weak.

25. Which one of the following is most closely influenced by school-related achievement?

a) individual performance tests

b) group verbal tests

c) group nonverbal tests

d) multiple-aptitude test batteries

e) creativity tests

ANSWERS TO CHAPTER TEST

1. d	10. c	18. a
2. b	11. c	19. d
3. a	12. a	20. a
4. d	13. a	21. e
5. a	14. no	22. e
6. a	15. a	23. c
7. c	16. c	24. c
8. c	17. a	25. b
9. a		

14

Standardized Achievement Tests

14.1 INTRODUCTION

Standardized achievement tests focus on general skills and content that are included among the educational objectives of virtually all school districts. Since they are ordinarily administered annually (or even less frequently), standardized achievement tests must span a much wider range of content than most teacher-constructed tests. Teacher-made examinations need to be given frequently to monitor and evaluate student and class progress, to identify the need for remediation, to motivate students, and so on. Teacher-made tests focus on a much more restricted range of content than standardized tests; they usually reflect a particular unit of study or a semester of study.

14.2 ADVANTAGES OF STANDARDIZED TESTS

The norms provided by standardized tests offer the user a comparison with a nationally representative group of educational peers; this comparison is important for such purposes as quality control, curricular evaluation, academic and vocational guidance and counseling, and identification of exceptional students. External comparisons cannot be made with nonstandardized tests. Parents often feel that the percent correct on a test directly reflects the quality of teaching or learning; they fail to realize that a very poor teacher can construct a test that is so easy that almost all students receive perfect scores even if they have learned little. On the other hand, an excellent teacher may develop a very difficult and discriminating test on which the average score may be only 60 percent or less. As was emphasized in Chapter 7, the difficulty of a test is arbitrary—the class average will be much lower if there are many items at the upper level of Bloom's taxonomy (Section 7.5).

Standardized tests impose certain controls on testing conditions—the conditions under which the tests are taken are to be *standard* for all examinees. The directions, practice items, and time limits should be uniform for all students. Only when standard questions are given under uniform conditions is there a meaningful basis for evaluating and comparing performance.

The best standardized tests are carefully developed and refined by means of editorial writing and item analysis from a field testing so that every item functions well. Intrinsic ambiguity should be removed, and implausible distracters are modified or replaced. As a consequence, the reliability of standardized achievement tests is (and needs to be) much greater than for teacher-made tests. Some of the 1500 standardized achievement tests are not highly reliable, but they are the exception rather than the rule.

The number and frequency of teacher-made tests can easily compensate for the lack of high reliability in a single test. If each of ten weekly quizzes has a reliability of only .5, the reliability coefficient of scores summed (or averaged) over the ten measures will exceed .90. (See the Spearman-Brown formula, Equation 5.5.)

It should be clear that teacher-made and standardized achievement tests complement each other. They serve related but somewhat different purposes. Both kinds of test are needed for an adequate evaluation of educational achievement by individual students, schools, and school districts.

14.3   THE APTITUDE-ACHIEVEMENT CONTINUUM

Intelligence and aptitude tests are future-oriented—their focus is on potential subsequent performance in the future. Educational achievement tests are present and past oriented—they reflect the degree of learning or achievement for a common core of curricular knowledge and skills. Aptitude tests are designed to predict potential; achievement tests depict present proficiency. A valid music aptitude test administered prior to music instruction should predict with some degree of accuracy, the performance level on a music proficiency measure *after* some period of instruction. Aptitude tests attempt to indicate what a person *could learn* if opportunity and motivation are present; achievement tests represent what a student *has learned*. In practice, this distinction is not as clear-cut as described above, nevertheless there is a clear distinction in purpose. Academic aptitude tests reflect a great deal of general achievement, such as vocabulary, whereas some achievement tests assess factors that are usually associated with intelligence, such as abstract reasoning and deductive and inductive logic. Although standardized achievement tests predict subsequent achievement better than scholastic aptitude (or intelligence) tests (Bracht & Hopkins, 1970b), aptitude tests are attempting to assess what the student "could do" more than what the student "will do."

Both aptitude and achievement tests reflect developed ability; the primary difference between them is largely in the nature of the test content and its level of generality. An implicit assumption in an achievement test (but not in an aptitude test) is that all students have been directly exposed to the content—the universe of content is specifically defined. An achievement test does not indicate how or why students do or do not perform, but it does represent current proficiency level.

All cognitive tests can be ordered along an achievement-aptitude continuum (see Figure 14–1). At one extreme are teacher-made tests that represent course-specific and even teacher-specific content. Standardized achievement tests are broader in objectives and content, but their items are more school-oriented than college admissions tests (*ACT, SAT,*

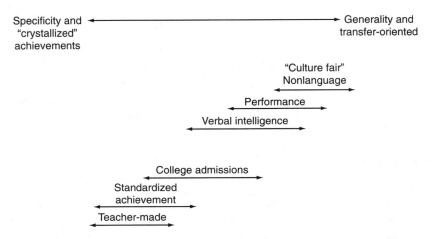

FIGURE 14–1 Spectrum of tests of cognitive abilities.

GRE). Even less related to the school curriculum are items on most verbal intelligence tests (e.g., the *Stanford-Binet*). More general still (i.e., less environmentally dependent) are performance, nonlanguage, and "culture-fair" tests that may be administered to people who are illiterate or have language restrictions associated with physical or cultural factors.

The concept of the continuum represented in Figure 14–1 is supported by research, showing that tests generally correlate most highly with their closest neighbors (in Figure 14–1) and progressively less as the separation increases. Some authorities maintain that standardized intelligence and achievement tests correlate so highly that they are essentially parallel forms of measures of the same abilities. Kelley consequently warned of the "jangle fallacy," the fallacy of assuming that tests with different labels measure different abilities. He also coined the phrase "jingle fallacy," the fallacy of assuming that tests with the same labels measure the same functions. Some scholastic aptitude tests have made the mistake (and hence have lower construct validity) of selecting items that maximize the correlation with achievement tests, rather than choosing items that are not dependent on formal schooling.

Figure 14–2 was constructed to illustrate the overlapping variance on well-constructed intelligence and achievement tests. Data are depicted for reading and math tests and for verbal and nonverbal intelligence measures, both for grades 3 and 8. The reliability coefficient (Section 5.8) of a test indicates what proportion of total variance is true variance and not measurement error. The area depicting true variance is indicated by slanting lines. The cross-hatched pattern shows the overlapping variance (r_{12}^2) for each set of tests. For example, the proportions of nonerror variance (i.e., the reliability coefficients) for the grade 3 verbal intelligence and reading tests were found to be .95 and .91. The verbal intelligence test correlates .68 with the reading test; thus, the variance in common for the two tests is $(.68)^2 = .46$. The figure in the upper left-hand corner of Figure 14–2 shows that 46 percent of the variance in the verbal (upper rectangle) and the reading (lower rectangle shifted to the right) tests is cross-hatched. By studying the figure, one sees that 49 percent [100% − (46% + 5%)] of the verbal test is independent of the reading test; 45 percent [100% − (46% + 9%)] of the true variance on the reading test is independent of the verbal test.

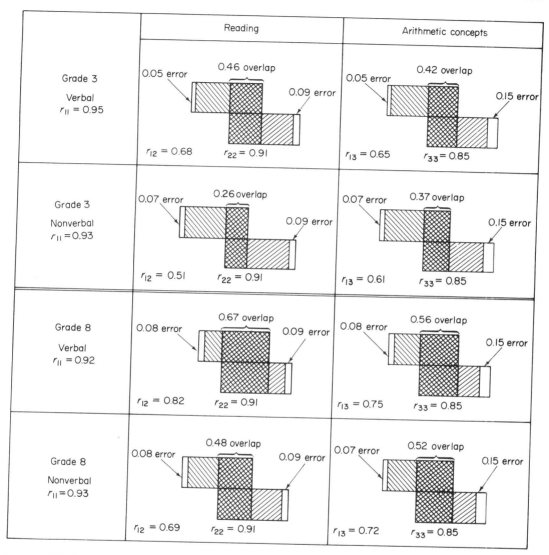

FIGURE 14–2 Common variance between standardized achievement test data (Iowa Test of Basic Skills, reading and math) and intelligence test data (Lorge-Thorndike Intelligence Test, verbal and non-verbal) at two grade levels. In each panel of this figure the upper horizontal rectangle represents the variance of the intelligence test; the lower rectangle represents the variance of the achievement test.

SOURCE: Based on data from the Technical Manual for the Lorge-Thorndike Intelligence Tests.

Figures 14–1 and 14–2 illustrate that, although there is a substantial relationship between the achievement and scholastic aptitude measures, each has considerable uniqueness. This could also be inferred from the environmental correlates (Table 13–3) or achievement and intelligence measures: Performance on achievement tests tends to be influenced by environmental factors much more than performance on scholastic aptitude measures.

14.4   CONTENT VALIDITY

The critical type of validity for achievement tests is content validity, sometimes called content relevance. Does the test reflect the reading or arithmetic objectives at a given grade level? Does the math test reflect the related curriculum? Ideally, the items on an achievement test should be a representative sample of the content and process objectives of a curriculum. If teachers assume that the *K-ABC* and *ITBS* arithmetic reasoning tests equally reflect arithmetic reasoning objectives and thus are equally valid measures, they are guilty of the "jingle fallacy." Often tests with the same label differ greatly in content, the taxonomy levels represented by their items, degree of speededness, and other important aspects. All items on one "Numerical Ability" test (the *DAT*) for high school students require only addition—none require subtraction, multiplication, or division; obviously this test has limited construct validity as a numerical ability test because it is only an "addition ability" measure.

Publishers of most current standardized achievement tests provide a classification of the skills and content assessed in their tests (see Figures 4–1 and 4–2 in Section 4.2). This type of content breakdown is especially useful in selecting tests for a particular school or school district.

14.5   NORMS ON STANDARDIZED ACHIEVEMENT TESTS

The pattern of a district's (or a student's) results from standardized tests is partially dependent on which test battery is being used. Several studies have shown that a school's average is influenced by the particular standardized test that is used. A portion of the disparity is attributable to differential content validity; that is, the fact that one test mirrors the district's objectives and instruction more completely than another. Some of the disparity can also result from differences in the tests' definitions of grade equivalent (GE). Some tests use medians to define GEs; others use means. When distributions are skewed, the mean and median will yield different averages. In addition, some tests have used "modal" norms—norms based only on students who are of the modal or usual age for their grade. When the underage and overage students are eliminated from the norm group, the norms become more demanding because more students are nonpromoted than are double promoted, and the inclusion of nonpromoted students tends to lower the average performance.

Another reason for the lack of correspondence between the norms on standardized achievement tests is that the norm groups are never completely comparable. Many school districts refuse to permit publishers to use their students for norming purposes; the percent of districts refusing to participate seems to be increasing—often almost one-half of the school districts contacted refuse to participate in the norming of standardized tests. Test publishers need to create a stronger incentive for participation.

14.6 CO-NORMED SCHOLASTIC APTITUDE AND ACHIEVEMENT TESTS

The lack of equivalence in norming populations is one of the principal reasons that it is best to select a companion (or co-normed) set of aptitude and achievement tests. For example, the *Cognitive Abilities Test* is co-normed with the *Iowa Tests of Basic Skills;* the *Metropolitan Achievement Test* and the *Stanford Achievement Test* are co-normed with the *Otis-Lennon School Ability Test*; the *Test of Cognitive Skills* is the companion aptitude test for the *Comprehensive Tests of Basic Skills* and the *California Achievement Tests.* The *WISC-III* was normed with the *Wechsler Individual Achievement Test* to allow a better assessment of aptitude-achievement discrepancies. The *Woodcock-Johns Psycho-Educational Battery* also includes both aptitude and achievement measures co-normed so that discrepancies can be used for diagnosis of educational problems. With dual standardization, the aptitude and achievement tests are on the same group of examinees; whatever bias there is in the norms is constant for both tests. Thus, the 50th percentile has the same *relative* meaning on all the tests in the companion set, even if perfect norms would yield a somewhat different percentile. For this reason, also, schools and school districts are advised to stay with the same achievement battery across grade levels. Otherwise, differences resulting from noncomparable norm groups can appear to be due to ineffective instruction at given grade levels.

Tables of comparable scores between various standardized achievement tests have been determined empirically but these quickly become outdated because the tests are revised and/or renormed every five to ten years. Norming is the weakest link in standardized testing. There are, however, some promising developments on the horizon.

14.7 ITEM NORMS FOR CLASS, SCHOOL, AND DISTRICT EVALUATIONS

Several publishers now furnish normative data for specific content strata/objectives. This information can have value for evaluating the success of a class, school (building), or district's curriculum and instruction. Figure 14–3 is an analysis of the fifth-grade results for "Johnson Elementary," a school in the "River Falls School District." Notice in section *C* that, in addition to average percent-correct scores for Johnson School in each of the major curricular areas, results for each content strata are also given for (1) the building, (2) the school system (school district), and (3) the nation. By comparing the building's average with that of the system, areas of strength and weakness can be identified. For example, relative to the system, the building was quite strong in math computations involving whole numbers but fell below the system in problems involving fractions and decimals. Relative to the nation, however, the system may be "robbing Peter to pay Paul"—the very high performance in "Fractions" and "Decimals" appears to come at the expense of "Whole Numbers." Information such as that given in Figure 14–3 can help diagnose instructional and curricular weaknesses of a class, school, and especially school district. Identifying areas of weakness is the first step

Iowa Tests of Basic Skills

Service 3: Building Criterion-Referenced Skills Analysis

Sample (A)

Building: **JOHNSON ELEM**
Bldg. Code:
System: RIVER FALLS ISD
Norms: SPRING 1992
Order No.: 000-005926-001 ===

Grade: 5
Level: 11
Form: K
Test Date: 05/93
Page: 42

N Tested = 63

Avg Standard Score
PR of Avg SS: Nat'l Student Norms
PR of Avg SS: Nat'l School Norms

Summary (top table)

	READING			LANGUAGE					MATHEMATICS			CORE TOTAL	SOURCES OF INFO.					COM-POSITE	MATH COMPU-TATION
	VOCAB-ULARY	COMPRE-HENSION	TOTAL	SPELL-ING	CAPITAL-IZATION	PUNC-TUATION	USAGE/EXPRESS	TOTAL	CON-CEPTS/ESTIM	PROBS/DATA INTERP	TOTAL		SOCIAL STUD-IES	SCI-ENCE	MAPS & DIA-GRAMS	REF-MATLS	TOTAL		
N	63	63	63	63	63	63	63	63	63	63	63	63	63	63	63	63	63	63	63
Avg Standard Score	215.5	207.9	211.7	203.8	200.4	214.3	216.8	208.5	206.2	208.5	204.9	208.8	212.6	217.1	209.8	205.8	207.8	210.5	202.0
PR Nat'l Student Norms	61	54	57	57	33	71	69	58	51	57	52	57	59	70	54	52	53	59	51
PR Nat'l School Norms	70	53	61	48															

* Includes Mathematics Computation

Skills (B)

Skills	Building Count	System Count	Number of Items	Avg Number Attempted Building	Avg Number Correct Building	Avg Percent Correct Building	Avg Percent Correct System	Avg Percent Correct Nation
VOCABULARY	63	152	37	36	22	59	63	56
READING COMPREHENSION	63	152	41	37	23	58	63	56
Construct Factual Meaning			15	14	9	57	57	57
Construct Inferential Meaning			14	12	7	51	56	57
Construct Evaluative Meaning			12	11	7	59	58	45
SPELLING	63	152	34	30 (C)	19	56	57	58
Root Words			12	18	12	57	52	58
Words with Affixes			21	8	7	49	52	50
Correct Spelling				5	5	60	53	73
CAPITALIZATION	63	152	27	26	16	59	62	62
Names and Titles				7	2	1	47	25
Dates and Holidays				3	3	63	66	66
Place Names				5	3	52	57	67
Names of Organizations and Groups				6	3	50	55	45
Linguistic and Literary Conventions				6	3	61	55	64
Overcapitalization/Correct Cap				5	3	49	56	60
PUNCTUATION	63	152	27	24	15	54	54	55
Terminal Punctuation				10	8	57	57	55
Comma				8	3	48	50	43
Other Punctuatin Mrks				6	3	53	53	48
Overuse/Correct Use				6	3	59	59	66
USAGE AND EXPRESSION	63	152	40	37	22	54	61	53
Usage			20	18	10	50	54	48
Verb Forms				8	2	41	45	27
Pronouns; Modifiers				6	3	45	38	40
Other Linguistic Conventions			13	6	3	72	72	78
Correct Usage				19	13	64	66	88
Expression				11	7	68	71	86
Conciseness & Clarity				10	5	62	62	85
Appropriate Use of Language				7	3	71	71	42
Organization of Ideas				8	4	55	55	58
MATH CONCEPTS & ESTIMATION	63	152	44	40	24	55	59	62
Concepts			26	23	15	58	51	62
Numeration and Operations				9	8	58	58	65
Geometry				3	2	52	52	60
Measurement				4	2	65	65	61
Fractions/Decimals/Percents				3	2	56	56	49
Probability and Statistics				3	2	67	67	68
Equations and Inequalities			18	13	9	63	60	66
Estimation				7	4	60	52	48
Standard Rounding				11	6	57	57	58
Order of Magnitude				4	4	49	58	58
Compensation				7	3	46	61	31

Skills (D)

Skills	Building Count	System Count	Number of Items	Avg Number Attempted Building	Avg Number Correct Building	Avg Percent Correct Building	Avg Percent Correct System	Avg Percent Correct Nation
PROBLEMS & DATA INTERP.	63	152	30	29	17	57	54	56
Problem-Solving			17	17	8	49	44	54
Single-Step: Add & Subtract				5	2	43	38	54
Single-Step: Multiply & Divide				6	1	48	25	52
Multiple-Step				4	3	48	55	52
Problem-Solving Strategies			13	12	9	50	43	54
Data Interpretation				4	3	71	81	54
Read Amounts				4	3	100	100	76
Compare Quantities				4	3	55	82	49
Interpret Relationships			38	5	3	64	85	58
SOCIAL STUDIES	63	152	40	4	3	64	64	58
History				11	7	48	54	53
Geography			12	5	3	61	35	62
Economics				4	1	51	63	64
Political Science				3	2	53	63	54
Sociology/Anthropology				4	3	100	80	54
Related Social Sciences			39	6	26	62	52	47
SCIENCE	63	152	40	6	6	54	52	53
Nature of Science			12	11	6	63	60	53
Life Science			12	11	7	61	59	55
Earth and Space			10	10	7	61	60	53
Physical Sciences			27	27	16	57	53	55
MAPS AND DIAGRAMS	63	152	13	13	7	38	35	55
Map Reading				5	1	51	48	55
Locate and Describe Places				5	2	49	70	44
Determine Direction and Distance				2	1	100	55	54
Interpret Data			14	14	3	65	64	56
Behavior and Living Conditions				6	3	59	59	57
Diagrams and Charts				5	4	75	72	59
Locate Information				3	2	68	77	74
Infer Processes or Products			32	18	18	58	53	60
Compare and Contrast Features				6	2	42	28	68
REFERENCE MATERIALS	63	152		6	2	39	23	57
Alphabetizing				7	4	61	59	53
Table of Contents				4	2	63	75	50
Dictionary				4	2	56	43	50
Library Card Catalog: Read				5	2	70	89	61
Encyclopedia			35	23	60	53	55	
General Reference Materials			25	16	58	44	82	
MATH COMPUTATION	63	152	39	29	6	63	63	78
Whole Numbers				6	4	63	63	61
Fractions			26	25	14	52	48	61
Decimals				26	16	55	51	58
THINKING SKILLS	63	152						
Focusing/Information-Gathering			81	58	47	58	56	55
Remembering			160	154	82	51	53	54
Organizing			63	61	31	49	54	53
Analyzing								
Generating			23	20	12	50	48	53
Integrating/Evaluating								

The Riverside Publishing Company — a Houghton Mifflin company toward correcting that weakness; by revealing such areas, the tests can serve an important educational and quality control function.

In addition to national norms, there are other important comparisons facilitated by standardized achievement tests. By comparing results on the same tests and grade levels from previous years, one has a basis for comparison that can be useful for detecting trends in gains and losses within a school or district. It is important not only to know how the students fare compared to a national sample but also whether progress is being made within the school and district.

14.8   SCHOOL VERSUS INDIVIDUAL NORMS

Some tests provide school norms as well as individual student norms, as in Figure 14–3. In Figure 14–4 the two distributions are compared: (1) the distributions of school averages versus (2) the distribution of the individual student scores. Note that the variability in students' scores is much greater than for school averages. For example, Figure 14–4 shows that for beginning fifth-grade students, a national grade equivalent (NGE) score in reading of 4.0 falls at the 22nd percentile in student norms. However, if a school has an average NGE reading of 4.0, it falls at the 3rd percentile. In other words, for students tested in the fall of grade five, 22 students in 100 earn scores of 4.0 or less, whereas only three schools in 100 have an average NGE of 4.0 or less.

School norms are of no interest for interpreting individual performance, but they are of great interest to the school and school district. Notice in Section A of Figure 14–3 that the percentile ranks for the average scores is given both in terms of the student and school norms. In reading vocabulary, the average student was at the 61st percentile, but this average placed the school at the 70th percentile in the school norms. On the capitalization test, however, the median student score was at the 45th percentile, but the school mean was at the 33rd percentile.

Later in this chapter, guidelines are given for selecting standardized tests for a school's testing program. In addition to the logical relevance of the items, the adequacy of the norms, and other technical considerations, one should appraise the kinds of service available, the time

---

FIGURE 14–3 (ON FACING PAGE)   A sample report of a school's and system's performance by content strata, together with corresponding national averages.

(by permission of the Riverside Publishing Company.)

In Figure 14–3, area

A gives summary data for each test and the composite. Percentile ranks indicate performance for the average student compared to other students in the nation and the performance of the school in comparison to other schools using school norms.

B gives the number of students who took each test in the building and district.

C gives, for each skill category, the number of items, the average number of items attempted, and the average number correct for the school, the district, and the nation.

D gives performance on the items across the entire battery that measure critical thinking skills.

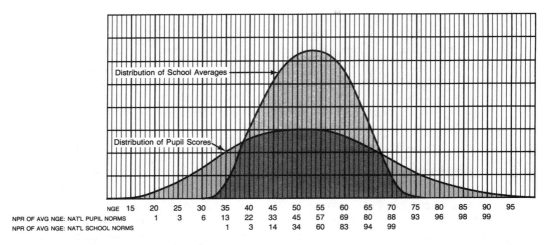

NGE	15	20	25	30	35	40	45	50	55	60	65	70	75	80	85	90	95
NPR OF AVG NGE: NAT'L PUPIL NORMS		1	3	6	13	22	33	45	57	69	80	88	93	96	98	99	
NPR OF AVG NGE: NAT'L SCHOOL NORMS					1	3	14	34	60	83	94	99					

FIGURE 14–4 A comparison of the Distribution of the Scores of Individual Students with the Distribution of School Averages, Grade 5 Reading. (by permission of the Riverside Publishing Company.)

lag between testing and results, and the types of student, parent, class, school, and district reports.

14.9 INTERPRETING GRADE EQUIVALENTS

The use of grade-equivalent (GE) norms is one of the most common methods for reporting results on standardized achievement tests in grades 1–8. To interpret grade-equivalent scores properly, one must understand how the grade equivalents are established. How can a fifth-grade child earn a reading score of 8.0 on a test? *Interpolation* and *extrapolation* are two procedures used in establishing grade equivalents.

Suppose that in the norming sample a reading test is given at the beginning of the school year to students in grades 4, 5, and 6. The medians (or means) for each of the three grade levels are determined—suppose the raw score means were 24, 40, and 47 (see Figure 14–5). By definition, the respective grade equivalents corresponding to these three scores are 4.0, 5.0, and 6.0. In other words, if a sixth grade student correctly answered only 24 of the reading items, the student's GE score is 4.0, since a raw score of 24 is the median score at the beginning of grade 4.0. How does one arrive at GE scores between 4.0 and 5.0, and between 5.0 and 6.0—how is a GE of 4.5 obtained? GE scores between 4.0 and 5.0, and 5.0 and 6.0 are determined by interpolation: The difference in the raw score means of 4.0 and 5.0 is divided into tenths; each tenth corresponds to a GE of .1 (one month). A raw score of 32 yields a GE of 4.5 because 32 is half the distance between 24 and 40. Using Figure 14–5, confirm that a raw score of 45 translates into a GE score of approximately 5.6.

This interpolation procedure assumes a constant rate of growth throughout the year. Empirical studies have demonstrated that this assumption only roughly approximates the true growth curves in various achievement areas. There are such marked discrepancies in math over the summer that the same group of students may average as much as 0.5 GE less at the

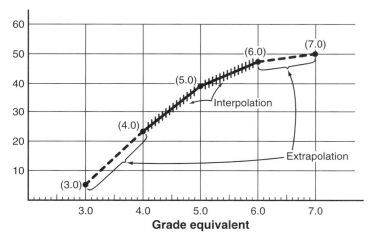

FIGURE 14–5 Illustration of interpolation and extrapolation in establishing grade-equivalent norms.

beginning of the school year than they did the previous June! The same phenomenon is evident, of course, irrespective of the particular norms used to describe performance—GEs, percentiles, NCEs, or standard scores. Fortunately, the rusty skills are quickly restored because beginning-of-year review is part of the instruction design in standard mathematics textbooks. *The best way to reduce interpolation artifacts from contaminating the meaning of scores from standardized achievement tests is to administer the tests during the same period in the school year that was employed in the standardization process.* If an unscrupulous administrator wanted to use the test results as propaganda to exaggerate the amount of achievement growth during the school year, pretests would be given during the first week of classes before there was much opportunity for review. It is not improbable that, according to the GE norms, it would appear that 1.5 years "growth" took place during the school year.

For a few standardized achievement tests the artifacts from interpolation are reduced by testing at the beginning, middle, and end of the school year in the norming process. Norms for most tests, however, were established from a single administration period during the school year; hence, they must rely more heavily on the validity of the interpolation process.

Extrapolation can result in even greater errors in the interpretation of scores on standardized achievement tests. Extrapolation is the most common method for establishing GE values at grade levels *outside* the range of grades to which the test was actually administered. It is simply a projection of the average performance at some grade levels from the performance of students at certain other grade levels. In our interpolation example (Figure 14–5), the raw score means were 24, 40, and 47 for the standardization sample at grades 4.0, 5.0, and 6.0, respectively. This pattern leads one to assume that the mean score at grade 7 would be approximately 50; hence, a raw score of 50 would receive a GE of 7.0. Similarly, a score of 5 might be predicted to correspond to the average performance at grade 3.0. Extrapolation is obviously a risky process. As the GE values extend beyond the grade levels actually sampled during the norming, their credibility is lessened. Fortunately, there is an increasing ten-

TABLE 14–1 Standard Deviations in Grade Equivalents for Various Subjects on the Iowa Test of Basic Skills at Grades 3, 5, and 8

Type of Test	Grade Level		
	3	5	8
Vocabulary	1.1	1.4	2.0
Reading	1.0	1.4	1.9
Spelling	1.2	1.6	2.2
Language total	1.1	1.4	2.0
Work-study total	.9	1.2	1.8
Arithmetic total	.8	1.1	1.7
Composite	.9	1.2	1.7

SOURCE: Based on data from *Test Manual, Iowa Test of Basic Skills.*

dency in test norming to administer a test above and below the actual grade levels for which it was designed to provide a more legitimate basis for attaching meaning to the GE scores.

A distinct advantage of GE scores at the elementary school level is that they help teachers realize the enormous extent of individual differences within a single grade level. Figure 14–6 depicts the actual distribution of performance for grades 2.6 to 10.6. Note the very large degree of overlap in adjacent distributions. For example, about one-sixth of third-grade students are performing better than the average fourth-grade student.

Table 14–1 shows that the variability in achievement increases with each successive grade level in each curricular area. Note how the standard deviations on the *Iowa Tests of Basic Skills* (*ITBS*) differ at grades 3, 5, and 8. Note, for example, that the standard deviation in Reading at grade 3 is 1.0, hence 16 percent of grade 3 students would be expected to earn GE scores of 4.0 or higher on this test. At grade 8, the standard deviation is approximately twice as large as at grade 3. This is to be expected, because the rate of growth of bright students is greater than the rate of growth of average and below average students.

One limitation of grade equivalent scores is that they can easily be misinterpreted, especially by parents. "If my fifth-grade child, Jane, tested near the end of grade 5, obtained a GE score of 7.5 in reading, why shouldn't she be allowed to skip sixth grade?" Parents, and some teachers, are unaware of the large degree of individual differences among the students within a given grade, as illustrated in Figure 14–6. They do not realize that 10 to 20 percent of the

FIGURE 14–6 (ON FACING PAGE) An illustration of the great degree of overlap in students' achievement performance among grade levels. (Note that approximately one-sixth of grade 2 students [i.e., @ 2.6] received better scores than one-half of grade 3 students [i.e., @ 3.6]. Similarly, approximately one-sixth of grade 3 students received lower scores than one-half of the students in grade 2.

SOURCE: Technical Memo, Expanded Standard Scale used in the CTBS. reprinted by permission of the publisher, CTB/McGraw-Hill, Monterey, Calif.

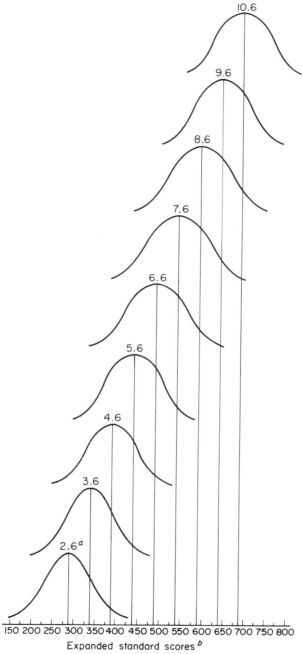

Expanded standard scores [b]

[a]Test administered during sixth month of school year; grade equivalents of corresponding
standard scores are given above the mean of each curve.
[b]Scale employs a mean of 600 and a standard deviation of 100 at grade 9.1.

students in the same fifth-grade class will have reading GE scores of 7.0 or more. The percentage will be even greater in schools in which the verbal aptitude is above average.

Currently there is much public support for setting minimum achievement standards for promotion from one grade to the next. The data given in Table 14–1 should be sufficient to show that the implications could be catastrophic if, for example, a seventh grade student is not promoted to grade 8 unless the reading score at the end of grade 7 is at least 7.0. Such a requirement would cause approximately 30 percent of the seventh grade students to repeat grade 7.

Another problem with GE scores is that the standard deviations in GE units are not uniform in all curricular areas. The variability in reading and language tends to be somewhat greater than in arithmetic. If a child in grade 3 (3.0) is at the 98th percentile (2σ above the mean, or a z-score of +2.0) on all areas on the *ITBS*, the GE scores will vary from about 5.4 for spelling to 4.6 for arithmetic. If percentile ranks are reported along with GEs, the chance of misinterpretation is reduced. Despite their technical flaws, percentile ranks are probably the preferred method of reporting achievement and aptitude test results to parents. Percentiles should not be used in statistical analyses, however, because of the great inequality in their units (for example, the percentile equivalent of the average score should be used, not the average percentile. Similarly, if a child's IQ scores on three aptitude tests (verbal, quantitative, and nonverbal) are 145, 100, and 130, the average score of 125 is near the 95th percentile, whereas the average percentile score is only 83 [(99.9 + 50 + 98)/3].

The classic statement by one of the prime movers in standardized achievement testing, John Flanagan, remains true today:

> In spite of their many limitations, they [grade equivalents] probably represent the best of available methods for rendering scores "comparable" for elementary school achievement tests . . . To date the consensus seems to be in favor of the use of grade equivalent scales below grade eight, and some type of [standard score] in high school and college. (Flanagan (1951, pp. 712–13)

The lack of continuity in subject matter after grade 8 is a major reason that the logical meaning of GE scores is greatly reduced beyond that grade. There is little growth in certain basic skills during high school; consequently, a small increment in performance often results in a large gain in grade placement units. For example, a raw score of 18 on the *CTBS Language-Mechanics Test* corresponds to a GE score of 10.1, but a raw score of only one point higher (19) corresponds to a GE score of 11.9! These data reflect the smallness of the improvement typically made in the eleventh grade on the type of language mechanics measured by this test.

14.10 LONGITUDINAL STUDY OF INDIVIDUAL PROGRESS

Most standardized tests are accompanied by "expanded" or "developmental" standard score scales that can be useful for evaluating student and school growth sequentially across several years. These are continuous scales that span several levels of a test. Figure 14–7 illustrates the growth curves of (1) a group and (2) a student from grade 2 to grade 12. Notice that at grade 8 the student begins to fall behind the class in performance. This type of report is particularly valuable in evaluating the progress of an individual or group.

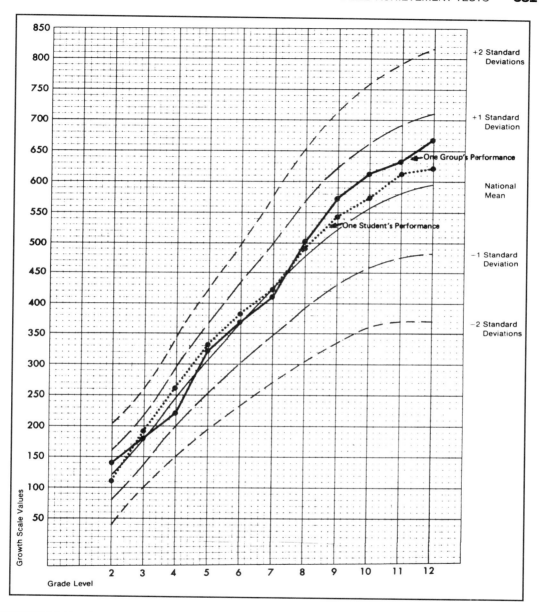

FIGURE 14–7   Growth curves for one class and for one student in the class for grades 2 through 12. Individual growth scale curves allow a student's performance to be compared both in relation to the group's performance and in relation to national performance.

SOURCE: Reproduced by permission of the publisher, Science Research Associates. Copyright by Science Research Associates, Inc.

When scores are to be compared statistically between two or more groups, raw scores or standard scores are preferable to GE scores because of possible artifacts associated with extrapolation. However, GE scores are better than percentile ranks (Section 3.4). Although it is always desirable when comparing two groups to report medians as well as means, it is especially important when GE or percentile scores are used.

14.11 DIAGNOSTIC USE OF TEST RESULTS

One of the principal uses of standardized achievement and academic aptitude tests is to identify students who need special education attention. Dual standardization (Section 14.6) is very common today—students in the norming population are given both a battery of achievement tests and a scholastic aptitude test. It is then possible to compare a student's achievement with that of students at the same grade level and with the same measured scholastic aptitude. The student's "expectancy" or "anticipated achievement" can be approached empirically. This method of identifying underachieving students is far superior to that of comparing a student's percentile ranks on an intelligence test with those on an achievement test—a procedure that will always find a large proportion of bright students to be "underachieving" and a corresponding proportion of students with low IQs to be achieving "well" in relation to their aptitude. Comparison of percentile ranks fails to acknowledge the universal regression effect (Hopkins, 1969; Shepard & Hopkins, 1977).

Figure 14–8 depicts a standard report form for "Joseph Lawrence, a fifth-grade student who took the *Iowa Tests of Basic Skills* (*ITBS*) and the *Cognitive Abilities Test* (*CogAT*). The tests were taken during April—the seventh month of the school year (actual grade placement of 5.7). In the lower left-hand corner his results on the three aptitude measures are given; his SAS (IQ) scores were 121, 102 and 93 for the Verbal, Quantitative, and Nonverbal tests, respectively. The national percentiles for these tests are expressed graphically, revealing above average performance in Verbal ability but below average performance in the other two ability tests.

Joseph's performance on the achievement (*ITBS*) is expressed in grade equivalents (GE), national stanines (NS), and national percentile ranks (NPR), and shown in the dark bars for each subtest. Joseph's anticipated or predicted scores, using as predictors the three aptitude measures (verbal, quantitative, and non-verbal) of the *CogAT,* are given in the first two columns in the *ITBS* panel. The average score on each subtest for persons like Joseph in the norming sample who are Joseph's statistical twins is the PGE score (predicted grade equivalent) and PNPR score(national percentile rank). When the discrepancy between the obtained and predicted GE scores is large enough to warrant special attention, the gray bar corresponding to the PNPR is graphed. Note that Joseph scored below expectation in Reading Comprehension, Usage & Expression, Core (the three Rs) Total, Science, and the Composite. Where no gray bar appears in the graph, the difference between the obtained and predicted performance is not large enough to be significant.

The report of a student's performance in such a complete and explicit form has become feasible only since computers became part of the test scoring and reporting process. This kind of test reporting can reduce over and under interpretation of standardized test results.

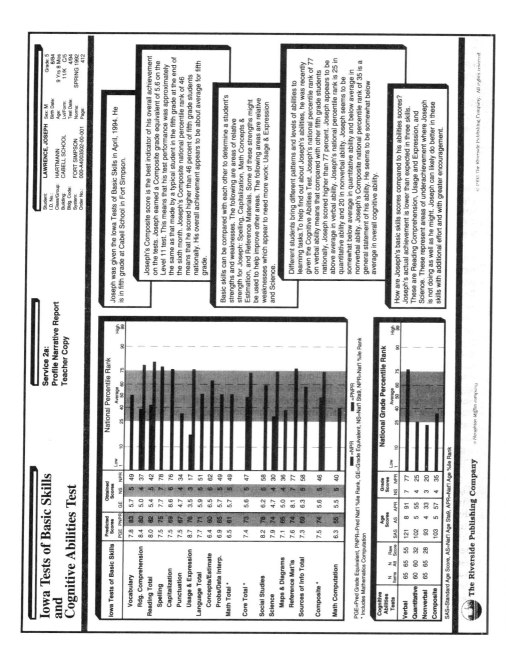

FIGURE 14–8 Sample Test Report Form to Describe Performance of a Student on a Battery of Standardized Achievement Tests and a Companion Academic Aptitude Battery. (Reproduced by permission of the publisher, the Riverside Publishing Company.)

14.12 CONTENT VALIDITY OF STANDARDIZED ACHIEVEMENT TESTS: THE SAMPLING OF THE CONTENT UNIVERSE

A test cannot have high content validity unless the items are a representative sample of the curricular objectives in skills and content (Chapter 7). The upper portion of Figure 14–9 shows that in certain curricular areas, such as reading, there exists a large common core of content, objectives, and sequence of instruction among school districts and states. The lower portion of the figure represents certain other curricular areas in which there is only a small common core. In social studies, for example, there are great differences in content and instructional approaches among states, among school districts, and even among schools within a district. This lack of curricular commonality has created severe obstacles to developing highly content-valid standardized tests (Freeman et al., 1983), especially in these areas. Test developers tend to assess only within the common core of content and objectives; hence, the items are not a representative sample for any school or district—the objectives measured are only a limited subset of the school's or district's objectives. This is especially true in social studies and science, which have the smallest degree of curricular commonality; for instance, it is common in grade 4 to study one's own state, which obviously cannot

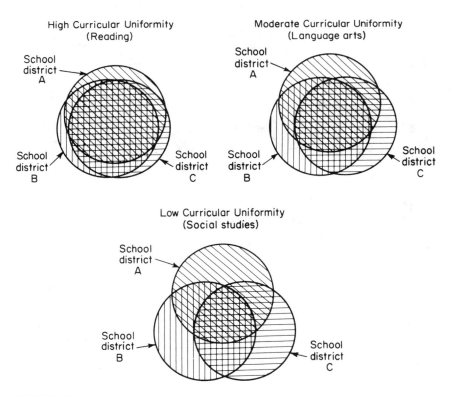

FIGURE 14–9 Graphic illustrations of the "core of curricular commonality" among American elementary schools for curricula with high, moderate, and low uniformity.

be included in a national test. Thus, standardized tests in social studies and science do not *represent* the school's curriculum as well as tests in reading and math do. This is the principal reason that standardized reading (and, to a lesser extent, math) tests have greater content validity than standardized achievement tests in other curricular areas (Hopkins, George & Williams, 1985).

14.13 TEACHERS' RATINGS AS VALIDATION CRITERIA

The differential validity pattern just described is corroborated when teachers' ratings of students' performance levels are employed as a criterion for validity. When teachers are properly oriented to rate (or rank) the extent to which their students have achieved curricular objectives in reading, the resulting ratings correlate very highly with scores obtained on reliable standardized reading tests. (Obviously, not all standardized tests are good tests.) These correlations often fall in the .7 to .8 range, which is extremely high, sometimes approaching the parallel-form reliability of the reading test (Farr & Roelke, 1971; Hopkins, Dobson & Oldridge, 1962; Pedulla, Airasian & Madaus, 1980). If these correlations are corrected for attenuation due to measurement error, they often approach .90 (Hopkins, George & Williams, 1985). In other words, in less than an hour the better standardized reading tests can provide an objective assessment that is confirmed by the assessment of a professional based on many hours of careful observation in a wide variety of contexts. Thus, to assert, as some critics have, that multiple-choice tests are only "guessing games" and that the tests have little validity is in the same breath an indictment of the professional competence of teachers and reading specialists (Farr & Roelke, 1971).

Correlations between standardized achievement tests and school marks tend to be substantial (.5 to .6); the correlations are considerably higher with teachers' ratings of proficiency levels, no doubt because marks are alloyed with grading philosophy, effort, deportment, and other factors that are irrelevant to the purposes of standardized achievement tests—the measurement of proficiency.

Using teachers' ratings as a validity criterion, reading tests have the greatest validity, followed by math, language arts, science, and social studies tests, in roughly that order. When interpreting results from standardized achievement tests, either at the student level or at the class, school, district, or state level, this factor must be considered—reading and math scores should be taken more seriously than scores in social studies and science.

14.14 "OUT-OF-LEVEL" TESTING

A standardized test designed for a particular grade level sometimes is inappropriate in difficulty for a given school, class, or student. If the average IQ score of a fourth-grade class is 85 or 90, more valid scores will result if the "out-of-level" test designed for grade 3 is used. When a test is too difficult for a class or a given student, gambling, speed-versus-accuracy response styles, and chance can result in misleading and invalid scores. In one large inner-city school district (Wick, 1983), when students were given the usual standardized test for their grade level, 42 percent of the students earned chance scores (Section 6.12) or below. Unfortunately, some students, without even reading the items on the test but who guess on all questions, will receive higher GE or percentile scores than they will if they were administered the test at the appropriate difficulty level (Hopkins, 1964a; Swan & Hopkins, 1965; Wick, 1983).

The user of standardized tests must realize that the entire educational story is not represented by the results from those tests. The widely used batteries of standardized achievement tests typically ignore one of the 3 Rs, writing, because of the difficulty and expense associated with essay tests. The important educational skill of listening is also missing from most tests. Neither are affective educational objectives. Standardized test data are important, but they are only fragments of the picture—and there are fewer fragments in certain curricular areas than in others.

14.15 SPECIAL PROBLEMS OF STANDARDIZED TESTING IN HIGH SCHOOL

The nature of the curriculum changes radically from elementary school to high school. In the elementary grades the curriculum is usually quite similar for all the students in a school district but at the high school level considerable *branching* occurs. There is great flexibility even in college preparatory programs. The common curriculum for all high school students has virtually disappeared, except perhaps in English, although there is some trend toward returning to certain core subjects. The lack of curricular uniformity is a major reason for the fact that there is little meaning in grade-equivalent units for most content areas after grade 8 or 9.

Two approaches have been initiated toward solving the problem of standardized testing in the secondary schools. One approach is represented by the *Iowa Tests of Educational Development* (*ITED*). The *ITED* are general education tests. They predict subsequent performance on the College Board examinations and academic success in college quite well. The tests in the *ITED* battery are the following:

1. Vocabulary
2. Content Area Reading
3. Expression Advanced Skills
4. Expression
5. Quantitative Advanced Skills
6. Quantitative Thinking
7. Literary Materials
8. Social Studies
9. Science
10. Sources of Information

The test titles indicate the general nature of the *ITED* tests. But this *general* nature is a two-edged sword. The ITED do not presuppose a fixed set of courses for the examinees; nevertheless, the general nature of the examination severely limits their value for the evaluation of the quality of learning and instruction in specific courses such as algebra I, American history, or chemistry.

The second approach to standardized testing at the high school level offers tailor-made tests for specific courses and subjects. These tests are less general and more content-oriented than the *ITED* tests. Examples of such tests are the *Nelson Biology Tests*, the *MLA Cooperative Foreign Language Tests*, the *Lankton First-Year Algebra Test*, the *Purdue High School English Test*, the *Anderson-Fisk Chemistry Test*, the *Crary American History Test*, and the College Entrance Examination Board achievement and advanced placement tests.

The two approaches can be used so that they are mutually complementary. The course-oriented examinations are of greater value in identifying specific weaknesses in a particular curriculum. They offer the teacher or department useful feedback on teaching success because norms on an external reference group are available. The general achievement tests are better as a *general* educational quality control measure, but they are not of great value in identifying specific educational deficiencies in a high school or a curriculum.

In addition to the tests mentioned, there is a set of standardized subject examinations for college courses (*CLEP,* the *College Level Examination Program*) used primarily to give people who have acquired their education by unconventional means a chance to receive advanced placement and college credit at many colleges. Tests are available in American government, general psychology, geology, Western civilization, English literature, and approximately 50 other subjects. Also, standardized achievement tests in most college majors—the GRE Advanced Tests—are widely used as one of the criteria for admission to graduate degree programs.

14.16   THE NATIONAL ASSESSMENT OF EDUCATIONAL PROGRESS

The U.S. Office of Education (now the Department of Education) was formed "for the purpose of collecting such statistics and facts as shall show the condition and progress of education in the several states . . . and of diffusing such information" (Act of Congress, March 2, 1867). Despite that century-old charge, the federal government only relatively recently began to collect meaningful data on the quality of education in U.S. schools.

In 1964, the Carnegie Corporation and the Ford Foundation were instrumental in the establishment of a committee under the chairmanship of Ralph Tyler to explore the feasibility of procedures for securing dependable information that could become a barometer of the progress of education. The committee developed a careful plan to assess achievement at four age levels: 9, following the primary grades; 13, following elementary school; 17, the last age before heavy dropout from school occurs; and young adults. In 1983, the National Assessment of Educational Progress (NAEP) began sampling by grade, as well as by age. Public and private schools are sampled. Not only are the achievements of the total U.S. population considered, but certain subpopulations in the country can be viewed separately. The large sample of students at each age and grade level is broken down by several factors such as sex, race/ethnicity, region (Northeast, Southeast, Central, and West), type of community (large city, smaller city, and rural small town), and socioeconomic level. Table 14–2 presents illustrative findings for a recent assessment in writing.

Selected curricular areas (reading, writing, science, mathematics, social studies, literature, music, art, citizenship, career and occupational development, and related affective

TABLE 14–2 Illustrative NAEP Findings: Writing. Percentiles and Standard Deviations for the Nation, Race/Ethnicity, and Gender, Grades 4, 8, and 12

				PERCENTILES				
	σ	5	10	25	50	75	90	9 5
GRADE 4								
Nation	41	153	169	195	**222**	250	273	287
White	38	166	180	204	**230**	256	279	291
Black	38	132	146	170	**196**	221	244	257
Hispanic	41	141	156	182	**209**	236	259	273
Asian	40	166	178	206	**235**	262	281	297
Am.Indian	40	154	166	188	**213**	241	265	279
Male	40	148	164	189	**216**	243	266	280
Female	41	159	176	202	**229**	256	280	293
GRADE 8								
Nation	38	198	213	236	**262**	288	310	323
White	36	208	221	244	**268**	293	314	327
Black	36	183	195	218	**242**	266	287	300
Hispanic	37	186	200	223	**248**	273	296	309
Asian	40	200	214	240	**268**	295	318	330
Am.Indian	39	177	194	221	**254**	276	297	307
Male	37	190	204	227	**252**	277	299	313
Female	36	211	225	248	**272**	296	317	330
GRADE 12								
Nation	40	218	233	259	**287**	314	338	351
White	39	225	240	265	**292**	318	341	354
Black	39	204	219	241	**268**	293	318	333
Hispanic	40	209	224	250	**278**	305	328	340
Asian	41	221	237	265	**294**	320	343	358
Am.Indian	42	199	214	240	**270**	298	324	338
Male	40	208	224	248	**276**	303	326	340
Female	38	232	246	271	**297**	223	345	358

SOURCE: National Assessment of Educational Progress (NAEP), 1992 Writing Assessment.

variables) are covered by means of a cycling approach; each subject matter field is assessed about every five years.

In order to prevent any invidious comparisons and pressures to teach for the tests, results are not pinpointed by class, school district, or states. The assessment reporting plan calls for the withholding of part of the exercises in each subject area so that they may be reused in the next assessment cycle for purposes of comparison. The NAEP promises "to provide useful indicators of educational progress." The NAEP data offer strong evidence for the "achievement decline."

14.17 THE SCHOOL TESTING PROGRAM

It is the exception rather than the rule when a school district invests the time and effort necessary for a sound program of evaluation and testing. The tests selected and used too often depend more on the quality of the publishers' salespeople than on the quality of the product. There is rarely a systematic program to help teachers properly interpret and use the results of the tests. It is not surprising that many teachers question the value of standardized testing. Tests are only tools. Measurement is always a means to an end, never an end in itself. Thus, the value of any testing program depends on the use made of results. An experienced educator was once heard to say that he had wondered for years what many people did with standardized tests after they had been given. At last he found out. They filed them! Little instructional use is often made of standardized test results above the elementary school level.

The initial step in planning a testing program is to make its purposes explicit. The most common purposes include the following:

1. *Quality control and public accountability.* National norms can provide a meaningful reference group for assessing the general level of academic achievement of a school or school district, especially when considered in relation to level of scholastic aptitude and socioeconomic factors. The taxpayers have a right to know the general level of academic achievement in their schools. The achievement trends within the district can also be monitored to determine, for example, whether the district is escaping the achievement decline. Annual reporting of test results can enhance professional credibility and public relations.

2. *Curricular and program evaluation.* Standardized tests can be a useful yardstick for identifying strengths and weaknesses in the curriculum and special programs. For example, parents of Spanish-speaking children in one bilingual program were concerned that the time spent in Spanish instruction might impede their children's progress in English. Comparing the students' test performance to that of similar students at the same school and grade levels for the previous year was useful in this regard. Another school found substantial gains in standardized test means in reading, English, and math following a new, more individualized instructional design (Klausmeier, 1982).

3. *Individual student assessment and diagnosis.* Standardized tests can serve as an objective measure of the general level of educational attainment of particular students. This level of attainment can be compared with that of students of similar aptitude nationwide in order to identify a student's strengths and deficiencies. Achievement trends over grade level can be studied for the student. Other related purposes include grouping, identifying underachievers, identifying the academically talented, and helping students make appropriate educational and vocational choices. Routinely, standardized test results should be communicated to the students' parents to help them

arrive at a realistic understanding of the child's achievement status and progress. Exemplary schools had a policy of school-home communication and disclosure of relevant information long before the Buckley Amendment was passed.[1]

The testing program should be a cooperative enterprise. Parents, teachers, and administrators should be made to feel that it is "their" program, as indeed it should be. This is not likely to occur if the principal, superintendent, or research department determines the program and then "hands it down" to classroom teachers. The entire staff and community should have a voice in determining the purpose of the program and in formulating the plans; they should have the opportunity to participate in it in every possible way from beginning to end. If this is not done, the teachers are not likely to understand the program fully or to appreciate what it is attempting to achieve. It is better to entrust the responsibility of planning the program to a committee representing all interested groups. The success of the program depends largely on cooperative action. An important part of the program is thus conducting a needs-assessment survey of parents, students, teachers, administrators, and school board members.

On the basis of the district's needs, a testing program should be proposed, including which curricular areas are to be tested at each grade level. Figure 14–10 represents the testing program of one outstanding school district.

14.18 SELECTING THE APPROPRIATE TEST(S)

After the purposes of the testing program have been determined, the test or tests must be selected. Tests with the same title may differ greatly in quality; beware of the "jingle fallacy" (Section 14.3).

Criteria for test selection should be established against which available tests will be screened. These criteria should include content validity (especially the taxonomy level of items), reliability, recency of norms, representativeness of norms, availability of item-level norms, testing time required, ease of administration, scoring, co-norming with a comparison scholastic aptitude test, types of converted scores available, articulation across grade levels, and costs and reporting aids and services.

---

[1]The Buckley Amendment (the Family Educational Rights and Privacy Act of 1974 and the Educational Amendments Act of 1974) demands that all public schools must, on request, make test results available to students and/or their parents. Specifically, parents are given the right to inspect and review any and all official records, files, and data directly related to their children, including all material that is incorporated into each student's cumulative record folder and intended for school use to be available to parties outside the school or school system, and specifically including, but not necessarily limited to, identifying data, academic work completed, level of achievement (grades, standardized achievement test scores), attendance data, scores on standardized intelligence, aptitude, and psychological tests, interest inventory results, health data, family background information, teacher or counselor ratings and observations, and verified reports of serious or recurrent behavior patterns. Although the federal government has no direct constitutional authority over educational agencies, the control is exerted indirectly through threats to discontinue federal funds to schools that do not operate according to federal prescriptions.

	Grade level											
	1	**2**	**3**	**4**	**5**	**6**	**7**	**8**	**9**	**10**	**11**	**12**
Reading	√	√	√	√	√	√	√		√		√	
Mathematics	√	√	√	√	√	√	√		√		√	
Language Arts			√	√	√	√	√		√		√	
Science						√	√	√	√		√		√
Social Studies					√	√	√	√		√		√	
Scholastic Aptitude			√	√	√	√	√		√		√	
*School-Related Attitudes					√			√		√		√	

*Results on these measures are not reported for individual students.

FIGURE 14–10 An illustrative standardized testing program for a school district.

Standardized tests differ considerably with respect to technical and nontechnical criteria. In one analysis, seven major achievement batteries varied in required testing time (from 161 to 480 minutes), average minutes per subtest (from 16 to 65 minutes), and cost (by a factor of 3 or more) (Stanley & Hopkins, 1972, p. 420).

14.19 LOCATING AVAILABLE STANDARDIZED TESTS

Users of standardized tests will find information in *Tests in Print* and *The Mental Measurements Yearbook* (MMY) to be of great value (see Appendix A). The breadth of available published measures is indicated by the ninth edition of MMY (1985); Table 14–3 gives the number of tests in each of its major categories.

The Mental Measurements Yearbook presents critical reviews on every published test. Unless a test is very new, it has probably been reviewed in the *MMY;* usually these reviews are very helpful. In addition to the *MMY,* the *Journal of Educational Measurement, Measurement and Evaluation in Guidance, Applied Psychological Measurement*, and several other professional journals publish reviews of new or revised tests.

The *MMY* makes it easier for a teacher, guidance counselor, or administrator to decide which tests to inspect. One can then send to the publishers for inexpensive specimen sets to compare and contrast.

Many aspects determine the suitability of a given test for a given purpose. Test specialists have offered various rating procedures designed to evaluate each of the tests being considered for use so that their characteristics will be considered properly. In this regard, consult *Standards for Educational and Psychological Testing* (AERA, 1985), produced by

TABLE 14–3   Number and Percentage of Published Tests in *The Mental Measurements Yearbook*, by Major Classification

Classification	Number	Percent
Personality	350	24.8
Vocation	295	20.9
Miscellaneous	139	9.9
Languages	134	9.5
Intelligence/Scholastic Aptitude	100	7.1
Reading	97	6.9
Achievement	68	4.8
Developmental	56	4.0
Mathematics	46	3.3
Speech and Hearing	39	2.8
Science	26	1.8
Motor/Visual Motor	23	1.6
Neuropsychological	14	1.0
Fine Arts	9	.6
Multi-Aptitude	8	.6
Social Studies	5	.4
Total	*1409*	*100*

a joint committee of the American Educational Research Association (AERA), the American Psychological Association (APA), and the National Council on Measurement in Education (NCME). Findley's (1963) "Impact and Improvement of School Testing Programs" will probably be even more useful.

14.20   TEST ADMINISTRATION AND SCORING

Fall or spring tests? There are advantages and disadvantages to each. Some students are entering the school for the first time, and their status in the group can best be determined by administering tests in the fall. A class roster of results can be reported for the class as a group, and, hence, the results are more conveniently organized for use by the teachers. The teachers then have the entire school year in which to remedy any deficiencies revealed by the tests. Testing in the fall reduces self-imposed pressure on teachers to make a good showing. Since the students in a given classroom have been in several different classes during the previous year, it is less likely that the results will be inappropriately used to evaluate individual teachers. End-of-year testing may encourage some teachers to teach toward the test rather than follow local curriculum guides (Tyler, 1960).

On the other hand, administering the tests near the end of the school year makes it possible for the information to serve several purposes. It can aid in making decisions about marking, promotions, educational guidance, and grouping. It seems likely that an analysis of the errors revealed in spring testing could serve as a basis for remedial teaching in the succeeding grade almost as well as data from fall testing, although sometimes changes may occur during the summer vacation. Spring testing has greater value for program and curricular evaluation. A chief drawback of spring testing is that no information is available on students who move into the district during the summer, the period of greatest family mobility.

Test norms are most meaningful if the tests are scheduled during the same month as that in which they were normed, usually October-November or April-May. This reduces ambiguities resulting from interpolation. Of course, if norms are to be meaningful, standard administration conditions, directions, and timing must be followed exactly.

In recent years, testing in grades 11 and 12 by outside agencies such as the College Board (verbal and quantitative scholastic aptitude, plus as many as 14 high school achievement tests), the College Board Advanced Placement Program examinations (26), the American College Testing Program (4 achievement areas), and the National Merit Scholarship Corporation have provided high schools and colleges with a wealth of comparative information about students. This can be used wisely in guidance and selection, in helping the student make thoughtful and satisfying educational and vocational choices. Such information may reduce the need for extensive ability testing at the high school level. The major drawback is that students self-select themselves for these tests, so those taking any particular test are unlikely to be representative of the high school as a whole.

14.21 STATE ASSESSMENTS

In states that have a statewide assessment program, the district's testing program can often be integrated with that of the state. Figure 14–11 gives illustrative state assessment results for grade 3 at "Shamrock Elementary School" and the "Calwest Unified School District" in California for the last three school years in each of the three Rs. In the graphs to the right, the "diamonds" denote actual performance on the tests; the "bands" give the score intervals for schools (and school districts, in the "District Scores" section) that statistically match this school (and this school district) in SES. Note that the extraordinarily high reading scores (the diamond is to the right of the band) at Shamrock Elementary that were evident in previous years are no longer evident. Indeed, the score for the most recent year falls toward the low end of the band, suggesting the need for further diagnostic analysis. Could the explanation be teacher changes at grade 3 at this school? Yet note in panel B that the entire district has shown a decline in reading compared to previous years. Has there been a change in textbooks or curricula that might account for the trend?

Notice that Shamrock Elementary (Figure 14–11) also had a mediocre showing in writing and mathematics. The California Assessment Program also provides results at a more diagnostic level. Figure 14–12 gives a "Diagnostic Display" for the grade 3 mathematics results. Notice to the far right of the figure that relative strength (RS) and relative weakness (RW) are identified for each of the past three years. This year-by-year comparison of relative strengths and weaknesses can be useful in assessing a school's annual educational progress. This type of analysis is even more useful at the district level, where numbers of students would be larger.

Survey of Basic Skills: Grade 3 — 1985

California Assessment Program

Part 1 - CONTENT AREA SUMMARY

School: **SHAMROCK ELEMENTARY**
District: CALWEST UNIFIED
County: CALIFORNIA
CDS: 99-12345-6789012

Students Tested 117   **NES** 0   **Total** 117

Scaled scores allow you to compare scores from year-to-year. For example, your scaled score for Reading is lower than the previous year's score of 298.

Scaled scores also allow you to compare scores between content areas. For example, your Reading score of 251 is lower than your score of 256 for Written Language.

The bands indicate typical performance of schools or districts which, statistically, are like yours. For example, in Reading, the scores for schools like yours range from 247 to 275.

You can compare your school scores to district scores. For example, your school's score of 251 for Reading is lower than the district score.

A. SCHOOL SCORES

Your scaled score is shown as a diamond (◊) and the comparison score band as a line (—).

Content Areas	Years	Scaled Scores	Comparison Score Bands
Reading	1982 - 83	278	238-271
	1983 - 84	298	247-281
	1984 - 85	251	247-275
Written Language	1982 - 83	247	245-272
	1983 - 84	271	254-282
	1984 - 85	256	253-279
Mathematics	1982 - 83	247	242-268
	1983 - 84	260	250-281
	1984 - 85	250	249-275

B. DISTRICT SCORES

Content Areas	Years	Scaled Scores	Comparison Score Bands
Reading	1982 - 83	254	240-262
	1983 - 84	261	248-269
	1984 - 85	259	256-274
Written Language	1982 - 83	257	246-261
	1983 - 84	268	252-271
	1984 - 85	268	260-277
Mathematics	1982 - 83	254	244-261
	1983 - 84	262	252-271
	1984 - 85	260	258-276

FIGURE 14–11 Sample profile for a school and district from the California Assessment Program. (The author is grateful to William Padia and Beth Breneman for providing figures 14–11 and 14–12.)

Survey of Basic Skills: Grade 3 — 1985

PROGRAM DIAGNOSTIC DISPLAY
MATHEMATICS

California Assessment Program

School:	**SHAMROCK ELEMENTARY**
District:	CALWEST UNIFIED
County:	CALIFORNIA
CDS:	99-12345-6789012

The questions on the *Survey* and the reporting of scores reflect a central concern of the *Mathematics Framework* that problem solving/applications serve as an umbrella for all mathematics strands. As shown below, the scores in all skill areas are broken down into skills and applications components. The "Applications" score under Problem Solving is an aggregation of scores for all application categories.

Interpretive Example

Your total Mathematics score of 250 is expressed below as a bold vertical line, and each skill area score is displayed as a bar. Your score in Counting and Place Value is identified as neither a relative strength nor weakness because the bar overlaps the vertical line.

See Part IV for an illustrative description of the Mathematics skill areas tested.

Your total Mathematics score of **250** is represented by the bold vertical line.

Scale: 100 150 200 250 300 350 400

MATHEMATICS SKILL AREAS	Scaled Score and Standard Error	Relative Strength/Weakness 82/83	83/84	84/85
Counting and Place Value				
Skills	242 ±13			
Applications	243 ±16		RW	
	239 ±22			
Operations				
Basic facts	258 ±9			
Addition	235 ±20	RW	RW	
Subtraction	244 ±20	RW	RW	
Multiplication	248 ±17	RS	RS	
Applications	284 ±18			
Basic facts	270 ±15			RS
Addition/subtraction	263 ±25	RS	RS	
Multiplication	279 ±25	RW	RW	RS
Nature of Numbers and Properties				
Properties and relationships	252 ±15	RS	RS	
Money and fractions	191 ±20	RW	RW	RW
Applications	291 ±27			RS
	276 ±25	RW	RW	
Geometry				
Skills	214 ±14			RW
Applications	199 ±17			RW
	243 ±24	RS	RS	
Measurement				
Linear measures	245 ±14			
Other measures	212 ±21	RW	RW	RW
Applications	250 ±23		RS	RS
	288 ±31			RS
Patterns and Graphs				
Skills	257 ±17			
Applications	258 ±23	RS		
	255 ±23			
Problem Solving				
Analysis and models	262 ±10			RS
Applications	256 ±23			
	263 ±10			RS

FIGURE 14–12 Sample diagnostic display profile for a school from the California Assessment Program.

14.22 INTERPRETATION OF DISTRICT RESULTS IN RELATION TO SCHOLASTIC APTITUDE

Graphic portrayals of test results (see Figure 14–12) are more functional than tables of numbers. The accompanying illustration of the interpretation of test results is taken from a school district's annual testing report.

The results in reading for the students in the district are given in Figure 14–13. The figure shows the district pattern of reading achievement for grades 1 through 11 in comparison with national averages, along with "expected" or anticipated scores (from scholastic aptitude tests) shown as a broken line.

The actual grade levels (year and month) of the students at the time of testing are indicated by the black triangles along the baseline (horizontal axis) of the upper portion of the figure. Testing was done in April, the seventh month of the school year, so the actual grade levels at the time of testing were 1.7, 2.7, 3.7, and so on, as indicated by the triangles.

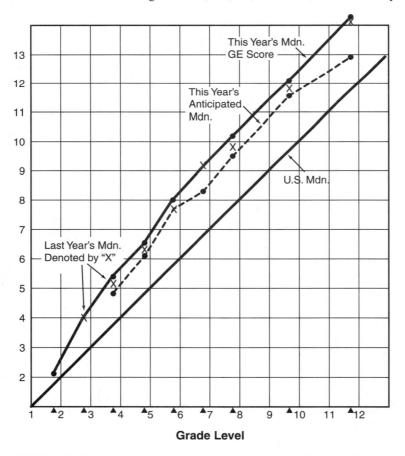

FIGURE 14–13 Graphic Representation of a School District's Results on a Standardized Reading Test.

Total reading performance in grade-equivalent units is shown on the vertical axis.

The 45-degree diagonal line labeled "U.S. Md." represents the median (i.e., the 50th percentile) in the national standardization sample. Scores falling above this line represent a performance better than the average U.S. performance, while scores falling below the U.S. median line are below the U.S. average.

The median performance of the students in the district at each grade level is shown by the solid, uppermost line. Figure 14–13 shows that the median reading GE score of the district's first-grade students (1.7, i.e., seventh month of grade 1) was approximately 2.1. Similarly, the median GE scores of the district's second-graders (2.7) was 4.0; at grade 3 (3.7), the median GE score was 5.4; and so forth.

Figure 14–13 shows that the levels of reading achievement of the students in the district are much higher than those of typical students at the same grade levels nationwide. High achievement is not surprising in view of the fact that the students are well above the national median in academic aptitude. The more important question is, Are the students doing as well as students across the nation who are comparable in terms of academic aptitude? Because of the dual norming of the standardized achievement test and a companion academic aptitude measure, the performance of each student can be compared with the performance of similar students throughout the nation on each test. The performance of similar students is termed *anticipated achievement* or *expected achievement*. The anticipated achievement of any student is the average score achieved by students throughout the nation who are of the same sex, age, grade, and academic aptitude. In other words, if Jane Smith is 11.9 years old, is a sixth-grade student with an aptitude score at the 91st percentile, and has an anticipated GE score in reading of 10.6, then 10.6 is the average reading GE obtained by a nationally representative sample of girls at age 11.9 who obtained an aptitude score at the 91st percentile and were tested in the seventh school month of grade 6. If Jane obtained a GE score of 8.0, her performance would be below expectation for her, even though her score would be higher than the national average (i.e., 6.7) for sixth-grade students.

Anticipated achievement scores are informative both for interpreting the performance of individual students and for evaluating achievement results for the school district. The dashed line in Figure 14–13 gives the median anticipated achievement grade equivalent (AAGE) in reading for students in the district. For example, at grade 3.7, the median AAGE score in total reading for students throughout the nation who are similar to the median student for the district in grade level, age, sex, and academic aptitude is 4.8. This value is more than a year above the national median of 3.7. The *actual* third-grade district median GE score of 5.4 was six months above the median *anticipated* achievement GE of 4.8.

The performance (median actual GE score) of the preceding year's students is shown in Figure 14–13 by small cross marks, ×. The district performance in reading differs little between the two years.

The overall interpretation of Figure 14–13 can be summarized briefly: Reading performance in the district is well above the U.S. median. More significantly, the district's median GE score in reading exceeded the median anticipated achievement GE score by three or more months (.3 GE) at every grade level for which this comparison could be made. (The companion academic aptitude test was not given in grades 1 and 2.) In other words, on the average, the students in the district scored somewhat higher in reading than equally bright students in the national norming group. In addition, the reading performance of this year's students was slightly higher than that of last year's students at corresponding grade levels.

14.23   ACHIEVEMENT STABILITY

Although considerable attention has been given to the issue of IQ stability, the related phenomenon of stability and change among individuals in scholastic attainment has been essentially ignored. Do "slow starters" continue to have ignition trouble, or do they mature and eventually achieve normally? Are early differences in achievement only a result of age or maturation differences that eventually disappear? Do children who achieve poorly in the early grades continue to be poor achievers? In other words, how stable is academic achievement? Bracht and Hopkins (1970b) studied a large number of children who were given standardized achievement tests during grades 1 to 7, 9, and 11. They found a high degree of stability and predictability in general academic achievement. The findings indicate that, for most students, success or failure in grade 1 is not likely to represent a temporary pattern or developmental stage. However, a small percentage of individual students may make radical changes in their achievement level, just as some do in IQ.

General academic achievement at the grade 1 level correlated above .6 with general academic achievement ten years later. By grade 3, the relationship increased to about .75, and by the end of the elementary school period a further increase to above .8 was observed. These relationships would be even higher if they were corrected for measurement error. Similar findings have been reported for other samples (Hilton, 1979).

14.24   BIAS AND ACHIEVEMENT TESTS

> . . . some tests have been viewed as sexually, ethnically, or socioeconomically biased because some groups perform less well on the tests than others . . . It is now commonly understood among measurement experts that the mere existence of such group differences in performance is not evidence of bias. (NCME, 1980, p. 5)

The question of cultural bias is much different when one is considering achievement tests than when one is dealing with scholastic aptitude tests. The relevant type of validity is content validity, not construct validity (Linn, 1988). The focus of standardized achievement tests is on common course objectives, as illustrated in Figure 14–9. A reading test is biased against a social or ethnic group only if items are included that will result in a particular group's having a relatively higher or lower mean than it has in the content universe of course objectives. Whether there are differences among groups in mean universe scores is irrelevant to the test's validity. Is the test measuring the intended curricular objectives? Do the items represent the intended content universe? An achievement test is biased if a given cultural or social group would be expected to perform differently on this set of items than it would on a representative set of items from the same content universe. Perhaps certain bilingual students can read in a language other than English better than they can in English. In bilingual programs one might wish to test students' reading ability in both languages. Certain standardized tests such as the *Comprehensive Tests of Basic Skills* (CTBS) are available in both English and Spanish.

Gardner (1978, p. 2) has observed, "Lower scores *alone* on an achievement test do not signify bias. If they did, then every . . . typing test is biased against persons who have never learned to type." No reading expert holds that reading tests are biased against boys because boys perform less well on them than girls. To attack tests because they indicate group differences is like breaking a thermometer because it indicates a nonnormal condition (Anastasi, 1988).

Efforts to reduce cultural bias on standardized tests are often misguided. Attempting to select items on which ethnic groups do not differ does a great disservice to minority groups. Such "bootstrapping" serves to gloss over or minimize a serious educational problem. The bald reality as shown by NAEP, as well as numerous other studies and statewide testing programs such as the California Assessment Program, is that, on the average, students who are Black or Hispanic American are considerably below (by more than one-half standard deviation) the norms in educational achievement, although the gap is being reduced in certain areas (NAEP, 1982). Misdiagnosing this problem and attributing the differences to test bias might make us feel better in the short run, but in the long run it does not serve the best interests of anyone but particularly not those of the low-scoring students. When the issue is innate aptitude or potential, the degree of cultural bias is moot; not so in the domain of educational achievement, unless the test focuses on content that is less germane to the curriculum of some groups. Bias is most likely on social studies tests and is least likely in reading and math, where curricular commonality among schools and districts is greatest (see Figure 14–9).

Obviously, the items on achievement tests should not promulgate racial or gender stereotypes; the authors of recently developed or revised standardized achievement tests have been careful to minimize this problem (see, e.g., Jensen & Beck, 1979; Wittig & Peterson, 1979). There are all ranges of cognitive aptitude, from mentally disabled to genius, in every ethnic and racial group. Stereotypical assessments and thinking need to give way to equal opportunity and fairness (Linn, 1988).

Bias can contaminate the results of nonreading standardized tests if the tests require a near-grade level reading proficiency. Obviously, reading is critically important, but it should not be the crucial factor in a science, social studies, or math reasoning test. The following section deals with assessing the reading difficulty of written materials generally, of which tests are a subset.

14.25 MEASURING THE DIFFICULTY OF READING MATERIAL

In order to measure, quantify, and describe the *readability* (reading difficulty) of books, tests, and other reading material, many different readability formulas have been devised. The subjective judgments of teachers of the grade level for which reading selections are intended have been found to be quite unreliable (Jorgenson, 1975). Readability formulas use such factors as percent of common words, average word length, average sentence length, average number of syllables per word, percent of words that are prepositions, and more recently, syntactic complexity (DiStefano & Valencia, 1980).

Research (Klare, 1975) suggests that the highly complex formulas add little to the use of the two factors that most highly correlate with reading difficulty: a word or semantic factor and a sentence or syntactic factor. The semantic factor seems to be the single most significant determinant of readability.

One of the most popular methods of assessing readability is described in Figure 14–14. Fry's Readability Graph uses two factors: average number of syllables per 100 words (word complexity) and average number of sentences per 100 words (sentence complexity). For example, a 100-word sample from *Tom Sawyer* contains 4.5 sentences and 126 syllables. The intersection of these points in Fry's readability graph indicates a seventh-grade level. On a specific topic (Mexico), the selection in the *World Book* was written at the eighth-grade level, whereas the *Encyclopaedia Britannica*'s selection was written at the eleventh-grade level.[2]

In addition to their obvious curricular use, measures of reading difficulty can be useful in describing the "reading load" of standardized achievement tests in subjects other than reading. Except when measuring reading ability, the readability of test content should be kept as simple as possible so that the students who are, for example, good in math and science but whose reading skills are lagging are not penalized unfairly. As Gardner (1978, p. 2) has observed, "A test designed to measure achievement in elementary science, and in which the items are presented in language and syntax far above the level of the pupils tested, is biased, especially against the poor readers." The reading level needed to "decipher" non-reading standardized achievement tests varies considerably among tests, and often reduces the validity of those tests (Hopkins, 1965). A formula for measuring the readability of single sentences, which can be used to assess the reading difficulty of individual test items is now available (Homan, Hewitt & Linder, 1994).

---

[2]Two other widely used readability formulas are the Dale-Chall (Klare, 1975) and Flesh (1948) reading ease (RE) formulas. Flesh's RE formulas use the same two factors as Fry's but are combined and weighted differently: $RE = 206.84 - 84.6X_{SL/W} - 1.015X_{W/S}$,

where $X_{SL/W}$ is the average number of syllables per word and

$X_{W/S}$ is the average number of words per sentence.

RE values are scaled such that they range from 30 or below for very difficult material to 90 or above for very easy reading matter such as comics.

The Dale-Chall readability formula is one of the most accurate for reading material intended for grades 3 to 8 (Klare, 1975). It predicts the grade level, G, of the students who will be able to answer 50 percent of the comprehension test questions on the reading passage correctly: $G = .116X\% + .060X_{W/S} + 3.27$, where $X\%$ is the percent of words that are not on a list of the most common 3000 words (the Dale-Chall list), and $X_{W/S}$ is defined as in the Flesh formula.

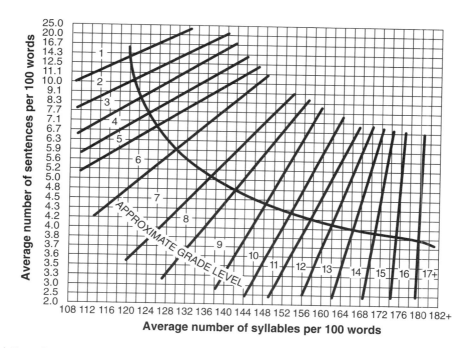

Expanded Directions for Working Readability Graph

1. Randomly select three (3) sample passages and count out exactly 100 words each, beginning with the beginning of a sentence. Do count proper nouns, initializations, and numerals.
2. Count the number of sentences in the hundred words, estimating length of the fraction of the last sentence to the nearest one-tenth.
3. Count the total number of syllables in the 100-word passage. If you don't have a hand counter available, an easy way is to simply put a mark above every syllable over one in each word, then when you get to the end of the passage, count the number of marks and add 100. Small calculators can also be used as counters by pushing numeral 1, then push the + sign for each word or syllable when counting.
4. Enter graph with *average* sentence length and *average* number of syllables; plot dot where the two lines intersect. Area where dot is plotted will give you the approximate grade level.
5. If a great deal of variability is found in syllable count or sentence count, putting more samples into the average is desirable.
6. A word is defined as a group of symbols with a space on either side; thus, *Joe, IRA, 1945,* and *&* are each one word.
7. A syllable is defined as a phonetic syllable. Generally, there are as many syllables as vowel sounds. For example, *stopped* is one syllable and *wanted* is two syllables. When counting syllables for numerals and initializations, count one syllable for each symbol. For example, *1945* is four syllables, *IRA* is three syllables, and *&* is one syllable.

Note: This "extended graph" does not outmode or render the earlier (1968) version inoperative or inaccurate; it is an extension.

FIGURE 14–14 Graph for estimating readability-extended.

SOURCE: Edward Fry, Rutgers University Reading Center, New Brunswick, N.J. 08904.

SUMMARY

Standardized achievement tests measure important educational objectives, but like any tool, they can be misused. *The results from standardized tests should be viewed as only one indicator among many of the quality of education within the district.* Standardized achievement batteries are composed of general survey tests. These tests are built around the curricula and objectives that are presumably common to all school districts and students across the nation. *Unique local objectives and content are not represented.* Good standardized measures are unavailable in certain curricular areas (e.g., music, art, and physical education), and these areas are not assessed in school districts' testing programs.

Most high school courses are only indirectly and incidentally sampled by survey-type achievement tests, if they are sampled at all. Little curricular commonality exists among high school students across the nation. Considerable variation in curriculum often exists, even among high schools within the same district, owing to differences in school size and student characteristics. Tests to assess a common core of educational experiences are less feasible at the high school level because of the highly elective nature of high school curricula and the diversity in students' objectives and courses of study. Consequently, *batteries of standardized tests reflect high school curricula only to a very limited extent.* Tests are available for specific high school and college courses, but these tests are not widely used. Many of these tests are less useful as a yardstick of educational quality at the secondary level than at the elementary and middle school levels. At the high school level, standardized tests often measure what is retained from the earlier grades more than what is learned in high school. The tests are measures of what a student knows or can do at a given point in time, even though the knowledge and skills tested may not be closely related to recent educational experiences. Standardized achievement tests are available for specific high school courses, but few courses are so standardized in content that the tests represent the particular emphasis of a given course.

Standardized tests have more validity in some subjects than in others. When there is much uniformity in curricula across school districts and states, the tests have substantial validity. This occurs in subjects with more limited content and a uniform skill sequence. Consequently, *reading and math tests tend to have much higher validity than tests of science and of social studies*, areas in which there is considerable interdistrict and interstate variation in content emphasis and sequencing. Therefore, reading and math results have the greatest validity and significance; the findings in other curricular areas are much less definitive.

Tests should be selected for a district's testing program only after careful study of the content validity of the available tests and batteries. Achievement tests with the same label may differ substantially in what they actually measure (the jingle fallacy). Conversely, tests with differing titles may actually measure little that is unique (the jangle fallacy).

Standardized achievement tests tend to be more general in scope, more process-oriented, and less oriented toward specific content than are the typical teacher-made tests. The norms on standardized tests usually offer a comparison with a nationally representative sample of students at the same grade levels and in the same courses.

There is no discrete point at which a test measures achievement and no longer measures scholastic aptitude; scholastic aptitude tests are general achievement tests, but they represent an even broader type of achievement than standardized achievement tests do.

Although there is considerable overlap between various types of scholastic aptitude tests, each is usually sufficiently unique to justify its use.

It is generally preferable to use a scholastic aptitude test and an achievement battery that have been standardized on the same students so that aptitude-achievement comparisons can be made with less error.

Presenting normative data for each item or item group—a trend among test publishers—promises to be of much greater value for the evaluation of instruction (or curriculum) for a class, school, or district than reporting only total scores. Item-level data for individual students are less useful and must be interpreted with greater caution.

Grade equivalents are useful units for reporting test results below high school. GE scores should be supplemented by standard scores or percentile ranks. The latter are most useful in reporting to parents. Extrapolation of norms attenuates the meaning that can be attached to GE scores that deviate greatly from a student's present grade level. Interpolation of norms also creates serious problems in curricular evaluation; for norms to have their clearest meaning, tests should be administered at the same time in the school year that was used in the norming process.

In the planning of a school testing program, all interested parties should be represented in the decision-making process. The three main purposes of school testing programs are educational quality control and public accountability, curricular and program evaluation, and individual student assessment and diagnosis.

The Mental Measurements Yearbook can be very useful in locating and evaluating published measures.

IMPORTANT TERMS AND CONCEPTS

aptitude versus achievement

survey versus diagnostic achievement tests

jingle versus jangle fallacies

crystallized versus transfer-oriented cognitive measures

achievement stability

expectancy, predicted, or anticipated achievement

MMY

survey versus course-specific standardized achievement tests

content validity

grade-equivalent (GE) scores

readability

National Assessment of Educational Progress (NAEP)

school versus individual norms

common-core content universe

differential content validity

interpolation and extrapolation

"out-of-level" testing

cultural or gender bias on achievement tests

CHAPTER TEST

1. Using Figure 14–2, which of these conclusions is *not* supported?
   a) The verbal intelligence tests correlated more highly with reading tests than the nonverbal tests did.
   b) The arithmetic concept tests were less reliable than the reading tests.
   c) The nonverbal intelligence tests correlated more highly with the arithmetic concepts than the verbal intelligence tests did.
   d) The observed correlation between the intelligence and achievement tests was higher at grade 8 than at grade 3.

2. The influence of the environment on standardized scholastic aptitude and achievement tests is
   a) greater on achievement tests.
   b) greater on scholastic aptitude tests.
   c) about equal on both types of tests.
   d) negligible on both types of tests.

3. On which one of the following types of tests is content *least* related to school content?
   a) verbal intelligence tests
   b) nonlanguage intelligence tests
   c) college admissions tests
   d) standardized achievement tests

4. The assumption that two tests measure different abilities because one is labeled an intelligence test and the other a scholastic aptitude test is an example of the
   a) jingle fallacy. b) jangle fallacy.

5. "Reading tests are reading tests, take your pick" illustrates the
   a) jingle fallacy. b) jangle fallacy.

6. Standardized achievement tests do *not* have
   a) a standard that defines acceptable performance.
   b) a standard time limit.
   c) a standard set of directions.
   d) norms.

7. Compared to a standardized achievement test, a typical teacher-made test tends to
   a) be more difficult, if raw scores are converted to percents.
   b) have higher reliability.
   c) cover large domains of content.
   d) allow more flexibility in administration.

8. Compared to aptitude tests, achievement tests tend to
   a) be more future oriented.
   b) be more transfer oriented.
   c) focus on a more clearly defined universe of content.
   d) be less able to predict subsequent performance.

9. Which one of the following is the major reason that the norms on standardized reading vocabulary tests are not interchangeable?
   a) They have different curricular objectives.
   b) They have different types of test items.
   c) They have noncomparable norm groups.
   d) There is a low correlation between the two reading tests.

10. Suppose a school's median on a standardized achievement test is at the 90th percentile using *school norms* (see Figure 14–4). If *individual student norms* are used, the average student would be expected to be
    a) above the 90th percentile in the individual student norms.
    b) at the 90th percentile in the individual student norms.
    c) below the 90th percentile in the individual student norms.
    d) No accurate predictions can be made.

11. If test norms were developed by sampling students at grades 4.6, 5.6, 6.6, 7.6, 8.6, and 9.6, the grade-equivalent scores between 4.6 and 9.6 are established using _____, whereas those below 4.6 and above 9.6 use the process of _____.
    a) interpolation . . . extrapolation   b) extrapolation . . . interpolation

12. Which one of the following is likely to result in more serious errors in grade-equivalent scores?
    a) interpolation   b) extrapolation

13. Mabel is in the fourth grade and obtained a GE score in math fundamentals of 9.8. Therefore, we know that she
    a) should be promoted to the fifth or sixth grade in mathematics.
    b) knows more math than most ninth-grade students.
    c) was very lucky on the test.
    d) is very advanced in math compared to other fourth-grade students.

14. In reading, which one of the following differences in reading ability would probably be greatest? (See Figure 14–6.) The differences between
    a) the median fourth-grade students and the median sixth-grade students.
    b) the 5th and 95th percentile in grade 5.
    c) GE scores of 5.6 and 7.6.
    d) the 75th percentile in grade 4 and the 25th percentile in grade 6.

15. At which one of the following grade levels will the standard deviation in GE scores be greatest?
    a) 2   b) 4   c) 6   d) 8   e) standard deviation will be equal at all grade levels

16. The variability (standard deviation) of GE scores tends to (see Table 14–1)
    a) increase as grade level increases.
    b) be greater in reading than in math.
    c) (among the separate tests) be least in math computations.
    d) Two of the above
    e) All of the above

17. In Figure 14–7,
   a) the group's performance consistently exceeded the national mean at grade 8 and thereafter.
   b) the individual's performance (One student's performance) consistently exceeded the national mean at grade 8 and thereafter.
   c) the individual's performance fell below the group's performance at grade 8 and thereafter.
   d) Two of the above
   e) All of the above

18. Joseph Lawrence (see Figure 14–8)
   a) scored below the national average in total reading.
   b) scored above "expectancy" in language expression.
   c) fell below "expectancy" in total mathematics.
   d) Two of the above
   e) All of the above

19. The diagnostic value of a survey achievement test is least definitive at the
   a) individual student level.
   b) class level.
   c) school level.
   d) district level.
   e) state level.

20. Which one of the following curricular areas has the largest common core of content and objectives?
   a) language arts   b) science   c) social studies   d) math   e) reading

21. In which one of the following areas will standardized achievement tests probably have the least content validity ?
   a) language mechanics   b) listening   c) social studies   d) math   e) reading

22. If a fifth-grade class has an average IQ of 90, which one of the following standardized reading achievement tests would probably yield the most valid scores for the students? A test designed for a typical class of students in grade
   a) three.   b) four.   c) five.   d) six.

23. Standardized achievement test batteries tend to have greatest content validity and usefulness at which school level?
   a) elementary school   b) middle school   c) high school

24. Using Table 14–2, which of the following conclusions is *not* supported by the NAEP reading data for the nationally representative sample?
   a) The means of students who are Black or Hispanic American were very close.
   b) Female students did better than male students.
   c) The Northeast did better than the Southeast.
   d) The gap between Caucasians and the two other ethnic groups didn't change much across grade level.
   e) The gain in scores between grade 3 and grade 11 was greater for Caucasians.

25. A standardized achievement test is certainly culturally biased if
    a) there is a difference among the medians of the various cultural groups.
    b) the test is based on a small common core of objectives.
    c) it has a nonrepresentative norm group.
    d) not all cultural groups were represented in its norming.
    e) the differences among the medians of the various culture groups are relatively greater on the test than for the entire content universe.

26. Which one of the following is *not* a common aim of school testing programs?
    a) evaluation of individual students
    b) program evaluation
    c) curricular evaluation
    d) teacher evaluation
    e) accountability

27. Which one of these is not a common criterion for the selection of standardized tests for a school testing program?
    a) content validity
    b) reliability
    c) adequacy of norms.
    d) ease of hand scoring
    e) amount of testing time

28. Which one of these sources provides critical reviews of published tests?
    a) *Tests in Print*   b) NAEP   c) *MMY*

ANSWERS TO CHAPTER TEST

1. c	11. a	20. e
2. a	12. b	21. c
3. b	13. d	22. b
4. b	14. b	23. a
5. a	15. d	24. e
6. a	16. e	25. e
7. d	17. e	26. d
8. c	18. d	27. d
9. c	19. a	28. c
10. c		

15

Standard Interest, Personality, and Social Measures

15.1 INTRODUCTION

In addition to informal methods of affective measurement (discussed in Chapter 11), there are hundreds of published measures of personal and social characteristics (see Table 14–3). Their principal use in schools pertains to personal and vocational counseling, in which interests and personality as well as aptitudes and abilities are important considerations.

Standardized measures of affective characteristics should not be administered by classroom teachers unless they have received special training; the dangers and likelihood of misinterpreting them, especially the personality inventories, are much greater than with standardized ability tests. If teachers have some general understanding of measures of typical performance, however, they can work more effectively with counselors and school psychologists.

Most high school and college students are anxious to know more about themselves so that they can better define their academic or vocational futures. Many have become familiar with self-report interest inventories. Students want *scientific* information regarding kinds of vocational activities they will enjoy and in which they will be successful. "Are my scientific interests stronger than my literary interests?" "Are my interests similar to those of schoolteachers, chemists, automobile mechanics, or forest rangers?" These are the kinds of questions standardized interest inventories can help answer. Note, for example, that the *ACT Student Profile* (see Figure 13–3) provides interest data, not for occupations but for each of six curricular areas: science, arts, social service, business contact, business operations, and technical.

15.2   VOCATIONAL INTEREST INVENTORIES

The first systematic effort to measure interests appears to have been made in 1915 at the Carnegie Institute of Technology, where James Miner developed a questionnaire to assist students in their vocational choices. Giant steps forward were taken in 1927 when E. K. Strong published the first edition of his *Vocational Interest Blank* (*SVIB*) and in 1939 when Kuder made available the initial form of the *Kuder Preference Record* (*KPR*). There are many different published measures of vocational interests, but the Strong and Kuder inventories have dominated the field for half a century.

15.3   THE STRONG INTEREST INVENTORY

The Strong inventory was designed to distinguish men who were successful in a given occupational group from men in general. Strong thought that the interests typical of any one occupational group would differ from those of people in general and at least a little from those of any other occupational group. He collected items in which examinees can indicate their interests and preferences in a wide range of activities. Instead of grouping items in similar-interest clusters, Strong simply gave the test to the members of many different occupational groups. For each group he determined which items were chosen more (or less) frequently than they were by men in general. From these differences he derived *empirically based scoring scales* for each group. Consequently, an individual taking the test can ascertain whether his interests resemble those of artists, architects, printers, morticians, and so on. Scoring scales have been developed for occupations ranging from artist to production manager and from minister to real estate salesman. Strong was not prejudicial in choosing which items would make up each given scale; the *actual* interest choices of the different groups decided the weights of the items for each scale. The success and prestige of the Strong inventory are due largely to the extensive research involved in its formulation. It has few competitors. It is interesting that Kuder adopted a rather similar scoring approach in the development of his second interest test, the *Kuder Occupational Interest Survey* (*KOIS*).

The current version of the Strong inventory, the *Strong Interest Inventory*, merges the men's and women's forms into a single test. The 207 Occupational Scales are also integrated into 23 Basic Interest Scales, which are grouped into six General Occupational Themes based on Holland's (1985) theory of vocational choice, in which each occupation can be classified as representing one or more of the following six themes: realistic, investigative, artistic, social, enterprising, and conventional.

Although examinees are asked to choose between competing activities, most of the 325 items on the *Strong* require the individual to indicate his or her preference by marking a phrase *D* for "dislike," *I* for "indifferent," or *L* for "like," as in the following three examples (not from the *Strong* itself):

Moving a piano	D I L
Multiplying one number by another	D I L
Purchasing a new automobile	D I L

How *should* successful computer programmers, say, respond to "moving a piano"? We might make a guess that more programmers than people in general would mark it *D* but only actual data will tell whether they, in fact, do. Each item is scored once for each occupational scale to which it contributes. The *Strong* must be scored separately for each occupation; hence, handscoring is impractical. The scoring must be done by computer at certain scoring centers. Scoring weights are determined by the discrepancies between the markings of the occupational group and the group of people in general. In the computer programmer scale, for example, a positive weight for a response is indicated when it occurs significantly more frequently among computer programmers than among people in general, and a negative weight indicates that it occurs significantly less frequently. Responses that do not differentiate between computer programmers and people in general do not carry any weight on the computer programmer scale, regardless of how frequently they were chosen by computer programmers. An examinee's total raw score on each occupation scale is the sum of the weights of his or her various responses. The raw scores for each scale are converted into *T*-scores (mean = 50, standard deviation = 10). Fortunately for the constructors of interest scales, the interests held by members of various vocations appear to be relatively stable for the past 30 or 40 years (Campbell, 1966a, 1966b); also, interest patterns within occupations appear very similar for Western cultures (Lonner & Adams, 1972). There are more than 100 occupations on which scales have been developed.

15.4   THE KUDER INTEREST INVENTORIES

There are three principal Kuder scales: the original *Kuder Preference Record-Vocational* (*KPR-V*), the *Kuder Occupational Interest Survey* (*KOIS*), and the *Kuder General Interest Survey* (*KGIS*). The Kuder scales consist of many sets of three phrases of the "You like most to . . ." variety, such as this item:

> R. Play a game that requires mental arithmetic.
> S. Play checkers.
> T. Work mechanical puzzles.

The examinee indicates which one of the three activities is most liked and which one is least liked. This is equivalent to ranking the three activities in order of preference, because obviously the one not marked ranks in the middle. Each of the Kuder items has this forced-choice triad form.

Empirical keying is employed on the *KOIS,* similar to the *Strong.* Let us examine the scoring of the sample item above for five scoring keys. First, this item does not contribute to the Verification (sincerity versus faking) scale. Not surprisingly, by empirical scoring you get one point on the bank cashier scale if you most like to "play a game that requires mental arithmetic." You get one point on the Librarian scale if you most like to "play checkers." You get one point on the X-ray Technician scale if you most like to "work mechanical puzzles." You get one point on the Pharmaceutical Salesman if you *least* like to "work mechanical puzzles." Thus, these four occupational scales use four of the six possible like-most and like-least responses to the item. Other occupational scales use the like-least responses for mental arithmetic and checkers, too.

The chief methodological difference between Strong's approach and Kuder's forced-choice scheme is that the former uses a considerable number of items of the rating scale type that one may mark as one pleases—all *L*, for instance, or all *I*—whereas the Kuder uses a triadic (forced-choice) item type that appears to be more resistant to response sets caused by the tendency to prefer one of the categories on the rating scale. Kuder requires, in effect, that the examinee mark exactly 100 "mosts" (one per item) and exactly 100 "leasts" (one per item). The *Strong* does not require the examinee to mark one-third of the 400 items *D*, one-third *I*, and one-third *L*, although some forced-choice items are used elsewhere in the *Strong*. The long history and research and predictive-validity information available for the *Strong* give it a distinct advantage over the *KOIS* at the present time.

15.5 IPSATIVE VERSUS NORMATIVE SCALES

The Kuder is an *ipsative* rather than a *normative* measure; that is, it shows relative *intra-individual* interests, not absolute degrees of interest. Whether Mary has more scientific interest than Martha cannot be ascertained from the Kuder scores; they show only the relative standing of the interest areas *within* each person. The failure to recognize this ipsative property frequently creates consternation for those who attempt to resolve differences in results when an examinee has taken both the *Strong* and the *Kuder*. In other words, if Jane is a person of many interests, she can be more interested in social work than Mary, even though Mary's greatest vocational interest is social work and yet social work is not among Jane's greatest interests.

The *Kuder General Interest Survey* (*KGIS*) is a downward extension of the *KPR-V*. Norms are available for grades 6 to 12. Correlations between corresponding *KGIS* and *KPR-V* scales are high when allowance is made for measurement error.

15.6 RELIABILITY AND VALIDITY OF INTEREST INVENTORIES

For some published interest tests, little or no adequate information is available concerning their validity and reliability. The critical test reviews found in the *Mental Measurements Yearbook*s provide invaluable guidance and an important quality control function for prospective users. Our comments will deal exclusively with the *Strong* (Hansen & Campbell, 1985) and *Kuder* (1977) inventories and therefore may or may not be characteristic of other instruments.

Although internal-consistency reliability estimates are satisfactory evidence of short-term stability in interest profiles, interest measurement over a long period cannot be expected to be stable until interests themselves have crystallized. Consequently, there is considerable fluctuation in the interest profiles of students below age 17 or 18 on the *Strong* and on the *KPR* (Crites, 1969). Moderate stability is achieved by college age, and fairly high stability is achieved by the end of the college years. (Hansen & Campbell, 1985). The median retest reliability coefficients for Occupational Scales, Basic Interest Scales, and General Occupational Themes are .87, .82, and .81, respectively. Long-term stability up to more than 20 years is also quite high (.60 or more).

15.7 FAKABILITY

The results of several studies have shown that response to the Kuder and Strong inventories can be faked and that the "accuracy" of the faked responses is correlated (about 0.4) with IQ. Thus, efforts to use these measures for personnel selection purposes have not been very successful. Falsification of interest is unlikely in an educational context, however, since there would rarely be a motive for faking. Like other self-report affective measures, their validity depends even more on the context—for example, on removing incentives to prevaricate—than to the content validity of the items. This fact also has an important bearing on the usefulness of available validity and reliability data: Data obtained in a research or counseling context cannot be safely generalized to other contexts such as admissions and selection decisions. If there are strong self-interest consequences to affective measures, their validity cannot be assumed. On the other hand, it is generally safe to assume that normal people are truthful unless they perceive it in their best interest to be otherwise.

15.8 MEASURED VERSUS EXPRESSED INTERESTS

Although there is a considerable relationship (rs of about .5) between expressed and measured interests, they are far from interchangeable. Super and Overstreet (1960) found that more than half of a sample of ninth-grade boys wished to enter occupations that appeared inappropriate for them in terms of the intellectual level required.

In Project Talent, approximately 14,000 representative grade 12 students were asked about their career plans (Flanagan et al., 1962), which were then classified into the broad categories of college-science (31%), college-nonscience (19%), noncollege-technical (22%), and noncollege-nontechnical (29%). Five years later a follow-up study was conducted to determine the careers those individuals were pursuing. The percentages of people in each original group who continued in the same broad categories were 31, 56, 51, and 55 percent, respectively (Flanagan, 1969, p. 138).

Expressed interests are not necessarily less valid than measured interests; in fact, some studies show expressed interests to be the better predictor of ultimate occupation. Such evidence does not attenuate the validity of measured interest because many factors other than interest determine one's occupation. For students from the upper social class, in which prestige factors limit the "acceptable" occupations that one may pursue, expressed interests predicted better than measured interests; for middle-class subjects, the reverse was true.

The likelihood of being dissatisfied with one's work has been reported to be much greater for those who choose a line of work that is inconsistent with their measured interests than for those whose occupation and measured interests are consistent, although recent studies have not supported this conclusion. Zytowski (1976), in a 12- to 19-year follow-up, found that people whose occupations were not consistent with their early interest profiles did not report less job satisfaction than those whose occupations were consistent with their measured interests.

15.9   INTERESTS, ABILITIES, AND GRADES

Contrary to popular opinion, little relationship exists between abilities and corresponding interests. Interests are, however, related to perceived abilities, which suggests the need for systematic feedback to students about their performance on standardized tests. Table 15–1 shows the correlations between the *KPR-V* interests and the various abilities measured by the *Differential Aptitude Tests* (*DAT*) for a group of male high school seniors. Although a moderate relationship exists in the mechanical and computational-numerical areas, the other interrelationships are low. Note the *r* of only .05 between clerical interest and ability!

Interests generally correlate poorly (below .3) with grades in relevant courses or fields. Even the Academic Orientation (Ao) scale of the *Strong* has very little relationship (*r*s in the .1 to .3 range) with academic grades (Campbell, 1974, p. 79). Measured interests do predict students' ratings of satisfaction with a field of study, but these factors have little relationship to grades.

Scores on vocational interest tests have been shown to be more highly related to the curriculum college students selected than were achievement, aptitude, or personality tests; personality tests were the poorest indicator of college major. Many studies have shown that measured interests have considerable validity for predicting occupations.

In a review of predictive validity studies on the *Strong* (Dolliver, Irwin & Bigley, 1972), it was found that the chances are even (one out of two) that a person will end up in an occupation in which he or she received a high interest score. The chances are eight out of nine *against* a person's ending up in an occupation in which he or she received a very low interest score. Results for the *KOIS* appear to be comparable (Zytowski, 1976).

TABLE 15–1   Correlation Coefficients Among Various Interests (*Kuder Preference Record*) and Abilities (*Differential Aptitude Tests*)

| | Differential Aptitude Tests | | | | | | | |
	Verbal	*Numerical*	*Abstract*	*Space*	*Mechanical*	*Clerical*	*Spelling*	*Sentences*
Kuder Scales								
Mechanical	.13	−.09	.06	.19	.38	−.32	−.28	−.05
Computational	.18	.54	.32	.12	.08	.27	.21	.22
Scientific	.16	.17	.25	.20	.44	−.09	.17	.07
Persuasive	−.05	−.06	−.06	−.15	−.15	.01	.16	.04
Artistic	−.03	−.36	.00	.15	.11	.05	−.18	−.15
Literary	.10	.06	−.28	−.21	−.24	.05	.27	.14
Musical	.02	.28	.12	.12	− .02	.41	−.05	.03
Social Service	−.12	−.14	−.12	−.27	−.37	.00	−.04	−.09
Clerical	−.02	.24	.11	.08	−.12	.05	−.02	.19

SOURCE: G. K. Bennett, H. G. Seashore, and A. G. Wesman, *Differential aptitude tests*, Forms L and M, Fourth Edition Manual (New York: Psychological Corporation), p. A–17. Reprinted by permission of the publisher. The Psychological Corporation, New York. All rights reserved. (Data are based on a relatively small sample).

The limited information on racial differences and interest inventories suggests that this factor is not significant in the assessment of interests, although the more general issues pertaining to the development of interests within a social or cultural group are critically important.

The prediction of occupational *success* is somewhat different from the prediction of occupational tenure. In the few studies that have been done in this area, low positive correlations have been reported between measured interests and vocational success.

An interest scale especially oriented to the skilled and semiskilled occupations is the *Minnesota Vocational Interest Inventory* (*MVII*), which follows the Strong approach. Keys have been developed for 21 specific occupations such as truck driver, electrician, and baker. This inventory may have greater value for non-college-bound students with less scholastic aptitude (Hall, 1966) than the *Strong* and the *KOIS,* although there seems to be much less interest differentiation among blue-collar workers.

In interpreting any interest profile, one must remember that (1) the nature of the duties of some jobs change with time, (2) many jobs with the same name differ considerably, and (3) there is a wide diversity of activities within most occupations that allow opportunity for interest differentiation within the occupations with the same job title. The "jingle" and "jangle" fallacies are about as apparent in job titles as they are in test labels.

In summary, interest tests are of little practical value by themselves, but when considered together with aptitude and achievement patterns, they can be a useful aid in helping a motivated student select a career pattern or course of study.

15.10   THE MEASUREMENT OF PERSONALITY VARIABLES: CONCEPTUALIZING THE HUMAN PERSONALITY

People have always categorized and evaluated the personalities of their contemporaries. The simplest form of personality evaluation uses some *typology* under which individuals can be classified. The four temperaments of ancient times—sanguine, melancholy, phlegmatic, and choleric—made up a classification based on a supposed predominance in an individual of one of the four bodily "humours," or fluids—blood, bile, phlegm, or choler. The introversion-extraversion typology suggested by the Swiss psychoanalyst C. G. Jung in 1921 is still popular today. Traces of typological psychology remain in personality theory, but more elaborate methods of assessment have been devised in a growing effort to capture the diversity of human personality. Measurement procedures have naturally accompanied the development of personality theory.

There are hundreds of standardized personality tests; they are exceeded in number only by achievement tests.

15.11   TRAITS ASSESSED BY DIRECT AND NATURALISTIC OBSERVATION

Via direct, unobtrusive observation a sample of behavior that manifests various personality and other affective traits can be observed and assessed. In Hartshorne and May's (1928) classic study, the Character Education Inquiry of Yale University, such traits as truthfulness, honesty, and persistence in children were studied by subjecting them to *situational tests* of these traits. Hartshorne and May found that most of the traits investigated depended strongly on the situation. For example, a child might cheat on an examination but not steal pennies.

The wartime Office of Strategic Services (OSS, 1948) was interested in selecting highly qualified men for risky undercover operations. The assessment staff felt that such traits as energy, initiative, effective intelligence, emotional stability, and leadership would be indispensable in this sort of work; consequently, a number of situational tests were devised to measure the degree of these and other attributes. In one situation the subject had to build a five-foot cube of giant Tinkertoys with the aid of two workers. Unknown to the subject, the two "helpers" were participant-observers (psychologists) who did everything possible to obstruct his progress and to belittle him. His reactions under such conditions were later evaluated in terms of the traits being sought.

In another trial called the stress interview, the candidate was given a short time to invent a story to cover the fact that he had been caught going through secret governmental papers. In a subsequent third-degree grilling, his reactions were evaluated again.

Although situational tests are very expensive and rarely practicable, the use of naturalistic observation is an extremely valuable assessment procedure. The teacher can periodically shift from "participant" mode to "observation" mode and be sensitive to individual and group behaviors and attitudes that would otherwise go unnoticed. A wholly subject-centered teacher is in sharp contrast to the teacher who uses naturalistic observation. Naturalistic observation differs from casual observation in that it is planned, disciplined, and systematically recorded. If a teacher has a periodic observation scheduled for each student, the teacher almost certainly will have a better understanding of that student in terms of interests and attitudes and with respect to social interrelationships. Obviously, naturalistic observation lends itself more to the self-contained classroom culture of the elementary school than to the separate-course culture of the secondary school.

15.12 TRAIT MEASUREMENT THROUGH SELF-REPORT

Most personality tests are of the paper-and-pencil, self-report variety; the examinee is presented with a series of questions describing typical behaviors or attitudes. The examinee's score will consist of the number of questions answered in the direction that supposedly displays those traits. Sometimes a self-report test measures only one trait dimension, such as security-insecurity or high anxiety-low anxiety. At other times a test can be devised and scored to measure several traits at once. For example, the *California Psychological Inventory* (*CPI*) yields 18 different scores on such traits as sociability, dominance, sense of well-being, self-control, tolerance, and flexibility.

The forerunner of all such devices was the *Woodworth Personal Data Sheet*, devised during World War I to facilitate the psychiatric screening of draftees. It consisted of 116 *yes-no* questions describing typical symptoms of neurotic behavior. *Normals* averaged about 10 psychoneurotic answers, but those with neurotic complications averaged close to 40 such answers (Franz, 1919). High scorers would be interviewed and evaluated more intensively. The first 36 items from the *Woodworth Personal Data Sheet* are shown in Figure 15–1. By

1.	Do you usually feel well and strong?	yes	*no*
2.	Do you usually sleep well?	yes	*no*
3.	Are you frightened in the middle of the night?	*yes*	no
4.	Are you troubled with dreams about your work?	*yes*	no
5.	Do you have nightmares?	*yes*	no
6.	Do you have too many sexual dreams?	*yes*	no
7.	Do you ever walk in your sleep?	*yes*	no
8.	Do you ever have the sensation of falling when going to sleep?	*yes*	no
9.	Does you heart ever thump in your ears so that you cannot sleep?	*yes*	no
10.	Do ideas run through your head so that you cannot sleep?	*yes*	no
11.	Do you feel well rested in the morning?	yes	*no*
12.	Do your eyes often pain you?	*yes*	no
13.	Do things ever seem to swim or get misty before your eyes?	*yes*	no
14.	Do you often have the feeling of suffocating?	*yes*	no
15.	Do you have continual itching in the face?	*yes*	no
16.	Are you bothered much by blushing?	*yes*	no
17.	Are you bothered by fluttering of the heart?	*yes*	no
18.	Do you feel tired most of the time?	*yes*	no
19.	Have you ever had fits of dizziness?	*yes*	no
20.	Do you have queer, unpleasant feelings in any part of the body?	*yes*	no
21.	Do you ever feel an awful pressure in or about the head?	*yes*	no
22.	Do you often have bad pains in any part of the body?	*yes*	no
23.	Do you have a great many bad headaches?	*yes*	no
24.	Is your head apt to ache on one side?	*yes*	no
25.	Have you *ever* fainted away?	*yes*	no
26.	Have you *often* fainted away?	*yes*	no
27.	Have you ever been blind, half-blind, deaf, or dumb for a time?	*yes*	no
28.	Have you ever had an arm or leg paralyzed?	*yes*	no
29.	Have you ever lost your memory for a time?	*yes*	no
30.	Did you have a happy childhood?	yes	*no*
31.	Were you happy when 14 to 18 years old?	yes	*no*
32.	Were you considered a bad boy?	*yes*	no
33.	As a child did you like to play alone better than to play with other children?	*yes*	no
34.	Did the other children let you play with them?	yes	*no*
35.	Were you shy with other boys?	*yes*	no
36.	Did you ever run away from home?	*yes*	no

FIGURE 15–1   The first 36 items of the Woodworth Personal Data Sheet. The "neurotic" response to each item is italicized here, but of course not on the inventory itself.

SOURCE: P. M. Symonds, *Diagnosing personality and conduct* (New York: Century, 1931), p. 175. Reprinted by permission of Prentice Hall, Inc.

role playing and taking the inventory yourself, you can gain insight into some of the difficulties encountered in assessing personality.

A number of purported "unidimensional" inventories were developed in the 1920s and 1930s to determine the strength of a variety of personality traits. It remained for psychologist Robert Bernreuter to demonstrate that *one* test could measure a number of personality traits simultaneously. To do this, he gathered a great number of self-report questions and determined which of them discriminated between high and low scorers on each of four tests, which respectively measured "introversion-extraversion," "ascendance-submission," "neurotic tendency," and "self-sufficiency." He found that a given item might correlate well with more than one of the unidimensional tests; through judicious selection he was able to produce a 125-item test, the responses to which could be variously combined to produce four separate scores, each of which correlated highly with the unidimensional test it was expected to replace.

Further refinement of self-report personality scales was introduced by John C. Flanagan, who maintained that since the four Bernreuter scales showed significant intercorrelations (e.g., people scoring very high on the introversion scale tended to score similarly on the neuroticism scale), the traits could not be called independent, and that, therefore, each separate scale did not necessarily have a unique psychological meaning. Flanagan overcame this difficulty by subjecting the Bernreuter test to a sophisticated statistical procedure, factor analysis, which sheds light on the dynamics underlying a table of intercorrelations. After examining the correlations among the items, he proposed that only two separate factors were needed to account for the score patterns. He defined these two factors as the continuum from self-confident, socially aggressive-self-conscious, to emotional instability and the sociable-nonsociable continuum.

This method of defining personality traits is analogous to the factors analytic method of determining separate mental abilities and has become a popular technique for producing multidimensional personality tests. Four of the more prominent tests are the *Guilford-Zimmerman Temperament Survey* (which yields ten scores on such traits as general activity, ascendance, sociability, emotional stability, and friendliness), Cattell's *Sixteen Personality Factor Questionnaire* (which yields scores on such trait pairs as aloof-warm, confident-insecure, tough-sensitive, conventional-eccentric, conservative-experimenting), the *Edwards Personal Preference Schedule* (which yields scores on 15 personality needs— need for achievement, order, autonomy, affiliation, change, aggression, and so on), the *California Psychological Inventory*, and the *Eysenck Personality Inventory*.

One of the most promising and widely used personality inventories is the *Myers-Briggs Type Indicator*. An individual is profiled using four continuums of bipolar adjectives: Extraversion—Introversions (where you like to focus your attention), Sensing—Intuition (the way you gather information), Thinking—Feeling (the way you make decisions), and Judging—Perceiving (how you deal with the outside world). Viewing each scale as a dichotomy results in sixteen different personality types.

15.13 SPECIAL PROBLEMS IN PERSONALITY MEASURES

In addition to the general problems in affective assessment (Sections 11.13–11.17), a number of things plague those who try to treat self-report personality items the same way they treat ability items. The "jingle" and "jangle" fallacies are a much greater problem when dealing with personality variables.

> The emotional stability factor appears in the literature under such aliases as anxiety, neuroticism, emotionality, lack of ego resiliency, and lack of confidence [the jangle fallacy]. Contrariwise, authors use the *same* word differently [the jingle fallacy]. "Introversion" represents for one author a brooding neurotic; for another, anyone who would rather be a clerk than a carnival barker. (Cronbach, 1984, p. 462)

15.14 TRAIT INSTABILITY

If a personality inventory (or a parallel form) is administered to the same individuals after a *short* interval, the correlation between the scores for the first and second times tells how stable the scores are over this time interval. If the scores fluctuate wildly from one time to another, they cannot be useful for making inferences over time. Unlike cognitive tests, many self-report devices can be expected to show considerable fluctuations within the individual, even when errors of measurement and situationally distorting aspects are small. This is especially true for traits such as depression and other mood-related variables. One can have a valid measure at time one but lack the ability to predict the status of the trait at time two.

15.15 THE SOCIAL DESIRABILITY RESPONSE STYLE

In an attempt to reduce the faking problem, various "lie" and "social-desirability" (see Section 11.14) scales have been devised to be integrated into personality inventories and other attitudinal measures. The typical procedure inserts items to which a particular response very likely indicates the intent to deceive, such as "Have you ever deliberately deceived someone?" Since virtually every mortal has done so, a "no" response by Bob Jones suggests that he is being phony in an effort to look good. If Bob also answers the other social-desirability (or lie) scale items in like manner, it follows that his answers to the other items are also suspect. Bob is either deliberately distorting the truth to give a favorable impression, is playing games, or is so seriously emotionally disturbed that he lacks self-insight.

Some personality and interest tests have social-desirability items built into them to help identify people who give invalid information either willfully (lying) or because they are deluded. The use of such scales in comparing groups for research and evaluation purposes can also increase the credibility of findings with attitudinal measures (Hopkins, 1986).

15.16 THE *MINNESOTA MULTIPHASIC PERSONALITY INVENTORY (MMPI)*

The most thoroughly studied paper-and-pencil personality inventory is the *Minnesota Multiphasic Personality Inventory (MMPI)*, which first appeared in 1940. Its 550 items are psychiatrically oriented declarative sentences to which the individual responds "true," "false," or "cannot say." Scores are obtained for a number of psychiatric categories (depression, hypochondriasis, schizophrenia, paranoia, psychopathic deviate, and so on). Many additional scales have been developed for normal traits that do not deal with psychopathology. The scores are based on empirical keying, similar to the *Strong*. An enormous amount of research (more than 8000 articles) has been done on the *MMPI* since its appearance. Because the *MMPI* is a complex instrument, the consequences of misinterpretation on this inventory can be very serious. Perhaps more than any other self-report personality test, the *MMPI* should not be used by school personnel. Ethical issues such as invasion of privacy are involved.[1]

In the *MMPI*, one's responses are compared with those of various psychiatric groups, which themselves are not well defined. Despite the extensive developmental work on this instrument, it has been shown to have no validity for predicting relevant criteria such as success in student teaching or performance in clinical psychology training. It has been found to have meager validity for predicting delinquent behavior among high school students.

Recently, a system for scoring and interpreting *MMPI* profiles by computer has become operational. Critical evaluations of these can be found in the *Mental Measurements Yearbooks* and in an article by Eyde (1987). This type of interpretation can be a two-edged sword—it encourages the use of the *MMPI*, especially by persons without the extensive training necessary for understanding the limited validity of the *MMPI*.

Some of the *MMPI* scales have inadequate reliabilities (in the .50s). In addition, the norms are not based on a representative sample of persons. This problem is compounded by the fact that there are substantial social and cultural correlates of test scores (Anastasi, 1988); any *MMPI* profile must be interpreted in relation to the age, sex, ethnicity, and socioeconomic status of the examinee. The *MMPI* is a clinical instrument; it should be used only by persons with special psychometric and psychological training so that its many limitations and pitfalls can be taken into account.

15.17 *CALIFORNIA PSYCHOLOGICAL INVENTORY*

Whereas the *MMPI* is oriented toward the abnormal, the *California Psychological Inventory* (*CPI*) was developed for use with normal adolescents and adults. The 462 items (*true-false*) in the 1987 revision of the *CPI* yield scores on seventeen scales (e.g., dominance, sociability, self-acceptance, responsibility) and three additional scales to assess response

---

[1]In the 1960s, investigative reporters accused psychologists of violating human dignity. At one point the U. S. Senate voted that no test dealing with a student's personality, home life, family relationships, economic status, or psychological or sociological problems could be given in schools. Attacks came from the political right and the political left. Opposition was caused by (1) the exaggerated validity claims made by some psychologists, (2) the low validity of clinical interpretations of findings, (3) the unfair use by denying equal opportunity on the basis of test results, (4) unfair treatment of nonconformers, and (5) possible improper entrapment. The school has a right to ask students about their emotions, family, and social life only if that information will lead to better education for the student (Cronbach, 1984).

integrity, two of which are designed to detect examinees who are "faking good" or "faking bad" (the latter is the reverse of social desirability, needed, for example, to identify those who want to be in some special program for the emotionally disturbed or who do not want to be drafted). Most of the scales are based on empirical keying, using peer ratings as criteria. All scores are reported using *T*-scores. The *CPI* has been found to have at least some degree of validity for predicting delinquency and dropping out of high school. Test-retest reliability estimates for high school students over a one-year interval average about .67, suggesting the need for considerable caution in individual use of the inventory. As with the *MMPI*, computerized reporting and interpretation services are available.

A measure similar in approach designed for assessing children 6 to 16, is the *Personality Inventory for Children (PIC)*. The child does not answer the questions, but a knowledgeable adult responds to describe the child. The 600 *true-false* questions yield scores on 16 scales. Since the scale is technically not a self-report inventory, it is free from some of the limitations of the *CPI* and the *MMPI*. It appears to have potential for identifying children in need of further psychological evaluation (Wirt & Lachar, 1981).

15.18 THE *MINNESOTA TEACHER ATTITUDE INVENTORY*

The *Minnesota Teacher Attitude Inventory (MTAI)* has been widely used to study teacher attitudes and has frequently been recommended in selecting prospective teachers. Each item is empirically weighted on how it discriminates between 100 "superior" and 100 "inferior" teachers (according to principals' ratings), who responded anonymously to many Likert-type items, such as "Without children life would be dull," "Children should be seen and not heard," "A teacher should acknowledge his ignorance of a topic in the presence of his pupils," and so on. Correlations above .4 were reported between *MTAI* results and the ratings of principals and students . A critical flaw in the research design that restricts the external validity or generalizability of Leeds's findings for teacher selection or evaluation was that participating teachers responded anonymously; consequently, a "need" or motive to fake was greatly reduced. Rabinowitz (1954) showed that education students have no difficulty simulating the attitudes of permissive or authoritative teachers when motivated to do so. When anonymity was not involved, subsequent studies generally failed to find any relationship between *MTAI* scores and teaching success that was great enough to be of any practical value.

A statistically significant relationship between *MTAI* and certain criteria has been reported in a few studies, but statistical significance does not ensure practical significance. Popham and Trimble (1960) reported a significant difference in *MTAI* means of 72 "superior" and 72 "inferior" student teachers. This difference represented a correlation of only .24. Studies have found low validity (predictive) coefficients of .18 to .28, for the *MTAI* and principals' ratings.

The *MTAI* has little apparent promise in teacher selection. In a research context in which the anonymity of the respondents can be preserved, the *MTAI* may have some utility, especially as a way to help teacher trainees consider some of their school-related attitudes. For this, however, the empirical scoring system (based on too few cases, anyway) can be abandoned.

15.19 EVALUATION OF SELF-REPORT MEASURES

Self-report personality measures are afflicted with the difficulties of affective assessment described in Chapter 11 (see Sections 11.13–11.17) to a greater extent than cognitive or psychomotor tests. Virtually all are fakable, although several inventories contain scales for detecting the self-deceived or the flagrant prevaricator. Job applicants and others responding when self-interests are served by a "good showing" describe themselves much more favorably than persons responding anonymously or when the incentive to look good is absent. The difficulty with self-report inventories is not reliability but validity; fakers tend to fake consistently (reliably).

Semantic problems and criterion inadequacy are very serious drawbacks to successful self-report personality assessment. A survey of 113 studies in which personality inventories were used for employment selection found a median validity coefficient of only .25, which is too low to be of much real practical value for personnel selection.

Current personality inventory scores have generally been of little or no value for predicting future success either in school, on the job, or in personal life. They have more validity for research and evaluation purposes when they can be administered anonymously.

15.20 THE ASSESSMENT OF MOTIVES: PROJECTIVE TECHNIQUES

Psychologists have not been very successful in assessing motivations. A *motive* is a psychological state of the individual that is inferred from behavior. Thus, if people begin to eat, the motive of hunger is assumed; if they struggle for success, the motive is said to be ambition; if they act uncharitably, the motive is selfishness. Psychologists suggest that, aside from physiological needs such as those for food, air, and rest, the motivation concept is ambiguous. The minimum assumption to be made in explaining human action is that the individual will set goals whose attainment provides satisfaction, pleasure, or gratification, either consciously or unconsciously. The particular goals of persons, however, will depend partly on their history of rewards and punishments; these in turn probably are influenced by the value systems of that person's environment—parents, social groups, and general culture. Thus, if a culture reinforces academic success, the behavior leading to such goals will be rewarded and there should be many "educated" individuals. If this formulation has validity, it suggests the importance of changes of the value system of some minority groups as a starting point if improved academic performance is a desired goal.

In this formulation the motive concept differs from the trait concept only in degree of generality. Motives predict behavior in a wide variety of environments; traits refer to more specific responses in highly specified conditions. For our purposes the most important question concerns the measurement of human motives.

15.21 THE RORSCHACH

Clinical psychologists have made extensive use of two instruments, the Rorschach inkblot test and the *TAT,* or variants of them, in many of their personality assessments. Such unstructured techniques are called *projective tests* because examinees are expected to *project* into inkblots, ambiguous pictures, or other stimuli and reveal their needs, wants, desires, aversions, fears, anxieties, and so on. The procedures for administering, scoring, and interpreting the two tests are quite different, but they have in common ambiguous stimuli—the amorphous inkblots or ambiguously provocative pictures. The subject is shown one blot at a time and is asked what is "seen." The examiner notes not only the content of the responses but also such things as use of the whole blot instead of details, injection of movement into the blots, and use of color and white spaces in making a response. Elaborate scoring systems attempt to relate the various perceptual modes to such personality variables as impulsiveness, sensitivity, and emotional stability. Although some of the data yielded by the Rorschach have shown some slight validity in comparing groups, their utility in individual clinical evaluations has not been sufficiently established (Anastasi, 1988, p. 599). Since its appearance in 1921, the Rorschach technique has stimulated much controversial literature; there are more than 5000 references pertaining to the Rorschach. There has, however, been a sharp decline in research using the Rorschach in the last decade, as its scientific value as a yardstick of personality is equivocal.

The *Holtzman Inkblot Technique (HIT)* is an attempt to bring the Rorschach technique in line with technical psychometric standards (Holtzman, 1975). The subject is asked to give only one response to each of 45 cards. The administration and scoring are standardized; scores are yielded on 22 variables. Interscorer agreement appears to be satisfactory, but stability of the scores over even a one-week interval is quite low (median stability coefficient of .65) for use with individuals, although it is sufficient for research use. It is not yet known whether the more structured projective technique will be useful. There are insufficient data on the *HIT* to assess its predictive validity and diagnostic utility adequately (Dush, 1985, p. 662).

Guilford (1959, p. 313) reviewed the status of Rorschach validity and concluded that

> in spite of the widespread popularity and use of the Rorschach ink blots, the reliabilities of scores tend to be relatively low, and validities, although quite varied, are generally near zero. This statement regarding validity applies to use of the instrument in discriminating pathological from normal individuals, for diagnosis of more particular pathologies such as anxiety, for indicating degree of maladjustment in the general population, and for predicting academic and vocational success.

Later, after reviewing the research on the *Rorschach,* Jensen (1965, p. 509) concluded that "the rate of scientific progress in clinical psychology might well be measured by the speed and thoroughness with which it gets over the *Rorschach.*" Peterson (1978, p. 1045), in his *MMY* review, concluded that "the general lack of predictive validity for the Rorschach raises serious questions about its continued use in clinical practice."

15.22 THE THEMATIC APPERCEPTION TEST

Henry Murray and his associates (1938) proposed that motives are a person's "inner concerns" and that if we learn what those concerns are, we may predict much of that person's behavior. We can learn of the concerns by listening to a person tell spontaneous, imaginative stories in response to picture cues, such as those used in Murray's *Thematic Apperception Test (TAT)*. By analyzing the content of a series of these spontaneous, imaginative stories according to well-defined rules, the investigator hopes to identify the presence or absence, as well as the strength, of one or more "motives."

We shall not discuss how the *TAT* is scored. There are several scoring procedures, although it typically is not scored as such, but instead provides an opportunity for clinical impressions. Much background in the psychology of personality and in clinical psychology is required before one is sufficiently well equipped to attempt to use projective techniques. Most measurement specialists have far less confidence in the validity of projective techniques than many clinical psychologists do. Validity is not well established psychometrically even for the Rorschach and the *TAT,* much less for less widely used projective techniques.

15.23   OTHER PROJECTIVE TECHNIQUES

Another very popular projective technique is the *Draw-a-Person Test* presented by Machover (1949). The examinee is provided with paper and pencil and asked to draw a person. Next the examinee is asked to draw a person of the gender opposite to that of the person in the first drawing. Every aspect of the drawings is purported to have psychological significance: size, position, order of drawing persons and parts of the body, clothing, shading, omission, background, and so on. Reliability and validity data on such measures are very poor. "The interpretive guide for the Draw-a-Person Test abound in sweeping generalizations . . . but no evidence is provided in support of these statements" (Anastasi, 1988, p. 611).

15.24   COPYING TECHNIQUES

Several "copying" measures have become popular in recent years. Their use is primarily for perceptual visual-motor assessment. Most are derivatives of the *Bender Visual Motor Gestalt Test* illustrated in Figure 15–2. The subject is asked simply to copy each design. There are several different scoring procedures for this test, but rotation of figures, omission, and distortion are the principal factors in its evaluation. "Copying" measurements appear to have some validity for predicting reading failure and identifying people with perceptual difficulty and certain types of brain damage. Significant differences between normal and neurologically disabled children have been found; consequently, the Bender test appears to have value as a screening test for brain damage, though some persons with known brain damage do well on it (Bigler & Ehrfurth, 1981). The value of the Bender for personality appraisal, however, has not been convincingly demonstrated.

An extensive standardization of the Bender-Gestalt was published in 1975 (Koppitz, 1975). Norms are available for ages five to ten. Retest reliabilities over a four-month interval are on the order of .6. Using the Koppitz scoring system, scores correlate moderately to substantially with IQ scores until age nine or ten, when most normal individuals obtain near-perfect scores. Performance also correlates significantly with academic achievement and cognitive aptitude measures in the primary grades.

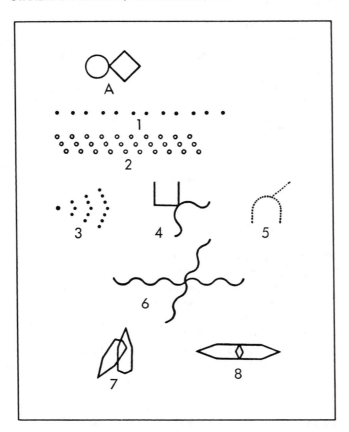

FIGURE 15–2 The Bender Visual Motor Gestalt Test.

SOURCE: Dr. Lauretta Bender, *A Visual Motor Gestalt Test and Its Clinical Use,* American Orthopsychiatric Association, Research Monographs (1938), p. 41. Reprinted by permission of the author and the American Orthopsychiatric Association, Inc. Copyright 1938 by the American Orthopsychiatric Association, Inc.

15.25 EVALUATION OF PROJECTIVE TECHNIQUES

Despite their widespread use by clinical and school psychologists, the validity of projective techniques for clinical personality assessment is equivocal. The scientific status of unstructured projective techniques is little better today than it was when they were critically evaluated by Eysenck (1959, pp. 276–277), who reached the following conclusions:

- There is no consistent meaningful and testable theory underlying modern projective devices.
- The actual practice of projective experts frequently contradicts the putative hypotheses on which their tests are built.

- On the empirical level, there is no indisputable evidence showing any kind of marked relationship between global projective test interpretation by experts and psychiatric diagnosis.
- There is no evidence of any marked relationship between Rorschach scoring categories combined in any approved statistical fashion into a scale, and diagnostic categories, when the association between the two is tested on a population other than that from which the scale was derived.
- There is no evidence for the great majority of the postulated relationships between projective test indicators and personality traits.
- There is no evidence for any marked relationship between projective test indicators of any kind and intellectual qualities and abilities as measured, estimated, or rated independently.
- There is no evidence for the predictive power of projective techniques with respect to success or failure in a wide variety of fields where personality qualities play an important part.
- There is no evidence that conscious or unconscious conflicts, attitudes, fears, or fantasies in patients can be diagnosed by means of projective techniques in such a way as to give congruent results with assessments made by psychiatrists independently.
- There is ample evidence to show that the great majority of studies in the field of projective techniques are inadequately designed, have serious statistical errors in the analysis of the data, and are subject to damaging criticisms on the grounds of contamination between test and criterion.

15.26 MEASURING SCHOOL AND INSTITUTIONAL CLIMATE

In the assessment of educational environment, the perceptions of people within the milieu are commonly used. The difficulty in clearly defining school climate is reflected in the diversity of climate typologies that have evolved (Anderson, 1982). One of the most widely used measures for appraising the organizational climate of schools is the *Organizational Climate Description Questionnaire (OCDQ)*, devised by Halpin (1966). Teachers and administrators respond to 64 Likert-type items such as "Teachers at this school stay to themselves"; "The morale of teachers is high"; and "The principal goes out of his way to help teachers." The items are grouped into four subtests that describe the group—disengagement, hindrance, esprit, and intimacy—and four subtests that describe the administration—aloofness, production emphasis, thrust, and consideration. Considerable difference among schools is evidenced in the various *OCDQ* scales.

The *CFK School Climate profile* (Phi Delta Kappan, 1973) is a similar measure but has the advantage of being able to be administered to students and parents in addition to teachers and administrators, thus affording a more comprehensive assessment. Respondents rate each item twice, in terms of "what is" and again in terms of "what should be," so that significant discrepancies can be identified. Preliminary research findings regarding the instrument's reliability and validity are encouraging (Dennis, 1979). For example, Dennis obtained school climate ratings by administrators, teachers, and students in ten high schools as shown in Figure 15–3. Notice how low the morale appears to be among the teachers and administrators in school C. Notice, also, that, except in school *C,* administrators perceived the school climate to be highest and students perceived it to be lowest. The up-and-down profile for administrators tended to be roughly parallel but with little correspondence to students' perceptions.

The *College Characteristics Index (CCI)* is designed to measure the environmental climate of colleges (Stern, 1970). Statements like "There would be a capacity audience for

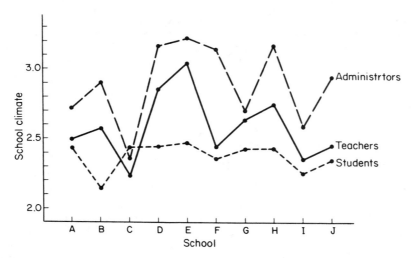

FIGURE 15–3 School climate ratings for ten high schools by administrators, teachers, and students in those schools.

SOURCE: P. Dennis, "An assessment of the validity and reliability of the CFK Ltd. School Climate Profile" (doctoral dissertation, University of Colorado, 1979).

a lecture by an outstanding philosopher or theologian" and "Professors here really care whether students learn" are answered by a representative sample of students. An institutional profile is then constructed using the percent of students subscribing to the statements. The *CCI* yields scores on 30 subtests, such as theoretical-practical orientation, conformity, extracurricular participation, and achievement-versus-relaxed pressure. A companion measure oriented toward individuals rather than institutions is the *Activities Index (AI)*. By comparing the respective *CCI* and *AI* profiles on the 30 scales, areas of compatibility and dissonance can be identified. A more general form of the *CCI*, the *Organizational Climate Index (OCI)*, is designed to apply to any organization.

The *College and University Environment Scale (CUES)* is a relative of the *CCI*; it uses students' perceptions to describe the institution in terms of five factors: practicality, community, awareness, propriety, and scholarship.

The *Social Climate Scales* (Moos, 1974, 1975) also measure ecological climate. They include nine scales that are applicable in a variety of environments, such as a family, a school classroom (e.g., the classroom environment scale [Moos, 1979]), or a residence hall. The scales show considerable ability to differentiate, and they appear to remain quite stable over time.

Climate measures can be useful, especially to administrators and other decision makers, for identifying areas of satisfaction and dissatisfaction, and they can give direction to needed institutional changes. Their reliability and validity are closely tied to the conditions of administration. In most instances, anonymity is a crucial prerequisite for validity.

15.27 MATRIX SAMPLING

Rather than having each respondent answer all items, when a school or other institution is to be assessed on many variables requiring many items, *matrix sampling* can be employed to reduce greatly the assessment time required and/or to increase greatly the number of variables that can be measured. It is not essential that every person respond to every question (as is the case with clinical appraisal) but, rather, that a representative sample of persons respond to a representative subset of the items. Matrix sampling is widely used in state assessment programs (Section 14.21) but can also be used when measuring the perceptions of a large number of individuals about an organization or group, as with the scales described in Section 15.26.

15.28 SOCIOMETRIC TECHNIQUES

Sociometry is the study of interrelationships among members of a group—that is, its social structure, or how each individual is perceived by the group. Sociometry was launched in 1934 with the publication of Moreno's *Who Shall Survive*. Bonney (1960, p. 1319) described the rationale as follows:

> The major assumption underlying sociometric method is that within all groups, such as a school class or teaching staff, in which considerable interaction is allowed, there emerges an informal organization among the members based on varying degrees of positive and negative interpersonal feelings, and that these preferences and aversions are significant factors in the morale and efficiency of this group.

Various techniques that were considered in Chapter 11, such as Q-sort, the semantic differential, and rating scales, can be used to rate others as well as oneself. Special sociometric techniques have been devised for the social appraisal of individuals and groups.

15.29 SOCIOMETRY AND PEER RATINGS

Teachers may study the social structure of a classroom by asking students to make *meaningful* choices like the following: With which student would you rather study tomorrow's arithmetic lesson? With which three persons would you rather play at recess? Which two classmates would be the most fun at a party at your home?

A more complex variation is to present the personality sketch of a hypothetical student and ask each youngster to name the three members of the class who seem most like the individual described.

We illustrate the sociometric process with actual data from a fourth-grade class of 14 girls and 17 boys. The teacher gave each child a sheet that read as follows:

My three best friends in this class are:
1. My very best friend _____
2. My second best friend _____
3. My third best friend _____

The results are shown in the *sociogram* in Figure 15–4; the capital letters from *A* through *N* designate girls, and the small letters from *a* through *q* represent boys.

How does one read Figure 15–4? Begin with girl *A*. In row A, we see that she chose girl *D* as her very best friend, because there is the number 1 at the intersection of row A and column D. Girl *A* selected girl *C* as her second-best friend. Girl *A* listed boy *c* as her third-best friend.

Who chose girl *A*? Look at column A, where you see (from top to bottom) the following numbers: 1 (first choice of girls *D* and *N* and boy *k*), 2 (second choice of girls *C, F,* and *G* and boy *d*), and 3 (third choice of boys *c* and *f*). Thus, girl *A* was named by nine students—three times as first choice, four times as second choice, and twice as third choice. You will find the numbers 3, 4, and 2 in column A of the first three rows below the choices.

In the lower left quadrant of Figure 15–4 you can see that girl *A* was chosen by four boys, whereas no other girl was chosen by more than one boy. You can also determine that no girl chose only boys but boy *k* chose only girls. Did any girl choose boy *k*? No, but *k* was the *first* choice of boy *o*.

If we give 3 points for being chosen as "very best friend," 2 points for "second best friend," and 1 point for "third best friend," the most popular students are girl *A* and boy *a,* each with 19 points, even though girl *A* was chosen by two more students than boy *a*. This happens because boy *a* was chosen as very best friend by five students, resulting in 15 points, whereas girl *A* was chosen as very best friend by only three students, yielding 9 points. For girl *A,* the computation is $(3 \times 3) + (4 \times 2) + (2 \times 1) = 19$. For boy *a,* it is $(5 \times 3) + (2 \times 2) = 19$.

The lowest scorers, whom nobody chose, are girls *L, M,* and *N* and boys *p* and *q*. They may be the fourth- or fifth-best friends of some of the students, but they weren't listed as first, second, or third. In Figure 15–4 the girls (and boys) are arranged in order of total number of points, from *A,* with the most, to *L, M,* and *N,* with the least.

Every girl listed three names, but boys *e, l,* and *q* did not. Inspect rows e, l, and q to see which choices they omitted. (Do you suppose that fourth-grade boys typically are less careful about such tasks than fourth-grade girls, or is it that some of the boys have fewer close friends than the girls have?)

The 31 very-best-friend choices went to just 15 students. How many of these were mutual choices—in which, for example, Mary listed Susan as her very best friend and Susan listed Mary as hers? By examining Figure 15–4 we can see that *A* chose *D* and was chosen by *D,* that *B* chose *f* and was chosen by *f,* that *C* chose *c* but was not chosen by *c,* and so on. The five mutual first-choice pairs are *AD, Bf, ag, bc,* and *eh.*

Girl *A,* the most popular student, has perfect mutuality with all three of her choices. She listed girl *D* as her very best friend, and girl *D* listed her likewise. She chose girl *C* as her second-best friend, and girl *C* reciprocated. She named boy *c* as her third-best friend, and he named her as his third-best friend.

Girl *B*'s three choices all named her as very best friend. Girl *C* listed boy *c* as her very best friend, but he did not choose her at all, instead choosing boys for first and second and designating her second-best friend, *A,* as his third-best friend.

We have illustrated how a study of these 89 "chose" and "was chosen by" listings can offer insight into a variety of interesting relationships.

The *target sociogram* shown in Figure 15–5 is a simple way of depicting sociometric data from groups as large as those found in most classrooms. It portrays the same data

Girls Chosen (columns A–N) — **Boys Chosen** (columns a–q)

Girls Chose = rows A–N; *Boys Chose* = rows a–q.

	A	B	C	D	E	F	G	H	I	J	K	L	M	N	a	b	c	d	e	f	g	h	i	j	k	l	m	n	o	p	q
A			2	1													3														
B				2			3									1															
C	2				3											1															
D	1		3		2																										
E		1			2													3													
F	2			1																			3								
G	2		3																		1										
H		1					3		2																						
I		1		3																			2								
J				2		1																				3					
K		2	1															3													
L						2										1		3													
M				2											1								3								
N	1			2	3																										
a																				2	1				3						
b																	1	2					3								
c	3																1	2													
d	2																1					3									
e					2																1										
f	3	1													2																
g															1							2						3			
h							2																						3		
i															2		1			3											
j															1	2				3											
k	1		3	2																											
l							2								1																
m																2		3					1								
n																2	1									3					
o																		3				2		1							
p															1			3	2												
q																				1											
1st choice	3	4	1	2				1							5	3	3	1	2	2	1	1		1	1						
2nd choice	4	1	1	1	2	3	2	1	1	1	1				2	3		2	1	2		1	1								
3rd choice	2		3		2		1		2								3	3	2		2		2	1		2	1	1	1		
Times chosen	9	5	4	3	4	3	3	2	3	1	1				7	6	6	6	5	4	3	2	3	2	1	2	1	1	1		
"Score"	19	14	8	8	6	6	5	5	4	2	2	0	0	0	19	15	12	10	10	10	5	5	4	4	3	2	1	1	1	0	0
	A	B	C	D	E	F	G	H	I	J	K	L	M	N	a	b	c	d	e	f	g	h	i	j	k	l	m	n	o	p	q

FIGURE 15–4 Choices of three best friends by a fourth-grade class of 14 girls and 17 boys.

School___Central___

Teacher___Williams___

Level or Grade___4___

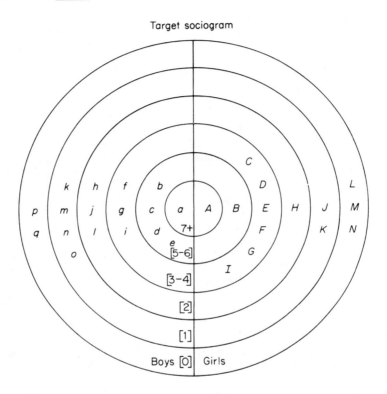

FIGURE 15–5 A "target sociogram" based on data in Figure 15–4.

Times chosen	Boys	Girls	Total
7+	1	1	2
5–6	4	1	5
3–4	3	6	9
3–2	3	1	4
5–6	4	2	6
0	2	3	5

as for the sociogram in Figure 15–4 but without using the ranks. Four concentric circles distinguish among the students; roughly one-fourth of them are represented in each of the four areas. Typically, boys are placed in one half, girls in the other. The "stars" are found near the center, the "isolates" and "fringers" near the periphery.

15.30 THE "GUESS WHO" TECHNIQUE

This nomination technique is one of the simplest methods of obtaining peer judgments. Each student is asked to indicate the student or students (if any) who match a series of brief descriptions that may include negative as well as positive characteristics. When negative descriptions are included, it is important that the response be optional.

Hartshorne and May (1928) originated this technique as a guessing game for young children—hence its name. Some excellent sample directions are given by Cunningham et al. (1951):

> Below are some word pictures of members of your class. Read each statement and write down the names of the persons whom you think the descriptions fit.
>
> REMEMBER: One description *may* fit several persons. You may write as many names as you think belong under each. The same person may be nominated for more than one description. If you cannot think of anyone to match a particular description, go on to the next one. You will have as much time as you need to finish. Do not hurry.

A series of behavior descriptions follows, such as

> Someone who always seems rather sad, worried, or unhappy.
> Someone who is very friendly, who is nice to everybody.

Torrance (1962) suggested using the Guess Who approach to evaluate different aspects of creative thinking. Sample items include "Who in your class has the most original or unusual ideas?" "Who does the most inventing or developing of new ideas, gadgets, and such?"

The results from an actual Guess Who application in a sixth-grade class are shown in Figure 15–6. The assessment was a part of a case study of student 36, who, because of her maladaptive behavior, had been referred by her teacher for a psychological appraisal. The teacher's suspicions were dramatically confirmed by the peer judgments obtained by the Guess Who technique. Note that student 36 was listed as "not liked" by all but one of her classmates. No other student was so identified by even one student. Her one nomination for "best friend" was from her own ballot!

From such a self-portrait of a class, the teacher can identify students in need of special attention. Notice the "quiet" pupils, 2, 6, 12, and 17. Although pupil 6 (L.J.) was perceived as the quietest, L.J. was listed as "best friend" by two other students; the other three quiet students were not nominated by any peer. Only one of the four received a single identification with "happy" by a peer, whereas each of the four was deemed "unhappy" by at least one peer.

This Guess Who chart differs in several important ways from the sociogram depicted in Figure 15–4. The gender of the student is not indicated, although this could be done readily by, for example, circling the student number of each female. Also, *which* student rated which student in what way is not indicated. To do so would be extremely cumbersome, but not having that information (which the sociogram provided) leaves the user of the chart unable to plan student interactions specifically designed to improve the classroom's social atmosphere.

The principal advantage of the Guess Who technique over the sociograms illustrated in Figs. 15–4 and 15–5 is its comprehensiveness (more than one characteristic) and usability. It requires only a few minutes to administer and tabulate and can assess several important dimensions within a group. Sociograms are typically limited to a single question—a separate figure or table is required for each item.

A variant of the Guess Who technique is The School Play, which gives 11 "roles" (e.g., a bully—someone who picks on smaller boys and girls). Each student nominates the class member who could best play the part. This might, however, confuse life role (actually a bully) with *acting* ability (e.g., big and menacing looking, but actually not a bully).

Specific *action* questions may elicit better responses than general ones do. "Whom would you most like to help you with a difficult arithmetic problem?" or "With whom would you prefer to share your lunch at the class picnic next week?" might, if used by the teacher at least partly for assigning arithmetic tutors or partners at the picnic, elicit more valid responses than more general questions such as "Who in this class is best in arithmetic?" or "Who is your best friend?" At the least, the action type may provide the teacher a firmer basis for trying to improve classroom interactions than the latter usually does.

15.31 RELIABILITY AND VALIDITY OF SOCIOMETRIC DATA

Test-retest reliability coefficients of approximately .75 have been found for sociometric choices over a 4 to 6 month interval for elementary school children. From his extensive study of sociometric literature, Bonney (1960, p. 1321) reported that "it seems fair to conclude that there is indeed a strong tendency for the members of a group to maintain quite similar sociometric ranks over several weeks or several months . . ."

Internal-consistency reliability is also evidenced in Figure 15–6; note the high degree of agreement between the independently rated characteristics, "quiet" and "silent." (The classification of "quiet" as a positive characteristic and "silent" as a negative characteristic is obviously inappropriate, they are the same in the minds of the raters.)

The immediate validity of sociometric data appears to be quite satisfactory (Cronbach, 1984, pp. 534-626) when certain precautions are taken. The confidentiality of the information must be perceived by the respondent; otherwise, many negative perceptions and interrelationships will not be expressed. A second requirement is that the members of the group must know each other quite well. This requirement reduces the value of sociometric data in large schools in which students change classes each period. Sociometric data have had, and will probably continue to have, their greatest utility in the educational context at the elementary school level.

Pupil No.	Quiet	Most Active in Games	Best Liked	Not Bossy	Polite	Works Well with Others	Happy	Tidy	Takes Care of Things	Best Friend	Restless	Talkative	Silent	Not Liked	Bossy	Not Polite	Does Not Take Care of Things	Unhappy	Untidy	Wastes Time	Does Not Work Well with Others	Sum of Positive Traits	Sum of Negative Traits
Positive Characteristics (10)											Negative Characteristics (11)												
1 T.R.		16	15	2	7	4	3		1	4	1											52	1
2 O.S.	6		1	3	6		1	9	2				2		1			1				28	4
3 A.B.		14	2	1		2		1	2							1			1			22	2
4 G.P.		2	5	2	2	3	7	2	2	3	2				9						2	28	13
5 R.P.		2	5	1	4	1	2	7							6	1	1					22	8
6 L.J.	13			7	4	1		3	3	2			17						2			33	19
7 B.C.				2		4		1	2	3								1				12	1
8 B.S.				2	4	1		2	4	1				1	1			1				14	3
9 E.J.	1	1		2				1	2	2												9	0
10 S.V.			5			1	3	2	1	3	1				1	1		1		2		15	6
11 M.E.				1	1	2	4	1	2			1				1					1	11	3
12 M.C.	6			3	2			1	1					3					2			13	5
13 T.B.				1	1	2	3		1									1				8	1
14 R.D.						1	8			1	1							1	1	1		10	4
15 B.B.			4	1	1		1												3	1		7	4
16 T.K.						1	1	1	2	1	1							1				5	2
17 D.C.	9		3	4	1								10				1	3				17	14
18 B.L.						1	1	1							1							3	1
19 J.J.						2																2	0
20 M.S.			1			3	1		1	2					2	2			1	1		8	6
21 S.D.								2		2					3							4	3
22 W.B.			1			2										1		1				3	2
23 M.M.						1	1													1	1	2	2
24 H.C.							1	1										1	1		1	2	3
25 O.R.						1					1				1							1	2
26 M.E.				1	1	1				1					1		1		3	1		4	6
27 F.J.			1								1		1		1	1						1	4
28 C.R.							1	1		1					1	1		1			1	2	5
29 E.T.			1								1					1	1	2		1		1	6
30 N.R.			1					1	1						1	1			5		3	3	10
31 A.E.									1						1	1			3		3	1	8
32 C.J.									1		1	1			3	1			2	1		1	9
33 S.M.									1						1	1	2	2			3	1	9
34 E.R.									1		4				6	2	1	2	3	2		0	21
35 H.S.						1			1		23				5	2	2	2	7	4		2	45
36 H.C.			1					3		1	14	2	34	5	6	22	17	9	15		9	5	133

FIGURE 15–6 Results of a typical Guess-Who sociometric assessment with a sixth-grade class. Numbers indicate the frequency with which each student was associated with the Guess-Who description by his or her classmates.

SOURCE: Courtesy of Frank Thompson, principal of Hillgrove School, La Puente, CA.

Sociometric techniques should be meaningful to the students and provide useful data for the teacher. Nothing beneficial can be expected to happen merely because each student has been asked, for example, to list his or her three best friends. Responses to this kind of question constitute the starting point from which an ingenious teacher studies the social structure of the classroom and devises ways to help it facilitate his or her teaching. The teacher may try to alter the structure in carefully thought-out ways, such as by forming study groups of low mutuality in the hope that this will permit the "friendless" to make friends. The teacher needs to understand the social psychology of the group rather well in order to do this extensively or radically. It is advisable to proceed with caution, but to proceed, nevertheless.

When properly obtained, according to Bonney (1960, p. 1323), sociometric data have validity for the following classroom uses:

1. To form subgroups which are composed of persons who have indicated preferences for each other,
2. To study changes in interpersonal relations and in the social structure of a group over a particular time interval,
3. To determine the extent to which students of different racial, religious, and social-class groupings accept each other,
4. To locate individuals and small groups of individuals who are outstanding centers of influence in a particular population in order to utilize their social prestige in the management of the group, and
5. To locate individuals who are isolates or fringers in order to plan some kind of assistance for them so that they may achieve some degree of recognition and feeling of belonging.

Sociometric information can also be useful in parent conferences, in enabling parents to understand better how their child is perceived by peers.

15.32 APPRAISING SOCIOECONOMIC STATUS

The concept of socioeconomic status (SES) is widely used in education, sociology, and psychology. SES is related to many educational characteristics of students, such as achievement motivation, dropping out of school and college, and academic achievement. The relationship between SES and academic achievement is only at most .3 for *individuals*, however—much less than is commonly assumed (White, 1982). For group comparisons, the mean differences tend to be large.

Occupation is an important ingredient of SES; its relationship to intelligence is graphically illustrated in Figure 13–12. Since the concept of SES is so pervasive, it is useful to understand how it is measured, even though it is rarely assessed formally in education except in research studies.

Methods of assessing SES have evolved largely from sociology and social psychology. Several different SES measures have been devised; all of them employ some combination of the following: educational level, occupational level, kind of residence, amount of income, source of income, and dwelling area.

15.33 THE WARNER-MEEKER-EELLS SCALE

The classic SES measure is the *Index of Status Characteristics (ISC)* (Warner, Meeker, and Eells, 1949), which uses four factors to arrive at an *ISC* score that is then converted into one of five social classes. (More detailed explanation of each category can be found in Bonjean et al., 1967.)

Occupation

1. Professionals and proprietors (such as established physicians, lawyers, certified public accountants, major executives, and "gentlemen" farmers)
2. Minor professionals and proprietors (such as beginning or less successful physicians, lawyers, and so on, and owners of large farms)
3. Semiprofessionals (such as salespeople and cashiers)
4. Skilled workers (such as bookkeepers, factory forepersons, sheriffs, and railroad engineers)
5. Medium-skilled workers (such as telephone operators, carpenters, plumbers, barbers, and firefighters)
6. Semiskilled workers (such as taxi and truck drivers, gas station attendants, and waiters)
7. Unskilled workers (such as laborers, miners, and janitors)

Source of Income

1. Inherited wealth
2. Earned wealth
3. Profits and professional fees
4. Salary and commissions
5. Wages, determined by an hourly rate
6. Private relief
7. Public relief and nonrespectable income

Housing

1. Excellent houses: very large single-family dwellings surrounded by large landscaped yards
2. Very good houses, but not as large as those in the first category
3. Good houses, more conventional and less ostentatious than those in the first two categories
4. Average houses, conventional single-family dwellings
5. Fair houses, smaller houses whose condition is not quite as good as that of the houses in category 4
6. Poor, badly run-down houses
7. Very poor houses surrounded by debris

Dwelling Area

1. Very high-status area
2. High-status area
3. Above-average area
4. Average area containing workers' homes
5. Below-average area; close to factories or railroads
6. Low-status area; run-down and semi-slum
7. Very low-status area; slum

Earlier, Warner had included amount of education and amount of income, but since these factors were found to be largely redundant with the four just listed, they were eliminated from the scale.

The *ISC* is arrived at by using the category ratings from the four factors in the following equation:

$$ISC = (4 \times \text{Occupation}) + (3 \times \text{Source of income}) + (3 \times \text{House type}) + (2 \times \text{Dwelling area})$$

15.34 THE HOLLINGSHEAD INDEX

Because of the difficulty and cost of obtaining residential information, more efficient SES scales have been devised that agree very closely with those obtained from more laborious methods such as the *ISC*. The *Hollingshead Two-Factor Index of Social Position* (Hollingshead & Redlich, 1957) is perhaps the most widely used measure of SES in the behavioral sciences. Its popularity is due in large part to its ease of use—the index requires only an occupation scale and a parental education scale, each of which is divided into seven levels.

Occupation Scale

1. Major executives of large concerns, major professionals, and proprietors
2. Lesser professions and proprietors, and business managers
3. Administrative personnel, small business owners, and minor professionals
4. Clerical and sales workers, and technicians
5. Skilled trades
6. Machine operators and semiskilled workers
7. Unskilled employees

Education Scale

1. Professionals (master's degree, doctorate, or professional degree)
2. College graduates
3. 1–3 years college or business school
4. High school graduates
5. 10–11 years of schooling
6. 7–9 years of schooling
7. Less than 7 years of schooling

A total index of social position (*ISP*) score is arrived at by using the following equation:

$$ISP = (7 \times \text{Occupation Rating}) + (4 \times \text{Education Rating})$$

Thus, a carpenter (5 on the Occupation Scale) with nine years of schooling (6 on the Education Scale) would have a total *ISP* score of: $ISP = (7 \times 5) + (4 \times 6) = 59$. Hollingshead uses the categorization below to group scores into five social classes:

Social Class	Scores
I	11–17
II	18–27
III	28–43
IV	44–60
V	61–77

SES scales based only on occupation have been devised (Stricker, 1985); obviously, the construct validity of the measures is less than for measures that use multiple relevant sources of information.

SUMMARY

The value of standardized interest tests is most apparent for vocational guidance purposes. The major tests of this kind are the Strong-Campbell and the Kuder.

During the high school years there is considerable fluctuation in interests; this must be considered in interpreting students' profiles. Measured interests have little relationship to abilities, although they are related to occupational choice and job satisfaction.

Personality assessment is difficult and imprecise with current tests and techniques. Self-report personality inventories are vulnerable to semantic difficulties, self-deception, faking "good" or "poor," and criterion inadequacy. Such measures have rarely been shown to yield information of any practical clinical value. Projective techniques are not easily faked, but their unique assessment difficulties greatly limit their usefulness for personality appraisal.

Sociometric techniques can help one understand the status and dynamics of groups such as a class of students. The Guess Who technique is particularly useful since it yields quantified information on several dimensions and requires little time to administer and tabulate.

Measures of socioeconomic status are often useful in research studies but have limited value for individual or classroom use.

IMPORTANT TERMS AND CONCEPTS

situation test
self-report inventory
empirical keying
SES
projective techniques

target diagram
sociometric measure
matrix sampling
Guess-Who technique

social desirability
lie scales
institutional climate
  measure

CHAPTER TEST

1. What are the two principal names associated with the major interest inventories?

2. The scoring of the *Strong* is based on
   a) content validity.   b) criterion-related validity.   c) construct validity.

3. Which one of the Kuder interest inventories is most similar to the *Strong*?
   a) *Kuder General Interest Survey (KGIS)*
   b) *Kuder Preference Record-Vocational (KPR-V)*
   c) *Kuder Occupational Interest Survey (KOIS)*

4. _____ is to normative as Kuder is to _____.

5. With an ipsative interest measure,
   a) examinees can be compared in absolute degree of interest.
   b) examinees are not forced to choose among options.
   c) an intra-individual interpretation is essential.
   d) percentile ranks can be interpreted in the same way as when a normative measure is used.

6. What is the primary source for obtaining critical reviews of published tests?

7. Which one of the following statements about the stability of interests is true?
   a) Interests are more stable for adolescents than for adults.
   b) Interests at age 17 or 18 correlate substantially with interests 15 to 20 years later.
   c) Interests have virtually no stability until people are in their mid-20s.
   d) Test-retest *rs* for interest tests of .9 or higher are common for a one-year interval.

8. In order to obtain a valid interest profile, which of the following factors is most important?
   a) giving the *Strong* rather than the *KOIS*
   b) admonishing the examinee to answer truthfully
   c) administering the interest inventory individually rather than in a group
   d) removing incentives to fake

9. In which of the following situations is the validity of a personality inventory *least* suspect?
   a) The inventory is administered to applicants for a job.
   b) The inventory is administered to people who are seeking counseling.
   c) The inventory is taken and scored by the examinee as part of a class assignment and results are reported to the instructor.
   d) The inventory is required by the court as part of a probation decision process.

10. Which one of the following is the most helpful for detecting lying and exaggeration by examinees?
    a) ipsative scales
    b) normative scales
    c) social-desirability scales
    d) scales based on empirical scoring

11. Measured interests have been shown to be more valid than expressed interests for nearly all groups studied. (*T* or *F*)

12. Abilities and corresponding interests (e.g., clerical ability and clerical interest) tend to be
    a) very highly correlated.
    b) highly correlated.
    c) substantially correlated.
    d) not highly correlated.

13. Which one of the following conclusions is most strongly supported by research on interest measurement?
    a) People tend to end up in occupations for which they have very high scores.
    b) People tend *not* to end up in occupations for which they have very low scores.
    c) Options *a* and *b* are equally strongly supported.

14. Which one of the following is more blue-collar-oriented and may be a more appropriate interest measure than the *Strong* for non-college-bound individuals?
    a) *MVII* b) *WAIS* c) *KOIS*

15. In interpreting interest inventories, one must bear in mind that
    a) there is a wide diversity of activities within most occupations.
    b) there is considerable variation among jobs with the same label.
    c) the duties of many jobs change with time because of automation and the like.
    d) Two of the above
    e) All of the above

16. Which one of the following is *not* a self-report personality inventory?
    a) *Guilford-Zimmerman Temperament Survey*
    b) *CPI*
    c) *TAT*
    d) *MMPI*

17. Which one of the following is *least* appropriate for use in schools?
    a) *MTAI* b) *MMPI* c) *CPI* d) *Strong*

18. Criterion-related validity is poorest for measures of
    a) personality. b) interest. c) achievement. d) scholastic aptitude.

19. Which of these is *not* a serious deficiency of almost all personality inventories?
    a) low internal-consistency reliability coefficients
    b) low criterion-related validity
    c) semantic problems
    d) faking
    e) self-deception

20. One advantage projective techniques have over personality inventories is that projective techniques
    a) are more valid.
    b) are more reliable.
    c) have better norms.
    d) are less fakable.

21. Which one of the following measures has some validity for detecting perceptual difficulties and correlates with academic performance in the primary grades?
    a) Rorschach b) *TAT* c) *Draw-a-Person* d) Bender Gestalt

22. Current research supports the
    a) validity of the theory underlying most projective techniques.
    b) predictive validity of projective techniques.
    c) relationship between performance on projective techniques and psychiatric diagnoses.
    d) Two or more of the above
    e) None of the above

23. In the sociogram results in Figure 15–5, which children appear to be "isolates" (received no votes)? Which boy chose only girls? Did the two girl "stars" select any boys? Did the two most popular boys select any girls?

24. In the Guess Who results in Figure 15–6, which student appears to be most highly regarded by the class? Which two students in the class appear to be having the greatest difficulty with peer acceptance? Which child is considered the quietest?

25. Which one of the following types of measures tends to have the greatest validity?
    a) sociometric techniques b) projective techniques c) personality inventories

26. The magnitude of the relationship between individual student's academic achievement and their socioeconomic status (SES) is
    a) very high (.80+). b) high (.60 – .80). c) moderate (.40 – .60). d) less than .40.

27. Which one of the following is *not* used in the *Hollingshead Two-Factor Index of Social Position?*
    a) housing b) education c) occupation

28. Which one of the following is a more comprehensive SES measure?
    a) Hollingshead's Index b) Warner-Meeker-Eells Scale

29. In order for measures of organizational climate to have high validity, which one of the following factors would be most important?
    a) an inventory of 100 questions or more
    b) a sample of 100 people or more
    c) up-to-date and representative norms
    d) anonymity for the respondents
    e) the use of matrix sampling

30. The sociogram of Figure 15–5 differs importantly from the Guess Who chart of Figure 15–4 in that the latter
    a) shows the gender of each student.
    b) depicts only negative characteristics.
    c) does not indicate which student rated which other student.
    d) yields a weighted composite score for each student, with each positive mark counted +1 and each negative mark –1.

ANSWERS TO CHAPTER TEST

1. Kuder, Strong
2. b
3. c
4. Strong, ipsative
5. c
6. *Mental Measurement Yearbooks*
7. b
8. d
9. b
10. c

11. F
12. d
13. b
14. a
15. e
16. c
17. b
18. a
19. a
20. d

21. d
22. e
23. L, M, N, p, q; k; yes; no
24. 1; 35 and 36;6
25. a
26. d
27. a
28. b
29. d
30. c

APPENDIX A

Resources for the Development and Selection of Measuring Instruments

AMERICAN ALLIANCE FOR HEALTH, PHYSICAL EDUCATION, AND RECREATION. *Testing for impaired, disabled, and handicapped individuals.* Washington, DC: American Alliance for Health, Physical Education, and Recreation, n.d. This monograph contains information about 60 instruments designed for handicapped persons. Types of measures included are motor ability, perceptual-motor development, physical fitness, and developmental profiles.

BEATTY, W. H. *Improving educational assessment and an inventory of measures of affective behavior.* Washington, DC: Association for Supervision and Curriculum Development, NEA, 1969. Section II gives a very brief description of approximately 130 instruments classified in eight categories: attitude, creativity, interaction, motivation, personality, readiness, self-concept, and miscellaneous. Instruments are not critically evaluated, although some reliability and validity are reported for about half the measures. Sample items are given for some instruments.

BEERE, C. A. *Women and women's issues: A handbook of tests and measures.* San Francisco: Jossey-Bass, 1979. A handbook designed to help locate suitable instruments for scientifically studying children's sex role behavior, women's attitudes toward marriage and work, men's and women's attitudes toward women's issues, and other related topics.

BONJEAN, C. M., R. J. HILL, and S. D. MCLEMORE. *Sociological measurement: An inventory of scales and indices.* San Francisco: Chandler, 1967. Contains bibliographic information on approximately 2000 sociological scales used in sociological research published between 1954 and 1965. The scales and indexes are divided into 78 categories; 47 measures that were used or cited more than five times are described in detail. Information in these detailed descriptions includes classification, title, bibliographic information, variables measured, developmental procedures, scoring procedures, validity and reliability data (when available), and a description of the sample with which the measure was used. Copies of some of the instruments are included. Section M of Miller (1977) extends this compendium through 1974.

BORICH, G. D., and S. K. MADDEN. *Evaluating classroom instruction: A sourcebook of instruments.* Reading, MA: Addison-Wesley, 1977. Describes approximately 175 measures classified using a two-dimensional grid: what is being evaluated (teacher, pupil, or classroom) and by whom it is being evaluated (teacher, pupil, or observer). Instruments are described in terms of type of measure, availability, reliability, validity, norms, and procedures for use. Copies of the instruments are not included, although sample items are provided.

BOYER, E. G., A. SIMON, and G. R. KARAFIN, (Eds.). *Measures of maturation: An anthology of early childhood observation instruments*. Philadelphia: Research for Better Schools, 1973. A three-volume anthology that describes 73 observational systems for recording children's behavior. (See listing for Simon & Boyer, 1970.)

CATTELL, R. B., and F. WARBURTON. *Objective personality and motivation tests*. Urbana: University of Illinois Press, 1967. The major portion of this volume is a compendium of personality measures. Each measure is described as follows: test title, author's designation and age range of tests, administration time, formal structure of test (e.g., ability, performance, opinionnaire, projective), variables derived from test, techniques for reducing fakability, theory supporting the test, design (positive and negative features), sample test items, and procedures for administration and scoring. No psychometric data are provided on validity or other technical qualities of the instruments.

CHUN, K., S. COBB, and J. FRENCH. *Measures for psychological assessment: A guide to 3,000 original sources and their application*. Ann Arbor: University of Michigan, Institute for Social Research, 1975. Developed to provide a comprehensive bibliography on all measures of mental health and related concepts, the volume entries are based on a search of 26 measurement-related journals in psychology and sociology from 1960 to 1970. Information that is relevant to a particular test includes a bibliographic reference to the first source that described the device, the test's title, key words that describe its content, bibliographic data referencing an article or in which the test has been used, and a set of terms indicating the type of information available in the article.

CLARKE, H. *Physical and motor tests in the Medford boys' growth study*. Englewood Cliffs, NJ: Prentice-Hall, 1971. A useful resource for psychomotor and physical measures of physical maturity, physique type, body size, muscular strength and endurance, motor ability, and athletic ability.

COMPTON, C. A. *A guide to 65 tests for special education*. Belmont, CA: Pitman Learning, 1980. Commonly used measures are described and briefly evaluated in the following areas of special education: academic achievement (reading, mathematics, language), perception and memory (comprehension, auditory, visual and visual-motor), speech and language (articulation, language), gross motor; preschool and kindergarten, and intelligence and developmental.

COMREY, A. L., T. E. BACKER, and E. M. GLASER. *A sourcebook for mental health measures*. Los Angeles: Human Interaction Research Institute, 1973. Includes 1100 abstracts of mental health-related psychological measures classified into 45 categories (e.g., alcoholism, drugs, marriage and divorce, racial attitudes, suicide and death). Each abstract gives title of the measure, source of the measure, author's name and address, and an abstract of 300 words or less providing the following information: purpose of the measure, target population, administration time, number of items, types of items, response modes, available reliability and validity data, and findings of the major research application of the measure. Also furnished is information on how to obtain a copy of the measure.

EPSTEIN, I. *Measuring attitudes toward reading*. New York: LaGuardia Community College, City University of New York, 1981. Thirteen self-report and one projective measure are given, along with information on administration, scoring, and additional references. No reliability or validity data are given.

ERIC/TME. American Institute of Research (AIR), 1055 Thomas Jefferson St., N.W., Washington, DC 20007 (202-342-5060) has a federal grant to operate the Educational Resources Information Clearinghouse on Tests, Measurement, and Evaluation (ERIC/TME). AIR acquires, selects, abstracts, and disseminates published and unpublished documents pertaining to all aspects of educational testing, evaluation, measurement, and learning theory. More than 200 test bibliographies on such topics as teacher attitudes, item pools, and tests for the hearing-impaired are available. Access is through usual ERIC channels.

ETS TEST COLLECTION CATALOG. Four volumes of descriptive guides to tests and inventories:

1. *Achievement Tests and Measurement Devices*—Over 2000 tests for all ages and grade levels.
2. *Vocational Tests and Measurement Devices*—lists 1400 vocational, aptitude, work sample, and career planning tests, including behavior rating scales, biographical inventories, and Piagetian measures.
3. *Tests for Special Populations*—Over 1700 tests and measures designed for use with the physically disabled, emotionally disturbed, culturally disadvantaged, learning disabled, and Spanish speaking.

4. *Cognitive Aptitude and Intelligence Tests*—Over 1500 tests for cognitive ability, cognitive style, creative thinking, memory, abstract reasoning, and spatial ability.

5. *Attitude Tests*—Over 1200 attitude measures are described, arranged by subject linked to the *Thesaurus of ERIC*, including such topics as stereotypes, honesty, life style, life satisfaction, child rearing, academic subjects.

FERNEAU, E. W. *Drug abuse research instrument inventory.* Cambridge, MA: Social Systems Analysts, 1973. A list of instruments, divided into six categories: attitudes, characteristics of abusers, effects of drugs, access and extent, knowledge about drugs, and evaluation of drug programs. No psychometric data are provided.

GOODWIN, W. L., and L. A. DRISCOLL. *Handbook for measurement and evaluation in early childhood education.* San Francisco: Jossey-Bass, 1980. Contains information on many scales and measures that are especially appropriate for preschoolers.

GOLDMAN, B. A., and J. C. BUSCH. *Directory of unpublished experimental measures*, vol. 2. New York: Human Sciences Press, 1979. An extension of the Goldman-Saunders work, paralleling it in content and organization.

GOLDMAN, B. A., and J. L. SAUNDERS. *Directory of unpublished experimental measures*, vol. 1. New York: Behavioral Publications, 1974. A very brief description (purpose, number of items, format, source) of 339 unpublished measures classified into achievement (21), adjustment-educational (6), adjustment-psychological (16), adjustment-social (27), aptitude (5), attitudes (22), communication (8), concept meaning (20), creativity (8), development (7), family (9), institutional information (44), interests (10), motivation (7), personality (16), perception (30), preference (11), status (10), trait measurement (22), values (5), and vocational education (34). Instruments are those used in studies published in 29 journals in 1970.

GOODWIN, W. L. and L. A. DRISCOLL. *Handbook for measurement and evaluation in early childhood education.* San Francisco: Jossey-Bass, 1980. Includes a compendium containing detailed yet concise information on measurement concepts, observation procedures, tests and other measures, evaluation designs, and assessment techniques appropriate for preschool levels.

HOEPFNER, R., et al.
1971. *CSE-ECR Preschool/kindergarten test evaluations*
1972. *CSE-RBS test evaluations: Tests of higher-order cognitive, affective, and interpersonal skills*
1974. *CSE secondary school test evaluations: Grades 7 and 8*
1974. *CSE secondary school test evaluations: Grades 9 and 10*
1974. *CSE secondary school test evaluations: Grades 11 and 12*
1976. *CSE elementary school test evaluations*
Los Angeles: UCLA, Center for the Study of Evaluation. Hundreds of published cognitive, affective, and psychomotor instruments are classified into categories and numerically rated in tabular format with respect to approximately 40 characteristics, which are subsets of the four major criteria: measurement validity, examinee appropriateness, administrative usability, and normed technical excellence. Ratings are useful in identifying measures for more careful review. Tests are keyed to a list of specific educational goals and indexed by goal and test title. Much of the information needs to be updated.

INDIK, B. P., M. HOCKMEYER, and C. CASTORE. *A compendium of measures of individuals, groups, and organizations relevant to the study of organizational behavior.* Technical Report No. 16. New Brunswick, NJ: Rutgers, The State University, 1968. Several hundred measures are briefly described. Technical data are provided for only a few of the measures.

JOHNSON, O. G., et al. *Tests and measurements in child development: Handbooks I and II.* San Francisco: Jossey-Bass, 1971, 1976. A comprehensive guide to noncommercial or unpublished measures in child development covering the age group from birth to 18 and the years 1956–75. Instruments are classified into ten categories. Each description provides the following information: title, author(s), age of subjects for whom the instrument is suitable, variable(s), type of measure, administration and scoring, source from which the tool may be obtained, description of the tool, reliability and validity data, and bibliographic citations.

KAPES, J. T., and M. M. MASTIE. *A counselor's guide to career assessment instruments* (2nd ed.). Alexandria, VA: American Association for Counseling and Development, 1982. Forty commonly used career assessment instruments are reviewed, and descriptions of an additional 125 are included. Measures include multiple aptitude batteries, interest inventories, work values instruments, and career development measures.

KEGAN, D. L. *SCALES/RIQS: An inventory of research instruments.* Evanston, IL: Northwestern University, Technological Institute, 1970. Contains more than 350 instruments measuring variables that are relevant to organizational theory, stored and retrieved by computer. Information includes author, reference, date, reliability and validity, variables measured, and author comments in 100 to 150 words. An associated computer file, PROPS/RIQS, is used to retrieve associated empirical studies.

KEYSER, D. J., and R. C. SWEETLAND (Eds.). *Test critiques*, volumes I–VI. Kansas City, MO: Westport Publishers, 1984. The volumes contain critical reviews of over 600 psychological, educational, and business tests. Compliments *The Mental Measurements Yearbooks.* The publisher publishes many similar (sometimes redundant) volumes, such as *Test Critiques Compendium, Test Critiques Applied Topics: Academic Achievement and Aptitude, TCAT: Special Education and Rehabilitation, TCAT: Business and Industry, An International Directory of Spatial Tests,* and *Testing Young Children.*

KNAPP, J. *An omnibus of measures related to school based attitudes.* Princeton, NJ: Educational Testing Service, Center for Statewide Educational Assessment, 1972. Sixteen self-report inventories are described and briefly evaluated in terms of content, subjects, mode of response, and scoring procedures.

LAKE, D., M. MILES, and R. EARLE. *Measuring human behavior.* New York: Teachers College Press, 1973. Provides systematic reviews of 84 different instruments that meet certain criteria in the following categories: personal variable (38), interpersonal (24), groups (10), and organizational relationships (12). Information provided on each instrument includes title, author, availability, variable measured, format, administration, scoring, development, critique (i.e., psychometric data), general comments (usefulness, cautions, etc.), references, and "uniterms" (key words). The volume also contains reviews of other compendia of instruments.

LYERLY, S. B. *Handbook of psychiatric rating scales.* Rockville, MD: National Institute of Mental Health, 1973. Contains descriptions of 38 published and unpublished rating scales that are being used or have been used in psychiatric settings with adults and children, as well as some that are general social and vocational adjustment. The basic descriptive format on each scale includes title, source, general description, patients, rater information, source of scale items, reliability and validity data, and related references. Also included is a listing and brief description of 23 additional scales that have not been used often in recent years but are of historical significance.

MARDELL, C. D., and D. S. GOLDENBERG. *Learning disabilities/early childhood research project.* Springfield: Illinois State Office of the Superintendent of Public Instruction, 1972. (Also available in ERIC, ED 082 408.) Over 900 instruments for identifying preschool children with potential learning disabilities are evaluated using the criteria of age-appropriateness, administration conditions, cost, and range of behaviors assessed. Critiques of 90 instruments are included.

MILLER, D. C. *Handbook of research design and social measurement,* (5th ed.). New York: D. McKay, 1991. Part 4 describes approximately 50 measures divided into 12 categories: social status; group structure, and dynamics; social indicators; organizational structure; organizational effectiveness; community; social participation; leadership in the work organization; morale and job satisfaction; scales of attitudes, values, and norms; family and marriage; and personality measurements. Each review includes title, author, variables(s) measured, description of the measure, where published, reliability and validity data, utility of the measure, and bibliographic data denoting instances of the measure's use in research. In most instances a copy of the measure itself is also included.

MILLER, R. I. *The assessment of college performance: A handbook of techniques and measures for institutional self-evaluation.* San Francisco: Jossey-Bass, 1979. A guide to the task of institution-wide evaluation. The handbook provides the measurement forms needed to appraise institutions. Areas included are faculty, learning, curriculum, administration, financial management, and evaluation. An annotated bibliography of key literature on institutional assessment is provided.

KRAMER, J. J., and J. C. CONOLEY (Eds.). *The Eleventh Mental Measurements Yearbook*. 1992. Lincoln, NE: Buros Institute for Mental Measurement. Contains critical reviews of virtually all current, commercially available tests (and measurement textbooks) in the fields of education and psychology. Copies of the tests are not included, but publishers are identified. Extensive bibliographies for the tests are provided. Test reviews are now included in the online computer service for the Buros Institute database, which is offered through Bibliographic Retrieval Services (BRS).

MURPHY, L. L., J. C. CONOLEY, and J. C. IMPARA. *Tests in print IV*. Lincoln, NE: Buros Institute of Mental Measurements. 1994. Contains 14 major sections: (1) a comprehensive bibliography of all known tests published for use with English-speaking subjects; (2) a classified index to the contents of the test sections of the *Mental Measurements Yearbook*s (*MMYs*) published to date; (3) comprehensive bibliographies on the construction, use, and validity of certain specific tests; (4) a name index covering all authors of tests, reviews, excerpts, and references in the *MMYs*; (5) a publishers' directory with a complete listing of each publisher's test titles; (6) a classified scanning list that describes the population for which each test is intended; (7) identification of foreign tests and journals, with the country of origin in brackets immediately after a test entry or journal; (8) listing of test titles at the foot of each page to permit immediate identification of pages consisting only of references or names; and (9) directions on how to use the book and an expanded table of contents.

MORROW, J. R., A. W. JACKSON, J. G. DISCH, and D. P. MOOD. *Measurement and Evaluation in Human Performance*. Champaign, IL: Human Kinetics, 1995. A comprehensive survey of methods and measures for assessing psychomotor performance, with special emphasis on measures related to sport and exercise measures.

NEWMARK, C. S. *Major psychological assessment instruments*. Newton, MA: Allyn and Bacon, 1985. Extensive information on the "ten most widely used" psychological tests: *MMPI*, Rorschach, *TAT, HTP, DAP, Bender-Gestalt, K-ABC, WISC-R, WAIS-R*, and the *Halstead-Reitan*.

PRICE, J. L. *Handbook of organizational measurement*. Lexington, MA: Heath, 1972. Contains descriptions of measures for 22 concepts relative to organizations. Descriptive information about each measure includes format, definition, data collection procedures, validity, reliability, comments, source of the measure, and further sources of information.

REEDER, L. G., L. RAMACHER, and S. GORELNIK. *Handbook of scales and indices of health behavior*. Pacific Palisades, CA: Goodyear, 1976. Focuses on scales and indexes within a defined segment of health services behavior research—health status, health behavior, health orientations, and utilization of health services. Descriptive information includes author(s); title; major health concept investigated; research design; theoretical framework; research hypotheses and/or questions; model used; conceptualization and operationalization of independent, intervening, and dependent variables; description of population, sample, and analysis units; and major findings and interpretation. Copies of the scales and indexes are also included.

ROBINSON, J. P., R. ATHANASIOU, and K. B. HEAD. *Measures of occupational attitudes and occupational characteristics*. Ann Arbor: University of Michigan, Institute for Social Research, 1969. Provides a systematic review and evaluation of approximately 80 instruments relevant to the study of variables that pertain to occupations. Instruments are classified into nine categories: general job satisfaction (13), job satisfaction for particular occupations (5), satisfaction with specific job features (8), concepts related to job satisfaction (8), occupational values (7), leadership styles (8), other work-relevant attitudes (10), vocational interest measures (4), and occupational status measures (8). Typical items are provided. No scale was included without some data on the measure.

ROBINSON, J. P., J. G. RUSK, and K. B. HEAD. *Measures of political attitudes*. Ann Arbor: University of Michigan, Institute for Social Research, Social Research Center, 1968. Approximately 100 measures are classified by domain assessed: liberalism-conservatism (17), democratic principles (6), domestic government policies (5), racial and ethnic attitudes (13), international affairs (12), hostility-related national attitudes (11), community-based political attitudes (6), political information (4), political participation (7), attitudes toward political process (14), and miscellaneous (9). Instruments are described in 300 to 500 words in terms of sample used, reliability, validity, source, administration, and results and comments. Copies of instruments are included.

ROBINSON, J. P., and P. SHAVER. *Measures of social psychological attitudes* (rev. ed.). Ann Arbor: University of Michigan, 1973. Approximately 100 scales are reviewed in 300 to 500 words under the headings of self-esteem, alienation/anomia, authoritarianism/dogmatism, sociopolitical values, attitudes toward people, religious attitudes, and methodological scales (e.g., social desirability).

ROSEN, P. *Attitudes toward school and school adjustment, grades 4–6*. Princeton, NJ: Educational Testing Service, 1973. Includes an annotated bibliography of 31 attitude measures, including both observational and self-report instruments.

SHAW, M. E., and J. M. WRIGHT. *Scales for the measurement of attitudes*. New York: McGraw-Hill, 1967. In addition to chapters on the nature of attitudes and methods of scale construction, includes descriptions of 176 attitude scales that deal with social issues and practices, international issues, abstract concepts, political and religious attitudes, ethnic and national groups, significant others, and social institutions. Descriptive material about each scale includes title, description, subjects, response mode, reliability and validity, and comments on strengths and/or weaknesses. An exhibit of each instrument accompanies the description. Evaluative comments on the adequacy of the scales are presented.

SIMON, A., and E. G. BOYER. *Mirrors for behavior: An anthology of observation instruments*, 14 vols. Philadelphia: Research for Better Schools, 1970. Approximately 100 "systems" and instruments for measuring variables in the school setting via observation are described; most pertain specifically to classroom observation. A given system is classified with respect to content focus (affective, cognitive, psychomotor [body movement], activity, content, sociological structure, and physical environment), coding units used (e.g., time unit, speaker change), collecting and coding methods (video/audio required, number of observers), setting focus (classroom versus nonclassroom, counseling, group dynamics, subject matter), population observed (teacher, student, family, small group, counselor, administrator), number of subjects observed, and purpose of observation (research, feedback, evaluation). Abstracts of each instrument/system are contained in a "summary" volume.

STRAUSS, M. A. *Family measurement techniques*: *Abstracts of published instruments, 1935–1965*. Minneapolis: University of Minnesota Press, 1969. Educational, psychological and sociological professional journal literature from 1935 to 1965 was searched; 319 family behavior measures were classified into adolescent, child, family, parent, premarital, and spousal categories and described in this volume. Each abstract contains the following material on the measure described: author, title, variables measured, instrument description, a sample item, validity data, sample size, sampling method, sample characteristics, reliability, norms, administration and scoring, availability, and references. Evaluative comments are few but can be found elsewhere (Strauss, 1964).

SWEETLAND, R. C., and D. J. KEYSER (Eds.). *Tests: A comprehensive reference for assessments in psychology, education, and business* (2nd ed.). Kansas City, MO: Test Corporation of America, 1983. Supplies information on over 3100 assessment instruments in three primary classifications: psychology, education, and business. There are 73 subsections to help identify tests for particular groups or purposes. The instruments are not reviewed or evaluated.

THOMAS, H. 1970. "Psychological assessment instruments for use with human infants." *Merrill-Palmer Quarterly*. 16:179-223, Review of nine instruments, together with related research: variables assessed, format, administration procedures, test content, standardization procedures, and validity.

WALKER, D. K. *Socioemotional measures for preschool and kindergarten children*. San Francisco: Jossey-Bass, 1973. Lists and describes 143 commercial and noncommercial, published and unpublished, measures that focus on the social and emotional behavioral areas of children aged three to six. The measures are divided into six categories—attitudes, general personality and emotional adjustment, interest or preferences, personality or behavior traits, self-concept, and social skills or competency. For each measure, Walker provides title, author(s), age range of appropriate respondents, measurement technique involved, sources in which measure is described, where measure can be obtained, administration and scoring information, norms, reliability, and validity data.

WARD, M. J., and M. E. FETLER. *Instruments for use in nursing education research.* Boulder, CO: Western Interstate Commission for Higher Education, 1979. Descriptions and brief critiques of approximately 75 previously unpublished instruments used in nursing education research. Approximately 50 published instruments are also described.

WARD, M. J., C. LINDEMAN, and D. BLOCH (Eds.) *Instruments for measuring nursing and other health care variables*: Psychosocial and Physiological. Washington, DC: Government Printing Office, 1978. Contains descriptions of 138 instruments for measuring psychosocial variables and 19 pieces of apparatus for measuring human physiological variables. Headings for descriptions of psychosocial instruments include title, author(s), variables measured, nature and content, administration and scoring, development (rationale, source of items, procedure for development), reliability and validity, use in research, comments, references, sources of additional information, and copyright information. Copies of 133 of the instruments are included. The headings for the physiological instrument descriptions are title, variable(s), parameters, research application, description, and comments. Indexed by author, title, and key concepts.

WYLIE, R. C. *The self-concept: A review of methodological considerations and measuring instruments.* Lincoln, NE: University of Nebraska Press, 1974. This comprehensive volume extends and updates the author's previous work: *The self concept: A critical survey of pertinent research* (1961, same publisher). A critical analysis of conceptual and theoretical issues in the measurement of self-concept, self-regard, self-acceptance, and related constructs. Widely used instruments of many formats (Q-sort, questionnaires, rating scales, adjective checklists) are evaluated.

OTHER RESOURCES

Psychological Abstracts gives a brief summary of current articles relative to educational and psychological tests. Relevant articles tend to be classified under such headings as "psychometrics and statistics," "test construction and validation," "educational psychology," and "applied psychology." It is also possible to obtain a computer search of articles indexed by key terms.

Education Index deals with the general field of education but organizes material by topic (e.g., ability tests, educational measurement, mental tests).

Periodicals that are useful in applied educational and psychological measurement include *Educational Measurement: Issues and Practice*, *Educational and Psychological Measurement*, *Applied Measurement in Education*, *Journal of Educational Measurement*, *Applied Psychological Measurement*, and *Measurement and Evaluation in Guidance*.

Occasional articles in *Psychological Bulletin, Review of Educational Research, Annual Review of Psychology, Journal of Experimental Education, Annual Review of Research in Education,* and *American Educational Research Journal* pertain to measurement and assessment.

APPENDIX B

Major Publishers of Standardized Tests

All will provide catalogues of current tests. A comprehensive listing of all other publishers is available in the latest volume of the *Mental Measurements Yearbook.*

AMERICAN COLLEGE TESTING PROGRAM, P.O. Box 168, Iowa City, IA 52243; (319) 337-1051

AMERICAN GUIDANCE SERVICES, INC., Publishers Building, Circle Pines, MN; (800) 328-2560

AUSTRALIAN COUNCIL FOR EDUCATIONAL RESEARCH, P.O. Box 210, Hawthorn, Victoria, 3122 Australia

COLLEGE BOARD PUBLICATIONS, 45 Columbus Ave., New York, NY 10023; (212) 713-8000

CONSULTING PSYCHOLOGISTS PRESS, INC., P.O. Box 60070, 577 College Avenue, Palo Alto, CA 94306 (415) 857-1444

CTB/MCGRAW-HILL, Del Monte Research Park, 2500 Garden Rd., Monterey, CA 93940; (800) 538-9547

EDUCATIONAL TESTING SERVICE (ETS), Rosedale Rd., Princeton, NJ 08540; (609) 921-9000

HODDER & STROUGHTON EDUCATIONAL SERVICES, P. O. Box 702, Dunton Green, Sevenoaks, Kent TN13 2YD, England

HUMAN SCIENCES RESEARCH COUNCIL, Private Bag 41, Pretoria, Republic of South Africa

INSTITUTE FOR PERSONALITY and ABILITY TESTING, 1602 Coronado Drive, Champaign, IL 6l820; (217) 352-4739

NATIONAL INSTITUTE FOR PERSONNEL RESEARCH, P.O. Box 10319, Johannesburg, Republic of South Africa

NFER PUBLISHING COMPANY, Darvelle House, 2 Oxford Rd. East, Windsor, Berkshire. SL4 1DF, England

PSYCHOLOGICAL ASSESSMENT RESOURCES (PAR), P.O. Box 998, Odessa, FL 33556; (813) 977-3395

PSYCHOLOGICAL CORPORATION, 555 Academic Court, San Antonio, TX 78204; (800) 228-0752

PSYCHOMETRIC AFFILIATES, P.O. Box 807, Murfreesboro, TN 37133; (615) 890-6296

RIVERSIDE PUBLISHING COMPANY, 8420 Bryn Mawr Ave., Chicago, IL 60631; (800) 323-9540

SCHOLASTIC TESTING SERVICE, P.O. Box 1056, 480 Meyer Rd., Bensenville, IL 60106; (312) 766-7150

SCIENCE RESEARCH ASSOCIATES, INC. (SRA), 155 North Wacker Drive, Chicago, IL 60606; (312) 984-7000

SHERIDAN PSYCHOLOGICAL SERVICES, P.O. Box 6101, Orange, CA 92667; (714) 639-2595

STOELTING COMPANY, 620 Wheat Lane, Wood Dale, IL 60191; (708) 860-9700

WESTERN PSYCHOLOGICAL SERVICES, 12031 Wilshire Blvd., Los Angeles, CA 90025; (213) 478-2061

Bibliography

ABRAMOWITZ, S., and A. I. LAW. 1978. The California High School Proficiency Exam: A study of student choice. *AERA 1978 annual meeting: Abstracts of papers.* Washington, DC: AERA.

ABRAMSON, T. 1969. The influence of examiner race on first-grade and kindergarten subjects' Peabody Picture Vocabulary Test scores. *Journal of Educational Measurement, 6,* 241–246.

ACE, M. C., and R. V. DAWIS. 1973. Item structure as a determinant of item difficulty in verbal analogies. *Educational and Psychological Measurement, 33,* 143–149.

ACT. 1984. Using the ACT assessment and high school grades to predict college freshman grade-point average. *Activity, 22,* 11.

AIKEN, L. R., Jr., 1963. The grading behavior of a college faculty. *Educational and Psychological Measurement, 23,* 319–322.

———. 1985. Review of ACT assessment program. *Ninth Mental Measurements Yearbook,* 29–31.

AIRASIAN, P. W. 1979. A perspective on the uses and misuses of standardized achievement tests. *NCME Measurement in Education, 10,* 1–12.

AIRASIAN, P. W., and G. F. MADAUS. 1972. Criterion-referenced testing in the classroom. *NCME Measurement in Education, 3,* 1–8.

AITKEN, K. 1977. Using cloze procedure as an overall language proficiency test. *TESOL Quarterly, 11,* 59–67.

ALBANESE, M. A. 1986. The correction for guessing: A further analysis of Angoff and Schrader. *Journal of Educational Measurement, 23,* 225–235.

ALDERMAN, D. L., and D. E. POWERS. 1980. The effects of special preparation on SAT-Verbal Scores. *American Educational Research Journal, 17,* 239–251.

ALEAMONI, L. 1978. Development and factorial validation of the Arizona counsel instructor evaluation questionnaire. *Educational and Psychological Measurement, 38,* 1063–67.

ALLISON, D. E. 1970. Test anxiety, stress, and intelligence-test performance. *Canadian Journal of Behavioral Science, 2,* 26–37.

———. 1984. The effect of item-difficulty sequence, intelligence, and sex on test performance, reliability, and item difficulty and discrimination. *Measurement and Evaluation in Guidance, 16,* 211–217.

AMERICAN ALLIANCE FOR HEALTH, PHYSICAL EDUCATION, AND RECREATION. n.d. *Testing for impaired, disabled, and handicapped individuals.* Washington, DC: American Alliance for Health, Physical Education, and Recreation.

THE AMERICAN COLLEGE. 1978. *Test wiseness: Test-taking skills for adults.* New York: McGraw-Hill.

AMERICAN COLLEGE TESTING PROGRAM. 1973. *Technical report for the ACT assessment program.* Iowa City.

AMERICAN EDUCATIONAL RESEARCH ASSOCIATION, AMERICAN PSYCHOLOGICAL ASSOCIATION, AND NATIONAL COUNCIL ON MEASUREMENT IN EDUCATION. 1985. *Standards for educational and psychological testing.* Washington, DC: American Psychological Association.

AMERICAN PERSONNEL AND GUIDANCE ASSOCIATION. 1972. The responsible use of tests: A position paper of AMEG, APGA, and NCME. *Measurement and Evaluation in Guidance, 5,* 385–388.

AMMONS, M. 1969. Objectives and outcomes. In R. L. Ebel (Ed.), *Encyclopedia of Educational Research* (4th ed.) (pp. 908–914). New York: Macmillan.

ANASTASI, A. 1958. Heredity, environment, and the question "how?" *Psychological Review, 65,* 197–208.

———. 1968, 1976. *Psychological testing* (3rd and 4th eds.). New York: Macmillan.

———. 1981. Coaching, test sophistication, and developed abilities. *American Psychologist, 36,* 1086–1093.

———. 1985a. Some emerging trends in psychological measurement: A fifty-year perspective. *Applied Psychological Measurement, 9,* 121–138.

———. 1985b. Review of theKaufman Assessment Battery for Children. In J. V. Mitchell, Jr. (Ed.), *Ninth mental measurement Yearbook.* Lincoln, NE: University of Nebraska Press.

———. 1988. *Psychological testing* (6th ed.). New York: Macmillan.

ANDERSON, C. S. 1982. The search for school climate: A review of research. *Review of Educational Research, 52,* 368–420.

ANDERSON, J. H. 1974. Cloze measures as indices of achievement comparison when learning from extended prose. *Journal of Educational Measurement, 11,* 83–92.

ANDERSON, R. 1970. Comments on Professor Gagne's paper entitled "Instructional variables and learning outcomes." In M. C. Wittrock and D. E. Wiley (Eds.), *The evaluation of instruction.* New York: Holt, Rinehart & Winston.

ANDERSON, R. H. 1966. The importance and purposes of reporting. *National Elementary School Principal, 45,* 6–11.

ANGOFF, W. H. 1971. Scales, norms, and equivalent scores. In R. L. Thorndike (Ed.), *Educational measurement* (2nd ed.) Chapter 15. Washington, DC.: American Council on Education.

ANGOFF, W. H., and E. G. JOHNSON. 1990. The differential impact of curriculum on aptitude test scores. *Journal of Educational Measurement, 27,* 291–305.

ARMITAGE, J. H. 1967. Analysis of citizenship goals in social studies instruction. Doctoral dissertation, University of Colorado. University Microfilms No. 68–10,601. *Dissertation Abstracts, 29,* 396–A, 397–A (August 1968).

ARMSTRONG, R. J., and R. F. MOONEY. 1969. Confidence testing: Is it reliable? Paper read at the annual meeting of the National Council on Measurement in Education, Los Angeles.

ASHBURN, R. R. 1938. An experiment in the essay-type question. *Journal of Experimental Education, 7,* 1–3.

ASTIN, A. W. 1970. *Predicting academic performance in college.* New York: Free Press.

ATKINSON, J. W. 1983. Motivational psychology and mental measurement. Chapter 2 in S. B. Anderson and J. S. Helmick (Eds.), *On educational testing: Intelligence, performance standards, test anxiety, and latent traits.* San Francisco: Jossey-Bass.

AYRES, L. P. 1912. *Measuring scale for handwriting,* Gettysburg edition. Bureau of Educational Research, Iowa City, IA: University of Iowa.

———. 1918. History and present status of educational measurements. *Seventeenth yearbook of the national society for the study of education,* Part II. Bloomington, IL: Public School Publishing.

BAGERT-DROWNS, R. L., J. A. KULIK, and C. C. KULIK. 1983. Effects of coaching programs on achievement test performance. *Review of Educational Research, 53,* 571–585.

BAGLEY, W. C. 1900. On the correlation of mental and motor ability in school children. *American Journal of Psychology. 12,* 193–205.

BAILEY, R. L. 1977. The test of standard written English: Another look. *Measurement and Evaluation in Guidance, 10,* 70–74.

BAIRD, L. L., and W. J. FEISTER. 1972. Grading standards: The relation of changes in average student ability to the average grades awarded. *American Educational Research Journal, 9,* 431–442.

BAJTELSMIT, J. 1977. Test-wiseness and systematic desensitization programs for increasing adult test-taking skills. *Journal of Educational Measurement, 14,* 335–342.

BAYLEY, N. 1955. On the growth of intelligence. *American Psychologist, 10,* 805–817.

BEERE, C. A. 1979. *Women and women's issues: A handbook of tests and measures.* San Francisco: Jossey-Bass.

BEJAR, I. I., and E. O. BLEW. 1981. Grade inflation and the validity of the scholastic aptitude test. *American Educational Research Journal, 18,* 143–156.

BENNETT, R. E., and W. C. WARD (Eds.). 1993. *Construction versus choice in cognitive measurement.* Lawrence Erlbaum.

BENNETT, R. E., D. A. ROCK, and B. A. KAPLAN. 1987. SAT differential item performance for nine handicapped groups. *Journal of Educational Measurement, 24,* 41–55.

BEN-SHAKHAR, G., and Y. SINAI. 1991. Gender differences in multiple-choice tests: The role of differential guessing tendencies. *Journal of Educational Measurement, 28,* 23–35.

BERG, H. D. 1958. Suggestions for increasing the thought content of objective test items. Mimeo. 9 pp.

———. 1961. Evaluation in social science. In P. L. Dressel (Ed.), *Evaluation in higher education.* Chapter 4. Boston: Houghton Mifflin.

BETEBENNER, D., and K. D. HOPKINS. 1997. Estimating Cronbach's Alpha from KR-21. Paper presented to the American Educational Research Association, Chicago.

BEUCHERT, A. K., and J. L. MENDOZA. 1979. A Monte Carlo comparison of ten item discrimination indices. *Journal of Educational Measurement, 16,* 109–118.

BIGLER, E. D., and J. W. EHRFURTH. 1981. The continued inappropriate single use of the Bender Visual Motor Gestalt Test. *Professional Psychology, 12,* 562–569.

BINET, A. 1911. *Les idees modernes sur les enfants.* Paris: Flammarion.

BINET, A., and T. SIMON. 1916. *The development of intelligence in children.* Translated by Elizabeth S. Kite. Baltimore: Williams & Wilkins.

BLESSUM, W. T. 1969. *Annual report 1968–1969, medical computer facility.* Irvine: University of California, Irvine, California College of Medicine.

BLOCK, J. 1961. *The Q-sort method in personality assessment and psychiatric research.* Springfield, IL: Chas. C. Thomas.

BLOCK, J. H. (Ed.). 1971. *Mastery learning: Theory and practice.* New York: Holt, Rinehart & Winston.

BLOOM, B. S. 1956. The 1955 normative study of the tests of general educational development. *School Review, 64,* 110–124.

———. 1961. Quality control in education. In *Tomorrow's teaching* (pp. 54–61). Oklahoma City: Frontiers of Science Foundation.

———. 1964. *Stability and change in human characteristics.* New York: John Wiley.

——— (Ed.). 1956, 1984. *Taxonomy of educational objectives: The classification of educational goals: Book I, The cognitive domain.* New York: D. McKay Company, Inc.

BOLDT, R. F. 1986. *Generalization of SAT validity across colleges.* College Board Report. New York: College Entrance Examination Board.

BOLDT, R. F., J. A. CENTRA, and R. G. COURTNEY. 1986. *The validity of various methods of treating multiple SAT scores.* College Board Report. New York: College Entrance Examination Board.

BOND, L. 1988. The effects of special preparation on measures of scholastic ability. In R. L. Linn (Ed.), *Educational measurement.* Chapter 11. Washington, DC: American Council on Education.

BONJEAN, C. M., R. J. HILL, and S. D. McLEMORE. 1967. *Sociological measurement: An inventory of scales and indices.* San Francisco: Chandler Publishing.

BONNEY, M. E. 1960. Sociometric methods. In C. W. Harris (Ed.), *Encyclopedia of Educational Research* (3rd ed.) (pp. 1319–1324). New York: Macmillan.

BORMUTH, J. R. 1967. Comparable cloze and multiple-choice comprehension test scores. *Journal of Reading, 10,* 291–299.

———. 1969. Factor validity of cloze tests as measures of reading comprehension ability. *Reading Research Quarterly, 4,* 358–365.

BOYER, E. G., A. SIMON, and G. R. KARAFIN (Eds.). 1973. *Measures of maturation: An anthology of early childhood observation instruments.* Philadelphia: Research for Better Schools.

BRACHT, G. H. 1967. The comparative values of objective and essay testing in undergraduate education: Implications for valid assessment of instruction. Unpublished master's thesis, University of Colorado.

BRACHT, G. H., and K. D. HOPKINS. 1968. Comparative validities of objective tests. Research Paper No. 20. Boulder: University of Colorado, Laboratory of Educational Research.

———. 1970a. The commonality of essay and objective tests of academic achievement. *Educational and Psychological Measurement, 30,* 359–364.

———. 1970b. Stability of General Academic Achievement. Paper presented at the annual meeting of the National Council on Measurement in Education, Minneapolis, March. Reprinted in G. H. Bracht, K. D. Hopkins, and J. C. Stanley (Eds.), *Perspectives in Educational and Psychological Measurement.* Selection 25. Englewood Cliffs, NJ: Prentice-Hall, 1972.

BRELAND, H. M. 1978. *Population validity and college entrance measures.* Princeton, NJ: Educational Testing Service.

———. 1979. *Population validity and college entrance measures.* Princeton, NJ: College Board Publications.

BRELAND, H. M., R. CAMP, R. J. JONES, M. M. MORRIS, and D. A. ROCK. 1987. *Assessing writing skill.* New York: College Entrance Examination Board.

BRELAND, H. M., and J. L. GAYNOR. 1979. A comparison of direct and indirect assessments of writing skill. *Journal of Educational Measurement, 16,* 119–128.

BRENNER, M. H. 1964. Test difficulty reliability and discrimination as functions of item difficulty order. *Journal of Applied Psychology, 48,* 98–100.

Brickman, W. W. 1961. Ethics, examinations and education. *School and Society, 89,* 412–415.

BRIDGES, K. R. 1985. Test-completion speed: Its relationship to performance on three course-based objective examinations. *Educational and Psychological Measurement, 45,* 29–35.

BRIDGMAN, C. S. 1964. The relation of the upper-lower item discrimination index, D, to the bivariate normal correlation coefficient. *Educational and Psychological Measurement, 24,* 85–90.

BUCKLEY, M. 1987. *Report card and grades survey: Colorado elementary schools.* Doctoral dissertation, University of Colorado.

BUDESCU, D., and M. BAR-HILLEL. 1993. To guess or not to guess: A decision-theoretical view of formula scoring. *Journal of Educational Measurement, 30,* 277–291.

BURACK, B. 1967. Relationship between course examination scores and time taken to finish the examination, revisited. *Psychological Reports, 20,* 1–164.

BUROS, O. K. (Ed.). 1938–1978. *The mental measurements yearbooks* (1ST–8TH eds.). Highland Park, NJ: Gryphon Press.

———. 1977. Fifty years in testing: Some reminiscences, criticisms, and suggestions. *Educational Researcher, 6,* 9–15.

BURR, W. L. 1963. Empirical relationships among modes of testing, modes of instruction and reading levels in sixth-grade social studies. *Journal of Experimental Education, 31,* 433–435.

BURSTEIN, L. 1983. A word about this issue. *Journal of Educational Measurement, 20,* 99–101.

BURTON, N. W. 1978. Societal standards. *Journal of Educational Measurement, 15,* 263–271.

———. 1980. Stability of the national assessment scoring methods. *Journal of Educational Measurement, 17,* 95–106.

BUSHWAY, A., and W. R. NASH. 1977. School cheating behavior. *Review of Educational Research, 47,* 623–632.

CALDWELL, E., and R. HARTNETT. 1967. Sex bias in college grading. *Journal of Educational Measurement, 4,* 129–132.

CALLENBACH, C. 1973. The effects of instruction and practice in content-independent test-taking techniques upon the standardized reading test scores of selected second-grade students. *Journal of Educational Measurement, 10,* 25–30.

CAMP, A. L., C. MENA, and J. CLINTON. 1987. A high school equivalency program: Meeting the needs of migrant dropouts. *Journal of the Southeastern Association of Educational Opportunity Program Personnel, 6,* 29–39.

CAMPBELL, D. P. 1966a. Stability of interest within an occupation over 30 years. *Journal of Applied Psychology, 50,* 51–56.

———. 1966b. Stability of vocational interests within occupations over long time spans. *Personnel and Guidance Journal, 44,* 1012–1019.

———. 1968. The Strong Vocational Interest Blank: 1927–1967. In P. McReynolds (Ed.), *Advances in psychological assessment.* Vol. 1 (pp. 105–130). Palo Alto, CA: Science and Behavior Books.

———. 1974. *Manual for the Strong-Campbell Interest Inventory.* Stanford, CA: Stanford University Press.

CAMPBELL, D. T. 1969. Reforms as experiments. *American Psychologist, 24,* 409–429.

CAMPBELL, D. T., and D. W. FISKE. 1959. Convergent and discriminant validation by the multitrait-multimethod matrix. *Psychological Bulletin, 56,* 81–105.

CAMPBELL, J. T., T. L. HILTON, and B. PITCHER. 1967. *Effects of repeating on test scores of the graduate record examinations.* Graduate Record Examinations Special Report 67–1. Princeton, NJ: Educational Testing Service.

CARTER, K. 1986. Test-wiseness for teachers and students. *Educational Measurement: Issues and Practice, 5,* 20–23.

CASSERLY, P. L. 1986. *Advanced placement revisited.* College Board Report No. 86–6. Princeton, NJ: Educational Testing Service.

CATTELL, R. B., and F. WARBURTON. 1967. *Objective personality and motivation tests.* Urbana, IL: University of Illinois Press.

CHADWICK, E. 1864. Statistics of educational results. *Museum, 3,* 480–484.

CHAMBERS, A. C., K. D. HOPKINS, and B. R. HOPKINS. 1972. Anxiety, physiologically and psychologically measured: Its effects on mental test performance. *Psychology in the Schools, 9,* 198–206.

CHASE, C. I. 1964. Relative length of options and response set in multiple choice items. *Educational and Psychological Measurement, 24,* 861–866.

———. 1968. The impact of some obvious variables on essay test scores. *Journal of Educational Measurement, 5,* 315–318.

———. 1979a. The impact of achievement expectations and handwriting quality on scoring essay tests. *Journal of Educational Measurement, 16,* 39–42.

———. 1979b. Students and faculty view the grading system. Paper presented at the annual meeting of the National Council on Measurement in Education, San Francisco, April.

———. 1983. Essay test scores and reading difficulty. *Journal of Educational Measurement, 20,* 293–297.

———. 1986. Essay test scoring: Interaction of relevant variables. *Journal of Educational Measurement, 23,* 33–41.

CHAUNCEY, H., and J. E. DOBBIN. 1963. *Testing: Its place in education today.* New York: Harper & Row.

CHAUNCEY, H., and T. L. HILTON. 1965. Are aptitude tests valid for the highly able? *Science, 148,* 1297–1304.

CHOPPIN, B. H. 1974. *The correction for guessing on objective tests.* IEA Monograph Studies No. 4. University of Stockholm, International Association for the Evaluation of Educational Achievement.

CHUN, K., S. COBB, and J. FRENCH. 1975. *Measures for psychological assessment:* A guide to 3,000 original sources and their application. Ann Arbor, MI: University of Michigan, Institute for Social Research.

CHURCHILL, W. D., and S. E. SMITH. 1966. The relationship of the 1960 Revised Stanford-Binet Intelligence Scale to intelligence and achievement test scores over a three-year period. *Educational and Psychological Measurement, 26,* 1015–1020.

CLARK, D. C. 1972. *Using instructional objectives in teaching.* Glenview, IL: Scott Foresman.

CLARKE, H. 1971. *Physical and motor tests in the Medford boys' growth study.* Englewood Cliffs, NJ: Prentice-Hall.

CLEARY, T. A., and T. L. HILTON. 1968. An investigation of item bias. *Educational and Psychological Measurement, 28,* 61–75.

CLIFFORD, P. I., and J. A. FISHMAN. 1963. The impact of testing programs on college preparation and attendance. In *The impact and improvement of school testing programs.* Sixty-second yearbook of the National Society for the Study of Education. Chicago: University of Chicago Press.

COFFMAN, W. E. 1969. Achievement tests. In R. L. Ebel (Ed.), *Encyclopedia of Educational Research* (4th ed.). New York: Macmillan.

———. 1971. Essay examinations. In R. L. Thorndike (Ed.), *Educational measurement* (2nd ed.). Washington, DC: American Council on Education. Chapter 10.

———. 1972. On the reliability of ratings of essay examinations. *NCME Measurement in Education, 3,* 1–7.

COFFMAN, W. E., and D. KURFMAN. 1968. A comparison of two methods of reading essay examinations. *American Educational Research Journal, 5,* 99–107.

COLE, N. 1982. The implications of coaching for ability testing. In A. K. Wigdor and W. R. Garner (Eds.), *Ability testing: Uses, consequences, and controversies.* Washington, DC: National Academy Press.

COLEMAN, J. S., et al. 1966. *The equality of educational opportunity.* Washington, DC: U. S. Department of Health, Education and Welfare, Office of Education.

COLLEGE ENTRANCE EXAMINATION BOARD. 1968. *Effects of coaching on Scholastic Aptitude Test.* Princeton, NJ.

CONGRESS OF THE UNITED STATES. 1987. *Educational achievement: Explanations and implications of recent trends.* Government Printing Office.

COLLER, A. R. 1971. *Self-concept measures: An annotated bibliography.* Princeton, NJ: Educational Testing Service.

COMPTON, A. 1980. *A guide to 65 tests for special education.* Belmont, CA: Pitman.

COMREY, A. S., T. E. BACKER, and E. M. GLASER. 1973. *A sourcebook for mental health measures.* Los Angeles: Human Interaction Research Institute.

CONRAD, L., D. TRISMEN, and R. MILLER (Eds.). 1977. *Graduate Record Examinations technical manual.* Princeton, NJ: Educational Testing Service.

COOK, T. D., and D. T. CAMPBELL. 1979. *Quasi-experimentation.* New York: Rand McNally.

COOPER, H. M. 1979. Pygmalion grows up: A model for teacher expectation communication and performance influence. *Review of Educational Research, 49,* 389–410.

COOPERSMITH, S. 1967. *The antecedents of self-esteem.* San Francisco: W. H. Freeman.

COPELAND, D. A. 1972. Should chemistry students change answers on multiple-choice tests? *Journal of Chemical Education, 49,* 258.

CORNEHLSEN, V. H. 1965. Cheating attitudes and practices in a suburban high school. *Journal of the National Association of Women Deans and Counselors, 28,* 106–109.

CRANDALL, V. C., V. J. CRANDALL, and W. KATKOVSKY. 1965. A children's social desirability questionnaire. *Journal of Consulting Psychology, 29,* 27–36.

CRITES, J. O. 1969. Interests. In R. L. Ebel (Ed.), *Encyclopedia of Educational Research* (4th ed.) (pp. 678–686). New York: Macmillan.

CROCKENBERG, S. B. 1972. Creativity test: Boon or boondoggle? *Review of Educational Research, 42,* 27–48.

CROCKER, L., and J. BENSON. 1976. Achievement, guessing, and risk-taking under norm referenced and criterion referenced testing conditions. *American Educational Research Journal, 13,* 207–215.

CRONBACH, L. J. 1942. Studies of acquiescence as a factor in true-false tests. *Journal of Educational Psychology, 33,* 401–415

———. 1946. Response sets and test validity. *Educational and Psychological Measurement, 6,* 475–494.

———. 1950. Further evidence on response sets and test design. *Educational and Psychological Measurement, 10,* 3–31.

———. 1951. Coefficient alpha and the internal structure of tests. *Psychometrika, 16,* 297–334.

———. 1970. *Essentials of psychological testing* (3rd ed.). New York: Harper & Row.

———. 1971. Test validation. In R. L. Thorndike (Ed.), *Educational measurement* (2nd ed.). Chapter 14. Washington, DC: American Council on Education.

———. 1984. *Essentials of psychological testing* (4th ed.). New York: Harper & Row.

———. 1989. Educational measurement. Book review in *Educational Measurement Issues And Practices, 8,* 22–25.

CRONBACH, L. J., and H. AZUMA. 1962. Internal-consistency reliability formulas applied to randomly sampled single-factor tests: An empirical comparison. *Educational and Psychological Measurement, 22,* 45–65.

CRONBACH, L. J., and L. FURBY. 1970. How we should measure change—Or should we? *Psychological Bulletin, 74,* 68–80.

CRONBACH, L. J., and P. E. MEEHL. 1955. Construct validity in psychological tests. *Psychological Bulletin, 52,* 281–302.

CRONBACH, L. J., N. RAJARATNAM, and G. C. GLESER. 1963. Theory of generalizability: A liberalization of reliability theory. *British Journal of Statistical Psychology, 16,* 281–302.

CROSS, L. H., and R. FRARY. 1977. An empirical test of Lord's theoretical results regarding formula scoring of multiple-choice tests. *Journal of Educational Measurement, 17,* 313–322.

CROWNE, D. P., and D. MARLOWE. 1964. *The Approval Motive.* New York: John Wiley.

CUNNINGHAM, R., et al. 1951. *Group behavior of boys and girls.* New York: Columbia University Press.

CURETON, E. E. 1969. Measurement theory. In R. L. Ebel (Ed.), *Encyclopedia of Educational Research* (4th ed.) (pp. 785–804). New York: Macmillan.

CURETON, L. W. 1971. The history of grading practices. *NCME Measurement in Education, 2,* 1–8.

CURTIS, F. D., W. C. DARLING, and N. H. SHERMAN. 1943. A study of the relative values of two modifications of the true-false test. *Journal of Educational Research, 36,* 517–527.

Curtis, H. A., and R. P. KROPP. 1961. A comparison of scores obtained by administering a test normally and visually. Journal of Experimental Education, 29, 249–260.

DADOURIAN, H. M. 1925. Are examinations worth the price? *School and Society, 21,* 442–443.

DALY, J. A., and F. DICKERSON-MARKMAN. 1982. Contrasts effects in evaluating essays. *Journal of Educational Measurement, 19,* 309–316.

DELANDSHEERE, V. 1977. On defining educational objectives. In *Evaluation in education: International progress.* Elmsford, NY: Pergamon Press.

DENNIS, P. 1979. An assessment of the validity and reliability of the CFK Ltd. School Climate Profile. Doctoral dissertation, University of Colorado.

DIAMOND, J. J. 1975. A preliminary study of the reliability and validity of a scoring procedure based upon confidence and partial information. *Journal of Educational Measurement, 12,* 129–134.

DI STEFANO, P., and S. VALENCIA. 1980. The effects of syntactic maturity on comprehension of graded reading passages. *Journal of Educational Research, 73,* 247–251.

DOLLIVER, R. H., J. A. IRWIN, and S. E. BIGLEY. 1972. Twelve-year follow-up of the Strong Vocational Interest Blank. *Journal of Counseling Psychology, 19,* 212–217.

DONLON, T. F. 1984. *The College Board technical handbook for the Scholastic Aptitude Test and achievement tests.* New York: College Entrance Examination Board.

DRISCOLL, L. A., and W. L. GOODWIN. 1979. The effects of varying information about use and disposition of results on university students' evaluation of faculty and courses. *American Educational Research Journal, 16,* 25–37.

DUBOIS, P. H. 1966. A test-dominated society: China, 1115 BC.–1905 AD. In A. Anastasi (Ed.), *Testing problems in perspective.* Washington, DC: American Council on Education.

DUDYCHA, A. L., and J. B. CARPENTER. 1973. Effects of item format on item discrimination and difficulty. *Journal of Applied Psychology, 58,* 11–121.

DUSEK, J. B. 1975. Do teachers bias children's learning? *Review of Educational Research, 45,* 661–684.

DUSH, D. M. 1985. Review of the Holtzman Inkblot Technique. In J. V. Mitchell (Ed.), *The Ninth Mental Measurements Yearbook.* Lincoln, NE: University of Nebraska Press.

EBEL, R. L. 1961. Improving the competence of teachers in educational measurement. *Clearing House, 36,* 67–71.

———. 1965a. Confidence weighting and test reliability. *Journal of Educational Measurement, 2,* 49–57.

———. 1965b, 1979. *Measuring educational achievement* (2nd ed. & 3rd ed.). Englewood Cliffs, NJ: Prentice-Hall.

————. 1968. The value of internal consistency in classroom examinations. *Journal of Educational Measurement, 5,* 71–73.

————. 1970. The case for true-false test items. *School Review, 78,* 373–389.

————. 1971. How to write true-false items. *Educational and Psychological Measurement, 31,* 417–426.

————. 1972. Some limitations of criterion-referenced measurement. Reprinted in G. H. Bracht, K. D. Hopkins, and J. C. Stanley (Eds.), *Perspectives in educational and psychological measurement.* Selection 14. Englewood Cliffs, NJ: Prentice-Hall.

————. 1974. Shall we get rid of grades? *NCME Measurement in Education, 5,* 1–5.

————. 1978. The case for non-referenced measurements. *Educational Researcher, 7,* 3–5.

————, and D. A. FRISBIE. 1986. *Measuring educational achievement* (4th ed.). Englewood Cliffs, NJ: Prentice-Hall.

EDUCATIONAL POLICIES COMMISSION. 1961. *The Central Purpose Of American Education.* Washington, DC: National Education Association.

EDUCATIONAL TESTING SERVICE. 1961. Judges disagree on qualities that characterize good writing. *ETS Developments, 9,* 2.

————. 1980a. *Test Use And Validity.* Princeton, NJ: Educational Testing Service.

————. 1988. *A summary of data collected from Graduate Record Examinations test-takers during 1986–87:* Data summary report number 12. Princeton, NJ: Educational Testing Service.

EDWARDS, A. L. 1957. *The social desirability variability in personality assessment and research.* New York: Dryden Press.

ENGELHART, M. D. 1964. *Improving classroom testing: What research says to the teacher.* Booklet No. 31. Washington, DC: National Education Association.

EPSTEIN, J. L. 1985. A question of merit: Principals' and Parents' evaluations of teachers. *Educational Researcher, 14,* 3–10.

ESCALONA, S. K., and A. MORIARTY. 1961. Prediction of school age intelligence from infant tests. *Child Development, 32,* 597–605.

ESTES, W. K. 1982. Learning, memory, and intelligence. In Sternberg, R. J. (Ed.), *Handbook of human intelligence.* Chapter 4. Cambridge: Cambridge University Press.

ETAUGH, A. F., C. F. ETAUGH, and D. HURD. 1972. Reliability of college grades and grade-point averages: Some implications for predicting academic performance. *Educational and Psychological Measurement, 32,* 1045–1105.

EYDE, L. D. 1987. Computerized psychological testing. *Applied psychology: An international review, 36.*

EYSENCK, H. J. 1959. Rorschach review. In O. K. Buros (Ed.), *The fifth mental measurements yearbook* (pp. 276–278). Highland Park, NJ: Gryphon Press.

FAIRBROTHER, R. 1975. The reliability of teachers' judgments of the abilities being tested by multiple choice items. *Educational Research, 17,* 202–210.

FARGO, G. A., D. C. CROWELL, M. H. NOYES, R. Y. FUCHIGAMI, J. M. Gordon, and P. DUNN-RANKIN. 1967. Comparability of group television and individual administration of the Peabody Picture Vocabulary Test: Implications for screening. *Journal of Educational Psychology, 58,* 137–140.

FARLEY, E. J., C. E. WEINHOLD, and A. P. CRABTREE. 1967. *High school certification through the G.E.D. tests.* New York: Holt, Rinehart & Winston.

FARR, R., and P. ROELKE. 1971. Measuring subskills of reading: Intercorrelations between standardized reading tests, teachers' ratings, and reading specialists' ratings. *Journal of Educational Measurement, 8,* 27–32.

FELDT, L. S., and R. L. BRENNAN. 1988. Reliability, Chapter 2 in R. L.Linn (Ed.), *Educational measurement* (3rd ed.). Washington, DC: American Council on Education.

FINDLEY, W. G. (Ed.). 1963. The impact and improvement of school testing programs. *Sixty-second yearbook of the National Society for the Study of Education, Part II.* Chicago: University of Chicago Press.

FISCHER, D. G., D. HUNT, and B. S. RANDHAWA. 1978. Empirical validity of Ertl's brain-wave analyzer. *Educational and Psychological Measurement, 38,* 1017–1030.

FISHMAN, J. A., et al. 1964. Guidelines for testing minority group children. *Journal of Social Issues, 20,* 127–145.

FLANAGAN, J. C. 1937. A proposed procedure for increasing the efficiency of objective tests. *Journal of Educational Psychology, 28,* 17–21.

———. 1951. Units, scores, and norms. In E. F. Lindquist (Ed.), *Educational measurement.* Washington, DC: American Council on Education.

———. 1952. The effectiveness of short methods for calculating correlation coefficients. *Psychological Bulletin, 49,* 342–348.

———. 1969. Student characteristics: Elementary and secondary. In R. L. Ebel (Ed.), *Encyclopedia of Educational Research* (4th ed.) (pp. 1330–1339). New York: Macmillan.

FLANAGAN, J. C., et al. 1962. *Design for a study of American youth. Vol. 1, The talents of American youth.* Boston: Houghton Mifflin.

FLEMING, E. S., and R. G. ANTTONEN. 1970. Teacher expectancy or my fair lady. In John Pilder (Ed.), *Abstracts one: 1970 annual meeting paper session.* Washington, DC: American Educational Research Association.

FLESH, R. 1948. A new readability yardstick. *Journal of Applied Psychology, 34,* 384–390.

FOOTE, R., and C. BELINKY. 1972. It pays to switch? Consequences of changing answers on multiple-choice examinations. *Psychological Reports, 31,* 667–673.

FRANKEL, E. 1960. Effects of growth, practice, and coaching on Scholastic Aptitude Test scores. *Personnel and Guidance Journal, 38,* 713–719.

FRANZ, S. I. 1919. *Handbook of mental examination methods.* New York: Macmillan.

FRARY, R. B., L. H. CROSS, and S. R. LOWRY. 1977. Random guessing, correction for guessing, and reliability of multiple-choice test scores. *Journal of Experimental Education, 46,* 9–15.

FREEMAN, D. J., G. M. BELLI, A. C. PORTER, R. E. FLODEN, W. H. SCHMIDT, and J. R. SCHWILLE. 1983. The influence of different styles of textbook use on instructional validity of standardized tests. *Journal of Educational Measurement, 20,* 259–266.

FRENCH, J. W. 1962. Effect of anxiety on verbal and mathematical examination scores. *Educational and Psychological Measurement, 22,* 553–564.

FRIEDLAND, D. L., and W. B. MICHAEL. 1987. The reliability of a promotional job knowledge examination scored by a number of items right and by four confidence weighting. *Educational and Psychological Measurement, 47,* 179–192.

FRISBEE, D. A. 1973. Multiple-choice versus true-false: A comparison of reliabilities and concurrent validities. *Journal of Educational Measurement, 10,* 297–304.

FUCHS, D., and L. S. FUCHS. 1986a. Test procedure bias: A meta-analysis examiner familiarity effects. *Review of Educational Research, 56,* 243–262.

FUCHS, L. S., and D. FUCHS. 1986b. Effects of systematic formative evaluation: A meta-analysis. *Exceptional Children, 53,* 199–208.

GAGE, N. L., P. J. RUNKEL, and B. B. CHATTERJEE. 1960. Equilibrium Theory and Behavior Change: An Experiment in Feedback from Pupils to Teachers. Urbana, IL: University of Illinois, Bureau of Educational Research.

GARBER, H. 1967. The digital computer simulates human rating behavior. In J. T. Flynn and H. Garber, *Assessing behavior: Readings in Educational and Psychological Measurement.* Reading, MA: Addison-Wesley.

GARDNER, E. G. 1978. Bias. *NCME Measurement News, 21,* 2.

GARLOCK, J., R. S. DOLLARHIDE, and K. D. HOPKINS. 1965. Comparability of scores on the Wide Range and the Gilmore Oral Reading tests. *California Journal of Educational Research, 16,* 54–57.

GAY, L. R. 1980. The comparative effects of multiple-choice versus short-answer tests on retention. *Journal of Educational Measurement, 17,* 45–50.

GILMAN, D. A., and P. FERRY. 1972. Increasing test reliability through self-scoring procedures. *Journal of Educational Measurement, 9,* 205–208.

GLASER, R. 1963. Instructional technology and the measurement of learning outcomes: Some questions. *American Psychologist, 18,* 519–521.

————. 1994. Criterion-referenced tests: Part I. Origins. *Educational Measurement: Issues and Practice, 13,* 9–11.

GLASS, G. V 1978a. Standards and criteria. *Journal of Educational Measurement, 15,* 237–261.

————. 1978b. Minimum competence and incompetence in Florida. *Phi Delta Kappan, 59,* 602–605.

————. 1978c. Matthew Arnold and minimal competency. *The Educational Forum, 42,* 139–144.

GLASS, G. V, and K. D. HOPKINS. 1996. *Statistical methods in education and psychology* (3RD ed.). Boston: Allyn & Bacon.

GLASS, G. V, B. MCGAW, and M. L. SMITH. 1981. *Meta-analysis in Social Research.* Beverly Hills: Sage Publications.

GLASS, G. V, and D. E. WILEY. 1964. Formula scoring and test reliability. *Journal of Educational Measurement, 1,* 43–47.

GLASSER, W. 1969. *Schools without failure.* New York: Harper & Row.

GLUTTING, J. J., P. A. MCDERMOTT, and J. C. STANLEY. 1987. Resolving differences among methods of establishing confidence limits for test scores. *Educational and Psychological Measurement, 47,* 607–611.

GODSHALK, F. I., F. SWINEFORD, W. E. COFFMAN, and EDUCATIONAL TESTING SERVICE. 1966. *The measurement of writing ability.* New York: College Entrance Examination Board.

GOLDMAN, B. A., and R. RICHARDS. 1974. The SAT prediction of grades for Mexican-American students versus Anglo-American students at the University of California, Riverside. *Journal of Educational Measurement, 11,* 129–136.

GOLDMAN, R. D., and R. E. SLAUGHTER. 1976. Why college grade-point average is difficult to predict. *Journal of Educational Psychology, 68,* 9–14.

GOODWIN, W. L. 1966. Effect of selected methodological conditions on dependent measures taken after classroom experimentation. *Journal of Educational Psychology, 57,* 350–358.

GORDON, R. A. 1975. Examining labelling theory: The case of mental retardation. In W. R. Gove (Ed.). *The labelling of deviance: Evaluating a perspective.* New York: Halsted Press.

GOTTFREDSON, L. S. (Ed.). 1986. The g factor in employment. *Journal of Vocational Behavior, 29,* 293–450.

GOZALI, J., and E. L. MEYER. 1970. The influence of the teacher expectancy phenomenon on the academic performance of educable mentally retarded pupils in special classes. *Journal of Special Education, 4,* 417–424.

GRAFF, K. 1965. The high school equivalency program. *Vocational Guidance Quarterly, 13,* 297–299.

GREEN, D. R. (Ed.). 1974. *The Aptitude-achievement distinction.* New York: CTB/McGraw-Hill.

GRONLUND, N. E 1974. *Improving marking and reporting in classroom instruction.* New York: Macmillan.

GUILFORD, J. P. Creativity. 1950. *American Psychologist, 14,* 469–479.

————. 1959. *Personality.* New York: McGraw-Hill.

————. 1965. Fundamental statistics in psychology and education (4th ed.). New York: McGraw-Hill.

————. 1967. *The nature of human intelligence.* New York: McGraw-Hill.

————. 1968. The structure of intelligence. In D. K. Whitla (Ed.), *Handbook of measurement and assessment in behavioral sciences.* Chapter 7. Reading, MA: Addison-Wesley.

GULLICKSON, A. R. 1984. Teach perspectives of their instructional use of tests. *Journal of Educational Research, 77,* 244–248.

————. 1985. Student evaluation techniques and their relationship to grade and curriculum. *Journal of Educational Research, 79,* 96–100.

GULLICKSON, and K. D. HOPKINS. 1976. Interval estimation of correlation coefficients corrected for restriction of range. *Educational and Psychological Measurement, 36,* 9–25.

————. 1987. Perspectives on Educational Measurement Instruction for Preservice Teachers. *Educational Measurement: Issues and Practice, 6,* 12–16.

GULLIKSEN, H. 1987. *Theory of Mental Tests.* Hillsdale, NJ: Lawrence Erlbaum Associates.

GUSTAV, A. 1963. Response sets in objective achievement tests. *Journal of Psychology, 56,* 421–427.

HABERMAN, M. 1970. The relationship of bogus expectations to success in student teaching (or, Pygmalion's illegitimate son). In *Abstract one: 1970 annual meeting paper sessions* (p. 66). Washington, DC: American Educational Research Association.

HAKSTIAN, A. R. 1971. The effect on study methods and test performance of objective and essay examinations. *Journal of Educational Research, 64,* 319–324.

HAKSTIAN, A. R., and W. KANSUP. 1975. A comparison of several methods of assessing partial knowledge in multiple-choice tests: II. Testing procedures. *Journal of Educational Measurement, 12,* 231–240.

HALES, L. W., and E. TOKAR. 1975. The effect of the quality of preceding responses on the grades assigned to subsequent responses to an essay question. *Journal of Educational Measurement, 12,* 115–118.

HALL, D. W. 1966. The Minnesota Vocational Interest Inventory. *Journal of Educational Measurement, 3,* 337–341.

HALPIN, A. W. 1966. *Theory and research in administration.* New York: Macmillan.

HAMAKER, C. 1986. The effects of adjunct questions on prose learning. *Review of Educational Research, 56,* 212–242.

HAMBLETON, R. K. 1978. Criterion-referenced testing and measurement: A review of technical issues and developments. *Review of Educational Research, 4,* 1–48.

HAMBLETON, R. K., and R. W. JONES. 1993. Comparison of classical test theory and item response theory and their applications to test development. *Educational Measurement: Issues and Practice, 12,* 38–47.

HAMBLETON, R. K., and R. E. TRAUB. 1974. The effects of item order on test performance and stress. *Journal of Experimental Education, 43,* 40–46.

HANNA, G. S. 1975. Incremental reliability and validity of multiple-choice tests with an answer-until-correct procedure. *Journal of Educational Measurement, 12,* 175–178.

HANNA, G. S., and R. E. OWENS. 1973. Incremental validity of confidence weighting of items. *California Journal of Educational Research, 24,* 165–168.

HANSEN, J. C., and D. P. CAMPBELL. 1985. *Manual for the SVIB-SCII* (4th ed.). Stanford, CA: Stanford University Press.

HARRIS, C. W. (Ed.). 1963. *Problems in measuring change.* Madison: University of Wisconsin Press.

HARROW, A. J. 1972. *A Taxonomy of the Psychomotor Domain.* New York: D. McKay.

HARTSHORNE, H., and M. A. MAY. 1928. *Studies in deceit.* New York: Macmillan.

HASHIMOTO, J. 1959. no yokoku koka ni tsuite (The effect of announcement of the coming test). *Japanese Journal of Educational Psychology, 6,* 217–222.

HAVIGHURST, R. J., and B. C. NEUGARTEN. 1975. *Society and education* (4th ed.). Boston: Allyn & Bacon.

HAWKES, H. E., E. F. LINDQUIST, and C. R. MANN. 1936. *The construction and use of achievement examinations.* Boston: Houghton Mifflin.

HEDGES, W. D. 1966. *Testing and evaluation for the secondary school.* Belmont, CA: Wadsworth.

HENSLEY, H., and R. A. DAVIS. 1952. What high-school teachers think and do about their examinations. *Educational Administration and Supervision, 38,* 219–28.

HICKLIN, J. J. 1962. A study of long-range techniques for predicting patterns of scholastic behavior. Unpublished Ph.D. thesis, University of Chicago.

HILLS, J. R. 1971. Use of measurement in selection and placement. In R. L. Thorndike (Ed.), *Educational measurement* (2nd ed.). Chapter 19. Washington, DC: American Council on Education.

HILLS, J. R., and J. STANLEY. 1970. Easier test improves prediction of black students' college grades. *Journal of Negro Education, 39,* 320–324.

HILTON, T. L. 1979. ETS study of academic prediction and growth. In J. E. Milholland (Ed.), *New directions for testing and measurement.* San Francisco: Jossey-Bass.

HOEPFNER, J., and M. O'SULLIVAN. 1968. Social intelligence and IQ. *Journal of Psychological Measurement, 28,* 339–344.

HOFFMAN, R. A., and E. W. ZIEGLER. 1978. The use of a standard language test to identify college students with deficient writing skills. *Measurement and Evaluation in Guidance, 11,* 159–161.

HOFFMAN, B. 1962. *The tyranny of testing.* New York: Crowell-Collier and Macmillan.

———. 1967a. Psychometric scientism. *Phi Delta Kappan, 48,* 381–386.

———. 1967b. Multiple-choice tests. *Physics Education, 2,* 247–251.

HOGAN, T. P., and C. MISHLER. 1980. Relationship between essay tests and objective tests of language skills for elementary school students. *Journal of Educational Measurement, 17,* 219–228.

HOLLAND, J. L. 1985. *Making vocational choices: A theory of vocational personalities and work environments* (2nd ed.). Englewood Cliffs, NJ: Prentice-Hall.

HOLLINGSHEAD, A. B., and F. C. REDLICH. 1957. *Two-factor index of social position.* New Haven, CT: The authors.

HOLLY, K. A., and W. B. MICHAEL. 1972. The relationship of structure-of-intellect factor abilities to performance in high school modern algebra. *Educational and Psychological Measurement, 32,* 447–450.

———. 1973. Comparative validities and testing times for composites of structure-of-intellect tests and previous mathematics grades. *Educational and Psychological Measurement, 33,* 915–919.

HOLT, J. 1968. *How children fail.* New York: Pitman.

HOLTZMAN, W. H. 1975. New developments in Holtzman Inkblot technique. In P. McReynolds (Ed.), *Advances in psychological assessment.* Vol. 3. San Francisco: Jossey-Bass.

HOMAN, S., M. HEWITT, and J. LINDER. 1994. The development and validation of a formula for measuring single-sentence test item readability. *Journal of Educational Measurement, 31,* 349–358.

HOPKINS, K. D. 1964a. Extrinsic reliability: Estimating and attenuating variance from response styles, chance, and other irrelevant sources. *Educational and Psychological Measurement, 24,* 271–281. Reprinted in G. H. Bracht, K. D. Hopkins, and J. C. Stanley (Eds.), *Perspectives in Educational and Psychological Measurement.* Selection 10. Englewood Cliffs, NJ: Prentice-Hall, 1972.

———. 1964b. An empirical analysis of the efficacy of the WISC in the diagnosis of organicity of children of normal intelligence. *Journal of Genetic Psychology, 105,* 163–172.

———. 1965. The readability of standardized achievement tests for the elementary school. M.S. thesis, University of Southern California, Los Angeles.

———. 1969. Regression and the matching fallacy in quasi-experimental research. *Journal of Special Education, 3,* 329–336.

———. 1975. Ten-year stability of verbal and nonverbal IQ scores. *American Educational Research Journal, 12,* 469–477.

———. 1986. Affective dependent measures: The use of a response integrity scale to enhance the validity of experimental and quasi-experimental research. *Journal of Special Education, 20,* 43–47.

HOPKINS, K. D., and M. BIBELHEIMER. 1971. Five-year stability IQ's from language and nonlanguage group tests. *Child Development, 42,* 645–649.

HOPKINS, K. D., and G. H. BRACHT. 1971. The stability and change of language and nonlanguage IQ scores. Final Report, Project No. O-H-024. Washington, DC: U.S. Department of Health, Education, and Welfare, Office of Education, Bureau of Research.

———. 1975. Ten-year stablity of verbal and nonverbal IQ scores. *American Educational Research Journal, 12,* 469–477.

HOPKINS, K. D., J. C. DOBSON, and O. A. OLDRIDGE. 1962. The concurrent and congruent validities of the Wide Range Achievement Test. *Educational and Psychological Measurement, 22,* 791–793.

HOPKINS, K. D., C. A. GEORGE, and D. D. WILLIAMS. 1985. The concurrent validity of standardized achievement tests by content area using teachers' ratings as criteria. *Journal of Educational Measurement, 22,* 177–182.

HOPKINS, K. D., A. R. HAKSTIAN, and B. R. HOPKINS. 1973. Validity and reliability consequences of confidence weighting. *Educational and Psychological Measurement, 33,* 135–141.

HOPKINS, K. D., and S. E. HODGE. 1984. Review of the Kaufman Assessment Battery (K-ABC) for Children. *Journal of Counseling Development, 63,* 105–107.

HOPKINS, K. D., and B. R. HOPKINS. 1964. Intraindividual and interindividual positional preference response styles in ability tests. *Educational and Psychological Measurement, 24,* 801–805.

HOPKINS, K. D., B. R. HOPKINS, and G. V. GLASS. 1996. *Basic statistics for the behavioral sciences* (3RD ed.). Boston: Allyn & Bacon.

HOPKINS, K. D., and G. KRETKE. 1978, 1979, 1983, 1984. *District testing report.* Boulder, CO: Boulder Valley School District.

HOPKINS, K. D., D. W. LEFEVER, and B. R. HOPKINS. 1967. TV vs. teacher administration of standardized tests: Comparability of scores. *Journal of Educational Measurement, 4,* 35–40.

HOPKINS, K. D., and L. MCGUIRE. 1966. Mental measurement of the blind: The validity of the Wechsler Intelligence Scale for Children. *International Journal for Education of the Blind, 15,* 65–73.

HOPKINS, K. D., J. C. STANLEY, and B. R. HOPKINS. 1990. *Educational and Psychological Measurement and Evaluation* (7TH ed.). Englewood Cliffs: Prentice Hall.

HORN, J. L. 1966. Some characteristics of classroom examinations. *Journal of Educational Measurement, 3,* 293–295.

HORN, J. L., and R. B. CATTELL. 1966. Refinement and test of the theory of fluid and crystallized general intelligence. *Journal of Educational Psychology, 57,* 253–270.

HORN, J. L., and J. R. KNAPP. 1973. On the subjective character of the empirical base of Guilford's structure-of-intellect model. *Psychological Bulletin, 80,* 33–43.

HOYT, D. P., and L. A. MUNDAY. 1966. *Your college freshmen.* Iowa City: American College Testing Program.

HUGHES, D. C., B. KEELING, and B. F. TUCK. 1980. The influence of context position and scoring method on essay scoring. *Journal of Educational Measurement, 17,* 131–136.

HUNKINS, F. P. 1969. Effects of analysis and evaluation questions on various levels of achievement. *Journal of Experimental Education, 38,* 45–58.

HUNT, J. 1961. *Intelligence and experience.* New York: Ronald.

INGLE, R. B., and G. DE AMINO. 1969. The effect of physical conditions of the room on standardized achievement test scores. *Journal of Educational Measurement, 6,* 237–240.

IRVIN, L. K., A. S. HALPERN, and J. T. LANDMAN. 1980. Assessment of retarded student achievement with standardized true-false and multiple-choice tests. *Journal of Educational Measurement, 17,* 51–58.

JACKSON, R. A. 1955. Guessing and test performance. *Educational and Psychological Measurement, 15,* 74–79.

JACOBS, S. S. 1972. Answer changing on objective tests: Some implications for test validity. *Educational and Psychological Measurement, 32,* 1039–1044.

JAEGER, R. M. 1988. Certification of student competence. In R. L. Linn (Ed.), *Educational measurement.* Chapter 14. Washington, DC: American Council on Education.

JENCKS, C. 1972. *Inequality: A reassessment of the effect of family and schooling in America.* New York: Basic Books.

JENSEN, A. R. 1965. Review of the Rorschach. In O. K. Buros (Ed.), *The sixth mental measurements yearbook.* Highland Park, NJ: Gryphon Press. Reprinted in G. H. Bracht, K. D. Hopkins, and J. C. Stanley (Eds.), *Perspectives in Educational and Psychological Measurement.* Selection 30. Englewood Cliffs, NJ: Prentice-Hall.

———. 1968. Social class, race, and genetics: Implications for education. *American Educational Research Journal, 5,* 1–42.

———. 1973a. *Genetics and education.* New York: Harper & Row.

———. 1973b. *Educability and group differences.* New York: Harper & Row.

———. 1980. *Bias in mental testing.* New York: Free Press.

———. 1981. *Straight talk about mental tests.* New York: Free Press.

JENSEN, M., and M. D. BECK. 1979. Gender balance analysis on the Metropolitan Achievement Tests, 1978 edition. *Measurement and Evaluation in Guidance, 12,* 25–34.

JESSEL, J. C., and W. L. SULLINS. 1975. The effect of keyed response sequencing of multiple-choice items on performance and reliability. *Journal of Educational Measurement, 12,* 45–48.

JOHNSON, F. W. 1911. A study of high school grades. *School Review, 19,* 13–24.

JONZ, J. 1976. Improving on the basic egg: The M-C cloze. *Language Learning, 26,* 255–265.

JORGENSON, G. W. 1975. An analysis of teacher judgments of reading level. *American Educational Research Journal, 12,* 67–75.

JOSE, J., and J. J. CODY. 1971. Teacher-pupil interaction as it relates to attempted changes in teacher expectancy of academic ability and achievement. *American Educational Research Journal, 8,* 39–50.

JURGENSEN, C. E. 1966. Advisory panel appraises suitability of USES testing. *Industrial Psychologist, 4,* 41–44.

KAISER, H. F. 1958. A modified stanine scale. *Journal of Experimental Education, 26,* 261.

KANE, J., and J. MALONEY. 1978. The effect of guessing on item reliability under answer-until-correct scoring. *Applied Psychological Measurement, 2,* 41–49.

KEEVES, J. P. (Ed.). 1988. *Educational research, methodology, and measurement: An international handbook.* New York: Pergamon Press.

KELLAHAN, T., G. F. MADAUS, and P. W. AIRASIAN. 1983. The effects of standardized testing: The Irish study. *Educational Measurement: Issues and Practice, 2,* 21–25.

KEMPTHORNE, O. 1978. Logical, epistemological and statistical aspects of nature-nurture data interpretations. *Biometrics, 34,* 1–23.

KENDRICK, S. A., and C. L. THOMAS. 1970. Education for socially disadvantaged children: Transition from school to college. *Review of Educational Research, 40,* 151–179.

KERLINGER, F. N. 1986. *Foundations of behavioral research* (3rd ed.). New York: Holt, Rinehart & Winston.

KEYSOR, R. E., and D. D. WILLIAMS. 1977. The effect of "test-wiseness" on professional school screening test scores. *NCME Measurement News, 20.*

KIFER, W. 1985. Review of ACT Assessment Program. *Ninth mental measurements yearbook,* 31–36.

KLARE, G. R. 1975. Assessing readability. *Reading Research Quarterly, 10,* 62–102.

KLAUSMEIER H. J. 1982. A research strategy for educational improvement. *Educational Researcher, 11,* 8–13.

KLEIN, S. P., and F. M. HART. 1968. The nature of essay grades in law school. Research Bulletin 68-6. Princeton, NJ: Educational Testing Service.

KLEINKE, D. 1979. Systematic errors in approximations to the standard error of measurement and reliability. *Applied Psychological Measurement, 3,* 161–164.

KNAPP, R. R. 1968. The effects of time limits on the intelligence test performance of Mexican-American subjects. *Journal of Educational Psychology, 51,* 14–20.

KOEHLER, R. A. 1971. A comparison of the validities of conventional choice testing and various confidence marking procedures. *Journal of Educational Measurement,* 8, 297–303.

———. 1974. Overconfidence on probabilistic tests. *Journal of Educational Measurement, 11,* 1101–1104.

KOPPITZ, E. M. 1975. *The Bender Gestalt Test for young children: Research and application, 1963–1973.* New York: Grune & Stratton.

KORETZ, D., B. STECHER, S. KLEIN, and D. McCAFFREY. 1994. The Vermont portfolio assessment program: Findings and implications. *Educational Measurement: Issues and Practice, 13,* 5–16.

KRAFT, R. S. 1978. Inside Chinese education. *School and University Review, 8,* 4–8.

KRAMER, J. J., and J. C. CONOLEY. (Eds.). *The Eleventh Mental Measurements Yearbook.* 1992. Lincoln, NE: Buros Institute for Mental Measurement.

KRATHWOHL, D. R., and D. PAYNE. 1971. Defining and assessing educational objectives. In R. L. Thorndike (Ed.), *Educational measurement* (2nd ed.). Chapter 2. Washington, DC: American Council on Education.

KRATHWOHL, D. R., et al. 1964. *Taxonomy of educational objectives: Handbook II, affective domain.* New York: D. McKay.

KRATHWOHL, D. R. 1965. Stating objectives appropriately for program, for curriculum, and for instructional materials development. *Journal of Teacher Education, 16,* 83–92.

KREIT, L. H. 1968. The effects of test-taking practice on pupil test performance. *American Educational Research Journal, 5,* 616–625.

KRUEGER, W. C. F. 1929. The effect of overlearning on retention. *Journal of Experimental Psychology, 12,* 71–78.

KUDER, G. F. 1977. *Activity, interests, and occupational choice.* Chicago: Science Research Associates.

KUDER, G. F., and M. W. RICHARDSON. 1937. The theory of the estimation of test reliability. *Psychometrika, 2,* 151–160.

KULIK, J. A., C. C. KULIK, and R. L. BANGERT. 1984. Effects of practice on aptitude and achievement test scores. *American Educational Research Journal, 21,* 435–447.

KULIK, J. A., and W. J MCKEACHIE. 1975. The evaluation of teachers in higher education. In F. N. Kerlinger (Ed.), *Review of Research in Education* (pp. 210–240).

LAFAVE, L. 1964. Essay tests can be standardized. *Science, 146,* 171.

LAVIN, D. E. 1967. *The prediction of academic performance.* New York: John Wiley.

LEHMANN, I. J., and S. E. PHILLIPS. 1987. A survey of state teacher-competency examination programs. *Educational Measurement: Issues and Practice, 6,* 14–18.

LENS, W. 1983. Fear of failure and performance on ability tests. In S. B. Anderson and J. S. Helmick (Eds.), *On educational testing: Intelligence, performance standards, test anxiety, and latent traits.* Chapter 9. San Francisco: Jossey-Bass.

LEVINE, R. S., and W. H. ANGOFF. 1958. The effects of practice and growth on scores on the Scholastic Aptitude Test. *Statistical Report 58–6.* Princeton, NJ: Educational Testing Service.

LEWIS, M., and H. MCGURK. 1972. Evaluation of infant intelligence. *Science, 178,* 1174–1177.

LIKERT, R. A. 1934. A technique for the measurement of attitudes. *Archives of Psychology.* No. 140.

LINDQUIST, E. F. 1944. The use of tests of accreditation of military experience and in the educational placement of war veterans. *Educational Record, 25,* 357–376.

LINN, R. L. 1983. Pearson selection formulas: Implications for studies of predictive bias and estimates of educational effects in selected samples. *Journal of Educational Management, 20,* 1–16.

———. 1988. Educational testing and assessment: Research needs and policy issues. *American Psychologist, 41,* 1153–1160.

LINN, R. L. and E. BURTON. 1994. Performance-based assessments: Implications of task specificity. *Educational Measurement: Issues and Practice, 13,* 5–8, 15.

LITTLE, E., and J. CREASER. 1966. Uncertain responses on multiple-choice examinations. *Psychological Reports, 18,* 801–802.

LIVINGSTON, S. A. 1972. Criterion-referenced applications of classical test theory. *Journal of Educational Measurement, 9,* 13–26.

LOEHLIN, H. C., G. LINDZEY, and J. N. SPUHLER. 1975. *Race differences in intelligence.* San Francisco: W. H. Freeman.

LONNER, W. J., and H. L. ADAMS. 1972. Interest patterns of psychologists in nine Western nations. *Journal of Applied Psychology, 56,* 141–151.

LORD, F. M. 1952. The relation of the reliability of multiple-choice tests to the distribution of item difficulties. *Psychometrika, 17,* 181–194.

———. 1955. A survey of observed test-score distribution with respect to skewness and kurtosis. *Educational and Psychological Measurement, 15,* 383–389.

———. 1956. A study of speed factors in tests and academic grades. *Psychometrika, 21,* 31–50.

———. 1959a. Test norms and sampling theory. *Journal of Experimental Education, 27,* 247–263.

———. 1959b. Tests of the same lengths do have the same standard error of measurement. *Educational and Psychological Measurement, 19,* 233–239.

———. 1963. Formula scoring and validity. *Educational and Psychological Measurement, 23,* 663–672.

———. 1971a. The self-scoring flexilevel test. *Journal of Educational Measurement, 8,* 147–151.

———. 1971b. A theoretical study of the measurement effectiveness of flexilevel tests. *Educational and Psychological Measurement, 31,* 805–814.

———. 1975. Formula scoring and number-right scoring. *Journal of Educational Measurement, 12,* 7–12.

———. 1976. Invited discussion. In *Proceedings of the first conference on computerized adaptive testing.* Washington, DC: U.S. Civil Service Commission.

———, and M. R. NOVICK. 1968. *Statistical theories of mental test scores.* Reading, MA: Addison-Wesley.

LYMAN, H. B. 1978. *Test scores and what they mean.* Englewood Cliffs, NJ: Prentice-Hall.

LYNCH, D. O., and B. C. SMITH. 1975. Item response changes: Effects on test scores. *Measurement and Evaluation in Guidance, 7,* 220–224.

MACHOVER, K. 1949. *Personality projection in the drawing of the human figure: A method of personality investigation*. Springfield, IL: Chas. C Thomas.

MADAUS, G. F., and J. T. MCDONAGH. 1979. Minimum competency testing: Unexamined assumptions and unexplored negative outcomes. In R. T. Lennon (Ed.), *New directions for testing and measurement: Impactive changes on measurement*. San Francisco: Jossey-Bass.

MAGNUSSON, D., and G. BACKTEMAN. 1978. Longitudinal stability of person characteristics: Intelligence and creativity. *Applied Psychological Measurement, 2,* 481–490.

MANN, H. 1845. Report of the annual examining committee of the Boston grammar and writing schools. *Common School Journal, 7,* 326–336.

MARKHAM, L. R. 1976. Influences of handwriting quality on teacher evaluation of written work. *American Educational Research Journal, 13,* 277–284.

MARSH, H. W. 1977. The validity of students' evaluations: Classroom evaluations of instructors by graduating seniors. *American Educational Research Journal, 14,* 441–447.

MARSHALL, J. C. 1967. Composition errors and essay examination grades re-examined. *American Educational Research Journal, 4,* 375–385.

MARSHALL, J. C., and J. M. POWERS. 1969. Writing readability, composition errors, and essay grades. Paper presented at the annual meeting of the National Council on Measurement in Education, Los Angeles.

MARSO, R. N. 1970. Test item arrangement, testing time and performance. *Journal of Educational Measurement, 7,* 113–118.

MASLING, J. 1959. The effects of warm and cold interaction on the administration and scoring of an intelligence test. *Journal of Consulting Psychology, 23,* 336–341.

MCASKIE, M., and A. M. CLARKE. 1976. Parent-offspring resemblances in intelligence: Theories and evidence. *British Journal of Psychology, 67,* 243–273.

MCMILLAN, J. H. 1977. The effect of effort and feedback on the formation of student attitudes. *American Educational Research Journal, 14,* 317–330.

MCNEMAR, Q. 1964. Lost: our intelligence. Why? *American Psychologist, 19,* 871–882.

MEEHL, P. E. 1954. *Clinical versus statistical prediction: A theoretical analysis and a review of the evidence*. Minneapolis, MN: University of Minnesota Press.

MEHRENS, W. A., and I. J. LEHMANN. 1984. *Measurement and evaluation in education and psychology* (3rd ed.). New York: Holt, Rinehart & Winston.

MENDELS, G. E., and J. P. FLANDERS. 1973. Teachers' expectations and pupil performance. *American Educational Research Journal, 10,* 203–212.

MERCER, J. 1977. *System of multicultural pluralistic assessment* (SOMPA). New York: Psychological Corporation.

MESSICK, S. 1980. The effectiveness of coaching for the SAT: Review and analysis of research from the fifties to the FTC. *ETS RR 80–81*. Princeton, NJ: Educational Testing Service.

———. 1989. Validity. In R. L. Linn (Ed.). *Educational Measurement* (3RD ed.). New York: American Council on Education and Macmillan.

METFESSEL, N. S., and G. SAX. 1957. Response set patterns in published instructors' manuals in education and psychology. *California Journal of Educational Research, 8,* 195–197.

MEYER, M. 1908. The grading of students. *Science, 27,* 243–250.

MICHAEL, J. J. 1968a. The reliability of a multiple-choice examination under various test-taking instructions. *Journal of Educational Measurement, 5,* 307–314.

———. 1968b. Structure of intellect theory and the validity of achievement examinations. *Educational and Psychological Measurement, 28,* 1141–1149.

MICHAEL, W. B., T. COOPER, P. SHAFFER, and E. WALLIS. 1980. A comparison of the reliability and validity of ratings of student performance on essay examinations by professors of English and by professors in other disciplines. *Educational and Psychological Measurement, 40,* 183–195.

MICHAEL, J. J., and W. B. MICHAEL. 1969. The relationship of performance on objective achievement examinations to the order in which students complete them. *Educational and Psychological Measurement, 29,* 511–513.

MILLER, P. M, N. S. FAGLEY, and D. S. LANE. 1988. Stability of the Gibb experimental test of testwiseness. *Educational and Psychological Measurement, 48,* 1123–1127.

MILLMAN, J. 1961. Multiple-choice test item construction rules. Ithaca, NY: Cornell University Press, mimeo. 7 pp.

———. 1974. Criterion-referenced measurement. In W. J. Popham (Ed.), *Evaluation in education: Current applications.* Berkeley, CA: McCutchan.

———. 1981a. *Handbook of teacher evaluation.* Beverly Hills, CA: Sage.

———. 1981b. Protesting the detesting of PRO testing, *NCME Measurement in Education, 12,* 1–6.

MILLMAN, J., C. H. BISHOP, and R. EBEL. 1965. An analysis of test-wiseness. *Educational and Psychological Measurement, 25,* 707–726.

MILLMAN, J., and J. GREENE. 1985. *The specification and development of tests of achievement and ability.* Department of Educational Psychology, Cornell University.

MILLMAN, J., and W. PAUK. 1969. *How to take tests.* New York: McGraw-Hill.

MILLS, C. N. 1991. Defining minimal Competence. *Educational Measurement: Issues and Practice, 10,* 7–10.

MIYAZAKI, I. 1976. *China's examination hell: The civil service examinations of imperial China.* Trans. by C. Schirokauer. New York and Tokyo: Weatherhill.

MOLLENKOPF, W. G. 1960. Time limits and the behavior of test takers. *Educational and Psychological Measurement, 20,* 223–230.

MONROE, W. S., and R. E. CARTER. 1923. *The use of different types of thought questions in secondary schools and their relative difficulty for students.* Bulletin No. 14. Urbana: University of Illinois, Bureau of Educational Research.

MONTEI, M. S. 1996. Validity of scores on the attitudes toward diversity scale (ATDS). *Educational and Psychological Measurement, 56,* 293–303.

MOORE, J. C., R. E. SCHUTZ, and R. L. BAKER. 1966. The application of a self-instructional technique to develop a test-taking strategy. *American Educational Research Journal, 3,* 13–17.

MOOS, R. H. 1974. *The social climate scales: An overview.* Palo Alto, CA: Consulting Psychologists Press.

———. 1975. Assessment and impact of social climate. In P. McReynolds (Ed.), *Advances in psychological assessment.* Vol. 3. Chapter 1. San Francisco: Jossey-Bass.

———. 1979. *Evaluating educational environments: Procedures, measures, findings, and policy implications.* San Francisco: Jossey-Bass.

MORROW, J. R. 1977. Some statistics regarding the reliability and validity of student ratings of teacher. *The Research Quarterly, 48,* 372–375.

MOYNIHAN, P. 1971. Seek parity of educational achievement, Moynihan urges. *Report on Educational Research, 3,* 4.

MUCHINSKY, P. M. 1996. The correction for attenuation. *Educational and Psychological Measurement, 56,* 63–75.

MUELLER, D. J., and A. SHWEDEL. 1975. Some correlates of net gain from answer changing on objective test items. *Journal of Educational Measurement, 12,* 251–254.

MUELLER, D. J., and V. WASSER. 1977. Implications of changing answers on objective test items. *Journal of Educational Measurement, 14,* 9–14.

MURPHY, L. L., J. C. CONOLEY, and J. C. IMPARA. 1994. *Tests in print IV.* Lincoln, NB: Buros Institute of Mental Measurements.

MURRAY, H. A., et al. 1938. *Explorations in Personality.* New York: Oxford University Press.

MYERS, C. T. 1960. Symposium: The effects of time limits on test scores. *Educational and Psychological Measurement, 20,* 221–222.

NATIONAL ASSESSMENT OF EDUCATIONAL PROGRESS. 1976. Minimal Competency Tests. *NAEP Newsletter, 9.*
———. 1978. *Update on Education.* Denver, CO.
NATIONAL COUNCIL ON MEASUREMENT IN EDUCATION. 1976. On bias in selection. *Journal of Educational Measurement, 13,* 1–99.
———. 1980. NCME statement on educational admissions testing. *NCME Measurement News, 23,* 4–6.
NATIONAL EDUCATION ASSOCIATION. 1967. National Education Association report to parents. *NEA Research BUlletin, 45,* 51–53.
NATIONAL INSTITUTE OF EDUCATION. 1979. *Testing, teaching, and learning.* Washington, DC: NIE.
NELL, W. 1963. A comparative investigation of teacher assigned grades and academic achievement in the Aztec Junior High, New Mexico. *Educational Research Bulletin.* (Society for the Study of Education), 15–16.
NILSSON, I. 1975. The occurrence of test-wiseness and the possibility of inducing it via instruction. *Educational Reports* UMEA No. 8.
NITKO, T. 1988. Designing tests that are integrated with instruction. In Linn, R. (Ed.), *Educational measurement* (3rd ed.). Chapter 12 . Washington, DC: American Council on Education.
NORMAN, R. D. 1954. The effects of a forward-retention set on an objective achievement test presented forwards or backwards. *Educational and Psychological Measurement, 14,* 487–498.
NOVICK, M. R., and C. LEWIS. 1967. Coefficient alpha and the reliability of composite measurements. *Psychometrika, 32,* 1–13.
OLDRIDGE, O. A. 1963. An experimental study of two guidance emphases in the elementary school. Doctoral dissertation, University of Southern California. *Dissertation Abstracts, 24,* 632–633.
OLSON, M. C., and P. DISTEFANO. 1980. Describing and testing the effectiveness of a contemporary model for in-service education in teaching composition. *English Education, 12,* 69–76.
OSGOOD, C. E., G. J. SUCI, and P. H. TANNENBAUM. 1957. *The measurement of meaning.* Urbana, IL: University of Illinois.
OSS ASSESSMENT STAFF. 1948. *Assessment of men: Selection of personnel for the office of strategic services.* New York: Rinehart.
OSTERLUND, B. L., and K. CHENEY. 1978. A holistic essay-reading composite as a criterion for the validity of the test of standard written English. *Measurement and Evaluation in Guidance, 11,* 155–158.
O'SULLIVAN, M., and J. P. GUILFORD. 1975. Six factors of behavioral cognition: Understanding other people. *Journal of Educational Measurement, 12,* 255–272.
OWEN, D. 1985. *None of the above: Behind the myth of the scholastic aptitude.* Boston: Houghton Mifflin.
OWENS, W. A. 1953. Age and mental abilities: A longitudinal study. *Genetic Psychology Monographs, 48,* 3–54.
———. 1966. Age and mental abilities: A second adult follow-up. *Journal of Educational Psychology, 57,* 311–325.
PADEN, P. A. 1986. The potential dual effect of context effects and score level effects on the assignments of scores to essays. Research Report, 1–18. Princeton, NJ: Educational Testing Service.
PAGE, A. 1960. To grade or retrograde. *College English, 21,* 213–216.
———. 1963. Socrates on cheating. *Liberal Education, 49,* 193–197.
PAGE, E. B. 1985. Review of the Kaufman Assessment Battery for Children. In J. V. Mitchell, Jr. (Ed.). *Ninth Mental Measurement Yearbook.* Lincoln, NE: University of Nebraska Press.
PAGE, E. B. 1958. Teacher comments and student performance: A seventy-four classroom experiment in school motivation. *Journal of Educational Psychology, 49,* 173–181.
———. 1966. The imminence of grading essays by computer. *Phi Delta Kappan, 47,* 238–243.
———. 1972. Miracle in Milwaukee: Raising the IQ. *Educational Research, 1,* 8–16.
PAGE, E. B., and T. F. BREEN. 1973. Educational values for measurement technology: Some theory and data. In W. E. Coffman (Ed.), *Frontiers of educational measurement and information systems.* Proceedings of the Invitational Conference on the Occasion of the Dedication of the Lindquist Center for Measurement. Boston: Houghton Mifflin.

PAGE, E. B., and H. FEIFS. 1985. *SAT* scores and American states: Seeking for useful meaning. *Journal of Educational Measurement, 22,* 305–312.

PALLAS, A. M., and K. L. ALEXANDER. 1983. Sex differences in quantitative SAT performance: New evidence on the differential coursework hypothesis. *American Educational Research Journal, 20,* 165–182.

PANACKAL, A. A., and C. S. HEFT. 1978. Cloze technique and multiple-choice technique: Reliability and validity. *Educational and Psychological Measurement, 38,* 917–932.

PASCALE, P. J. 1974. Changing answers on multiple-choice achievement tests. *Measurement and Evaluation in Guidance, 6,* 236–238.

PAYNE, D. A. 1963. A note on skewness and internal consistency reliability estimates. *Journal of Experimental Education, 32,* 43–46.

PEAK, H., and E. G. BORING. 1926. The factor of speed in intelligence. *Journal of Experimental Psychology, 9,* 71.

PEARSON, P. D., and D. D. JOHNSON. 1978. *Teaching reading comprehension.* New York: Holt, Rinehart & Winston.

PEDULLA, J. J., P. W. AIRASIAN, and G. F. MADAUS. 1980. Do teacher ratings and standardized test results of students yield the same information. *American Educational Research Journal, 17,* 303–307.

PETERS, F. R. 1956. Measurement of informal educational achievement by the GED tests. *School Review, 64,* 227–232.

PETERSEN, N. S., M. J. KOLEN, and H. D. HOOVER. 1988. Scaling, norming, and equating. In R. L. Linn (Ed.), *Educational measurement* (3rd. ed.). Chapter 6 . Washington, DC: American Council on Education.

PETERSON, R. A. 1978. Review of the Rorschach. In O. K. Buros (Ed.), *The eighth mental measurement yearbook* (pp. 1042–1045). Highland Park, NJ: Gryphon Press.

PEZZULLO, T. R., E. E. THORSEN, and G. F. MADAUS. 1972. The heritability of Jensen's Level I and II and divergent thinking. *American Educational Research Journal, 9,* 539–546.

PHI DELTA KAPPA. 1973. *School climate improvement.* Bloomington: Phi Delta Kappa Educational Foundation.

PIDGEON, D. A., and A. YATES. 1957. Experimental inquiries into the use of essay-type English papers. *British Journal of Educational Psychology, 27,* 37–47.

PIKE, L. W. 1978. *Short-term instruction, test-wiseness, and the Scholastic Aptitude Test: A literature review with research recommendations.* Research Bulletin RB-78-2. Princeton, NJ: Educational Testing Service.

PINCHAK, B. M., and H. M. BRELAND. 1974. Grading practices in American high schools: National longitudinal study of high school class of 1972. *Educational Digest, 39,* 21–23.

POOLE, R. L. 1972. Characteristics of the taxonomy of educational objectives: Cognitive domain, a replication. *Psychology in the Schools, 9,* 83–88.

POPHAM, W. J. 1978a. The case for criterion-referenced measurement. *Educational Research, 7,* 6–10.

———. 1978b. *Criterion-referenced measurement.* Englewood Cliffs, NJ: Prentice-Hall.

POPHAM, W. J., and R. R. TRIMBLE. 1960. The Minnesota Teacher Attitude Inventory as an index of general teaching competence. *Educational and Psychological Measurement, 20,* 509–572.

POWERS, D. E. 1985. Effects of coaching on GRE aptitude test scores. *Journal of Educational Measurement, 22,* 121–136.

POWERS, D. E., and D. L. ALDERMAN. 1983. Effects of test familiarization on *SAT* performance. *Journal of Educational Measurement, 20,* 71–80.

PRINSELL, C. P., P. H. RAMSEY, and P. P. RAMSEY. 1994. Score gains, attitudes, and behavior changes due to answer changing instruction. *Journal of Educational Measurement, 31,* 227–338.

PYRCZAK, F. 1973. Validity of the discrimination index as a measure of item quality. *Journal of Educational Measurement, 10,* 227–231.

QUIRK, T. J., B. J. WITTEN, and S. F. WEINBERG. 1973. Review of studies of the concurrent and predictive validity of the Naional Teachers Examinations. *Review of Educational Research, 43,* 89–113.

RABINOWITZ, F. M. 1970. Characteristic sequential dependencies in multiple-choice situations. *Psychological Bulletin, 74,* 141–148.

RABINOWITZ, W. 1954. The fakability of the Minnesota Teacher Attitude Inventory. *Educational and Psychological Measurement, 14,* 657–664.

RAMOS, R. A., and J. STERN. 1973. Item behavior associated with changes in the number of alternatives in multiple-choice items. *Journal of Educational Measurement, 10,* 305–310.

REILING, E., and R. TAYLOR, 1972. A new approach to the problem of changing initial responses to multiple-choice questions. *Journal of Educational Measurement, 9,* 67–70.

RICHARDS, J. M., JR., and S. W. LUTZ. 1968. Predicting student achievement in college from the ACT assessment. *Journal of Educational Measurement, 5,* 17–29.

RIGOL, G. W. 1989. Why do women score lower than men on the SAT? *College Prep,* Number 4.

RIMLAND, B., and H. MUNSINGER. 1977. Burt's IQ data. *Science, 195,* 248.

RINDLER, S. E. 1980. The effects of skipping over more difficult items on time-limited tests: Implications for test validity. *Educational and Psychological Measurement, 40,* 989–998.

ROELFS, R. M. 1955. Trends in junior high school progress reporting. *Journal of Educational Research, 49,* 241–249.

ROSENTHAL, R., and L. JACOBSON. 1969. *Pygmalion in the classroom: Teacher expectation and pupils' intellectual development.* New York: Holt, Rinehart & Winston. Reviewed by R. R. Snow in *Contemporary Psychology, 14,* 197–199.

ROTEM, A., and N. S. GLASMAN. 1979. On the effectiveness of students' evaluative feedback to university instructors. *Review of Educational Research, 49,* 497–511.

RULON, P. J. 1939. A simplified procedure for determining the reliability of a test by split halves. *Harvard Educational Review, 9,* 99–103.

RYANS, D. G. 1960. *Characteristics of teachers.* Washington, DC: American Council on Education.

SADLER, D. R. 1983. Evaluation and the improvement of academic learning. *Journal of Higher Education, 54,* 60–79.

SARASON, S. B., et al. 1960. *Anxiety in elementary school children.* New York: John Wiley.

SARASON, S. S., G. MANDLER, and P. G. CRAIGHILL. 1952. The effect of differential instructions on anxiety and learning. *Journal of Abnormal and Social Psychology, 47,* 561–565.

SAX, G., and A. CARR. 1962. An investigation of response set on altered parallel forms. *Educational and Psychological Measurement, 22,* 371–376.

SAX, G., and L. S. COLLET. 1968. The effects of differing instructions and guessing formulas on reliability and validity. *Educational and Psychological Measurement, 28,* 1127–1136.

SAX, G., and T. R. CROMACK. 1966. The effects of various forms of item arrangements on test performance. *Journal of Educational Measurement, 3,* 309–311.

SAX, G., and M. READE. 1964. Achievement as a function of test difficulty level. *American Educational Research Journal, 1,* 22–25.

SCANNELL, D. P., and J. C. MARSHALL. 1966. The effect of selected composition errors on grades assigned to essay examinations. *American Educational Research Journal, 3,* 125–130.

SCARR, S., A., and L. CARTER-SALTZMAN 1982. Genetics and intelligence. In R. J. Sternberg (Ed.), *Handbook of human intelligence.* Chapter 13. Cambridge: Cambridge Univeristy Press.

SCHOENFELDT, L. F., and D. H. BRUSH. 1975. Patterns of college grades across curricular areas: Some implications for GPA as a criterion. *American Educational Research Journal, 12,* 313–321.

SCHON, I., K. D. HOPKINS, and C. VOJIR. 1980. The effects of special curricular study of Mexican culture on Anglo and Mexican-American students' perceptions of Mexican-Americans. Paper presented to the American Educational Research Association, Boston.

SCHRIESHEIM, C. A., and K. D. HILL. 1981. Controlling acquiescence response bias by item reversals: The effect on questionable validity. *Educational and Psychological Measurement, 41,* 1101–1114.

SCHUMACHER, C. F., and H. H. GEE. 1961. The relationship between initial and retest scores on the Medical College Admission Test. *Journal of Medical Education, 36,* 129–133.

SCHWARZ, J. C. 1967. A new procedure for administering objective tests to large classes. *Journal of Educational Measurement, 4,* 167–168.

SCHWARZ, S. P., R. F. McMORRIS, and L. P. DeMERS. 1991. Reasons for changing answers: An evaluation using personal interviews. *Journal of Educational Measurement, 28,* 163–171.

SCRIVEN, M. 1970. *Proceedings of the 1969 invitational conference on testing problems* (pp. 112–117). Princeton, NJ: Educational Testing Service.

SEASHORE, C. E. 1899. Some psychological statistics. *University of Iowa Studies in Psychology, 2,* 1–84.

SECOLSKY, C. 1983. Using examinee judgments for detecting invalid items on teacher-made criterion-referenced tests. *Journal of Educational Measurement, 20,* 51–64.

SELLTIZ, C., L. S. WRIGHTSMAN, and S. W. COOK. 1981. *Research methods in social relations* (4th ed.). New York: Holt, Rinehart & Winston.

SESNOWITZ, M., K. L. BERNHARDT, and D. M. KNAIN. 1982. An analysis of the impact of commercial test preparation courses on SAT scores. *American Educational Research Journal, 19,* 429–441.

SHANKER, A. 1977. AFT position paper on testing. *American Education, 62,* 15.

SHAW, M. E., and J. M. WRIGHT. 1967. *Scales for the measurement of attitudes.* New York: McGraw-Hill.

SHELDON, M.S., and A.G. Sorenson. 1960. On the use of Q-techniques in educational evaluation and research. *Journal of Experimental Education, 29,* 143–151.

SHEPARD, L. A. 1976. Setting standards and living with them *Florida Journal of Educational Research, 18,* 28–32.

———. 1979a. Setting standards. In M. A. Bunda and J. R. Sanders (Eds.) *Practices and problems in competency-based measurement.* Washington, DC: National Council on Measurement in Education.

———. 1979b. Norm-referenced vs. criterion-referenced tests. *Educational Horizons, 58,* 26–32.

———. 1980. Technical issues in minimum competency testing. *Review of Research in Education, 8,* 30–82.

———. 1993. Evaluating test validity. *Review of Research in Education, 19,* 405–450. ,

SHEPARD, L. A., and K. D. HOPKINS. 1977. Regression and the matching fallacy in quasi-experimental research. *National Association for Business Teachers Education Review, 4,* 11–15.

SHEPHERD, E. M. 1929. The effect of the quality of penmanship on grades. *Journal of Educational Research, 19,* 102–105.

SHORTLAND, R. L., and W. G. BERGER. 1970. Behavioral validation of several values. *Journal of Applied Psychology, 54,* 433–435.

SILVERSTEIN, A. B., P. J. MOHAN, R. E. FRANKEN, and D. E. RHONE. 1964. Test anxiety and intellectual performance in mentally retarded school children. *Child Development, 35,* 1137–1146.

SIMPSON, E. J. 1972. The classification of educational objectives in the psychomotor domain. *The Psychological Domain.* (Vol. 3). Washington: Gryphon House.

SLAKTER, M. J. 1967. Risk taking on objective examinations. *American Educational Research Journal, 4,* 31–43.

———. 1969. Generality of risk taking on objective examinations. *Educational and Psychological Measurement, 29,* 115–128.

SLAKTER, M. J., R. A. KOEHLER, and S. H. HAMPTON. 1970. Grade level, sex, and selected aspects of testwiseness. *Journal of Educational Measurement, 7,* 119–122.

SMITH, A., and J. C. MOORE. 1976. The effects of changing answers on scores of non-test-sophisticated examinees. *Measurement and Evaluation in Guidance, 8,* 252–256.

SMITH, M., K. P. WHITE, and R. H. COOP. 1979. The effect of item type on the consequences of changing answers on multiple-choice tests. *Journal of Educational Measurement, 16,* 203–208.

SMITH, P. L. 1979. The generalizability of student ratings of courses: Asking the right questions. *Journal of Educational Measurement, 16,* 77–88.

SNOW, R. E. 1969. Unfinished pygmalion: A review of Rosenthal and Jacobson's *Pygmalion in the classroom. Contemporary Psychology, 14,* 197–199.

SODERQUIST, H. 1936. A new method of weighting scores in a true-false test. *Journal of Educational Research, 30,* 290–292.

SPANDEL, V. S. 1984. *Direct measures of writing skill: Issues and applications.* Portland, OR.: Clearinghouse for Applied Performance Testing, Northwest Regional Educational Laboratory.

SPEARMAN, C. 1927. *The abilities of man.* New York: Macmillan.

STAFFORD, R. E. 1971. The speededness quotient: A new descriptive statistic for tests. *Journal of Educational Measurement, 8,* 275–277.

STAFFORD, R. E., and D. D. SJOGRAN. 1964. Activity level and learning effectiveness. NDEA Title VII, Project No. 753. Lincoln: University of Nebraska, 1964.

STALNAKER, J. M. 1936. The problem of the English examination. *Educational Record, 17,* 41.

STANLEY, J. C. 1954. Psychological correction for chance. *Journal of Experimental Education, 22,* 297–298.

———. 1957. K-R 20 as the stepped-up mean item intercorrelation. *Yearbook of the National Council on Measurements Used in Education, 14,* 78–92.

———. 1960. College studies and college life in Belgium. *College Board Review, 40,* 10–14.

———. 1971a. Predicting college success of the educationally disadvantaged. *Science, 171,* 640–647.

———. 1980. On educating the gifted. *Educational Researcher, 9,* 8–12.

———. 1984. Use of general and specific aptitude measures in identification: Some principles and certain cautions. *Gifted Child Quarterly, 28,* 177–180.

———. 1971b. Reliability of test scores and other measurements. In L. C. Deighton (Ed.), *The encyclopedia of education.* New York: Macmillan. Reprinted in G. H. Bracht, K. D. Hopkins, and J. C. Stanley (Eds.) *Perspectives in Educational and Psychological Measurement.* Selection 6. Englewood Cliffs, NJ: Prentice-Hall, 1972.

STANLEY, J. C., and E. Y. BEEMAN. 1956. Interaction of major field of study with kind of test. *Psychological Reports, 2,* 333–336.

STANLEY, J. C., and BENBOW. 1986. Youths who reason exceptionally well mathematically. In R. J. Sternberg and J. E. Davidson (Eds.). *Conceptions of giftedness* (pp. 361–387). Cambridge: Cambridge University Press.

STANLEY, J. C., and K. D. HOPKINS. 1972. *Educational and Psychological Measurement* and evaluation. Englewood Cliffs, NJ: Prentice-Hall.

STANLEY, J. C., and A. C. PORTER. 1967. Correlation of Scholastic Aptitude Test score with college grades for Negroes versus whites. *Journal of Educational Measurement, 4,* 199–218.

STANLEY, J. C., and M. D. WANG. 1970. Weighting test items and test-item options: An overview of the analytical and empirical literature. *Educational and Psychological Measurement, 30,* 21–35.

STARCH, D., and E. C. ELLIOT. 1912. Reliability of grading high school work in English. *Scholastic Review, 20,* 442–457.

———. 1913. Reliability of grading high school work in mathematics. *Scholastic Review, 21,* 254–259.

STECKLEIN, J. E. 1955. *Bulletins on classroom testing.* Minneapolis, MN: Bureau of Institutional Research, University of Minnesota.

STEININGER, M., R. E. JOHNSON, and D. K. KIRTS. 1964. Cheating on college examinations as a function of situationally aroused anxiety and hostility. *Journal of Educational Psychology, 55,* 317–324.

STEPHENSEN, W. 1953. *The study of behavior: Q-technique and its methodology.* Chicago: University of Chicago Press.

STERN, G. G. 1970. *People in context: Measuring person-environment congruence in education and industry.* New York: John Wiley.

STERNBERG, R. J. 1982. *Handbook of human intelligence.* Cambridge: Cambridge Univeristy Press.

———. 1996. Myths, countermyths, and truths about intelligence. *Educational Researcher, 25,* 11–18.

STEVENSON, H. W. 1961. Social reinforcement with children as a function of CA, sex of examiner, and sex of subject. *Journal of Abnormal and Social Psychology, 63,* 147–154.

STIGGINS, R., and N. J. BRIDGEFORD. 1986. Classroom assessment: A key to effective education. *Educational Measurement: Issues and Practice, 5,* 5–17.

STOREY, A. G. 1968. The versatile multiple- choice item. *Journal of Educational Research, 62,* 169–172.

STRANG, H. R. 1977. The effects of technical and unfamiliar options upon guessing on multiple choice test items. *Journal of Educational Measurement, 14,* 253–260.

STRICKER, L. J. 1985. Test disclosure and retest performance on the SAT. *Applied Psychological Measurement, 8,* 81–87.

SUPER, D. E., W. F. BRAASCH, and J. B. SHAY. 1947. The effect of distractions on test results. *Journal of Educational Psychology, 38,* 373–377.

SUPER, D. E., and P. L. OVERSTREET. 1960. *The vocational maturity of ninth grade boys.* New York: Columbia University, Teachers College.

SWAN, R. J., and K. D. HOPKINS. 1965. An investigation of theoretical and empirical chance scores on selected standardized group tests. *California Journal of Educational Research, 16,* 34–41.

SWINEFORD, F. 1938. The measurement of a personality trait. *Journal of Educational Psychology, 29,* 295–300.

———. 1941. Analysis of a personality trait. *Journal of Educational Psychology, 32,* 438–444.

TAYLOR, C., and K. R. WHITE. 1982. The effect of reinforcement and training on group standardized test behavior. *Journal of Educational Measurement, 19,* 199–210.

TAYLOR, W. L. 1953. Cloze procedure: A new tool for measuring readability. *Journalism Quarterly, 30,* 415–433.

———. 1956. Recent developments in the cloze procedure. *Journalism Quarterly, 33,* 42–48.

TERMAN, and M. A. MERRILL. 1937. *Measuring intelligence.* Boston: Houghton Mifflin.

———. 1960. *Stanford-Binet Intelligence Scale.* Boston: Houghton Mifflin.

———. 1972. *Stanford-Binet Intelligence Scale*: Manual for third revision. Boston: Houghton Mifflin.

TERWILLIGER, J. S. 1971. *Assigning grades to students.* Glenview, IL: Scott, Foresman.

THOMAS, C. L., and J. C. STANLEY. 1969. Effectiveness of high school grades for predicting college grades of black students: A review and discussion. *Journal of Educational Measurement, 6,* 203–215.

THORNDIKE, E. L. 1910. *Handwriting.* New York: Columbia University, Teachers College.

———. 1918. The nature, purposes, and general methods of measurements of educational products (p. 16). In *The seventh yearbook of the national society for the study of education,* Part II.

THORNDIKE, R. L. 1949. *Personnel selection.* New York: John Wiley.

———. 1963a. *The concepts of over- and under-achievement.* New York: Columbia University, Teachers College.

———. 1963b. Some methodological issues in the study of creativity. In *Proceedings of the 1962 invitational conference on testing problems.* Princeton, NJ: Educational Testing Service. Reprinted in G. H. Bracht, K. D. Hopkins, and J. C. Stanley (Eds.) *Perspectives in Educational and Psychological Measurement* Selection 21. Englewood Cliffs, NJ: Prentice-Hall, 1972.

———. 1968. Review of Rosenthal and Jacobson's *Pygmalion in the classroom. American Educational Research Journal, 5,* 708–711.

———. 1969. Marks and marking systems. In R. L. Ebel (Ed.), *Encyclopedia of Educational Research* (4th ed.) (pp. 759–766). New York: Macmillan. Reprinted in G. H. Bracht, K. D. Hopkins, and J. C. Stanley (Eds.), *Perspectives in Educational and Psychological Measurement* Selection 17. Englewood Cliffs, NJ: Prentice-Hall, 1972.

———. 1974. *Technical manual: Cognitive Abilities Test.* New York: Houghton Mifflin.

THORNDIKE, R. M. and E. HAGEN. 1974. *Technical manual: Cognitive abilities test.* New York: Houghton Mifflin.

———. 1977. *Measurement and evaluation in psychology and education* (4th ed.). New York: John Wiley.

THORNDIKE, R. L., and E. HAGEN. 1997. *CogAT Research Hndbook..* Itasca, IL: Riverside Publishing.

THORNDIKE, R. L., E. P. HAGEN, and J. M. SATTLER. 1986. *Stanford-Binet Intelligence Scale* (4th ed.): Technical manual. Chicago, IL: The Riverside Publishing Co.

THORNDIKE, R. M. 1997. *Measurement and evaluation in psychology and education* (6th ed.). New York: Prentice-Hall.

THURSTONE, L. L. 1955. The differential growth of mental abilities. Paper No. 14. University of North Carolina, Psychometric Laboratory.

TOLLEFSON, N. 1978. Effect of item-difficulty arrangement and state anxiety on achievement test performance. In *AERA 1978 annual meeting: Abstracts of papers.* Washington, DC: AERA.

TORRANCE, E. P. 1962. *Guiding creative talent.* Englewood Cliffs, NJ: Prentice-Hall.

TRAUB, R. E., and C. W. FISHER. 1977. *On the equivalence of constructed-response and multiple-choice tests.* Toronto: Ontario Institute for Studies in Educatiion.

TRAUB, R. E., and R. K. HAMBLETON. 1972. The effect of scoring instructions and degree of speededness on the validity and reliability of multiple-choice tests. *Educational and Psychological Measurement, 32,* 737–758.

TRAUB, R. E., R. K. HAMBLETON, and B. SINGH. 1968. Effects of promised reward and threatened penalty on performance of a multiple-choice vocabulary test. Unpublished manuscript. Toronto: Ontario Institute for Studies in Education.

TRAUB, R. E., and G. L. ROWLEY. 1991. Understanding reliability. *Educational Measurement: Issues and Practice, 10,* 37–45.

TRENTHAM, L. L. 1975. The effect of distractions on sixth-grade students in a testing situation. *Journal of Educational Measurement, 12,* 13–18.

TYLER, L. E. 1956. Friends or foes? *California Journal of Educational Research, 3,* 66–71.

———. 1958. The stability of patterns of primary mental abilities among grade school children. *Educational and Psychological Measurement, 18,* 769–774.

TYLER, R. W. 1960. What testing does to teachers and students. *The 1959 invitational conference on testing problems.* Princeton, NJ: Educational Testing Service.

TYLER, R. W. 1973. Assessing educational achievement in the affective domain. *NCME Measurement in Education, 4,* 1–8.

TYLER, R. W., and R. M. WOLF (Eds.). 1974. *Crucial issues in testing.* Berkeley, CA: McCutchan.

VEAL, S. R., and E. F. BIESBROCK. 1971. Primary essay tests. *Journal of Educational Measurement, 8,* 45–46.

VECCHIO, R., and F. COSTIN. 1977. Predicting teacher effectiveness from graduate admissions predictors. *American Educational Research Journal, 14,* 169–176.

VERNON, P. E. 1950. *The structure of human abilities.* London: Methuen.

———. 1962. The determinants of reading comprehension. *Educational and Psychological Measurement, 22,* 269–286.

———. 1964. Creativity and intelligence. *Journal of Educational Research, 6,* 163–169.

WAHLSTROM, M., and F. J. BOERSMA. 1968. The influence of test-wiseness upon achievement. *Educational and Psychological Measurement, 27,* 413–420.

WALBERG, H. J. 1967. Scholastic aptitude, the National Teacher Examinations, and teaching success. *Journal of Educational Research, 61,* 129–131.

WANG, M. D., and J. C. STANLEY. 1970. Differential weighting: A review of methods and empirical studies. *Review of Educational Research, 40,* 663–705.

WARD, W. C. 1982. A comparison of free-response and multiple-choice forms of verbal aptitude tests. *Applied Psychological Measurement, 6,* 1–11.

WARD, W. C., N. FREDERIKSEN, and S. B. CARLSON. 1980. Construct validity of free-response and machine-scorable forms of a test. *Journal of Educational Measurement, 17,* 11–30.

WARNER, W. L., M. MEEKER, and K. EELLS. 1949. *Social class in America.* Chicago: Science Research Associates.

WARREN, G. R. 1975. The continuing controversy over grades. T. M. Report 51, ERIC Clearinghouse on Tests, Measurements, and Evaluation. Princeton, NJ: Educational Testing Service.

WATERS, L. K. 1967. Effects of perceived scoring formula on some aspects of test performance. *Educational and Psychological Measurement, 27,* 1005–1010.

WEIDEMANN, C. C. 1933. Written examination procedures. *Phi Delta Kappan, 16,* 78–83.

———. 1941. Review of essay test studies. *Journal of Higher Education, 12,* 41–44.

WEISS, D. J. 1976. *Computerized ability testing 1972–1975.* University of Minnesota, Psychometric Methods Program.

WHITE, E. E. 1886. *The elements of pedagogy.* New York: American Book.

WHITE, K. R. 1982. The relationship between socioeconomic status and academic achievement. *Psychological Bulletin, 91,* 461–481. Doctoral dissertation, University of Colorado.

WICK, J. W. 1983. Reducing proportion of chance scores in inner-city standardized testing results: Impact on average scores. *American Educational Research Journal, 20,* 461–463.

WILEY, D. E., J. R. COLLINS, and G. V GLASS. 1970. *Sources of variation in multiple-choice test performance.* Research Paper 37. Boulder: University of Colorado, Laboratory of Educational Research.

WILLIAMS, R. G., and J. E. WARE. 1976. Validity of student ratings of instruction under different incentive conditions. *Journal of Educational Psychology, 68,* 48–56.

WILLIAMSON, M. L., and K. D. HOPKINS. 1967. The use of "none-of-these" versus homogeneous alternatives on multiple-choice tests: Experimental reliability and validity comparisons. *Journal of Educational Measurement, 4,* 53–58.

WILSON, K. M. 1978. *Predicting the long-term performance in college of minority and nonminority students.* Research Bulletin RB-78-6. Princeton, NJ: Educational Testing Service.

WINEBURG, S. S. 1987. The self-fulfillment of the self-fulfilling prophecy. *Educational Researcher, 16,* 28–37.

WINFIELD, L. F. 1987. *The relationship between minimum competency testing programs and students' reading proficiency.* Research Report 87–15. Princeton, NJ: Educational Testing Service.

WIRT, R. D., and D. LACHAR. 1981. The Personality Inventory for Children: Development and clinical applications. In P. McReynolds (Ed.), *Advances in Psychological Assessment, 5,* 353–393. San Francisco: Jossey-Bass.

WISEMAN, S., and S. WRIGLEY. 1958. Essay-reliability: The effect of choice of essay-title. *Educational and Psychological Measurement, 18,* 129–138.

WISSLER, C. 1901. The correlation of mental and physical tests. *Psychological Review*, Monograph Supplements, *8,* 1–62.

WITTIG, M. E., and A. C. PETERSEN (Eds.). 1979. *Sex-related differences in cognitive functioning: Developmental issues.* Series in Cognition and Perception. New York: Academic Press.

WOOD, R. 1976. Inhibiting blind guessing: The effect of instructions. *Journal of Educational Measurement, 13,* 297–307.

———. 1977. Multiple-Choice: A state of the art report. *Evaluation in Education, 1,* 191–280.

WRIGHT, W. H. E. 1944. The modified true-false item applied to testing in chemistry. *School Science and Mathematics, 44,* 637–639.

WRINKLE, W. L. 1956. *Improving marking and reporting practices in elementary and secondary schools.* New York: Holt, Rinehart & Winston, Inc.

ZASTROW, C. H. 1970. Cheating among college graduate students. *Journal of Educational Research, 64,* 157–160.

ZILLER, R. C. 1957. A measure of the gambling response set in objective tests. *Psychometrika, 22,* 289–292.

ZYTOWSKI, D. G. 1976. Predictive validity of the Kuder Occupational Interest Survey: A 12- to 19-year follow-up. *Journal of Counseling Psychology, 23,* 221–233.

Author Index

Subject Index